W9-DAF-944

THE OUTLINE
OF HISTORY

BEING A PLAIN HISTORY OF
LIFE AND MANKIND BY

H. G. WELLS

REVISED AND BROUGHT UP TO THE END
OF THE SECOND WORLD WAR BY
RAYMOND POSTGATE

With Maps and Plans by
J. F. HORRABIN

VOLUME II

GARDEN CITY BOOKS
Garden City, New York

THE OUTLINE OF HISTORY

MUHAMMAD AND ISLAM

§ 6

ABU BEKR and Omar I are the two master figures in the history of Islam. It is not within our scope here to describe the wars by which in a hundred and twenty-five years Islam spread itself from the Indus to the Atlantic and Spain, and from Kashgar, on the borders of China, to Upper Egypt. Two maps must suffice to show the limits to which the vigorous impulse of the new faith carried the Arab idea and the Arabic scriptures, before worldliness, the old trading and plundering spirit, and the glamour of the silk robe had completely recovered their paralyzing sway over the Arab intelligence and will. The reader will note how the great tide swept over the footsteps of Yuan Chwang, and how easily in Africa the easy conquests of the Vandals were repeated in the reverse direction. And if the reader entertains any delusions about a fine civilization, either Persian, Roman, Hellenic, or Egyptian, being submerged by this flood, the sooner he dismisses such ideas the better. Islam prevailed because it was the best social and political order the times could offer. It prevailed because everywhere it found politically apathetic peoples robbed, oppressed, bullied, uneducated, and unorganized, and it found selfish and unsound governments out of touch with any people at all. It was the broadest, freshest, and cleanest political idea that had yet come into actual activity in the world, and it offered better terms than any other to the mass of mankind. The capitalistic and slaveholding system of the Roman Empire and the literature and culture and social tradition of Europe had altogether decayed and broken down before Islam arose; it was only when mankind lost faith in the sincerity of its representatives that Islam, too, began to decay.

The larger part of its energy spent itself in conquering and assimilating Persia and Turkestan; its most vigorous thrusts were northwardly from Persia and westwardly through Egypt. Had it concentrated its first vigour upon the Byzantine Empire there can be little doubt that by the eighth century it would have taken Constantinople and come through into Europe as easily as it reached the Pamirs. The Caliph Moawiya, it is true, besieged the capital for seven years (672–678), and Suleiman in 717 and 718; but the pressure was not sustained, and for three or four centuries longer the Byzantine Empire remained the crazy bulwark of Europe. In the newly Christianized or still pagan Avars, Bulgars, Serbs, Slavs, and Saxons, Islam would certainly have found as ready converts as it did in the Turks of Central Asia. And though, instead of insisting upon Constantinople, it first came round into Europe by the circuitous route of Africa and Spain, it was only in France, at the end of a vast line of communications from Arabia, that it encountered a power sufficiently vigorous to arrest its advance.

From the outset the Bedouin aristocrats of Mecca dominated the new empire. Abu Bekr, the first Caliph, was in an informal shouting way elected at Medina, and so were Omar I and Othman, the third Caliph, but all three were Meccans of good family. They were not men of Medina. And though Abu Bekr and Omar were men of stark simplicity and righteousness, Othman was of a baser quality, a man quite in the vein of those silk robes, to whom conquest was not conquest for Allah but for Arabia, and especially for Mecca in Arabia, and more particularly for himself and for the Meccans and for his family, the Omayyads. He was a worthy man, who stood out for his country and his town and his "people." He was no early convert as his two predecessors had been; he had joined the Prophet for reasons of policy in fair give and take. With his accession the Caliph ceases to be a strange man of fire and wonder, and becomes an Oriental monarch, like many Oriental monarchs before and since, a fairly good monarch by Eastern standards as yet but nothing more.

The rule and death of Othman brought out the consequences of Muhammad's weaknesses as clearly as the lives of Abu Bekr and Omar had witnessed to the divine fire in his teaching. Muhammad had been politic at times when Abu Bekr would have been firm, and the new element of aristocratic greediness that came in with Othman was one fruit of those politic movements. And the legacy of that carelessly compiled harem of the Prophet, the family complications and jealousies which had lurked in the background of Moslem affairs during the rule of the first two Caliphs, was now coming out into the light of day. Ali, who was the nephew, the adopted son, and the son-in-law of the Prophet—he was the husband of the Prophet's daughter Fatima—had considered himself the rightful Caliph. His claims formed an undertow to the resentment of Medina and of the rival families of Mecca against the advancement of the Omayyads. But Ayesha, the favourite wife of the Prophet, had always been jealous of Fatima and hostile to Ali. She supported Othman. . . . The splendid opening of the story of Islam collapses suddenly into this squalid dispute and bickering of heirs and widows.

In 656 Othman, an old man of eighty, was stoned in the streets of Medina by a mob, chased to his house, and murdered; and Ali became at last Caliph, only to be murdered in his turn (661). In one of the battles in this civil war, Ayesha, now a gallant mischievous old lady, distinguished herself by leading a charge, mounted on a camel. She was taken prisoner and treated well.

While the armies of Islam were advancing triumphantly to the conquest of the world, this sickness of civil war smote at its head. What was the rule of Allah in the world to Ayesha when she could score off the detested Fatima, and what heed were the Omayyads and the partisans of Ali likely to take of the unity of mankind when they had a good hot feud of this sort to entertain them, with the caliphate as a prize? The world of Islam was rent in twain by the spites, greeds, and partisan silliness of a handful of men and women in Medina. That quarrel still lives. To this day one main division of the Moslems, the Shiites, maintain the hereditary right of Ali to be Caliph *as an article of faith!* They prevail in Persia and India.

But an equally important section, the Sunnites, with whom it is difficult for a disinterested observer not to agree, deny this peculiar addendum to Muhammad's simple creed. So far as we can gather at this length of time, Ali was an entirely commonplace individual.

To watch this schism creeping across the brave beginnings of Islam is like watching a case of softening of the brain. To the copious literature of the subject we must refer the reader who wishes to learn how Hasan, the son of Ali, was poisoned by his wife, and how Husein, his brother, was killed. We do but name them here, because they still afford a large section of mankind scope for sentimental partisanship and mutual annoyance. They are the two chief Shiite martyrs. Amidst the coming and going of their conflicts the old Kaaba at Mecca was burnt down, and naturally there began endless disputation whether it should be rebuilt in exactly its ancient form or on a much larger scale.

In this and the preceding sections we have seen once more the inevitable struggle of this newest and latest unifying impulse in the world's affairs against the everyday worldliness of mankind, and we have seen also how from the first the complicated household of Muhammad was like an evil legacy to the new faith. But as this history now degenerates into the normal crimes and intrigues of an Oriental dynasty, the student of history will realize a third fundamental weakness in the world-reforms of Muhammad. He was an illiterate Arab, ignorant of history, totally ignorant of all the political experiences of Rome and Greece, and almost as ignorant of the real history of Judea; and he left his followers with no scheme for a stable government embodying and concentrating the general will of the faithful, and no effective form to express the very real spirit of democracy (using the word in its modern sense) that pervades the essential teaching of Islam. His own rule was unlimited autocracy, and autocratic Islam has remained. Politically, Islam was not an advance, but a retrogression from the traditional freedoms and customary laws of the desert. The breach of the pilgrims' truce that led to the battle of Badr is the blackest mark against early Islam. Nominally, Allah is its chief ruler—but, practically, its master has always been whatever man was vigorous and unscrupulous enough to snatch and hold the caliphate—and, subject to revolts and assassinations, its final law has been that man's will.

For a time, after the death of Ali, the Omayyad family was in the ascendant, and for nearly a century they gave rulers to Islam.

The Arab historians are so occupied with the dynastic squabbles and crimes of the time, that it is difficult to trace the external history of the period. We find Moslem shipping upon the seas defeating the Byzantine fleet in a great sea-fight off the coast of Lycia (A.D. 655), but how the Moslems acquired this victorious fleet thus early we do not clearly know. It was probably chiefly Egyptian. For some years Islam certainly controlled the Eastern Mediterranean, and in 669 and again in 674, during the reign of Muawiya (661–680), the first great Omayyad Caliph made two sea attacks upon Constantinople. They had to be sea attacks because Islam, so long as it was under Arab rule, never surmounted the barrier of the Taurus Mountains. During the same period the Moslems were also pressing their conquests further and further into Central Asia. While Islam was already decaying at its centre, it was yet making great hosts of new adherents and awakening a new spirit among the hitherto divided and aimless Turkish peoples. Medina was no longer a possible centre for its vast enterprises in Asia, Africa, and the Mediterranean, and so Damascus became the usual capital of the Omayyad Caliphs.

Chief among these, as for a time the clouds of dynastic intrigue clear, are Abdal Malik (685–705) and Walid I (705–714), under whom the Omayyad line rose to the climax of its successes. The western boundary was carried to the Pyrenees, while to the east the domains of the Caliph marched with China. The son of Walid, Suleiman (715), carried out a second series of Moslem attacks upon Constantinople which his father had planned and proposed. As with the Caliph Muawiya half a century before, the approach was by sea—for Asia Minor, as we have just noted, was still unconquered—and the shipping was drawn chiefly from Egypt. The emperor, a usurper, Leo the Isaurian, displayed extraordinary skill and obstinacy in the defence; he burnt most of the Moslem shipping in a brilliant sortie, cut up the troops they had landed upon the Asiatic side of the Bosphorus, and after a campaign in Europe of two years (716–717), a winter of unexampled severity completed their defeat.

From this point onward the glory of the Omayyad line decays. The first tremendous impulse of Islam was now spent. There was no further expansion and a manifest decline in religious zeal. Islam had made millions of converts, and had digested those millions very imperfectly. Cities, nations, whole sects and races, Arab pagans, Jews, Christians, Manichæans, Zoroastrians, Turanian pagans had been swallowed up into this new vast empire of Muhammad's successors. It has hitherto been the common characteristic of all the great unifying religious initiators of the world, the common oversight, that they have accepted the moral and theological ideals to which the first appeal was made, as though they were universal ideals. Muhammad's appeal, for example, was to the traditional chivalry and underlying monotheistic feelings of the intelligent Arabs of his time. These things were latent in the mind and conscience of Mecca and Medina; he did but call them forth.

Then, as the new teaching spread and stereotyped itself, it had to work on a continually more uncongenial basis, it had to grow in soil that distorted and perverted it. Its sole textbook was the Koran. To minds untuned to the melodies of Arabic, this book seemed to be, as it seems to many European minds to-day, a mixture of fine-spirited rhetoric with—to put it plainly—formless and unintelligent gabble. Countless converts missed the real thing in it altogether. To that we must ascribe the readiness of the Persian and Indian sections of the faith to join the Shiite schism upon a quarrel that they could at least understand and feel. And to the same attempt to square the new stuff with old prepossessions was due such extravagant theology as presently disputed whether the Koran was and always had been co-existent with God.[1] We should

---

[1] Sir Mark Sykes.

be stupefied by the preposterousness of this idea if we did not recognize in it at once the well-meaning attempt of some learned Christian convert to Islamize his belief that "In the beginning was the Word, and the Word was with God, and the Word was God."[1]

None of the great unifying religious initiators of the world hitherto seems to have been accompanied by any understanding of the vast educational task, the vast work of lucid and varied exposition and intellectual organization involved in its propositions. They all present the same history of a rapid spreading like a little water poured over a great area, and then of superficiality and corruption.

In a little while we hear stories of an Omayyad Caliph, Walid II (743–744), who mocked at the Koran, ate pork, drank wine, and did not pray. Those stories may have been true or they may have been circulated for political reasons. There began a puritan reaction in Mecca and Medina against the levity and luxury of Damascus. Another great Arab family, the Abbas family, the Abbasids, had long been scheming for power, and was making capital out of the general discontent. The feud of the Omayyads and the Abbasids was older than Islam; it had been going on before Muhammad was born. These Abbasids took up the tradition of the Shiite "martyrs," Ali and his sons Hasan and Husein, and identified themselves with it. The banner of the Omayyads was white; the Abbasids adopted a black banner, black in mourning for Hasan and Husein, black because black is more impressive than any colour; moreover, the Abbasids declared that all the Caliphs after Ali were usurpers. In 749 they accomplished a carefully prepared revolution, and the last of the Omayyad Caliphs was hunted down and slain in Egypt. Abul Abbas was the first of the Abbasid Caliphs, and he began his reign by collecting into one prison every living male of the Omayyad line upon whom he could lay hands and causing them all to be massacred. Their bodies, it is said, were heaped together, a leathern carpet was spread over them, and on this gruesome table Abul Abbas and his councillors feasted. Moreover, the tombs of the Omayyad Caliphs were rifled, and their bones burnt and scattered to the four winds of heaven. So the grievances of Ali were avenged at last, and the Omayyad line passed out of history.

There was, it is interesting to note, a rising on behalf of the Omayyads in Khorasan which was assisted by the Chinese emperor.

§ 7

But the descendants of Ali were not destined to share in this triumph for long. The Abbasids were adventurers and rulers of an older school than Islam. Now that the tradition of Ali had served its purpose, the next proceeding of the new Caliph was to hunt down and slaughter the surviving members of his family, the descendants of Ali and Fatima.

Clearly the old traditions of Sassanid Persia and of Persia before the Greeks

---

[1] St. John's Gospel, chap. i, 1.

were returning to the world. With the accession of the Abbasids the control of the sea departed from the Caliph, and with it went Spain and North Africa, in which, under an Omayyad survivor in the former case, independent Moslem states now arose.

The centre of gravity of Islam shifted across the desert from Damascus to Mesopotamia. Mansur, the successor of Abul Abbas, built himself a new capital at Bagdad near the ruins of Ctesiphon, the former Sassanid capital. Turks and Persians as well as Arabs became Emirs, and the army was reorganized upon Sassanid lines. Medina and Mecca were now only of importance as pilgrimage centres, to which the faithful turned to pray. But because it was a fine language, and because it was the language of the Koran, Arabic continued to spread until presently it had replaced Greek and become the language of educated men throughout the whole Moslem world.

Of the Abbasid monarchs after Abul Abbas we need tell little here. A bickering war went on year by year in Asia Minor, in which neither Byzantium nor Bagdad made any permanent gains, though once or twice the Moslems raided as far as the Bosphorus. A false prophet, Mokanna, who said he was God, had a brief but troublesome career. There were plots, there were insurrections; they lie flat and colourless now in the histories, like dead flowers in an old book. One other Abbasid Caliph only need be named, and that quite as much for his legendary as for his real importance, Haroun-al-Raschid (786–809). He was not only the Caliph of an outwardly prosperous empire in the world of reality, but he was also the Caliph of an undying empire in the deathless world of fiction, he was the Haroun-al-Raschid of the *Arabian Nights*.

Sir Mark Sykes[1] gives an account of the reality of his empire from which we will quote certain passages. He says: "The Imperial Court was polished, luxurious, and unlimitedly wealthy; the capital, Bagdad, a gigantic mercantile city surrounding a huge administrative fortress, wherein every department of state had a properly regulated and well-ordered public office; where schools and colleges abounded; whither philosophers, students, doctors, poets, and theologians flocked from all parts of the civilized globe. . . . The provincial capitals were embellished with vast public buildings, and linked together by an effective and rapid service of posts and caravans; the frontiers were secure and well garrisoned, the army loyal, efficient, and brave; the governors and ministers honest and forbearing. The empire stretched with equal strength and unimpaired control from the Cilician gates to Aden, and from Egypt to Central Asia. Christians, Pagans, Jews, as well as Moslems, were employed in the government service. Usurpers, rebellious generals, and false prophets seemed to have vanished from the Moslem dominions. Traffic and wealth had taken the place of revolution and famine. . . . Pestilence and disease were met by Imperial hospitals and government physicians. . . . In government business the rough-and-ready methods of Arabian administration had given place to a complicated system of Divans, initiated partly from the Roman, but chiefly

---

[1] *The Caliph's Last Heritage.*

taken from the Persian system of government. Posts, Finance, Privy Seal, Crown Lands, Justice, and Military Affairs were each administered by separate bureaux in the hands of ministers and officials; an army of clerks, scribes, writers and accountants swarmed into these offices and gradually swept the whole power of the government into their own hands by separating the Commander of the Faithful from any direct intercourse with his subjects. The Imperial Palace and the entourage were equally based on Roman and Persian precedents. Eunuchs, closely veiled 'harems' of women, guards, spies, go-betweens, jesters, poets, and dwarfs clustered around the person of the Commander of the Faithful, each, in his degree, endeavouring to gain the royal favour and indirectly distracting the royal mind from affairs of business and state. Meanwhile the mercantile trade of the East poured gold into Bagdad, and supplemented the other enormous stream of money derived from the contributions of plunder and loot despatched to the capital by the commanders of the victorious raiding forces which harried Asia Minor, India, and Turkestan. The seemingly unending supply of Turkish slaves and Byzantine specie added to the richness of the revenues of Irak and, combined with the vast commercial traffic of which Bagdad was the centre, produced a large and powerful moneyed class, composed of the sons of generals, officials, landed proprietors, royal favourites, merchants, and the like, who encouraged the arts, literature, philosophy, and poetry as the mood took them, building palaces for themselves, vying with each other in the luxury of their entertainments, suborning poets to sound their praises, dabbling in philosophy, supporting various schools of thought, endowing charities, and, in fact, behaving as the wealthy have always behaved in all ages.

"I have said that the Abbasid Empire in the days of Haroun-al-Raschid was weak and feeble to a degree, and perhaps the reader will consider this a foolish proposition when he takes into consideration that I have described the Empire as orderly, the administration definite and settled, the army efficient, and wealth abundant. The reason I make the suggestion is that the Abbasid Empire had lost touch with everything original and vital in Islam, and was constructed entirely by the reunion of the fragments of the empires Islam had destroyed. There was nothing in the empire which appealed to the higher instinct of the leaders of the people; the holy war had degenerated into a systematic acquisition of plunder. The Caliph had become a luxurious Emperor or King of Kings; the administration had changed from a patriarchal system to a bureaucracy. The wealthier classes were rapidly losing all faith in the religion of the state; speculative philosophy and high living were taking the place of Koramic orthodoxy and Arabian simplicity. The solitary bond which could have held the empire together, the sternness and plainness of the Moslem faith, was completely neglected by both the Caliph and his advisers. . . . Haroun-al-Raschid himself was a wine-bibber, and his palace was decorated with graven images of birds and beasts and men. . . .

"For a moment we stand amazed at the greatness of the Abbasid dominion; then suddenly we realize that it is but as a fair husk enclosing the dust and ashes of dead civilizations."

Haroun-al-Raschid died in 809. At his death his great empire fell immediately into civil war and confusion, and the next great event of unusual importance in this region of the world comes two hundred years later when the Turks, under the chiefs of the great family of the Seljuks, poured southward out of Turkestan, and not only conquered the empire of Bagdad, but Asia Minor also. Coming from the north-east as they did, they were able to outflank the great barrier of the Taurus Mountains, which had hitherto held back the Moslems. They were still much the same people as those of whom Yuan Chwang gave us a glimpse four hundred years earlier, but now they were Moslems, and Moslems of the primitive type, men whom Abu Bekr would have welcomed to Islam. They caused a great revival of vigour in Islam, and they turned the minds of the Moslem world once more in the direction of a religious war against Christendom. For there had been a sort of truce between these two great religions after the cessation of the Moslem advance and the decline of the Omayyads. Such warfare as had gone on between Christianity and Islam had been rather border-bickering than sustained war. It became only a bitter fanatical struggle again in the eleventh century.

§ 8

But before we go on to tell of the Turks and the Crusaders, the great wars that began between Christendom and Islam, and which have left a quite insane intolerance between these great systems right down to the present time, it is necessary to give a little more attention to the intellectual life of the Arabic-speaking world which was now spreading more and more widely over the regions which Hellenism had once dominated. For some generations before Muhammad, the Arab mind had been, as it were, smouldering, it had been producing poetry and much religious discussion; under the stimulus of the national and racial successes, it presently blazed out with a brilliance second only to that of the Greeks during their best period. It revived the human pursuit of science. If the Greek was the father, then the Arab was the foster-father of the scientific method. Through the Arabs it was, and not by the Latin route, that the modern world received that gift of light and power.

But when we write Arab here, we must write it with a certain reservation. The Arabic culture of Islam has something of the same relation to the original Arab as the Hellenic culture after the days of Alexander had to the original European Greek. It was no longer racially pure. It had incorporated with it a group of pre-existing cultures, the Persian of the Arsacid dynasty, and the Coptic of Hellenized Egypt. Persia and Egypt learnt to talk Arabic with great promptitude, but they remained in quality Persia and Egypt.

The early conquests of the Arabs had brought the Arabic culture into close contact with the Greek literary tradition—not, it is true, in the original Greek, but through the Syrian translations of the Greek writer. The Nestorian Christians, the Christians to the east of orthodoxy, seem to have been much more intelligent and active-minded than the court theologians of Byzantium, and at a much higher level of general education than the Latin-speaking Christians of the west. They had been tolerated during the latter days of the Sassanids, and they were tolerated by Islam until the ascendancy of the Turks in the eleventh century. They were the intellectual backbone of the Persian world. They had preserved much of the Hellenic medical science, and had even added to it. In the Omayyad times most of the physicians in the Caliph's dominions were Nestorians, and no doubt many learned Nestorians professed Islam without any serious compunction or any great change in their work and thoughts. They had preserved much of Aristotle both in Greek and in Syrian translations. They had a considerable mathematical literature. Their equipment makes the contemporary resources of Saint Benedict or Cassiodorus seem very pitiful. To these Nestorian teachers came the fresh Arab mind out of the desert, keen and curious, and learnt much and improved upon its teaching. It learnt much and acquired much. Persia had been for many centuries a country of intense and subtle theological and speculative activity. These activities now clothed themselves in Arabic phrases and became a process of heresy and schism in the Moslem Church. The Shiite schism was essentially Persian.

But the Persians with the Hellenic learning were not the only teachers available for the Arabs. Throughout all the rich cities of the East the kindred Jews were scattered with their own distinctive literature and tradition, and the Arab and the Jewish mind reacted upon one another to a common benefit. The Arab was informed and the Jew sharpened to a keener edge. The Jews have never been pedants in the manner of their language; we have already noted that a thousand years before Islam they spoke Greek in Hellenized Alexandria, and now all over this new Moslem world they were speaking and writing Arabic. Some of the greatest of Jewish literature was written in Arabic, the religious writings of Maimonides, for example. Indeed, it is difficult to say, in the case of this Arabic culture, where the Jew ends and the Arab begins, so important and essential were its Jewish factors.

Moreover, there was a third source of inspiration, more particularly in mathematical science, to which at present it is difficult to do justice—India. There can be little doubt that the Arab mind during its period of splendour was in close and effective contact with Sanskrit literature and with Indo-Persian physical science.

The distinctive activities of the Arab mind were already manifest under the Omayyads, although it was during the Abbasid time that it made its best display. History is the beginning and core of all sound philosophy and all great literature, and the first Arab writers of distinction were historians, biographers, and quasi-historical poets. Romantic fiction and the short story followed as a reading public developed, willing to be amused. And as reading ceased to be a special accomplishment, and became necessary to every man of affairs and to every youth of breeding, came the systematic growth of an educational system and an educational literature. By the ninth and tenth centuries there are not only grammars but great lexicons, and a mass of philological learning in Islam.

And a century or so in advance of the West, there grew up in the Moslem world at a number of centres, at Basra, at Kufa, at Bagdad and Cairo, and at Cordoba, out of what were at first religious schools dependent upon mosques, a series of great universities. The light of these universities shone far beyond the Moslem world, and drew students to them from east and west. At Cordoba in particular there were great numbers of Christian students, and the influence of Arab philosophy coming by way of Spain upon the universities of Paris, Oxford, and North Italy, and upon Western European thought generally, was very considerable indeed. The name of Averroes (Ibnrushd) of Cordoba (1126–1198) stands out as that of the culminating influence of Arab philosophy upon European thought. He developed the teachings of Aristotle upon lines that made a sharp division between religious and scientific truth, and so prepared the way for the liberation of scientific research from the theological dogmatism that restrained it both under Christianity and under Islam. Another great name is that of Avicenna (Ibnsina), the Prince of Physicians (980–1037), who was born at the other end of the Arabic world at Bokhara, and who travelled in Khorasan. . . . The book-copying industry flourished at Alexandria, Damascus, Cairo, and Bagdad, and about the year 970 there were twenty-seven free schools open in Cordoba for the education of the poor.

"In mathematics," say Thatcher and Schwill,[1] "the Arabs built on the foundations of the Greek mathematicians. The origin of the so-called Arabic numerals is obscure. Under Theodoric the Great, Boëthius made use of certain signs which were in part very like the nine digits which we now use." One of the pupils of Gerbert also used signs which were still more like ours; but the zero, it is stated, was unknown until the ninth century, when it was invented by a Moslem mathematician named Muhammad-Ibn-Musa, who also was the first to use the decimal notation, and who gave the digits the value of position. This, however, is disputed by many Indians, who claim the zero and the decimal system as a distinctly Indian contribution.

"In geometry the Arabs did not add much to Euclid, but algebra is practically their creation; also, they developed spherical trigonometry, inventing the sine, tangent, and cotangent. In physics they invented the pendulum, and produced works on optics. They made progress in the science of astronomy. They built several observatories, and constructed many astronomical instruments which are still in use. They calculated the angle of the ecliptic and the precession of the equinoxes. Their knowledge of astronomy was undoubtedly considerable.

"In medicine they made great advances over the work of the Greeks. They studied physiology and hygiene, and their *materia medica* was practically the same as ours to-day. Many of their methods of treatment are still in use among us. Their surgeons understood the use of anæsthetics, and performed some of the most difficult operations known. At the time when in Europe the practice of medicine was forbidden by the Church, which expected cures to be effected by religious rites performed by the clergy, the Arabs had a real science of medicine.

---

[1] *A General History of Europe.*

"In chemistry they made a good beginning. They discovered many new substances, such as potash, nitrate of silver, corrosive sublimate, and nitric and sulphuric acid." The word "alcohol" is Arabic, though the substance was known under the name of "spirits of wine" to Pliny (A.D. 100). ". . . In manufactures they outdid the world in variety and beauty of design and perfection of workmanship. They worked in all the metals—gold, silver, copper, bronze, iron and steel. In textile fabrics they have never been surpassed. They made glass and pottery of the finest quality. They knew the secrets of dyeing, and they manufactured paper. They had many processes of dressing leather, and their work was famous throughout Europe. They made tinctures, essences and syrups. They made sugar from the cane, and grew many fine kinds of wine. They practised farming in a scientific way, and had good systems of irrigation. They knew the value of fertilizers, and adapted their crops to the quality of the ground. They excelled in horticulture, knowing how to graft and how to produce new varieties of fruit and flowers. They introduced into the West many trees and plants from the East, and wrote scientific treatises on farming."

One item in this account must be underlined here because of its importance in the intellectual life of mankind, the manufacture of paper. This the Arabs seemed to have learnt from the Chinese by way of Central Asia. The Europeans acquired it from the Arabs. Until that time books had to be written upon parchment or papyrus, and after the Arab conquest of Egypt Europe was cut off from the papyrus supply. Until paper became abundant, the art of printing was of little use, and newspapers and popular education by means of books was impossible. This was probably a much more important factor in the relative backwardness of Europe during the dark ages than historians seem disposed to admit. . . .

And all this mental life went on in the Moslem world in spite of a very considerable amount of political disorder. From first to last the Arabs never grappled with the problem, the still unsolved problem, of the stable progressive state; everywhere their form of government was absolutist and subject to the convulsions, changes, intrigues, and murders that have always characterized the extremer forms of monarchy. But for some centuries, beneath the crimes and rivalries of courts and camps, the spirit of Islam did preserve a certain general decency and restraint in life; the Byzantine Empire was impotent to shatter this civilization, and the Turkish danger in the north-east gathered strength only very slowly. Until the Turk fell upon it, the intellectual life of Islam continued. Perhaps it secretly flattered itself that it would always be able to go on, in spite of the threat of violence and unreason in its political direction. Hitherto, in all countries, that has been the characteristic attitude of science and literature. The intellectual man has been loth to come to grips with the forcible man. He has generally been something of a courtier and time-server. Possibly he has never yet been quite sure of himself. Hitherto men of reason and knowledge have never had the assurance and courage of the religious fanatic. But there can be little doubt that they have accumulated settled convictions and gathered confidence during the last few centuries; they have slowly found a means to power through the development of popular education and popular literature, and to-day they are far more disposed to say things plainly and to claim a dominating voice in the organization of human affairs than they have ever been before in the world's history.

§ 9

The Moslem conquests are associated with new types of architecture, called variously Saracenic, Mohammedan and Arabic. But the true Arab, says Gayet, was never an artist. He built, because he had to build, mosques, palaces, tombs, cities, but he found his workmen and architects among the Egyptians, Syrians, and Persians he had conquered. Arabic art in Persia was a mere continuation of Persian art, but in Egypt and Syria there was a real adaptation to new conditions and a new type and character of building and decoration appeared. This was "Arab" art strictly speaking. To the west in North Africa and Spain was developed a special variation characterized by the horseshoe arch. Syria and Egypt, long before the coming of the Arabs, had diverged from Byzantine forms by replacing the round arch by the pointed arch, and had gone far beyond Byzantine art in the disuse of modelled forms. For Hellenic realism they were substituting patterning, and the Arab temperament, contemplative and ecstatic, was all for enhancing this process. "Not to obey a religious precept," says Gayet—for there are many early Arab representative paintings—"but through an instinct." In the common matters of life, and apart from any culture, the Arab displays an extreme disinclination to strip his body or look upon a body. Gradually in the evolution of Arab art the decoration passes from conventionalized animal and vegetable forms to geometrical interlacings, "arabesques." Roofs and vaults become more and more deeply encrusted, pierced screens multiply, and even the outward form becomes polyhedral. The vaults are covered with circular and polygonal studs which descend at last like stalactites. A new mysterious beauty is produced by these suppressions and sublimations, like the beauty of crystals and ripples and the subtle and obscure rhythms of inanimate things, a beauty diametrically opposed to the unrestricted freedoms, the glorious vulgarities, the exuberant vitality, of Hellenic art.

Associated in our minds with these structural developments as characteristically Arabic are the minaret and the bulbous cupola, and a brilliant use of glazed and often richly ornamented tiles. An enormous use is made in decoration of texts and phrases from the Koran in the beautiful sweeping Arabic writing.

XXXI

CHRISTENDOM AND THE CRUSADES

§ 1. *The Western World at its Lowest Ebb.* § 2. *The Feudal System.*
§ 3. *The Frankish Kingdom of the Merovingians.* § 4. *The Christianization of the Western Barbarians.* § 5. *Charlemagne becomes Emperor of the West.* § 6. *The Personality of Charlemagne.* § 7. *Romanesque Architecture and Art.* § 8. *The French and the Germans become Distinct.*
§ 9. *The Normans, the Saracens, the Hungarians and the Seljuk Turks.*
§ 10. *How Constantinople Appealed to Rome.* § 11. *The Crusades.*
§ 12. *The Crusades a Test of Christianity.* § 13. *The Emperor Frederick II.* § 14. *Defects and Limitations of the Papacy.* § 15. *A List of Leading Popes.* § 16. *Gothic Architecture and Art.* § 17. *Mediæval Music.*

§ 1

LET us turn again now from this intellectual renascence in the cradle of the ancient civilizations to the affairs of the Western world.

We have described the complete economic, social, and political break-up of the Roman imperial system in the West, the confusion and darkness that followed in the sixth and seventh centuries, and the struggles of such men as Cassiodorus to keep alight the flame of human learning amidst these windy confusions. For a time it would be idle to write of states and rulers. Smaller or greater adventurers seized a castle or a countryside and ruled an uncertain area. The British Islands, for instance, were split up amidst a multitude of rulers; and numerous Keltic chiefs in Ireland and Scotland and Wales and Cornwall fought and prevailed over and succumbed to each other: the English invaders were also divided into a number of fluctuating "kingdoms," Kent, Wessex, Essex, Sussex, Mercia, Northumbria and East Anglia, which were constantly at war with one another.

So it was over most of the Western world. Here a bishop would be the monarch, as Gregory the Great was in Rome; here a town or a group of towns would be under the rule of the duke or prince of this or that. Amidst the vast ruins of the city of Rome, half-independent families of quasi-noble adventurers and their retainers maintained themselves. The Pope kept a sort of general predominance there, but he was sometimes more than balanced by a "Duke of Rome." The great arena of the Colosseum had been made into a privately-owned castle, and so, too, had the vast circular tomb of the Emperor Hadrian; and the adventurers who had possession of these strongholds and their partisans waylaid each other and fought and bickered in the ruinous streets of the once imperial city. The Tomb of Hadrian was known after the days of Gregory the Great as the Castle of St. Angelo, the Castle of the Holy Angel, because, when he was crossing the bridge over the Tiber, on his way to St. Peter's to pray against the great pestilence which was devastating the city, he had had a vision of a great angel standing over the dark mass of the mausoleum and sheathing a sword, and he had known then that his prayers would be answered. This Castle of St. Angelo played a very important part in Roman affairs during this age of disorder.

Spain was in much the same state of political fragmentation as Italy or France or Britain; and in Spain the old feud of Carthaginian and Roman was still continued in the bitter hostility of their descendants and heirs, the Jew and the Christian. So that when the power of the Caliph had swept along the North African coast to the Straits of Gibraltar, it found in the Spanish Jews ready helpers in its invasion of Europe. A Moslem army of Arabs and of Berbers, the nomadic Hamitic people of the African desert and mountain hinterland who had been converted to Islam, crossed and defeated the West Goths in a great battle in 711. In a few years the whole country was in their possession.

In 720 Islam had reached the Pyrenees, and had pushed round their eastern end into France; and for a time it seemed that the faith was likely to subjugate Gaul as easily as it had subjugated the Spanish peninsula. But presently it struck against something hard, a new kingdom of the Franks, which had been consolidating itself for some two centuries in the Rhineland and North France.

Of this Frankish kingdom, the precursor of France and Germany, which formed the western bulwark of Europe against the faith of Muhammad, as the Byzantine Empire behind the Taurus Mountains formed the eastern, we shall now have much to tell; but first we must give some account of the new system of social groupings out of which it arose.

§ 2

It is necessary that the reader should have a definite idea of the social condition of Western Europe in the eighth century. It was not a barbarism. Eastern Europe was still barbaric and savage; things had progressed but little beyond the state of affairs described by Gibbon in his account of the mission of Priscus to Attila (see ch. 27, § 6). But Western Europe was a shattered civilization without law, without administration, with roads destroyed and education disorganized, but still with great numbers of people with civilized ideas and habits and traditions.

It was a time of confusion, of brigandage, of crimes unpunished and universal insecurity. It is very interesting to trace how, out of the universal mêlée, the beginnings of a new order appeared. In a modern breakdown there would probably be the formation of local vigilance societies, which would combine and restore a police administration and a roughly democratic rule. But in the broken-down Western Empire of the sixth, seventh, and eighth centuries, men's ideas turned rather to leaders than to committees, and the centres about which affairs crystallized were here barbaric chiefs, here a vigorous bishop or some surviving claimant to a Roman official position, here a long-recognized landowner or man of ancient family, and here again some vigorous usurper of power. No solitary man was safe.

So men were forced to link themselves with others, preferably people stronger than themselves. The lonely man chose the most powerful and active person in his district and became *his* man. The freeman or the weak lordling of a petty territory linked himself to some more powerful lord. The protection of that lord (or the danger of his hostility) became more considerable with every such accession. So very rapidly they went on a process of political crystallization in the confused and lawless sea into which the Western Empire had liquefied. These natural associations and alliances of protector and subordinates grew very rapidly into a sort of system, *the feudal system,* traces of which are still to be found in the social structure of every European community west of Russia. It varied enormously in its manifestations.

This process speedily took on technical forms and laws of its own. In such a country as Gaul it was already well in progress in the days of insecurity *before* the barbarian tribes broke into the empire as conquerors. The Franks when they came into Gaul brought with them an institution, which we have already noted in the case of the Macedonians, and which was probably of very wide distribution among the Nordic people, the gathering about the chief or war king of a body of young men of good family, the companions or *comitatus,* his counts or captains. It was natural in the case of invading peoples that the relations of a weak lord to a strong lord should take on the relations of a count to his king, and that a conquering chief should divide seized and confiscated estates among his companions. From the side of the decaying empire that came to feudalism the idea of the grouping for mutual protection of men and estates; from the Teutonic side came the notions of knightly association, devotion, and personal service. The former was the economic side of the institution, the latter the chivalrous.

The analogy of the aggregation of feudal groupings with crystallization is a very close one. As the historian watches the whirling and eddying confusion of the fourth and fifth centuries in Western Europe, he begins to perceive the appearance of these pyramidal growths of heads and subordinates and subsubordinates, which jostle against one another, branch, dissolve again, or coalesce. "We use the term 'feudal system' for convenience' sake, but with a degree of impropriety if it conveys the meaning 'systematic.' Feudalism in its most flourishing age was anything but systematic. It was confusion roughly organized. Great diversity prevailed everywhere, and we should not be surprised to find some different fact or custom in every lordship. Anglo-Norman feudalism attained in the eleventh and twelfth centuries a logical completeness and a uniformity of practice which, in the feudal age proper, can hardly be found elsewhere through so large a territory. . . .

"The foundation of the feudal relationship proper was the *fief,* which was usually land, but might be any desirable thing, as an office, a revenue in money or kind, the right to collect a toll, or operate a mill. In return for the fief, the man became the *vassal* of his lord; he knelt before him, and, with his hands between his lord's hands, promised him fealty and service. . . . The faithful performance of all the duties he had assumed in homage constituted the vassal's right and title to his fief. So long as they were fulfilled, he, and his heir after him, held the fief as his property, practically and in relation to all under tenants as if he were the owner. In the ceremony of homage and investiture, which is the creative contract of feudalism, the obligations assumed by the two parties were, as a rule, not specified in exact terms. They were determined by local custom. . . . In many points of detail the vassal's services differed widely in different parts of the feudal world. We may say, however, that they fall into two classes, general and specific. The general included all that might come under the idea of loyalty, seeking the lord's interests, keeping

his secrets, betraying the plans of his enemies, protecting his family, etc. The specific services are capable of more definite statement, and they usually received exact definition in custom and sometimes in written documents. The most characteristic of these was the military service, which included appearance in the field on summons with a certain force, often armed in a specified way, and remaining a specified length of time. It often included, also, the duty of guarding the lord's castle, and of holding one's own castle subject to the plans of the lord for the defence of his fief. . . . Theoretically regarded, feudalism covered Europe with a network of these fiefs, rising in graded ranks one above the other from the smallest, the knight's fee, at the bottom, to the king at the top, who was the supreme landowner, or who held the kingdom from God. . . ."[1]

But this was the theory that was superimposed upon the established facts. The reality of feudalism was its voluntary co-operation.

"The feudal state was one in which, it has been said, private law had usurped the place of public law." But rather is it truer that public law had failed and vanished and private law had come in to fill the vacuum. Public duty had become private obligation.

§ 3

We have already mentioned various kingdoms of the barbarian tribes who set up a more or less flimsy dominion over this or that area amidst the debris of the empire, the kingdoms of the Suevi and West Goths in Spain, the East-Gothic kingdom in Italy, and the Italian Lombard kingdom which succeeded the Goths after Justinian had expelled the latter and after the great pestilence had devastated Italy.

The Frankish kingdom was another such barbarian power which arose first in what is now Belgium, and which spread southward to the Loire, but it developed far more strength and solidarity than any of the others. It was the first real state to emerge from the universal wreckage. It became at last a wide and vigorous political reality, and from it are derived two great powers of modern Europe, France and the German Empire. Its founder was Clovis (481–511), who began as a small king in Belgium and ended with his southern frontiers nearly at the Pyrenees. He divided his kingdom among his four sons, but the Franks retained a tradition of unity in spite of this division, and for a time fraternal wars for a single control united rather than divided them. A more serious split arose, however, through the Latinization of the Western Franks, who occupied Romanized Gaul and who learnt to speak the corrupt Latin of the subject population, while the Franks of the Rhineland retained their Low German speech. At a low level of civilization, differences in language cause very powerful political strains. For a hundred and fifty years the Frankish world was split in two, Neustria, the nucleus of France, speaking a Latinish speech, which became at last the French language we know, and Austrasia, the Rhineland, which remained German. The Franks differed from the Swabians and South Germans, and came much nearer the Anglo-Saxons in that they spoke a "Low German" and not a "High German" dialect. Their language resembled Plattdeutsch and Anglo-Saxon, and was the direct parent of Dutch and Flemish. In fact, the Franks where they were not Latinized became Flemings and "Dutchmen" of South Holland (North Holland is still Friesisch—i.e., Anglo-Saxon). The "French" which the Latinized Franks and Burgundians spoke in the seventh to the tenth centuries was remarkably like the Rumansch language of Switzerland, judging from the vestiges that remain in old documents.

---

[1] *Encyclopædia Britannica* Twelfth Edition, article "Feudalism," by Professor G. B. Adams.

We will not tell here of the decay of the dynasty, the Merovingian dynasty, founded by Clovis; nor how in Austrasia a certain court official, the Mayor of the Palace, gradually became the king *de facto* and used the real king as a puppet. The position of Mayor of the Palace also became hereditary in the seventh century, and in 687 a certain Pepin of Heristhal, the Austrasian Mayor of the Palace, had conquered Neustria and reunited all the Franks. He was followed in 721 by his son, Charles Martel, who also bore no higher title than Mayor of the Palace. (His poor little Merovingian kings do not matter in the slightest degree to us here.) It was this Charles Martel who stopped the Moslems. They had pushed as far as Tours when he met them, and in a great

Area more or less under FRANKISH dominion in the time of CHARLES MARTEL

battle between that place and Poitiers (732) utterly defeated them and broke their spirit. Thereafter the Pyrenees remained their utmost boundary; they came no further into Western Europe.

Charles Martel divided his power between two sons, but one resigned and went into a monastery, leaving his brother Pepin sole ruler. This Pepin it was who finally extinguished the descendants of Clovis. He sent to the Pope to ask who was the true king of the Franks, the man who held the power or the man who wore the crown; and the Pope, who was in need of a supporter, decided in favour of the Mayor of the Palace. So Pepin was chosen king at a gathering of the Frankish nobles in the Merovingian capital, Soissons, and anointed and crowned. That was in 751. The Franco-Germany he united was consolidated

by his son Charlemagne. It held together until the death of his grandson Louis
(840), and then France and Germany broke away again—to the great injury
of mankind. It was not a difference of race or temperament, it was a difference
of language and tradition that split these Frankish peoples asunder.

That old separation of Neustria and Austrasia still works out in bitter consequences. In 1916 the ancient conflict of Neustria and Austrasia had broken
out into war once more. In the August of that year the present writer visited
Soissons, and crossed the temporary wooden bridge that had been built by
the English after the battle of the Aisne from the main part of the town to
the suburb of Saint Médard. Canvas screens protected passengers upon the
bridge from the observation of the German sharpshooters who were sniping
from their trenches down the curve of the river. He went with his guides across
a field and along by the wall of an orchard in which a German shell exploded
as he passed. So he reached the battered buildings that stand upon the site of
the ancient Abbey of St. Médard, in which the last Merovingian was deposed
and Pepin the Short was crowned in his stead. Beneath these ancient buildings
there were great crypts, very useful as dug-outs—for the German advanced
lines were not more than a couple of hundred yards away. The sturdy French
soldier lads were cooking and resting in these shelters, and lying down to
sleep among the stone coffins that had held the bones of their Merovingian
kings.

§ 4

The populations over which Charles Martel and King Pepin ruled were at
very different levels of civilization in different districts. To the west and south
the bulk of the people consisted of Latinized and Christian Kelts; in the central
regions these rulers had to deal with such more or less Christianized Germans
as the Franks and Burgundians and Alemanni; to the north-east were still pagan Frisians and Saxons; to the east were the Bavarians, recently Christianized
through the activities of St. Boniface, and to the east of them again pagan
Slavs and Avars. The "paganism" of the Germans and Slavs was very similar
to the primitive religion of the Greeks; it was a manly religion in which temple,
priest, and sacrifices played a small part, and its gods were like men, a kind
of "school prefects" of more powerful beings who interfered impulsively and
irregularly in human affairs. The Germans had a Jupiter in Odin, a Mars in
Thor, a Venus in Freya, and so on. Throughout the seventh and eighth centuries a steady process of conversion to Christianity went on amidst these German and Slavonic tribes.

It will be interesting to English-speaking readers to note that the most zeal-
ous and successful missionaries among the Saxons and Frisians came from
England. Christianity was twice planted in the British Isles. It was already
there while Britain was a part of the Roman Empire; a martyr, St. Alban,
gave his name to the town of St. Albans, and nearly every visitor to Canterbury
has also visited little old St. Martin's Church which was used during the Roman times. From Britain, as we have already said, Christianity spread beyond

the imperial boundaries into Ireland—the chief missionary was St. Patrick—and there was a vigorous monastic movement with which are connected the names of St. Columba and the religious settlements of Iona. Then in the fifth and sixth centuries came the fierce and pagan English, and they cut off the early Church of Ireland from the main body of Christianity. In the seventh century Christian missionaries were converting the English, both in the north from Ireland and in the south from Rome. The Rome mission was sent by Pope Gregory the Great just at the close of the sixth century. The story goes that he saw English boys for sale in the Roman slave market, though it is a little difficult to understand how they got there. They were very fair and good-looking. In answer to his inquiries, he was told that they were Angles. "Not Angles, but Angels," said he, "had they but the gospel."

The mission worked through the seventh century. Before that century was over, most of the English were Christians; though Mercia, the central English kingdom, held out stoutly against the priests and for the ancient faith and ways. And there was a swift progress in learning upon the part of these new converts. The monasteries of the kingdom of Northumbria in the north of England became a centre of light and learning. Theodore of Tarsus was one of the earliest archbishops of Canterbury (668–690). "While Greek was utterly unknown in the west of Europe, it was mastered by some of the pupils of Theodore. The monasteries contained many monks who were excellent scholars. Most famous of all was Bede, known as the Venerable Bede (673–735), a monk of Jarrow (on Tyne). He had for his pupils the six hundred monks of that monastery, besides the many strangers who came to hear him. He gradually mastered all the learning of his day, and left at his death forty-five volumes of his writings, the most important of which are 'The Ecclesiastical History of the English' and his translation of the Gospel of John into English. His writings were widely known and used throughout Europe. He reckoned all dates from the birth of Christ, and through his works the use of Christian chronology became common in Europe. Owing to the large number of monasteries and monks in Northumbria that part of England was for a time far in advance of the south in civilization."[1]

In the seventh and eighth centuries we find the English missionaries active upon the eastern frontiers of the Frankish kingdom. Chief among these was St. Boniface (680–755), who was born at Crediton, in Devonshire, who converted the Frisians, Thuringians, and Hessians, and who was martyred in Holland.

Both in England and on the Continent the ascendant rulers seized upon Christianity as a unifying force to cement their conquests. Christianity became a banner for aggressive chiefs—as it did in Uganda in Africa in the bloody days before that country was annexed to the British Empire.

After Pepin, who died in 768, came two sons, Charles and another, who divided his kingdom; but the brother of Charles died in 771, and Charles then became sole king (771–814) of the growing realm of the Franks. This

---

[1] *A General History of Europe,* Thatcher and Schwill.

Charles is known in history as Charles the Great, or Charlemagne. As in the case of Alexander the Great and Julius Cæsar, posterity has enormously exaggerated his memory. He made his wars of aggression definitely religious wars. All the world of North-western Europe which is now Great Britain, France, Germany, Denmark, and Norway and Sweden, was in the ninth century an arena of bitter conflict between the old faith and the new. Whole na-

tions were converted to Christianity by the sword, just as Islam in Arabia, Central Asia, and Africa had converted whole nations a century or so before.

With fire and sword Charlemagne preached the Gospel of the Cross to the Saxons, Bohemians, and as far as the Danube into what is now Hungary; he carried the same teaching down the Adriatic coast, through what is now Dalmatia, and drove the Moslems back from the Pyrenees as far as Barcelona.

Moreover, he it was who sheltered Egbert, an exile from Wessex, in England, and assisted him presently to establish himself as king in Wessex (802). Egbert subdued the Britons in Cornwall, as Charlemagne conquered the Britons of Brittany, and, by a series of wars, which he continued after the death of his Frankish patron, made himself at last the first King of all England (828).

But the attacks of Charlemagne upon the last strongholds of paganism pro-

voked a vigorous reaction on the part of the unconverted. The Christianized English had retained very little of the seamanship that had brought them from the mainland, and the Franks had not yet become seamen. As the Christian propaganda of Charlemagne swept towards the shores of the North and Baltic seas, the pagans were driven to the sea. They retaliated for the Christian persecutions with plundering raids and expeditions against the northern coasts of France and against Christian England.

These pagan Saxons and English of the mainland and their kindred from Denmark and Norway are the Danes and Northmen of our national histories. They were also called Vikings,[1] which means "inletmen," because they came from the deep inlets of the Scandinavian coast. They came in long black galleys, making little use of sails. Most of our information about these wars and invasions of the pagan Vikings is derived from Christian sources, and so we have abundant information of the massacres and atrocities of their raids and very little about the cruelties inflicted upon their pagan brethren, the Saxons, at the hands of Charlemagne. Their animus against the Cross and against monks and nuns was extreme. They delighted in the burning of monasteries and nunneries and the slaughter of their inmates.

Throughout the period between the fifth and the ninth centuries these Vikings or Northmen were learning seamanship, becoming bolder, and ranging further. They braved the northern seas until the icy shores of Greenland were a familiar haunt, and by the ninth century they had settlements (of which Europe in general knew nothing) in America. The Northmen had no permanent settlement in America. Somewhere about 1,000 there was an attempt to settle in some part of America called "Vinland," but the land was held only for two years. A skin canoe appeared one day full of painted Indians, who struck the Northmen as very ugly customers. There seems to have been a silent, mutual inspection, but no trade nor conflict. The new world stared at the old. Later there was trouble, and the Northmen, outnumbered and far from home, packed up and re-embarked. No other Northmen settlement upon American soil is recorded. In the twelfth century many of their sagas began to be written down in Iceland. They saw the world in terms of valiant adventure. They assailed the walrus, the bear, and the whale. In their imaginations, a great and rich city to the south, a sort of confusion of Rome and Byzantium, loomed large. They called it "Miklagard" (the great city—compare Icelandic Miklabaer "the great farm") or Micklegarth. The magnetism of Micklegarth was to draw the descendants of these Northmen down into the Mediterranean by two routes, by the west and also across Russia from the Baltic, as we shall tell later. By the Russian route went also the kindred Swedes.

So long as Charlemagne and Egbert lived, the Vikings were no more than raiders; but as the ninth century wore on, these raids developed into organized invasions. In several districts of England the hold of Christianity was by no means firm as yet. In Mercia, in particular, the pagan Northmen found sympathy and help. By 886 the Danes had conquered a fair part of England, and the English king, Alfred the Great, had recognized their rule over their conquests, the Dane-law, in the pact he made with Guthrum their leader.

A little later, in 911, another expedition under Rolf the Ganger established itself upon the coast of France in the region that was known henceforth as Normandy (=Northman-dy).

But of how there was presently a fresh conquest of England by the Danes, and how finally the Duke of Normandy became King of England, we cannot

---

[1] N. B.—Vik-ings, not Vi-kings: Vik = a fiord or inlet.

tell at any length. There were very small racial and social differences between Angle, Saxon, Jute, Dane, or Norman; and though these changes loom large in the imaginations of the English, they are seen to be very slight rufflings indeed of the stream of history when we measure them by the standards of a greater world.

The issue between Christianity and paganism vanished presently from the struggle. By the Treaty of Wedmore the Danes agreed to be baptized if they were assured of their conquests; and the descendants of Rolf in Normandy were not merely Christianized, but they learnt to speak French from the more civilized people about them, forgetting their own Norse tongue. Of much greater significance in the history of mankind are the relations of Charlemagne with his neighbours to the south and east, and to the imperial tradition.

§ 5

Through Charlemagne the tradition of the Roman Cæsar was revived in Europe. The Roman Empire was dead and decaying; the Byzantine Empire was far gone in decline; but the education and mentality of Europe had sunken to a level at which new creative political ideas were probably impossible. In all Europe there survived not a tithe of the speculative vigour that we find in the Athenian literature of the fifth century B.C. There was no power to postulate a new occasion or to conceive and organize a novel political method.

Official Christianity had long overlaid and accustomed itself to ignore those strange teachings of Jesus of Nazareth from which it had arisen. The Roman Church, clinging tenaciously to its possession of the title of *pontifex maximus*, had long since abandoned its appointed task of achieving the Kingdom of Heaven. It was preoccupied with the revival of Roman ascendancy on earth, which it conceived of as its inheritance. It had become a political body, using the faith and needs of simple men to forward its schemes. It clung to the tradition of the Roman Empire and to the idea that it was the natural method of European unity. Europe, in a series of attempts to restore it, drifted towards a dreary imitation and revival of the misconceived failures of the past.

For eleven centuries, from Charlemagne onwards, "Emperors" and "Cæsars" of this line and that come and go in the history of Europe like fancies in a disordered mind. We shall have to tell of a great process of mental growth in Europe, of enlarged horizons and accumulating power, but it was a process that went on independently of, and in spite of, the political forms of the time, until at last it shattered those forms altogether. Europe, during those eleven centuries of the imitation Cæsars which began with Charlemagne, and which closed only in the monstrous bloodshed of 1914–1918, has been like a busy factory owned by a somnambulist, who is sometimes quite unimportant and sometimes disastrously in the way. Or, rather than a somnambulist, let us say by a corpse that magically simulates a kind of life. The Roman Empire staggers, sprawls, is thrust off the stage, and reappears, and—if we may carry the image one step further—it is the Church of Rome which plays the part of the magician and keeps this corpse alive.

And throughout the whole period there is always a struggle going on for the control of the corpse between the spiritual and various temporal powers. We have already noted the spirit of St. Augustine's *City of God*. It was a book which we know Charlemagne read, or had read to him—for his literary accomplishments are rather questionable. He conceived of this Christian Empire as being ruled and maintained in its orthodoxy by some such great Cæsar as himself. He was to rule even the Pope.

But at Rome the view taken of the revived empire differed a little from that. There the view taken was that the Christian Cæsar must be anointed and guided by the Pope—who would even have the power to excommunicate and depose him. Even in the time of Charlemagne this divergence of view was apparent. In the following centuries it became acute.

The idea of the revived Empire dawned only very gradually upon the mind of Charlemagne. At first he was simply the ruler of his father's kingdom of the Franks, and his powers were fully occupied in struggles with the Saxons and Bavarians, and with the Slavs to the east of them, with the Moslem in Spain, and with various insurrections in his own dominions. And as the result of a quarrel with the King of Lombardy, his father-in-law, he conquered Lombardy and North Italy. We have noted the establishment of the Lombards in North Italy about 570 after the great pestilence, and after the overthrow of the East Gothic kings by Justinian. These Lombards had always been a danger and a fear to the Popes, and there had been an alliance between Pope and Frankish King against them in the time of Pepin. Now Charlemagne completely subjugated Lombardy (774), sent his father-in-law to a monastery, and carried his conquests beyond the present north-eastern boundaries of Italy into Dalmatia in 776. In 781 he caused one of his sons, Pepin, who did not outlive him, to be crowned King of Italy in Rome.

There was a new Pope, Leo III, in 795, who seems from the first to have resolved to make Charlemagne emperor. Hitherto the Court at Byzantium had possessed a certain indefinite authority over the Pope. Strong emperors like Justinian had bullied the Popes and obliged them to come to Constantinople; weak emperors had annoyed them ineffectively. The idea of a breach, both secular and religious, with Constantinople had long been entertained at the Lateran,[1] and in the Frankish power there seemed to be just the support that was necessary if Constantinople was to be defied.

So at his accession Leo III sent the keys of the tomb of St. Peter and a banner to Charlemagne as the symbols of his sovereignty in Rome as King of Italy. Very soon the Pope had to appeal to the protection he had chosen. He was unpopular in Rome; he was attacked and ill-treated in the streets during a procession, and obliged to fly to Germany (799). Eginhard says his eyes were gouged out and his tongue cut off; he seems, however, to have had both eyes and tongue again a year later. Charlemagne brought him back and reinstated him (800).

Then occurred a very important scene. On Christmas Day in the year 800,

---

[1] The Lateran was the earlier palace of the Popes in Rome. Later they occupied the Vatican.

as Charles was rising from prayer in the Church of St. Peter, the Pope, who had everything in readiness, clapped a crown upon his head and hailed him Cæsar and Augustus. There was great popular applause. But Eginhard, the friend and biographer of Charlemagne, says that the new emperor was by no means pleased by this coup of Pope Leo's. If he had known this was to happen, he said, "he would not have entered the church, great festival though it was."

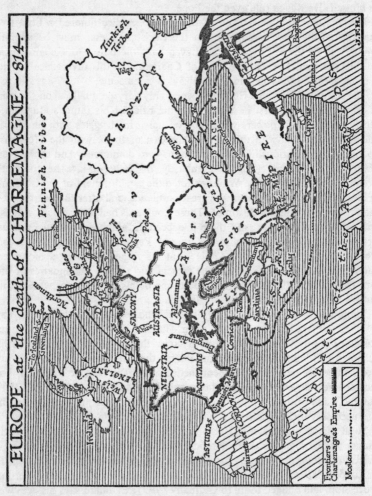

No doubt he had been thinking and talking of making himself emperor, but he had evidently not intended that the Pope should make him emperor. He had had some idea of marrying the Empress Irene, who at that time reigned in Constantinople, and so becoming monarch of both Eastern and Western Empires. He was now obliged to accept the title in the manner that Leo III had adopted, as a gift from the Pope, and in a way that estranged Constantinople and secured the separation of Rome from the Byzantine Church. At first Byzantium was unwilling to recognize the imperial title of Charlemagne. But in 811 a great disaster fell upon the Byzantine Empire. The pagan Bulgarians, under their Prince Krum (802–815), defeated and destroyed the armies of the Emperor Nicephorus, whose skull became a drinking-cup for Krum. The great part of the Balkan peninsula was conquered by these people. (The Bulgarian and the English nations thus became established as political unities almost simultaneously.) After this misfortune Byzantium did not dispute this revival of the empire in the West, and in 812 Charlemagne was formally recognized by Byzantine envoys as Emperor and Augustus.

Thus the Empire of Rome, which had died at the hands of Odoacer in 476, rose again in 800 as the "Holy Roman Empire." While its physical strength lay north of the Alps, the centre of its idea was Rome. It was, therefore, from the beginning a divided thing of uncertain power, a claim and an argument rather than a necessary reality. The German sword was always clattering over the Alps into Italy, and missions and legates toiling over in the reverse direction. But the Germans could never hold Italy permanently, because they could not stand the malaria that the ruined, neglected, undrained country fostered. And in Rome, as well as in several other of the cities of Italy, there smouldered a more ancient tradition, the tradition of the aristocratic republic, hostile to both Emperor and Pope.

§ 6

In spite of the fact that we have a life of him written by his contemporary, Eginhard,[1] the character and personality of Charlemagne are difficult to visualize. Eginhard lacks vividness; he tells many particulars, but not the particulars that make a man live again in the record. Charlemagne, he says, was a tall man, with a rather feeble voice; and he had bright eyes and a long nose. "The top of his head was round," whatever that may mean, and his hair was "white." He had a thick, rather short neck, and "his belly too prominent." He wore a tunic with a silver border, and gartered hose. He had a blue cloak, and was always girt with his sword, hilt and belt being of gold and silver.

He was evidently a man of great activity—one imagines him moving quickly—and his numerous love affairs did not interfere at all with his incessant military and political labours. He had numerous wives and mistresses. He took much exercise, was fond of pomp and religious ceremonies, and gave generously. He was a man of very miscellaneous activity and great intellectual enterprise, and with a self-confidence that is rather suggestive of William II, the ex-German Emperor—the last, perhaps for ever, of this series of imitation Cæsars in Europe which Charlemagne began.

The mental life that Eginhard records of him is interesting, because it not only gives glimpses of a curious character, but serves as a sample of the intellectuality of the time. He could read; probably, at meals he "listened to

---

[1] Eginhard's *Life of Karl the Great*.

music or reading," but we are told that he had not acquired the art of writing; "he used to keep his writing-book and tablets under his pillow, that when he had leisure he might practise his hand in forming letters, but he made little progress in an art begun too late in life." He had, however, a real respect for learning and a real desire for knowledge, and he did his utmost to attract men of learning to his Court. Among others who came was Alcuin, a learned Englishman.

All those learned men were, of course, clergymen, there being no other learned men, and naturally they gave a strongly clerical tinge to the information they imparted to their master. At his Court, which was usually at Aix-la-Chapelle or Mayence, he maintained in the winter months a curious institution called his "school," in which he and his erudite associates affected to lay aside all thoughts of worldly position, assumed names taken from the classical writers or from Holy Writ, and discoursed upon theology and literature. Charlemagne himself was "David." He developed a considerable knowledge of theology, and it is to him that we must ascribe the proposal to add the words *filio que* to the Nicene Creed—an addition that finally split the Latin and Greek churches asunder. But it is more than doubtful if he had any such separation in mind. He wanted to add a word or so to the creed, just as the Emperor William II wanted to write operas and paint pictures, and he took up what was originally a Spanish innovation. It was not accepted until much later; Pope Leo discreetly opposed it. When at last it was accepted, it was probably taken with the deliberate intention of making a breach with the Greek Church. The point involved is a subtle but vital one, upon which the writer can offer no opinion. Latin Christendom believes that the Holy Ghost proceeds from the Father *and the Son;* Greek and Eastern Christians, that the Holy Spirit proceeds from the Father, without any mention of the Son. The latter attitude seems to incline a little towards the Arian point of view. Of the organization of the empire by Charlemagne there is little to be said here. He was far too restless and busy to consider the quality of his successor or the condition of political stability, and the most noteworthy thing in this relationship is that he particularly schooled his son and successor, Louis the Pious (814–840), to take the crown from the altar and *crown himself*. But Louis the Pious was too pious to adhere to those instructions when the Pope made an objection.

The legislation of Charlemagne was greatly coloured by Bible-reading; he knew his Bible well, as the times went; and it is characteristic of him that after he had been crowned emperor he required every male subject above the age of twelve to renew his oath of allegiance, and to undertake to be not simply a good subject but a good Christian. To refuse baptism and to retract after baptism were crimes punishable by death.

He did much to encourage architecture, and imported many Italian architects, chiefly from Ravenna, to whom we owe many of the pleasant buildings that still at Worms and Cologne and elsewhere delight the tourist in the Rhineland. He did much to develop that Romanesque architecture which we shall describe in the next section. He founded a number of cathedrals and monastic schools, did much to encourage the study of classical Latin, and was a distinguished amateur of church music. The possibility of his talking Latin and understanding Greek is open to discussion; probably he talked French-Latin. Frankish, however, was his habitual tongue. He made a collection of old German songs and tales, but these were destroyed by his successor, Louis the Pious, on account of their paganism.

He corresponded with Haroun-al-Raschid, the Abbasid Caliph at Bagdad, who was not, perhaps, the less friendly to him on account of his vigorous handling of the Omayyad Arabs in Spain. Gibbon supposes that this "public correspondence was founded on vanity," and that "their remote situation left no room for a competition of interest." But with the Byzantine Empire between them in the East, and the independent caliphate of Spain in the West, and a common danger in the Turks of the great plains, they had three very excellent reasons for cordiality. Haroun-al-Raschid, says Gibbon, sent Charlemagne by his ambassadors a splendid tent, a water-clock, an elephant, and the keys of the Holy Sepulchre. The last item suggests that Charlemagne was to some extent regarded by the Saracen monarch as the protector of the Christians and Christian properties in his dominions. Some historians declare explicitly that there was a treaty to that effect.

§ 7

While in the East, under Christian influence, the floridly balanced and stereotyped architecture of the Roman Empire, the architecture of Palmyra and Baalbek, was being modified rapidly and profoundly into the stiff unfleshly richness of the Byzantine style, in the West it was undergoing similar but not exactly parallel developments. The name "Romanesque" has been spread over a great variety of buildings which show a common quality because they derived from the Roman tradition, attenuated and restrained by the general impoverishment of the world, but which everywhere testify also to new racial influences and new social necessities. There were no more amphitheatres, no great aqueducts, no triumphal arches, no temples to the gods. There were fortresses and castles, round or square and massive, churches and towers. The tower now for the first time becomes important in Europe. Architecture ascends. Hitherto we have had to note towers only in Mesopotamia. Buildings in the Egyptian and Hellenic and Roman world did not attempt to scale the heavens. In Roman and Hellenic fortifications and in the Great Wall of China there are towers, parts of the defences, but that is almost all there is to tell of until the Christian era. Then in a world raided by Huns, Arabs, sea pirates of all sorts—we shall tell of the Northmen, Saracens and Hungarians in another section—the tower becomes a necessity. The church for the new congregational religion is another necessity, and the two come naturally together.

The new book and idea religions, Christianity and Islam, had this in common: they sought to reach the mind of everyone. The people had to be got together into the place of worship and sacrifice; they had to be reminded of prayer and belief. So Islamic architecture shot up its most delicate flower, the minaret, from which the people could be called and exhorted. Christianity could no longer do with the small dark temple of the older gods; churches had to be built big, to hold all the believers in the countryside. And the people had to be summoned from the bell tower, the campanile. The type of the imperial temple was abandoned; the need for a roomy building turned the Christian architects to the model of the Roman law courts, the basilicas.

It is impossible in the space at our disposal to trace the wide variations of "Romanesque" as it merged into Byzantine art to the east and was modified by Norman, Saxon, and Frank. But the phase of stability under Charlemagne gathered together the artistic forces of Western Europe under his protection, and it is in such buildings as the Cathedral of Aix-la-Chapelle that the Romanesque style reaches its most distinctive expression.

A parallel but not so complete a disappearance of the modelled reality which we have noted in Byzantine and Arabic art went on in Western Europe in these insecure ages. The sculptor who could deal vigorously with the poses of man or beast was no longer to be found on earth west of India. Painting had taken refuge in the monasteries. The illumination of books had been carried to high levels in the Roman and Hellenic empires, and it never altogether died out. The coming and going of the Christian monks kept it alive and freshened it by an exchange of methods and ideas. The Irish monasteries were producing manuscripts of great beauty as early as the seventh century. The *Book of Kells,* a copy of the Gospels, in Trinity College, Dublin, is of this date. Celtic work is curiously parallel to early Arabic work in its decorative suppression of living forms. Its colour and design are marvelous; its drawing contemptible. Celtic influences mingled with classical and Byzantine in the artistic revival at the Court of Charlemagne. There the illuminated MS. loaded with gold rose to its most brilliant levels.

A disposition to representative art and outline figures appears rebelliously in some of the English and Norman work and presently breaks away towards miniature pictures. But the gradual deterioration of MS. illumination and the disappearance of initiative therein, due to the diversion of artistic energy to other media, became marked only in the twelfth and thirteenth centuries.

§ 8

The Empire of Charlemagne did not outlive his son and successor, Louis the Pious. It fell apart into its main constituents. The Latinized Keltic and Frankish population of Gaul begins now to be recognizable as France, though this France was broken up into a number of dukedoms and principalities, often with no more than a nominal unity; the German-speaking peoples between the Rhine and the Slavs to the east similarly begin to develop an even more fragmentary intimation of Germany. When at length a real emperor reappears in Western Europe (962) he is not a Frank, but a Saxon; the conquered in Germany have become the masters.

We see here the first intimations of a new sort of political aggregation in Europe, the dawn of what we now call nationalism. It is like the beginning of a process of crystallization, a separation out, in the entirely confused medley which has followed the shattering of the imperial order.

It is impossible here to trace the events of the ninth and tenth centuries in any detail, the alliances, the treacheries, the claims and acquisitions. Everywhere there was lawlessness, war, and a struggle for power. In 987 the nominal kingdom of France passed from the hands of the Carlovingians, the last descendants of Charlemagne, into the hands of Hugh Capet, who founded a new dynasty. Most of his alleged subordinates were in fact independent, and willing to make war on the king at the slightest provocation. The dominions of the Duke of Normandy, for example, were more extensive and more powerful than the patrimony of Hugh Capet. Almost the only unity of this France over which the king exercised a nominal authority lay in the common resolution of its great provinces to resist incorporation in any empire dominated either by a German ruler or by the Pope. Apart from the simple organization dictated by that common will, France was a mosaic of practically independent nobles. It was an era of castle-building and fortification, and what was called "private war," throughout all Europe.

The state of Rome in the tenth century is almost indescribable. The decay of the Empire of Charlemagne left the Pope without a protector, threatened by Byzantium and the Saracens (who had taken Sicily), and face to face with the unruly nobles of Rome. Among the most powerful of these were two women, Theodora and Marozia, mother and daughter,[1] who in succession held the Castle of St. Angelo (§ 1), which Theophylact, the patrician husband of Theodora, had seized together with most of the temporal power of the Pope. These two women were as bold, unscrupulous, and dissolute as any male prince of the time could have been, and they are abused by historians as though they were ten times worse. Marozia seized and imprisoned Pope John X (928), who speedily died under her care. Her mother, Theodora, had been his mistress. Marozia subsequently made her illegitimate son Pope under the title of John XI.

After him, her grandson, John XII, filled the chair of St. Peter. Gibbon's account of the manners and morals of John XII takes refuge at last beneath a veil of Latin footnotes. This Pope, John XII, was finally degraded by the new German Emperor Otto, who came over the Alps and down into Italy to be crowned in 962.

This new line of Saxon emperors, which thus comes into prominence, sprang from a certain Henry the Fowler, who was elected King of Germany by an assembly of German nobles, princes and prelates in 919. In 936 he was succeeded as King by his son, Otto I, surnamed the Great, who was also elected to be his successor at Aix-la-Chapelle, and who finally descended upon Rome at the invitation of John XII, to be crowned Emperor in 962. His subsequent degradation of John was forced upon him by that Pope's treachery. With his assumption of the imperial dignity, Otto I did not so much overcome Rome as restore the ancient tussle of Pope and Emperor for ascendancy to

---

[1] Gibbon mentions a second Theodora, the sister of Marozia.

something like decency and dignity again. Otto I was followed by Otto II (973–983), and he again by a third Otto (983–1002).

There were, we may note here, three dynasties of emperors in the early Middle Ages—Saxon: Otto I (962) to Henry II, ending 1024; Salian: Conrad II to Henry V, ending about 1125; and Hohenstaufen: Conrad III to Frederick II, ending in 1250. The Hohenstaufens were Swabian in origin. Then came the Habsburgs, with Rudolph I in 1273, who lasted until 1918. We speak of

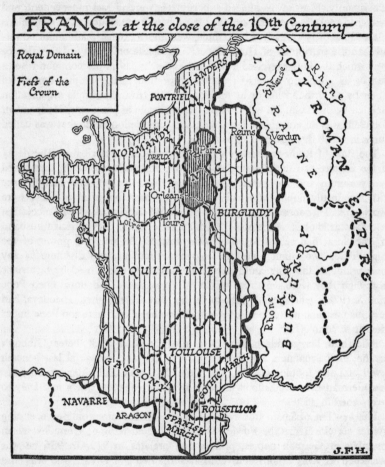

dynasties here, but there was a parade of electing the emperor at each accession.

The struggle between the Emperor and the Pope for ascendancy over the Holy Roman Empire plays a large part in the history of the early Middle Ages, and we shall have presently to sketch its chief phases. Though the Church never sank quite to the level of John XII again, the story fluctuates through phases of great violence, confusion, and intrigue.

Yet the outer history of Christendom is not the whole history of Christendom. That the Lateran was as cunning, foolish, and criminal as most other contemporary Courts has to be recorded; but, if we are to keep due proportions in this history, it must not be unduly emphasized. We must remember that through all those ages, leaving profound consequences, but leaving no conspicuous records upon the historian's page, countless men and women were touched by that Spirit of Jesus which still lived and lives still at the core of Christianity, that they led lives that were on the whole gracious and helpful, and that they did unselfish and devoted deeds. Through those ages such lives cleared the air, and made a better world possible. Just as in the Moslem world the Spirit of Islam generation by generation produced its crop of courage, integrity, and kindliness.

§ 9

While the Holy Roman Empire and the nations of France and England were thus appearing amidst the extreme political fragmentation of the civilization of Western Europe, both that civilization and the Byzantine Empire were being subjected to a threefold attack—from the Saracen powers, from the Northmen, and, more slowly developed and most formidable of all, from a new westward thrust of the Turkish peoples through South Russia, and also by way of Armenia and the Empire of Bagdad from Central Asia.

After the overthrow of the Omayyads by the Abbasid dynasty, the strength of the Saracenic impulse against Europe diminished. Islam was no longer united: Spain was under a separate Omayyad Caliph; North Africa, though nominally subject to the Abbasids, was really independent; and presently (699) Egypt became a separate power with a Shiite Caliph of its own, a pretender claiming descent from Ali and Fatima (the Fatimite Caliphate). These Egyptian Fatimites, the green flag Moslems, were fanatics in comparison with the Abbasids, and did much to embitter the genial relations of Islam and Christianity. They took Jerusalem and interfered with the Christian access to the Holy Sepulchre. On the other side of the shrunken Abbasid domain there was also a Shiite kingdom in Persia. The chief Saracen conquest in the ninth century was Sicily; but this was not overrun in the grand old style in a year or so, but subjugated tediously through a long century, and with many set-backs. The Spanish Saracens disputed in Sicily with the Saracens from Africa. In Spain the Saracens were giving ground before a renascent Christian effort. Nevertheless, the Byzantine Empire and Western Christendom were still so weak upon the Mediterranean Sea that the Saracen raiders and pirates from North Africa were able to raid almost unchallenged in South Italy and the Greek Islands.

But now a new force was appearing in the Mediterranean. We have already remarked that the Roman Empire never extended itself to the shores of the Baltic Sea, nor had ever the vigour to push itself into Denmark. The Nordic Aryan peoples of these neglected regions learnt much from the empire that was unable to subdue them; as we have already noted, they developed the

art of shipbuilding and became bold seamen; they spread across the North
Sea to the west, and across the Baltic and up the Russian rivers into the very
heart of what is now Russia. One of their earliest settlements in Russia was
Novgorod the Great.

There is the same trouble and confusion for the student of history with
these northern tribes as there is with the Scythians of classical times, and
with the Hunnish Turkish peoples of Eastern and Central Asia. They appear
under a great variety of names, they change and intermingle. In the case of

Britain, for example, the Angles, the Saxons, and Jutes conquered most of what is now England in the fifth and sixth centuries; the Danes, a second wave of practically the same people, followed in the eighth and ninth; and in 1016 a Danish king, Canute the Great, reigned in England, and not only over England, but over Denmark and Norway. His subjects sailed to Iceland, Greenland, and perhaps to the American continent. For a time, under Canute and his sons, it seemed possible that a great confederation of the Northmen might have established itself.

Then in 1066 a third wave of the same people flowed over England from the "Norman" State in France, where the Northmen had been settled since the days of Rolf the Ganger (911), and where they had learnt to speak French. William, Duke of Normandy, became the William the Conqueror (1066) of English history.

Practically, from the standpoint of universal history, all these peoples were the same people, waves of one Nordic stock. These waves were not only flowing westward but eastward. Already we have recorded a very interesting earlier movement of the same peoples under the name of Goths from the Baltic to the Black Sea. We have traced the splitting of these Goths into the Ostrogoths and the Visigoths, and the adventurous wanderings that ended at last in the Ostrogoth kingdom in Italy and the Visigoth states in Spain. In the ninth century a second movement of the Northmen across Russia was going on at the same time that their establishments in England and their dukedom of Normandy were coming into existence.

The populations of South Scotland, England, East Ireland, Flanders, Normandy, and the Russias have more elements in common than we are accustomed to recognize. All are fundamentally Gothic and Nordic peoples. Even in their weights and measures the kinship of Russians and English is to be noted; both have the Norse inch and foot, and many early Norman churches in England are built on a scale that shows the use of the sajene (7 ft.) and quarter-sajene, a Norse measure still used in Russia. These "Russian" Norsemen travelled in the summertime, using the river routes that abounded in Russia; they carried their ships by portages from the northward-running rivers to those flowing southward. They appeared as pirates, raiders, and traders both upon the Caspian and the Black Sea. The Arabic chroniclers noted their apparition upon the Caspian, and learnt to call them Russians. They raided Persia, and threatened Constantinople with a great fleet of small craft (in 865, 904, 941 and 1043[1]).

One of these Northmen, Rurik (*circa* 850), established himself as the ruler of Novgorod, and his successor, the Duke Oleg, took Kieff and laid the foundations of modern Russia. The fighting qualities of the Russian Vikings were speedily appreciated at Constantinople; the Greeks called them Varangians, and an Imperial Varangian bodyguard was formed. After the conquest of England by the Normans (1066), a number of Danes and English were driven

---

[1] These dates are from Gibbon. Beazley gives 865, 904–7, 935, 944, 971–2 (*History of Russia,* Clarendon Press).

into exile and joined these Russian Varangians, apparently finding few obstacles to intercourse in their speech and habits.

Meanwhile the Normans from Normandy were also finding their way into the Mediterranean from the West. They came first as mercenaries, and later as independent invaders; and they came mainly, not, it is to be noted, by sea, but in scattered bands by land. They came through the Rhineland and Italy, partly in the search for warlike employment and loot, partly as pilgrims. For the ninth and tenth centuries saw a great development of pilgrimage.

These Normans, as they grew powerful, discovered themselves such rapacious and vigorous robbers that they forced the Eastern Emperor and the Pope into a feeble and ineffective alliance against them (1053). They defeated and captured and were pardoned by the Pope; they established themselves in Calabria and South Italy, conquered Sicily from the Saracens (1060–1090), and under Robert Guiscard, who had entered Italy as a pilgrim adventurer and began his career as a brigand in Calabria, threatened the Byzantine Empire itself (1081). His army, which contained a contingent of Sicilian Moslems, crossed from Brindisi to Epirus in the reverse direction to that in which Pyrrhus had crossed to attack the Roman Republic, thirteen centuries before (273 B.C.). He laid siege to the Byzantine stronghold of Durazzo.

Robert captured Durazzo (1082), but the pressure of affairs in Italy recalled him, and ultimately put an end to this first Norman attack upon the Empire of Byzantium, leaving the way open for the rule of a comparatively vigorous Commenian dynasty (1081–1204).

In Italy, amidst conflicts too complex for us to tell here, it fell to Robert Guiscard to besiege and sack Rome (1084); and the anti-Christian Gibbon notes with quiet satisfaction the presence of that contingent of Sicilian Moslems amongst the looters. There were in the twelfth century three other Norman attacks upon the Eastern power, one by the son of Robert Guiscard, and the two others directly from Sicily by sea. . . .

But neither the Saracens nor the Normans pounded quite so heavily against the old empire at Byzantium or against the Holy Roman Empire, the vamped-up Roman Empire of the West, as did the double thrust from the Turanian centres in Central Asia, of which we must now tell.

We have already noted the westward movement of the Avars, and the Turkish Magyars who followed in their track. From the days of Pepin I onward, the Frankish power and its successors in Germany were in conflict with these Eastern raiders along all the Eastern borderlands. Charlemagne held and punished them, and established some sort of overlordship as far east as the Carpathians; but, amidst the enfeeblement that followed his death, these peoples, more or less blended now in the accounts under the name of Hungarians, led by the Magyars, re-established their complete freedom again, and raided yearly, often as far as the Rhine. They destroyed, Gibbon notes, the monastery of St. Gall in Switzerland, and the town of Bremen. Their great raiding period was between 900 and 950. Their biggest effort, through Germany right into France, thence over the Alps and home again by North Italy, was in 938–9. Robbers abroad, these people had very considerable freedom at home. They are said to have already had a traditional political constitution in the tenth century.

Thrust southward by these disturbances, and by others to be presently noted, the Bulgarians, as we have already noted, established themselves under Krum, between the Danube and Constantinople. Originally a Turkish people, the Bulgarians, since their first appearance in the east of Russia, had become, by repeated admixture, almost entirely Slavonic in race and language. For some time after their establishment in Bulgaria they remained pagan. Their king, Boris (852–884), entertained Moslem envoys, and seems to have contemplated an adhesion to Islam, but finally he married a Byzantine princess, and handed himself and his people over to the Christian faith.

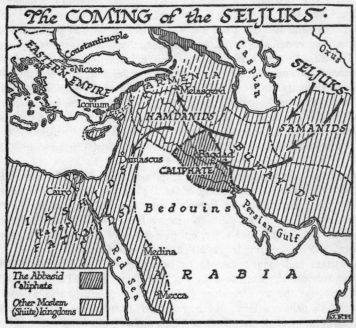

The Hungarians were drubbed into a certain respect for western civilization by Henry the Fowler, the elected King of Germany, and Otto the First, the first Saxon emperor, in the tenth century. But they did not decide to adopt Christianity until about A.D. 1000. Though they were Christianized, they retained their own Turko-Finnic language (Magyar), and they retain it to this day. They retained, too, a certain freedom under the monarchy imposed upon them. Their written constitution, the "Golden Seal," dates from 1222, and is an Eastern parallel to the English Magna Charta in its limitations of the king's absolute power. King Stephen, the first king of the Magyars, stipulated, when he formally accepted Christianity, that Hungary, unlike Bohemia and Poland, should not be incorporated with the Holy Roman Empire.

Bulgarians and Hungarians do not, however, exhaust the catalogue of the peoples whose westward movements embodied the Turkish thrust across South Russia. Behind the Hungarians and Bulgarians thrust the Khazars, a Turkish people, with whom were mingled a very considerable proportion of Jews who had been expelled from Constantinople, and who had mixed with them and made many proselytes. To these Jewish Khazars are to be ascribed the great settlements of Jews in Poland and Russia. Behind the Khazars again, and overrunning them, were the Petschenegs (or Patzinaks), a savage Turkish people who are first heard of in the ninth century, and who were destined to dissolve and vanish as the kindred Huns did five centuries before.

And while the trend of all these peoples was westward, we have, when we are thinking of the present population of these South Russian regions, to remember also the coming and going of the Northmen between the Baltic and the Black Sea, who interwove with the Turkish migrants like warp and woof, and bear in mind also that there was a considerable Slavonic population, the heirs and descendants of Scythians, Sarmatians, and the like, already established in these restless, lawless, but fertile areas. All these races mixed with and reacted upon one another. The universal prevalence of Slavonic languages, except in Hungary, shows that the population remained predominantly Slav. And in what is now Roumania, for all the passage of peoples, and in spite of conquest after conquest, the tradition and inheritance of the Roman provinces of Dacia and Mœsia Inferior still kept a Latin speech and memory alive.

But this direct thrust of the Turkish peoples against Christendom to the north of the Black Sea was, in the end, not nearly so important as their indirect thrust south of it through the empire of the Caliph. We cannot deal here with the tribes and dissensions of the Turkish peoples of Turkestan, nor with the particular causes that brought to the fore the tribes under the rule of the Seljuk clan. In the eleventh century these Seljuk Turks broke with irresistible force, not in one army, but in a group of armies, and under two brothers, into the decaying fragments of the Moslem Empire.

For Islam had long ceased to be one empire. The orthodox Sunnite Abbasid rule had shrunken to what was once Babylonia; and even in Bagdad the Caliph was the mere creature of his Turkish palace guards. A sort of mayor of the palace, a Turk, was the real ruler. East of the Caliph, in Persia, and west of him, in Palestine, Syria, and Egypt, were Shiite heretics.

The Seljuk Turks were orthodox Sunnites; they now swept down upon and conquered the Shiite rulers and upstarts, and established themselves as the protectors of the Bagdad Caliph, taking over the temporal powers of the mayor of the palace. Very early they conquered Armenia from the Greeks, and then, breaking the bounds that had restrained the power of Islam for four centuries, they swept on to the conquest of Asia Minor, almost to the gates of Constantinople. The mountain barrier of Cilicia that had held the Moslem so long had been turned by the conquest of Armenia from the north-east. Under Alp Arslan, who had united all the Seljuk power in his own hands, the Turks utterly smashed the Byzantine army at the battle of Manzikert, or Melasgird (1071). The effect of this battle upon people's imaginations was very great. Islam, which had appeared far gone in decay, which had been divided religiously and politically, was suddenly discovered to have risen again, and it was the secure old Byzantine Empire that seemed on the brink of dissolution.

The loss of Asia Minor was very swift. The Seljuks established themselves at Iconium (Konia), in what is now Anatolia. In a little while they were in possession of the fortress of Nicæa over against the capital.

§ 10

We have already told of the attack of the Normans upon the Byzantine Empire from the west, and of the battle of Durazzo (1082); and we have noted that Constantinople had still vivid memories of the Russian sea raids (1043). Bulgaria, it is true, had been tamed and Christianized, but there was heavy and uncertain warfare going on with the Petschenegs. North and west, the emperor's hands were full. Now came this final crowning threat from the east. This swift advance of the Turks into country that had been so long securely Byzantine must have seemed like the approach of final disaster. The Byzantine Emperor Michael VII, under the pressure of these convergent dangers, took a step that probably seemed both to himself and to Rome of the utmost political significance. The Greek world turned to her renascent Latin sister. He appealed to the Pope, Gregory VII, for assistance. His appeal was repeated still more urgently by his successor, Alexius Comnenus, to Pope Urban II.

To the counsellors of Rome this must have presented itself as a supreme opportunity for the assertion of the headship of the Pope over the entire Christian world.

In this history we have traced the growth of this idea of a religious government of Christendom—and through Christendom of mankind—and we have shown how naturally and how necessarily, because of the tradition of world empire, it found a centre at Rome. The Pope of Rome was the only Western patriarch; he was the religious head of a vast region in which the ruling tongue was Latin; the other patriarchs of the Orthodox Church spoke Greek, and so were inaudible throughout his domains; and the two words *filio que*, which had been added to the Latin creed, had split off the Byzantine Christians by one of those impalpable and elusive doctrinal points upon which there is no reconciliation. (The final rupture was in 1054.)

The life of the Lateran changed in its quality with every occupant of the chair of St. Peter; sometimes papal Rome was a den of corruption and uncleanness, as it had been in the days of John XII; sometimes it was pervaded by the influence of widely thinking and nobly thinking men. But behind the Pope was the assembly of the cardinals, priests, and a great number of highly educated officials, who never, even in the darkest and wildest days, lost sight altogether of the very grand idea of a divine world dominion, of a peace of Christ throughout the earth that St. Augustine had expressed. Through all the Middle Ages that idea was the guiding influence in Rome. For a time, perhaps, mean minds would prevail there, and in the affairs of the world Rome would play the part of a greedy, treacherous, and insanely cunning old woman;

followed a phase of masculine and quite worldly astuteness, perhaps, or a phase of exaltation. Came an interlude of fanaticism or pedantry, when all the pressure was upon exact doctrine. Or there was a moral collapse, and the Lateran became the throne of some sensuous or æsthetic autocrat, ready to sell every hope or honour the Church could give for money to spend upon pleasure or display. Yet, on the whole, the papal ship kept its course, and came presently before the wind again.

In this period to which we have now come, the period of the eleventh century, we discover a Rome dominated by the personality of an exceptionally great statesman, Hildebrand, who occupied various official positions under a succession of Popes, and finally became Pope himself under the name of Gregory VII (1073–1085). We find that under his influence, vice, sloth, and corruption have been swept out of the Church, that the method of electing the Popes has been reformed, and that a great struggle has been waged with the Emperor upon the manifestly vital question of "investitures," the question whether Pope or temporal monarch should have the decisive voice in the appointment of the bishops in their domains. How vital that question was we can better realize when we bear in mind that in many kingdoms more than a quarter of the land was clerical property. Hitherto the Roman clergy had been able to marry; but now, to detach them effectually from the world and to make them more completely the instruments of the Church, celibacy was imposed upon all priests. . . .

Gregory VII had been prevented by his struggle over the investitures from any effectual answer to the first appeal from Byzantium; but he had left a worthy successor in Urban II (1088–1099); and when the letter of Alexius came to hand, Urban seized at once upon the opportunity it afforded for drawing together all the thoughts and forces of Western Europe into one passion and purpose. Thereby he might hope to end the private warfare that prevailed, and find a proper outlet for the immense energy of the Normans. He saw, too, an opportunity of thrusting the Byzantine power and Church aside, and extending the influence of the Latin Church over Syria, Palestine, and Egypt.

The envoys of Alexius were heard at a church council, hastily summoned at Piacenza (=Placentia), and next year (1095), at Clermont, Urban held a second great council, in which all the slowly gathered strength of the Church was organized for a universal war propaganda against the Moslems. Private war, all war among Christians, was to cease until the infidel had been swept back and the site of the Holy Sepulchre was again in Christian hands.

The fervour of the response enables us to understand the great work of creative organization that has been done in Western Europe in the previous five centuries. In the beginning of the seventh century we saw Western Europe as a chaos of social and political fragments, with no common idea nor hope, a system shattered almost to a dust of self-seeking individuals. Now, in the close of the eleventh century, there is everywhere a common belief, a linking idea, to which men may devote themselves, and by which they can co-operate together in a universal enterprise. We realize that, in spite of much weakness and intellectual and moral unsoundness, to this extent the Christian Church has *worked*. We are able to measure the evil phases of tenth-century Rome, the scandals, the filthiness, the murders and violence, at their proper value by the scale of this fact. No doubt, also, all over Christendom there had been many lazy, evil, and foolish priests, but it is manifest that this task of teaching and co-ordination had been accomplished only through a great multitude of right-living priests and monks and nuns. A new and greater amphictyony, the amphictyony of Christendom, had come into the world, and it had been built by thousands of anonymous, faithful lives.

And this response to the appeal of Urban II was not confined only to what we should call educated people. It was not simply knights and princes who were willing to go upon this crusade. Side by side with the figure of Urban we must put the figure of Peter the Hermit, a type novel to Europe, albeit a little reminiscent of the Hebrew prophets. This man appeared preaching the crusade to the common people. He told a story—whether truthful or untruthful hardly matters in this connection—of his pilgrimage to Jerusalem, of the wanton destruction at the Holy Sepulchre by the Seljuk Turks, who took it somewhen about 1075—the chronology of this period is still very vague—and of the exactions, brutalities, and deliberate cruelties practised upon the Christian pilgrims to the Holy Places. Barefooted, clad in a coarse garment, riding on an ass, and bearing a huge cross, this man travelled about France and Germany, and everywhere harangued vast crowds in church or street or market-place.

Here for the first time we discover Europe with an idea and a soul! Here is a universal response of indignation at the story of a remote wrong, a swift understanding of a common cause for rich and poor alike. You cannot imagine this thing happening in the Empire of Augustus Cæsar, or, indeed, in any previous state in the world's history. Something of the kind might perhaps have been possible in the far smaller world of Hellas, or in Arabia before Islam. But this movement affected nations, kingdoms, tongues, and peoples. It is clear that we are dealing with something new that has come into the world, a new clear connection of the common interest with the consciousness of the common man.

§ 11

From the very first this flaming enthusiasm was mixed with baser elements. There was the cold and calculated scheme of the free and ambitious Latin Church to subdue and replace the emperor-ruled Byzantine Church; there was the freebooting instinct of the Normans, who were tearing Italy to pieces, which turned readily enough to a new and richer world of plunder; and there was something in the multitude who now turned their faces east, something deeper than love in the human composition, namely, fearborn hate, that the impassioned appeals of the propagandists and the exaggeration of the horrors and cruelties of the infidel had fanned into flame.

And there were still other forces; the intolerant Seljuks and the intolerant

Fatimites lay now an impassable barrier across the eastward trade of Genoa and Venice that had hitherto flowed through Bagdad and Aleppo, or through Egypt. They must force open these closed channels, unless Constantinople and the Black Sea route were to monopolize Eastern trade altogether. Moreover, in 1094 and 1095 there had been a pestilence and famine from the Scheldt to Bohemia, and there was great social disorganization.

"No wonder," says Mr. Ernest Barker, "that a stream of emigration set towards the East, such as would in modern times flow towards a newly discovered goldfield—a stream carrying in its turbid waters much refuse, tramps and bankrupts, camp followers and hucksters, fugitive monks and escaped villeins, and marked by the same motley grouping, the same fever of life, the same alternations of affluence and beggary, which mark the rush for a goldfield to-day."

But these were secondary contributory causes. The fact of predominant interest to the historian of mankind is this *will to crusade* suddenly revealed as a new mass possibility in human affairs.

The story of the crusades abounds in such romantic and picturesque detail that the writer of an Outline of History must ride his pen upon the curb through this alluring field. The first forces to move eastward were great crowds of undisciplined people rather than armies, and they sought to make their way by the valley of the Danube, and thence southward to Constantinople. This was the "people's crusade." Never before in the whole history of the world had there been such a spectacle as these masses of practically leaderless people moved by an idea. It was a very crude idea. When they got among foreigners, they did not seem to have realized that they were not already among the infidel. Two great mobs, the advance guard of the expedition, committed such excesses in Hungary, where the language must have been incomprehensible to them, as to provoke the Hungarians to destroy them. They were massacred. A third host began with a great pogrom of the Jews in the Rhineland—for the Christian blood was up—and this multitude was also dispersed in Hungary. Two other hosts under Peter got through and reached Constantinople, to the astonishment and dismay of the Emperor Alexius. They looted and committed outrages as they came, and at last he shipped them across the Bosphorus, to be massacred rather than defeated by the Seljuks (1096).

This first unhappy appearance of the "people" as people in modern European history, was followed in 1097 by the organized forces of the First Crusade. They came by diverse routes from France, Normandy, Flanders, England, Southern Italy and Sicily, and the will and power of them were the Normans. They crossed the Bosphorus and captured Nicæa, which Alexius snatched away from them before they could loot it.

Then they went on by much the same route as Alexander the Great, through the Cilician Gates, leaving the Turks in Konia unconquered, past the battlefield of the Issus, and so to Antioch, which they took after nearly a year's siege. Then they defeated a great relieving army from Mosul.

A large part of the crusaders remained in Antioch, a smaller force under Godfrey of Bouillon (in Belgium) went on to Jerusalem. "After a little more than a month's siege, the city was finally captured (July 15, 1099). The slaughter was terrible; the blood of the conquered ran down the streets, until men splashed in blood as they rode. At nightfall, 'sobbing for excess of joy,' the crusaders came to the Sepulchre from their treading of the winepress, and put their blood-stained hands together in prayer. So, on that day of July, the First Crusade came to an end."[1]

The authority of the Patriarch of Jerusalem was at once seized upon by the Latin clergy with the expedition, and the Orthodox Christians found themselves in rather a worse case under Latin rule than under the Turk. There

Map to illustrate the FIRST CRUSADE

States set up by the Crusaders . . .

Eastern Empire . . .

Seljuks . . . . . .

Route of Crusaders

were already Latin principalities established at Antioch and Edessa, and there began a struggle for ascendancy between these various courts and kings, and an unsuccessful attempt to make Jerusalem a property of the Pope. These are complications beyond our present scope.

Let us quote, however, a characteristic passage from Gibbon:—

"In a style less grave than that of history, I should perhaps compare the Emperor Alexius to the jackal, who is said to follow the steps and to devour the leavings of the lion. Whatever had been his fears and toils in the passage of the First Crusade, they were amply recompensed by the subsequent benefits which he derived from the exploits of the Franks. His dexterity and vigilance

---

[1] E. Barker, art. "Crusades," *Encyclopædia Britannica.*

secured their first conquest of Nicæa, and from this threatening station the Turks were compelled to evacuate the neighbourhood of Constantinople.

"While the crusaders, with blind valour, advanced into the midland countries of Asia, the crafty Greek improved the favourable occasion when the emirs of the sea coast were recalled to the standard of the Sultan. The Turks were driven from the isles of Rhodes and Chios; the cities of Ephesus and Smyrna, of Sardes, Philadelphia, and Laodicea, were restored to the empire, which Alexius enlarged from the Hellespont to the banks of the Mæander and the rocky shores of Pamphylia. The churches resumed their splendour; the towns were rebuilt and fortified; and the desert country was peopled with colonies of Christians, who were gently removed from the more distant and dangerous frontier.

"In these paternal cares we may forgive Alexius, if we forget the deliverance of the holy sepulchre; but, by the Latins, he was stigmatized with the foul reproach of treason and desertion. They had sworn fidelity and obedience to his throne; but *he* had promised to assist their enterprise in person, or, at least, with his troops and treasures; his base retreat dissolved their obligations; and the sword, which had been the instrument of their victory, was the pledge and title of their just independence. It does not appear that the emperor attempted to revive his obsolete claims over the kingdom of Jerusalem, but the borders of Cilicia and Syria were more recent in his possession and more accessible to his arms. The great army of the crusaders was annihilated or dispersed; the principality of Antioch was left without a head, by the surprise and captivity of Bohemond; his ransom had oppressed him with a heavy debt; and his Norman followers were insufficient to repel the hostilities of the Greeks and Turks.

"In this distress, Bohemond embraced a magnanimous resolution, of leaving the defence of Antioch to his kinsman, the faithful Tancred; of arming the West against the Byzantine Empire, and of executing the design which he inherited from the lessons and example of his father Guiscard. His embarkation was clandestine; and if we may credit a tale of the Princess Anna, he passed the hostile sea closely secreted in a coffin. (Anna Comnena adds that, to complete the imitation, he was shut up with a dead cock; and condescends to wonder how the barbarian could endure the confinement and putrefaction. This absurd tale is unknown to the Latins.) But his reception in France was undignified by the public applause and his marriage with the king's daughter; his return was glorious, since the bravest spirits of the age enlisted under his veteran command; and he repassed the Adriatic at the head of five thousand horse and forty thousand foot, assembled from the most remote climates of Europe. The strength of Durazzo and prudence of Alexius, the progress of famine and approach of winter, eluded his ambitious hopes; and the venal confederates were seduced from his standard. A treaty of peace suspended the fears of the Greeks."

We have dealt thus lengthily with the First Crusade, because it displays completely the quality of all these expeditions. The reality of the struggle between the Latin and the Byzantine system became more and more nakedly apparent.

In 1101 came reinforcements, in which the fleet of the mercantile republics of Venice and Genoa played a prominent part, and the power of the kingdom of Jerusalem was extended.

The year 1147 saw a Second Crusade, in which both the Emperor Conrad III and King Louis of France participated. It was a much more stately and far less successful and enthusiastic expedition than its predecessor. It had been provoked by the fall of Edessa to the Moslems in 1144. One large division of Germans, instead of going to the Holy Land, attacked and subjugated the still pagan Wends east of the Elbe. This, the Pope agreed, counted as crusading, and so did the capture of Lisbon, and the foundation of the Christian kingdom of Portugal by the Flemish and English contingents.

In 1169 a Kurdish adventurer named Saladin became ruler of Egypt, in which country the Shiite heresy had now fallen before a Sunnite revival. This Saladin reunited the efforts of Egypt and Bagdad, and preached a Jehad, a Holy War, a counter-crusade, of all the Moslems against the Christians. This Jehad excited almost as much feeling in Islam as the First Crusade had done in Christendom. It was now a case of crusader against crusader; and in 1187 Jerusalem was retaken.

This provoked the Third Crusade (1189). This also was a grand affair, planned jointly by the Emperor Frederick I (known better as Frederick Barbarossa), the King of France, and the King of England (who at that time owned many of the fairest French provinces). The papacy played a secondary part in this expedition; it was in one of its phases of enfeeblement; and the crusade was the most courtly, chivalrous, and romantic of all. Religious bitterness was mitigated by the idea of knightly gallantry, which obsessed both Saladin and Richard I (1189–1199) of England (Cœur de Lion), and the lover of romance may very well turn to the romances about this period for its flavour. The crusade saved the principality of Antioch for a time, but failed to retake Jerusalem. The Christians, however, remained in possession of the sea coast of Palestine.

By the time of the Third Crusade, the magic and wonder had gone out of these movements altogether. The common people had found them out. Men went, but only kings and nobles straggled back; and that often only after heavy taxation for a ransom.

The idea of the crusades was cheapened by their too frequent and trivial use. Whenever the Pope quarrelled with anyone now, or when he wished to weaken the dangerous power of the emperor by overseas exertions, he called for a crusade, until the word ceased to mean anything but an attempt to give flavour to an unpalatable war. There was a crusade against the heretics in the south of France, one against John (King of England), one against the Emperor Frederick II. The Popes did not understand the necessity of dignity to the papacy. They had achieved a moral ascendancy in Christendom. Forthwith they began to fritter it away. They not only cheapened the idea of the crusades, but they made their tremendous power of excommunication, of putting people outside all the sacraments, hopes, and comforts of religion ridiculous by using it in mere disputes of policy. Frederick II was not only crusaded against, but excommunicated—without visible injury. He was excommunicated again in 1239, and this sentence was renewed by Innocent IV in 1245.

The bulk of the Fourth Crusade never reached the Holy Land at all. It started from Venice (1202), captured Zara, encamped at Constantinople (1203), and finally, in 1204, stormed the city. It was frankly a combined attack on the Byzantine Empire. Venice took much of the coast and islands of the empire, and a Latin, Baldwin of Flanders, was set up as emperor in Constantinople. The Latin and Greek Churches were declared to be reunited, and Latin emperors ruled as conquerors in Constantinople from 1204 to 1261.

In 1212 occurred a dreadful thing, a children's crusade. An excitement that could no longer affect sane adults was spread among the children in the south of France and in the Rhone valley. A crowd of many thousands of French boys marched to Marseilles; they were then lured on board ship by slave-traders, who sold them into slavery in Egypt. The Rhineland children tramped into Italy, many perishing by the way, and there dispersed.

Pope Innocent III made great capital out of this strange business. "The very children put us to shame," he said; and sought to whip up enthusiasm for a Fifth Crusade. This crusade aimed at the conquest of Egypt, because Jerusalem was now held by the Egyptian Sultan; its remnants returned in 1221, after an inglorious evacuation of its one capture, Damietta, with the Jerusalem vestiges of the True Cross as a sort of consolation concession on the part of the victor. We have already noted the earlier adventures of this venerable relic before the days of Muhammad, when it was carried off by Chosroes II to Ctesiphon, and recovered by the Emperor Heraclius. Fragments of the True Cross, however, had always been in Rome at the church of S. Croce-in-Gerusalemme, since the days of the Empress Helena (the mother of Constantine the Great), to whom, says the legend, its hiding-place had been revealed in a vision during her pilgrimage to the Holy Land.

"The custody of the *True Cross*," says Gibbon, "which on Easter Sunday was solemnly exposed to the people, was entrusted to the Bishop of Jerusalem; and he alone might gratify the curious devotion of the pilgrims by the gift of small pieces, which they encased in gold or gems, and carried away in triumph to their respective countries. But, as this gainful branch of commerce must soon have been annihilated, it was found convenient to suppose that the marvellous wood possessed a secret power of vegetation, and that its substance, though continually diminished, still remained entire and unimpaired."

The Sixth Crusade (1228) was a crusade bordering upon absurdity. The Emperor Frederick II had promised to go upon a crusade, and evaded his vow. He had made a false start and returned. He was probably bored by the mere idea of a crusade. But the vow had been part of the bargain by which he secured the support of Pope Innocent III in his election as emperor. He busied himself in reorganizing the government of his Sicilian kingdom, though he had given the Pope to understand that he would relinquish those possessions if he became emperor; and the Pope was anxious to stop this process of consolidation by sending him to the Holy Land. The Pope did not want Frederick II, or any German emperor at all, in Italy, because he himself wished to rule Italy. As Frederick II remained evasive, Gregory IX excommunicated him, proclaimed a crusade against him, and invaded his dominions in Italy (1228). Whereupon the Emperor sailed with an army to the Holy Land. There he had a meeting with the Sultan of Egypt (the Emperor spoke six languages freely, including Arabic); and it would seem these two gentlemen, both of sceptical opinions, exchanged views of a congenial sort, discussed the Pope in a worldly spirit, debated the Mongolian rush westward, which threatened them both alike, and agreed finally to a commercial convention, and the surrender of a part of the kingdom of Jerusalem to Frederick.

This, indeed, was a new sort of crusade, a crusade by private treaty. As this astonishing crusader had been excommunicated, he had to indulge in a purely secular coronation in Jerusalem, taking the crown from the altar with his own hand, in a church from which all the clergy had gone. Probably there was no one to show him the Holy Places; indeed, these were presently all put under an interdict by the Patriarch of Jerusalem and locked up; manifestly, the affair differed altogether in spirit from the red onslaught of the First Crusade. It had not even the kindly sociability of the Caliph Omar's visit six hundred years before.

Frederick II rode out of Jerusalem almost alone, returned from this unromantic success to Italy, put his affairs there in order very rapidly, chased the papal armies out of his possessions, and obliged the Pope to give him absolution from his excommunication (1230). This Sixth Crusade was, indeed, not only the *reductio ad absurdum* of crusades, but of papal excommunications. Of this Frederick II we shall tell more in a later section because he was very typical of certain new forces that were coming into European affairs.

The Christians lost Jerusalem again in 1244; it was taken from them very easily by the Sultan of Egypt when they attempted an intrigue against him. This provoked the Seventh Crusade, the Crusade of St. Louis, King of France (Louis IX), who was taken prisoner in Egypt and ransomed in 1250. Not until 1918, when it fell to a mixed force of French, British, and Indian troops did Jerusalem slip once more from the Moslem grasp. . . .

One more crusade remains to be noted, an expedition to Tunis by this same Louis IX, who died of fever there.

§ 12

The essential interest of the crusades for the historian of mankind lies in the wave of emotion, of unifying feeling, that animated the first. Thereafter these expeditions became more and more an established process, and less and less vital events. The First Crusade was an occurrence like the discovery of America; the later ones were more and more like a trip across the Atlantic. In the eleventh century, the idea of the crusade must have been like a strange and wonderful light in the sky; in the thirteenth, one can imagine honest burghers saying in tones of protest, "What! *another* crusade!"

The experience of St. Louis in Egypt is not like a fresh experience for mankind; it is much more like a round of golf over some well-known links, a round that was dogged by misfortune. It is an insignificant series of events. The interest of life had shifted to other directions.

The beginning of the crusades displays all Europe saturated by a naïve Christianity, and ready to follow the leading of the Pope trustfully and simply. The scandals of the Lateran during its evil days, with which we are all so familiar now, were practically unknown outside Rome. And Gregory VII and Urban II had redeemed all that. But intellectually and morally their successors at the Lateran and the Vatican[1] were not equal to their opportunities. The strength of the papacy lay in the faith men had in it, and it used that faith so carelessly as to enfeeble it. Rome has always had too much of the shrewdness of the priest and too little of the power of the prophet. So that while the eleventh century was a century of ignorant and confiding men, the thirteenth was an age of knowing and disillusioned men. It was a far more civilized and profoundly sceptical world.

The bishops, priests, and the monastic institutions of Latin Christendom before the days of Gregory VII had been perhaps rather loosely linked together and very variable in quality; but it is clear that they were, as a rule, intensely intimate with the people among whom they found themselves, and with much of the spirit of Jesus still alive in them; they were trusted, and they had enormous power *within the conscience of their followers*. The church, in comparison with its later state, was more in the hands of local laymen and the local ruler; it lacked its later universality.

The energetic bracing up of the church organization by Gregory VII, which was designed to increase the central power of Rome, broke many subtle filaments between priest and monastery on the one hand, and the countryside about them on the other. Men of faith and wisdom believe in growth and their fellow men; but priests, even such priests as Gregory VII, believe in the false "efficiency" of an imposed discipline. The squabble over investitures made every prince in Christendom suspicious of the bishops as agents of a foreign power; this suspicion filtered down to the parishes. The political enterprises of the papacy necessitated an increasing demand for money. Already in the thirteenth century it was being said everywhere that the priests were not good men, that they were always hunting for money.

In the days of ignorance there had been an extraordinary willingness to believe the Catholic priesthood good and wise. Relatively it was better and wiser in those days. Great powers beyond her spiritual functions had been entrusted to the church, and very extraordinary freedoms. Of this confidence the fullest advantage had been taken. In the Middle Ages the church had become a state within the state. It had its own law courts. Cases involving not merely priests, but monks, students, crusaders, widows, orphans, and the helpless, were re-

---

[1] The Popes inhabited the palace of the Lateran until 1309, when a French Pope set up the papal Court at Avignon. When the Pope returned to Rome in 1377 the Lateran was almost in ruins, and the palace of the Vatican became the seat of the papal court. It was, among other advantages, much nearer to the papal stronghold, the Castle of St. Angelo.

served for the clerical courts; and whenever the rites or rules of the church were involved, there the church claimed jurisdiction over such matters as wills, marriages, oaths, and, of course, over heresy, sorcery, and blasphemy. There were numerous clerical prisons in which offenders might pine all their lives. The Pope was the supreme lawgiver of Christendom, and his court at Rome the final and decisive court of appeal. And the church levied taxes; it had not only vast properties and a great income from fees, but it imposed a tax of a tenth, the tithe, upon its subjects. It did not call for this as a pious benefaction; it demanded it as a right. The clergy on the other hand, were now claiming exemption from lay taxation.

This attempt to trade upon their peculiar prestige and evade their share in fiscal burdens was certainly one very considerable factor in the growing dissatisfaction with the clergy. Apart from any question of justice, it was impolitic. It made taxes seem ten times more burthensome to those who had to pay. It made everyone feel the immunities of the church.

And a still more extravagant and unwise claim made by the church was the claim to the power of *dispensation*. The Pope might in many instances set aside the laws of the church in individual cases; he might allow cousins to marry, permit a man to have two wives, or release anyone from a vow. But to do such things is to admit that the laws affected are not based upon necessity and an inherent righteousness; that they are in fact restrictive and vexatious. The lawgiver, of all beings, most owes the law allegiance. He of all men should behave as though the law compelled him. But it is the universal weakness of mankind that what we are given to administer we presently imagine we own.

§ 13

The Emperor Frederick II is a very convenient example of the sort of doubter and rebel the thirteenth century could produce. It may be interesting to tell a little of this intelligent and cynical man. He was the son of the German Emperor Henry VI; and grandson of Frederick Barbarossa, and his mother was the daughter of Roger I, the Norman King of Sicily. He inherited this kingdom in 1198, when he was four years old; his mother was his guardian for six months, and when she died, Pope Innocent III (1198–1216) became regent and guardian.

He seems to have had an exceptionally good and remarkably mixed education, and his accomplishments earned him the flattering title of *Stupor mundi*, the amazement of the world. The result of getting an Arabic view of Christianity, and a Christian view of Islam, was to make him believe that all religions were impostures, a view held perhaps by many a stifled observer in the Age of Faith. But he talked about his views; his blasphemies and heresies are on record.

Growing up under the arrogant rule of Innocent III, who never seems to have realized that his ward had come of age, he developed a humorous evasiveness. It was the papal policy to prevent any fresh coalescence of the power of Germany and Italy, and it was equally Frederick's determination to get whatever he could. When presently opportunity offered him the imperial crown of Germany, he secured the Pope's support by agreeing, if he were elected, to relinquish his possessions in Sicily and South Italy, and to put down heresy in Germany. For Innocent III was one of the great persecuting Popes, an able, grasping, and aggressive man. (For a Pope, he was exceptionally young. He became Pope at thirty-seven.) It was Innocent who had preached a cruel crusade against the heretics in the south of France, a crusade that presently became a looting expedition beyond his control.

So soon as Frederick was elected emperor (1212), Innocent pressed for the performance of the vows and promises he had wrung from his dutiful ward. The clergy were to be freed from lay jurisdiction and from taxation, and exemplary cruelties were to be practised upon the heretics. None of which things Frederick did. As we have already told, he would not even relinquish Sicily. He liked Sicily as a place of residence better than he liked Germany.

Innocent III died baffled in 1216, and his successor, Honorius III, effected nothing. Innocent III had not crowned Frederick, but Honorius did so in 1220. Honorius was succeeded by Gregory IX (1227), who evidently came to the papal throne with a nervous resolution to master this perplexing young Emperor. He excommunicated him at once for failing to start upon his promised crusade, which was now twelve years overdue; and he denounced his vices, heresies, and general offences in a public letter (1227). To this Frederick replied in a far abler document, which either he wrote or had written for him, addressed to all the princes of Europe, a document of extreme importance in history, because it is the first clear statement of the issue between the pretensions of the Pope to be absolute ruler of all Christendom, and the claims of the secular rulers. This conflict had always been smouldering; it had broken out here in one form, and there in another; but now Frederick put it in clear general terms upon which men could combine together.

Having delivered this blow, he departed upon the pacific crusade of which we have already told. In 1239 Gregory IX was excommunicating him for a second time, and renewing that warfare of public abuse in which the papacy had already suffered severely. The controversy was revived after Gregory IX was dead, when Innocent IV was Pope; and again a devastating letter, which men were bound to remember, was written by Frederick against the church. He denounced the pride and irreligion of the clergy, and ascribed all the corruptions of the time to their pride and wealth. He proposed to his fellow princes a general confiscation of church property—for the good of the church. It was a suggestion that never afterwards left the imagination of the European princes.

We will not go on to tell of his last years or of the disasters due to his carelessness, which cast a shadow of failure over his end. The particular events of his life are far less significant than its general atmosphere. It is possible to piece together something of his court life in Sicily. He is described towards the end of his life as "red, bald, and short-sighted"; but his features were good and pleasing. He was luxurious in his way of living, and fond of beautiful things. He is described as licentious. But it is clear that his mind was not satisfied by religious scepticism, and that he was a man of very effectual curiosity and inquiry. He gathered Jewish and Moslem as well as Christian philosophers at his Court, and he did much to irrigate the Italian mind with Saracenic influences. Through him Arabic numerals and algebra were introduced to Christian students, and among other philosophers at his Court was Michael Scott, who translated portions of Aristotle and the commentaries thereon of the great Arab philosopher Averroes (of Cordoba).

In 1224 Frederick founded the University of Naples, and he enlarged and enriched the great medical school at Salerno University, the most ancient of universities. He also founded a zoological garden. He left a book on hawking, which shows him to have been an acute observer of the habits of birds, and he was one of the first Italians to write Italian verse. Italian poetry was, indeed, born at his Court. He has been called by an able writer "the first of the moderns," and the phrase expresses aptly the unprejudiced detachment of his intellectual side. His was an all-round originality. During a gold shortage he introduced and made a success of a coinage of stamped leather or parchment, bearing his promise to pay in gold, a sort of leather bank-note issue. This revived a monetary method such as the world had not seen since Carthaginian days.

In spite of the torrent of abuse and calumny in which Frederick was drenched, he left a profound impression upon the popular imagination. He is still remembered in South Italy almost as vividly as is Napoleon I by the peasants of France; he is the "Gran Frederigo." And German scholars declare that, in spite of Frederick's manifest dislike for Germany, it is he, and not Frederick I, Frederick Barbarossa, to whom that German legend originally attached—that legend which represents a great monarch slumbering in a deep cavern, his beard grown round a stone table, against a day of awakening when the world will be restored by him from an extremity of disorder to peace. Afterwards, it seems, the story was transferred to the Crusader Barbarossa, the grandfather of Frederick II.

A difficult child was Frederick II for Mother Church, and he was only the precursor of many such difficult children. The princes and educated gentlemen throughout Europe read his letters and discussed them. The more enterprising university students found, marked, and digested the Arabic Aristotle he had made accessible to them in Latin. Salerno cast a baleful light upon Rome. All sorts of men must have been impressed by the futility of the excommunications and interdicts that were levelled at Frederick.

§ 14

We have said that Innocent III never seemed to realize that his ward, Frederick II, was growing up. It is equally true that the papacy never seemed to realize that Europe was growing up. It is impossible for an intelligent modern student of history not to sympathize with the underlying idea of the papal court, with the idea of one universal rule of righteousness keeping the peace of the earth, and not to recognize the many elements of nobility that entered into the Lateran policy. Sooner or later mankind must come to one universal peace, unless our race is to be destroyed by the increasing power of its own destructive inventions; and that universal peace must needs take the form of a government, that is to say, a law-sustaining organization, in the best sense of the word religious—a government ruling men through the educated co-ordination of their minds in a common conception of human history and human destiny.

The papacy we must now recognize as the first clearly conscious attempt to provide such a government in the world. We cannot too earnestly examine its deficiencies and inadequacies, for every lesson we can draw from them is necessarily of the greatest value to us in forming our ideas of our own international relationships. We have tried to suggest the main factors in the breakdown of the Roman Republic, and it now behoves us to attempt a diagnosis of the failure of the Roman Church to secure and organize the good-will of mankind.

The first thing that will strike the student is the intermittence of the efforts of the church to establish the world-City of God. The policy of the church was not whole-heartedly and continuously set upon that end. It was only now and then that some fine personality or some group of fine personalities dominated it in that direction. The kingdom of God that Jesus of Nazareth had preached was overlaid, as we have explained, almost from the beginning by the doctrines and ceremonial traditions of an earlier age, and of an intellectually inferior type. Christianity, almost from its commencement, ceased to be purely prophetic and creative. It entangled itself with archaic traditions of human sacrifice, with Mithraic blood-cleansing, with priestcraft as ancient as human society, and with elaborate doctrines about the structure of the divinity. The gory forefinger of the Etruscan *pontifex maximus* emphasized the teachings of Jesus of Nazareth; the mental complexity of the Alexandrian Greek entangled them. In the inevitable jangle of these incompatibles the church had become dogmatic. In despair of other solutions to its intellectual discords it had resorted to arbitrary authority.

Its priests and bishops were more and more men moulded to creeds and dogmas and set procedures; by the time they became cardinals or popes they were usually oldish men, habituated to a politic struggle for immediate ends and no longer capable of world-wide views. They no longer wanted to see the Kingdom of God established in the hearts of men—they had forgotten about that; they wanted to see the power of the church, which was their own power, dominating men. They were prepared to bargain even with the hates and fears and lusts in men's hearts to ensure that power. And it was just because many of them probably doubted secretly of the entire soundness of their vast and elaborate doctrinal fabric that they would brook no discussion of it. They were intolerant of questions or dissent, not because they were sure of their faith, but because they were not. They wanted conformity for reasons of policy.

By the thirteenth century the church was evidently already morbidly anxious about the gnawing doubts that might presently lay the whole structure of its pretensions in ruins. It had no serenity of soul. It was hunting everywhere for heretics, as timid old ladies are said to look under beds and in cupboards for burglars before retiring for the night.

We have already referred to the Persian Mani, who was crucified and flayed in the year 277. His way of representing the struggle between good and evil was as a struggle between a power of light which was, as it were, in rebellion against a power of darkness inherent in the universe. All these profound mysteries are necessarily represented by symbols and poetic expressions, and the ideas of Mani still find a response in many intellectual temperaments to-day. One may hear Manichæan doctrines from many Christian pulpits. But the orthodox Catholic symbol was a different one.

These Manichæan ideas have spread very widely in Europe, and particularly in Bulgaria and the south of France. In the south of France the people who held them were called the Cathars or Albigenses. Their ideas jarred so little with the essentials of Christianity, that they believed themselves to be devout Christians. As a body they lived lives of conspicuous virtue and purity in a violent, undisciplined, and vicious age. But they questioned the doctrinal soundness of Rome and the orthodox interpretation of the Bible. They thought Jesus was a rebel against the cruelty of the God of the Old Testament, and not his harmonious son.

Closely associated with the Albigenses were the Waldenses, the followers of a man called Waldo, who seems to have been quite soundly Catholic in his theology, but equally offensive to the church because he denounced the riches and luxury of the clergy. This was enough for the Lateran, and so we have the spectacle of Innocent III preaching a crusade against these unfortunate sectaries, and permitting the enlistment of every wandering scoundrel at loose ends to carry fire and sword and rape and every conceivable outrage among the most peaceful subjects of the King of France. The accounts of the cruelties and abominations of this crusade are far more terrible to read than any account of Christian martyrdoms by the pagans, and they have the added horror of being indisputably true.

This black and pitiless intolerance was an evil spirit to be mixed into the project of a rule of God on earth. This was a spirit entirely counter to that of Jesus of Nazareth. We do not hear of his smacking the faces or wringing the wrists of recalcitrant or unresponsive disciples. But the Popes during their centuries of power were always raging against the slightest reflection upon the intellectual sufficiency of the church.

And the intolerance of the church was not confined to religious matters. The shrewd, pompous, irascible, and rather malignant old men who manifestly constituted a dominant majority in the councils of the church resented any knowledge but their own knowledge, and distrusted any thought at all that they did not correct and control. They set themselves to restrain science, of which they were evidently jealous. Any mental activity but their own struck them as being insolent. Later on they were to have a great struggle upon the question of the earth's position in space, and whether it moved round the sun or not. This was really not the business of the church at all. She might very well have left to reason the things that are reason's, but she seems to have been impelled by an inner necessity to estrange the intellectual conscience in men.

Had this intolerance sprung from a real intensity of conviction it would have been bad enough, but it was accompanied by a scarcely disguised contempt for the intelligence and mental dignity of the common man that makes it far less acceptable to our modern judgments, and which no doubt made it far less acceptable to the free spirits of the time. We have told quite dispassionately the policy of the Roman church towards her troubled sister in the East. Many of the tools and expedients she used were abominable. In her treatment of her own people a streak of real cynicism is visible. She destroyed her prestige by disregarding her own teaching of righteousness. Of dispensations we have already spoken. Her crowning folly in the sixteenth century was the sale of *indulgences,* whereby the sufferings of the soul in purgatory could be commuted for a money payment. But the spirit that led at last to this shameless and, as it proved, disastrous proceeding was already very evident in the twelfth and thirteenth centuries.

Long before the seed of criticism that Frederick II had sown had germinated in men's minds and produced its inevitable crop of rebellion, there was apparent a strong feeling in Christendom that all was not well with the spiritual atmosphere. There began movements—movements that nowadays we should call "revivalist"—within the church, that implied rather than uttered a criticism of the sufficiency of her existing methods and organization. Men sought fresh forms of righteous living outside the monasteries and priesthood.

One notable figure is that of St. Francis of Assisi (1181–1226). We cannot tell here in any detail of how this pleasant young gentleman gave up all the amenities and ease of his life and went forth to seek God; the opening of the story is not unlike the early experiences of Gautama Buddha. He had a sudden conversion in the midst of a life of pleasure, and, taking a vow of extreme poverty, he gave himself up to an imitation of the life of Christ, and to the service of the sick and wretched, and more particularly to the service of the lepers who then abounded in Italy.

He was joined by great multitudes of disciples, and so the first Friars of the Franciscan Order came into existence. An order of women devotees was set up beside the original confraternity, and in addition great numbers of men and women were brought into less formal association. He preached, unmolested by the Moslems, be it noted, in Egypt and Palestine, though the Fifth Crusade was then in progress. His relations with the church are still a matter for discussion. His work had been sanctioned by Pope Innocent III, but while he was in the East there was a reconstitution of his order, intensifying discipline and substituting authority for responsive impulse, and as a consequence of these changes he resigned its headship. To the end he clung passionately to the ideal of poverty, but he was hardly dead before the order was holding property through trustees and building a great church and monastery to his memory at Assisi. The disciplines of the order that were applied after his death to his immediate associates are scarcely to be distinguished from a persecution; several of the more conspicuous zealots for simplicity were scourged, others were imprisoned, one was killed while attempting to escape, and Brother Bernard, the "first disciple," passed a year in the woods and hills, hunted like a wild beast.

This struggle within the Franciscan Order is a very interesting one, because it foreshadows the great troubles that were coming to Christendom. All through the thirteenth century a section of the Franciscans were straining at the rule of the church, and in 1318 four of them were burnt alive at Marseilles as incorrigible heretics. There seems to have been little difference between the teaching and the spirit of St. Francis and that of Waldo in the twelfth century, the founder of the murdered sect of Waldenses. Both were passionately enthusiastic for the spirit of Jesus of Nazareth. But while Waldo rebelled against the church, St. Francis did his best to be a good child of the church, and his comment on the spirit of official Christianity was only implicit. But both were instances of an outbreak of conscience against authority and the ordinary procedure of the church. And it is plain that in the second instance, as in the first, the church scented rebellion.

A very different character to St. Francis was the Spaniard St. Dominic (1170–1221), who was, of all things, orthodox. He had a passion for the argumentative conversion of heretics, and he was commissioned by Pope Innocent III to go and preach to the Albigenses. His work went on side by side with the fighting and massacres of the crusade; whom Dominic could not convert, Innocent's crusaders slew; yet his very activities and the recognition and encouragement of his order by the Pope witness to the rising tide of discussion, and to the persuasion even of the papacy that force was no remedy.

In several respects the development of the Black Friars or Dominicans— the Franciscans were the Grey Friars—shows the Roman church at the parting of the ways, committing itself more and more deeply to organized dogma, and so to a hopeless conflict with the quickening intelligence and courage of mankind. She whose one duty was to lead, chose to compel. The last discourse of St. Dominic to the heretics he had sought to convert is preserved to us. It is a signpost in history. It betrays the fatal exasperation of a man who had lost his faith in the power of truth because *his* truth has not prevailed.

"For many years," he said, "I have exhorted you in vain, with gentleness, preaching, praying, and weeping. But according to the proverb of my country, 'Where blessing can accomplish nothing, blows may avail,' we shall rouse against you princes and prelates, who, alas! will arm nations and kingdoms against this land. . . . and thus blows will avail where blessings and gentleness have been powerless."[1]

The thirteenth century saw the development of a new institution in the church, the papal Inquisition. Before this time it had been customary for the Pope to make occasional inquests or inquiries into heresy in this region or that, but now Innocent III saw in the new order of the Dominicans a powerful instrument of suppression. The Inquisition was organized as a standing inquiry

---

[1] *Encyclopædia Britannica*, art. "Dominic."

under their direction, and with fire and torment the church set itself, through
this instrument, to assail and weaken the human conscience in which its sole
hope of world dominion resided. Before the thirteenth century the penalty of
death had been inflicted but rarely upon heretics and unbelievers. Now in a
hundred market-places in Europe the dignitaries of the church watched the
blackened bodies of its antagonists, for the most part poor and insignificant
people, burn and sink pitifully, and their own great mission to mankind burn
and sink with them into dust and ashes.

The beginnings of the Franciscans and the Dominicans were but two among
many of the new forces that were arising in Christendom, either to help or
shatter the church, as its own wisdom might decide. Those two orders the
church did assimilate and use, though with a little violence in the case of the
former. But other forces were more frankly disobedient and critical. A century and a half later came Wycliffe (1320–1384). He was a learned doctor
at Oxford; for a time he was Master of Balliol; and he held various livings
in the church. Quite late in his life he began a series of outspoken criticisms
of the corruption of the clergy and the unwisdom of the church.

He organized a number of poor priests, the Wycliffites, to spread his ideas
throughout England; and in order that people should judge between the church
and himself, he translated the Bible into English.

He was a more learned and far abler man than either St. Francis or St.
Dominic. He had supporters in high places and a great following among the
people; and though Rome raged against him and ordered his imprisonment,
he died a free man, still administering the Sacraments as parish priest of
Lutterworth.

But the black and ancient spirit that was leading the Catholic church to its
destruction would not let his bones rest in his grave. By a decree of the Council
of Constance, in 1415, his remains were ordered to be dug up and burnt, an
order which was carried out, at the command of Pope Martin V, by Bishop
Fleming in 1428. This desecration was not the act of some isolated fanatic; it
was the official act of the church.

§ 15

The history of the papacy is confusing to the general reader because of the
multitude and abundance of the Popes. They mostly began to reign as old
men, and their reigns were short, averaging less than two years each.

But certain of the Popes stand out and supply convenient handles for the
student to grasp. Such were Gregory I the Great (590–604), the first monkish
Pope, the friend of Benedict, the sender of the English mission.

Other noteworthy Popes are Leo III (795–816), who crowned Charlemagne, the scandalous Popes John XI (931–936) and John XII (955–963),
which latter was deposed by the Emperor Otto I, and the great Hildebrand,
who ended his days as Pope Gregory VII (1073–1085), and who did so
much, by establishing the celibacy of the clergy, and insisting upon the suprem-

acy of the church over kings and princes, to centralize the power of the church in Rome.

There was a great struggle between Hildebrand and the emperor-elect, Henry IV, upon the question of investitures. The emperor attempted to depose the Pope; the Pope excommunicated the emperor and released his subject princes from their allegiance. The emperor was obliged to go in penitence to the Pope at Canossa (1077), and to await forgiveness for three days, clad in sackcloth and barefooted in the snow in the courtyard of the castle. But later on Henry asserted himself, being greatly aided by the vigorous attacks of the Norman adventurer, Robert Guiscard, upon the papal power.

The next Pope but one after Gregory VII was Urban II (1087–1099), the Pope of the First Crusade.

The period from the time of Gregory VII onward for a century and a half was the great period of ambition and effort for the church. There was a real sustained attempt to unite all Christendom under a purified and reorganized church.

The setting up of Latin kingdoms in Syria and the Holy Land in religious communions with Rome, after the First Crusade, marked the opening stage of a conquest of Eastern Christianity by Rome that reached its climax during the Latin rule in Constantinople (1204–1261).

In 1177, at Venice, the Emperor Frederick Barbarossa (Frederick I) knelt to the Pope Alexander III, recognized his spiritual supremacy and swore fealty to him. But after the death of Alexander III, in 1181, the peculiar weakness of the papacy, its liability to fall to old and enfeebled men, became manifest. Five Popes tottered to the Lateran to die within the space of ten years. Only with Innocent III (1198–1216) did another vigorous Pope take up the great policy of the City of God.

Under Innocent III, the guardian of that Emperor Frederick II whose career we have already studied, and the five Popes who followed him, the Pope of Rome came nearer to being the monarch of a united Christendom than he had ever been before, and was ever to be again. The empire was weakened by internal dissensions, Constantinople was in Latin hands, from Bulgaria to Ireland and from Norway to Sicily and Jerusalem the Pope was supreme. Yet his supremacy was more apparent than real. For, as we have seen, while in the time of Urban the power of faith was strong in all Christian Europe, in the time of Innocent III the papacy had lost its hold upon the hearts of princes, and the faith and conscience of the common people were turning against a merely political and aggressive church.

The church in the thirteenth century was extending its legal power in the world, and losing its grip upon men's consciences. It was becoming less persuasive and more violent. No intelligent man can tell of this process, or read of this process of failure without very mingled feelings. The church had sheltered and formed a new Europe throughout the long ages of European darkness and chaos; it had been the matrix in which the new civilization had been cast. But this new-formed civilization was impelled to grow by its own inherent vitality, and the church lacked sufficient power of growth and accommodation. The time was fast approaching when this matrix was to be broken.

The first striking intimation of the decay of the living and sustaining forces of the papacy appeared when presently the Popes came into conflict with the growing power of the French king. During the lifetime of the Emperor Frederick II, Germany fell into disunion, and the French king began to play the rôle of guard, supporter, and rival to the Pope that had hitherto fallen to the Hohenstaufen emperors. A series of Popes pursued the policy of supporting the French monarchs, French princes were established in the kingdom of Sicily and Naples, with the support and approval of Rome, and the French kings saw before them the possibility of restoring and ruling the Empire of Charlemagne. When, however, the German interregnum after the death of Frederick II, the last of the Hohenstaufens, came to an end and Rudolf of Habsburg was elected first Habsburg Emperor (1273), the policy of the Lateran began to fluctuate between France and Germany, veering about with the sympathies of each successive Pope.

In 1294 Boniface VIII became Pope. He was an Italian, hostile to the French, and full of a sense of the great traditions and mission of Rome. For a time he carried things with a high hand. In 1300 he held a jubilee, and a vast multitude of pilgrims assembled in Rome. "So great was the influx of money into the papal treasury, that two assistants were kept busy with rakes collecting the offerings that were deposited at the tomb of St. Peter."[1] But this festival was a delusive triumph. It is easier to raise a host of excursionists than a band of crusaders. Boniface came into conflict with the French king in 1302; and in 1303, as he was about to pronounce sentence of excommunication against that monarch, he was surprised and arrested in his own ancestral palace at Anagni, by Guillaume de Nogaret. This agent from the French king forced an entrance into the palace, made his way into the bedroom of the frightened Pope—he was lying in bed with a cross in his hands—and heaped threats and insults upon him. The Pope was liberated a day or so later by the townspeople, and returned to Rome; but there he was seized upon and again made prisoner by some members of the Orsini family, and in a few weeks' time the shocked and disillusioned old man died a prisoner in their hands.

The people of Anagni did resent the first outrage and rose against Nogaret to liberate Boniface, but then Anagni was the Pope's native town. The important point to note is that the French king, in this rough treatment of the head of Christendom, was acting with the full approval of his people; he had summoned a council of the Three Estates of France (lords, church, and commons) and gained their consent before proceeding to extremities. Neither in Italy, Germany, nor England was there the slightest general manifestation of disapproval at this free handling of the sovereign pontiff. The idea of Christendom had decayed until its power over the minds of men had gone.

In the East, in 1261, the Greeks recaptured Constantinople from the Latin emperors, and the founder of the new Greek dynasty, Michael Palæologus,

---

[1] J. H. Robinson.

Michael VIII, after some unreal tentatives of reconciliation with the Pope, broke away from the Roman communion altogether, and with that and the fall of the Latin kingdoms in Asia the eastward ascendancy of the Popes came to an end.

Throughout the fourteenth century the papacy did nothing to recover its moral sway. The next Pope but one, Clement V, was a Frenchman, the choice of King Philip of France. He never came to Rome. He set up his Court in the town of Avignon, which then belonged not to France, but to the Papal See, though embedded in French territory; and there his successors remained until 1377, when Pope Gregory XI returned to the Vatican palace in Rome. But Gregory XI did not take the sympathies of the whole church with him. Many of the cardinals were of French origin, and their habits and associations were rooted deep at Avignon. When in 1378 Gregory XI died, and an Italian, Urban VI, was elected, these dissentient cardinals declared the election invalid, and elected another Pope, the anti-Pope Clement VII.

This split is called the Great Schism. The Popes remained in Rome, and all the anti-French powers, the Emperor, the King of England, Hungary, Poland, and the North of Europe, were loyal to them. The anti-Popes, on the other hand, continued in Avignon, and were supported by the King of France, his ally the King of Scotland, Spain, Portugal, and various German princes. Each Pope excommunicated and cursed the adherents of his rival, so that by one standard or another all Christendom was damned soundly and completely during this time (1378–1417).

The lamentable effect of this split upon the solidarity of Christendom it is impossible to exaggerate. Is it any marvel that such men as Wycliffe began to teach men to think on their own account, when the fountain of truth thus squirted against itself?

In 1417 the Great Schism was healed at the Council of Constance, the same council that dug up and burnt Wycliffe's bones, and which, as we shall tell later, caused the burning of John Huss; at this council, Pope and anti-Pope resigned or were swept aside, and Martin V became the sole Pope of a formally reunited but spiritually very badly strained Christendom.

How, later on, the Council of Basel (1439) led to a fresh schism, and to further anti-Popes, we cannot relate here.

Such, briefly, is the story of the great centuries of papal ascendancy and papal decline. It is the story of the failure to achieve the very noble and splendid idea of a unified and religious world. We have pointed out in the previous section how greatly the inheritance of a complex dogmatic theology encumbered the church in this its ambitious adventure. It had too much theology, and not enough religion. But it may not be idle to point out here how much the individual insufficiency of the Popes also contributed to the collapse of its scheme and dignity. There was no such level of education in the world as to provide a succession of cardinals and popes with the breadth of knowledge and outlook needed for the task they had undertaken; they were not sufficiently educated for their task, and only a few, by sheer force of genius, transcended that defect. And, as we have already pointed out, they were, when at last they got to power, too old to use it. Before they could grasp the situation they had to control, most of them were dead.

It would be interesting to speculate how far it would have tilted the balance in favour of the church if the cardinals had retired at fifty, and if no one could have been elected Pope after fifty-five. This would have lengthened the average reign of each Pope, and enormously increased the continuity of the policy of the church. And it is perhaps possible that a more perfect system of selecting the cardinals, who were the electors and counsellors of the Pope, might have been devised. The rules and ways by which men reach power are of very great importance in human affairs. The psychology of the ruler is a science that has still to be properly studied. We have seen the Roman Republic wrecked, and here we see the church failing in its world mission very largely through ineffective electoral methods.

§ 16

Certain architectural and artistic developments mark the phases in the history of Christianity from the Romanesque period to the age of doubt and declining faith of which Frederick II was the precursor. There was a great outbreak of cathedral-building in the eleventh and twelfth centuries, and a rapid development of western Romanesque architecture into what is called, in the stricter sense, Gothic. The steep roof of the Romanesque towers elongated and became a spire; the cross-groined vaulted roof was introduced, and the pointed arch—which had already prevailed in Arabic art for two hundred years or more—swept away the rounded arch. With these features came a great development and elaboration of windows, and of stained glass.

It was probably the growth and enrichment of the monastic orders that released the flow of artistic energy that gave the world the Church of Notre Dame in Paris, for example, the Cathedral of Chartres, Amiens Cathedral, the magnificent beginning of Beauvais. And for several centuries the Gothic impulse was sustained. In the thirteenth century the traceried window was reaching its highest degree of development. In the fourteenth, Gothic became for a time exuberant and then in reaction severe. The English struck out a line of their own in the high austere "Perpendicular." Over large areas of Northern and Eastern Germany, where building-stone was rare or inaccessible, the Gothic forms took on a new quality with the use of brick. With the onset of the fifteenth century Gothic architecture waned. The great days of the church in Europe were past, and new social conditions had to express themselves in novel forms. In some towns of Belgium and Holland we still have the cathedral incomplete, and beside it some great municipal building which robbed the church of its constructive resources. In Ypres, for example, before the destruction of the war, the great Cloth Hall completely overshadowed the Cathedral.

In Spain, the Gothic followed the Christians as province by province they won back the peninsula from the Moors. The Mauresque Arabic and the Spanish Gothic developed each in its own confines. In Seville, close to the

Mauresque palace of the Alcazar rises a great Gothic cathedral, whose towering interior seems to be exulting in sombre triumph over the conquered conquerors.

The Gothic never penetrated deeply into Italy. The most prominent example is Milan Cathedral. But Italy, during the Gothic period in Western Europe, was a battleground of ancient traditions and conflicting styles. The Byzantine St. Mark's at Venice balances the Gothic of Milan Cathedral, and Norman and Saracen mingle their spirit with the Roman in such buildings as the Cathedral at Amalfi. The Cathedral and Baptistery and Campanile at Pisa compose a most expressive group of Italian buildings dating from round and about the twelfth century.

Throughout the Gothic period the passion for representative art, so strong in both Aryan and Hamitic peoples, is very evidently struggling against the instinctive disposition to suppress that appeared in the Western world after the first prevalence of Christianity and Islam. There was, it must be understood, no expressed hostility to representative art among the Christians. Classical Roman painting died out in the Catacombs and adorned Christian graves. A certain amount of mural painting of inferior quality struggled on through the Middle Ages and increased in the tenth and eleventh centuries.

With increased security came a growing desire to beautify churches and monastic buildings. Paintings spread from the cramped work of the illuminator to walls and modern panels. The stiff saints became more flexible; backgrounds became visible behind them, and gave the painter scope for naturalistic detail. The painted panel, which was made in one place, and taken to, and fixed up, in another, was the ancestor of the independent picture. For a time, in the twelfth and thirteenth centuries, France and Germany were ahead of Italy in this revival of pictorial art. Simultaneously the stone-mason was infusing his laborious decoration of the Gothic building with an increasing animation and realism. He turned the water-spout into a grimacing gargoyle; he put faces and figures upon capital and pinnacle; he brought the sculptured saint from relief into solidity. Here also Germany led. This creeping back of imitation is the most interesting general fact in the artistic history of the Middle Ages.

We have already noted a similar previous disappearance and reappearance of imitation in human history. The later Palæolithic man carved and drew realities with freedom and vigour, but the early Neolithic man has left us neither good drawings nor good carvings of living things. Plastic art scarcely reappeared until the Bronze Age. Exactly the same thing on a larger scale happened between the great days of the Roman Empire and the Middle Ages, not only under Christianity but under Islam. There has never been a full and satisfactory explanation of these alternations. Art retreated from reality and devoted itself to formal elaboration. Since then there has been another great wave of vivid imitativeness, culminating, perhaps, a little while ago. Both pictures and sculpture were, generally speaking, more fully imitative and representative, less symbolical and indicative, fifty years ago than they are now. Here we can offer no satisfactory explanation for these waves in the general artistic impulse, these alternations of exultant, intensely-rendered reality with aloofness and austerity. It is as if excessive realism, excessive delight in the body and in movement and excitement, and circumstantial detail, produced at last reaction and an instinctive resort to abstraction and formality.

§ 17

In the days of the Crusades very great changes were happening to music. Hitherto there had been no harmony recognized; music had been a simple affair of rhythm and melody; now began an entirely new development—first a primitive part-singing, and then the complication of more and more elaborately interwoven melodies. The different voices were made to sing simultaneously different airs which harmonized. Concurrently a notation was evolved capable of expressing and recording the new polyphonic music. The notation was as necessary to the free development of music as writing was to the appearance of a growing and varying literature.

It would seem that the first beginnings of this re-making of music were in Western Europe and probably in Wales and the English Midlands. For there it is that we have the first recorded cases of part-singing. It may have begun as early as the ninth century; it was certainly established and practised by the end of the twelfth century. A fine piece of English part-writing dating from about 1240 is still extant. It is the *rota*, "Sumer is i-cumen in." It was probably written by John of Forneste, a Reading monk, and, says Sir W. H. Hadow, "its part-writing is astonishingly sound and satisfying, and it can be heard with great pleasure at the present day. . . . It is the first voice in the development of our Western art which can still speak to us in friendly and familiar accents."

Those days of wandering adventurers were also days of wandering music. The Troubadours went from castle to castle; there were many mendicant minstrels, and the new conception of harmony spread through France and Italy and into Central Europe. Most of the compositions were unaccompanied vocal polyphony, the development of instrumentation came later with the lute, the virginal, the viol, and the greater use and range of the organ as the skill of the organ-builders increased. The castle and court had yet to reach such a pitch of luxury and elaboration as was necessary for the production of more than mainly vocal and mainly popular secular music; the chief laboratories of the new music were at first the great monastic cathedral choirs. There the innovating choir-masters struggled against a very conservative religiosity, and struggled far.

The dominant form of the phase of mainly vocal harmony was the madrigal. Palestrina (1526–1594), the Italian composer, was the culminating master of this period of choral music. In the sixteenth century the Italian makers were already perfecting the violin, the modern organ was being evolved, new social conditions were arising, new feelings were seeking expression, and new methods were being developed that were to render possible a still broader type of musical composition in which instrumentation was to play the greater part.

BOOK VII

THE MONGOL EMPIRES OF THE LAND WAYS AND THE NEW EMPIRES OF THE SEA WAYS

XXXII

THE GREAT EMPIRE OF JENGIS KHAN AND HIS SUCCESSORS

(The Age of the Land Ways)

§ 1. *Asia at the End of the Twelfth Century.* § 2. *The Rise and Victories of the Mongols.* § 3. *The Travels of Marco Polo.* § 4. *The Ottoman Turks and Constantinople.* § 5. *Why the Mongols were not Christianized.* § 6. *The Yuan and Ming Dynasties in China.* § 7. *The Mongols Revert to Tribalism.* § 8. *The Kipchak Empire and the Tsar of Muscovy.* § 9. *Timurlane.* § 10. *The Mongol Empire of India.* § 11. *The Gipsies.*

§ 1

WE HAVE to tell now of the last and greatest of all the raids of nomadism upon the civilizations of the East and West. We have traced in this history the development side by side of these two ways of living, and we have pointed out that, as the civilizations grew more extensive and better organized, the arms, the mobility, and the intelligence of the nomads also improved. The nomad was not simply an uncivilized man, he was a man specialized and specializing along his own line. From the very beginning of history the nomad and the settled people have been in reaction. We have told of the Semitic and Elamite raids upon Sumer; we have seen the Western empire smashed by the nomads of the great plains and Persia conquered and Byzantium shaken by the nomads of Arabia. The Mongol aggression, which began with the thirteenth century, was the latest thus far of these destructive reploughings of human association.

From entire obscurity the Mongols came very suddenly into history towards the close of the twelfth century. They appeared in the country to the north of China, in the land of origin of the Huns and Turks, and they were manifestly of the same strain as these peoples. They were gathered together under a chief, with whose name we will not tax the memory of the reader; under his son Jengis Khan their power grew with extraordinary swiftness.

The reader will already have an idea of the gradual breaking up of the original unity of Islam. In the beginning of the thirteenth century there were a number of separate and discordant Moslem states in Western Asia. There was

Egypt (with Palestine and much of Syria) under the successors of Saladin, there was the Seljuk power in Asia Minor, there was still an Abbasid caliphate in Bagdad, and to the east of this again there had grown up a very considerable empire, the Kharismian empire, that of the Turkish princes from Khiva who had conquered a number of fragmentary Seljuk principalities and reigned from the Ganges valley to the Tigris. They had but an insecure hold on the Persian and Indian populations.

The state of the Chinese civilization was equally inviting to an enterprising invader. Our last glimpse of China in this history was in the seventh century during the opening years of the Tang dynasty, when that shrewd and able emperor Tai-tsung was weighing the respective merits of Nestorian Christianity, Islam, Buddhism, and the teachings of Lao Tse, and on the whole inclining to the opinion that Lao Tse was as good a teacher as any. We have described his reception of the traveller Yuan Chwang. Tai-tsung tolerated all religions, but several of his successors conducted a pitiless persecution of the Buddhist faith; it flourished in spite of these persecutions, and its monasteries played a somewhat analogous part in at first sustaining learning and afterwards retarding it, that the Christian monastic organization did in the West.

By the tenth century the mighty Tang dynasty was in an extreme state of decay; the usual degenerative process through a series of voluptuaries and incapables had gone on, and China broke up again politically into a variable number of contending states, "The Age of the Ten States," an age of confusion that lasted through the first half of the tenth century. Then arose a dynasty, the Northern Sung (960–1127), which established a sort of unity, but which was in constant struggle with a number of Hunnish peoples from the north who were pressing down the eastern coast. For a time one of these peoples, the Khitan, prevailed. In the twelfth century these people had been subjugated and had given place to another Hunnish empire, the empire of the Kin, with its capital at Peking and its southern boundary south of Hwang-ho.

The Sung empire shrank before this Kin empire. In 1138 the capital was shifted from Nankin, which was now too close to the northern frontier, to the city of Han Chau on the coast. From 1127 onward to 1295 the Sung dynasty is known as the Southern Sung. To the north-west of its territories there was now the Tartar empire of the Hsia, to the north the Kin empire, both states in which the Chinese population was under rulers in whom nomadic traditions were still strong. So that here on the east, also, the main masses of Asiatic mankind were under uncongenial rulers and ready to accept, if not to welcome, the arrival of a conqueror.

Northern India we have already noted was also a conquered country at the opening of the thirteenth century. It was at first a part of the Khivan empire, but in 1206 an adventurous ruler, Kutub, who had been a slave and who had risen as a slave to be governor of the Indian province, set up a separate Moslem state of Hindustan in Delhi. Brahminism, as we have already noted, had long since ousted Buddhism from India, but the converts to Islam were still but a small ruling minority in the land.

Such was the political state of Asia when Jengis Khan began to consolidate

Map of
EUROPE and ASIA
about 1200 A.D.

his power among the nomads in the country between the lakes Balkash and Baikal in the beginning of the thirteenth century.

§ 2

The career of conquest of Jengis Khan and his immediate successors astounded the world, and probably astounded no one more than these Mongol Khans themselves.

The Mongols were in the twelfth century a tribe subject to those Kin who had conquered North-east China. They were a horde of nomadic horsemen living in tents, and subsisting mainly upon mare's milk products and meat. Their occupations were pasturage and hunting, varied by war. They drifted northward as the snows melted for summer pasture, and southward to winter pasture after the custom of the steppes. Their military education began with a successful insurrection against the Kin. The empire of Kin had the resources of half China behind it, and in the struggle the Mongols learnt very much of the military science of the Chinese. By the end of the twelfth century they were already a fighting tribe of exceptional quality.

The opening years of the career of Jengis were spent in developing his military machine, in assimilating the Mongols and the associated tribes about them into one organized army. His first considerable extension of power was westward, when the Tartar Kirghis and the Uighurs[1] (who were the Tartar

---

[1] The Uighurs first appear in the 6th century, when they were known as the Kao-ku or High Carts, one of the two main divisions of the Turks in and around Northern Mongolia. Their period of independent greatness covered A.D. 750–850, corresponding with the height of the glory of the famous T'ang Dynasty.

The Uighurs attained a very high level of culture, and recent archæological research has brought to light a vast amount of Uighur literature and art from which we learn that Christianity, Buddhism and Manichænism were all practised in their kingdom, the utmost tolerance being observed while Manichænism was the state religion. The Uighurs were certainly the most civilized of all the northern neighbours of China, and though their kingdom was destroyed in 850 by a northern Turkish tribe, the Khirgiz, the Uighurs by no means disappear from history, and up to the 15th century we constantly find small Uighur principalities and states springing up, while during the whole of this period the Uighurs were extensively employed in Muhammadan chancelleries, playing much the same rôle in the government offices of Turkestan as the Hindus under the Delhi Moguls and the Bengalis under the British in India.

The period of Oriental history beginning with the appearance of Jengis Khan in the 13th century and ending with the conquest of Constantinople by the Ottoman Turks, tells us of the rise and fall of a great number of Turkish dynasties in Central Asia, India and Persia; and it is curious to note that in most cases these dynasties were founded by men who had begun life as slaves. In an unpublished Persian MS. of the 13th century the following curious account of the Turks occurs:—

"It is common knowledge that all races and classes while they remain among their own people and in their own country are honoured and respected; but when they go abroad they become miserable and abject. The Turks, on the contrary, while they remain among their own people are merely a tribe among many tribes, and enjoy no particular power or status. But when they leave their own country and come to a Muhammadan country (the more remote they are from their own homes and relatives, the more highly they are valued and appreciated) they become Amirs and Generalissimos. Now from the days of Adam down to

people of the Tarim basin) were not so much conquered as induced to join
his organization. He then attacked the Kin empire and took Peking (1214).

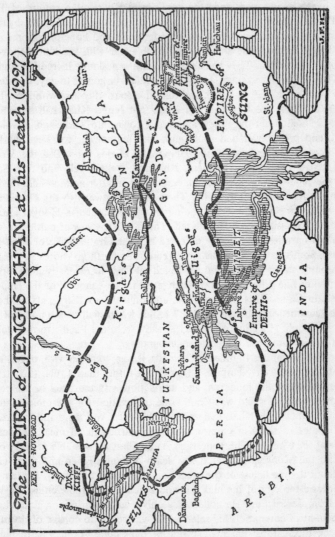

The Khitan people, who had been so recently subdued by the Kin, threw in
their fortunes with his, and were of very great help to him. The settled Chinese

---

the present day no slave bought at a price has ever become king except among
the Turks; and among the sayings of Afrasyab, who was king of the Turks, and
was extraordinarily wise and learned, was his dictum, that the Turk is like a
pearl in its shell at the bottom of the sea, which only becomes valuable when it
leaves the sea and adorns the diadems of kings and the ears of brides."

(Note by Sir Denison Ross)

population went on sowing and reaping and trading during this change of masters without lending its weight to either side.

We have already mentioned the very recent Kharismian empire of Turkestan, Persia and North India. This empire extended eastward to Kashgar, and it must have seemed one of the most progressive and hopeful empires of the time. Jengis Khan, while still engaged in this war with the Kin empire, sent envoys to Kharismia. They were put to death—an almost incredible stupidity. The Kharismian government, to use the political jargon of to-day, had decided not to "recognize" Jengis Khan, and took this spirited course with him. Thereupon (1218) the great host of horsemen that Jengis Khan had consolidated and disciplined swept over the Pamirs and down into Turkestan. It was well armed, and probably it had some guns and gunpowder for siege work—for the Chinese were certainly using gunpowder at this time, and the Mongols learnt its use from them. Kashgar, Khokand, Bokara fell, and then Samarkand, the capital of the Kharismian empire. Thereafter nothing held the Mongols in the Kharismian territories. They swept westward to the Caspian, and southward as far as Lahore. To the north of the Caspian a Mongol army encountered a Russian force from Kieff. There was a series of battles, in which the Russian armies were finally defeated and the Grand Duke of Kieff taken prisoner. So it was the Mongols appeared on the northern shores of the Black Sea. A panic swept Constantinople, which set itself to reconstruct its fortifications. Meanwhile other armies were engaged in the conquest of the empire of the Hsia in China. This was annexed, and only the southern part of the Kin empire remained unsubdued. In 1227 Jengis Khan died in the midst of a career of triumph. His empire reached already from the Pacific to the Dnieper. And it was an empire still vigorously expanding.

Like all the empires founded by nomads, it was, to begin with, purely a military and administrative empire, a framework rather than a rule. It centred on the personality of the monarch, and its relation with the mass of the populations over which it ruled was simply one of taxation for the maintenance of the horde. But Jengis Khan had called to his aid a very able and experienced administrator of the Kin empire, who was learned in all the traditions and science of the Chinese. This statesman, Yeliu Chutsai, was able to carry on the affairs of the Mongols long after the death of Jengis Khan and there can be little doubt that he is one of the great political heroes of history. He tempered the barbaric ferocity of his masters, and saved innumerable cities and works of art from destruction. He collected archives and inscriptions, and when he was accused of corruption his sole wealth was found to consist of documents and a few musical instruments. To him perhaps quite as much as to Jengis is the efficiency of the Mongol military machine to be ascribed. Under Jengis, we may note further, we find the completest religious toleration established across the entire breadth of Asia.

At the death of Jengis the capital of the new empire was still in the great barbaric town of Karakorum in Mongolia. There an assembly of Mongol leaders elected Ogdai Khan, the son of Jengis, as his successor. The war against the vestiges of the Kin empire was prosecuted until Kin was altogether subdued (1234). The Chinese empire to the south under the Sung dynasty helped the Mongols in this task, so destroying their own bulwark against the universal conquerors. The Mongol hosts then swept right across Asia to Russia (1235), an amazing march; Kieff was destroyed in 1240, and nearly all Russia became tributary to the Mongols. Poland was ravaged, and a mixed army of Poles and Germans was annihilated at the battle of Liegnitz in Lower Silesia in 1241. The Emperor Frederick II does not seem to have made any great efforts to stay the advancing tide.

"It is only recently," says Bury in his notes to Gibbon's *Decline and Fall of the Roman Empire,* "that European history has begun to understand that the successes of the Mongol army which overran Poland and occupied Hungary in the spring of A.D. 1241 were won by consummate strategy and were not due to a mere overwhelming superiority of numbers. But this fact has not yet become a matter of common knowledge; the vulgar opinion which represents the Tartars as a wild horde carrying all before them solely by their multitude, and galloping through Eastern Europe without a strategic plan, rushing at all obstacles and overcoming them by mere weight, still prevails. . . .

"It was wonderful how punctually and effectually the arrangements of the commander were carried out in operations extending from the Lower Vistula to Transylvania. Such a campaign was quite beyond the power of any European army of the time, and it was beyond the vision of any European commander. There was no general in Europe, from Frederick II downwards, who was not a tyro in strategy compared to Subutai. It should also be noticed that the Mongols embarked upon the enterprise with full knowledge of the political situation of Hungary and the condition of Poland—they had taken care to inform themselves by a well-organized system of spies; on the other hand, the Hungarians and Christian powers, like childish barbarians, knew hardly anything about their enemies."

But though the Mongols were victorious at Liegnitz, they did not continue their drive westward. They were getting into woodlands and hilly country, which did not suit their tactics; and so they turned southward and prepared to settle in Hungary, massacring or assimilating the kindred Magyar, even as these had previously massacred and assimilated the mixed Scythians and Avars and Huns before them. From the Hungarian plain they would probably have made raids west and south as the Hungarians had done in the ninth century, the Avars in the seventh and eighth, and the Huns in the fifth. But in Asia the Mongols were fighting a stiff war of conquest against the Sung, and they were also raiding Persia and Asia Minor; Ogdai died suddenly, and in 1242 there was trouble about the succession and, recalled by this, the undefeated hosts of Mongols began to pour back across Hungary and Rumania towards the east.

To the great relief of Europe the dynastic troubles at Karakorum lasted for some years, and this vast new empire showed signs of splitting up. Mangu Khan became the Great Khan in 1251, and he nominated his brother Kublai Khan as Governor-General of China. Slowly but surely the entire Sung empire was subjugated, and as it was subjugated the eastern Mongols became more and more Chinese in their culture and methods. Tibet was invaded and devastated by Mangu, and Persia and Syria were invaded in good earnest. Another brother of Mangu, Hulagu, was in command of this latter war. He turned his arms against the caliphate and captured Bagdad, in which city he perpetrated a massacre of the entire population. Bagdad was still the religious capital of Islam, and the Mongols had become bitterly hostile to the Moslems. This hostility exacerbated the natural discord of nomad and townsman. In 1259 Mangu died, and in 1260—for it took the best part of a year for the Mongol leaders to gather from the extremities of this vast empire, from Hungary and Syria and Scind and China—Kublai was elected Great Khan. He was already deeply interested in Chinese affairs; he made his capital Peking instead of Karakorum, and Persia, Syria, and Asia Minor became virtually independent under his brother Hulagu; while the hordes of Mongols in Russia and Asia next to Russia, and various smaller Mongol groups in Turkestan, became also practically separate. Kublai died in 1294, and with his death even the titular supremacy of the Great Khan disappeared.

At the death of Kublai there was a main Mongol empire, with Peking as its capital, including all China and Mongolia; there was a second great Mongol empire, that of Kipchak, in Russia; there was a third in Persia, that founded by Hulagu, the Ilkhan empire, to which the Seljuk Turks in Asia Minor were tributary; there was a Siberian state between Kipchak and Mongolia; and another separate state, "Great Turkey," in Turkestan. It is particularly remarkable that India beyond the Punjab was never invaded by the Mongols during this period, and that an army under the Sultan of Egypt completely defeated Ketboga, Hulagu's general, in Palestine (1260), and stopped them from entering Africa. By 1260 the impulse of Mongol conquest had already passed its zenith. Thereafter the Mongol story is one of division and decay.

The Mongol dynasty that Kublai Khan had founded in China, the Yuan dynasty, lasted from 1280 until 1368. Later on a recrudescence of Mongolian energy in Western Asia was destined to create a still more enduring monarchy in India. But in the thirteenth and fourteenth centuries the Afghans and not the Mongols were masters of North India, and an Afghan empire extended into the Deccan.

§ 3

Now, this story of Mongolian conquests is surely one of the most remarkable in all history. The conquests of Alexander the Great cannot compare with them in extent. Their effect in diffusing and broadening men's ideas and stimulating their imaginations was enormous. For a time all Asia and Western Europe enjoyed an open intercourse; all the roads were temporarily open, and representatives of every nation appeared at the Court of Karakorum.

The barriers between Europe and Asia set up by the religious feud of Christianity and Islam were lowered. Great hopes were entertained by the papacy for the conversion of the Mongols to Christianity. Their only religion so far had been Shamanism, a primitive paganism. Envoys of the Pope, Buddhist priests from India, Parisian and Italian and Chinese artificers, Byzantine and Armenian merchants, mingled with Arab officials and Persian and Indian astronomers and mathematicians at the Mongol Court. We hear too much in history of the campaigns and massacres of the Mongols, and not enough of

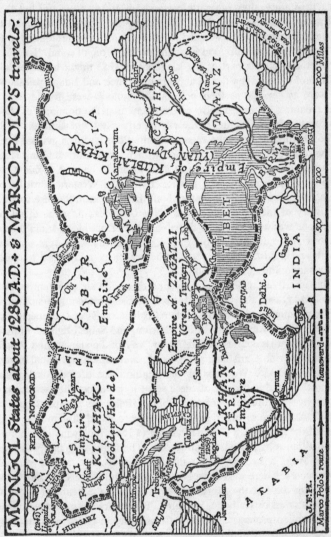

their curiosity and desire for learning. Not perhaps as an originative people, but as transmitters of knowledge and method their influence upon the world's history has been very great. And everything one can learn of the vague and romantic personalities of Jengis and Kublai tends to confirm the impression that these men were at least as understanding and creative monarchs as either that flamboyant but egotistical figure Alexander the Great, or that raiser of political ghosts, that energetic but illiterate theologian Charlemagne.

The missionary enterprises of the papacy in Mongolia ended in failure. Christianity was losing its persuasive power. The Mongols had no prejudice against Christianity; they evidently preferred it at first to Islam; but the missions that came to them were manifestly using the power in the great teachings of Jesus to advance the vast claims of the Pope to world dominion. Christianity so vitiated was not good enough for the Mongol mind. To make the empire of the Mongols part of the kingdom of God might have appealed to them; but not to make it a fief of a group of French and Italian priests, whose claims were as gigantic as their powers and outlook were feeble, who were now the creatures of the Emperor of Germany, now the nominees of the King of France, and now the victims of their own petty spites and vanities.

In 1269 Kublai Khan sent a mission to the Pope with the evident intention of finding some common mode of action with Western Christendom. He asked that a hundred men of learning and ability should be sent to his Court to establish an understanding. His mission found the Western world popeless, and engaged in one of those disputes about the succession that are so frequent in the history of the papacy. For two years there was no pope at all. When at last a pope was appointed, he dispatched two Dominican friars to convert the greatest power in Asia to his rule! Those worthy men were appalled by the length and hardship of the journey before them, and found an early excuse for abandoning the expedition.

But this abortive mission was only one of a number of attempts to communicate, and always they were feeble and feeble-spirited attempts, with nothing of the conquering fire of the earlier Christian missions. Innocent IV had already sent some Dominicans to Karakorum, and Saint Louis of France had also dispatched missionaries and relics by way of Persia; Mangu Khan had numerous Nestorian Christians at his Court, and subsequent papal envoys actually reached Pekin. We hear of the appointment of various legates and bishops to the East, but many of these seem to have lost themselves and perhaps their lives before they reached China. There was a papal legate in Peking in 1346, but he seems to have been a mere papal diplomatist. With the downfall of the Mongolian (Yuan) dynasty (1368), the dwindling opportunity of the Christian missions passed altogether. The house of Yuan was followed by that of Ming, a strongly nationalist Chinese dynasty, at first very hostile to all foreigners. There may have been a massacre of the Christian missions. Until the later days of the Mings (1644) little more is heard of Christianity, whether Nestorian or Catholic, in China. Then a fresh and rather more successful attempt to propagate Catholic Christianity in China was made by the Jesuits, but this second missionary wave reached China by the sea.

In the year 1298 a naval battle occurred between the Genoese and the Venetians, in which the latter were defeated. Among the 7,000 prisoners taken by the Genoese was a Venetian gentleman named Marco Polo, who had been a great traveller, and who was very generally believed by his neighbours to be given to exaggeration. He had taken part in that first mission to Kublai

Khan, and had gone on when the two Dominicans turned back. While this Marco Polo was a prisoner in Genoa, he beguiled his tedium by talking of his travels to a certain writer named Rusticiano, who wrote them down. We will not enter here into the vexed question of the exact authenticity of Rusticiano's story—we do not certainly know in what language it was written—but there can be no doubt of the general truth of this remarkable narrative, which became enormously popular in the fourteenth and fifteenth centuries with all men of active intelligence. *The Travels of Marco Polo* is one of the great books of history. It opens this world of the thirteenth century to our imaginations—this century which saw the reign of Frederick II and the beginnings of the Inquisition—as no mere historian's chronicle can do. It led directly to the discovery of America.

It begins by telling of the journey of Marco's father, Nicolo Polo, and uncle, Maffeo Polo, to China. These two were Venetian merchants of standing, living in Constantinople, and somewhere about 1260 they went to the Crimea and thence to Kazan; from that place they journeyed to Bokhara, and at Bokhara they fell in with a party of envoys from Kublai Khan in China to his brother Hulagu in Persia. These envoys pressed them to come on to the Great Khan, who at that time had never seen men of the "Latin" peoples. They went on; and it is clear they made a very favourable impression upon Kublai, and interested him greatly in the civilization of Christendom. They were made the bearers of that request for a hundred teachers and learned men, "intelligent men acquainted with the Seven Arts, able to enter into controversy, and able clearly to prove to idolators and other kinds of folk that the Law of Christ was best," to which we have just alluded. But when they returned Christendom was in a phase of confusion, and it was only after a delay of two years that they got their authorization to start for China again in the company of those two faint-hearted Dominicans. They took with them young Marco, and it is due to his presence and the boredom of his subsequent captivity at Genoa that this most interesting experience has been preserved to us.

The three Polos started by way of Palestine, and not by the Crimea as in the previous expedition. They had with them a gold tablet and other indications from the Great Khan that must have greatly facilitated their journey. The Great Khan had asked for some oil from the lamp that burns in the Holy Sepulchre at Jerusalem; and so thither they first went, and then by way of Cilicia into Armenia. They went thus far north because the Sultan of Egypt was raiding the Ilkhan domains at this time. Thence they came by way of Mesopotamia to Ormuz, on the Persian Gulf, as if they contemplated a sea voyage. At Ormuz they met merchants from India. For some reason they did not take ship, but instead turned northward through the Persian deserts, and so by way of Balkh over the Pamir to Kashgar, and by way of Kotan and the Lob Nor (so following in the footsteps of Yuan Chwang) into the Hwang-ho valley and on to Peking. Peking, Polo calls "Cambaluc"; Northern China, "Cathay" (=Khitan); and Southern China of the former Sung dynasty, "Manzi."

At Peking was the Great Khan, and they were hospitably entertained. Marco particularly pleased Kublai; he was young and clever, and it is clear he had mastered the Tartar language very thoroughly. He was given an official position and sent on several missions, chiefly in South-west China. The tale he had to tell of vast stretches of smiling and prosperous country, "all the way excellent hostelries for travellers," and "fine vineyards, fields and gardens," of "many abbeys" of Buddhist monks, of manufactures of "cloth of silk and gold and many fine taffetas," a "constant succession of cities and borough," and so on, first roused the incredulity and then fired the imagination of all Europe.

He told of Burmah, and of its great armies with hundreds of elephants, and how these animals were defeated by the Mongol bowmen, and also of the Mongol conquest of Pegu. He told of Japan, and greatly exaggerated the amount of gold in that country. And still more wonderful, he told of Christians and Christian rulers in China, and of a certain "Prester John," John the Priest, who was the "king" of a Christian people. Those people he had not seen. Apparently they were a tribe of Nestorian Tartars in Mongolia. An understandable excitement probably made Rusticiano over-emphasize what must have seemed to him the greatest marvel of the whole story, and Prester John became one of the most stimulating legends of the fourteenth and fifteenth centuries. It encouraged European enterprise enormously to think that far away in China was a community of their co-religionists, presumably ready to welcome and assist them. For three years Marco ruled the city of Yang-chow as governor, and he probably impressed the Chinese inhabitants as being very little more of a foreigner than any Tartar would have been. He may also have been sent on a mission to India. Chinese records mention a certain Polo attached to the imperial council in 1277, a very valuable confirmation of the general truth of the Polo story.

The Polos had taken about three and a half years to get to China. They stayed there upwards of sixteen. Then they began to feel homesick. They were the protégés of Kublai, and possibly they felt that his favours roused a certain envy that might have disagreeable results after his death. They sought his permission to return. For a time he refused it, and then an opportunity occurred. Argon, the Ilkhan monarch of Persia, grandson of Hulagu, Kublai's brother, had lost his Mongol wife, and on her death-bed had promised not to wed any other woman but a Mongol of her own tribe. He sent ambassadors to Peking, and a suitable princess was selected, a girl of seventeen. To spare her the fatigues of the caravan route, it was decided to send her by sea with a suitable escort. The "Barons" in charge of her asked for the company of the Polos because these latter were experienced travellers and sage men, and the Polos snatched at this opportunity of getting homeward.

The expedition sailed from some port on the east of South China; they stayed long in Sumatra and South India, and they reached Persia after a voyage of two years. They delivered the young lady safely to Argon's successor—for Argon was dead—and she married Argon's son. The Polos then went by Tabriz to Trebizond, sailed to Constantinople, and got back to Venice about 1295.

It is related that the returned travellers, dressed in Tartar garb, were refused admission to their own house. It was some time before they could establish their identity. Many people who admitted that, were still inclined to look askance at them as shabby wanderers; and in order to dispel such doubts they gave a great feast, and when it was at its height they had their old padded suits brought to them, dismissed the servants, and then ripped open these garments, whereupon an incredible display of "rubies, sapphires, carbuncles, emeralds, and diamonds" poured out before the dazzled company. Even after this, Marco's accounts of the size and population of China were received with much furtive mockery. The wits nicknamed him *Il Milione* because he was always talking of millions of people and millions of ducats.

Such was the story that raised eyebrows first in Venice and then throughout the Western world. The European literature, and especially the European romance of the fifteenth century, echoes with the names in Marco Polo's story, with Cathay and Cambaluc and the like.

§ 4

These travels of Marco Polo were only the beginning of a very considerable intercourse. Before we go on, however, to describe the great widening of the mental horizons of Europe that was now beginning, and to which his book of travels was to contribute very materially, it will be convenient first to note a curious side-consequence of the great Mongol conquests, the appearance of the Ottoman Turks upon the Dardanelles, and next to state in general terms the breaking-up and development of the several parts of the empire of Jengis Khan.

The Ottoman Turks were a little band of fugitives who fled south-westerly before the first invasion of Western Turkestan by Jengis. They made their long way from Central Asia, over deserts and mountains and through alien populations, seeking some new lands in which they might settle. "A small band of alien herdsmen," says Sir Mark Sykes, "wandering unchecked through crusades and counter-crusades, principalities, empires, and states. Where they camped, how they moved and preserved their flocks and herds, where they found pasture, how they made their peace with the various chiefs through whose territories they passed, are questions which one may well ask in wonder."

They found a resting-place at last and kindred and congenial neighbours on the table-lands of Asia Minor among the Seljuk Turks. Most of this country, the modern Anatolia, was now largely Turkish in speech and Moslem in religion, except that there was a considerable proportion of Greeks, Jews, and Armenians in the town populations. No doubt the various strains of Hittite, Phrygian, Trojan, Lydian, Ionian Greek, Cimmerian, Galatian, and Italian (from the Pergamus times) still flowed in the blood of the people, but they had long since forgotten these ancestral elements. They were, indeed, much the same blend of ancient Mediterranean dark-whites, Nordic Aryans, Semites, and Mongolians as were the inhabitants of the Balkan peninsula, but they believed themselves to be a pure Turanian race and altogether superior to the Christians on the other side of the Bosphorus.

Gradually the Ottoman Turks became important, and at last dominant among the small principalities, into which the Seljuk empire, the empire of "Roum," had fallen. Their relations with the dwindling empire of Constantinople remained for some centuries tolerantly hostile. They made no attack upon the Bosphorus, but they got a footing in Europe at the Dardanelles, and, using this route—the route of Xerxes and not the route of Darius—they pushed their way steadily into Macedonia, Epirus, Illyria, Yugo-Slavia, and Bulgaria.

In the Serbs (Yugo-Slavs) and Bulgarians the Turks found people very like themselves in culture and, though neither side recognized it, probably very similar in racial admixture, with a little less of the dark Mediterranean and Mongolian strains than the Turks and a trifle more of the Nordic element. But these Balkan peoples were Christians, and bitterly divided among themselves. The Turks, on the other hand, spoke one language; they had a greater sense of unity, they had the Moslem habits of temperance and frugality, and they were on the whole better soldiers. They converted what they could of the conquered people to Islam; the Christians they disarmed, and conferred upon them the monopoly of tax-paying. Gradually the Ottoman princes consolidated an empire that reached from the Taurus Mountains in the east to the boundaries of Hungary and Rumania in the west. Adrianople became their chief city. They surrounded the shrunken empire of Constantinople on every side. It was not Constantinople which was the bulwark of Europe at the time; it was Hungary—a Christian Turkish people defended Europe against the Moslem Turks.

The Ottomans organized a standing military force, the Janissaries, rather on the lines of the Mamelukes who dominated Egypt.

"These troops were formed of levies of Christian youths to the extent of one thousand per annum, who were affiliated to the Bektashi order of dervishes, and though at first not obliged to embrace Islam, were one and all strongly imbued with the mystic and fraternal ideas of the confraternity to which they were attached. Highly paid, well disciplined, a close and jealous secret society, the Janissaries provided the newly formed Ottoman state with a patriotic force of trained infantry soldiers, which, in an age of light cavalry and hired companies of mercenaries, was an invaluable asset. . . .

"The relations between the Ottoman Sultans and the Emperors has been singular in the annals of Moslem and Christian states. The Turks had been involved in the family and dynastic quarrels of the Imperial City, were bound by ties of blood to the ruling families, frequently supplied troops for the defence of Constantinople, and on occasion hired parts of its garrison to assist them in their various campaigns; the sons of the Emperors and Byzantine statesmen even accompanied the Turkish forces in the field, yet the Ottomans never ceased to annex Imperial territories and cities both in Asia and Thrace. This curious intercourse between the House of Osman and the Imperial government had a profound effect on both institutions; the Greeks grew more and more debased and demoralized by the shifts and tricks that their military weakness obliged them to adopt towards their neighbours; the Turks were corrupted by the alien atmosphere of intrigue and treachery which crept into their domestic life. Fratricide and parricide, the two crimes which most frequently stained the annals of the Imperial Palace, eventually formed a part of the policy of the Ottoman dynasty. One of the sons of Murad I embarked on an intrigue with Andronicus, the son of the Greek Emperor, to murder their respective fathers. . . .

"The Byzantine found it more easy to negotiate with the Ottoman Pasha than with the Pope. For years the Turks and Byzantines had intermarried and hunted in couples in strange bypaths of diplomacy. The Ottoman had played the Bulgar and the Serb of Europe against the Emperor, just as the

Emperor had played the Asiatic Amir against the Sultan; the Greek and the Turkish Royal Princes had mutually agreed to hold each other's rivals as prisoners and hostages; in fact, Turk and Byzantine policy had so intertwined that it is difficult to say whether the Turks regarded the Greeks as their allies, enemies, or subjects, or whether the Greeks looked upon the Turks as their tyrants, destroyers, or protectors. . . ."[1]

It was in 1453, under the Ottoman Sultan Muhammad II, that Constantinople at last fell to the Moslems. He attacked it from the European side, and with a great power of artillery. The Greek Emperor was killed, and there was much looting and massacre. The Great Church of Saint Sophia, which Justinian the Great had built (532), was plundered of its treasures and turned at once into a mosque. This event sent a wave of excitement throughout Eu-

---

[1] Sir Mark Sykes, *The Caliphs' Last Heritage.*

rope, and an attempt was made to organize a crusade; but the days of the crusades were past.

Says Sir Mark Sykes: "To the Turks the capture of Constantinople was a crowning mercy and yet a fatal blow. Constantinople had been the tutor and polisher of the Turks. So long as the Ottomans could draw science, learning, philosophy, art, and tolerance from a living fountain of civilization in the heart of their dominions, so long had the Ottomans not only brute force but intellectual power. So long as the Ottoman Empire had in Constantinople a free port, a market, a centre of world finance, a pool of gold, an exchange, so long did the Ottomans never lack for money and financial support. Muhammad was a great statesman; the moment he entered Constantinople he endeavoured to stay the damage his ambition had done; he supported the patriarch, he conciliated the Greeks, he did all he could to continue Constantinople the city of the Emperors . . . but the fatal step had been taken; Constantinople as the city of the Sultans was Constantinople no more; the markets died away, the culture and civilization fled, the complex finance faded from sight; and the Turks had lost their governors and their support. On the other hand, the corruptions of Byzantium remained, the bureaucracy, the eunuchs, the palace guards, the spies, the bribers, go-betweens—all these the Ottomans took over, and all these survived in luxuriant life. The Turks, in taking Stambul, let slip a treasure and gained a pestilence. . . ."

Muhammad's ambition was not sated by the capture of Constantinople. He set his eyes also upon Rome. He captured and looted the Italian town of Otranto, and it is probable that a very vigorous and perhaps successful attempt to conquer Italy—for the peninsula was divided against itself—was averted only by his death (1481). His sons engaged in fratricidal strife. Under Bayezid II (1481–1512), his successor, war was carried into Poland, and most of Greece was conquered. Selim (1512–1520), the son of Bayezid, extended the Ottoman power over Armenia and conquered Egypt. In Egypt, the last Abbasid Caliph was living under the protection of the Mameluke Sultan—for the Fatimite caliphate was a thing of the past. Selim bought the title of Caliph from this last degenerate Abbasid, and acquired the sacred banner and other relics of the Prophet. So the Ottoman Sultan became also Caliph of all Islam. Selim was followed by Suleiman the Magnificent (1520–1566), who conquered Bagdad in the east and the greater part of Hungary in the west, and very nearly captured Vienna. For three centuries Hungary had stood out against the Sultan, but the disaster at Mohacs (1526), in which the king of Hungary was killed, laid that land at the feet of the conqueror. His fleets also took Algiers, and inflicted a number of reverses upon the Venetians. In most of his warfare with the Empire he was in alliance with the French. Under him the Ottoman power reached its zenith.

§ 5

Let us now very briefly run over the subsequent development of the main masses of the empire of the Great Khan. In no case did Christianity succeed in capturing the imagination of these Mongol states. Christianity was in a phase of moral and intellectual insolvency, without any collective faith, energy, or honour; we have told of the wretched brace of timid Dominicans which was the Pope's reply to the appeal of Kublai Khan, and we have noted the general failure of the overland missions of the thirteenth and fourteenth centuries.

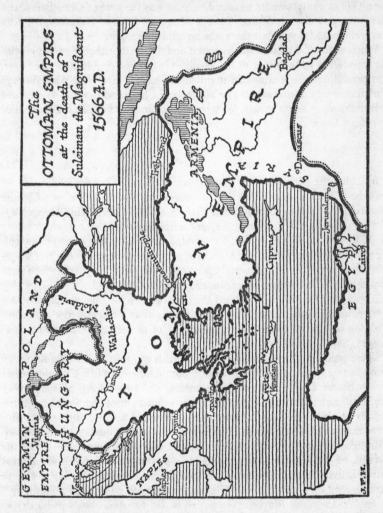

The OTTOMAN EMPIRE at the death of Suleiman the Magnificent 1566 A.D.

That apostolic passion which could win whole nations to the Kingdom of Heaven was dead in the church.

In 1305, as we have told, the Pope became the kept pontiff of the French king. All the craft and policy of the Popes of the thirteenth century to oust the Emperor from Italy had only served to let in the French to replace him. From 1309 to 1377 the Popes remained at Avignon; and such slight missionary effort as they made was merely a part of the strategy of Western European politics. In 1377 the Pope Gregory XI did indeed re-enter Rome and die there, but the French cardinals split off from the others at the election of his successor, and two Popes were elected, one at Avignon and one at Rome. This split, the Great Schism, lasted from 1378 to 1418. Each Pope cursed the other and put all his supporters under an interdict. Such was the state of Christianity, and such were now the custodians of the teachings of Jesus of Nazareth. All Asia was white unto harvest, but there was no effort to reap it.

When at last the church was reunited and missionary energy returned with the foundation of the order of the Jesuits, the days of opportunity were over. The possibility of a world-wide moral unification of East and West through Christianity had passed away. The Mongols in China and Central Asia turned to Buddhism; in South Russia, Western Turkestan and the Ilkhan Empire they embraced Islam.

§ 6

In China the Mongols were already saturated with Chinese civilization by the time of Kublai. After 1280 the Chinese annals treated Kublai as a Chinese monarch, the founder of the Yuan dynasty (1280–1368). This Mongol dynasty was finally overthrown by a Chinese nationalist movement which set up the Ming dynasty (1368–1644), a cultivated and artistic line of emperors, ruling until a northern people, the Manchus, who were the same as the Kin whom Jengis had overthrown, conquered China and established a dynasty which gave way only to a native republican form of government in 1912.

It was the Manchus who obliged the Chinese to wear Manchu pigtails as a mark of submission. The pigtailed Chinaman is quite a recent figure in history. With the coming of the republic the wearing of the pigtail ceased to be compulsory, and is now wholly unknown.

These political changes in the far east which we must needs note so briefly here went on over the surface of a multitudinous civilized life. Chinese art has always chosen fragile and perishable media, and so we have no such bulky wealth of material to testify to the artistic refinement of the Sung and Yuan periods as we have of the far less highly developed art of contemporary Europe. But we have enough to convince us of the fine quality of the period. Although the Sung dynasty marks a period of political recession under the pressure of the Khitan and Kin and Hsia powers, it was a period of great artistic activity. During the Southern Sung period Chinese painting is said to have reached its highest levels. "Glorious in art as in poetry and philosophy," writes Mr. Laurence Binyon, "the period which for Asia stands in history as the Periclean age in Europe. . . . With a passion for nature unmatched in Europe until Wordsworth's day, the Sung artists portrayed their delight in mountains, mists, plunging torrents, the flight of the wild geese from the reed beds, the moonlit reveries of sages in forest solitudes, the fisherman in his boat on lake or stream."

The Sung impetus in painting went on without any great change throughout the Yuan dynasty, but when the Ming rule began a certain weakening and elaboration appeared. With the Mings we come to a period which has left abundant monuments. Much wood and ivory carving remains; bowls and carvings of jade and rock crystal and a multitude of fine bronzes. The avenues of colossal stone statues leading to the Ming tombs, though by no means representative of the best of Chinese sculpture, are well known. Gradually a fussy over-elaboration invaded Chinese carving until it was smothered under a profusion of dragons, flowers, and symbolical figures.

Although "something worthy of the name of porcelain," says William Burton, was made as early as the Tang period, the earliest surviving Chinese porcelain dates from the Sung period. Porcelain began to travel westward with silk, and it is recorded that Saladin sent a present of forty pieces to the sultan of Damascus. With the coming of the Ming dynasty the manufacture of pottery received the stimulus of direct imperial patronage and was developed with extraordinary energy and success. Painted decoration began to be used, and it was in the fifteenth century that the finest blue and white porcelain was achieved. Astonishingly fine porcelain, perforated porcelain, and a marvellous under-glaze red are among the triumphs of this, the supreme period of Chinese ceramics.

§ 7

In the Pamirs, in much of Eastern and Western Turkestan, and to the north, the Mongols presently dropped back towards the tribal conditions from which they had been lifted by Jengis. It is possible to trace the dwindling succession of many of the small Khans, who became independent during this period, almost down to the present time. The Kalmucks in the seventeenth and eighteenth centuries founded a considerable empire, but dynastic troubles broke it up before it had extended its power beyond Central Asia. The Chinese recovered Eastern Turkestan from them about 1757.

Tibet was more and more closely linked with China, and became the great home of Buddhism and Buddhist monasticism.

Over most of the area of Western Central Asia and Persia and Mesopotamia the ancient distinction of nomad and settled population remains to this day. The townsmen despise and cheat the nomads, the nomads ill-treat and despise the townsfolk.

§ 8

The Mongols of the great realm of Kipchak remained nomadic, and grazed their stock across the wide plains of South Russia and Western Asia adjacent to Russia. They became not very devout Moslems, retaining many traces of their earlier barbaric Shamanism. Their chief khan was the Khan of the Golden Horde. To the west, over large tracts of open country, and more particularly in what is now known as Ukrainia, the old Scythian population, Slavs with a Mongol admixture, reverted to a similar nomadic life. These Christian nomads, the Cossacks, formed a sort of frontier screen against the Tartars, and their free and adventurous life was so attractive to the peasants of Poland and Lithuania that severe laws had to be passed to prevent a vast migration from the ploughlands to the steppes. The serf-owning landlords of Poland regarded the Cossacks with considerable hostility on this account, and war was as frequent between the Polish chivalry and the Cossacks as it was between the latter and the Tartars.

In the empire of Kipchak, as in Turkestan almost up to the present time, while the nomads roamed over wide areas, a number of towns and cultivated regions sustained a settled population which usually paid tribute to the nomad Khan. In such towns as Kieff, Moscow, and the like, the pre-Mongol, Christian town life went on under Russian dukes or Tartar governors, who collected the tribute for the Khan of the Golden Horde. The Grand Duke of Moscow gained the confidence of the Khan, and gradually, under his authority, obtained an ascendancy over many of his fellow tributaries. In the fifteenth century, under its Grand Duke Ivan III, Ivan the Great (1462–1505), Moscow threw off its Mongol allegiance and refused to pay tribute any longer (1480). The successors of Constantine no longer reigned in Constantinople, and Ivan took possession of the Byzantine double-headed eagle for his arms. He claimed to be the heir to Byzantium because of his marriage (1472) with Zoe Palæologa of the imperial line. This ambitious grand dukedom of Moscow assailed and subjugated the ancient Northman trading republic of Novgorod to the north, and so the foundations of the modern Russian Empire were laid and a link with the mercantile life of the Baltic established. Ivan III did not, however, carry his claim to be the heir of the Christian rulers of Constantinople to the extent of assuming the imperial title. This step was taken by his grandson, Ivan IV (Ivan the Terrible, because of his insane cruelties; 1533–1584). Although the ruler of Moscow thus came to be called Tsar (Cæsar), his tradition was in many respects Tartar rather than European; he was autocratic after the unlimited Asiatic pattern, and the form of Christianity he affected was the Eastern, court-ruled, "orthodox" form, which had reached Russia long before the Mongol conquest, by means of Bulgarian missionaries from Constantinople.

To the west of the domains of Kipchak, outside the range of Mongol rule, a second centre of Slav consolidation had been set up during the tenth and eleventh centuries in Poland. The Mongol wave had washed over Poland, but had never subjugated it. Poland was not "orthodox," but Roman Catholic in religion; it used the Latin alphabet instead of the strange Russian letters, and its monarch never assumed an absolute independence of the Emperor. Poland was, in fact, in its origins an outlying part of Christendom and of the Holy Empire; Russia never was anything of the sort.

§ 9

The nature and development of the empire of the Ilkhans in Persia, Mesopotamia, and Syria is perhaps the most interesting of all the stories of these

Mongol powers, because in this region nomadism really did attempt, and really did to a very considerable degree succeed in its attempt, to stamp a settled civilized system out of existence. When Jengis Khan first invaded China, we are told that there was a serious discussion among the Mongol chiefs whether all the towns and settled populations should not be destroyed. To these simple practitioners of the open-air life the settled populations seemed corrupt, crowded, vicious, effeminate, dangerous, and incomprehensible; a detestable human efflorescence upon what would otherwise have been good pasture. They had no use whatever for the towns. The early Franks and the Anglo-Saxon conquerors of South Britain seem to have had much the same feeling towards townsmen. But it was only under Hulagu in Mesopotamia that these ideas seem to have been embodied in a deliberate policy. The Mongols here did not only burn and massacre; they destroyed the irrigation system that had endured for at least eight thousand years, and with that the mother civilization of all the Western world came to an end. Since the days of the priest-kings of Sumer there had been a continuous cultivation in these fertile regions, an accumulation of tradition, a great population, a succession of busy cities—Eridu, Nippur, Babylon, Nineveh, Ctesiphon, and Bagdad. Now the fertility ceased. Mesopotamia became a land of ruins and desolation, through which great waters ran to waste, or overflowed their banks to make malarious swamps. Later on Mosul and Bagdad revived feebly as second-rate towns. . . .

But for the defeat and death of Hulagu's general Ketboga in Palestine (1260), the same fate might have overtaken Egypt. But Egypt was now a Turkish sultanate; it was dominated by a body of soldiers, the Mamelukes, whose ranks, like those of their imitators, the Janissaries of the Ottoman Empire, were recruited and kept vigorous by the purchase and training of boy slaves. A capable Sultan such men would obey; a weak or evil one they would replace. Under this ascendancy Egypt remained an independent power until 1517, when it fell to the Ottoman Turks.

The first destructive vigour of Hulagu's Mongols soon subsided, but in the fifteenth century a last tornado of nomadism arose in Western Turkestan under the leadership of a certain Timur the Lame, or Timurlane. He was descended in the female line from Jengis Khan. He established himself in Samarkand, and spread his authority over Kipchak (Turkestan to South Russia), Siberia, and southward as far as the Indus. He assumed the title of Great Khan in 1369. He was a nomad of the savage school, and he created an empire of desolation from North India to Syria. Pyramids of skulls were his particular architectural fancy; after the storming of Ispahan he made one of 70,000.

His ambition was to restore the empire of Jengis Khan as he conceived it, a project in which he completely failed. He spread destruction far and wide; the Ottoman Turks—it was before the taking of Constantinople and their days of greatness—and Egypt paid him tribute; the Punjab he devastated; and Delhi surrendered to him. After Delhi had surrendered, however, he made a frightful massacre of its inhabitants. At the time of his death (1405) very little remained to witness to his power but a name of horror, ruins and desolated countries, and a shrunken and impoverished domain in Persia.

The dynasty founded by Timur in Persia was extinguished by another Turkoman horde fifty years later.

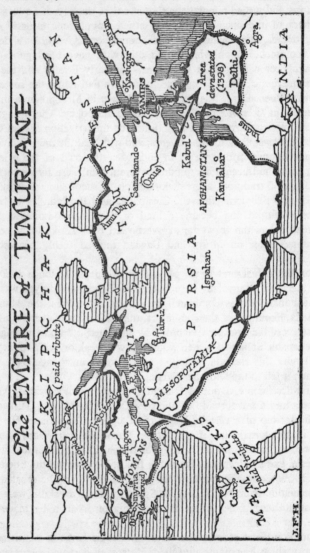

§ 10

In 1505 a small Turkoman chieftain, Baber, a descendant of Timur and therefore of Jengis, was forced after some years of warfare and some temporary successes—for a time he held Samarkand—to fly with a few followers over the Hindu Kush to Afghanistan. There his band increased, and he made himself master of Cabul. He assembled an army, accumulated guns, and then laid claim to the Punjab because Timur had conquered it a hundred and seven years before. He pushed his successes beyond the Punjab. India was in a state of division, and quite ready to welcome any capable invader who promised peace and order. After various fluctuations of fortune Baber met the Sultan of Delhi at Panipat (1525), ten miles north of that town, and though he had but 25,000 men, provided, however, with guns, against a thousand elephants and four times as many men—the numbers, by the by, are his own estimate—he gained a complete victory. He ceased to call himself King of Cabul, and assumed the title of Emperor of Hindustan. "This," he wrote, "is quite a different world from our countries." It was finer, more fertile, altogether richer. He conquered as far as Bengal, but his untimely death in 1530 checked the tide of Mongol conquest for a quarter of a century, and it was only after the accession of his grandson Akbar that it flowed again. Akbar subjugated all India as far as Berar, and his great-grandson Aurungzeb (1658–1707) was practically master of the entire peninsula. This great dynasty of Baber (1526–1530), Humayun (1530–1556), Akbar (1556–1605), Jehangir (1605–1627), Shah Jehan (1628–1658), and Aurungzeb (1658–1707), in which son succeeded father for six generations, this "Mogul (=Mongol) dynasty," marks the most splendid age that had hitherto dawned upon India. Akbar, next perhaps to Asoka, was one of the greatest of Indian monarchs, and one of the few royal figures that approach the stature of great men.

To Akbar it is necessary to give the same distinctive attention that we have shown to Charlemagne or Constantine the Great. He is one of the hinges of history. Much of his work on consolidation and organization in India survives to this day. It was taken over and continued by the British when they became the successors of the Mogul emperors. The British monarch, indeed, used as his Indian title the title of the Mogul emperors, *Kaisar-i-Hind*. All the other great administrations of the descendants of Jengis Khan, in Russia, throughout Western and Central Asia and in China, have long since dissolved away and given place to other forms of government. Their governments were, indeed, little more than taxing governments; a system of revenue-collecting to feed the central establishment of the ruler, like the Golden Horde in South Russia or the imperial city at Karakorum or Peking. The life and ideas of the people they left alone, careless how they lived—so long as they paid. So it was that, after centuries of subjugation, a Christian Moscow and Kieff, a Shiite Persia, and a thoroughly Chinese China rose again from their Mongol submergence. But Akbar made a new India. He gave the princes and ruling classes of India some inklings at least of a common interest. If India is now anything more than a sort of ragbag of incoherent states and races, a prey to every casual raider from the north, it is very largely due to him.

His distinctive quality was his openness of mind. He set himself to make every sort of able man in India, whatever his race or religion, available for the public work of Indian life. His instinct was the true statesman's instinct for synthesis. His empire was to be neither a Moslem nor a Mongol one, nor was it to be Rajput or Aryan, or Dravidian, or Hindu, or high or low caste; it was to be *Indian*. "During the years of his training he enjoyed many opportunities of noting the good qualities, the fidelity, the devotion, often the nobility of soul, of those Hindu princes, whom, because they were followers of Brahma, his Moslem courtiers devoted mentally to eternal torments. He noted that these men, and men who thought like them, constituted the vast majority of his subjects. He noted, further, of many of them, and those the most trustworthy, that though they had apparently much to gain from a worldly point of view by embracing the religion of the Court they held fast to their own. His reflective mind, therefore, was unwilling from the outset to accept the theory that because he, the conqueror, the ruler, happened to be born a Muhammadan, therefore Muhammadanism was true for all mankind. Gradually his thoughts found words in the utterance: 'Why should I claim to guide men before I myself am guided?' and, as he listened to other doctrines and other creeds, his honest doubts became confirmed, and, noting daily the bitter narrowness of sectarianism, no matter of what form of religion, he became more and more wedded to the principle of toleration for all."

"The son of a fugitive emperor," says Dr. Emil Schmit, "born in the desert, brought up in nominal confinement, he had known the bitter side of life from his youth up. Fortune had given him a powerful frame, which he trained to support the extremities of exertion. Physical exercise was with him a passion; he was devoted to the chase, and especially to the fierce excitement of catching the wild horse or elephant or slaying the dangerous tiger. On one occasion, when it was necessary to persuade the Raja of Jodhpore to abandon his intention of forcing the widow of his deceased son to mount the funeral pyre, Akbar rode two hundred and twenty miles in two days. In battle he displayed the utmost bravery. He led his troops in person during the dangerous part of a campaign, leaving to his generals the lighter task of finishing the war. In every victory he displayed humanity to the conquered, and decisively opposed any exhibition of cruelty. Free from all those prejudices which separate society and create dissension, tolerant to men of other beliefs, impartial to men of other races, whether Hindu or Dravidian, he was a man obviously marked out to weld the conflicting elements of his kingdom into a strong and prosperous whole.

"In all seriousness he devoted himself to the work of peace. Moderate in all pleasures, needing but little sleep and accustomed to divide his time with the utmost accuracy, he found leisure to devote himself to science and art after the completion of his State duties. The famous personages and scholars who adorned the capital he had built for himself at Fatepur-Sikri were at the same time his friends; every Thursday evening a circle of these was collected for intellectual conversation and philosophical discussion. His closest friends were two highly talented brothers, Faizi and Abul Fazl, the sons of a learned freethinker. The elder of these was a famous scholar in Hindu literature; with his help, and under his direction, Akbar had the most important of the Sanskrit works translated into Persian. Fazl, on the other hand, who was an especially close friend of Akbar, was a general, a statesman, and an organizer, and to his activity Akbar's kingdom chiefly owed the solidarity of its internal organization."[1]

Like Charlemagne and like Tai-tsung, Akbar dabbled in religion, and had long discussions, that are still on record, with Jesuit missionaries.

(Such was the quality of the circle that used to meet in the palaces of Fatepur-Sikri—buildings which still stand in the Indian sunlight, but empty now and desolate. Fatepur-Sikri, like the city of Ambar, is now a dead city. A few years ago the child of a British official was killed by a panther in one of its silent streets.)

Akbar, like all men, great or petty, lived with the limitations of his period and its circles of ideas. And a Turkoman, ruling in India, was necessarily ignorant of much that Europe had been painfully learning for a thousand years. He knew nothing of the growth of a popular consciousness in Europe, and little or nothing of the wide educational possibilities that the church had been working out in the West. Something more than an occasional dispute with a Christian missionary was needed for that. His upbringing in Islam and his native genius made it plain to him that a great nation in India could only be cemented by common ideas upon a religious basis, but the knowledge of how such a solidarity could be created and sustained by universal schools, cheap books, and a university system at once organized and free to think, to which the modern state is still feeling its way, was as impossible to him as a knowledge of steamboats or aeroplanes. The form of Islam he knew best was the narrow and fiercely intolerant form of the Turkish Sunnites. The Moslems were only a minority of the population. The problem he faced was, indeed, very parallel to the problem of Constantine the Great. But it had peculiar difficulties of its own. He never got beyond an attempt to adapt Islam to a wider appeal by substituting for "There is one God, and Muhammad is his prophet," the declaration, "There is one God, and the Emperor is his regent." This he thought might form a common platform for every variety of faith in India, that kaleidoscope of religions. With this faith he associated a simple ritual borrowed from the Persian Zoroastrians (the Parsees), who still survived, and survive to-day, in India. This new state religion, however, died with him, because it had no roots in the minds of the people about him.

The essential factor in the organization of a living state, the world is coming to realize, is the organization of an education. This Akbar never understood. And he had no class of men available who would suggest such an idea to him or help him to carry it out. The Moslem teachers in India were not so much teachers as conservators of an intense bigotry; they did not want a common mind in India, but only a common intolerance in Islam. The Brahmins, who had the monopoly of teaching among the Hindus, had all the conceit and slackness of hereditary privilege. Yet, though Akbar made no general educational scheme for India, he set up a number of Moslem and Hindu schools.

The artistic and architectural remains of the Moguls are still very abundant,

---

[1] Dr. Schmit in Helmolt's *History of the World.*

and when people speak of Indian art without any qualification it is usually this great period that they have in mind. The painting of the time is fine and beautiful, and in type and quality very close to contemporary Persian work.

In building it has always been the lot of India to import the seed of highly developed methods and to impose upon them modifications and elaborations of her own. It was only after the Hellenic invasion that stone architecture became prevalent, and the outbreak of stupas, memorial pillars and other erections under Asoka shows everywhere the presence of Persian and Hellenic artists. The Buddhist art that has left such remarkable remains in the Gandhara district upon the north-west frontier, dating from the first four centuries A.D., is also strongly Hellenic. One finds façades represented with normal Corinthian columns.

It was only under the Gupta dynasty and in the fifth and sixth centuries A.D. that architecture and sculpture in India became distinctively Hindu, with a quality and dignity of its own. Dravidian influence from the south restrained the prevalence of vertical lines and steadied the building with horizontal mouldings and a storied pyramidalism. The Black Pyramid of Kanarak is one of the finest and most characteristic of pre-Moslem Hindu temples.

The Moslem conquest brought in the chief forms of the Saracenic style, the minaret, the pointed arch; and upon this new basis India wrought with exquisitely elaborate carving, window tracery and pierced screens. The Jama Masjid of Ahmedabad (fifteenth century) is one of the finest of Indian mosques, but perhaps the most splendid and typical specimen of all this Mogul architecture is the Taj Mahal, the tomb built by Shah Jehan (1627–1658) for his wife. Italian architects and workmen collaborate with Indians upon this gracious building.

§ 11

A curious side result of these later Mongol perturbations—those of the fourteenth century, of which Timurlane was the head and centre—was the appearance of drifting batches of a strange refugee Eastern people in Europe, the Gipsies. They appeared somewhen about the end of the fourteenth and early fifteenth centuries in Greece, where they were believed to be Egyptians (hence Gipsy), a very general persuasion which they themselves accepted and disseminated. Their leaders, however, styled themselves "Counts of Asia Minor."

They had probably been drifting about Western Asia for some centuries before the massacres of Timurlane drove them over the Hellespont. They may have been dislodged from their original homeland—as the Ottoman Turks were —by the great cataclysm of Jengis, or even earlier. They had drifted about as the Ottoman Turks had drifted about, but with less good fortune. They spread slowly westward across Europe; strange fragments of nomadism in a world of plough and city, driven off their ancient habitat of the Bactrian steppes to harbour upon European commons and by hedgerows and in wild woodlands and neglected patches. The Germans called them "Hungarians" and "Tartars," and the French "Bohemians."

They do not seem to have kept the true tradition of their origin, but they have a distinctive language which indicates their lost history; it contains many North Indian words, and is probably in its origin North Indian or Bactrian. There are also considerable Armenian and Persian factors in their speech.

They are found in all European countries to-day; they are tinkers, pedlars, horse-dealers, showmen, fortune-tellers, and beggars. To many imaginative minds their wayside encampments, with their smoking fires, their rounded tents, their hobbled horses, and their brawl of sunburnt children, have a very strong appeal.

Civilization is so new a thing in history, and has been for most of the time so very local a thing, that it has still to conquer and assimilate most of our instincts to its needs. In most of us, irked by its conventions and complexities, there stirs the nomad strain. We are but half-hearted homekeepers. The blood in our veins was brewed on the steppes as well as on the ploughlands.

Among other infections that the Gipsies have carried from land to land is the quality of the folk-music in the countries through which they have passed. They have always been enthusiastic if not very original musicians; everywhere they have carried a popular minstrelsy, giving it a gusto all their own. They have stolen people's airs as they sometimes stole their children and made gipsies of them. They never used any musical notation, but their tradition has been a strong one, and to-day the gipsy song has abundant offspring in the music of Hungary, Spain and Russia.

XXXIII

THE RENASCENCE OF WESTERN CIVILIZATION

(Land Ways Give Place to Sea Ways)

§ 1. *Christianity and Popular Education.* § 2. *Europe Begins to Think for Itself.* § 3. *The Great Plague and the Dawn of Communism.* § 4. *How Paper Liberated the Human Mind.* § 5. *Protestantism of the Princes and Protestantism of the Peoples.* § 6. *The Reawakening of Science.* § 7. *The New Growth of European Towns.* § 8. *The Literary Renaissance.* § 9. *The Artistic Renaissance.* § 10. *America Comes into History.* § 11. *What Machiavelli Thought of the World.* § 12. *The Republic of Switzerland.* § 13A. *The Life of the Emperor Charles V.* § 13B. *Protestants if the Prince Wills It.* § 13C. *The Intellectual Undertow.*

§ 1

Judged by the map, the three centuries from the beginning of the thirteenth to the end of the fifteenth century were an age of recession for Christendom. These centuries were the Age of the Mongolian peoples. Nomadism from Central Asia dominated the known world. At the crest of this period there were rulers of Mongol or the kindred Turkish race and tradition in China, India, Persia, Egypt, North Africa, the Balkan peninsula, Hungary, and Russia.

The Ottoman Turk had even taken to the sea, and fought the Venetian upon his own Mediterranean waters. In 1529 the Turks besieged Vienna, and were defeated rather by the weather than by the defenders. The Habsburg empire of Charles V paid the Sultan tribute. It was not until the battle of Lepanto, in 1571—the battle in which Cervantes, the author of *Don Quixote,* lost his left arm, that Christendom, to use his words, "broke the pride of the Osmans and undeceived the world which had regarded the Turkish fleet as invincible."

The sole region of Christian advance was Spain. A man of foresight surveying the world in the early sixteenth century might well have concluded that it was only a matter of a few generations before the whole world became Mongolian—and probably Moslem. Just as in 1900 most people seemed to take it for granted that European rule and a sort of liberal Christianity were destined to spread over the whole world. Few people seem to realize how recent and probably how temporary a thing is this European ascendancy. It was only as the fifteenth century drew to its close that any indications of the real vitality of Western Europe became clearly apparent.

Our history is now approaching our own times, and our study becomes more

and more a study of the existing state of affairs. The European or Europeanized system in which the reader is living is the same system that we see developing in the crumpled-up, Mongol-threatened Europe of the early fifteenth
century. Its problems then were the embryonic form of the problems of to-day.
It is impossible to discuss that time without discussing our own time. We become political in spite of ourselves. "Politics without history has no root,"
said Sir J. R. Seely; "history without politics has no fruit."

Let us try, with as much detachment as we can achieve, to discover what
the forces were that were dividing and holding back the energies of Europe
during this tremendous outbreak of the Mongol peoples, and how we are to
explain the accumulation of mental and physical energy that undoubtedly
went on during this phase of apparent retrocession, and which broke out so
impressively at its close.

Now, just as in the Mesozoic Age, while the great reptiles lorded it over
the earth, there were developing in odd out-of-the-way corners those hairy
mammals and feathered birds who were finally to supersede that tremendous
fauna altogether by another far more versatile and capable, so in the limited
territories of Western Europe of the Middle Ages, while the Mongolian monarchies dominated the world from the Danube to the Pacific and from the
Arctic seas to Madras and Morocco and the Nile, the fundamental lines of a
new and harder and more efficient type of human community were being laid
down. This type of community, which is still only in the phase of formation,
which is still growing and experimental, we may perhaps speak of as the "modern state." This is, we must recognize, a vague expression, but we shall endeavour to get meaning into it as we proceed.

We have noted the appearance of its main root ideas in the Greek republics
and especially in Athens, in the great Roman republic, in Judaism, in Islam,
and in the story of Western Catholicism. Essentially this modern state, as we
see it growing under our eyes to-day, is a tentative combination of two apparently contradictory ideas, the idea of a *community of faith and obedience,*
such as the earliest civilizations undoubtedly were, and the idea of a *community of will,* such as were the primitive political groupings of the Nordic
and Hunnish peoples. For thousands of years the settled civilized peoples, who
were originally in most cases dark-white Caucasians, or Dravidian or Southern
Mongolian peoples, seem to have developed their ideas and habits along the
line of worship and personal subjection, and the nomadic peoples theirs along
the line of personal self-reliance and self-assertion. Naturally enough, under
the circumstances, the nomadic peoples were always supplying the civilizations
with fresh rulers and new aristocracies. That is the rhythm of all early history.
It was only after thousands of years of cyclic changes between refreshment
by nomadic conquest, civilization, decadence, and fresh conquest, that the
present process of a mutual blending of "civilized," or obedient labouring,
and "free," or aristocratic and adventurous, tendencies into a new type of
community, that now demands our attention and which is the substance of
contemporary history, began.

We have traced in this history the slow development of larger and larger "civilized" human communities from the days of the primitive Palæolithic family tribe. We have seen how the advantages and necessities of cultivation, the fear of tribal gods, the ideas of the priest-king and the god-king, played their part in consolidating continually larger and more powerful societies in regions of maximum fertility. We have watched the interplay of priest, who was usually native, and monarch, who was usually a conqueror, in these early civilizations, the development of a written tradition and its escape from priestly

control, and the appearance of novel forces, at first apparently incidental and secondary, which we have called the free intelligence and the free conscience of mankind. We have seen the rulers of the primitive civilizations of the river valleys widening their area and extending their sway, and simultaneously over the less fertile areas of the earth we have seen mere tribal savagery develop into a more and more united and politically competent nomadism.

Steadily and divergently mankind pursued one or other of these two lines. For long ages all the civilizations grew and developed along monarchist lines, upon lines of absolute monarchy and in every monarchy and dynasty we have watched, as if it were a necessary process, efficiency and energy give way to pomp, indolence, and decay, and finally succumb to some fresher lineage from the desert or the steppe.

The story of the early cultivating civilizations and their temples and courts and cities bulks large in human history, but it is well to remember that the scene of that story was never more than a very small part of the land surface of the globe. Over the greater part of the earth until quite recently, until the last two thousand years, the hardier, less numerous tribal peoples of forest and parkland and the nomadic peoples of the seasonal grasslands maintained and developed their own ways of life.

The primitive civilizations were, we may say, "communities of obedience": obedience to god-kings or kings under gods was their cement; the nomadic tendency, on the other hand, has always been towards a different type of association which we shall here call a "community of will." In a wandering, fighting community the individual must be at once self-reliant and disciplined. The chiefs of such communities must be chiefs who are followed, not masters who compel. This community of will is traceable throughout the entire history of mankind; everywhere we find the original disposition of all the nomads alike, Nordic, Semitic, or Mongolian, was individually more *willing* and more *erect* than that of the settled folk. The Nordic peoples came into Italy and Greece under leader kings; they did not bring any systematic temple cults with them, they found such things in the conquered lands and adapted as they adopted them. The Greeks and Latins lapsed very easily again into republics, and so did the Aryans in India. There was a tradition of election also in the early Frankish and German kingdoms, though the decision was usually taken between one or other members of a royal caste or family. The early Caliphs were elected, the Judges of Israel and the "kings" of Carthage and Tyre were elected, and so was the Great Khan of the Mongols until Kublai became a Chinese monarch.

Equally constant in the settled lands do we find the opposite idea, the idea of a non-elective divinity in kings and of their natural and inherent right to rule.

As our history has developed we have noted the appearance of new and complicating elements in the story of human societies; we have seen that nomad turned go-between, the trader, appear, and we have noted the growing importance of shipping in the world. It seems as inevitable that voyaging should make men free in their minds as that settlement within a narrow horizon should make men timid and servile. . . . But, in spite of all such complications, the broad antagonism between the method of obedience and the method of will runs through history down into our own times. To this day their reconciliation is incomplete.

Civilization even in its most servile forms has always offered much that is enormously attractive, convenient, and congenial to mankind; but something restless and untamed in our race has striven continually to convert civilization from its original reliance upon unparticipating obedience into a community of participating wills. And to the lurking nomadism in our blood, and particularly in the blood of monarchs and aristocracies, which have no doubt contributed in a large proportion to the begetting of later generations, we must ascribe also that incessant urgency towards a wider range that forces every state to extend its boundaries if it can, and to spread its interests to the ends of the earth. The power of nomadic restlessness, that tends to bring all the earth under one rule, seems to be identical with the spirit that makes most of us chafe under direction and restraint, and seek to participate in whatever government we tolerate.

And this natural, this temperamental struggle of mankind to reconcile civilization with freedom has been kept alive age after age by the military and political impotence of every "community of obedience" that has ever existed. Obedience, once men are broken to it, can be very easily captured and transferred; witness the passive rôle of Egypt, Mesopotamia, and India, the original and typical lands of submission, the "cradles of civilization," as they have passed from one lordship to another. A servile civilization is a standing invitation to predatory free men.

But, on the other hand, a "community of will" necessitates a fusion of intractable materials; it is a far harder community to bring about, and still more difficult to maintain. The story of Alexander the Great displays the community of will of the Macedonian captains gradually dissolving before his demand that they should worship him. The incident of the murder of Clitus is quite typical of the struggle between the free and the servile tradition that went on whenever a new conqueror from the open lands and the open air found himself installed in the palace of an ancient monarchy.

In the case of the Roman Republic, history tells of the first big community of will in the world's history, the first free community much larger than a city, and how it weakened with growth and spent itself upon success until at last it gave way to a monarchy of the ancient type, and decayed swiftly into one of the feeblest communities of servitude that ever collapsed before a handful of invaders. We have given some attention in this book to the factors in that decay, because they are of primary importance in human history. One of the most evident was the want of any wide organization of education to base the ordinary citizens' minds upon the idea of service and obligation to the republic, to keep them *willing*, that is: another was the absence of any medium of general information to keep their activities in harmony, to enable them to *will* as one body. The community of will is limited in size by the limitations set upon the possibilities of a community of knowledge. The concentration of property in a few hands and the replacement of free workers by slaves were rendered possible by the decay of public spirit and the confusion of the public intelligence that resulted from these limitations.

There was, moreover, no efficient religious idea behind the Roman state; the dark Etruscan liver-peering cult of Rome was as little adapted to the political needs of a great community as the very similar Shamanism of the Mongols. It is in the fact that both Christianity and Islam, in their distinctive ways, did at least promise to supply, for the first time in human experience, this patent gap in the Roman republican system as well as in the nomadic system, to give a common moral education for a mass of people, and to supply them with a common history of the past and a common idea of a human purpose and destiny, that their enormous historical importance lies. Both Plato and Aristotle, as we have noted, had set a limit to the ideal community of a few thousand citizens, because they could not conceive how a larger multitude could be held together by a common idea. They had had no experience of any sort of education beyond the tutorial methods of their time. Greek education was almost purely *viva-voce* education; it could reach, therefore, only to a limited aristocracy. Both the Christian church and Islam demonstrated the unsoundness of this limitation. We may think they did their task of education in their vast fields of opportunity crudely or badly, but the point of interest to us is that they did it at all. Both sustained almost world-wide propaganda of idea and inspiration. Both relied successfully upon the power of the written word to link great multitudes of diverse men together in common enterprises.

By the eleventh century, as we have seen, the idea of Christendom had been imposed upon all the vast warring miscellany of the smashed and pulverized Western empire, and upon Europe far beyond its limits, as a uniting and inspiring idea. It had made a shallow but effective community of will over an unprecedented area and out of an unprecedented multitude of human beings. The Jews were already holding their community together by systematic education at least as early as the beginning of the Christian era. Only one other thing at all like this ever happened to any great section of mankind before, and that was the idea of a community of good behaviour that the *literati* had spread throughout China.

The Catholic Church provided what the Roman Republic had lacked, a system of popular teaching, a number of universities and methods of intellectual intercommunication. By this achievement it opened the way to the new possibilities of human government that now became apparent in this Outline, possibilities that are still being apprehended and worked out in the world in which we are living. Hitherto the government of states had been either authoritative, under some uncriticized and unchallenged combination of priest and monarch, or it had been a democracy, uneducated and uninformed, degenerating with any considerable increase of size, as Rome and Athens did, into a mere rule by mob and politician. But by the thirteenth century the first intimations had already dawned of an ideal of government which is still making its way to realization, the modern ideal, the ideal of a world-wide *educational government*, in which the ordinary man is neither the slave of an absolute monarch nor of a demagogue-ruled state, but an informed, inspired, and consulted part of the community. It is upon the word educational that stress must be laid, and upon the idea that information must precede consultation.

It is in the practical realization of this idea, that education is a collective function and not a private affair, that one essential distinction of the "modern state" from any of its precursors lies. The modern citizen, men are coming to realize, must be informed first and then consulted. Before he can vote he must hear the evidence; before he can decide he must know. It is not by setting up polling-booths, but by setting up schools and making literature and knowledge and news universally accessible, that the way is opened from servitude and confusion to that willingly co-operative state which is the modern ideal. Votes in themselves are worthless things. Men had votes in Italy in the time of the Gracchi. Their votes did not help them. Until a man has education, a vote is a useless and dangerous thing for him to possess. The ideal community towards which we move is not a community of will simply; it is *a community of knowledge and will,* replacing *a community of faith and obedience.* Education is the adapter which will make the nomadic spirit of freedom and self-reliance compatible with the co-operations and wealth and security of civilization.

§ 2

But though it is certain that the Catholic Church, through its propaganda, its popular appeals, its schools and universities, opened up the prospect of the modern educational state in Europe, it is equally certain that the Catholic Church never intended to do anything of the sort. It did not send out knowledge with its blessing; it let it loose inadvertently. It was not the Roman Republic whose heir the Church esteemed itself, but the Roman Emperor. Its conception of education was not release, not an invitation to participate, but the subjugation of minds. Two of the greatest educators of the Middle Ages were, indeed, not churchmen at all, but monarchs and statesmen, Charlemagne and Alfred the Great of England, who made use of the church organization. But it was the Church that had provided the organization. Church and monarch in their mutual grapple for power were both calling to their aid the thoughts of the common man. In response to these conflicting appeals appeared the common man, the unofficial outside independent man, thinking for himself.

Already in the thirteenth century we have seen Pope Gregory IX and the Emperor Frederick II engaging in a violent public controversy. Already then there was a sense that a new arbitrator greater than pope or monarchy had come into the world, that there were readers and a public opinion. The exodus of the Popes to Avignon, and the divisions and disorders of the papacy during the fourteenth century, stimulated this free judgment upon authority throughout Europe enormously.

At first the current criticism upon the church concerned only moral and material things. The wealth and luxury of the higher clergy and the heavy papal taxation were the chief grounds of complaint. And the earlier attempts to restore Christian simplicity, the foundation of the Franciscans for example, were not movements of separation, but movements of revival. Only later did a deeper and more destructive criticism develop, which attacked the central fact of the church's teaching and the justification of priestly importance, namely, the sacrifice of the Mass.

We have sketched in broad outlines the early beginnings of Christianity, and we have shown how rapidly that difficult and austere conception of the Kingdom of God, which was the central idea of the teachings of Jesus of

Nazareth, was overlaid by a revival of the ancient sacrificial idea, a doctrine more difficult indeed to grasp, but easier to reconcile with the habits and dispositions and acquiescences of everyday life in the Near East. We have noted how a sort of theocrasia went on between Christianity and Judaism and the cult of the Serapeum and Mithraism and other competing cults, by which the Mithraist Sunday, the Jewish idea of blood as a religious essential, the Alexandrian importance of the Mother of God, the shaven and fasting priest, self-tormenting asceticism, and many other matters of belief and ritual and practice, became grafted upon the developing religion. These adaptations, no doubt, made the new teaching much more understandable and acceptable in Egypt and Syria and the like. They were things in the way of thought of the dark-white Mediterranean race; they were congenial to that type. But, as we have shown in our story of Muhammad, these acquisitions did not make Christianity more acceptable to the Arab nomads; to them these features made it disgusting. And so, too, the robed and shaven monk and nun and priest seem to have roused something like an instinctive hostility in the Nordic barbarians of the North and West. We have noted the peculiar bias of the early Anglo-Saxons and Northmen against the monks and nuns. They seem to have felt that the lives and habits of these devotees were queer and unnatural.

The clash between what we may call the "dark-white" factors and the newer elements in Christianity was no doubt intensified by Pope Gregory VII's imposition of celibacy upon the Catholic priests in the eleventh century. The East had known religious celibates for thousands of years; in the West they were regarded with scepticism and suspicion.

And now in the thirteenth and fourteenth centuries, as the lay mind of the Nordic peoples began to acquire learning, to read and write and express itself, and as it came into touch with the stimulating activities of the Arab mind, we find a much more formidable criticism of Catholicism beginning, an intellectual attack upon the priest as priest, and upon the ceremony of the Mass as the central fact of the religious life, coupled with a demand for a return to the personal teachings of Jesus as recorded in the Gospels.

We have already mentioned the career of the Englishman Wycliffe (c. 1320–1384), and how he translated the Bible into English in order to set up a counter-authority to that of the Pope. He denounced the doctrines of the church about the Mass as disastrous error, and particularly the teaching that the consecrated bread eaten in that ceremony becomes in some magical way the actual body of Christ. We will not pursue the question of transubstantiation, as this process of the mystical change of the elements in the sacrament is called, into its intricacies. These are matters for the theological specialist. But it will be obvious that any doctrine, such as the Catholic doctrine, which makes the consecration of the elements in the sacrament a miraculous process performed by the priest, and only to be performed by the priest, and which makes the sacrament the central necessity of the religious system, enhances the importance of the priestly order enormously.

On the other hand, the view, which was the typical "Protestant" view, that this sacrament is a mere eating of bread and drinking of wine as a personal remembrance of Jesus of Nazareth, does away at last with any particular need for a consecrated priest at all.

Wycliffe himself did not go to this extremity; he was a priest, and he remained a priest to the end of his life; he held that God was spiritually if not substantially present in the consecrated bread, but his doctrine raised a question that carried men far beyond his positions. From the point of view of the historian, the struggle against Rome that Wycliffe opened became very speedily a struggle of what one may call rational or layman's religion, making its appeal to the free intelligence and the free conscience in mankind, against authoritative, traditional, ceremonial, and priestly religion. The ultimate tendency of this complicated struggle was to strip Christianity as bare as Islam of every vestige of ancient priestcraft, to revert to the Bible documents as authority, and to recover, if possible, the primordial teachings of Jesus. Most of its issues are still undecided among Christians to this day.

Wycliffe's writings had nowhere more influence than in Bohemia. About 1396 a learned Czech, John Huss, delivered a series of lectures in the University of Prague based upon the doctrines of the great Oxford teacher. Huss became rector of the university, and his teachings roused the church to excommunicate him (1412).

This was at the time of the Great Schism, just before the Council of Constance (1414–1418) gathered to discuss the scandalous disorder of the church. We have already told how the schism was ended by the election of Martin V. The council aspired to reunite Christendom completely. But the methods by which it sought this reunion jar with our modern consciences. Wycliffe's bones were condemned to be burnt. Huss was decoyed to Constance under promise of a safe conduct, and he was then put upon his trial for heresy. He was ordered to recant certain of his opinions. He replied that he could not recant until he was convinced of his error. He was told that it was his duty to recant if his superiors required it of him, whether he was convinced or not. He refused to accept this view. In spite of the emperor's safe conduct, he was burnt alive (1415), a martyr not for any specific doctrine, but for the free intelligence and free conscience of mankind.

It would be impossible to put the issue between priest and anti-priest more clearly than it was put at this trial of John Huss, or to demonstrate more completely the evil spirit in priestcraft. A colleague of Huss, Jerome of Prague, was burnt in the following year.

These outrages were followed by an insurrection of the Hussites in Bohemia (1419), the first of a series of religious wars that marked the breaking-up of Christendom. In 1420 the Pope, Martin V, issued a bull proclaiming a crusade "for the destruction of the Wycliffites, Hussites, and all other heretics in Bohemia," and, attracted by this invitation, the unemployed soldiers of fortune and all the drifting blackguardism of Europe converged upon that valiant country. They found in Bohemia, under its great leader Ziska, more hardship and less loot than crusaders were disposed to face. The Hussites were conducting their affairs upon extreme democratic lines, and the whole country was aflame with enthusiasm. The crusaders beleaguered Prague but failed to take it, and they experienced a series of reverses that ended in their retreat from Bohemia. A second crusade (1421) was no more successful. Two other crusades failed. Then, unhappily, the Hussites fell into internal dissensions. Encouraged by this, a fifth crusade (1431) crossed the frontier under Frederick, Margrave of Brandenburg.

The army of these crusaders, according to the lowest estimates, consisted of 90,000 infantry and 40,000 horsemen. Attacking Bohemia from the west, they first laid seige to the town of Tachov, but failing to capture the strongly fortified city, they stormed the little town of Most, and here, as well as in the surrounding country, committed the most horrible atrocities on a population a large part of which was entirely innocent of any theology whatever.

The crusaders, advancing by slow marches, penetrated farther into Bohemia, till they reached the neighborhood of the town of Domazlice (Tauss). "It was at three o'clock on August 14th, 1431, that the crusaders, who were encamped in the plain between Domazlice and Horsuv Tyn, received the news that the Hussites, under the leadership of Prokop the Great, were approaching. Though the Bohemians were still four miles off, the rattle of their war-wagons and the song, 'All ye warriors of God,' which their whole host was chanting, could already be heard." The enthusiasm of the crusaders evaporated with astounding rapidity. Lützow[1] describes how the papal representative and the Duke of Saxony ascended a convenient hill to inspect the battlefield. It was, they discovered, not going to be a battlefield. The German camp was in utter confusion. Horsemen were streaming off in every direction, and the clatter of empty wagons being driven off almost drowned the sound of that terrible singing. The crusaders were abandoning even their loot. Came a message from the Margrave of Brandenburg advising flight; there was no holding any of their troops. They were dangerous now only to their own side, and the papal representative spent an unpleasant night hiding from them in the forest. . . . So ended the Bohemian crusade.

In 1434 civil war again broke out among the Hussites, in which the extreme and most valiant section was defeated, and in 1436 an agreement was patched up between the Council of Basel and the moderate Hussites, in which the Bohemian church was allowed to retain certain distinctions from the general Catholic practice, which held good until the German Reformation in the sixteenth century.

§ 3

The split among the Hussites was largely due to the drift of the extremer section towards a primitive communism, which alarmed the wealthier and more influential Czech noblemen. Similar tendencies had already appeared among the English Wycliffites. They seem to follow naturally enough upon the doctrines of equal human brotherhood that emerge whenever there is an attempt to reach back to the fundamentals of Christianity.

---

[1] Lützow's *Bohemia*.

The development of such ideas had been greatly stimulated by a stupendous misfortune that had swept the world and laid bare the foundations of society, a pestilence of unheard-of virulence. It was called the Black Death, and it came nearer to the extirpation of mankind than any other evil has ever done. It was far more deadly than the plague of Pericles, or the plague of Marcus Aurelius, or the plague waves of the time of Justinian and Gregory the Great that paved the way for the Lombards in Italy. It arose in South Russia or Central Asia, and came by way of the Crimea and a Genoese ship to Genoa and Western Europe. It passed by Armenia to Asia Minor, Egypt, and North Africa. It reached England in 1348. Two-thirds of the students at Oxford died, we are told; it is estimated that between a quarter and a half of the whole population of England perished at this time. Throughout all Europe there was as great a mortality. Hecker estimates the total as twenty-five million dead. It spread eastward to China, where, the Chinese records say, thirteen million people perished. Dr. C. O. Stallybrass says that this plague reached China thirty or forty years after its first appearance in Europe. Ibn Batuta, the Arab traveller, who was in China from 1342 to 1346, first met with it on his return to Damascus. The Black Death is the human form of a disease endemic among the jerboas and other small rodents in the districts round the head of the Caspian Sea. In China the social disorganization led to a neglect of the river embankments, and as a consequence great floods devastated the crowded agricultural lands.

Never was there so clear a warning to mankind to seek knowledge and cease from bickering, to unite against the dark powers of nature. All the massacres of Hulagu and Timurlane were as nothing to this. "Its ravages," says J. R. Green, "were fiercest in the greater towns, where filthy and undrained streets afforded a constant haunt to leprosy and fever. In the burial-ground which the piety of Sir Walter Manny purchased for the citizens of London, a spot whose site was afterwards marked by the Charter House, more than fifty thousand corpses are said to have been interred. Thousands of people perished at Norwich, while in Bristol the living were hardly able to bury the dead.

"But the Black Death fell on the villages almost as fiercely as on the towns. More than one-half of the priests of Yorkshire are known to have perished; in the diocese of Norwich two-thirds of the parishes changed their incumbents. The whole organization of labour was thrown out of gear. The scarcity of hands made it difficult for the minor tenants to perform the services due for their lands, and only a temporary abandonment of half the rent by the land-owners induced the farmers to refrain from the abandonment of their farms. For a time cultivation became impossible. 'The sheep and cattle strayed through the fields and corn,' says a contemporary, 'and there were none left who could drive them.' "

It was from these distresses that the peasant wars of the fourteenth century sprang. There was a great shortage of labour and a great shortage of goods, and the rich abbots and monastic cultivators who owned so much of the land, and the nobles and rich merchants, were too ignorant of economic laws to understand that they must not press upon the toilers in this time of general distress. They saw their property deteriorating, their lands going out of cultivation, and they made violent statutes to compel men to work without any rise in wages, and to prevent their straying in search of better employment. Naturally enough this provoked "a new revolt against the whole system of social inequality which had till then passed unquestioned as the divine order of the world. The cry of the poor found a terrible utterance in the words of 'a mad priest of Kent,' as the courtly Froissart calls him, who for twenty years (1360–1381) found audience for his sermons, in defiance of interdict and imprisonment, in the stout yeomen who gathered in the Kentish churchyards. 'Mad,' as the landowners called him, it was in the preaching of John Ball that England first listened to a declaration of natural equality and the rights of man. 'Good people,' cried the preacher, 'things will never go well in England so long as goods be not in common, and so long as there be villeins and gentlemen. By what right are they whom we call lords greater folk than we? On what grounds have they deserved it? Why do they hold us in serfage? If we all came of the same father and mother, of Adam and Eve, how can they say or prove that they are better than we, if it be not that they make us gain for them by our toil what they spend in their pride? They are clothed in velvet and warm in their furs and their ermines, while we are covered with rags. They have wine and spices and fair bread; and we oat-cake and straw, and water to drink. They have leisure and fine houses; we have pain and labour, the rain and the wind in the fields. And yet it is of us and of our toil that these men hold their state.' A spirit fatal to the whole system of the Middle Ages breathed in the popular rhyme which condensed the levelling doctrine of John Ball: 'When Adam delved and Eve span, who was then the gentleman?' "

Wat Tyler, the leader of the English insurgents, was assassinated by the Mayor of London, in the presence of the young King Richard II (1381), and his movement collapsed.

The communist side of the Hussite movement was a part of the same system of disturbance. A little earlier than the English outbreak had occurred the French "Jacquerie" (1358), in which the French peasants had risen, burnt chateaux, and devastated the countryside. A century later the same urgency was to sweep Germany into a series of bloody Peasant Wars. These began late in the fifteenth century. Economic and religious disturbance mingled in the case of Germany even more plainly than in England.

One conspicuous phase of these German troubles was the Anabaptist outbreak. The sect of the Anabaptists appeared in Wittenberg in 1521 under three "prophets," and broke out into insurrection in 1525. Between 1532 and 1535 the insurgents held the town of Münster in Westphalia, and did their utmost to realize their ideas of a religious communism. They were besieged by the Bishop of Münster, and under the distresses of the siege a sort of insanity ran rife in the town; cannibalism is said to have occurred, and a certain John of Leyden seized power, proclaimed himself the successor of King David, and followed that monarch's evil example by practising polygamy.

After the surrender of the city the victorious bishop had the Anabaptist leaders tortured very horribly and executed in the market-place, their mutilated bodies being hung in cages from a church tower to witness to all the world that decency and order were now restored in Münster. . . .

These upheavals of the common labouring men of the Western European countries in the fourteenth and fifteenth centuries were more serious and sustained than anything that had ever happened in history before. The nearest previous approach to them were certain communistic Muhammadan movements in Persia. There was a peasant revolt in Normandy about A.D. 1,000, and there were revolts of peasants (Bagaudæ) in the later Roman Empire, but these were not nearly so formidable. They show a new spirit growing in human affairs, a spirit altogether different from the unquestioning apathy of the serfs and peasants in the original regions of civilization or from the anarchist hopelessness of the serf and slave labour of the Roman capitalists.

All these early insurrections of the workers that we have mentioned were suppressed with much cruelty, but the movement itself was never completely stamped out. From that time to this there has been a spirit of revolt in the lower levels of the pyramid of civilization. There have been phases of insurrection, phases of repression, phases of compromise and comparative pacification; but from that time until this, the struggle has never wholly ceased. We shall see it flaring out during the French Revolution at the end of the eighteenth century, insurgent again in the middle and at the opening of the last quarter of the nineteenth century, and achieving vast proportions in the world of to-day. The socialist movement of the nineteenth century was only one version of that continuing revolt.

In many countries, in France and Germany and Russia, for example, this labour movement has assumed at times an attitude hostile to Christianity, but there can be little doubt that this steady and, on the whole, growing pressure of the common man in the West against a life of toil and subservience is closely associated with Christian teaching. The church and the Christian missionary may not have intended to spread equalitarian doctrines, but behind the church was the unquenchable personality of Jesus of Nazareth, and even in spite of himself the Christian preacher brought the seeds of freedom and responsibility with him, and sooner or later they shot up where he had been.

"We haue the payne and trauayle, rayne and wynd in the feldes," . . . John Ball's speech

This steady and growing upheaval of "Labour," its development of a consciousness of itself as a class and of a definite claim upon the world at large, quite as much as the presence of schools and universities, quite as much as abundant printed books and a developing and expanding process of scientific research, mark off our present type of civilization the "modern civilization," from any pre-existing state of human society, and mark it, for all its incidental successes, as a thing unfinished and transitory. It is an embryo or it is something doomed to die. It may be able to solve this complex problem of co-ordinated toil and happiness, and so adjust itself to the needs of the human soul, or it may fail and end in a catastrophe as the Roman system did. It may be the opening phase of some more balanced and satisfying order of society, or it may be a system destined to disruption and replacement by some differently conceived method of human association.

Like its predecessor, our present civilization may be no more than one of those crops farmers sow to improve their land by the fixation of nitrogen from the air; it may have grown only that, accumulating certain traditions, it may be ploughed into the soil again for better things to follow. Such questions as these are the practical realities of history, and in all that follows we shall find them becoming clearer and more important, until in our last chapter we shall end, as all our days and years end, with a recapitulation of our hopes and fears—and a note of interrogation.

§ 4

The development of free discussion in Europe during this age of fermentation was enormously stimulated by the appearance of printed books. It was the introduction of paper from the East that made practicable the long latent method of printing. It is still difficult to assign the honour of priority in the use of the simple expedient of printing for multiplying books. It is a trivial question that has been preposterously debated. Apparently the glory, such as it is, belongs to Holland. In Haarlem, one Coster was printing from movable type somewhen before 1446. Gutenberg was printing at Mainz about the same time. There were printers in Italy by 1465, and Caxton set up his press in Westminster in 1477. The first book printed in Hungary is dated 1473. But long before this time there had been a partial use of printing. Manuscripts as early as the twelfth century displayed initial letters that may have been printed from wooden stamps.

Far more important is the question of the manufacture of paper. It is scarcely too much to say that paper made the revival of Europe possible. Paper originated in China, where its use probably goes back to the second century B.C. In 751 the Chinese made an attack upon the Arab Moslems in Samarkand; they were repulsed, and among the prisoners taken from them were some skilled paper-makers, from whom the art was learnt. Arabic paper manuscripts, from the ninth century onward, still exist. The manufacture entered Christendom either through Greece or by the capture of Moorish paper-mills during the Christian reconquest of Spain. But under the Christian

Spanish the product deteriorated sadly. Good paper was not made in Christian Europe until near the end of the thirteenth century, and then it was Italy which led the world. Only by the fourteenth century did the manufacture reach Germany, and not until the end of that century was it abundant and cheap enough for the printing of books to be a practicable business proposition. Thereupon printing followed naturally and necessarily, and the intellectual life of the world entered upon a new and far more vigorous phase. It ceased to be a little trickle from mind to mind; it became a broad flood, in which thousands and, presently, scores and hundreds of thousands of minds participated.

One immediate result of this achievement of printing was the appearance of an abundance of Bibles in the world. Another was a cheapening of schoolbooks. The knowledge of reading spread swiftly. There was not only a great increase of books in the world, but the books that were now made were plainer to read and so easier to understand. Instead of toiling at a crabbed text and then thinking over its significance, readers now could think unimpeded as they read. With this increase in the facility of reading, the reading public grew. The book ceased to be a highly decorated toy or a scholar's mystery. People began to write books to be read as well as looked at by ordinary people.

With the fourteenth century the real history of the European literatures begins. We find a rapid replacement of local dialects by standard Italian, standard English, standard French, standard Spanish, and, later, standard German. These languages became literary languages in their several countries; they were tried over, polished by use, and made exact and vigorous. They became at last as capable of the burden of philosophical discussion as Greek or Latin.

§ 5

Here we devote a section to certain elementary statements about the movement in men's religious ideas during the fifteenth and sixteenth centuries. They are a necessary introduction to the political history of the seventeenth and eighteenth centuries that follows.

We have to distinguish clearly between two entirely different systems of opposition to the Catholic Church. They intermingled very confusingly. The church was losing its hold upon the consciences of princes and rich and able people; it was also losing the faith and confidence of common people. The effect of its decline of spiritual power upon the former class was to make them resent its interference, its moral restrictions, its claims to overlordship, its claim to tax and to dissolve allegiances. They ceased to respect its power and its property. This insubordination of princes and rulers was going on throughout the Middle Ages, but it was only when in the sixteenth century the church began to side openly with its old antagonist the Emperor, when it offered him its support and accepted his help in its campaign against heresy, that princes began to think seriously of breaking away from the Roman communion and setting up fragments of a church. And they would never have done so if they had not perceived that the hold of the church upon the masses of mankind had relaxed.

The revolt of the princes was essentially an irreligious revolt against the world-rule of the church. The Emperor Frederick II, with his epistles to his fellow-princes, was its forerunner. The revolt of the people against the church, on the other hand, was as essentially religious. They objected not to the church's power but to its weaknesses. They wanted a deeply righteous and fearless church to help them and organize them against the wickedness of powerful men. Their movements against the church, within it and without, were movements not for release from a religious control but for a fuller and more abundant religious control. They did not want less religious control but more—but they wanted to be assured that it was religious. They objected to the Pope not because he was the religious head of the world but because he was not; because he was a wealthy earthly prince when he ought to have been their spiritual leader.

The contest in Europe from the fourteenth century onward, therefore, was a three-cornered contest. The princes wanted to use the popular forces against the Pope, but not to let those forces grow too powerful for their own power and glory. For a long time the church went from prince to prince for an ally without realizing that the lost ally it needed to recover was popular veneration.

Because of this triple aspect of the mental and moral conflicts that were going on in the fourteenth and fifteenth and sixteenth centuries, the series of ensuing changes, those changes that are known collectively in history as the Reformation, took on a three-fold aspect. There was the Reformation according to the princes, who wanted to stop the flow of money to Rome, and to seize the moral authority, the educational power, and the material possessions of the church within their dominions. There was the Reformation according to the people, who sought to make Christianity a power against unrighteousness, and particularly against the unrighteousness of the rich and powerful. And finally there was the Reformation within the church, of which St. Francis of Assisi was the precursor, which sought to restore the goodness of the church and, through its goodness, to restore its power.

The Reformation according to the princes took the form of a replacement of the Pope by the prince as the head of the religion and the controller of the consciences of his people. The princes had no idea and no intention of letting free the judgments of their subjects, more particularly with the object-lessons of the Hussites and the Anabaptists before their eyes; they sought to establish national churches dependent upon the throne. As England, Scotland, Sweden, Norway, Denmark, North Germany, and Bohemia broke away from the Roman communion, the princes and other ministers showed the utmost solicitude to keep the movement well under control. Just as much reformation as would sever the link with Rome they permitted; anything beyond that, any dangerous break towards the primitive teachings of Jesus or the crude direct interpretation of the Bible, they resisted. The Established Church of England is one of the most typical and successful of the resulting compromises. It is still sacramental and sacerdotal; but its organization centres in the Court and the Lord Chancellor; and though subversive views may, and do, break out in the lower and less prosperous ranks of its priesthood, it is rare for them to struggle up to any position of influence and authority.

The Reformation according to the common man was very different in spirit from the princely Reformation. We have already told something of the popular attempts at Reformation in Bohemia and Germany. The wide spiritual upheavals of the time were at once more honest, more confused, more enduring, and less immediately successful than the reforms of the princes. Very few religious-spirited men had the daring to break away or the effrontery to confess that they had broken away from all authoritative teaching, and that they were now relying entirely upon their own minds and consciences. That required a very high intellectual courage. The general drift of the common man in this period in Europe was to set up his new acquisition, the Bible, as a counter-authority to the church. This was particularly the case with the great leader of German Protestantism, Martin Luther (1483–1546). All over Germany, and, indeed, all over Western Europe, there were now men spelling over the black-letter pages of the newly-translated and printed Bible, over the Book of Leviticus and the Song of Solomon and the Revelation of St. John the Divine—strange and perplexing books—quite as much as over the simple and inspiring record of Jesus in the Gospels. Naturally, they produced strange views and grotesque interpretations. It is surprising that they were not stranger and grotesquer. But the human reason is an obstinate thing, and will criticize and select in spite of its own resolutions. The bulk of these new Bible students took what their consciences approved from the Bible and ignored its riddles and contradictions.

All over Europe, wherever the new Protestant churches of the princes were set up, a living and very active residuum of Protestants remained who declined to have their religion made over for them in this fashion. These were the Nonconformists, a medley of sects, having nothing in common but their resistance to authoritative religion, whether of the Pope or the State. In Germany Nonconformity was for the most part stamped out by the princes; in Great Britain it remained powerful and various. Much of the differences in the behaviour of the German and British peoples seems to be traceable to the relative suppression of the free judgment in Germany.

Most, but not all, of these Nonconformists held to the Bible as a divinely inspired and authoritative guide. This was a strategic rather than an abiding position, and the modern drift of Nonconformity has been onward away from this original Bibliolatry towards a mitigated and sentimentalized recognition of the bare teachings of Jesus of Nazareth. Beyond the range of Nonconformity, beyond the range of professed Christianity at all, there is also now a great and growing mass of equalitarian belief and altruistic impulse in the modern civilizations, which certainly owes, as we have already asserted, its spirit to Christianity.

Let us say a word now of the third phase of the Reformation process, the Reformation within the church. This was already beginning in the twelfth and thirteenth centuries with the appearance of the Black and Grey Friars (chap. xxxi, § 14). In the sixteenth century, and when it was most needed, came a fresh impetus of the same kind. This was the foundation of the Society of Jesus by Inigo Lopez de Recalde, better known to the world of to-day as Saint Ignatius of Loyola.

Ignatius began his career as a very tough and gallant young Spaniard. He was clever and dexterous and inspired by a passion for pluck, hardihood, and rather showy glory. His love affairs were free and picturesque. In 1521 the French took the town of Pampeluna, in Spain, from the Emperor Charles V, and Ignatius was one of the defenders. His legs were smashed by a cannon-ball, and he was taken prisoner. One leg was badly set and had to be broken again, and these painful and complex operations nearly cost him his life. He received the last sacraments. In the night, thereafter, he began to mend, and presently he was convalescent and facing the prospect of a life in which he would perhaps always be a cripple. His thoughts turned to the adventure of religion. Sometimes he would think of a certain great lady, and how, in spite of his broken state, he might yet win her admiration by some amazing deed; and sometimes he would think of being in some especial and personal way the Knight of Christ. In the midst of these confusions, one night as he lay awake, he tells us, a new great lady claimed his attention; he had a vision of the Blessed Virgin Mary carrying the Infant Christ in her arms. "Immediately a loathing seized him for the former deeds of his life." He resolved to give up all further thoughts of earthly women, and to lead a life of absolute chastity and devotion to the Mother of God. He projected great pilgrimages and a monastic life.

His final method of taking his vows marks him the countryman of Don Quixote. He had regained his strength, and he was riding out into the world rather aimlessly, a penniless soldier of fortune with little but his arms and the mule on which he rode, when he fell into company with a Moor. They went on together and talked, and presently disputed about religion. The Moor was the better-educated man; he had the best of the argument, he said offensive things about the Virgin Mary that were difficult to answer, and he parted triumphantly from Ignatius. The young Knight of Our Lady was boiling with shame and indignation. He hesitated whether he should go after the Moor and kill him or pursue the pilgrimage he had in mind. At a fork in the road he left things to his mule, which spared the Moor.

He came to the Benedictine Abbey of Montserrat near Manresa, and here he imitated that peerless hero of the mediæval romance, Amadis de Gaul, and kept an all-night vigil before the Altar of the Blessed Virgin. He presented his mule to the abbey, he gave his worldly clothes to a beggar, he laid his sword and dagger upon the altar, and clothed himself in a rough sackcloth garment and hempen shoes. He then took himself to a neighbouring hospice and gave himself up to scourgings and austerities. For a whole week he fasted absolutely. Thence he went on a pilgrimage to the Holy Land.

For some years he wandered, consumed with the idea of founding a new order of religious knighthood, but not knowing clearly how to set about this

Loyola

enterprise. He became more and more aware of his own illiteracy, and the Inquisition, which was beginning to take an interest in his proceedings, forbade him to attempt to teach others until he had spent at least four years in study. So much cruelty and intolerance is laid at the door of the Inquisition that it is pleasant to record that in its handling of this heady, imaginative young enthusiast it showed itself both sympathetic and sane. It recognized his vigour and possible uses; it saw the dangers of his ignorance. He studied at Salamanca and Paris, among other places. He was ordained a priest in 1538, and a year later his long-dreamt-of Order was founded under the title of the "Society of Jesus." Like the Salvation Army of modern England, it made the most direct attempt to bring the generous tradition of military organization and discipline to the service of religion.

This Ignatius of Loyola who founded the Order of Jesuits was a man of forty-seven; he was a very different man, much wiser and steadier, than the rather absurd young man who had aped Amadis de Gaul and kept vigil in the Abbey of Manresa; and the missionary and educational organization he now created and placed at the disposal of the Pope was one of the most powerful instruments the church had ever handled.

These men gave themselves freely and wholly to be used by the church. It was the Order of the Jesuits which carried Christianity to China again after the downfall of the Ming dynasty, and Jesuits were the chief Christian missionaries in India and North America. To their civilizing work among the Indians in South America we shall presently allude. But their main achievement lay in raising the standard of Catholic education. Their schools became and remained for a long time the best schools in Christendom. Says Lord Verulam (Sir Francis Bacon): "As for the pedagogic part . . . consult the schools of the Jesuits, for nothing better has been put in practice." They raised the level of intelligence, they quickened the conscience of all Catholic Europe, they stimulated Protestant Europe to competitive educational efforts.

Some day it may be we shall see a new Order of Jesuits, vowed not to the service of the Pope, but to the service of mankind.

And concurrently with this great wave of educational effort, the tone and quality of the church was also greatly improved by the clarification of doctrine and the reforms in organization and discipline that were made by the Council of Trent. This council met intermittently either at Trent or Bologna between the years 1545 and 1563, and its work was at least as important as the energy of the Jesuits in arresting the crimes and blunders that were causing state after state to fall away from the Roman communion. The change wrought by the Reformation within the Church of Rome was as great as the change wrought in the Protestant churches that detached themselves from the mother body. There are henceforth no more open scandals or schisms to record. But, if anything, there has been an intensification of doctrinal narrowness, and such phases of imaginative vigour as are represented by Gregory the Great, or by the group of Popes associated with Gregory VII and Urban II, or by the group that began with Innocent III, no longer enliven the sober and pedestrian narrative. The church settled down to what it is to-day, a religious organization apart from statecraft, a religious body among religious bodies. The sceptre had departed from Rome.

§ 6

The reader must not suppose that the destructive criticism of the Catholic Church and of Catholic Christianity, and the printing and study of the Bible, were the only or even the most important of the intellectual activities of the fourteenth and fifteenth centuries. That was merely the popular and most conspicuous aspect of the intellectual revival of the time. Behind this conspicuous and popular awakening to thought and discussion, other less immediately striking but ultimately more important mental developments were in progress. Of the trend of these developments we must now give some brief indications. They had begun long before books were printed, but it was printing that released them from obscurity.

We have already told something of the first appearance of the free intelligence, the spirit of inquiry and plain statement, in human affairs. One name is central in the record of that first attempt at systematic knowledge, the name of Aristotle. We have noted, also, the brief phase of scientific work at Alexandria. From that time onward the complicated economic and political and religious conflicts of Europe and Western Asia impeded further intellectual progress. These regions, as we have seen, fell for long ages under the sway of the Oriental type of monarchy and of Oriental religious traditions. Rome tried and abandoned a slave-system of industry. The first great capitalistic system developed, and fell into chaos through its own inherent weaknesses. Europe relapsed into universal insecurity. The Semite rose against the Aryan, and replaced Hellenic civilization throughout Western Asia and Egypt by an Arabic culture. All Western Asia and half of Europe fell under Mongolian rule. It is only in the twelfth and thirteenth centuries that we find the Aryan intelligence struggling through again to clear expression.

We then find in the growing universities of Paris, Oxford, and Bologna an increasing amount of philosophical discussion going on. In form it is chiefly a discussion of logical questions. As the basis of this discussion we find part of the teachings of Aristotle, not the whole mass of writings he left behind him, but his logic only. Later on his work became better known through the Latin translations of the Arabic edition annotated by Averroes. Except for these translations of Aristotle, and they were abominably bad translations, very little of the Greek philosophical literature was read in Western Europe until the fifteenth century.

The creative Plato—as distinguished from the scientific Aristotle—was almost unknown. Europe had the Greek criticism without the Greek impulse. Some neo-Platonic writers were known, but neo-Platonism had much the same relation to Plato that Christian Science has to orthodox Christianity.

It has been the practice of recent writers to decry the philosophical discussion of the mediæval "schoolmen" as tedious and futile. It was nothing of the sort. It had to retain a severely technical form because the dignitaries of the church, ignorant and intolerant, were on the watch for heresy. It lacked the sweet clearness, therefore, of fearless thought. It often hinted what it dared not say. But it dealt with fundamentally important things, it was a long and necessary struggle to clear up and correct certain inherent defects of the human mind, and many people to-day blunder dangerously through their neglect of the issues the schoolmen discussed.

There is a natural tendency in the human mind to exaggerate the differences and resemblances upon which classification is based, to suppose that things called by different names are altogether different, and that things called by the same name are practically identical. This tendency to exaggerate classification produces a thousand evils and injustices. In the sphere of race or nationality, for example, a "European" will often treat an "Asiatic" almost as if he were a different animal, while he will be disposed to regard another "European" as necessarily as virtuous and charming as himself. He will, as a matter of course, take sides with Europeans against Asiatics. But, as the reader of this history must realize, there is no such difference as the opposition of these names implies. It is a phantom difference created by two names. . . .

The main mediæval controversy was between the "Realists" and the "Nominalists," and it is necessary to warn the reader that the word "Realist" in mediæval discussion has a meaning almost diametrically opposed to "Realist" as it is used in the jargon of modern criticism. The modern "Realist" is one who insists on materialist details; the mediæval "Realist" was far nearer what nowadays we should call an Idealist, and his contempt for incidental detail was profound. The Realists outdid the common human tendency to exaggerate the significance of class. They held that there was something in a name, in a common noun that is, that was essentially real. For example, they held there was a typical "European," an ideal European, who was far more real than any individual European. Every European was, as it were, a failure, a departure, a flawed specimen of this profounder reality. On the other hand, the Nominalist held that the only realities in the case were the individual Europeans, that the name "European" was merely a name, and nothing more than a name, applied to all these instances.

Nothing is quite so difficult as the compression of philosophical controversies, which are by their nature voluminous and various and tinted by the mental colours of a variety of minds. With the difference of Realist and Nominalist stated baldly, as we have stated it here, the modern reader unaccustomed to philosophical discussion may be disposed to leap at once to the side of the Nominalist. But the matter is not so simple that it can be covered by one instance, and here we have purposely chosen an extreme instance. Names and classifications differ in their value and reality. While it is absurd to suppose that there can be much depth of class difference between men called Thomas and men called William, or that there is an ideal and quintessential Thomas or William, yet, on the other hand, there may be much profounder differences between a white man and a Hottentot, and still more between *Homo sapiens* and *Homo Neanderthalensis*. While again the distinction between the class of pets and the class of useful animals is dependent upon very slight differences of habit and application, the difference of a cat and dog is so profound that the microscope can trace it in a drop of blood or a single hair. While some classifications are trivial, others seem to be fundamental and real. When this aspect of the question is considered, it becomes understandable how Nominalism had ultimately to abandon the idea that names were as insignificant as labels, and how, out of a revised and amended Nominalism, there grew up that systematic attempt to find the *true*—the most significant and fruitful—classification of things and substances which is called Scientific Research.

And it will be almost as evident that while the tendency of Realism, which is the natural tendency of every untutored mind, was towards dogma, harsh divisions, harsh judgments, and uncompromising attitudes, the tendency of earlier and later Nominalism was towards qualified statements, towards an examination of individual instances, and towards inquiry and experiment and scepticism.

So, while in the market-place and the ways of the common life men were questioning the morals and righteousness of the clergy, the good faith and propriety of their celibacy, and the justice of papal taxation; while in theological circles their minds were set upon the question of transubstantiation, the question of the divinity or not of the bread and wine in the Mass, in studies and lecture-rooms a wider-reaching criticism of the methods of ordinary Catholic teaching was in progress.

We cannot attempt here to gauge the significance in this process of such names as Peter Abelard (1079–1142), Albertus Magnus (1193–1280), and Thomas Aquinas (1225–1274). These men sought to reconstruct Catholicism on a sounder system of reasoning; and they turned towards Nominalism. Chief among their critics and successors were Duns Scotus (?–1308), an Oxford Franciscan and, to judge by his sedulous thought and deliberate subtleties, a Scotchman, and Occam, an Englishman (?–1347).

Both these latter, like Averroes, made a definite distinction between theological and philosophical truth; they placed theology on a pinnacle, but they placed it where it could no longer obstruct research: Duns Scotus declared that it was impossible to prove by reasoning the existence of God or of the Trinity or the credibility of the act of Creation; Occam was still more insistent upon this separation of theology from practical truth—a separation which manifestly released scientific inquiry from dogmatic control. A later generation, benefiting by the freedoms towards which these pioneers worked, and knowing not the sources of its freedom, had the ingratitude to use the name of Scotus as a term for stupidity, and so we have our English word "Dunce." Says Professor Pringle Pattison[1]: "Occam, who is still a Scholastic, gives us the Scholastic justification of the spirit which had already taken hold upon Roger Bacon, and which was to enter upon its rights in the fifteenth and sixteenth centuries."

Standing apart by himself because of his distinctive genius is this Roger Bacon (about 1210 to about 1293), who was also English. He was a Franciscan of Oxford, and a very typical Englishman indeed, irritable, hasty, honest, and shrewd. He was two centuries ahead of his world. Says H. O. Taylor of him[2]:

"The career of Bacon was an intellectual tragedy, conforming to the old principles of tragic art: that the hero's character shall be large and noble, but not flawless, inasmuch as the fatal consummation must issue from character, and not happen through chance. He died an old man; as in his youth, so in his age, a devotee of tangible knowledge. His pursuit of a knowledge which was not altogether learning had been obstructed by the Order of which he was an unhappy and rebellious member; quite as fatally his achievement was deformed from within by the principles which he accepted from his time. But he was responsible for his acceptance of current opinions; and as his views roused the distrust of his brother Friars, his intractable temper drew their hostility on his head. Persuasiveness and tact were needed by one who would impress such novel views as his upon his fellows, or, in the thirteenth century, escape persecution for their divulgence. Bacon attacked dead and living worthies, tactlessly, fatuously, and unfairly. Of his life scarcely anything is known, save from his allusions to himself and others; and these are insufficient for the construction of even a slight consecutive narrative. Born; studied at Oxford; went to Paris, studied, experimented; is at Oxford again, and a Franciscan; studies, teaches, becomes suspect to his Order; is sent back to Paris, kept under surveillance, receives a letter from the Pope; writes, writes, writes—his three best-known works; is again in trouble, confined for many years, released, and dead, so very dead, body and fame alike, until partly unearthed after five centuries."

The bulk of these "three best-known works" is a hotly phrased and sometimes quite abusive but entirely just attack on the ignorance of the times, combined with a wealth of suggestions for the increase of knowledge. In his passionate insistence upon the need of experiment and of collecting knowledge the spirit of Aristotle lives again in him. "Experiment, experiment," that is the burthen of Roger Bacon.

Yet of Aristotle himself Roger Bacon fell foul. He fell foul of him because men, instead of facing facts boldly, sat in rooms and pored over the bad Latin translations which were then all that was available of the master. "If I had my way," he wrote, in his intemperate fashion, "I should burn all the books of Aristotle, for the study of them can only lead to a loss of time,

---

[1] *Encyclopædia Britannica* Twelfth Edition, article "Scholasticism."
[2] *The Medieval Mind*, by Henry Osborn Taylor.

produce error, and increase ignorance," a sentiment that Aristotle would probably have echoed could he have returned to a world in which his works were not so much read as worshipped—and that, as Roger Bacon showed, in these most untrustworthy translations.

Throughout his books, a little disguised by the necessity of seeming to square it all with orthodoxy for fear of the prison and worse, Roger Bacon shouted to mankind, "Cease to be ruled by dogmas and authorities; *look at the world!*"

Four chief sources of ignorance he denounced; respect for authority, custom, the sense of the ignorant crowd, and the vain, proud unteachableness of our dispositions. Overcome but these, and a world of power would open to men. "Machines for navigating are possible without rowers, so that great ships suited to river or ocean, guided by one man, may be borne with greater speed than if they were full of men. Likewise, cars may be made so that without a draught animal they may be moved *cum impetu inæstimabili,* as we deem the scythed chariots to have been from which antiquity fought. And flying machines are possible, so that a man may sit in the middle turning some device by which artificial wings may beat the air in the manner of a flying bird."

Occam, Roger Bacon, these are the early precursors of a great movement in Europe away from "Realism" towards reality. For a time the older influences fought against the naturalism of the new Nominalists. In 1339 Occam's books were put under a ban and Nominalism solemnly condemned. As late as 1473 an attempt, belated and unsuccessful, was made to bind teachers of Paris by an oath to teach Realism. It was only in the sixteenth century, with the printing of books and the increase of intelligence, that the movement from absolutism towards experiment became massive, and that one investigator began to co-operate with another.

Throughout the thirteenth and fourteenth centuries experimenting with material things was on the increase, items of knowledge were being won by men, but there was no inter-related advance. The work was done in a detached, furtive, and inglorious manner. A tradition of isolated investigation came into Europe from the Arabs, and a considerable amount of private and secretive research was carried on by the alchemists, for whom modern writers are a little too apt with their contempt. These alchemists were in close touch with the glass and metal workers and with the herbalists and medicine-makers of the times; they pried into many secrets of nature, but they were obsessed by "practical" ideas; they sought not knowledge, but power; they wanted to find out how to manufacture gold from cheaper materials, how to make men immortal by the elixir of life, and such-like vulgar dreams. Incidentally in their researches they learnt much about poisons, dyes, metallurgy and the like; they discovered various refractory substances, and worked their way towards clear glass and so to lenses and optical instruments; but as scientific men tell us continually, and as "practical" men still refuse to learn, it is only when knowledge is sought for her own sake that she gives rich and unexpected gifts in any abundance to her servants.

The world of to-day is still much more disposed to spend money on technical research than on pure science. Half the men in our scientific laboratories still dream of patents and secret processes. We live to-day largely in the age of alchemists, for all our sneers at their memory. The "business man" of to-day still thinks of research as a sort of alchemy.

Closely associated with the alchemists were the astrologers, who were also a "practical" race. They studied the stars—to tell fortunes. They lacked that broader faith and understanding which induces men simply to study the stars.

Not until the fifteenth century did the ideas which Roger Bacon expressed begin to produce their first-fruits in new knowledge and a widening outlook. Then suddenly, as the sixteenth century dawned, and as the world recovered from the storm of social trouble that had followed the pestilences of the fourteenth century, Western Europe broke out into a galaxy of names that outshine the utmost scientific reputations of the best age of Greece. Nearly every nation contributed, the reader will note, for science knows no nationality.

One of the earliest and most splendid in this constellation is the Florentine, Leonardo da Vinci (1452–1519), a man with an almost miraculous vision for reality. He was a naturalist, an anatomist, an engineer, as well as a very great artist. He was the first modern to realize the true nature of fossils, he made note-books of observations that still amaze us, he was convinced of the practicability of mechanical flight. Another great name is that of Copernicus, a Pole (1473–1543), who made the first clear analysis of the movements of the heavenly bodies and showed that the earth moves round the sun. Tycho Brahe (1546–1601), a Dane working at the University of Prague, rejected this latter belief, but his observations of celestial movements were of the utmost value to his successors, and especially to the German, Kepler (1571–1630). Galileo Galilei (1564–1642) was the founder of the science of dynamics. Before his time it was believed that a weight a hundred times greater than another would fall a hundred times as fast. Galileo denied this. Instead of arguing about it like a scholar and a gentleman, he put it to the coarse test of experiment by dropping two unequal weights from an upper gallery of the leaning tower of Pisa—to the horror of all erudite men.

Galileo made what was almost the first telescope, and he developed the astronomical views of Copernicus; but the church, struggling gallantly against the light, decided that to believe that the earth was smaller and inferior to the sun, made man and Christianity of no account; so Galileo was induced to recant this view and put the earth back in its place as the immovable centre of the universe. Seven cardinals condemned him to a period of imprisonment and he was ordered to recite the seven penitential psalms once a week for three years.

Newton (1642–1727) was born in the year of Galileo's death. By his discovery of the law of gravitation he completed the clear vision of the starry universe that we have to-day. But Newton carries us into the eighteenth century. He carries us too far for the present chapter.

Among the earlier names, that of Dr. Gilbert (1540–1603), of Colchester, is pre-eminent. Roger Bacon had preached experiment, Gilbert was one of the first to practise it. There can be little doubt that his work, which was chiefly upon magnetism, helped to form the ideas of Francis Bacon, Lord Verulam (1561–1626), Lord Chancellor to James I of England. This Francis Bacon has been called the "Father of Experimental Philosophy," but of his share in the development of scientific work far too much has been made.[1] He was, says Sir R. A. Gregory, "not the founder but the apostle" of the scientific method. His greatest service to science was a fantastic book, *The New Atlantis*. "In his *New Atlantis*, Francis Bacon planned in somewhat fanciful language a palace of invention, a great temple of science, where the pursuit of knowledge in all its branches was to be organized on principles of the highest efficiency."

From this Utopian dream arose the Royal Society of London, which received a Royal Charter from Charles II of England in 1662. The essential use and virtue of this society was and is *publication*. Its formation marks a definite step from isolated inquiry towards co-operative work, from the secret and solitary investigations of the alchemist to the frank report and open discussion which is the life of the modern scientific process. For the true scientific method is this: to make no unnecessary hypotheses, to trust no statements without verification, to test all things as rigorously as possible, to keep no secrets, to attempt no monopolies, to give out one's best modestly and plainly, serving no other end but knowledge.

The long-slumbering science of anatomy was revived by Harvey (1578–1657), who demonstrated the circulation of the blood. Presently the Dutchman, Leeuwenhoek (1632–1723), brought the first crude microscope to bear upon the hidden minutiæ of life.

These are but some of the brightest stars amidst that increasing multitude of men who have from the fifteenth century to our own time, with more and more collective energy and vigour, lit up our vision of the universe, and increased our power over the conditions of our lives.

§ 7

We have dealt thus fully with the recrudescence of scientific studies in the Middle Ages because of its ultimate importance in human affairs. In the long run, Roger Bacon is of more significance to mankind than any monarch of his time. But the contemporary world, for the most part, knew nothing of this smouldering activity in studies and lecture-rooms and alchemists' laboratories that was presently to alter all the conditions of life. The church did, indeed, take notice of what was afoot, but only because of the disregard of her conclusive decisions. She had decided that the earth was the very centre of God's creation, and that the Pope was the divinely appointed ruler of the earth. Men's ideas on these essential points, she insisted, must not be disturbed by any contrary teaching. So soon, however, as she had compelled Galileo to say that the world did not move she was satisfied; she does not seem to

---

[1] See Gregory's *Discovery*, chap. vi.

have realized how ominous it was for her that, after all, the earth did move.

Very great social as well as intellectual developments were in progress in Western Europe throughout this period of the later Middle Ages. But the human mind apprehends events far more vividly than changes; and men for the most part, then as now, kept on in their own traditions in spite of the shifting scene about them.

In an Outline such as this it is impossible to crowd in the clustering events of history that do not clearly show the main process of human development, however bright and picturesque they may be. We have to record the steady growth of towns and cities, the reviving power of trade and money, the gradual re-establishment of law and custom, the extension of security, the supersession of private warfare that went on in Western Europe in the period between the first crusade and the sixteenth century.

Of much that looms large in our national histories we cannot tell anything. We have no space for the story of the repeated attempts of the English kings to conquer Scotland and set themselves up as kings of France, nor of how the Norman English established themselves insecurely in Ireland (twelfth century), and how Wales was linked to the English crown (1282). All through the Middle Ages the struggle of England with Scotland and France was in progress; there were times when it seemed that Scotland was finally subjugated and when the English king held far more land in France than its titular sovereign. In the English histories this struggle with France is too often represented as a single-handed and almost successful attempt to conquer France. In reality it was a joint enterprise undertaken in concert first with the Flemings and Bavarians and afterwards with the powerful French vassal state of Burgundy to conquer and divide the patrimony of Hugh Capet.

Of the English rout by the Scotch at Bannockburn (1314), and of William Wallace and Robert the Bruce, the Scottish national heroes; of the battles of Crècy (1346) and Poitiers (1356) and Agincourt (1415) in France, which shine like stars in the English imagination, little battles in which sturdy bowmen through some sunny hours made a great havoc among French knights in armour; of the Black Prince and Henry V of England, and of how a peasant girl, Joan of Arc, the Maid of Orleans, drove the English out of her country again (1429–1430)—this history relates nothing. For every country has such cherished national events. They are the ornamental tapestry of history, and no part of the building. Rajputana or Poland, Hungary, Russia, Spain, Persia, and China can all match or outdo the utmost romance of Western Europe, with equally adventurous knights and equally valiant princesses and equally stout fights against the odds.

Nor can we tell in any detail how Louis XI of France (1461–1483), the son of Joan of Arc's Charles VII, brought Burgundy to heel and laid the foundations of a centralized French monarchy. It signifies more that in the thirteenth and fourteenth centuries, gunpowder, that Mongol gift, came to Europe, so that the kings (Louis XI included) and the law, relying upon the support of the growing towns, were able to batter down the castles of the half-independent robber knights and barons of the earlier Middle Ages and consolidate a more centralized power.

The fighting nobles and knights of the barbaric period disappear slowly from history during these centuries; the Crusades consumed them, such dynastic wars as the English Wars of the Roses killed them off, the arrows from the English long-bow pierced them and stuck out a yard behind, infantry so armed swept them from the stricken field; they became reconciled to trade and changed their nature. They disappeared in everything but a titular sense from the west and south of Europe before they disappeared from Germany. The knight in Germany remained a professional fighting man into the sixteenth century.

Between the eleventh and the fifteenth centuries in Western Europe, and particularly in France and England, there sprang up like flowers a multitude of very distinctive and beautiful buildings, cathedrals, abbeys, and the like, the Gothic architecture. We have already noted its chief characteristics. This lovely efflorescence marks the appearance of a body of craftsmen closely linked in its beginnings to the church. In Italy and Spain, too, the world was beginning to build freely and beautifully again. At first it was the wealth of the church that provided most of these buildings; then kings and merchants also began to build. Beside the church and the castle appear the mansion and the house.

From the twelfth century onward, with the increase of trade, there was a great revival of town life throughout Europe. Prominent among these towns were Venice, with its dependents Ragusa and Corfu, Genoa, Verona, Bologna, Pisa, Florence, Naples, Milan, Marseilles, Lisbon, Barcelona, Narbonne, Tours, Orleans, Bordeaux, Paris, Ghent, Bruges, Boulogne, London, Oxford, Cambridge, Southampton, Dover, Antwerp, Hamburg, Bremen, Cologne, Mayence, Nuremberg, Munich, Leipzig, Magdeburg, Breslau, Stettin, Dantzig, Königsberg, Riga, Pskof, Novgorod, Wisby, and Bergen.

"A West German town, between 1400 and 1500,[1] embodied all the achievements of progress at that time, although from a modern standpoint much seems wanting. . . . The streets were mostly narrow and irregularly built, the houses chiefly of wood, while almost every burgher kept his cattle in the house, and the herd of swine which was driven every morning by the town herdsman to the pasture-ground formed an inevitable part of city life." Charles Dickens in his *American Notes* mentions swine in Broadway, New York, in the middle nineteenth century. "In Frankfort-on-Main it was unlawful after 1481 to keep swine in the Altstadt, but in the Neustadt and in Sachsenhausen this custom remained as a matter of course. It was only in 1645, after a corresponding attempt in 1556 had failed, that the swine-pens in the inner town were pulled down at Leipzig. The rich burghers, who occasionally took part in the great trading companies, were conspicuously wealthy land-owners, and had extensive courtyards with large barns inside the town walls. The most opulent of them owned those splendid patrician houses which we still admire even to-day.

---

[1] From Dr. Tille in Helmolt's *History of the World.*

"But even in the older towns most houses of the fifteenth century have disappeared; only here and there a building with open timber-work and over-hanging stories, as in Bacharach or Miltenburg, reminds us of the style of architecture then customary in the houses of burghers. The great bulk of the inferior population, who lived on mendicancy, or got a livelihood by the ex-ercise of the inferior industries, inhabited squalid hovels outside the town; the town wall was often the only support for these wretched buildings. The internal fittings of the houses, even amongst the wealthy population, were very defec-tive according to modern ideas; the Gothic style was as little suitable for the petty details of objects of luxury as it was splendidly adapted for the building of churches and town halls. The influence of the Renaissance added much to the comfort of the house.

"The fourteenth and fifteenth century saw the building of numerous Gothic town churches and town halls throughout Europe, which still in many cases serve their original purpose. The power and prosperity of the towns find their best expression in these and in the fortifications, with their strong towers and gateways. Every picture of a town of the sixteenth or later centuries shows conspicuously these latter erections for the protection and honour of the town.

"The town did many things which in our time are done by the State. Social problems were taken up by town administration or the corresponding munici-pal organization. The regulation of trade was the concern of the guilds in agreement with the council, the care of the poor belonged to the church, while the council looked after the protection of the town walls and the very neces-sary fire brigades. The council, mindful of its social duties, superintended the filling of the municipal granaries, in order to have supplies in years of scarcity. Such storehouses were erected in almost every town during the fifteenth cen-tury. Tariffs of prices for the sale of all wares, high enough to enable every artisan to make a good livelihood, and to give the purchaser a guarantee for the quality of the wares, were maintained. The town was also the chief capi-talist; as a seller of annuities on lives and inheritances it was a banker and enjoyed unlimited credit. In return it obtained means for the construction of fortifications or for such occasions as the acquisition of sovereign rights from the hand of an impecunious prince."

For the most part these European towns were independent or quasi-inde-pendent aristocratic republics. Most admitted a vague overlordship on the part of the church, or of the emperor or of a king. Others were parts of kingdoms, or even the capitals of dukes or kings. In such cases their internal freedom was maintained by a royal or imperial charter. In England the Royal City of Westminster on the Thames stood cheek by jowl with the walled city of Lon-don, into which the king came only with ceremony and permission.

The entirely free Venetian republic ruled an empire of dependent islands and trading ports, rather after the fashion of the Athenian republic. Genoa also stood alone.

The Germanic towns of the Baltic and North Sea from Riga to Middleburg in Holland, Dortmund, and Cologne were loosely allied in a confederation, the confederation of the Hansa towns, under the leadership of Hamburg,

Bremen, and Lübeck, a confederation which was still more loosely attached to the empire. This confederation, which included over seventy towns in all, and which had depots in Novgorod, Bergen, London, and Bruges, did much to keep the northern seas clean of piracy, that curse of the Mediterranean and of the Eastern seas.

The Eastern Empire throughout its last phase, from the Ottoman conquest of its European hinterland in the fourteenth and early fifteenth century until its fall in 1453, was practically only the trading town of Constantinople, a town state like Genoa or Venice, except that it was encumbered by a corrupt imperial court.

The fullest and most splendid developments of this city life of the later Middle Ages occurred in Italy. After the end of the Hohenstaufen line in the thirteenth century, the hold of the Holy Roman Empire upon North and Central Italy weakened, although, as we shall tell, German emperors were still crowned as kings and emperors in Italy up to the time of Charles V (*circa* 1530). There arose a number of quasi-independent city states to the north of Rome, the papal capital. South Italy and Sicily, however, remained under foreign dominion. Genoa and her rival, Venice, were the great trading seaports of this time; their noble palaces, their lordly paintings still win our admiration. Milan, at the foot of the St. Gothard Pass, also revived to wealth and power. Brightest perhaps of all the stars in the Italian constellation of cities was Florence, a trading and financial centre which, under the almost monarchical rule of the Medici family in the fifteenth century, enjoyed a second "Periclean age." Already, before the time of these cultivated Medici "bosses," Florence had produced much beautiful art. Giotto's tower (Giotto, 1266–1337) and the Duomo (by Brunelleschi, 1379–1446) already existed. Towards the end of the fourteenth century Florence became the centre of the rediscovery, restoration, and imitation of antique art. But of the Renaissance of Art, in which Florence played so large a part, it will be more convenient to speak in a later section.

§ 8

A great outbreak of creative literature is associated with this general reawakening of the Western European intelligence. We have already noted the appearance of literature in Italian under the initiatives of the Emperor Frederick II. Simultaneously the Troubadours in both Northern France and in Provence were setting people to the making of verse in the northern and southern dialects, love songs, narrative songs and the like. These things broke out, so to speak, beneath a general disposition to write and read Latin. They came from the popular mind and the relaxed mind and not from the learned. In Florence in 1265 was born Dante Alighieri, who, after vehement political activities, became an exile and wrote, among other works, an elaborate poem in rhymed Italian verse, the *Commedia*, a tapestry of allegory and sporadic incident and religious disquisition. It describes a visit to Hell, Purgatory and Paradise. Its relationship to the ancestral Latin literature is suggested by the fact that

Dante's guide in the lower regions is Virgil. In its various English translations it makes extremely dull reading, but those who are best qualified to speak in the matter are scarce able to express their perception of the exquisite beauty, interest and wisdom of the original. Dante also wrote in Latin upon political questions and upon the claims of the Italian tongue to be considered a literary language. He was severely criticized for his use of Italian and accused of an incapacity for Latin verse.

A little later Petrarch (1304–1374) was also writing sonnets and odes in Italian which arouse the enthusiasm of all who have been sufficiently cultivated to respond to them. For example, John Addington Symonds wrote: "The *Rime in Vita e Morte di Madonna Laura* cannot become obsolete, for perfectly metrical form has here been married to language of the choicest and purest." The poems leave us doubtful if Madonna Laura ever existed. Petrarch was one of the group of Italians who were strenuous to restore the glories of the Latin literature. In an Outline of History these glories are not perhaps so supreme as they seemed to be to a generation of Italians reawakening to the charms and excitement of literary beauty. Writing in Italian waned for a time before a revival of Latin authorship. Petrarch wrote an epic in Latin, *Africa*. There was a considerable output of pseudo-classical writing, epics and sham tragedies and sham comedies in Latin, no doubt very like the poems and rhetorical prose one receives in English from gifted young Indians. It was only later with Boiardo and Ariosto (1475–1533) that Italian poetry emerges again to distinction. Ariosto's *Orlando Furioso* was only the crowning specimen of a great multitude of romantic narrative poems that delighted the less erudite readers of the Renaissance. These narrative poems always paid the tribute of more or less allusion and imitation to the traditions of the artificial Virgilian epic, itself an imitative and scholarly exploit. Comedy and the narrative poem, shorter poems in various forms, constitute the bulk of this literature. Prose was not sufficiently artificial and genteel for critical approval.

The reawakening of literary life in the French-speaking community was also dominated by memories of the Latin literature. There was already a literature of merry songs in mediæval Latin in France, songs of the tavern and the road (the Goliardic poetry of the thirteenth century), and the spirit of this authentic writing lived in such true and native verse as that of Villon (1431–1463), but the revival of Latin studies flowed in from Italy and imposed artificiality upon all but the sturdiest minds. An elaborate style was established, with something of the dignity of monumental masonry, and splendid poems and classical plays were erected for the admiration rather than the pleasure of posterity. Yet the genius of French life was not altogether confined to these noble exercises; a fine and flexible prose appeared. Montaigne (1533–1592), the first of essayists, wrote pleasantly of life and unpleasantly about the learned, and Rabelais (1490?–1553), like a torrent of burning, shouting, laughing lava, burst through all the dignitaries and decencies of the pedants.

In Germany and in Holland the new intellectual impulses were more nearly simultaneous with the immense political and religious stresses of the Reformation, and they produced less purely artistic forms. Erasmus, says J. Addington Symonds, is the great representative in Holland of the Renaissance as Luther was in Germany, but he wrote not in Dutch but Latin.

There was an outbreak of literary activity in England as early as the fourteenth century. Geoffrey Chaucer (1340?–1400) produced delightful narrative poetry that derived very obviously from Italian models, and there was much pre-existing romantic narrative verse. But the Civil Wars, the Wars of the Roses, pestilence, and religious conflicts damped down the first beginning, and it was only with the sixteenth century and after the reign of Henry VIII that English literature broke into vigorous life. There was first a rapid spread of classical learning and a fertilizing torrent of translations from Latin, Greek and Italian. There came a sudden harvest of fine English writing. English was played with, tested, elaborated. Spenser wrote his *Faerie Queen*, a tedious allegorical work of great decorative beauty. But it was in the drama, in the days of Queen Elizabeth, that the English genius found its best expression. It never succumbed to the classical tradition; the Elizabethan drama was a new and fuller and looser, more vigorous and altogether more natural, literary form. It found its extreme exponent in Shakespeare (1564–1616), a man happily with "little Latin and less Greek," whose richest, subtlest passages are drawn from homely and even vulgar life. He was a man of keen humour and great sweetness of mind, who turned every sentence he wrote into melody. Eight years before the death of Shakespeare, Milton (1608–1674) was born. Early classical studies gave both his prose and verse a proud and pompous gait from which they never completely recovered. He went to Italy and saw the glories of Renaissance painting. He translated the paintings of Raphael and Michael Angelo into superb English verse in his great epics of *Paradise Lost* and *Paradise Regained*. It is well for English literature that Shakespeare lived to counterbalance Milton and save so much of its essential spirit from the classical obsession.

Portugal, at the touch of the literary Renaissance, produced an epic, the *Lusiad* of Camoens (1524–1580); but Spain, like England, was so fortunate as to find a man of supreme genius, unembarrassed by an excess of learning, to express its spirit. Cervantes (1547–1616) seized upon the humours and absurdities of a conflict between the mediæval tradition of chivalry in possession of the imagination of a lean, poor, half-crazy gentleman, and the needs and impulses of the vulgar life. His Don Quixote and Sancho Panza, like Shakespeare's Sir John Falstaff, Chaucer's wife of Bath, and Rabelais' Gargantua break through the dignity and heroics of formal literature to let in freedom and laughter. They break through as Roger Bacon and the scientific men broke through the bookish science of the scholars, and as the painters and sculptors we have next to tell about broke through the decorative restraints and religious decorum of mediæval art. The fundamental fact of the Renaissance was not classicism but release. The revival of Latin and Greek learning only contributed to the positive values of the Renaissance by their corrosive influence upon the Catholic, Gothic and Imperial traditions.

§ 9

It would be beyond our scale and compass to trace the multifarious revivals of domestic and decorative art in this great period of human recovery, or to tell how the northern Gothic was adapted to municipal and private buildings and modified, and to a large extent replaced by forms deriving from the Italian Romanesque, and the revival of classical traditions in Italy. Italy had never taken kindly to the Gothic that had invaded her from the north, or to the Saracenic forms that had come in from the south. The Latin writings in architecture of Vitruvius were unearthed in the fifteenth century, and had a very stimulating effect upon processes of change already in operation. The classical influences which were flowing strongly in literature spread into the already active world of artistic creation.

But, just as the literary revival preceded the revival of classical learning, so the artistic reawakening was in full progress before attention was drawn to classical representative art. The gradual reassertion of the desire for imitative representation rather than decoration has been going on in Europe ever since the days of Charlemagne. There was a vigorous development of painting, the painting of real things upon wood, in Germany in the twelfth and thirteenth centuries. In Italy, where the architectural forms gave more space than did the Gothic, mural painting also was increasing in importance. The first definite school of German painting was in Cologne (1360 onward). A little later came Hubert and Jan Van Eyck (*circa* 1380–1440) in Holland. Their work is bright and fresh and delightful; it is like the illustration of a missal taking the air in the larger spaces of the painted panel.

In Italy in the thirteenth century Cimabue was painting; he was the master of Giotto (1266–1337), who stands out as the early master figure of this first phase in the recovery of art. It was a phase that culminated and closed with Fra Angelico da Fiesole (1387–1455).

And now there began in Italy, and especially at Florence, a strictly scientific research into the artifices of realistic representation. It cannot be too strongly emphasized, because nothing is more steadfastly ignored in books about art, that the essence in the changes in art and sculpture that were happening in Europe in the Renaissance period was an abandonment of æsthetic for scientific considerations. In the place of design and patterning, formal, abstract and lovely, there was a research for reality that was at best bold and splendid and often harsh and brutal. The swing and sway of the crude human body that Saracenic art had suppressed and Byzantine frozen, came back upon wall and stone. Life returned to art and was presently sweating and gesticulating. The problems of perspective were studied and solved, and for the first time painters began with assurance to represent depth in the picture. Anatomy was acutely and minutely investigated. Art was for a time intoxicated with representation. There was a close, veracious rendering of details—flowers and jewels, folds of fabrics, and reflections in transparent objects. A phase of extreme decorative beauty was attained and passed.

We cannot trace here the sustained drive of these reawakened impulses through the various schools of the Italian and Low German cities, nor the mutual reactions of Flemish and Florentine and Umbrian and such-like groups of painters. We can but name among the fifteenth-century masters the Florentines, Filippo Lippi, Botticelli, Ghirlandajo, and the Umbrians Signorelli and Perugino and Mantegna. Mantegna (1431–1506) stands out because in his work more than that of any contemporary one traces the recovered leaven of the old classical art. He has at his best an inimitable austerity.

With the sixteenth century came Leonardo da Vinci (1452–1519), of whose scientific speculations we have already spoken. A kindred spirit in Nuremberg was Albrecht Dürer (1471–1528). Venetian art rose to its climax with Titian (1476?–1576), Tintoretto (1518–1594) and Paul Veronese (1528–1588). But it will mean little to the reader for us to catalogue names. The best reproductions would only give a few intimations of the quality of these masters; in print we can only state their general relationship to art and life as factors in a new attitude to the body and tangible things. The student must go to their pictures for his realizations of their quality. We may point him to the picture by Titian known by the inappropriate name of *Sacred and Profane Love*, or to various of the sibyls, and to the *Creation of Adam* painted by Michael Angelo on the roof of the Sistine Chapel, as among the supremely beautiful flowers of this growth. Painting went to England with the German, Hans Holbein (1497–1543), for England had been too torn by civil war to shelter any school of painting. It was a mere visit. Even the Elizabethan time, so rich in literature, so fertile of music, produced no English painting or sculpture to compare with that of Italy and France. War and political trouble presently checked the art of Germany, but the Flemish impulse went on to Rubens (1577–1640), Rembrandt (1606–1669), and to a great number of delightful genre and landscape painters who reproduced in oil in the extreme west of Europe, and without any possible connection or derivation, work curiously similar in spirit and subject to some of the most interesting Chinese work. The parallelism may be due to some obscure parallelism of social conditions.

From the end of the sixteenth century onward the painters of Italy declined in stature. The novelty and zest of painting the brightly lit human body in every possible contraction, extension and foreshortening against backgrounds of more than natural vividness faded, the justifications of sculpture and classical mythology for such illuminated physical exercises were largely exhausted, the representation of the virtues, vices, arts, sciences, cities, nations, and so forth by freely revealed feminine figures agreeably disposed ceased to provoke original minds, and a less strenuous type of practitioner was attracted to the practice of the art, content to paint pictures that did at the best merely vie with pictures already painted. The European sculpture that had developed slowly and naturally in Germany, France and North Italy from the eleventh century onward, and which had produced such fine works as the angels of the Sainte Chapelle in Paris, the equestrian monument of Can Grande in Verona, and the Colleoni statue at Venice (by Verrocchio and Leopardi), was presently carried away by attempts to revive the peculiar qualities of the classical

statuary that was now being disinterred and admired. Michael Angelo, drunk
with this inspiration, produced works of a towering force and dignity and unparalleled anatomical vigour that stunned his successors into imitation and decline. As the seventeenth century progressed European painting and sculpture
began to have the quality of an athlete who has overtrained and is stale; of a
rose that is overblown.

But architecture is sustained by material needs when less necessary arts decay, and through the sixteenth and seventeenth centuries a steady and various
production of gracious and beautiful buildings went on all over Europe. We
can but name Palladio (1518–1580), whose work abounds in his native town
of Vicenza, and whose books and teaching spread his revivified classical style
over nearly every European country. He was like a great fountain of architectural suggestions. We cannot trace here the intricate extensions and variations
of Renaissance architecture that have continued in a natural and continuous
evolution into our own times.

Painting in Spain was no such authentic growth of the soil as it was in Low
Germany and Italy. The Spanish painters went to Italy to learn, and brought
their art back thence. But in the opening half of the seventeenth century, at
the shrunken but still opulent Spanish Court, Spanish painting flowered in the
great and original personality of Velasquez (1599–1660). He had a novel
directness of vision, a new power in his brush. He, in company with the Dutch
Rembrandt, stands out from the rest of the Renaissance painters in spirit and
quality, and looks towards the most vigorous work of the later nineteenth century and of our own time.

§ 10

In 1453, as we have related, Constantinople fell. Throughout the next century the Turkish pressure upon Europe was heavy and continuous. The boundary line between Mongol and Aryan, which had lain somewhere east of the
Pamirs in the days of Pericles, had receded now to Hungary. Constantinople
had long been a mere island of Christians in a Turk-ruled Balkan peninsula.
Its fall did much to interrupt the trade with the East.

Of the two rival cities of the Mediterranean, Venice was generally on much
better terms with the Turks than Genoa. Every intelligent Genoese sailor
fretted at the trading monopoly of Venice, and tried to invent some way of
getting through it or round it. And there were now new peoples taking to the
sea trade, and disposed to look for new ways to the old markets because the
ancient routes were closed to them.

The Portuguese, for example, were developing an Atlantic coasting trade.
The Atlantic was waking up again after a vast period of neglect that dated
from the Roman murder of Carthage. It is rather a delicate matter to decide
whether the Western European was pushing out into the Atlantic or whether
he was being pushed out into it by the Turk, who lorded it in the Mediterranean until the battle of Lepanto (1571). The Venetian and Genoese ships
were creeping round to Antwerp, and the Hansa town seamen were coming

south and extending their range. And there were considerable developments of seamanship and shipbuilding in progress. The Mediterranean is a sea for galleys and coasting. But upon the Atlantic Ocean and the North Sea winds are more prevalent, seas run higher, the shore is often a danger rather than a refuge. The high seas called for the sailing ship, and in the fourteenth and fifteenth centuries it appears, keeping its course by the compass and the stars.

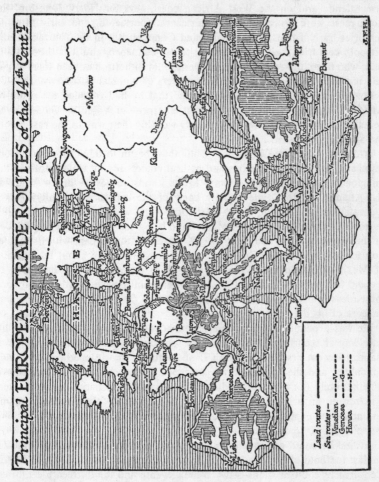

By the thirteenth century the Hansa merchants were already sailing regularly from Bergen across the grey cold seas to the Northmen in Iceland. In Iceland men knew of Greenland, and adventurous voyagers had long ago found a further land beyond, Vinland, where the climate was pleasant and where men could settle if they chose to cut themselves off from the rest of human kind. This Vinland was either Nova Scotia or, what is more probable, New England.

All over Europe in the fifteenth century merchants and sailors were speculating about new ways to the East. The Portuguese, unaware that Pharaoh Necho had solved the problem ages ago, were asking whether it was not possible to go round to India by the coast of Africa. Their ships followed (1445) in the course that Hanno took to Cape Verde. They put out to sea to the west and found the Canary Isles, Madeira, and the Azores. That was a fairly long stride across the Atlantic. In these maritime adventures in the eastern Atlantic and on the West African coast, says Sir Harry Johnston, the Portuguese were preceded in the thirteenth, fourteenth, and early fifteenth centuries by Normans, Catalonians, and Genoese. But in the fourteenth and fifteenth centuries their activities rose to pre-eminence, and it is they, at any rate, who fixed and established discoveries that hitherto had been mere vague and incidental visits. They were the pioneers of nautical astronomy. In 1486 a Portuguese, Bartolomeu Diaz, reported that he had rounded the south of Africa. So the way opened for the great enterprise of Vasco da Gama eleven years later. The Portuguese were already working their way to the east before the Spanish went west.

A certain Genoese, Christopher Columbus, began to think more and more of what is to us a very obvious and natural enterprise, but which strained the imagination of the fifteenth century to the utmost, a voyage due west across the Atlantic. At that time nobody knew of the existence of America as a separate continent. Columbus knew that the world was a sphere, but he underestimated its size; the travels of Marco Polo had given him an exaggerated idea of the extent of Asia, and he supposed, therefore, that Japan, with its reputation for a great wealth of gold, lay across the Atlantic in about the position of Mexico. He had made various voyages in the Atlantic; he had been to Iceland and perhaps heard of Vinland, which must have greatly encouraged these ideas of his, and this project of sailing into the sunset became the ruling purpose of his life.

He was a penniless man, some accounts say he was a bankrupt, and his only way of securing a ship was to get someone to entrust him with a command. He went first to King John II of Portugal, who listened to him, made difficulties, and then arranged for an expedition to start without his knowledge, a purely Portuguese expedition. This highly diplomatic attempt to steal a march on an original man failed, as it deserved to fail; the crew became mutinous, the captain lost heart and returned (1483). Columbus then went to the Court of Spain.

At first he could get no ship and no powers. Spain was assailing Granada, the last foothold of the Moslems in Western Europe. Most of Spain had been recovered by the Christians between the eleventh and the thirteenth centuries; then had come a pause; and now all Christian Spain, united by the marriage of Ferdinand of Aragon and Isabella of Castile, was setting itself to the completion of the Christian conquest. Despairing of Spanish help, Columbus sent his brother Bartholomew to Henry VII of England, but the adventure did not attract that canny monarch. Finally, in 1492, Granada fell—some slight compensation for the Christian loss of Constantinople fifty years before; and then, helped by some merchants of the town of Palos, Columbus got his ships—

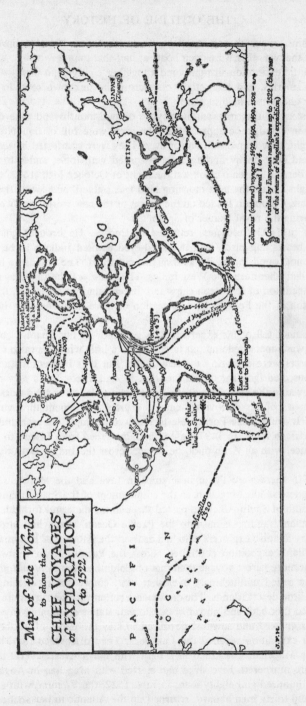

Map of the World
to show the
CHIEF VOYAGES
of EXPLORATION
(to 1522)

Columbus' (outward) voyages — 1492, 1493, 1498, 1502 = 1-4
numbered 1 to 4.

Coasts visited by European navigators up to 1522 (the year of the return of Magellan's expedition)

JAPAN (Zipangu)

CHINA

INDIA

Cape of Good Hope

Diaz 1486

V. da Gama 1497

Azores

Canary Is.

ICELAND

GREENLAND

North America (before 1600)

(Later) English & Dutch attempts to find a North East Passage

Labrador

Cabot 1498

Chanc. 1553

NEWFOUNDLAND

NORTH AMERICA

VINLAND

Cartier 1534

SOUTH AMERICA

Columbus

East of this line to Portugal.

West of this line to Spain.

The Pope's Line

Str. of Magellan

Magellan 1520

PACIFIC OCEAN

Ladrones

J.F.H.

three ships, of which only one, the *Santa Maria,* of 100 tons burthen, was decked; the two other were open boats of half that tonnage.

The little expedition—it numbered altogether eighty-eight men!—went south to the Canaries, and then stood out across the unknown seas, in beautiful weather and with a helpful wind.

The story of that momentous voyage of two months and nine days must be read in detail to be appreciated. The crew were full of doubts and fears; they might, they feared, sail on for ever. They were comforted by seeing some birds, and later on by finding a pole worked with tools, and a branch with strange berries. At ten o'clock, on the night of October 11th, 1492, Columbus saw a light ahead; the next morning land was sighted, and, while the day was still young, Columbus landed on the shores of the new world, richly apparelled and bearing the royal banner of Spain.

Early in 1493 Columbus returned to Europe. He brought gold, cotton, strange beasts and birds, and two wild-eyed painted Indians to be baptized. He had not found Japan, it was thought, but India. The islands he had found were called, therefore, the West Indies. The same year he sailed again with a great expedition of seventeen ships and fifteen hundred men, with the express permission of the Pope to take possession of these new lands for the Spanish crown.

We cannot tell of his experiences as governor of this Spanish colony, nor how he was superseded and put in chains. In a little while a swarm of Spanish adventurers were exploring the new lands. But it is interesting to note that Columbus died ignorant of the fact that he had discovered a new continent. He believed to the day of his death that he had sailed round the world to Asia.

The news of his discoveries caused a great excitement through Western Europe. It spurred the Portuguese to renewed attempts to reach India by the South African route. In 1497 Vasco da Gama sailed from Lisbon to Zanzibar, and thence, with an Arab pilot, he struck across the Indian Ocean to Calicut in India.

In 1515 there were Portuguese ships in Java and the Moluccas. In 1519 a Portuguese sailor, Magellan, in the employment of the Spanish king, coasted to the south of South America, passed through the dark and forbidding "Strait of Magellan," and so came into the Pacific Ocean, which had already been sighted by Spanish explorers who had crossed the Isthmus of Panama.

Magellan's expedition continued across the Pacific Ocean westward. This was a far more heroic voyage than that of Columbus; for *eight and ninety days* Magellan sailed unflinchingly over that vast, empty ocean, sighting nothing but two little desert islands. The crews were rotten with scurvy; there was little water and that bad, and putrid biscuit to eat. Rats were hunted eagerly; cowhide was gnawed and sawdust devoured to stay the pangs of hunger. In this state the expedition reached the Ladrones. They discovered the Philippines, and here Magellan was killed in a fight with the natives. Several other captains were murdered. Five ships had started with Magellan in August, 1519, and two hundred and eighty men; in July, 1522, the *Victoria,* with a remnant of one-and-thirty men aboard, returned up the Atlantic to her anchorage near the Mole of Seville, in the river Guadalquivir—the first ship that ever circumnavigated this planet.

The English and French and Dutch and the sailors of the Hansa towns came rather late into this new adventure of exploration. They had not the same keen interest in the eastern trade. And when they did come in, their first efforts were directed to sailing round the north of America as Magellan had sailed round the south, and to sailing round the north of Asia as Vasco da Gama had sailed round the south of Africa. Both these enterprises were doomed to failure by the nature of things. Both in America and the East, Spain and Portugal had half a century's start of England and France and Holland.

And Germany never started. The King of Spain was Emperor of Germany in those crucial years, and the Pope had given the monopoly of America to Spain, and not simply to Spain but to the kingdom of Castile. This must have restrained both Germany and Holland at first from American adventures. The Hansa towns were quasi-independent; they had no monarch behind them to support them, and no unity among themselves for so big an enterprise as oceanic exploration. It was the misfortune of Germany, and perhaps of the world, that, as we will presently tell, a storm of warfare exhausted her when all the Western powers were going to this newly-opened school of trade and administration upon the high seas.

Slowly throughout the sixteenth century the immense good fortune of Castile unfolded itself before the dazzled eyes of Europe. She had found a new world, abounding in gold and silver and wonderful possibilities of settlement. It was all hers, because the Pope had said so. The Court of Rome, in an access of magnificence, had divided this new world of strange lands, which was now opening out to the European imagination, between the Spanish, who were to have everything west of a line 370 leagues west of the Cape Verde Islands, and the Portuguese, to whom everything east of this line was given.

At first the only people encountered by the Spaniards in America were savages of a Mongoloid type. Many of these savages were cannibals. It is a misfortune for science that the first Europeans to reach America were these rather incurious Spaniards, without any scientific passion, thirsty for gold, and full of the blind bigotry of a recent religious war. They made few intelligent observations of the native methods and ideas of these primordial people. They slaughtered them, they robbed them, they enslaved them, and baptized them; but they made small note of the customs and motives that changed and vanished under their assault. They were as destructive and reckless as the early British settlers in Tasmania, who shot at sight the Palæolithic men who still lingered there and put out poisoned meat for them to find.

Great areas of the American interior were prairie land, whose nomadic tribes subsisted upon vast herds of the now practically extinct bison. In their manner of life, in their painted garments and their free use of paint, in their general physical characters, these prairie Indians showed remarkable resemblances to the Later Palæolithic men of the Solutrean age in Europe. But they had no horses. They seem to have made no very great advance from that primordial state, which was probably the state in which their ancestors had reached America. They had, however, a knowledge of metals, and most notably a free use of native copper, but no knowledge of iron.

As the Spaniards penetrated into the continent, they found and they attacked, plundered, and destroyed two separate civilized systems that had developed in America, perhaps quite independently of the civilized systems of the old world. One of them was the Aztec civilization of Mexico; the other, that of Peru. They may have arisen out of the Neolithic sub-civilization that had spread across the Pacific, island by island, step by step, age after age, from its region of origin round and about the Mediterranean. We have already noted one or two points of interest in these unique developments. They were thousands of years behind the Orient and Mediterranean. Along their own lines these civilized peoples of America had reached to a state of affairs roughly parallel with the culture of pre-dynastic Egypt or the early Sumerian cities. Before the Aztecs and the Peruvians there had been still earlier civilized beginnings which had either been destroyed by their successors, or which had failed and relapsed of their own accord.

The Aztecs seem to have been a conquering, less civilized people, dominating a more civilized community as the Aryans dominated Greece and North India. Their religion was a primitive, complex, and cruel system, in which human sacrifices and ceremonial cannibalism played a large part. Their minds were haunted by the idea of sin and the need for bloody propitiations. Their religion was like a dreadful and complete caricature of the primitive sacrificial religions of the old world.

The Aztec civilization was destroyed by an expedition under Cortez. He had eleven ships, four hundred Europeans, two hundred Indians, sixteen horses, and fourteen guns. But in Yucatan he picked up a stray Spaniard who had been a captive with the Indians for some years, and who had more or less learnt various Indian languages, and knew that the Aztec rule was deeply resented by many of its subjects. It was in alliance with these that Cortez advanced over the mountains into the valley of Mexico (1519).

How he entered Mexico, how its war-chief, Montezuma, was killed by his own people for favouring the Spaniards, how Cortez was besieged in Mexico and escaped with the loss of his guns and horses, and how after a terrible retreat to the coast he was able to return and subjugate the whole land, is a romantic and picturesque story which we cannot even attempt to tell here. The population of Mexico to this day is largely of native blood, but Spanish has replaced the native languages, and modern Mexican culture is Spanish in origin.

The still more curious Peruvian state fell a victim to another adventurer, Pizarro. He sailed from the Isthmus of Panama in 1530, with an expedition of a hundred and sixty-eight Spaniards. Like Cortez in Mexico, he availed himself of the native dissensions to secure possession of the doomed state. Like Cortez, too, who had made a captive and tool of Montezuma, he seized the Inca of Peru by treachery, and attempted to rule in his name.

Here again we cannot do justice to the tangle of subsequent events, the ill-planned insurrections of the natives, the arrival of Spanish reinforcements from Mexico, and the reduction of the state to a Spanish province. Nor can we tell much more of the swift spread of Spanish adventurers over the rest of America, outside the Portuguese reservation of Brazil. To begin with, each story is nearly always a story of adventurers and of cruelty and loot. The Spaniards ill-treated the natives, they quarrelled among themselves, the law and order of Spain were months and years away from them; it was only very slowly that the phase of violence and conquest passed into a phase of government and settlement. But long before there was much order in America, a

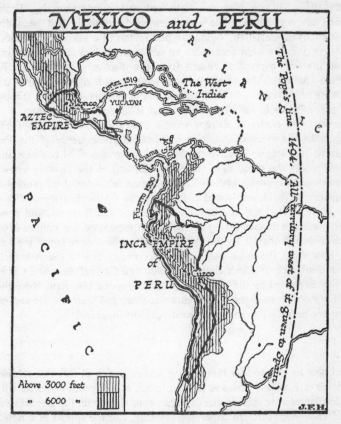

steady stream of gold and silver began to flow across the Atlantic to the Spanish government and people.

After the first violent treasure hunt came plantation and the working of mines. With that arose the earliest labour difficulty in the new world. At first the Indians were enslaved with much brutality and injustice; but to the honour of the Spaniards this did not go uncriticized. The natives found champions, and very valiant champions, in the Dominican Order and in a secular priest Las Casas, who was for a time a planter and slave-owner in Cuba until his conscience smote him. An importation of negro slaves from West Africa also began quite early in the sixteenth century. After some retrogression, Mexico, Brazil, and Spanish South America began to develop into great slave-holding, wealth-producing lands.

We cannot tell here, as we would like to do, of the fine civilizing work done in South America, and more especially among the natives, by the Franciscans, and presently by the Jesuits, who came into America in the latter half of the sixteenth century (after 1549).

So it was that Spain rose to a temporary power and prominence in the world's affairs. It was a very sudden and very memorable rise. From the eleventh century this infertile and corrugated peninsula had been divided against itself, its Christian population had sustained a perpetual conflict with the Moors; then by what seems like an accident it achieved unity just in time to reap the first harvest of benefit from the discovery of America. Before that time Spain had always been a poor country; it is a poor country to-day; almost its only wealth lies in its mines. For a century, however, through its monopoly of the gold and silver of America, it dominated the world.

The east and centre of Europe were still overshadowed by the Turk and Mongol; the discovery of America was itself a consequence of the Turkish conquests; very largely through the Mongolian inventions of compass and paper, and under the stimulus of travel in Asia and of the growing knowledge of eastern Asiatic wealth and civilization, came this astonishing blazing up of the mental, physical, and social energies of the "Atlantic fringe." For close in the wake of Portugal and Spain came France and England, and presently Holland, each in its turn taking up the rôle of expansion and empire overseas.

The centre of interest for European history, which once lay in the Levant, shifts now from the Alps and the Mediterranean Sea to the Atlantic. For some centuries the Turkish Empire, Russia and Central Asia and China are relatively neglected by the limelight of the European historian. Nevertheless, these central regions of the world remain central, and their welfare and participation are necessary to the permanent peace of mankind.

§ 11

And now let us consider the political consequences of this vast release and expansion of European ideas in the fourteenth and fifteenth centuries with the new development of science, the exploration of the world, the great dissemination of knowledge through paper and printing, and the spread of a new craving for freedom and equality. How was it affecting the mentality of the courts and kings that directed the formal affairs of mankind? We have already shown how the hold of the Catholic Church upon the consciences of men was weakening at this time. Only the Spaniards, fresh from a long and finally successfully religious war against Islam, had any great enthusiasm left for the church. The Turkish conquests and the expansion of the known world robbed the Roman Empire of its former prestige of universality. The old mental and moral framework of Europe was breaking up. What was happening to the dukes, princes, and kings of the old dispensation during this age of change?

In England, as we shall tell later, very subtle and interesting tendencies were leading towards a new method in government, the method of parliament, that was to spread later on over nearly all the world. But of these tendencies the world at large was as yet practically unconscious in the sixteenth century.

Few monarchs have left us intimate diaries; to be a monarch and to be frank are incompatible feats; monarchy is itself necessarily a pose. The historian is obliged to speculate about the contents of the head that wears a crown as best he can. No doubt regal psychology has varied with the ages. We have, however, the writings of a very able man of this period who set himself to study and expound the arts of kingcraft as they were understood in the latter fifteenth century.

This was the celebrated Florentine, Niccolo Machiavelli (1469–1527). He was of good birth and reasonable fortune, and he had entered the public employment of the republic by the time he was twenty-five. For eighteen years he was in the Florentine diplomatic service; he was engaged upon a number of embassies, and in 1500 he was sent to France to deal with the French king. From 1502 to 1512 he was the right-hand man of the gonfalonier (the life president) of Florence, Soderini. Machiavelli reorganized the Florentine army, wrote speeches for the gonfalonier, was, indeed, the ruling intelligence in Florentine affairs. When Soderini, who had leant upon the French, was overthrown by the Medici family, whom the Spanish supported, Machiavelli, though he tried to transfer his services to the victors, was tortured on the rack and expelled. He took up his quarters in a villa near San Casciano, twelve miles or so from Florence, and there entertained himself partly by collecting and writing salacious stories to a friend in Rome, and partly by writing books about Italian politics in which he could no longer play a part. Just as we owe Marco Polo's book of travels to his imprisonment, so we owe Machiavelli's *Prince,* his *Florentine History,* and *The Art of War* to his downfall and the boredom of San Casciano.

The enduring value of these books lies in the clear idea they give us of the quality and limitations of the ruling minds of this age. Their atmosphere was his atmosphere. If he brought an exceptionally keen intelligence to their business, that merely throws it into a brighter light.

His susceptible mind had been greatly impressed by the cunning, cruelty, audacity, and ambition of Cæsar Borgia, the Duke of Valentino, in whose camp he had spent some months as an envoy. In his *Prince* he idealized this dazzling person. Cæsar Borgia (1476–1507), the reader must understand, was the son of Pope Alexander VI, Rodrigo Borgia (1492–1503). The reader will perhaps be startled at the idea of a Pope having a son, but this, we must remember, was a pre-Reformation Pope. The Papacy at this time was in a mood of moral relaxation, and though Alexander was, as a priest, pledged to live unmarried, this did not hinder him from living openly with a sort of unmarried wife, and devoting the resources of Christendom to the advancement of his family. Cæsar was a youth of spirit even for the times in which he lived; he had early caused his elder brother to be murdered, and also the husband of his sister Lucrezia. He had, indeed, betrayed and murdered a number of people. With his father's assistance he had become duke of a wide area of Central Italy when Machiavelli visited him. He had shown little or no military ability, but considerable dexterity and administrative power. His magnificence was of the most temporary sort. When presently his father died, it collapsed like a pricked bladder. Its unsoundness was not evident to Machiavelli. Our chief interest in Cæsar Borgia is that he realized Machiavelli's highest ideals of a superb and successful prince.

Much has been written to show that Machiavelli had wide and noble intentions behind his political writings, but all such attempts to ennoble him will leave the sceptical reader, who insists on reading the lines instead of reading imaginary things between the lines of Machiavelli's work, cold towards him. This man manifestly had no belief in any righteousness at all, no belief in a God ruling over the world or in a God in men's hearts, no understanding of the power of conscience in men. Not for him were Utopian visions of world-wide human order, or attempts to realize the *City of God*. Such things he did not want. It seemed to him that to get power, to gratify one's desires and sensibilities and hates, to swagger triumphantly in the world, must be the crown of human desire. Only a prince could fully realize such a life. Some streak of timidity, or his sense of the poorness of his personal claims, had evidently made him abandon such dreams for himself; but at least he might hope to serve a prince, to live close to the glory, to share the plunder and the lust and the gratified malice. He might even make himself indispensable! He set himself, therefore, to become an "expert" in princecraft. He assisted Soderini to fail. When he was racked and rejected by the Medicis, and had no further hopes of being even a successful Court parasite, he wrote these handbooks of cunning to show what a clever servant some prince had lost. His ruling thought, his great contribution to political literature, was that the moral obligations upon ordinary men cannot bind princes.

There is a disposition to ascribe the virtue of patriotism to Machiavelli because he suggested that Italy, which was weak and divided—she had been invaded by the Turks and saved from conquest only by the death of the Sultan Muhammad, and she was being fought over by the French and Spanish as though she was something inanimate—might be united and strong; but he saw in that possibility only a great opportunity for a prince. And he advocated a national army only because he saw the Italian method of carrying on war by hiring bands of foreign mercenaries was a hopeless one. At any such time troops might go over to a better paymaster or decide to plunder the state they protected. He had been deeply impressed by the victories of the Swiss over the Milanese, but he never fathomed the secret of the free spirit that made those victories possible. The Florentine militia he created was a complete failure. He was a man born blind to the qualities that make peoples free and nations great.

Yet this morally blind man was living in a little world of morally blind men. It is clear that his style of thought was the style of thought of the Court of his time. Behind the princes of the new states that had grown up out of the wreckage of the empire and the failure of the church, there were every-

where chancellors and secretaries and trusted ministers of the Machiavellian
type. Cromwell, for instance, the minister of Henry VIII of England after his
breach with Rome, regarded Machiavelli's *Prince* as the quintessence of political wisdom. When the princes were themselves sufficiently clever they too
were Machiavellian. They were scheming to outdo one another, to rob weaker
contemporaries, to destroy rivals, so that they might for a brief interval swagger. They had little or no vision of any scheme of human destinies greater
than this game they played against one another.

§ 12

It is interesting to note that this Swiss infantry which had so impressed
Machiavelli was not part of the princely system of Europe. At the very centre

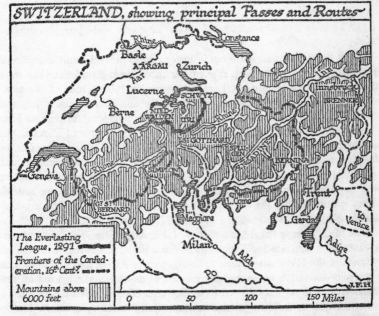

SWITZERLAND, showing principal Passes and Routes

The Everlasting League, 1291
Frontiers of the Confederation, 16th Cent.
Mountains above 6000 feet

0   50   100   150 Miles

of the European system there had arisen a little confederation of free states,
the Swiss Confederation, which, after some centuries of nominal adhesion to
the Holy Roman Empire, became frankly republican in 1499. As early as
the thirteenth century, the peasant farmers of three valleys round about the
Lake of Lucerne took it into their heads that they would dispense with an
overlord and manage their own affairs in their own fashion. Their chief trouble came from the claims of a noble family of the Aar valley, the Habsburg
family. In 1245 the men of Schwyz burnt the castle of New Habsburg which
had been set up near Lucerne to overawe them; its ruins are still to be seen
there.

This Habsburg family was a growing and acquisitive one; it had lands and possessions throughout Germany; and in 1273, after the extinction of the Hohenstaufen house, Rudolf of Habsburg was elected Emperor of Germany, a distinction that became at last practically hereditary in his family. None the less, the men of Uri, Schwyz, and Unterwalden did not mean to be ruled by any Habsburg; they formed an Everlasting League in 1291, and they held their own among the mountains from that time onward to this day, first as free members of the empire and then as an absolutely independent confederation. Of the heroic legend of William Tell we have no space to tell here, nor have we room in which to trace the gradual extension of the confederation to its present boundaries. Romanish, Italian, and French-speaking valleys were presently added to this valiant little republican group. The red-cross flag of Geneva has become the symbol of international humanity in the midst of warfare. The bright and thriving cities of Switzerland have been a refuge for free men from a score of tyrannies.

§ 13A

Most of the figures that stand out in history do so through some exceptional personal quality, good or bad, that makes them more significant than their fellows. But there was born at Ghent in Belgium, in 1500, a man of commonplace abilities and melancholy temperament, the son of a mentally defective mother who had been married for reasons of State, who was, through no fault of his own, to become the focus of the accumulating stresses of Europe. The historian must give him a quite unmerited and accidental prominence side by side with such marked individualities as Alexander and Charlemagne and Frederick II. This was the Emperor Charles V. For a time he had an air of being the greatest monarch in Europe since Charlemagne. Both he and his illusory greatness were the results of the matrimonial statecraft of his grandfather, the Emperor Maximilian I (1459–1519).

Some families have fought, others have intrigued their way to world power; the Habsburgs married their way. Maximilian began his career with the inheritance of the Habsburgs, Austria, Styria, part of Alsace and other districts; he married—the lady's name scarcely matters to us—the Netherlands and Burgundy. Most of Burgundy slipped from him after his first wife's death, but the Netherlands he held. Then he tried unsuccessfully to marry Brittany. He became Emperor in succession to his father, Frederick III, in 1493, and married the duchy of Milan. Finally he married his son to the weak-minded daughter of Ferdinand and Isabella, the Ferdinand and Isabella of Columbus, who not only reigned over a freshly united Spain, and over Sardinia and the kingdom of the two Sicilies, but, by virtue of the papal gifts to Castile, over all America west of Brazil. So it was that Charles, his grandson, inherited most of the American continent and between a third and a half of what the Turks had left of Europe. The father of Charles died in 1506, and Maximilian did his best to secure his grandson's election to the imperial throne.

Charles succeeded to the Netherlands in 1506; he became practically king of the Spanish dominions, his mother being imbecile, when his grandfather

Ferdinand died in 1516; and his grandfather Maximilian dying in 1519, he was in 1520 elected Emperor at the still comparatively tender age of twenty.

His election as Emperor was opposed by the young and brilliant French King Francis I, who had succeeded to the French throne in 1515 at the age of twenty-one. The candidature of Francis was supported by Leo X (1513),

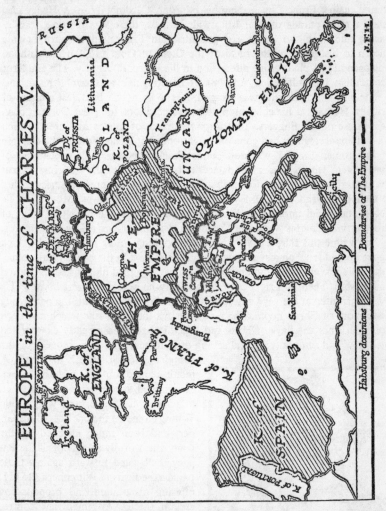

who also requires from us the epithet brilliant. It was, indeed, an age of brilliant monarchs. It was the age of Baber in India (1526–1530) and Suleiman in Turkey (1520). Both Leo and Francis dreaded the concentration of so much power in the hands of one man as the election of Charles threatened. The only other monarch who seemed to matter in Europe was Henry VIII, who had become King of England in 1509 at the age of eighteen. He also offered himself as a candidate for the empire, and the imaginative English reader may amuse himself by working out the possible consequences of such an election.

There was much scope for diplomacy in this triangle of kings. Charles on his way from Spain to Germany visited England and secured the support of Henry against Francis by bribing his minister, Cardinal Wolsey. Henry also made a great parade of friendship with Francis; there was feasting, tournaments, and such-like antiquated gallantries in France, in a courtly picnic known to historians as the Field of the Cloth of Gold (1520). Knighthood was becoming a picturesque affectation in the sixteenth century. The Emperor Maximilian I is still called "the last of the knights" by German historians.

The election of Charles was secured, it is to be noted, by a vast amount of bribery. He had, as his chief supporters and creditors, the great German business house of the Fuggers. That large treatment of money and credit which we call finance, which had gone out of European political life with the collapse of the Roman Empire, was now coming back to power. This appearance of the Fuggers, whose houses and palaces outshone those of the emperors, marks the upward movement of forces that had begun two or three centuries earlier in Cahors in France and in Florence and other Italian towns. Money, public debts, and social unrest and discontent re-enter upon the miniature stage of this *Outline*. Charles V was not so much a Habsburg as a Fugger emperor.

For a time this fair, not very intelligent-looking young man with the thick upper lip and long, clumsy chin was largely a puppet in the hands of his ministers. Able servants after the order of Machiavelli guided him at first in the arts of kingship. Then in a slow but effectual way he began to assert himself. He was confronted at the very outset of his reign in Germany with the perplexing dissensions of Christendom. The revolt against the papal rule which had been going on since the days of Huss and Wycliffe had been recently exasperated by a new and unusually cynical selling of indulgences to raise money for the

Luther
(after Cranach)

completion of St. Peter's at Rome. A monk named Luther, who had been consecrated as a priest, who had taken to reading the Bible, and who, while visiting Rome on the business of his Order, had been much shocked by the levity and worldly splendour of the Papacy, had come forward against these papal expedients at Wittenberg (1517), offering disputation and propounding certain theses. An important controversy ensued.

At first Luther carried on this controversy in Latin, but presently took to German, and speedily had the people in a ferment. Charles found this dispute raging when he came from Spain to

Germany. He summoned an assembly or "diet" of the empire at Worms on the Rhine. To this, Luther, who had been asked to recant his views by Pope Leo X, and who had refused to do so, was summoned. He came, and, entirely in the spirit of Huss, refused to recant unless he was convinced of his error by logical argument or by the authority of Scripture. But his protectors among the princes were too powerful for him to suffer the fate of John Huss.

Here was a perplexing situation for the young Emperor. There is reason to suppose that he was inclined at first to support Luther against the Pope. Leo X had opposed the election of Charles, and was friendly with his rival, Francis I. But Charles V was not a good Machiavellian, and he had acquired in Spain a considerable religious sincerity. He decided against Luther. Many of the German princes, and especially the Elector of Saxony, sided with the reformer. Luther went into hiding under the protection of the Saxon Elector, and Charles found himself in the presence of the opening rift that was to split Christendom into two contending camps.

Close upon these disturbances, and probably connected with them, there came a widespread peasants' revolt throughout Germany. This outbreak frightened Luther very effectually. He was shocked by its excesses, and from that time forth the Reformation he advocated ceased to be a Reformation according to the people and became a Reformation according to the princes. He lost his confidence in that free judgment for which he had stood up so manfully.

Meanwhile Charles realized that his great empire was in a very serious danger both from the west and from the east. On the west of him was his spirited rival, Francis I; to the east was the Turk in Hungary, in alliance with Francis and clamouring for certain arrears of tribute from the Austrian dominions. Charles had the money and army of Spain at his disposal, but it was extremely difficult to get any effective support in money from Germany. His grandfather had developed a German infantry on the Swiss model, very much upon the lines expounded in Machiavelli's *Art of War,* but these troops had to be paid and his imperial subsidies had to be supplemented by unsecured borrowings, which were finally to bring his supporters, the Fuggers, to ruin.

On the whole, Charles, in alliance with Henry VIII, was successful against Francis I and the Turk. Their chief battlefield was North Italy; the generalship was dull on both sides; their advances and retreats depended chiefly on the arrival of reinforcements. The German army invaded France, failed to take Marseilles, fell back into Italy, lost Milan, and was besieged in Pavia. Francis I made a long and unsuccessful siege of Pavia, was caught by fresh German forces, defeated, wounded, and taken prisoner. He sent back a message to his queen that all was "lost but honour," made a humiliating peace, and broke it as soon as he was liberated—so that even the salvage of honour was but temporary.

Henry VIII and the Pope, in obedience to the rules of Machiavellian strategy, now went over to the side of France in order to prevent Charles becoming too powerful. The German troops in Milan, under the Constable of Bourbon, being unpaid, forced rather than followed their commander into a raid upon

Rome. They stormed the city and pillaged it (1527). The Pope took refuge in the Castle of St. Angelo while the looting and slaughter went on. He bought off the German troops at last by the payment of four hundred thousand ducats. Ten years of such stupid and confused fighting impoverished all Europe and left the Emperor in possession of Milan. In 1530 he was crowned by the Pope —he was the last German Emperor to be crowned by the Pope—at Bologna. One thinks of the rather dull-looking blond face, with its long lip and chin, bearing the solemn expression of one who endures a doubtful though probably honourable ceremony.

Meanwhile the Turks were making great headway in Hungary. They had defeated and killed the King of Hungary in 1526, they held Buda and Pesth, in 1529, as we have already noted, Suleiman the Magnificent very nearly took

Vienna. The Emperor was greatly concerned by these advances, and did his utmost to drive back the Turks, but he found the greatest difficulty in getting the German princes to unite, even with his formidable enemy upon their very borders.

Francis I remained implacable for a time, and there was a new French war; but in 1538 Charles won his rival over to a more friendly attitude by ravaging the south of France. Francis and Charles then formed an alliance against the Turk, but the Protestant princes, the German princes who were resolved to break away from Rome, had formed a league, the Schmalkaldic League (named after the little town of Schmalkalden in Hesse, at which its constitution was arranged), against the Emperor, and, in the place of a great campaign to recover Hungary for Christendom, Charles had to turn his mind to the gathering internal struggle in Germany. Of that struggle he saw only the opening war. It was a struggle, a sanguinary irrational bickering of princes for ascendancy, now flaming into war and destruction, now sinking back to intrigues and diplomacies; it was a snake's sack of Machiavellian policies, that was to go on writhing incurably right into the nineteenth century, and to waste and desolate Central Europe again and again.

The Emperor never seems to have grasped the true forces at work in these gathering troubles. He was, for his time and station, an exceptionally worthy man, and he seems to have taken the religious dissensions that were tearing Europe into warring fragments as genuine theological differences. He gathered diets and councils in futile attempts at reconciliation. Formulæ and confessions were tried over. The student of German history must struggle with the details of the Religious Peace of Nuremberg, the settlement at the Diet of Ratisbon, the Interim of Augsburg, and the like. Here we do but mention them as details in the worried life of this culminating emperor.

As a matter of fact, hardly one of the multifarious princes and rulers in

Europe seems to have been acting in good faith. The widespread religious trouble of the world, the desire of the common people for truth and social righteousness, the spreading knowledge of the time, all those things were merely counters in the imaginations of princely diplomacy. Henry VIII of England, who had begun his career with a book written against heresy, and who had been rewarded by the Pope with the title of "Defender of the Faith," being anxious to divorce his first wife, because she was sonless, in favour of an animated young lady named Anne Boleyn, and wishing also to turn against the Emperor in favour of Francis I and to loot the vast wealth of the church of England, joined the company of Protestant princes in 1530. Sweden, Denmark and Norway had already gone over to the Protestant side.

Henry VIII.

The German religious war began in 1546, a few months after the death of Martin Luther. We need not trouble about the incidents of the campaign. The Protestant Saxon army was badly beaten at Lochau. By something very like a breach of faith, Philip of Hesse, the Emperor's chief remaining antagonist, was caught and imprisoned, and the Turks were bought off by the payment of an annual tribute. In 1547, to the great relief of the Emperor, Francis I died. So by 1547 Charles got to a kind of settlement, and made his last efforts to effect peace where there was no peace.

In 1552 all Germany was at war again, only a precipitate flight from Innsbruck saved Charles from capture, and, with the treaty of Passau, came another unstable equilibrium. Charles was now utterly weary of the cares and splendours of empire; he had never had a very sound constitution, he was naturally indolent, and he was suffering greatly from gout. He abdicated. He made over all his sovereign rights in Germany to his brother Ferdinand, and Spain and the Netherlands he resigned to his son Philip. Then in a sort of magnificent dudgeon he retired to a monastery at Yuste, among the oak and chestnut forests in the hills to the north of the Tagus valley, and there he died in 1558.

Much has been written in a sentimental vein of this retirement, this renunciation of the world by this tired, majestic Titan, world-weary, seeking in an austere solitude his peace with God. But his retreat was neither solitary nor austere; he had with him nearly a hundred and fifty attendants; his establishment had all the indulgences without the fatigues of a Court, and Philip II was a dutiful son to whom his father's advice was a command. As for his austerities, let Prescott witness: "In the almost daily correspondence between Quixada, or Gaztelu, and the Secretary of State at Valladolid, there is scarcely a letter that does not turn more or less on the Emperor's eating or his illness. The one seems naturally to follow like a running commentary on the other.

It is rare that such topics have formed the burden of communications with the department of State. It must have been no easy matter for the secretary to preserve his gravity in the perusal of dispatches in which politics and gastronomy were so strangely mixed together. The courier from Valladolid to Lisbon

was ordered to make a detour, so as to take Jarandilla in his route and bring supplies for the royal table. On Thursdays he was to bring fish to serve for the *jour maigre* that was to follow. The trout in the neighbourhood Charles thought too small; so others, of a larger size, were to be sent from Valladolid. Fish of every kind was to his taste, as, indeed, was anything that in its nature or habits at all approached to fish. Eels, frogs, oysters, occupied an important place in the royal bill of fare. Potted fish, especially anchovies, found great favour with him; and he regretted that he had not brought a better supply of these from the Low Countries. On an eel-pasty he particularly doted." . . .[1]

In 1554 Charles had obtained a bull from Pope Julius III granting him a dispensation from fasting, and allowing him to break his fast early in the morning even when he was to take the sacrament.

"That Charles was not altogether unmindful of his wearing apparel in Yuste may be inferred from the fact that his wardrobe contained no fewer than sixteen robes of silk and velvet, lined with ermine, or eider down, or soft hair of the Barbary goat. As to the furniture and upholstery of his apartments, how little reliance is to be placed on the reports so carelessly circulated about these may be gathered from a single glance at the inventory of his effects, prepared by Quixada and Gaztelu soon after their master's death. Among the items we find carpets from Turkey and Alcarez, canopies of velvet and other stuffs, hangings of fine black cloth, which since his mother's death he had always chosen for his own bedroom; while the remaining apartments were provided with no fewer than twenty-five suits of tapestry, from the looms of Flanders, richly embroidered with figures of animals and with landscapes. . . .

"Among the different pieces of plate we find some of pure gold, and others especially noted for their curious workmanship; and as this was an age in which the art of working the precious metals was carried to the highest perfection, we cannot doubt that some of the finest specimens had come into the Emperor's possession. The whole amount of plate was estimated at between twelve and thirteen thousand ounces in weight." . . .[2]

Charles had never acquired the habit of reading, but he would be read aloud to at meals after the fashion of Charlemagne, and would make what one nar-

---

[1] Prescott's Appendix to Robertson's *History of Charles V.*
[2] Ibid.

rator describes as a "sweet and heavenly commentary." He also amused himself with technical toys, by listening to music or sermons, and by attending to the imperial business that still came drifting in to him. The death of the Empress, to whom he was greatly attached, had turned his mind towards religion, which in his case took a punctilious and ceremonial form; every Friday in Lent he scourged himself with the rest of the monks with such good will as to draw blood.

These exercises and the gout released a bigotry in Charles that had been hitherto restrained by considerations of policy. The appearance of Protestant teaching close at hand in Valladolid roused him to fury. "Tell the grand inquisitor and his council from me to be at their posts, and to lay the axe at the root of the evil before it spreads further." . . . He expressed a doubt whether it would not be well, in so black an affair, to dispense with the ordinary course of justice, and to show no mercy, "lest the criminal, if pardoned, should have the opportunity of repeating his crime." He recommended, as an example, his own mode of proceeding in the Netherlands, "where all who remained obstinate in their errors were burned alive, and those who were admitted to penitence were beheaded."

And almost symbolical of Charles's place and rôle in history was his preoccupation with funerals. It was as if he felt the need to write Finis to something exhausted. He not only attended every actual funeral that was celebrated at Yuste, but he had services conducted for the absent dead, he held a funeral service in memory of his wife on the anniversary of her death, and, finally, he celebrated his own obsequies.

"The chapel was hung with black, and the blaze of hundreds of wax lights was scarcely sufficient to dispel the darkness. The brethren in their conventual dress, and all the Emperor's household clad in deep mourning, gathered round a huge catafalque, shrouded also in black, which had been raised in the centre of the chapel. The service for the burial of the dead was then performed; and, amidst the dismal wail of the monks, the prayers ascended for the departed spirit, that it might be received into the mansions of the blessed. The sorrowful attendants were melted to tears as the image of their master's death was presented to their minds—or they were touched, it may be, with compassion by this pitiable display of weakness. Charles, muffled in a dark mantle, and bearing a lighted candle in his hand, mingled with his household, the spectator of his own obsequies; and the doleful ceremony was concluded by his placing the taper in the hands of the priest, in sign of his surrendering up his soul to the Almighty."

Other accounts make Charles wear a shroud and lie in the coffin, remaining there alone until the last mourner had left the chapel.

Within two months of this masquerade he was dead. And the greatness of the Holy Roman Empire died with him. The Holy Roman Empire struggled on, indeed, to the days of Napoleon, but as an invalid and dying thing. To this day its unburied tradition poisons our political air.

§ 13b

Ferdinand, the brother of Charles V, took over his abandoned search for unity and met the German princes at Augsburg in 1555. Again there was an attempt to establish a religious peace. Nothing could better show the quality of that attempted settlement, and the blindness of the princes and statesmen concerned in it to the deeper and broader processes of the time, than the form that settlement took. The recognition of religious freedom was to apply to the states and not to individual citizens; *cujus regio ejus religio, "the confession of the subject was to be dependent on that of the territorial lord."*

§ 13c

We have given as much attention as we have done to the writings of Machiavelli and to the personality of Charles V because they throw a flood of light upon the antagonisms of the next period in our history. This present chapter has told the story of a vast expansion of human horizons and of a great increase and distribution of knowledge; we have seen the conscience of common men awakening and intimations of a new and profounder social justice spreading throughout the general body of the Western civilization. But this process of light and thought was leaving Courts and the political life of the world untouched. There is little in Machiavelli that might not have been written by some clever secretary in the Court of Chosroes I or Shi-Hwang-ti—or even of Sargon I or Pepi. While the world in everything else was moving forward, in political ideas, in ideas about the relationship of state to state and of sovereign to citizen, it was standing still. Nay, it was falling back. For the great idea of the Catholic Church as the world city of God had been destroyed in men's minds by the church itself, and the dream of a world imperialism had, in the person of Charles V, been carried in effigy through Europe to limbo. Politically the world seemed falling back towards personal monarchy of the Assyrian or Macedonian pattern.

It is not that the newly-awakened intellectual energies of Western European men were too absorbed in theological restatement, in scientific investigations, in exploration and mercantile development, to give a thought to the claims and responsibilities of rulers. Not only were common men drawing ideas of a theocratic or republican or communistic character from the now accessible Bible, but the renewed study of the Greek classics was bringing the creative and fertilizing spirit of Plato to bear upon the Western mind.

In England Sir Thomas More produced a quaint imitation of Plato's *Republic* in his *Utopia,* setting out a sort of autocratic communism. In Naples, a century later, a certain friar Campanella was equally bold in his *City of the Sun.* But such discussions were having no immediate effect upon political arrangements. Compared with the massiveness of the task, these books do, indeed, seem poetical and scholarly and flimsy. (Yet later on the *Utopia* was to bear fruit in the English Poor Laws.)

The intellectual and moral development of the Western mind and this drift towards Machiavellian monarchy in Europe were for a time going on concurrently in the same world, but they were going on almost independently. The statesmen still schemed and manœuvred as if nothing grew but the power of wary and fortunate kings.

It was only in the seventeenth and eighteenth centuries that these two streams of tendency—the stream of general ideas and the drift of traditional and egoistic monarchical diplomacy—interfered and came into conflict.

BOOK VIII

THE AGE OF THE GREAT POWERS

XXXIV

PRINCES, PARLIAMENTS AND POWERS

§ 1

IN THE preceding chapter we have traced the beginnings of a new civilization, the civilization of the "modern" type which becomes at the present time world-wide. It is still a vast unformed thing, still only in the opening phases of growth and development to-day. We have seen the mediæval ideas of the Holy Roman Empire and of the Roman Church, as forms of universal law and order, fade in its dawn. They fade out, as if it were necessary in order that these ideas of one law and one order for all men should be redrawn on world-wide lines. And while in nearly every other field of human interest there was advance, the effacement of these general political ideas of the Church and Empire led back for a time in things political towards merely personal monarchy and monarchist nationalism of the Macedonian type.

There came an interregnum, as it were, in the consolidation of human affairs, a phase of the type the Chinese annalists would call an "Age of Confusion." This interregnum has lasted as long as that between the fall of the Western Empire and the crowning of Charlemagne in Rome. We are living in it to-day. It may be drawing to its close; we cannot tell yet. The old leading ideas had broken down, a medley of new and untried projects and suggestions perplexed men's minds and actions, and meanwhile the world at large had to fall back for leadership upon the ancient tradition of an individual prince. There was no new way clearly apparent for men to follow, and the prince was there.

All over the world the close of the sixteenth century saw monarchy prevailing and tending towards absolutism. Germany and Italy were patchworks of autocratic princely dominions, Spain was practically autocratic, the throne had never been so powerful in England, and, as the seventeenth century drew on the French monarchy gradually became the greatest and most consolidated power in Europe. The phases and fluctuations of its ascent we cannot record here.

At every Court there were groups of ministers and secretaries who played a Machiavellian game against their foreign rivals. Foreign policy is the natural employment of courts and monarchies. Foreign offices are, so to speak, the leading characters in all the histories of the seventeenth and eighteenth centuries. They kept Europe in a fever of wars. And wars were becoming expensive. Armies were no longer untrained levies, no longer assemblies of feudal knights who brought their own horses and weapons and retainers with them; they needed more and more artillery; they consisted of paid troops who insisted on their pay; they were professional and slow and elaborate, conducting long sieges, necessitating elaborate fortifications. War expenditure increased everywhere and called for more and more taxation.

And here it was that these monarchies of the sixteenth and seventeenth centuries came into conflict with new and shapeless forces of freedom in the community. In practice the princes found they were not masters of their subjects' lives or property. They found an inconvenient resistance to the taxation that was necessary if their diplomatic aggressions and alliances were to continue. Finance became an unpleasant spectre in every council chamber. In theory the monarch owned his country. James I of England (1603) declared that "As it is atheism and blasphemy to dispute what God can do; so it is presumption and high contempt in a subject to dispute what a king can do, or say that a king cannot do this or that."

In practice, however, he found, and his son Charles I (1625) was to find still more effectually, that there were in his dominions a great number of landlords and merchants, substantial and intelligent persons, who set a very definite limit to the calls and occasions of the monarch and his ministers. They were prepared to tolerate his rule if they themselves might also be monarchs of their lands and businesses and trades and what not. But not otherwise.

Everywhere in Europe there was a parallel development. Beneath the kings and princes there were these lesser monarchs, the private owners, noblemen, wealthy citizens and the like, who were now offering the sovereign prince much the same resistance that the kings and princes of Germany had offered the emperor. They wanted to limit taxation so far as it pressed upon themselves, and to be free in their own houses and estates. And the spread of books and reading and intercommunication was enabling these smaller monarchs, these monarchs of ownership, to develop such a community of ideas and such a solidarity of resistance as had been possible at no previous stage in the world's history. Everywhere they were disposed to resist the prince, but it was not everywhere that they found the same facilities for an organized resistance. The economic circumstances and the political traditions of the Netherlands and England made those countries the first to bring this antagonism of monarchy and private ownership to an issue.

At first this seventeenth-century "public," this public of property owners, cared very little for foreign policy. They did not perceive at first how it affected them. They did not want to be bothered with it; it was, they conceded, the affairs of kings and princes. They made no attempt, therefore, to control foreign entanglements. But it was with the direct consequences of these entanglements that they quarrelled; they objected to heavy taxation, to interference with trade, to arbitrary imprisonment, and to the control of consciences by the monarch. It was upon these questions that they joined issue with the Crown.

§ 2

The breaking away of the Netherlands from absolutist monarchy was the beginning of a series of such conflicts throughout the sixteenth and seventeenth centuries. They varied very greatly in detail according to local and racial peculiarities, but essentially they were all rebellious against the idea of a predominating personal "prince" and his religious and political direction.

In the twelfth century all the lower Rhine country was divided up among a number of small rulers, and the population was a Low German one on a Celtic basis, mixed with subsequent Danish ingredients very similar to the English admixture. The south-eastern fringe of it spoke French dialects; the bulk, Frisian, Dutch and other Low German languages. The Netherlands figured largely in the crusades. Godfrey of Bouillon, who took Jerusalem (First Crusade), was a Belgian; and the founder of the so-called Latin Dynasty of emperors in Constantinople (Fourth Crusade) was Baldwin of Flanders. (They were called Latin emperors because they were on the side of the Latin Church.)

In the thirteenth and fourteenth centuries considerable towns grew up in the Netherlands: Ghent, Bruges, Ypres, Utrecht, Leyden, Haarlem, and so forth; and these towns developed quasi-independent municipal governments and a class of educated townsmen. We will not trouble the reader with the dynastic accidents that linked the affairs of the Netherlands with Burgundy (Eastern France), and which finally made their overlordship the inheritance of the Emperor Charles V.

It was under Charles that the Protestant doctrines that now prevailed in Germany spread into the Netherlands. Charles persecuted with some vigor, but in 1556, as we have told, he handed over the task to his son Philip (Philip II). Philip's spirited foreign policy—he was carrying on a war with France—presently became a second source of trouble between himself and the Netherlandish noblemen and townsmen, because he had to come to them for supplies. The great nobles, led by William the Silent, Prince of Orange, and the Counts of Egmont and Horn, made themselves the heads of a popular resistance, in which it is now impossible to disentangle the objection to taxation from the objection to religious persecution. The great nobles were not at first Protestants—they became Protestants as the struggle grew in bitterness. The people were already bitterly Protestant.

Philip was resolved to rule both the property and consciences of his Netherlanders. He sent picked Spanish troops into the country, and he made governor-general a nobleman named Alva, one of those ruthless "strong" men who wreck governments and monarchies. For a time he ruled the land with a hand of iron, but the hand of iron begets a soul of iron in the body it grips, and in 1567 the Netherlands were in open revolt. Alva murdered, sacked, and massacred—in vain. Counts Egmont and Horn were executed. William the Silent became the great leader of the Dutch, a king *de facto*.

For a long time, and with many complications, the struggle for liberty continued, and through it all it is noteworthy that the rebels continued to cling to the plea that Philip II was their king—if only he would be a reasonable and limited king. But the idea of limited monarchy was distasteful to the crowned heads of Europe at that time, and at last Philip drove the United Provinces, for which we now use the name of Holland, to the republican form of government. Holland, be it noted—not all the Netherlands; the southern Netherlands, Belgium as we now call that country, remained at the end of the struggle a Spanish possession and Catholic.

The siege of Alkmaar (1573), as Motley[1] describes it, may be taken as a sample of that long and hideous conflict between the little Dutch people and the still vast resources of Catholic Imperialism.

" 'If I take Alkmaar,' Alva wrote to Philip, 'I am resolved not to leave a single creature alive; the knife shall be put to every throat.' . . .

"And now, with the dismantled and desolate Haarlem before their eyes, a prophetic phantom, perhaps, of their own imminent fate, did the handful of people shut up within Alkmaar prepare for the worst. Their main hope lay in the friendly sea. The vast sluices called the Zyp, through which the inundation of the whole northern province could be very soon effected, were but a few miles distant. By opening these gates and by piercing a few dykes the ocean might be made to fight for them. To obtain this result, however, the consent of the inhabitants was requisite, as the destruction of all the standing crops would be inevitable. The city was so closely invested that it was difficult therefore, to find an envoy for this hazardous mission. At last, a carpenter in the city, Peter Van der Mey by name, undertook the adventure. . . .

"Affairs soon approached a crisis within the beleaguered city. Daily skirmishes, without decisive results, had taken place outside the walls. At last, on the 18th of September, after a steady cannonade of nearly twelve hours, Don Frederick, at three in the afternoon, ordered an assault. Notwithstanding his seven months' experience at Haarlem, he still believed it certain that he should carry Alkmaar by storm. The attack took place at once upon the Frisian gate and upon the red tower on the opposite side. Two choice regiments, recently arrived from Lombardy, led the onset, rending the air with their shouts and confident of an easy victory. They were sustained by what seemed an overwhelming force of disciplined troops. Yet never, even in the recent history of Haarlem, had an attack been received by more dauntless breasts. Every living man was on the walls. The storming parties were assailed with cannon,

---

[1] *Rise of the Dutch Republic.*

with musketry, with pistols. Boiling water, pitch and oil, molten lead, and unslaked lime were poured upon them every moment. Hundreds of tarred and burning hoops were skilfully quoited around the necks of the soldiers, who struggled in vain to extricate themselves from these fiery ruffs, while as fast as any of the invaders planted foot upon the breach they were confronted face to face with sword and dagger by the burghers, who hurled them headlong into the moat below.

"Thrice was the attack renewed with ever-increasing rage—thrice repulsed with unflinching fortitude. The storm continued four hours long. During all that period not one of the defenders left his post, till he dropped from it dead or wounded. . . . The trumpet of recall was sounded, and the Spaniards, utterly discomfited, retired from the walls, leaving at least one thousand dead in the trenches, while only thirteen burghers and twenty-four of the garrison lost their lives. . . . Ensign Solis, who had mounted the breach for an instant, and miraculously escaped with life after having been hurled from the battlements, reported that he had seen 'neither helmet nor harness' as he looked down into the city: only some plain-looking people generally dressed like fishermen. Yet these plain-looking fishermen had defeated the veterans of Alva. . . .

"Meantime, as Governor Sonoy had opened many of the dykes, the land in the neighbourhood of the camp was becoming plashy, although as yet the threatened inundation had not taken place. The soldiers were already very uncomfortable and very refractory. The carpenter-envoy had not been idle. . . ."

He returned with dispatches for the city. By accident or contrivance he lost these dispatches as he made his way into the town, so that they fell into Alva's hands. They contained a definite promise from the Duke of Orange to flood the country so as to drown the whole Spanish army. Incidentally this would also have drowned most of the Dutch harvest and cattle. But Alva, when he had read these documents, did not wait for the opening of any more sluices. Presently the stout men of Alkmaar, cheering and jeering, watched the Spaniards breaking camp. . . .

The form assumed by the government of liberated Holland was a patrician republic under the leadership of the House of Orange. The States-General was far less representative of the whole body of citizens than was the English Parliament, whose struggle with the Crown we shall next relate.

Though the worst of the struggle was over after Alkmaar, Holland was not effectively independent until 1609, and its independence was only fully and completely recognized by the Treaty of Westphalia in 1648.

§ 3

The open struggle of the private property owner against the aggressions of the "Prince" begins in England far back in the twelfth century. The phase in this struggle that we have to study now is the phase that opened with the attempts of Henry VII and VIII, and their successors, Edward VI, Mary, and

Elizabeth I to make the government of England a "personal monarchy" of the continental type. It became more acute when, by dynastic accidents, James, King of Scotland, became James I, King of both Scotland and England (1603), and began to talk in the manner we have already quoted of his "divine right" to do as he pleased.

But never had the path of English monarchy been a smooth one. In all the monarchies of the Northern and Germanic invaders of the empire there had been a tradition of a popular assembly of influential and representative men to preserve their general liberties, and in none was it more living than in England. France had her tradition of the assembly of the Three Estates, Spain

Central EUROPE after the Peace of Westphalia, 1648.

Boundary of the Empire ▬▬ Free Towns, thus: •Cologne Swedish territory.... French " .... Austrian Habsburgs.. Spanish Habsburgs Brandenburg (Prussia)....

her Cortes, but the English assembly was peculiar in two respects; that it had behind it a documentary declaration of certain elementary and universal rights, and that it contained elected "Knights of the Shire" as well as elected burghers from the towns. The French and Spanish assemblies had the latter but not the former elected element.

These two features gave the English Parliament a peculiar strength in its struggle with the Throne. The document in question was *Magna Charta*, the Great Charter, a declaration which was forced from King John (1199–1216), the brother and successor of Richard Cœur de Lion (1189–99), after a revolt of the Barons in 1215. It rehearsed a number of fundamental rights that made England a legal and not a regal state. It rejected the power of the king to control the personal property and liberty of every sort of citizen—save with the consent of that man's equals.

The presence of the elected shire representatives in the English Parliament —the second peculiarity of the British situation—came about from very simple and apparently innocuous beginnings. From the shires, or county divisions, knights seem to have been summoned to the national council to testify to the taxable capacity of their districts. They were sent up by the minor gentry, freeholders and village elders of their districts as early as 1254, two knights from each shire. This idea inspired Simon de Montfort, who was in rebellion against Henry III, the successor of John, to summon to the national council two knights from each shire and two citizens from each city or borough. Edward I, the successor to Henry III, continued this practice because it seemed a convenient way of getting into financial touch with the growing towns.

At first there was considerable reluctance on the parts of the knights and townsmen to attend Parliament, but gradually the power they possessed of linking the redress of grievances with the granting of subsidies was realized.

Quite early, if not from the first, these representatives of the general property owners in town and country, the Commons, sat and debated apart from the great Lords and Bishops. So there grew up in England a representative assembly, the Commons, beside an episcopal and patrician one, the Lords. There was no profound and fundamental difference between the personnel of the two assemblies; many of the knights of the shire were substantial men who might be as wealthy and influential as peers and also the sons and brothers of peers, but on the whole the Commons was the more plebeian assembly.

From the first these two assemblies, and especially the Commons, displayed a disposition to claim the entire power of taxation in the land. Gradually they extended their purview of grievances to a criticism of all the affairs of the realm.

We will not follow the fluctuations of the power and prestige of the English Parliament through the time of the Tudor monarchs (*i.e.*, Henry VII and VIII, Edward VI, Mary, and Elizabeth I), but it will be manifest from what has been said that when at last James Stuart made his open claim to autocracy, the English merchants, peers, and private gentlemen found themselves with a tried and honoured traditional means of resisting him such as no other people in Europe possessed.

Another peculiarity of the English political conflict was its comparative detachment from the great struggle between Catholic and Protestant that was now being waged all over Europe. There were, it is true, very distinct religious issues mixed up in the English struggle, but upon its main lines it was a political struggle of King against the Parliament embodying the class of private-property-owning citizens. But Crown and people were formally reformed and Protestant. It is true that many people on the latter side were Protestants of a Bible-respecting, non-sacerdotal type, representing the Reformation according to the peoples, and that the king was the nominal head of a special sacerdotal and sacramental church, the established Church of England, representing the Reformation according to the princes, but this antagonism never completely obscured the essentials of the conflict.

The struggle of King and Parliament had already reached an acute phase before the death of James I (1625), but only in the reign of his son Charles I did it culminate in civil war. Charles did exactly what one might have expected a king to do in such a position, in view of the lack of Parliamentary control over foreign policy; he embroiled the country in a conflict with both Spain and France, and then came to the country for supplies in the hope that patriotic feeling would override the normal dislike to giving him money. When Parliament refused supplies, he demanded loans from various subjects, and attempted similar illegal exactions.

This produced from Parliament in 1628 a very memorable document, the *Petition of Right,* citing the Great Charter and rehearsing the legal limitations upon the power of the English king, denying his right to levy charges upon, or to imprison or punish anyone, or to quarter soldiers on the people, without due process of law.

The Petition of Right stated the case of the English Parliament. The disposition to "state a case" has always been a very marked English characteristic. When President Wilson, during the first World War of 1914–18, prefaced each step in his policy by a "Note," he was walking in the most respectable traditions of the English.

Charles dealt with this Parliament with a high hand; he dismissed it in 1629, and for eleven years he summoned no Parliament. He levied money illegally, but not enough for his purpose; and realizing that the church could be used as an instrument of obedience, he made Laud, an aggressive high churchman, very much of a priest and a very strong believer in "divine right," Archbishop of Canterbury, and so head of the Church of England.

In 1638 Charles tried to extend the half-Protestant, half-Catholic characteristics of the Church of England to his other kingdom of Scotland, where the secession from Catholicism had been more complete, and where a non-sacerdotal, non-sacramental form of Christianity, Presbyterianism had been established as the national church. The Scotch revolted, and the English levies Charles raised to fight them mutinied.

Insolvency, at all times the natural result of a "spirited" foreign policy, was close at hand. Charles, without money or trustworthy troops, had to summon a Parliament at last in 1640. This Parliament, the Short Parliament, he dismissed in the same year; he tried a Council of Peers at York (1640), and then, in the November of that year, summoned his last Parliament.

This body, the Long Parliament, assembled in the mood for conflict. It seized Laud, the Archbishop of Canterbury, and charged him with treason. It published a "Grand Remonstrance," which was a long and full statement of its case against Charles. It provided by a Bill for a meeting of Parliament at least once in three years, whether the King summoned it or no. It prosecuted the King's chief ministers who had helped him to reign for so long without Parliament, and in particular the Earl of Strafford.

To save Strafford the King plotted for a sudden seizure of London by the army. This was discovered, and the Bill for Strafford's condemnation was hurried on in the midst of a vast popular excitement. Charles I, who was probably one of the meanest and most treacherous occupants the English throne has ever known, was frightened by the London crowds. Before Strafford could die by due legal process, it was necessary for the King to give his assent. Charles gave it—and Strafford was beheaded.

Meanwhile the King was plotting and looking for help in strange quarters —from the Catholic Irish, from treasonable Scotchmen. Finally, he resorted to a forcible-feeble display of violence. He went down to the Houses of Parliament to arrest five of his most active opponents. He entered the House of Commons and took the Speaker's chair. He was prepared with some bold speech about treason, but when he saw the places of his five antagonists vacant, he was baffled, confused, and spoke in broken sentences. He learnt that they had departed from his royal city of Westminster and taken refuge in the city of London, which had municipal autonomy. London defied him. A week later the Five Members were escorted back in triumph to the Parliament House in Westminster by the Trained Bands of London, and the King, to avoid the noise and hostility of the occasion, left Whitehall for Windsor.

Both parties then prepared openly for war.

The King was the traditional head of the army, and the habit of obedience in soldiers is to the King. The Parliament had the greater resources. The King set up his standard at Nottingham on the eve of a dark and stormy August day in 1642.

There followed a long and obstinate civil war, the King holding Oxford, the Parliament, London. Success swayed from side to side, but the King could never close on London nor Parliament take Oxford. Each antagonist was weakened by moderate adherents who "did not want to go too far."

There emerged among the Parliament commanders a certain Oliver Cromwell, who had raised a small troop of horse and who rose to the position of general. Lord Warwick, his contemporary, describes him as a plain man, in a cloth suit "made by an ill country tailor." He was no mere fighting soldier, but a military organizer; he realized the inferior quality of many of the Parliamentary forces, and set himself to remedy it. The Cavaliers of the King had the picturesque tradition of chivalry and loyalty on their side; Parliament was something new and difficult—without any comparable traditions. "Your troops are most of them old decayed serving men and tapsters," said Cromwell. "Do you think that the spirits of such base and mean fellows will ever be able to encounter gentlemen that have honour and courage and resolution in them?"

But there is something better and stronger than picturesque chivalry in the world, religious enthusiasm. So Cromwell set himself to get together a "godly" regiment. They were to be earnest, sober-living men. Above all, they were to be men of strong convictions. He disregarded all social traditions and drew his officers from every class. "I had rather have a plain, russet-coated captain *that knows what he fights for and loves what he knows,* than what you call a gentleman and is nothing else."

England discovered a new force, the Ironsides, in its midst, in which footmen, draymen, and ships' captains held high command, side by side with men of family. They became the type on which the Parliament sought to reconstruct its entire army. The Ironsides were the backbone of the "New Model." From Marston Moor to Naseby these men swept the Cavaliers before them. The King was at last a captive in the hands of Parliament.

There were still attempts at settlement that would have left the King a sort of king, but Charles was a man doomed to tragic issues, incessantly scheming, "so false a man that he is not to be trusted." The English were drifting towards a situation new in the world's history, in which a monarch should be formally tried for treason to his people and condemned.

Most revolutions are precipitated, as this English one was, by the excesses of the ruler, and by attempts at strength and firmness beyond the compass of the law; and most revolutions swing by a kind of necessity towards an extremer conclusion than is warranted by the original quarrel. The English revolution was no exception. The English are by nature a compromising and even a vacillating people, and probably the great majority of them still wanted the King to be King and the people to be free, and all the lions and lambs to lie down together in peace and liberty. But the army of the New Model could not go back. There would have been scant mercy for these draymen and footmen who had ridden down the King's gentlemen if the King came back. When Parliament began to treat again with this regal trickster, the New Model intervened; Colonel Pride turned out eight members from the House of Commons who favoured the King, and the illegal residue, the Rump Parliament, then put the King on trial.

But indeed the King was already doomed. The House of Lords rejected the ordinance for the trial, and the Rump then proclaimed "that the People are, under God, the original of all just power," and that "the Commons of England . . . have the supreme power in this nation," and—assuming that it was itself the Commons—proceeded with the trial. The King was condemned as a "tyrant, traitor, murderer, and enemy of his country." He was taken one January morning in 1649 to a scaffold erected outside the windows of his own banqueting-room at Whitehall. There he was beheaded. He died with piety and a certain noble self-pity—eight years after the execution of Strafford, and after six and a half years of a destructive civil war which had been caused almost entirely by his own lawlessness.

This was indeed a great and terrifying thing that Parliament had done. The like of it had never been heard of in the world before. Kings had killed each other times enough; parricide, fratricide, assassination, those are the privileged expedients of princes; but that a section of the people should rise up, try its king solemnly and deliberately for disloyalty, mischief, and treachery, and condemn and kill him, sent horror through every Court in Europe. The Rump Parliament had gone beyond the ideas and conscience of its time. It was as if a committee of jungle deer had taken and killed a tiger—a crime against nature. The Tsar of Russia chased the English Envoy from his Court. France and

Holland committed acts of open hostility. England, confused and conscience-stricken at her own sacrilege, stood isolated before the world.

But for a time the personal quality of Oliver Cromwell and the discipline and strength of the army he had created maintained England in the republican course she had taken. The Irish Catholics had made a massacre of the Protestant English in Ireland, and now Cromwell suppressed the Irish insurrection with great vigour. Except for certain friars at the storm of Drogheda, none but men with arms in their hands were killed by his troops; but the atrocities of the massacre were fresh in his mind, no quarter was given in battle, and so his memory still rankles in the minds of the Irish, who have a long memory for their own wrongs.

After Ireland came Scotland, where Cromwell shattered a Royalist army at the Battle of Dunbar (1650).

Then he turned his attention to Holland, which country had rashly seized upon the divisions among the English as an excuse for the injury of a trade rival. The Dutch were then the rulers of the sea, and the English fleet fought against odds; but after a series of obstinate sea fights the Dutch were driven from the British seas and the English took their place as the ascendant naval power. Dutch and French ships must dip their flags to them. An English fleet went into the Mediterranean—the first English naval force to enter these waters; it put right various grievances of the English shippers with Tuscany and Malta, and bombarded the pirate nest of Tunis and destroyed the pirate fleet—which in the lax days of Charles had been wont to come right up to the coasts of Cornwall and Devon to intercept ships and carry off slaves to Africa.

The strong arm of England also intervened to protect the Protestants in the south of France, who were being hunted to death by the Duke of Savoy. France, Sweden, Denmark, all found it wiser to overcome their first distaste for regicide and allied themselves with England. Came a war with Spain, and the great English Admiral Blake destroyed the Spanish Plate Fleet at Teneriffe in an action of almost incredible daring. He engaged land batteries. He was the first man "that brought ships to contemn castles on the shore." (He died in 1657, and was buried in Westminster Abbey, but after the restoration of the monarchy his bones were dug out by the order of Charles II, and removed to St. Margaret's, Westminster.) Such was the figure that England cut in the eyes of the world during her brief republican days.

On September 3rd, 1658, Cromwell died in the midst of a great storm that did not fail to impress the superstitious. Once his strong hand lay still, England fell away from this premature attempt to realize a righteous commonweal of free men. In 1660 Charles II, the son of Charles the "Martyr," was welcomed back to England with all those manifestations of personal loyalty dear to the English heart, and the country relaxed from its military and naval efficiency as a sleeper might wake and stretch and yawn after too intense a dream. The Puritans were done with. "Merrie England" was herself again, and in 1667 the Dutch, once more masters of the sea, sailed up the Thames to Gravesend and burnt an English fleet in the Medway.

"On the night when our ships were burnt by the Dutch," says Pepys, in his diary, "the King did sup with my Lady Castelmaine, and there they were all mad, hunting a poor moth."

Charles, from the date of his return, 1660, took control of the foreign affairs of the State, and in 1670 concluded a secret treaty with Louis XIV of France by which he undertook to subordinate entirely English foreign policy to that of France for an annual pension of £100,000. Dunkirk, which Cromwell had taken, had already been sold back to France. The King was a great sportsman; he had the true English love for watching horse-races, and the racing centre at Newmarket is perhaps his most characteristic monument.

While Charles lived, his easy humour enabled him to retain the British crown, but he did so by wariness and compromise, and when in 1685 he was succeeded by his brother James II, who was a devout Catholic, and too dull to recognize the hidden limitation of the monarchy in Britain, the old issue between Parliament and Crown became acute.

James set himself to force his country into a religious reunion with Rome. In 1688 he was in flight to France. But this time the great lords and merchants and gentlemen were too circumspect to let this revolt against the King fling them into the hands of a second Pride or a second Cromwell. They had already called in another king, William, Prince of Orange, to replace James. The change was made rapidly. There was no civil war—except in Ireland—and no release of any deeper revolutionary forces in the country.

Of William's claim to the throne, or rather to his wife Mary's claim, we cannot tell here, its interest is purely technical, nor how William III and Mary ruled, nor how, after the widower William had reigned alone for a time, the throne passed on to Mary's sister Anne (1702-14). Anne seems to have thought favourably of a restoration of the Stuart line, but the Lords and the Commons, who now dominated English affairs, preferred a less competent king. Some sort of claim could be made out for the Elector of Hanover, who became King of England as George I (1714-27). He was entirely German, he could speak no English, and he brought a swarm of German women and German attendants to the English Court; a dullness, a tarnish, came over the intellectual life of the land with his coming, but this isolation of the Court from English life was his conclusive recommendation to the great landowners and the commercial interests that chiefly brought him over.

England entered upon a phase which Lord Beaconsfield has called the "Venetian oligarchy" stage; the supreme power resided in Parliament, dominated now by the Lords, for the art of bribery and a study of the methods of working elections, carried to a high pitch by Sir Robert Walpole, had robbed the House of Commons of its original freedom and vigour. By ingenious devices the parliamentary vote was restricted to a shrinking number of electors, old towns with little or no population would return one or two members (old Sarum had one non-resident voter, no population, and two members), while newer populous centres had no representation at all. And by insisting upon a high property qualification for members, the chance of the

Commons speaking in common accents of vulgar needs was still more restricted.

George I was followed by the very similar George II (1727–60), and it was only at his death that England had again a king who had been born in England, and one who could speak English fairly well, his grandson George III. On this monarch's attempt to recover some of the larger powers of monarchy we shall have something to say in a later section.

Such briefly is the story of the struggle in England during the seventeenth and eighteenth centuries between the three main factors in the problem of the "modern state"; between the Crown, the private property owners, and that vague power, still blind and ignorant, the power of the quite common people. This latter factor appears as yet only at moments when the country is most deeply stirred; then it sinks back into the depths. But the end of the story, thus far, is a very complete triumph of the British private property owner over the dreams and schemes of Machiavellian absolutism. With the Hanoverian Dynasty, England became—as *The Times* recently styled her—a "crowned republic." She had worked out a new method of government, Parliamentary government, recalling in many ways the Senate and Popular Assembly of Rome, but more steadfast and efficient because of its use, however restricted, of the representative method. Her assembly at Westminster was to become the "Mother of Parliaments" throughout the world.

Towards the Crown the English Parliament has held and still holds much the relation of the mayor of the palace to the Merovingian kings. The king is conceived of as ceremonial and irresponsible, a living symbol of the royal and imperial system.

But much power remains latent in the tradition and prestige of the Crown, and the succession of the six Hanoverian Georges, William IV (1830), Victoria (1837), Edward VII (1901), George V (1910), Edward VIII (1936), George VI (1936), and Elizabeth II (1952), is of a quite different strain from the feeble Merovingian monarchs. In the affairs of the church, the military and naval organizations, and the foreign office, these sovereigns have all in various degrees exercised an influence which is none the less important because it is indefinable.

§ 4

Upon no part of Europe did the collapse of the idea of a unified Christendom bring more disastrous consequences than to Germany. Naturally one would have supposed that the Emperor, being by origin a German, both in the case of the earlier lines, and in the case of the Habsburgs, would have developed into the national monarch of a united German-speaking state. It was the accidental misfortune of Germany that her emperors never remained German. Frederick II, the last Hohenstaufen, was, as we have seen, a half-Orientalized Sicilian; the Habsburgs, by marriage and inclination, became, in the person of Charles V, first Burgundian and then Spanish in spirit. After the death of Charles V, his brother Ferdinand took Austria and the empire, and his son Philip II took Spain, the Netherlands, and South Italy; but the Austrian line, obstinately Catholic, holding its patrimony mostly on the eastern frontiers, deeply entangled, therefore, with Hungarian affairs and paying tribute, as Ferdinand and his two successors did, to the Turk, retained no grip upon the north Germans with their disposition towards Protestantism, their Baltic and westward affinities, and their ignorance of or indifference to the Turkish danger.

The sovereign princes, dukes, electors, prince bishops and the like, whose domains cut up the map of the Germany of the Middle Ages into a crazy patchwork, were really not the equivalent of the kings of England and France. They were rather on the level of the great land-owning dukes and peers of France and England. Until 1701 none of them had the title of "King." Many of their dominions were less both in size and value than the larger estates of the British nobility. The German Diet was like the States-General or like a parliament without the presence of elected representatives. So that the great civil war in Germany that presently broke out, the Thirty Years' War (1618–48) was in its essential nature much more closely akin to the civil war in England (1643–49) and to the war of the Fronde (1648–55), the league of feudal nobles against the Crown in France, than appears upon the surface.

In all these cases the Crown was either Catholic or disposed to become Catholic, and the recalcitrant nobles found their individualistic disposition tending to a Protestant formula. But while in England and Holland the Protestant nobles and rich merchants ultimately triumphed, and in France the success of the Crown was even more complete, in Germany neither was the Emperor strong enough, nor had the Protestant princes a sufficient unity and organization among themselves to secure a conclusive triumph. It ended there in a torn-up Germany.

Moreover, the German issue was complicated by the fact that various non-German peoples, the Bohemians and the Swedes (who had a new Protestant monarchy which had arisen under Gustavus Vasa as a direct result of the Reformation), were entangled in the struggle. Finally, the French monarchy, triumphant now over its own nobles, although it was Catholic, came in on the Protestant side with the evident intention of taking the place of the Habsburgs as the imperial line.

The prolongation of the war, and the fact that it was not fought along a determinate frontier, but all over an empire of patches, Protestant here, Catholic there, made it one of the most cruel and destructive that Europe had known since the days of the barbarian raids. Its peculiar mischief lay not in the fighting, but in the concomitants of the fighting. It came at a time when military tactics had developed to a point that rendered ordinary levies useless against trained professional infantry. Volley firing with muskets at a range of a few score yards had abolished the individualistic knight in armour, but the charge of disciplined masses of cavalry could still disperse any infantry that had not been drilled into a mechanical rigidity. The infantry with their muzzle-loading muskets could not keep up a steady enough fire to wither determined cavalry before it charged home. They had, therefore, to meet the shock standing or kneeling behind a bristling wall of pikes or bayonets. For this they needed great discipline and experience. Iron cannon were still of small size and not very abundant, and they did not play a decisive part as yet in warfare. They could "plough lanes" in infantry, but they could not easily smash and scatter it if it was sturdy and well drilled.

War under these conditions was entirely in the hands of seasoned professional soldiers, and the question of their pay was as important a one to the generals of that time as the question of food or munitions. As the long struggle dragged on from phase to phase, and the financial distress of the land increased, the commanders of both sides were forced to fall back upon the looting of towns and villages, both for supply and to make up the arrears of their soldiers' pay. The soldiers became, therefore, more and more mere brigands living on the country, and the Thirty Years' War set up a tradition of looting as a legitimate operation in warfare and of outrage as a soldier's privilege that has tainted the good name of Germany right down to the first World War of 1914.

The earlier chapters of Defoe's *Memoirs of a Cavalier,* with its vivid description of a massacre and burning of Magdeburg, will give the reader a far better idea of the warfare of this time than any formal history. So harried was the land that the farmers ceased from cultivation, what snatch crops could be harvested were hidden away, and great crowds of starving women and children became camp followers of the armies, and supplied a thievish tail to the rougher plundering. At the close of the struggle all Germany was ruined and desolate. Central Europe did not fully recover from these robberies and devastations for a century.

Here we can but name Tilly and Wallenstein, the great plunder captains on the Habsburg side, and Gustavus Adolphus, the King of Sweden, the Lion of the North, the champion of the Protestants, whose dream was to make the Baltic Sea a "Swedish Lake." Gustavus Adolphus was killed in his decisive victory over Wallenstein at Lützen (1632), and Wallenstein was murdered in 1634.

In 1648 the princes and diplomatists gathered amidst the havoc they had made to patch up the affairs of Central Europe at the Peace of Westphalia. By that peace the power of the Emperor was reduced to a shadow, and the acquisition of Alsace brought France up to the Rhine. And one German prince, the Hohenzollern Elector of Brandenburg, acquired so much territory as to become the greatest German power next to the Emperor, a power that presently (1701) became the kingdom of Prussia.

The treaty of Westphalia also recognized two long accomplished facts, the separation from the empire and the complete independence of both Holland and Switzerland.

§ 5

We have opened this chapter with the stories of two countries, the Netherlands and Britain, in which the resistance of the private citizen to this new

type of monarchy, the Machiavellian monarchy, that was arising out of the moral collapse of
Christendom, succeeded. But in
France, Russia, in many parts of
Germany and of Italy—Saxony
and Tuscany e.g.—personal monarchy was not so restrained and
overthrown; it established itself,
indeed, as the ruling European
system during the seventeenth
and eighteenth centuries. And
even in Holland and Britain, the
monarchy was recovering power
during the eighteenth century.

(In Poland conditions were peculiar, and they will be dealt with
in a later section.)

In France there had been no
Magna Charta, and there was
not quite so definite and effective
a tradition of parliamentary rule.
There was the same opposition of
interests between the crown on
the one hand and the landlords
and merchants on the other, but
the latter had no recognized gath-
ering-place, and no dignified

method of unity. They formed oppositions to the crown, they made leagues of
resistance—such was the "Fronde," which was struggling against the young
King Louis XIV and his great minister Mazarin, while Charles I was fighting
for his life in England—but ultimately (1652), after a civil war, they were
conclusively defeated; and while in England after the establishment of the
Hanoverians the House of Lords and their subservient Commons ruled the
country, in France, on the contrary, after 1652, the Court entirely dominated
the aristocracy. Cardinal Mazarin was himself building upon a foundation
that Cardinal Richelieu, the contemporary of King James I of England, had
prepared for him.

After the time of Mazarin we hear of no great French nobles unless they
are at Court as Court servants and officials. They have been bought and tamed
—but at a price, the price of throwing the burthen of taxation upon the voice-
less mass of the common people. From many taxes both the clergy and the
nobility—everyone indeed who bore a title—were exempt. In the end this injustice became intolerable, but for a while the French monarchy flourished
like the Psalmist's green bay tree. By the opening of the eighteenth century

English writers are already calling attention of the misery of the French lower classes and the comparative prosperity, *at that time,* of the English poor.

On such terms of unrighteousness, what we may call "Grand Monarchy" established itself in France. Louis XIV, styled the Grand Monarque, reigned for the unparalleled length of seventy-two years (1643–1715), and set a pattern for all the kings of Europe. At first he was guided by his Machiavellian minister, Cardinal Mazarin; after the death of the Cardinal he himself, in his

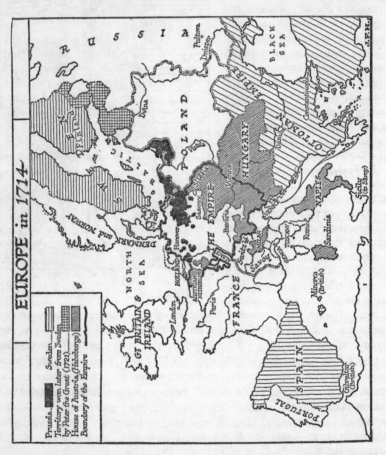

own proper person, became the ideal "Prince." He was, within his limitations, an exceptionally capable king; his ambition was stronger than his baser passions, and he guided his country towards bankruptcy through the complication of a spirited foreign policy with an elaborate dignity that still exhorts our admiration. His immediate desire was to consolidate and extend France to the Rhine and Pyrenees, and to absorb the Spanish Netherlands; his remoter view saw the French kings as the possible successors of Charlemagne in a recast Holy Roman Empire.

He made bribery a State method almost more important than warfare. Charles II of England was in his pay, and so were most of the Polish nobility, presently to be described. His money, or rather the money of the tax-paying classes in France, went everywhere. But his prevailing occupation was splendour. His great palace at Versailles, with its salons, its corridors, its mirrors, its terraces and fountains and parks and prospects, was the envy and admiration of the world.

He provoked a universal imitation. Every king and princelet in Europe was building his own Versailles as much beyond his means as his subjects and credits would permit. Everywhere the nobility rebuilt or extended their châteaux to the new pattern. A great industry of beautiful and elaborate fabrics and furnishings developed. The luxurious arts flourished everywhere; sculpture in alabaster, faience, gilt wood-work, metal work, stamped leather, much music, magnificent painting, beautiful printing and bindings, fine cookery, fine vintages. Amidst the mirrors and fine furniture went a strange race of "gentlemen" in vast powdered wigs, silks and laces, poised upon high red heels, supported by amazing canes; and still more wonderful "ladies," under towers of powdered hair and wearing vast expansions of silk and satin sustained on wire. Through it all postured the great Louis, the sun of his world, unaware of the meagre and sulky and bitter faces that watched him from those lower darknesses to which his sunshine did not penetrate.

We cannot give here at any length the story of the wars and doings of this monarch. In many ways Voltaire's *Siècle de Louis XIV* is still the best and most wholesome account. He created a French navy fit to face the English and Dutch; a very considerable achievement. But because his intelligence did not rise above the lure of that Fata Morgana, that crack in the political wits of Europe, the dream of a world-wide Holy Roman Empire, he drifted in his later years to the propitiation of the Papacy, which had hitherto been hostile to him. He set himself against those spirits of independence and disunion, the Protestant Princes, and he made war against Protestantism in France. Great numbers of his most sober and valuable subjects were driven abroad by his religious persecutions, taking arts and industries with them. The English silk manufacture, for instance, was founded by French Protestants. Under his rule were carried out the "dragonnades," a peculiarly malignant and effectual form of persecution. Rough soldiers were quartered in the houses of the Protestants, and were free to disorder the life of their hosts and insult their womankind as they thought fit. Men yielded to that sort of pressure who would not have yielded to rack and fire.

The education of the next generation of Protestants was broken up, and the parents had to give Catholic instruction or none. They gave it, no doubt, with a sneer and an intonation that destroyed all faith in it. While more tolerant countries became mainly sincerely Catholic or sincerely Protestant, the persecuting countries, like France and Spain and Italy, so destroyed honest Protestant teaching that these people became mainly Catholic believers or Catholic atheists, ready to break out into blank atheism whenever the opportunity offered. The next reign, that of Louis XV, was the age of that supreme mocker Voltaire (1694–1778), an age in which everybody in French society conformed to the Roman Church and hardly anyone believed in it.

It was part—and an excellent part—of the pose of Grand Monarchy to patronize literature and the sciences. Louis XIV set up an academy of sciences in rivalry with the English Royal Society of Charles II and the similar association at Florence. He decorated his Court with poets, playwrights, philosophers, and scientific men. If the scientific process got little inspiration from this patronage it did at any rate acquire resources for experiment and publication, and a certain prestige in the eyes of the vulgar.

The literary activities of France and England set the key of most of the literary activities of Europe during this period of big and little Grand Monarchs, of great country houses and of growing commercial powers. French conditions were much more monarchist than the English, more centralized and uniform. The French writers lacked the great tradition of such a free and undisciplined spirit as Shakespeare, French intellectual life centred upon the Court and was more conscious of control than the English; it never produced such literary "common men" as the English Bunyan, and in the seventeenth century it had no such release of the dissentient spirit as the Commonweal, to liberate a Milton. Its disposition was much more towards correctitude and limitation, it was more completely under the sway of the schoolmaster and the scholarly critic. It subordinated substance to style. The organization of an Academy still further restrained its already excessive restraints. As a consequence of these differences, this French literature before the nineteenth century was saturated with literary self-consciousness, and seems to have been written rather in the spirit of a good scholar who fears bad marks than in that of a man seeking frank expression. It is a literature of cold, correct and empty masterpieces, tragedies, comedies, romances and critical dissertations extraordinarily devoid of vitality. Eminent among the practitioners of dramatic correctitude were Corneille (1606–1684) and Racine (1639–1699). They were men of commanding genius; those who study them closely are most aware of their essential fire; but to those untrained in the conventions of the period they are at first almost as forbidding as monumental masonry (which also at times can conceal deep feeling). Molière (1622–73) also triumphed over his period with comedies that some authorities esteem the best in the world. Almost the only vein of easy, vivid and interesting reading to be found among this genteel and stately mental furniture of the French Grand Monarchy is to be found in the gossiping and scandalous memoirs of the time. There is that, and there is some lively social and political controversy.

Some of the brightest and best writing in French during this time was done out of France by Frenchmen in exile and in revolt. Descartes (1596–1650), the greatest of French philosophers, lived for most of his life in the comparative security of Holland. He is the central and dominant figure of a constellation of speculative minds which were active in undermining, modifying and dwarfing the genteel Christianity of their age. Towering above all these other exiles and above all other contemporary European writers is the great figure of Voltaire, of whose mental attitude we shall speak later. Jean Jacques Rousseau (1712–1778), another outcast spirit, with his sentimental attack on formal morals and his sentimental idealization of nature and freedom, stands out as the master novelist of his time and country. Of him, also, we shall have more to say.

The English literature of the seventeenth century reflected the less stable and centralized quality of English affairs and had more vigour and less polish than the French. The English Court and capital had not swallowed up the national life as the French had done. Against Descartes and his school one may put Bacon, of whom we have already told in our account of the scientific renaissance, and Hobbes and Locke. Milton (1608–1674) wore a mixed garment of Greek and Latin learning, Italian culture and Puritanical theology, with a glory all his own. There was a considerable free literature outside the range of classical influence finding perhaps its most characteristic expression in Bunyan's *Pilgrim's Progress* (1678). The still underrated creative work of Defoe (1659–1731) again, is manifestly addressed to a public innocent of the accomplishments and affectations of the academic world. His *Robinson Crusoe* is among the great inventions of literature. His *Moll Flanders* is an admirable study of manners, and both that and his fictitious developments of history are technically far in advance of any of his contemporaries. Nearly on a level with him was Fielding, the London magistrate, the author of *Tom Jones*. Samuel Richardson, the printer who wrote *Pamela* and *Clarissa,* was a third great figure among the living realities of English literature in the eighteenth century, the literature that did not trouble to be literary, and with these three it is the custom of criticism to associate the name of the far inferior Smollett. With these names and with that of J. J. Rousseau, the novel, the pseudo-real account of ways of living, of going about in the world, of the encounter with moral problems, comes back into importance. It disappeared in the decline of the Roman Empire. Its return marks the release of new, indeterminate sorts of people curious about life and conduct, people of some leisure, people anxious to supplement their own experience by stories of kindred adventures. Life has become less urgent and more interesting for them.

Here perhaps, before we end this literary parenthesis, we may note also as significant in English literature the graceful emptiness of Addison (1672 - 1719) and the lumpish lovableness of Dr. Samuel Johnson (1709–1784), the compiler of the first English dictionary. Of his actual writings scarcely anything except a few short lives of the poets remains readable, but his sayings and oddities have been preserved for all time in the inimitable biography of Boswell. Alexander Pope (1688–1744), classical in intention and French in spirit, translated Homer and transmuted a broadly Deistic philosophy into neatly polished verse. The most powerful writing of this age of polite and secondary men in England as in France came from a spirit in exasperated conflict with the current order, and, indeed, with the whole order of the world, Swift (1667–1745), the author of *Gulliver's Travels*. Laurence Sterne (1713–1768), the rather disreputable clergyman who wrote *Tristram Shandy* and taught later novelists a hundred turns and devices, drew his vitality from the greatness of the preclassical Frenchman Rabelais. Gibbon, the historian, we shall quote in a subsequent section, and then we will animadvert again upon the peculiar mental limitations of this gentlemanly age.

The Grand Monarque died in 1715. Louis XV was his great-grandson and an incompetent imitator of his predecessor's magnificence. He posed as a king, but his ruling passion was that common obsession of our kind, the pursuit of women, tempered by a superstitious fear of hell. How such women as the Duchess of Châteauroux, Madame de Pompadour, and Madame du Barry dominated the pleasures of the king, and how wars and alliances were made, provinces devastated, thousands of people killed, because of the vanities and spites of these creatures, and how all the public life of France and Europe was tainted with intrigue and prostitution and imposture because of them, the reader must learn from the memoirs of the time. The spirited foreign policy went on steadily under Louis XV towards its final smash.

In 1774 this Louis, Louis the Well-Beloved, as his flatterers called him, died of smallpox, and was succeeded by his grandson Louis XVI (1774–93), a dull, well-meaning man, an excellent shot, and an amateur locksmith of some ingenuity. Of how he came to follow Charles I to the scaffold we shall tell in a later section. Our present concern is with Grand Monarchy in the days of its glory.

Among the chief practitioners of Grand Monarchy outside France we may note first the Prussian kings, Frederick William I (1713–40), and his son and successor, Frederick II, Frederick the Great (1740–86). The story of the slow rise of the Hohenzollern family, which ruled the kingdom of Prussia, from inconspicuous beginnings is too tedious and unimportant for us to follow here. It is a story of luck and violence, of bold claims and sudden betrayals. It is told with great appreciation in Carlyle's *Frederick the Great*. By the eighteenth century the Prussian kingdom was important enough to threaten the empire; it had a strong, well-drilled army, and its king was an attentive and worthy student of Machiavelli. Frederick the Great perfected his Versailles at Potsdam. There the park of Sans Souci, with its fountains, avenues, statuary, aped its model; there, also, was the New Palace, a vast brick building erected at enormous expense, the Orangery in the Italian style, with a collection of pictures, a Marble Palace, and so on. Frederick carried culture to the pitch of authorship, and corresponded with and entertained Voltaire, to their mutual exasperation.

The Austrian dominions were kept too busy between the hammer of the French and the anvil of the Turks to develop the real Grand Monarch style until the reign of Maria Theresa (who, being a woman, did not bear the title of Empress) (1740–80). Joseph II, who was Emperor from 1765–90, succeeded to her palaces in 1780.

With Peter the Great (1682–1725) the empire of Muscovy broke away from her Tartar traditions and entered the sphere of French attraction. Peter shaved the Oriental beards of his nobles and introduced Western costume. These were but the outward and visible symbols of his westering tendencies. To release himself from the Asiatic feeling and traditions of Moscow, which, like Peking has a sacred inner city, the Kremlin, he built himself a new capital, Petrograd, upon the swamp of the Neva. And of course he built his Versailles, the Peterhof, about eighteen miles from this new Paris, employing a French architect and having a terrace, fountains, cascades, picture gallery, park, and all the recognized features. His more distinguished successors were Elizabeth (1741–62) and Catherine the Great, a German princess, who, after obtaining the crown in sound Oriental fashion through the murder of her husband, the legitimate Tsar, reverted to advanced Western ideals and ruled with great vigour from 1762 to 1796. She set up an academy, and corresponded with Voltaire. And she lived to witness the end of the system of Grand Monarchy in Europe and the execution of Louis XVI.

We cannot even catalogue here the minor Grand Monarchs of the time in Florence (Tuscany) and Savoy and Saxony and Denmark and Sweden. Versailles, under a score of names, is starred in every volume of Baedeker, and the tourist gapes in their palaces. Nor can we deal with the war of the Spanish Succession. Spain, overstrained by the imperial enterprises of Charles V and Philip II, and enfeebled by a bigoted persecution of Protestants, Moslems, and Jews, was throughout the seventeenth and eighteenth centuries sinking down from her temporary importance in European affairs to the level of a secondary power again.

These European monarchs ruled their kingdoms as their noblemen ruled their estates: they plotted against one another, they were politic and far-seeing in an unreal fashion, they made wars, they spent the substance of Europe upon absurd "policies" of aggression and resistance. At last there burst upon them a great storm out of the depths. That storm, the First French Revolution, the indignation of the common man in Europe, took their system unawares. It was but the opening outbreak of a great cycle of political and social storms that still continues, that will perhaps continue until every vestige of nationalist monarchy has been swept out of the world and the skies clear again for the great peace of the federation of mankind.

§ 6

The seventeenth and eighteenth centuries were a period of vigorous progress in music. The intellectual instrument had been elaborated; the major and minor scales with their fixed succession of notes, their adaptability to modulation and their possibilities of harmonic colour, were established. It was possible to define a musical intention clearly, to regulate the co-operation of diverse instruments with great exactitude. And social conditions, the growing towns, the Courts, the country houses were adding new fields of musical possibility to the older range of the church choirs. Masques and pageants had been popular in the sixteenth century; they gave opportunities for elaborate music; and with the seventeenth came a great development to operas and oratorios.

In Italy appeared the "Nuove Musiche." Lully (1635–1687), says Sir W. H. Hadow, "is the most important historically, not only for the dramatic power of his melody but for the close accuracy of his declamation." Beside him stands the Italian Monteverde. Music began to work upon a large scale in this period.

"The sixteenth-century Masses were written for the church choir, the sixteenth-century madrigals for a party of friends round the supper-table; only towards its end do the lutenists and the virginalists begin to introduce into executive art the conception of the virtuoso. . . . The vast improvement in organ building brought with it a succession of great performers: Bull and Philips the Englishmen, Sweelinck the Netherlander, Frescobaldi at Rome, Froberger in Vienna, Buxtehude in Lübeck, whom Bach travelled on foot to hear. . . . Along with this goes the development of virginal music. . . . Not less momentous was the arrival, and the tardy acceptance, of the violin and its family. Dating from Tieffenbrücker and the Amatis in the first half of the sixteenth century, it took nearly a hundred years to make its way into public favour; as late as 1676 Mace, the lutenist, can still inveigh against the 'scoulding violins,' and regret the quieter and more even tone of its ancestor the viol. But its wider compass, its greater agility and its more poignant power of expression made themselves felt in the long run. . . . In Italy, its natural home, though clumsily held and clumsily played, it came to be recognized as the only instrument which could rival the human voice."[1]

For a time, we are told, the display and adoration of the vocalist in Italian opera retarded musical development; the seventeenth-century singers, and especially the male sopranos, sustained almost as vulgar and terrible a fame as the modern film star, yet the period produced the abundant and beautiful music of Alessandro Scarlatti (1659–1725), the precursor of Mozart. In England a great outburst of musical activity followed a phase of quiescence during the Commonweal and culminated in Purcell (1658–1695). In Germany the little Courts and town-bands provided numberless centres of musical stimulation, and in 1685 in Saxony J. S. Bach and Handel were born, to carry German music to a pitch of supremacy it was to retain for a century and a half. "Of all composers," says Sir W. H. Hadow, "before the Viennese period they are the most closely related to our own day, their voices sound in our ears with the most familiar accents."

Palestrina, who marked a previous culmination in music, is by comparison, a being in a different world. He was the crowning master of choral music before the days of instrumental achievement. Following upon the names of Bach and Handel came others in a constellation; Haydn (1732–1809), Mozart (1756–1791), Beethoven (1770–1827), stand out among the brightest stars. The great stream of modern music was now flowing wide and deep. And still flows. Here we can but name composers and further on give, in a brief paragraph or so, a few compact generalizations about the music of the nineteenth century and our own days. At the time of its making this seventeenth- and eighteenth-century music was the privilege of a small cultivated world—people in Courts, people in provincial towns and country houses who could organize

---

[1] Sir W. H. Hadow, *Music*.

performances, people in cities large enough for opera-houses and concert-rooms. The peasant and the worker of Western Europe had less and less music in the seventeenth and eighteenth centuries while these new forms were developing. Folk singing had declined and seemed likely to be forgotten. A few popular songs, a few hymns, was all the musical life left to the generality of people. Religious revivals in those days probably owed something of their impetus to their release of the pent-up singing impulse. It is only to-day, with a vast development of the mechanical methods of musical reproduction that music, modernized, evolved and exalted, returns into the common life, and Bach and Beethoven become a part of the general culture of mankind.

§ 7

The painting and architecture of this period, like its music, reflect the social conditions of the time. It is a time of fragmentation for ideas and for power, and no longer do considerations of object and dignity dominate pictorial art. Religious subjects are relegated to a secondary place, and where they are dealt with they are dealt with as incidents in a narrative and not as great spectacular facts. Allegory and symbolic figures decline. The painter paints for the sake of the vision and neither for the idea nor the fact. The picture of reality re-places the heroic or devotional picture just as the novel replaces the epic and the fantastic romance. The two supreme masters in the painting of the sev-enteenth century are Velasquez (1599–1660) and Rembrandt (1606–1669). To them it would seem all life was equal except in so far as it gave them more or less scope for the realization of beauty, in atmosphere, in light, in sub-stance. Velasquez at the decaying Court of Spain painted popes and kings without flattery, and dwarfs and cripples without contempt. Minute, analytical and documentary drawing of objects gives place in the work of these, the first of the moderns, to a broad rendering of effect, to a concentration upon unity of impression at the cost of all secondary considerations. Hitherto, in the more centralized life of the past, the picture had been a witness, an ex-hortation, a flatterer, an embellishment; now, in a great many cases, it became a thing in itself, existing for the sake of itself. Pictures were hung up as pictures—collected into galleries. Landscape developed vigorously, also genre painting. The nude was painted pleasantly and excitingly, and in France Watteau, Fragonard and others delighted and flattered the gentlefolk with a delicate apotheosis of the facts of country life. One realizes in these things the evidences of a growing community of secure, prosperous and quite fine-spirited people, appreciative of life and a little detached from either its mag-nificences or its sufferings.

The Elizabethan period in England had no plastic enthusiasms to match its literary and musical activities. It imported its painters and architects. But in the seventeenth and eighteenth centuries the accumulating wealth and pros-perity of what had hitherto been a very marginal country in European civili-zation created conditions favourable to artistic effort, and in the eighteenth century such English painters as Reynolds (1723–1792), Gainsborough

(1727–1788) and Romney could challenge comparison with any contemporary effort.

This period of the monarchies and gentlefolk was also extremely favourable to the development of certain types of architecture. Processes already active in the sixteenth century were going on now with enhanced vigour. Everywhere monarchs were building and rebuilding palaces, and the nobles and gentry were demolishing their castles and replacing them with fine houses. The town house was being conceived upon an ampler scale. Ecclesiastical architecture had waned; municipal effort was relatively less important: it is the large prosperous individual in this as in all things who sets the key of the period. In England the burning of a large part of London in the Great Fire of 1666 gave peculiar opportunity to Sir Christopher Wren, and his Saint Paul's Cathedral and his London churches mark a culminating phase in the history of British architecture. Drawings were sent by him to America for various country houses erected there, and his peculiar genius stamped itself also upon early American design. Inigo Jones was a second great figure among the English architects of the early seventeenth century, and his Banqueting Hall—it was to have been part of an unfinished palace in Whitehall—makes his work familiar to every visitor to London. Both these men, and indeed all English, French and German architects of this period, were working upon the still living and developing lines of the Italian Renaissance, and many of the best buildings of these countries were the work of Italians. Gradually, as the eighteenth century drew to its end, the free and natural development of Renaissance architecture was checked by a wave of classical pedantry. The gradual coagulation of classical studies in the schools of Western Europe had its correlative in a growing tendency to imitate Greek and Roman models. What had once been a stimulant was now becoming a traditional and stupefying mental drug. Banks, churches, museums, were dressed up as Athenian temples, and even terraces of houses were subjected to the colonnade. But the worst excesses of this deadening tendency were in the nineteenth century and beyond the limits of our present period.

§ 8

We have seen how the idea of a world-rule and a community of mankind first came into human affairs, and we have traced how the failure of the Christian churches to sustain and establish those conceptions of its founder, led to a moral collapse in political affairs, and a reversion to egotism and want of faith. We have seen how Machiavellian monarchy set itself up against the spirit of brotherhood in Christendom and how Machiavellian monarchy developed throughout a large part of Europe into the Grand Monarchies and Parliamentary Monarchies of the seventeenth and eighteenth centuries. But the mind and imagination of man is incessantly active, and beneath the sway of the grand monarchs, a complex of notions and traditions was being woven as a net is woven, to catch and entangle men's minds, the conception of international politics not as a matter of dealings between princes but as a matter of dealings between a kind of immortal Beings, the Powers. The Princes came and went; a Louis XIV would be followed by a petticoat-hunting Louis XV, and he again by that dull-witted amateur locksmith, Louis XVI. Peter the Great gave place to a succession of empresses; the chief continuity of the Habsburgs after Charles V, either in Austria or Spain, was a continuity of thick lips, clumsy chins, and superstition; the amiable scoundrelism of a Charles II would make a mock of his own pretensions. But what remained much more steadfast were the secretariats of the foreign ministries and the ideas of people who wrote of State concerns. The ministers maintained a continuity of policy during the "off days" of their monarchs, and between one monarch and another.

So we find that the prince gradually became less important in men's minds than the "Power" of which he was the head. We begin to read less and less of the schemes and ambitions of King This or That, and more of the "Designs of France" or the "Ambitions of Prussia." In an age when religious faith was declining, we find men displaying a new and vivid belief in the reality of these personifications. These vast vague phantoms, the "Powers," crept insensibly into European political thought, until in the later eighteenth and in the nineteenth centuries they dominated it entirely. To this day they dominate it. European life remained nominally Christian, but to worship one God in spirit and in truth is to belong to one community with all one's fellow worshippers. In practical reality Europe does not do this, she has given herself up altogether to the worship of this strange State mythology. To these sovereign deities, to the unity of "Italy," to the hegemony of "Prussia," to the glory of "France," and the destinies of "Russia," she has sacrificed many generations of possible unity, peace, and prosperity and the lives of millions of men.

To regard a tribe or a state as a sort of personality is a very old disposition of the human mind. The Bible abounds in such personifications. Judah, Edom, Moab, Assyria figure in the Hebrew Scriptures as if they were individuals; it is sometimes impossible to say whether the Hebrew writer is dealing with a person or with a nation. It is manifestly a primitive and natural tendency. But in the case of modern Europe it is a retrocession. Europe, under the idea of Christendom, had gone far towards unification. And while such tribal persons as "Israel" or "Tyre" did represent a certain community of blood, a certain uniformity of type, and a homogeneity of interest, the European powers which arose in the seventeenth and eighteenth centuries were entirely fictitious unities. Russia was in truth an assembly of the most incongruous elements, Cossacks, Tartars, Ukrainians, Muscovites, and, after the time of Peter, Esthonians and Lithuanians; the France of Louis XV comprehended German Alsace and freshly assimilated regions of Burgundy; it was a prison of suppressed Huguenots and a sweating-house for peasants. In "Britain," England carried on her back the Hanoverian dominions in Germany, Scotland, the profoundly alien Welsh and the hostile and Catholic Irish. Such powers as Sweden, Prussia, and still more so Poland and Austria, if we watch them in a series of historical maps, contract, expand, thrust out extensions, and wander over the map of Europe as amœbæ do under the microscope. . . .

If we consider the psychology of international relationship as we see it manifested in the world about us, and as it is shown by the development of the "Power" idea in modern Europe, we shall realize certain historically very important facts about the nature of man. Aristotle said that man is a political animal, but in our modern sense of the word politics, which now covers world-politics, he is nothing of the sort. He has still the instincts of the family tribe, and beyond that he has a disposition to attach himself and his family to something larger, to a tribe, a city, a nation, or a state. But that disposition, left to itself, is a vague and very uncritical disposition. If anything, he is inclined to fear and dislike criticism of this something larger that encloses his life and to which he has given himself, and to avoid such criticism. Perhaps he has a subconscious fear of the isolation that may ensue if the system is broken or discredited. He takes the *milieu* in which he finds himself for granted; he accepts his city or his government, just as he accepts the nose or the digestion which fortune has bestowed upon him. But men's loyalties, the sides they take in political things, are not innate, they are educational results. For most men their education in these matters is the silent, continuous education of things about them. Men find themselves a part of Merry England or Holy Russia; they grow up into these devotions; they accept them as a part of their nature.

It is only slowly that the world is beginning to realize how profoundly the tacit education of circumstances can be supplemented, modified, or corrected by positive teaching, by literature, discussion, and properly criticized experience. The real life of the ordinary man is his everyday life, his little circle of affections, fears, hungers, lusts, and imaginative impulses. It is only when his attention is directed to political affairs as something vitally affecting this personal circle, that he brings his reluctant mind to bear upon them. It is scarcely too much to say that the ordinary man thinks as little about political matters as he can, and stops thinking about them as soon as possible. It is still only very curious and exceptional minds, or minds that have by example or good education acquired the scientific habit of wanting to know *why*, or minds shocked and distressed by some public catastrophe and roused to wide apprehensions of danger, that will not accept governments and institutions, however preposterous, that do not directly annoy them, as satisfactory. The ordinary human being, until he is so aroused, will acquiesce in any collective activities that are going on in this world in which he finds himself, and any phrasing or symbolization that meets his vague need for something greater to which his personal affairs, his individual circle, can be anchored.

If we keep these manifest limitations of our nature in mind, it no longer becomes a mystery how, as the idea of Christianity as a world brotherhood of men sank into discredit because of its fatal entanglement with priestcraft and the Papacy on the one hand and with the authority of princes on the other, and the age of faith passed into our present age of doubt and disbelief, men shifted the reference of their lives from the kingdom of God and the brotherhood of mankind to these apparently more living realities, France and England, Holy Russia, Spain, Prussia, which were at least embodied in active Courts, which maintained laws, exerted power through armies and navies, waved flags with a compelling solemnity and were self-assertive and insatiably greedy in an entirely human and understandable fashion.

Certainly such men as Cardinal Richelieu and Cardinal Mazarin thought of themselves as serving greater ends than their own or their monarch's; they served the quasi-divine France of their imaginations. And as certainly these habits of mind percolated down from them to their subordinates and to the general body of the population. In the thirteenth and fourteenth centuries the general population of Europe was religious and only vaguely patriotic; by the nineteenth it had become wholly patriotic. In a crowded English or French or German railway carriage of the later nineteenth century it would have aroused far less hostility to have jeered at God than to have jeered at one of those strange beings, England or France or Germany. To these things men's minds clung, and they clung to them because in all the world there appeared nothing else so satisfying to cling to. They were the real and living gods of Europe.

This idealization of governments and foreign offices, this mythology of "Powers" and their loves and hates and conflicts, has so obsessed the imaginations of Europe and Western Asia as to provide it with its "forms of thought." Nearly all the histories, nearly all the political literature of the last two centuries in Europe, have been written in its phraseology. Yet a time is coming when a clearer-sighted generation will read with perplexity how in the community of Western Europe, consisting everywhere of slight variations of a common racial mixture of Nordic and Iberian peoples and immigrant Semitic and Mongolian elements, speaking nearly everywhere modifications of the same Aryan speech, having a common past in the Roman Empire, common religious forms, common social usages, and a common art and science, and intermarrying so freely that no one could tell with certainty the "nationality" of any of his great-grandchildren, men could be moved to the wildest excitement upon the question of the ascendancy of "France," the rise and unification of "Germany," the rival claims of "Russia" and "Greece" to possess Constantinople. These conflicts will seem then as reasonless and insane as those dead, now incomprehensible feuds of the "greens" and "blues" that once filled the streets of Byzantium with shouting and bloodshed.

Tremendously as these phantoms, the Powers, rule our minds and lives to-day, they are, as this history shows clearly, things only of the last few centuries, a mere hour, an incidental phase, in the vast deliberate history of our kind. They mark a phase of relapse, a backwater, as the rise of Machiavellian monarchy marks a backwater; they are part of the same eddy of faltering faith, in a process altogether greater and altogether different in its general tendency, the process of the moral and intellectual reunion of mankind. For a time men have relapsed upon these national or imperial gods of theirs; it is but for a time. The idea of the world-State, the universal kingdom of righteousness of which every living soul shall be a citizen, was already in the world two thousand years ago, never more to leave it. Men know that it is present even when they refuse to recognize it. In the writings and talk of men about international affairs to-day in the current discussions of historians and political

journalists, there is an effect of drunken men growing sober, and terribly
afraid of growing sober. They still talk loudly of their "love" for France, of
their "hatred" of Germany, of the "traditional ascendancy of Britain at sea,"
and so on and so on, like those who sing of their cups in spite of the steadfast
onset of sobriety and a headache. These are dead gods they serve. By sea
or land men want no Powers ascendant, but only law and service. That silent
unavoidable challenge is in all our minds like dawn breaking slowly, shining
between the shutters of a disordered room.

§ 9

The seventeenth century in Europe was the century of Louis XIV; he and
French ascendancy and Versailles are the central motif of the story. The
eighteenth century was equally the century of the "rise of Prussia as a great

THE PARTITIONS OF POLAND

power," and the chief figure in the story
is Frederick II, Frederick the Great. Interwoven with his history is the story of
Poland.

The condition of affairs in Poland was
peculiar. Unlike its three neighbours
Prussia, Russia, and the Austro-Hungarian monarchy of the Habsburgs, Poland
had not developed a Grand Monarchy.
Its system of government may be best
described as republican with a king, an
elected life-president. Each king was separately elected. It was in fact rather
more republican than Britain, but its republicanism was more aristocratic in
form. Poland had little trade and few
manufactures; she was agricultural and
still with great areas of grazing, forest,
and waste; she was a poor country, and
her landowners were poor aristocrats.
The mass of her population was a downtrodden and savagely ignorant peasantry, and she also harboured great
masses of very poor Jews. She had remained Catholic. She was, so to speak,
a poor Catholic inland Britain, entirely
surrounded by enemies instead of by the
sea. She had no definite boundaries at all,
neither sea, nor mountain. And it added
to her misfortunes that some of her
elected kings had been brilliant and aggressive rulers. Eastward her power ex-

tended weakly into regions inhabited almost entirely by Russians; westward she overlapped a German subject population.

Because she had no great trade, she had no great towns to compare with those of Western Europe, and no vigorous universities to hold her mind to-gether. Her noble class lived on their estates, without much intellectual inter-course. They were patriotic, they had an aristocratic sense of freedom—which was entirely compatible with the systematic impoverishment of their serfs—but their patriotism and freedom were incapable of effective co-operation. While warfare was a matter of levies of men and horses, Poland was a comparatively strong power; but it was quite unable to keep pace with the development of military art that was making standing forces of professional soldiers the necessary weapon in warfare. Yet, divided and dis-abled as she was, she could yet count some notable victories to her credit. The last Turkish attack upon Vienna (1683) was defeated by the Polish cavalry under King John Sobiesky, King John III. (This same Sobiesky, before he was elected king, had been in the pay of Louis XIV, and had also fought for the Swedes against his native country.) Needless to say, this weak aristocratic re-public, with its recurrent royal elections, invited aggression from all three of its neighbours. "Foreign money," and every sort of exterior interference came into the country at each election. And like the Greeks of old, every disgruntled Polish patriot flew off to some foreign

THE PARTITIONS OF POLAND

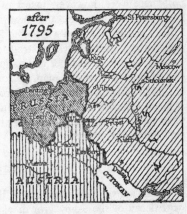

enemy to wreak his indignation upon his ungrateful country.

Even when the King of Poland was elected, he had very little power because of the mutual jealousy of the nobles. Like the English peers, they preferred a foreigner, and for much the same reason, because he had no roots of power in the land; but, unlike the British, their own government had not the solidarity which the periodic assembling of Parliament in London, the "coming up to town," gave the British peers. In London there was "Society," a continuous intermingling of influential persons and ideas. Poland had no London and no "Society." So, practically, Poland had no central government at all. The King of Poland could not make war nor peace, levy a tax nor alter the law, without the consent of the Diet, and *any single member of the Diet had the power of putting a veto upon any proposal before it*. He had merely to rise and say, "I disapprove," and the matter dropped. He could even carry his free veto, his *liberum veto,* further. He could object to the assembly of the Diet, and the Diet was thereby dissolved. Poland was not simply a crowned aristocratic republic like the British, it was a paralyzed crowned aristocratic republic.

To Frederick the Great, the existence of Poland was particularly provocative because of the way in which an arm of Poland reached out to the Baltic at Dantzig and separated his ancestral dominions in East Prussia from his territories with the empire. It was he who incited Catherine the Second of Russia and Maria Theresa of Austria, whose respect he had earned by depriving her of Silesia, to a joint attack upon Poland.

Let four maps of Poland tell the tale.

After this first outrage of 1772 Poland underwent a great change of heart. Poland was, indeed, born as a nation on the eve of her dissolution. There was a hasty but very considerable development of education, literature, and art; historians and poets sprang up, and the impossible constitution that had made Poland impotent was swept aside. The free veto was abolished, the crown was made hereditary to save Poland from the foreign intrigues that attended every election, and a Parliament in imitation of the British was set up. There were, however, lovers of the old order in Poland who resented these necessary changes, and these obstructives were naturally supported by Prussia and Russia, who wanted no Polish revival. Came the second partition, and, after a fierce patriotic struggle that began in the region annexed by Prussia and found a leader and national hero in Kosciusko, the final obliteration of Poland from the map. So for a time ended this Parliamentary threat to Grand Monarchy in Eastern Europe. But the patriotism of the Poles grew stronger and clearer with suppression. For a hundred and twenty years Poland struggled like a submerged creature beneath the political and military net that held her down. She rose again in 1918, at the end of the first World War.

§ 10

We have given some account of the ascendancy of France in Europe, the swift decay of the sappy growth of Spanish power and its separation from Austria, and the rise of Prussia. So far as Portugal, Spain, France, Britain, and Holland were concerned, their competition for ascendancy in Europe was extended and complicated by a struggle for dominion overseas.

The discovery of the huge continent of America, thinly inhabited, undeveloped, and admirably adapted for European settlement and exploitation, the simultaneous discovery of great areas of unworked country south of the torrid equatorial regions of Africa that had hitherto limited European knowledge, and the gradual realization of vast island regions in the Eastern seas, as yet untouched by Western civilization, was a presentation of opportunity to mankind unprecedented in all history. It was as if the peoples of Europe had come into some splendid legacy. Their world had suddenly quadrupled. There was more than enough for all; they had only to take these lands and continue to do well by them, and their crowded poverty would vanish like a dream. And they received this glorious legacy like ill-bred heirs; it meant no more to them than a fresh occasion for atrocious disputes. But what community of human beings has ever yet preferred creation to conspiracy? What nation in all our story has ever worked with another when, at any cost to itself, it could contrive to do that other an injury? The powers of Europe began by a frantic "claiming" of the new realms. They went on to exhausting conflicts. Spain, who claimed first and most, and who was for a time "mistress" of two-thirds of America, made no better use of her possession than to bleed herself nearly to death therein.

We have told how the Papacy in its last assertion of world dominion, instead of maintaining the common duty of all Christendom to make a great common civilization in the new lands, divided the American continent between Spain and Portugal. This naturally roused the hostility of the excluded nations. The seamen of England showed no respect for either claim, and set themselves particularly against the Spanish; the Swedes turned their Protestantism to a similar account. The Hollanders, so soon as they had shaken off their Spanish masters, also set their sails westward to flout the Pope and share in the good things of the New World. His Most Catholic Majesty of France hesitated as little as any Protestant. All these powers were soon busy staking out claims in North America and the West Indies.

Neither the Danish kingdom (which at that time included Norway and Iceland) nor the Swedes secured very much in the scramble. The Danes annexed some of the West Indian islands. Sweden got none. Both Denmark and Sweden at this time were deep in the affairs of Germany. We have already named Gustavus Adolphus, the Protestant "Lion of the North," and mentioned his campaigns in Germany, Poland and Russia. These Eastern European regions are great absorbents of energy, and the strength that might have given Sweden a large share in the new world reaped a barren harvest of glory in Europe. Such small settlements as the Swedes made in America presently fell to the Dutch.

The Hollanders, too, with the French monarchy under Cardinal Richelieu and under Louis XIV eating its way across the Spanish Netherlands towards their frontier, had not the undistracted resources that Britain, behind her "silver streak" of sea, could put into overseas adventures.

Moreover, the absolutist efforts of James I and Charles I, and the restoration of Charles II, had the effect of driving out from England a great number of sturdy-minded, republican-spirited Protestants, men of substance and character, who set up in America, and particularly in New England, out of reach, as they supposed, of the king and his taxes. The *Mayflower* was only one of the pioneer vessels of a stream of emigrants. It was the luck of Britain that they remained, though dissentient in spirit, under the British flag. The Dutch never sent out settlers of the same quantity and quality, first because their Spanish rulers would not let them, and then because they had got possession of their

own country. And though there was a great emigration of Protestant Huguenots from the dragonnades and persecution of Louis XIV, they had Holland
and England close at hand as refuges, and their industry, skill and sobriety
went mainly to strengthen those countries, and particularly England. A few

of them founded settlements in Carolina, but these did not remain French;
they fell first to the Spanish and finally to the English.

The Dutch settlements, with the Swedish, also succumbed to Britain; Nieuw
Amsterdam became British in 1674, and its name was changed to New York,

as the reader may learn very cheerfully in Washington Irving's *Knicker-bocker's History of New York*. The state of affairs in North America in 1750 is indicated very clearly by a map we have adapted from one in Robinson's *Medieval and Modern Times*. The British power was established along the east coast from Savannah to the St. Lawrence River, and Newfoundland and considerable northern areas, the Hudson Bay Company territories, had been acquired by treaty from the French. The British occupied Barbados (almost their oldest American possession) in 1605, and acquired Jamaica, the Bahamas, and British Honduras from the Spaniards. But France was pursuing a very dangerous and alarming game, a game even more dangerous and alarming on the map than in reality. She had made real settlements in Quebec and Montreal to the north and at New Orleans in the south, and her explorers and agents had pushed south and north, making treaties with the American Indians of the great plains and setting up claims—without setting up towns—right across the continent behind the British. But the realities of the case are not adequately represented in this way. The British colonies were being very solidly settled by a good class of people; they already numbered a population of over a million; the French at that time hardly counted a tenth of that. They had a number of brilliant travellers and missionaries at work, but no substance of population behind them.

Many old maps of America in this period are still to be found, maps designed to scare and "rouse" the British to a sense of the "designs of France" in America. War broke out in 1754, and in 1759 the British and Colonial forces under General Wolfe took Quebec and completed the conquest of Canada in the next year. In 1763 Canada was finally ceded to Britain. (But the western part of the rather indefinite region of Louisiana in the south, named after Louis XIV, remained outside the British sphere. It was taken over by Spain; and in 1800 it was recovered by France. Finally, in 1803, it was bought from France by the United States government. In this Canadian war the American colonists gained a considerable experience of the military art, and a knowledge of British military organization that was to be of great use to them a little later.

§ 11

It was not only in America that the French and British powers clashed. The condition of India at this time was one very interesting and attractive to European adventurers. The great Mongol Empire of Baber, Akbar, and Aurungzeb was now far gone in decay. What had happened to India was very parallel to what had happened to Germany. The Great Mogul at Delhi in India, like the Holy Roman Emperor in Germany, was still legally overlord, but after the death of Aurungzeb he exerted only a nominal authority except in the immediate neighbourhood of his capital. There had been a great revival of Hinduism and of the native spirit. In the south-west a Hindu people, the Mahrattas, had risen against Islam, restored Brahminism as the ruling religion, and for a time extended their power over the whole southern triangle of India.

In Rajputana, also, the rule of Islam was replaced by Brahminism, and at Bhurtpur and Jaipur there ruled powerful Rajput princes. In Oudh there was a Shiite kingdom, with its capital at Lucknow, and Bengal was also a separate (Moslem) kingdom. Away in the Punjab to the north had arisen a very interesting religious body, the Sikhs, proclaiming the universal rule of one God and assailing both the Hindu Vedas and the Moslem Koran. Originally a pacific sect, the Sikhs presently followed the example of Islam and sought—at first very disastrously to themselves—to establish the kingdom of God by the sword. And into this confused and disordered but very vital renascent Indian India there presently (1738) came an invader from the north, Nadir

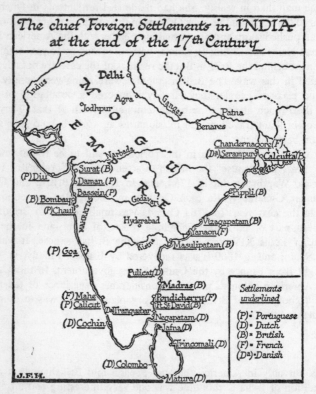

The chief Foreign Settlements in INDIA at the end of the 17th Century

Settlements underlined

(P) = Portuguese
(D) = Dutch
(B) = British
(F) = French
(Da) = Danish

Shah (1736–47), the Turcoman ruler of Persia, who swept down through the Khyber Pass, broke every army that stood in his way, and captured and sacked Delhi, carrying off an enormous booty. He left the north of India so utterly broken, that in the next twenty years there were no less than six other successful plundering raids into North India from Afghanistan, which had become an independent state at the death of Nadir Shah. For a time Mahrattas fought with Afghans for the rule of North India; then the Mahratta power broke up into a series of principalities, Indore, Gwalior, Baroda, and others. India in the eighteenth century was very like the Europe of the seventh and eighth centuries, a land of slow revival, distressed by foreign raiders. This was the India into which the French and English thrust themselves.

A succession of other European powers had been struggling for a commercial and political footing in India and the east ever since Vasco da Gama had made his memorable voyage round the Cape to Calicut. The sea trade of India had previously been in the hands of the Red Sea Arabs, and the Portuguese won it from them in a series of sea fights. The Portuguese ships were the bigger, and carried a heavier armament. For a time the Portuguese held the Indian trade as their own, and Lisbon outshone Venice as a mart for Oriental spices; the seventeenth century, however, saw the Dutch grasping at

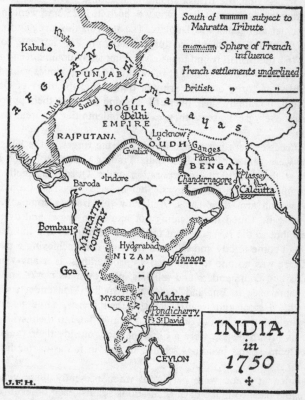

this monopoly. At the crest of their power the Dutch had settlements at the Cape of Good Hope, they held Mauritius, they had two establishments in Persia, twelve in India, six in Ceylon, and all over the East Indies they had dotted their fortified stations. But their selfish resolution to exclude traders of any other European nationality forced the Swedes, Danes, French, and English into hostile competition. The first effectual blows at their overseas monopoly were struck in European waters by the victories of Blake, the English republican admiral; and by the opening of the eighteenth century both the English and French were in vigorous competition with the Dutch for trade and privileges throughout India. At Madras, Bombay, and Calcutta the English established their headquarters; Pondicherry and Chandernagore were the chief French settlements.

At first all these European powers came merely as traders, and the only establishments they attempted were warehouses; but the unsettled state of the country, and the unscrupulous methods of their rivals, made it natural for them to fortify and arm their settlements, and this armament made them attractive allies of the various warring princes who now divided India. And it was entirely in the spirit of the new European nationalist politics that when the French took one side, the British should take another. The great leader upon the English side was Robert Clive, who was born in 1725, and went to India in 1743. His chief antagonist was Dupleix. The story of this struggle throughout the first half of the eighteenth century is too long and intricate to be told here. By 1761 the British found themselves completely dominant in the Indian peninsula. At Plassey (1757) and at Buxar (1764) their armies gained striking and conclusive victories over the army of Bengal and the army of Oudh. The Great Mogul, nominally their overlord, became in effect their puppet. They levied taxes over great areas; they exacted indemnities for real or fancied opposition.

These successes were not gained directly by the forces of the King of England; they were gained by the East India Trading Company, which had been originally at the time of its incorporation under Queen Elizabeth no more than a company of sea adventurers. Step by step they had been forced to raise troops and arm their ships. And now this trading company, with its tradition of gain, found itself dealing not merely in spices and dyes and tea and jewels, but in the revenues and territories of princes and the destinies of India. It had come to buy and sell, and it found itself achieving a tremendous piracy. There was no one to challenge its proceedings. Is it any wonder that its captains and commanders and officials, nay, even its clerks and common soldiers, came back to England loaded with spoils? Men under such circumstances, with a great and wealthy land at their mercy, could not determine what they might or might not do. It was a strange land to them with a strange sunlight; its brown people were a different race, outside their range of sympathy; its temples and buildings seemed to sustain fantastic standards of behaviour.

Englishmen at home were perplexed when presently these generals and officials came back to make dark accusations against each other of extortions and cruelties. Upon Clive Parliament passed a vote of censure. He committed suicide in 1774. In 1788 Warren Hastings, a second great Indian administrator, was impeached and acquitted (1792). It was a strange and unprecedented situation in the world's history. The English Parliament found itself ruling over a London trading company, which in its turn was dominating an empire far greater and more populous than all the domains of the British crown. To the bulk of the English people India was a remote, fantastic, almost inaccessible land, to which adventurous poor young men went out, to return after many years very rich and very choleric old gentlemen. It was difficult for the English to conceive what the life of these countless brown millions in the eastern sunshine could be. Their imaginations declined the task. India remained romantically unreal. It was impossible for the English, therefore, to exert any effective supervision and control over the company's proceedings.

§ 12

And while the great peninsula of the south of Asia was thus falling under the dominion of the English sea traders, an equally remarkable reaction of Europe upon Asia was going on in the north. We have told how the Christian states of Russia recovered their independence from the Golden Horde, and how the Tsar of Moscow became master of the republic of Novgorod; and in § 5 of this chapter we have told of Peter the Great joining the circle of Grand Monarchs and, as it were, dragging Russia into Europe. The rise of this great central power of the old world, which is neither altogether of the East nor altogether of the West, is one of the utmost importance to our human destiny. We have also told in the same chapter of the appearance of a Christian steppe people, the Cossacks, who formed a barrier between the feudal agriculture of Poland and Hungary to the west and the Tartar to the east. The Cossacks were the wild east of Europe, and in many ways not unlike the wild west of the United States in the middle nineteenth century. All who had made Russia too hot to hold them, criminals as well as the persecuted innocent, rebellious serfs, religious sectaries, thieves, vagabonds, murderers, sought asylum in the southern steppes and there made a fresh start and fought for life and freedom against Pole, Russian, and Tartar alike. Doubtless fugitives from the Tartars to the east also contributed to the Cossack mixture. Chief among these new nomad tribes were the Ukraine Cossacks on the Dnieper and the Don Cossacks on the Don. Slowly these border folks were incorporated in the Russian imperial service, much as the Highland clans of Scotland were converted into regiments by the British government. New lands were offered them in Asia. They became a weapon against the dwindling power of the Mongolian nomads, first in Turkestan and then across Siberia as far as the Amur.

The decay of Mongol energy in the seventeenth and eighteenth centuries is very difficult to explain. Within two or three centuries from the days of Jengis and Timurlane, central Asia had relapsed from a period of world ascendancy to extreme political impotence. Changes of climate, unrecorded pestilences, infections of a malarial type, may have played their part in this recession—which may be only a temporary recession measured by the scale of universal history—of the Central Asian peoples. Some authorities think that the spread of Buddhist teaching from China also had a pacifying influence upon them. At any rate, by the sixteenth century the Mongol Tartar and Turkish peoples were no longer pressing outward, but were being invaded, subjugated, and pushed back both by Christian Russia in the west and by China in the east.

All through the seventeenth century the Cossacks were spreading eastward from European Russia, and settling wherever they found agricultural conditions. Cordons of forts and stations formed a moving frontier to these settlements to the south, where the Turkomans were still strong and active; to the north-east, however, Russia had no frontier until she reached right to the Pacific. . . .

At the same time China was in a phase of expansion. The Manchu conquerors had brought a new energy into Chinese affairs, and their northern interests led to a considerable northward expansion of the Chinese civilization and influence into Manchuria and Mongolia. So it was that by the middle of the eighteenth century the Russians and Chinese were in contact in Mongolia. At this period China ruled eastern Turkestan, Tibet, Nepal, Burma, and Annam. . . .

The Manchu period in China was also one of considerable literary activity. Parallel with their European equivalents but quite independently, the Chinese novel and short story rose to high levels of style and interest, and there were important developments of the Chinese drama. Much fine landscape was painted, colour printing was invented, copper engraving learnt from the Jesuit missionaries, and the manufacture of Chinese porcelain was carried to unexampled heights. But as the eighteenth century wore on the æsthetic quality of this latter product declined through the readiness of the potters to adapt themselves to what they considered to be European taste. There was a steady exportation throughout all this century to the palaces, chateaux and country houses of the European nobility and gentry. European pottery imitated and competed with the Chinese product but never bettered it. The European tea trade also began.

We have mentioned a Japanese invasion of China (or rather of Korea). Except for this aggression upon China, Japan plays no part in our history before the nineteenth century. Like China under the Mings, Japan had set her face resolutely against the interference of foreigners in her affairs. She was a country leading her own civilized life, magically sealed against intruders. We have told little of her hitherto because there was little to tell. Her picturesque and romantic history stands apart from the general drama of human affairs. Her population was chiefly a Mongolian population, with some very interesting white people suggestive of a primitive Nordic type, the Hairy Ainu, in the northern islands. Her civilization seems to have been derived almost entirely from Korea and China; her art is a special development of Chinese art, her writing an adaptation of the Chinese script.

§ 13

In these preceding twelve sections we have been dealing with an age of division, of separated nationalities. We have already described this period of the seventeenth and eighteenth centuries as an interregnum in the progress of mankind towards a world-wide unity. Throughout this period there was no unifying idea in men's minds. The impulse of the Empire had failed until the Emperor was no more than one of a number of competing princes, and the dream of Christendom, also, was a fading dream. The developing "powers" jostled one another throughout the world; but for a time it seemed that they might jostle one another indefinitely without any great catastrophe to mankind. The great geographical discoveries of the sixteenth century had so enlarged human resources that, for all their divisions, for all the waste of their wars and policies, the people of Europe enjoyed a considerable and increasing prosperity. Central Europe recovered steadily from the devastation of the Thirty Years' War.

Looking back upon this period which came to its climax in the eighteenth century, looking back, as we can begin to do nowadays, and seeing its events in relation to the centuries that came before it and to the great movements of the present time, we are able to realize how transitory and provisional were its political forms and how unstable its securities. Provisional it was as no other age has been provisional, an age of assimilation and recuperation, a political pause, a gathering up of the ideas of men and the resources of science for a wider human effort. But the contemporary mind did not see it in that light. The failure of the great creative ideas as they had been formulated in the Middle Ages, had left human thought for a time destitute of the guidance of creative ideas; even educated and imaginative men saw the world undramatically; no longer as an interplay of effort and destiny but as a scene in which a trite happiness was sought and the milder virtues were rewarded. It was not simply the contented and conservative-minded who, in a world of rapid changes, were under the sway of this assurance of an achieved fixity of human conditions. Even highly critical and insurgent intelligences, in default of any sustaining movements in the soul of the community, betrayed the same disposition. Political life, they felt, had ceased to be the urgent and tragic thing it had once been; it had become a polite comedy. The eighteenth was a century of comedy—which at the end grew grim. It is inconceivable that that world of the middle eighteenth century could have produced a Jesus of Nazareth, a Gautama, a Francis of Assisi, an Ignatius of Loyola. If one may imagine an eighteenth-century John Huss, it is impossible to imagine anyone with sufficient passion to burn him. Until the stirrings of conscience in Britain that developed into the Methodist revival began, we can detect scarcely a suspicion that there still remained great tasks in hand for our race to do, that enormous disturbances were close at hand, or that the path of man through space and time was dark with countless dangers, and must to the end remain a high and terrible enterprise.

We have quoted again and again in this History from Gibbon's *Decline and Fall of the Roman Empire*. Now we shall quote from it for the last time and bid it farewell, for we have come to the age in which it was written. Gibbon was born in 1737, and the last volume of his history was published in 1787, but the passage we shall quote was probably written in the year 1780. Gibbon was a young man of delicate health and fairly good fortune; he had a partial and interrupted education at Oxford, and then he completed his studies in Geneva; on the whole his outlook was French and cosmopolitan rather than British, and he was much under the intellectual influence of that great Frenchman who is best known under the name of Voltaire (François Marie Arouet de Voltaire, 1694–1778). Voltaire was an author of enormous industry; seventy volumes of him adorn the present writer's shelves, and another edition of Voltaire's works runs to ninety-four; he dealt largely with history and public affairs, and he corresponded with Catherine the Great of Russia, Frederick the Great of Prussia, Louis XV, and most of the prominent people of the time. Both Voltaire and Gibbon had the sense of history strong in them; both have set out very plainly and fully their visions of human life; and it is clear that to both of them the system in which they lived, the system of monarchy, of leisurely and privileged gentlefolks, of rather despised industrial and trading people and of downtrodden and negligible labourers and poor and common people, seemed the most stably established way of living that the world has ever seen. They postured a little as republicans, and sneered at the divine pretensions of monarchy; but the republicanism that appealed to Voltaire was the crowned republicanism of the Britain of those days, in which the king was simply the official head, the first and greatest of the gentlemen.

The ideal they sustained was the ideal of a polite and polished world in which men—men of quality that is, for no others counted—would be ashamed to be cruel or gross or enthusiastic, in which the appointments of life would be spacious and elegant, and the fear of ridicule the potent auxiliary of the law in maintaining the decorum and harmonies of life. Voltaire had in him the possibility of a passionate hatred of injustice, and his interventions on behalf of a persecuted or ill-used men are the high lights of his long and complicated life-story. And this being the mental disposition of Gibbon and Voltaire, and of the age in which they lived, it is natural that they should find the existence of religion in the world, and in particular the existence of Christianity, a perplexing and rather unaccountable phenomenon. The whole of that side of life seemed to them a kind of craziness in the human make-up. Gibbon's great history is essentially an attack upon Christianity as the operating cause of the decline and fall. He idealized the crude and gross plutocracy of Rome into a world of fine gentlemen upon the eighteenth-century model, and told how it fell before the Barbarian from without because of the decay through Christianity within. In our history here we have tried to set that story in a better light. To Voltaire official Christianity was *"l'infâme"*; something that limited people's lives, interfered with their thoughts, persecuted harmless dissentients. And, indeed, in that period of the interregnum there was very little life or light in either the orthodox Christianity of Rome or in the orthodox tame churches of Russia and of the Protestant princes. In an interregnum incommoded with an abundance of sleek parsons and sly priests it was hard to realize what fires had once blazed in the heart of Christianity, and what fires of political and religious passion might still blaze in the hearts of men.

At the end of his third volume Gibbon completed his account of the breaking-up of the Western Empire. He then raised the question whether civilization might ever undergo again a similar collapse. This led him to review the existing state of affairs (1780) and to compare it with the state of affairs during the decline of imperial Rome. It will be very convenient to our general design to quote some passages from that comparison here, for nothing could better illustrate the state of mind of the liberal thinkers of Europe at the crest of the political interregnum of the age of the Great Powers before the first intimations of those profound political and social forces of disintegration that have produced at length the dramatic interrogations of our own times.

"This awful revolution," wrote Gibbon of the Western collapse, "may be usefully applied to the useful instruction of the present age. It is the duty of a patriot to prefer and promote the exclusive interest and glory of his native country; but a philosopher may be permitted to enlarge his views, and to consider Europe as one great republic, whose various inhabitants have attained almost the same level of politeness and cultivation. The balance of power will continue to fluctuate, and the prosperity of our own or the neighbouring kingdoms may be alternately exalted or depressed; but these partial events cannot essentially injure our general state of happiness, the system of arts, and laws and manners, which so advantageously distinguish, above the rest of mankind, the Europeans and their colonies. The savage nations of the globe are the common enemies of civilized society; and we may inquire with anxious curiosity whether Europe is still threatened with a repetition of those calamities which formerly oppressed the arms and institutions of Rome. Perhaps the same reflections will illustrate the fall of that mighty empire and explain the probable causes of our actual security.

"The Romans were ignorant of the extent of their danger, and the number of their enemies. Beyond the Rhine and Danube, the northern countries of Europe and Asia were filled with innumerable tribes of hunters and shepherds, poor, voracious, and turbulent; bold in arms, and impatient to ravish the fruits of industry. The Barbarian world was agitated by the rapid impulse of war; and the peace of Gaul or Italy was shaken by the distant revolutions of China. The Huns who fled before a victorious enemy, directed their march towards the west; and the torrent was swelled by the gradual accession of captives and allies. The flying tribes who yielded to the Huns assumed in *their* turn the spirit of conquest; the endless column of barbarians pressed on the Roman Empire with accumulated weight, and if the foremost were destroyed, the vacant space was instantly replenished by new assailants. Such formidable emigrations can no longer issue from the north; and the long repose, which has been imputed to the decrease of population, is the happy consequence of the progress of arts and agriculture. Instead of some rude villages, thinly scattered among its woods and morasses, Germany now produces a list of two thousand three hundred walled towns; the Christian kingdoms of Denmark, Sweden, and Poland have been successively established; and the Hansa merchants, with the Teutonic knights, have extended their colonies along the coast of the Baltic, as far as the Gulf of Finland. From the Gulf of Finland to the Eastern Ocean, Russia now assumes the form of a powerful and civilized empire. The plough, the loom, and the forge are introduced on the banks of the Volga, the Obi, and the Lena; and the fiercest of the Tartar hordes have been taught to tremble and obey. . . .

"The Empire of Rome was firmly established by the singular and perfect coalition of its members. . . . But this union was purchased by the loss of national freedom and military spirit; and the servile provinces, destitute of life and motion, expected their safety from the mercenary troops and governors, who were directed by the orders of a distant Court. The happiness of a hundred millions depended on the personal merit of one or two men, perhaps children, whose minds were corrupted by education, luxury, and despotic power. Europe is now divided into twelve powerful, though unequal kingdoms, three respectable commonwealths, and a variety of smaller, though independent, states; the chances of royal and ministerial talents are multiplied, at least with the number of its rulers; and a Julian[1] or Semiramis[2] may reign in the north, while Arcadius and Honorius[3] again slumber on the thrones of the House of Bourbon. The abuses of tyranny are restrained by the mutual influence of fear and shame; republics have acquired order and stability; monarchies have imbibed the principles of freedom, or, at least, of moderation; and some sense of honour and justice is introduced into the most defective constitutions by the general manners of the times. In peace, the progress of knowledge and industry is accelerated by the emulation of so many active rivals; in war, the European forces are exercised by temperate and undecisive contests. If a savage conqueror should issue from the deserts of Tartary, he must repeatedly vanquish the robust peasants of Russia, the numerous armies of Germany, the gallant nobles of France, and the intrepid freemen of Britain; who, perhaps, might confederate for their common defence. Should the victorious Barbarians carry slavery and desolation as far as the Atlantic Ocean, ten thousand vessels would transport beyond their pursuit the remains of civilized society; and Europe would revive and flourish in the American world which is already filled with her colonies and institutions.

"Cold, poverty, and a life of danger and fatigue fortify the strength and courage of Barbarians. In every age they have oppressed the polite and peaceful nations of China, India and Persia, who neglected, and still neglect to counterbalance these natural powers by the resources of military art. The warlike states of antiquity, Greece, Macedonia, and Rome, educated a race of soldiers; exercised their bodies, disciplined their courage, multiplied their forces by regular evolutions, and converted the iron which they possessed into strong and serviceable weapons. But this superiority insensibly declined with their laws and manners; and the feeble policy of Constantine and his successors armed and instructed, for the ruin of the empire, the rude valour of the Barbarian mercenaries. The military art has been changed by the invention of gunpowder; which enables man to command the two most powerful agents of nature, air and fire. Mathematics, chemistry, mechanics, architecture, have been applied to the service of war; and the adverse parties oppose to each other the most elaborate modes of attack and of defence. Historians may indignantly observe that the preparations of a siege would found and maintain a flourishing colony; yet we cannot be displeased that the subversion of a city

---

[1] Frederick the Great of Prussia.
[2] Catherine the Great of Russia.
[3] Louis XVI of France and Charles III of Spain.

should be a work of cost and difficulty, or that an industrious people should be protected by those arts, which survive and supply the decay of military virtue. Cannon and fortifications now form an impregnable barrier against the Tartar horse; and Europe is secure from any future irruption of Barbarians; since, before they can conquer, they must cease to be barbarous. . . .

"Should these speculations be found doubtful or fallacious, there still remains a more humble source of comfort and hope. The discoveries of ancient and modern navigators, and the domestic history, or tradition, of the most enlightened nations, represent the *human savage*, naked both in mind and body, and destitute of laws, of arts, of ideas, and almost of language. From this abject condition, perhaps the primitive and universal state of man, he has gradually risen to command the animals, to fertilize the earth, to traverse the ocean, and to measure the heavens. His progress in the improvement and exercise of his mental and corporeal faculties has been irregular and various, infinitely slow in the beginning, and increasing by degrees with redoubled velocity; ages of laborious ascent have been followed by a moment of rapid downfall; and the several climates of the globe have felt the vicissitudes of light and darkness. Yet the experience of four thousand years should enlarge our hopes, and diminish our apprehensions; we cannot determine to what height the human species may aspire in their advances towards perfection; but it may safely be presumed that no people, unless the face of nature is changed, will relapse into their original barbarism.

"Since the first discovery of the arts, war, commerce, and religious zeal have diffused among the savages of the Old and New World those inestimable gifts, they have been successively propagated; they can never be lost. We may therefore acquiesce in the pleasing conclusion that every age of the world has increased, and still increases, the real wealth, the happiness, the knowledge, and perhaps the virtue, of the human race."

§ 14

One of the most interesting aspects of this story of Europe in the seventeenth and earlier eighteenth century, during the phase of the Grand and Parliamentary Monarchies, is the comparative quiescence of the peasants and workers. The insurrectionary fires of the fourteenth and fifteenth and sixteenth centuries seem to have died down. The acute economic clashes of the earlier period had been mitigated by rough adjustments. The discovery of America had revolutionized and changed the scale of business and industry, had brought a vast volume of precious metal for money into Europe, had increased and varied employment. For a time life and work ceased to be intolerable to the masses of the poor. This did not, of course, prevent much individual misery and discontent; the poor we have always had with us, but this misery and discontent was divided and scattered. It became inaudible.

In the earlier period the common people had had an idea to crystallize upon, the idea of Christian communism. They had found an educated leadership in the dissentient priests and doctors of the Wycliffe type. As the movement for a revival in Christianity spent its force, as Lutheranism fell back for leadership from Jesus upon the Protestant Princes, this contact and reaction of the fresher minds of the educated class upon the illiterate mass was interrupted. However numerous a downtrodden class may be, and however extreme its miseries, it will never be able to make an effective protest until it achieves solidarity by the development of some common general idea. Educated men and women of ideas are more necessary to a popular political movement than to any other political process. A monarchy learns by ruling, and an oligarchy of any type has the education of affairs; but the common man, the peasant or toiler, has no experience in large matters, and can exist politically only through the services, devotion, and guidance of educated men. The Reformation, the Reformation that succeeded, the Reformation that is of the Princes, by breaking up educational facilities, largely destroyed the poor scholar and priest class whose persuasion of the crowd had rendered the Reformation possible.

The Princes of the Protestant countries when they seized upon the national churches early apprehended the necessity of gripping the universities also. Their idea of education was the idea of capturing young clever people for the service of their betters. Beyond that they were disposed to regard education as a mischievous thing. The only way to an education, therefore, for a poor man was through patronage. Of course, there was a parade of encouragement towards learning in all the Grand Monarchies, a setting up of Academies and Royal Societies, but these benefited only a small class of subservient scholars. The church also had learnt to distrust the educated poor man. In the great aristocratic "crowned republic" of Britain there was the same shrinkage of educational opportunity. "Both the ancient universities," says Hammond, in his account of the eighteenth century, "were the universities of the rich. There is a passage in Macaulay describing the state and pomp of Oxford at the end of the seventeenth century, 'when her Chancellor, the venerable Duke of Ormonde, sat in his embroidered mantle on his throne under the painted ceiling of the Sheldonian theatre, surrounded by hundreds of graduates robed according to their rank, while the noblest youths of England were solemnly presented to him as candidates for academical honours.' The university was a power, not in the sense in which that could be said of a university like the old university of Paris, whose learning could make Popes tremble, but in the sense that the university was part of the recognized machinery of aristocracy. What was true of the universities was true of the public schools. Education in England was the nursery not of a society, but of an order; not of a State, but of a race of owner-rulers." The missionary spirit had departed from education throughout Europe. To that, quite as much as to the amelioration of things by a diffused prosperity, this phase of quiescence among the lower classes is to be ascribed. They had lost brains and speech, and they were fed. The community was like a pithed animal in the hands of the governing class.

Moreover, there had been considerable changes in the proportions of class to class. One of the most difficult things for the historian to trace is the relative amount of the total property of the community held at any time by any particular class in that community. These things fluctuate very rapidly. The peasant wars of Europe indicate a phase of comparatively concentrated property when large masses of people could feel themselves expropriated and at a common disadvantage, and so take mass action. This was the time of the rise and prosperity of the Fuggers and their like, a time of international finance. Then with the vast importation of silver and gold and commodities into Europe from America, there seems to have been a restoration of a more diffused state of wealth. The poor were just as miserable as ever, but there were perhaps not so many poor relatively, and they were broken up into a variety of types without any ideas in common. In Great Britain the agricultural life which had been dislocated by the confiscations of the Reformation had settled down again into a system of tenant farming under great landowners. Side by side with the large estates there was still, however, much common land for pasturing the beasts of the poorer villagers, and much land cultivated in strips upon communal lines. The middling sort of man, and even the poorer sort of man upon the land, were leading an endurable existence in 1700. The standard of life, the idea, that is, of what is an endurable existence, was, however, rising during the opening phase of Grand Monarchy; after a time the process of the upward concentration of wealth seems to have been resumed, the large landowners began to acquire and crowd out the poorer free cultivators, and the proportion of poor people and of people who felt they were leading impoverished lives increased again. The bigger men were unchallenged rulers of Great Britain, and they set themselves to enact laws, the Enclosure Acts, that practically confiscated the unenclosed and common lands, mainly for the benefit of the larger landowners. The smaller men sank to the level of wage workers upon the land over which they had once possessed right of cultivation and pasture.

The peasant in France and upon the Continent generally was not so expropriated; his enemy was not the landlord, but the tax-gatherer; he was squeezed on his land instead of being squeezed off it.

As the eighteenth century progressed, it is apparent in the literature of the time that what to do with "the poor" was again exercising men's thoughts. We find such active-minded English writers as Defoe (1659–1731) and Fielding (1707–54) deeply exercised by this problem. But as yet there is no such revival of the communistic and equalitarian ideas of primitive Christianity as distinguished the time of Wycliffe and John Huss. Protestantism in breaking up the universal church had for a time broken up the idea of a universal solidarity. Even if the universal church of the Middle Ages had failed altogether to realize that idea, it had at any rate been the symbol of that idea.

Defoe and Fielding were men of a livelier practical imagination than Gibbon, and they realized something of the economic processes that were afoot in their time. So did Oliver Goldsmith (1728–74); his *Deserted Village* (1770) is a pamphlet on enclosures disguised as a poem. But Gibbon's circumstances had never brought economic facts very vividly before his eyes; he saw the world as a struggle between barbarism and civilization, but he perceived nothing of that other struggle over which he floated, the mute, unconscious struggle of the commonalty against able, powerful, rich, and selfish men. He did not perceive the accumulation of stresses that were presently to strain and break up all the balance of his "twelve powerful, though unequal, kingdoms," his "three respectable commonwealths," and their rag, tag, and bobtail of independent minor princes, reigning dukes, and so forth. Even the civil war that had begun in the British colonies in America did not arouse him to the nearness of what we now call "Democracy."

From what we have been saying hitherto, the reader may suppose that the squeezing of the small farmer and the peasant off the land by the great land-owners, the mere grabbing of commons and the concentration of property in the hands of a powerful privileged and greedy class, was all that was happening to the English land in the eighteenth century. So we do but state the worse side of the change. Concurrently with this change of ownership there was going on a great improvement in agriculture. There can be little doubt that the methods of cultivation pursued by the peasants, squatters, and small farmers were antiquated, wasteful, and comparatively unproductive, and that the larger private holdings and estates created by the Enclosure Acts were much more productive (one authority says twenty times more productive) than the old ways. The change was perhaps a necessary one, and the evil of it was not that it was brought about, but that it was brought about so as to increase both wealth and the numbers of the poor. Its benefits were intercepted by the bigger private owners. The community was injured to the great profit of this class.

And here we come upon one of the chief problems of our lives at the present time, the problem of the deflection of the profits of progress. For two hundred years there has been, mainly under the influence of the spirit of science and inquiry, a steady improvement in the methods of production of almost everything that humanity requires. If our sense of community and our social science were equal to the tasks required of them, there can be little question that this great increment in production would have benefited the whole community, would have given everyone an amount of education, leisure, and freedom such as mankind had never dreamt of before. But though the common standard of living has risen, the rise has been on a scale disproportionately small. The rich have developed a freedom and luxury unknown in the world hitherto, and there has been an increase in the proportion of rich people and stagnantly prosperous and unproductive people in the community; but that also fails to account for the full benefit. There has been much sheer waste. Vast accumulations of material and energy have gone into warlike preparations and warfare. Much has been devoted to the futile efforts of unsuccessful business competition. Huge possibilities have remained undeveloped because of the opposition of owners, forestallers, and speculators to their economical exploitation. The good things that science and organization have been bringing within the reach of mankind have not been taken methodically and used to their utmost, but they have been scrambled for, snatched at, seized upon by gambling adventurers and employed upon selfish and vain ends. The eighteenth century in Europe, and more particularly in Great Britain and Poland, was the age of private ownership. "Private enterprise," which meant in practice that everyone was entitled to get everything he could out of the business of the community, reigned supreme. No sense of obligation to the state in business matters is to be found in the ordinary novels, plays, and such-like representative literature of the time. Everyone is out "to make his fortune," there is no recognition that it is wrong to be an unproductive parasite on the community, and still less that a financier or merchant or manufacturer can ever be overpaid for his services to mankind. This was the moral atmosphere of the time, and those lords and gentlemen who grabbed the people's commons, assumed possession of the mines under their lands, and crushed down the yeoman farmers and peasants to the status of pauper labourers, had no idea that they were living anything but highly meritorious lives.

Concurrently with this change in Great Britain from traditional patch agriculture and common pasture to large and more scientific agriculture, very great changes were going on in the manufacture of commodities. In these changes Great Britain was, in the eighteenth century, leading the world. Hitherto, throughout the whole course of history from the beginnings of civilization, manufactures, building, and industries generally had been in the hands of craftsmen and small masters who worked in their own houses. They had been organized in guilds, and were mostly their own employers. They formed an essential and permanent middle class. There were capitalists among them, who let out looms and the like, supplied material, and took the finished product, but they were not big capitalists. There had been no rich manufacturers. The rich men of the world before this time had been great landowners or money-lenders and money manipulators or merchants. But in the eighteenth century, workers in certain industries began to be collected together into factories in order to produce things in larger quantities through a systematic division of labour, and the employer, as distinguished from the master worker, began to be a person of importance. Moreover, mechanical invention was producing machines that simplified the manual work of production, and were capable of being driven by water-power and presently by steam. In 1765 Watt's steam engine was constructed, a very important date in the history of industrialism.

The cotton industry was one of the first to pass into factory production (originally with water-driven machinery). The woolen industry followed. At the same time iron smelting, which had been restrained hitherto to small methods by the use of charcoal, resorted to coke made from coal, and the coal and iron industries also began to expand. The iron industry shifted from the wooded country of Sussex and Surrey to the coal districts. By 1800 this change-over of industry from a small scale business with small employers to a large scale production under big employers was well in progress. Everywhere there sprang up factories using first water, then steam power. It was a change of fundamental importance in human economy. From the dawn of history the manufacturer and craftsman had been, as we have said, a sort of middle-class townsman.

The machine and the employer now superseded his skill, and he either became an employer of his fellows, and grew towards wealth and equality with the other rich classes, or he remained a worker and sank very rapidly to the level of a mere labourer. This great change in human affairs is known as the Industrial Revolution. Beginning in Great Britain, it spread during the nineteenth century throughout the world.

As the Industrial Revolution went on, a great gulf opened between employer and employed. In the past every manufacturing worker had the hope of becoming an independent master. Even the slave craftsmen of Babylon and Rome were protected by laws that enabled them to save and buy their freedom and to set up for themselves. But now a factory and its engines and machines became a vast and costly thing measured by the scale of the worker's pocket. Wealthy men had to come together to create an enterprise; credit and plant, that is to say, "Capital," were required. "Setting up for oneself" ceased to be a normal hope for an artisan. The worker was henceforth a worker from the cradle to the grave. Besides the landlords and merchants and the money dealers who financed trading companies and lent their money to the merchants and the State, there arose now this new wealth of industrial capital—a new sort of power in the State.

Of the working out of these beginnings we shall tell later. The immediate effect of the Industrial Revolution upon the countries to which it came, was to cause a vast, distressful shifting and stirring of the mute, uneducated, leaderless, and now more and more propertyless common population. The small cultivators and peasants, ruined and dislodged by the Enclosure Acts, drifted towards the new manufacturing regions, and there they joined the families of the impoverished and degraded craftsmen in the factories. Great towns of squalid houses came into existence. Nobody seems to have noted clearly what was going on at the time. It is the keynote of "private enterprise" to mind one's own business, secure the utmost profit and disregard any other consequences. Ugly factories grew up, built as cheaply as possible, to hold as many machines and workers as possible. Around them gathered the streets of workers' homes, built at the cheapest rate, without space, without privacy, barely decent, and let at the utmost rent that could be exacted. These new industrial centres were at first without schools, without churches. . . . The English gentleman of the closing decades of the eighteenth century read Gibbon's third volume and congratulated himself that there was henceforth no serious fear of the Barbarians, with this new barbarism growing up, with this metamorphosis of his countrymen into something dark and desperate, in full progress, within an easy walk, perhaps, of his door.

XXXV

THE NEW DEMOCRATIC REPUBLICS OF
AMERICA AND FRANCE

§ 1. *Inconveniences of the Great Power System.* § 2. *The Thirteen Colonies before their Revolt.* § 3. *Civil War is Forced upon the Colonies.* § 4. *The War of Independence.* § 5. *The Constitution of the United States.* § 6. *Primitive Features of the United States Constitution.* § 7. *Revolutionary Ideas in France.* § 8. *The Revolution of the Year* 1789. § 9. *The French "Crowned Republic" of* '89–'91. § 10. *The Revolution of the Jacobins.* § 11. *The Jacobin Republic,* 1792–94. § 12. *The Directory.* § 13. *The Pause in Reconstruction, and the Dawn of Modern Socialism.*

§ 1

WHEN Gibbon, nearly a century and a half ago, was congratulating the world of refined and educated people that the age of great political and social catastrophies was past, he was neglecting many signs which we—in the wisdom of accomplished facts—could have told him portended far heavier jolts and dislocations than any he foresaw. We have told how the struggles of the sixteenth- and seventeenth-century princes for ascendancies and advantages developed into a more cunning and complicated struggle of foreign offices, masquerading as idealized "Great Powers," as the eighteenth century wore on. The intricate and pretentious art of diplomacy developed. The "Prince" ceased to be a single and secretive Machiavellian schemer, and became merely the crowned symbol of a Machiavellian scheme. Prussia, Russia, and Austria fell upon and divided Poland. France was baffled in profound schemes against Spain. Britain circumvented the "designs of France" and America and acquired Canada, and got the better of France in India. And then a remarkable thing occurred, a thing very shocking to European diplomacy. The British Colonies in America flatly refused to have any further part or lot in this game of "Great Powers." They objected that they had no voice and no great interest in these European schemes and conflicts, and they refused to bear any portion of the burthen of taxation these foreign policies entailed. "Taxation without representation is tyranny"—this was their dominant idea.

Of course, this decision to separate did not flash out complete and finished from the American mind at the beginning of these troubles. In America in the eighteenth century, just as in England in the seventeenth, there was an entire willingness, indeed a desire on the part of ordinary men, to leave foreign affairs in the hands of the king and his ministers. But there was an equally strong desire on the part of ordinary men to be neither taxed nor interfered with in their ordinary pursuits. These are incompatible wishes. Common men cannot shirk world-politics and at the same time enjoy private freedom; but it has taken them countless generations to learn this. The first impulse in the American revolt against the government in Great Britain was, therefore, simply a resentment against the taxation and interference that followed necessarily from "foreign policy," without any clear recognition of what was involved in that objection. It was only when the revolt was consummated that the people of the American colonies recognized at all clearly that they had repudiated the Great Power view of life. The sentence in which that repudiation was expressed was Washington's injunction to "avoid entangling alliances." For a full century the united colonies of Great Britain in North America, liberated and independent as the United States of America, stood apart altogether from the blood-stained intrigues and conflicts of the European foreign offices. Soon after (1801 to 1823) they were able to extend their principle of detachment to the rest of the continent, and to make all the New World "out of bounds" for the scheming expansionists of the old. When at length, in 1917, they were obliged to re-enter the arena of world politics, it was to bring into the tangle of international relationships the new spirit and new aims their aloofness had enabled them to develop. They were not, however, the first to stand aloof. Since the Treaty of Westphalia (1648) the confederated states of Switzerland, in their mountain fastnesses, had sustained their right to exclusion from the schemes of kings and empires.

But since the North American peoples are now to play an increasingly important part in our history, it will be well to devote a little more attention than we have hitherto given to their development. We have already glanced at this story in § 10 of the preceding chapter. We will now tell a little more fully—though still in the barest outline—what these colonies were, whose recalcitrance was so disconcerting to the king and ministers of Great Britain in their diplomatic game against the rest of mankind.

§ 2

The extent of the British colonies in America in the early half of the eighteenth century is shown in the accompanying map. The darker shading represents the districts settled in 1700, the lighter the growth of the settlements up to 1760. It will be seen that the colonies were a mere fringe of population along the coast, spreading gradually inland and finding in the Alleghany and Blue Mountains a very serious barrier. Among the oldest of these settlements was the colony of Virginia, the name of which commemorates Queen Elizabeth, the Virgin Queen of England. The first expedition to found a colony in Virginia was made by Sir Walter Raleigh in 1584, but there was no permanent settlement at that time, and the real beginnings of Virginia date from the foundation of the Virginia Company in 1606, in the reign of James I (1603–1625). The story of John Smith and the early founders of Virginia, and of how the Indian "princess" Pocahontas married one of his gentlemen, is an English classic.[1] In growing tobacco the Virginians found the beginning of

---

[1] *John Smith's Travels.*

prosperity. At the same time that the Virginia Company was founded, the Plymouth Company obtained a charter for the settlement of the country to the north of Long Island Sound, to which the English laid claim. But it was only in 1620 that the northern region began to be settled, and that under fresh charters. The settlers of the northern region (New England), which became Connecticut, New Hampshire, Rhode Island, and Massachusetts, were men

The AMERICAN Colonies, showing territories settled up to 1760

British settlements to 1700
ditto to 1760
● French settlements
★ " forts
N.H.= NEW HAMPSHIRE
M. = MASSACHUSETTS
C. = CONNECTICUT.
R.I.= RHODE IS.
N.J.= NEW JERSEY
M?= MARYLAND
D. = DELAWARE

of a different stamp to the Virginian people; they were Protestants discontented with the Anglican Church compromise, and republican-spirited men hopeless of resistance to the Grand Monarchy of James I and Charles I. Their pioneer ship was the *Mayflower,* which founded New Plymouth in 1620. The dominant northern colony was Massachusetts. Differences in religious methods and in ideas of toleration led to the separation of the three other Puritan colonies from Massachusetts. It illustrates the scale upon which things were done in those days that the whole state of New Hampshire was claimed as belonging to a certain Captain John Mason, and that he offered to sell it to the king (King Charles II, in 1671) in exchange for the right to import 300 tons of French wine free of duty—an offer which was refused. The present state of Maine was bought by Massachusetts from its alleged owner for twelve hundred and fifty pounds.

In the Civil War that ended with the decapitation of Charles I the sympathies of New England were for the Parliament, and Virginia was Cavalier; but two hundred and fifty miles separated these settlements, and there were no serious hostilities. With the return of the monarchy in 1660, there was a vigorous development of British colonization in America. Charles II and his associates were greedy for gain, and the British crown had no wish to make any further experiments in illegal taxation at home. But the undefined relations of the colonies to the crown and the British government seemed to afford promise of financial adventure across the Atlantic. There was a rapid development of plantations and proprietary colonies. Lord Baltimore had already in 1632 set up a colony that was to be a home of religious freedom for Catholics under the attractive name of Maryland, to the north and east of Virginia; and now the Quaker Penn (whose father had rendered valuable service to Charles II) established himself to the north of Philadelphia and founded the colony of Pennsylvania. Its main boundary with Maryland and Virginia was delimited by two men, Mason and Dixon, whose "Mason and Dixon's line" was destined to become a very important line indeed in the later affairs of the United States. Carolina, which was originally an unsuccessful French Protestant establishment and which owed its name not to Charles (Carolus) II of England, but to Charles IX of France, had fallen into English hands and was settled at several points. Between Maryland and New England stretched a number of small Dutch and Swedish settlements, of which the chief town was New Amsterdam. These settlements were captured from the Dutch by the British in 1664, lost again in 1673, and restored by treaty when Holland and England made peace in 1674. Thereby the whole coast from Maine to Carolina became in some form or other a British possession. To the south the Spanish were established; their headquarters were at Fort St. Augustine in Florida, and in 1733 the town of Savannah was settled by a philanthropist Oglethorpe from England, who had taken pity on the miserable people imprisoned for debt in England, and rescued a number of them from prison to become the founders of a new colony, Georgia, which was to be a bulwark against the Spanish. So by the middle of the eighteenth century we have these settlements along the American coastline: the New England group of Puritans and free Protestants—Maine (belonging to Massachusetts), New Hampshire, Connecticut, Rhode Island, and Massachusetts; the captured Dutch group, which was now, divided up into New York (New Amsterdam rechristened), New Jersey, and Delaware (Swedish before it was Dutch, and in its earliest British phase attached to Pennsylvania); then came Catholic Maryland; Cavalier Virginia; Carolina (which was presently divided into North and South) and Oglethorpe's Georgia. Later on, a number of Tyrolese Protestants took refuge in Georgia, and there was a considerable immigration of a good class of German cultivators into Pennsylvania.

Such were the miscellaneous origins of the citizens of the Thirteen Colonies. The possibility of their ever becoming closely united would have struck an impartial observer in 1760 as being very slight. Superadded to the initial differences of origin, fresh differences were created by climate. North of the Mason and Dixon line, farming was practised mainly upon British or Central European lines by free white cultivators. The settled country of New England took on a likeness to the English countryside; considerable areas of Pennsylvania developed fields and farmhouses like those of South Germany. The distinctive conditions in the north had, socially, important effects. Masters and men had to labour together as backwoodsmen, and were equalized in the process. They did not start equally; many "servants" are mentioned in the roster of the *Mayflower*. But they rapidly became equal under colonial conditions; there was, for instance, a vast tract of land to be had for the taking, and the "servant" went off and took land like his master. The English class system disappeared. Under colonial conditions there arose equality "in the faculties both of body and mind," and an individual independence of judgment impatient of interference from England. But south of the Mason and Dixon line tobacco-growing began, and the warmer climate encouraged the establishment of plantations with gang labour. Red Indian captives were tried but found to be too homicidal; Cromwell sent Irish prisoners of war to Virginia, which did much to reconcile the Royalist planters to republicanism; convicts were sent out, and there was a considerable trade in kidnapped children, who were "spirited away" to America to become apprentices or bond slaves. But the most convenient form of gang labour proved to be that of negro slaves. The first negro slaves were brought to Jamestown in Virginia by a Dutch ship as early as 1620. By 1700 negro slaves were scattered all over the states, but Virginia, Maryland, and the Carolinas were their chief regions of employment, and while the communities to the north were communities of not very rich and not very poor farming men, the south developed a type of large proprietor and a white community of overseers and professional men subsisting on slave labour. Slave labour was a necessity to the social and economic system that had grown up in the south; in the north the presence of slaves was unnecessary and in some respects inconvenient. Conscientious scruples about slavery were more free, therefore, to develop and flourish in the northern atmosphere. To this question of the revival of slavery in the world we must return when we come to consider the perplexities of American Democracy. Here we note it simply as an added factor in the heterogeneous mixture of the British Colonies.

But if the inhabitants of the Thirteen Colonies were miscellaneous in their origins and various in their habits and sympathies, they had three very strong antagonisms in common. They had a common interest against the Red Indians. For a time they shared a common dread of French conquest and dominion. And thirdly, they were all in conflict with the claims of the British crown and the commercial selfishness of the narrow oligarchy who dominated the British Parliament and British affairs.

So far as the first danger went, the Indians were a constant evil but never more than a threat of disaster. They remained divided against themselves. Yet they had shown possibilities of combination upon a larger scale. The five nations of the Iroquois (see map of 1760 colonies) were a very important league of tribes. But it never succeeded in playing off the French against the English to secure itself, and no Red Indian Jengis Khan ever arose among these nomads of the New World. The French aggression was a more serious threat. The French never made settlements in America on a scale to compete with the English, but their government set about the encirclement of the colonies and their subjugation in a terrifying systematic manner. The English in America were colonists; the French were explorers, adventurers, agents, missionaries, merchants, and soldiers. Only in Canada did they strike root. French statesmen sat over maps and dreamt dreams, and their dreams are to be seen in our map, in the chain of forts creeping southward from the Great Lakes and northward up the Mississippi and Ohio rivers. The struggle of France and Britain was a world-wide struggle. It was decided in India, in Germany, and on the high seas. In the Peace of Paris (1763) the French gave England Canada, and relinquished Louisiana to the inert hands of declining Spain. It was the complete abandonment of America by France. The lifting of the French danger left the colonists unencumbered to face their third common antagonist —the crown and government of their motherland.

§ 3

We have noted in the previous chapter how the governing class of Great Britain steadily acquired the land and destroyed the liberty of the common people throughout the eighteenth century, and how greedily and blindly the new industrial revolution was brought about. We have noted also how the British Parliament, through the decay of the representative methods of the House of Commons, had become both in its upper and lower houses merely the instrument of government through the big landowners. Both these big property-holders and the crown were deeply interested in America—the former as private adventurers, the latter partly as representing the speculative exploitations of the Stuart kings, and partly as representing the State in search of funds for the expenses of foreign policy; and neither lords nor crown were disposed to regard the traders, planters, and common people of the colonies with any more consideration than they did the yeomen and small cultivators at home. At bottom the interests of the common man in Great Britain, Ireland, and America were the same. Each was being squeezed by the same system. But while in Britain oppressor and oppressed were closely tangled up in one intimate social system, in America the crown and the exploiter were far away, and men could get together and develop a sense of community against their common enemy.

Moreover, the American colonist had the important advantage of possessing a separate and legal organ of resistance to the British government in the assembly or legislature of his colony that was necessary for the management of local affairs. The common man in Britain, cheated out of his proper representation in the Commons, had no organ, no centre of expression and action for his discontents.

It will be evident to the reader, bearing in mind the variety of the colonies, that here was the possibility of an endless series of disputes, aggressions and counter-aggressions. The story of the development of irritations between the colonies and Britain is a story far too intricate, subtle, and lengthy for the scheme of this *Outline*. Suffice it that the grievances fell under three main heads: attempts to secure for British adventurers or the British Government the profits of the exploitation of new lands; systematic restrictions upon trade designed to keep the foreign trade of the colonies entirely in British hands, so that the colonial exports all went through Britain and only British-made goods were used in America; and finally, attempts at taxation through the British Parliament as the supreme taxing authority of the empire. Under the pressure of this triple system of annoyances the American colonists were forced to do a very considerable amount of hard political thinking. Such men as Patrick Henry and James Otis began to discuss the fundamental ideas of government and political association very much as they had been discussed in England in the great days of Cromwell's Commonwealth. They began to deny both the divine origin of kingship and the supremacy of the British Parliament, and (James Otis, 1762) to say such things as—

"God made all men naturally equal.

"Ideas of earthly superiority are educational, not innate.

"Kings were made for the good of the people, and not the people for them.

"No government has a right to make slaves of its subjects.

"Though most governments are *de facto* arbitrary, and consequently the curse and scandal of human nature, yet none are *de jure* arbitrary."

Some of which propositions reach far.

This ferment in the political ideas of the Americans was started by English leaven. One very influential English writer was John Locke (1632–1704), whose *Two Treatises on Civil Government* may be taken, as much as one single book can be taken in such cases, as the point of departure for modern democratic ideas. He was the son of a Cromwellian soldier, he was educated at Christ Church, Oxford, during the republican ascendancy, he spent some years in Holland in exile, and his writings form a bridge between the bold political thinking of those earlier republican days and the revolutionary movement both in America and France.

But men do not begin to act upon theories. It is always some real danger, some practical necessity, that produces action; and it is only after action has destroyed old relationships and produced a new and perplexing state of affairs that theory comes to its own. Then it is that theory is put to the test. The discord in interests and ideas between the colonists was brought to a fighting issue by the obstinate resolve of the British Parliament after the peace of 1763 to impose taxation upon the American colonies. Britain was at peace and flushed with successes; it seemed an admirable opportunity for settling accounts with these recalcitrant settlers. But the great British property-owners found a power beside their own, of much the same mind with them, but a little divergent in its ends—the reviving crown. King George III, who had begun his reign in 1760, was resolved to be much more of a king than his two German predecessors. He could speak English; he claimed to "glory in the name of Briton"—and, indeed, it is not a bad name for a man with scarcely a trace of English, Welsh, or Scotch blood in his veins. In the American colonies and the overseas possessions generally, with their indefinite charters or no charters at all, it seemed to him that the crown might claim authority and obtain resources and powers absolutely denied to it by the strong and jealous aristocracy in Britain. This inclined many of the Whig noblemen to a sympathy with the colonists that they might not otherwise have shown. They had no objection to the exploitation of the colonies in the interests of British "private enterprise," but they had very strong objections to the strengthening of the crown by that exploitation so as to make it presently independent of themselves.

The war that broke out was, therefore, in reality not a war between Britain and the colonists, it was a war between the British government and the colonists, with a body of Whig noblemen and a considerable amount of public feeling in England on the side of the latter. An early move after 1763 was an attempt to raise revenue for Britain in the colonies by requiring that newspapers and documents of various sorts should be stamped. This was stiffly resisted, the British crown was intimidated, and the Stamp Acts were repealed (1766). Their repeal was greeted by riotous rejoicings in London, more hearty even than those in the colonies.

But the Stamp Act affair was only one eddy in a turbulent stream flowing towards civil war. Upon a score of pretexts, and up and down the coast, the representatives of the British government were busy asserting their authority and making British government intolerable. The quartering of soldiers upon the colonists was a great nuisance. Rhode Island was particularly active in defying the trade restrictions. The Rhode Islanders were "free traders"—that is to say, smugglers; a government schooner, the *Gaspee*, ran aground off Providence; she was surprised, boarded, and captured by armed men in boats, and burnt. In 1773, with a total disregard of the existing colonial tea trade, special advantages for the importation of tea into America were given by the British Parliament to the East India Company. It was resolved by the colonists to refuse and boycott this tea. When the tea importers at Boston showed themselves resolute to land their cargoes, a band of men disguised as Indians, in the presence of a great crowd of people, boarded the three tea ships and threw the tea overboard (December 16th, 1773).

All 1774 was occupied in the gathering up of resources on either side for the coming conflict. It was decided by the British Parliament in the spring of 1774 to punish Boston by closing her port. Her trade was to be destroyed unless she accepted that tea. It was a quite typical instance of that silly "firmness" which shatters empires. In order to enforce this measure, British troops were concentrated at Boston under General Gage. The colonists took counter-measures. The first colonial congress met at Philadelphia in September, at which twelve colonies were represented: Massachusetts, Connecticut, New Hampshire, Rhode Island, New York, New Jersey, Pennsylvania, Maryland, Delaware, Virginia, and North and South Carolina. Georgia was not present. True to the best English traditions, the congress documented its attitude by a "Declaration of Rights." Practically this congress was an insurrectionary government, but no blow was struck until the spring of 1775. Then came the first shedding of blood.

Two of the American leaders, Hancock and Samuel Adams, had been marked down by the British government for arrest and trial for treason; they were known to be at Lexington, about eleven miles from Boston; and in the night of April 8th, 1775, Gage set his forces in motion for their arrest.

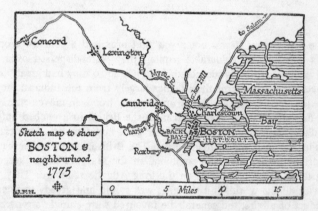

Sketch map to show BOSTON & neighbourhood 1775

That night was a momentous one in history. The movement of Gage's troops had been observed, signal lanterns were shown from a church tower in Boston, and two men, Dawes and Paul Revere, stole away in boats across the Back Bay to take horse and warn the country-side. The British were also ferried over the water, and as they marched through the night towards Lexington the firing of signal cannon and the ringing of church bells went before them. As they entered Lexington at dawn, they saw a little company of men drawn up in military fashion. It seems that the British fired first. There was a single shot and then a volley, and the little handful decamped, apparently without any answering shots, leaving eight dead and nine wounded upon the village green.

The British then marched on to Concord, ten miles further, occupied the village, and stationed a party on the bridge at that place. The expedition had failed in its purpose of arresting Hancock and Adams, and the British commander seems to have been at a loss what to do next. Meanwhile the colonial levies were coming up from all directions, and presently the picket upon the bridge found itself subjected to an increasing fire and finally to an assault.

A retreat to Boston was decided upon. It was a disastrous retreat. The country had risen behind; all the morning the colonials had been gathering. Both sides of the road were now swarming with sharpshooters firing from behind rock and fence and building, while occasionally they pressed up to bayonet distance. The soldiers were in conspicuous scarlet uniforms, with yellow facings and white gaiters and cravats; these must have stood out very vividly against the cold sharp colours of the late New England spring; the day was bright, hot, and dusty, and the men were already exhausted by a night march. Every few yards a man fell, wounded or killed. The rest tramped on, or halted to fire an ineffectual volley. At Lexington there were British reinforcements and two guns, and after a brief rest the retreat was resumed in better order. But the pursuit was pressed to the river, and after the British had crossed back into Boston, the colonial levies took up their quarters in Cambridge and prepared to blockade the city.

§ 4

So the war began. It was not a war that promised a conclusive end. The colonists had no one vulnerable capital; they were dispersed over a great country with a limitless wilderness behind it, and so they had great powers of resistance. They had learnt their tactics largely from the Indians; they could fight well in open order, and harry and destroy troops in movement. But they had no disciplined army that could meet the British in a pitched battle, and little military equipment; and their levies grew impatient at a long campaign, and tended to go home to their farms. The British, on the other hand, had a well-drilled army, and their command of the sea gave them the power of shifting their attack up and down the long Atlantic seaboard. They were at peace with all the world. But the king was stupid and greedy to interfere in the conduct of affairs; the generals he favoured were stupid "strong men" or flighty men of birth and fashion, and the heart of England was not in the business. He trusted rather to being able to blockade, raid and annoy the colonists into submission than to a conclusive conquest and occupation of the land. But the methods employed, and particularly the use of hired German troops, who still retained the cruel traditions of the Thirty Years' War, and of Indian auxiliaries, who harried the outlying settlers, did not so much weary the Americans of the war as of the British. The Congress, meeting for the second time in 1775, endorsed the actions of the New England colonists, and appointed George Washington the American commander-in-chief. In 1777 General Burgoyne, in an attempt to get down to New York from Canada, was defeated at Freeman's Farm on the Upper Hudson, and surrounded and obliged to capitulate at Saratoga with his whole army. This disaster encouraged the French and Spanish to come into the struggle on the side of the colonists. The French fleet did much to minimize the advantage of the British at sea. General Cornwallis was caught in the Yorktown peninsula in Virginia in 1781, and capitulated with his army. The British government, now heavily engaged with France and Spain in Europe, was at the end of its resources.

At the outset of the war the colonists in general seem to have been as little disposed to repudiate monarchy and claim complete independence as were the Hollanders in the opening phase of Philip II's persecutions and follies. The separatists were called radicals; they were mostly extremely democratic, as we should say in England to-day, and their advanced views frightened many of the steadier and wealthier colonists, for whom class privileges and distinctions had considerable charm. But early in 1776, an able and persuasive Englishman, Thomas Paine, published a pamphlet at Philadelphia with the title of *Common Sense,* which had an enormous effect on public opinion. Its style was rhetorical by modern standards. "The blood of the slain, the weeping voice of nature cries, ' 'Tis time to part,' " and so forth. But its effects were very great. It converted thousands to the necessity of separation. The turn-over of opinion, once it had begun, was rapid.

Only in the summer of 1776 did Congress take the irrevocable step of declaring for separation. "The Declaration of Independence," another of those exemplary documents which it has been the peculiar service of the English to produce for mankind, was drawn up by Thomas Jefferson; and after various amendments and modifications it was made the fundamental document of the United States of America. There were two noteworthy amendments to Jefferson's draft. He had denounced the slave trade fiercely, and blamed the home government for interfering with colonial attempts to end it. This was thrown out, and so, too, was a sentence about the British: "we must endeavour to forget our former love for them . . . we might have been a free and a great people together."

Towards the end of 1782 the preliminary articles of the treaty in which Britain recognized the complete independence of the United States were signed at Paris. The end of the war was proclaimed in April 19th, 1783, exactly eight years after Paul Revere's ride and the retreat of Gage's men from Concord to Boston. The Treaty of Peace was finally signed at Paris in September.

§ 5

From the point of view of human history, the way in which the Thirteen States became independent is of far less importance than the fact that they did become independent. And with the establishment of their independence came a new sort of community into the world. It was like something coming out of an egg. It was a Western European civilization that had broken free from the last traces of Empire and Christendom; and it had not a vestige of monarchy left and no State religion. It had no dukes, princes, counts, nor any sort of title-bearers claiming to ascendancy or respect as a right. Even its unity was as yet a mere unity for defence and freedom. It was in these respects such a clean start in political organization as the world had not seen before. The absence of any binding religious tie is especially noteworthy. It had a number of forms of Christianity, its spirit was indubitably Christian; but, as a State document of 1796 explicitly declared, "The government of the United

States is not in any sense founded on the Christian religion."[1] The new community had, in fact, gone right down to the bare and stripped fundamentals of human association, and it was building up a new sort of society and a new sort of state upon those foundations.

Here were about four million people scattered over a vast area with very slow and difficult means of intercommunication, poor as yet, but with the potentiality of limitless wealth, setting out to do in reality on a huge scale such a feat of construction as the Athenian philosophers twenty-two centuries before had done in imagination and theory.

This situation marks a definite stage in the release of man from precedent and usage, and a definite step forward towards the conscious and deliberate reconstruction of his circumstances to suit his needs and aims. It was a new method becoming practical in human affairs. The modern states of Europe have been evolved, institution by institution, slowly and planlessly out of preceding things. The United States were planned and made.

In one respect, however, the creative freedom of the new nation was very seriously restricted. This new sort of community and state was not built upon a cleared site. It was not even so frankly an artificiality as some of the later Athenian colonies which went out from the mother-city to plan and build brand-new city states with brand-new constitutions. The thirteen colonies by the end of the war had all of them constitutions either, like that of Connecticut and Rhode Island, dating from their original charters (1662) or, as in the case of the rest of the states, where a British governor had played a large part in the administration, re-made during the conflict. But we may well consider these reconstructions as contributory essays and experiments in the general constructive effort.

Upon the effort certain ideas stood out very prominently. One is the idea of political and social equality. This idea, which we saw coming into the world as an extreme and almost incredible idea in the age between Buddha and Jesus of Nazareth, is now asserted in the later eighteenth century as a practical standard of human relationship. Says the fundamental statement of Virginia: "All men are by nature equally free and independent," and it proceeds to rehearse their "rights," and to assert that all magistrates and governors are but "trustees and servants" of the commonweal. All men are equally entitled to the free exercise of religion. The king by right, the aristocrat, the "natural slave," the god-king, and the god have all vanished from this political scheme—so far as these declarations go. Most of the states produced similar preludes to government. The Declaration of Independence said that "all men are born equal." It is everywhere asserted in eighteenth-century terms that the new community is to be—to use the phraseology we have introduced in an earlier chapter—a community of will and not a community of obedience. But the thinkers of that time had a rather clumsier way of putting the thing, they imagined a sort of individual choice of and assent to citizenship that never in fact occurred—the so-called Social Contract. The

---

[1] The Tripoli Treaty, see Channing, vol. iii, chap. xviii.

Massachusetts preamble, for instance, asserts that the State is a voluntary association, "by which the whole people covenants with each citizen and each citizen with the whole people that all shall be governed by certain laws for the common good."

Now, it will be evident that most of these fundamental statements are very questionable statements. Men are not born equal, they are not born free; they are born a most various multitude enmeshed in an ancient and complex social net. Nor is any man invited to sign the social contract, or, failing that, to depart into solitude. These statements, literally interpreted, are so manifestly false that it is impossible to believe that the men who made them intended them to be literally interpreted. They made them in order to express certain elusive but profoundly important ideas—ideas that, after another century and a half of thinking, the world is in a better position to express. Civilization, as this *Outline* has shown, arose as a community of obedience, and was essentially a community of obedience. But generation after generation the spirit was abused by priests and rulers. There was a continual influx of masterful will from the forests, parklands and steppes. The human spirit had at last rebelled altogether against the blind obediences of the common life; it was seeking— and at first it was seeking very clumsily—to achieve a new and better sort of civilization that should also be a community of will. To that end it was necessary that every man should be treated as the sovereign of himself; his standing was to be one of fellowship and not of servility. His real use, his real importance, depended upon his individual quality. The method by which these creators of political America sought to secure this community of will was an extremely simple and crude one. They gave what was for the time, and in view of American conditions, a very wide franchise. Conditions varied in the different states; the widest franchise was in Pennsylvania, where every adult male taxpayer voted; but, compared with Britain, all the United States were well within sight of manhood suffrage by the end of the eighteenth century. These makers of America also made efforts, considerable for their times, but puny by more modern standards, to secure a widely diffused common education. The information of the citizens as to what was going on at home and abroad they left, apparently without any qualms of misgiving, to public meetings and the privately owned printing-press.

The story of the various state constitutions, and of the constitution of the United States as a whole, is a very intricate one, and we can only deal with it here in the broadest way. The most noteworthy point in a modern view is the disregard of women as citizens. The American community was a simple, largely agricultural community, and most women were married; it seemed natural that they should be represented by their menfolk. But New Jersey admitted a few women to vote on a property qualification. Another point of great interest is the almost universal decision to have two governing assemblies, confirming or checking each other, on the model of the Lords and Commons of Britain. Only Pennsylvania had a single representative chamber, and that was felt to be a very dangerous and ultra-democratic state of affairs. Apart from the argument that legislation should be slow as well as sure, it is difficult to establish any necessity for this "bi-cameral" arrangement. It seems to have been a fashion with constitution planners in the eighteenth century rather than a reasonable imperative. The British division was an old one: the Lords, the original parliament, was an assembly of "notables," the leading men of the kingdom; the House of Commons came in as a new factor, as the elected spokesmen of the burghers and the small landed men. It was a little too hastily assumed in the eighteenth century that the commonalty would be given to wild impulses and would need checking; opinion was for democracy, but for democracy with powerful brakes always on, whether it was going up hill or down. About all the upper houses there was, therefore, a flavour of selectness; they were elected on a more limited franchise. This idea of making an upper chamber which shall be a stronghold for the substantial man does not appeal to modern thinkers so strongly as it did to the men of the eighteenth century, but the bi-cameral idea in another form still has its advocates. They suggest that a community may with advantage consider its affairs from two points of view—through the eyes of a body elected to represent trades, industries, professions, public services, and the like, a body representing *function,* and through the eyes of a second body elected by localities to represent *communities.* For the members of the former a man would vote by his calling, for the latter by his district of residence. They point out that the British House of Lords is in effect a body representing function, in which the land, the law, and the church are no doubt disproportionately represented, but in which industrialism, finance, the great public services, art, science, and medicine also find places; and that the British House of Commons is purely geographical in its reference. It has even been suggested in Britain that there should be "labour peers," selected from among the leaders of the great industrial trade unions. But these are speculations beyond our present scope.

The Central Government of the United States was at first a very feeble body, a Congress of representatives of the thirteen governments, held together by certain Articles of Confederation. This Congress was little more than a conference of sovereign representatives; it had no control, for instance, over the foreign trade of each state, it could not coin money nor levy taxes by its own authority. When John Adams, the first minister from the United States to England, went to discuss a commercial treaty with the British foreign secretary, he was met by a request for thirteen representatives, one from each of the states concerned. He had to confess his inadequacy to make binding arrangements. The British presently began dealing with each state separately over the head of the Congress, and they retained possession of a number of posts in the American territory about the Great Lakes because of the inability of Congress to hold these regions effectually. In another urgent matter Congress proved equally feeble. To the west of the thirteen states stretched limitless lands into which settlers were now pushing in ever-increasing numbers. Each of the states had indefinable claims to expansion westward. It was evident to every clear-sighted man that the jostling of these claims must lead in the long run to war, unless the Central Government could take on their apportionment. The feebleness of the Central Government, its lack of concentration, became so much of an inconvenience and so manifest a danger that there was some secret discussion of a monarchy, and Nathaniel Gorham of Massachusetts, the president of Congress, caused Prince Henry of Prussia, the brother of Frederick the Great, to be approached on the subject. Finally a constitutional convention was called in 1787 at Philadelphia, and there it was that the present

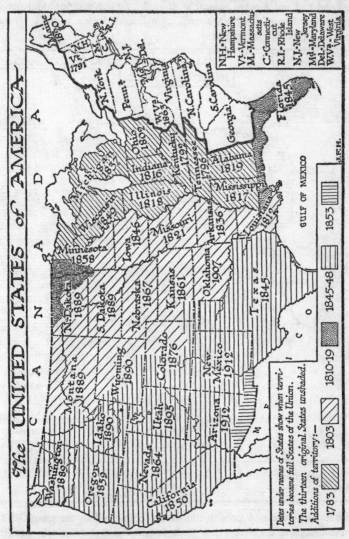

constitution of the United States was on its broad lines hammered out. A great change of spirit had gone on during the intervening years, a widespread realization of the need of unity.

When the Articles of Confederation were drawn up, men had thought of the people of Virginia, the people of Massachusetts, the people of Rhode Island, and the like; but now there appears a new conception, "the people of the United States." The new government, with the executive President, the senators, congressmen, and the Supreme Court, that was now created, was declared to be the government of "the people of the United States"; it was a synthesis and not a mere assembly. It said "we the people," and not "we the states," as Lee of Virginia bitterly complained. It was to be a "federal" and not a confederate government.

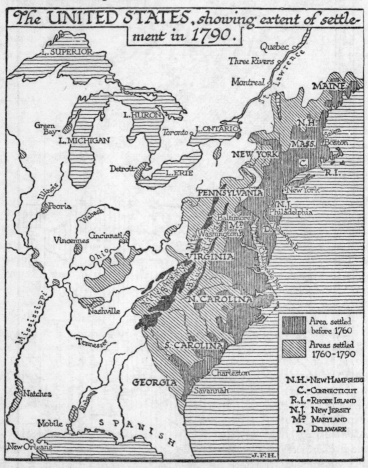

The UNITED STATES, showing extent of settlement in 1790.

| Area settled before 1760 |
| Areas settled 1760–1790 |

N.H. = New Hampshire
C. = Connecticut
R.I. = Rhode Island
N.J. = New Jersey
M? = Maryland
D. = Delaware

State by state the new constitution was ratified, and in the spring of 1788 the first Congress upon the new lines assembled at New York, under the presidency of George Washington, who had been the national commander-in-chief throughout the War of Independence. The constitution then underwent considerable revision, and Washington upon the Potomac was built as the Federal capital.

§ 6

In an earlier chapter we have described the Roman republic, and its mixture of modern features with dark superstition and primordial savagery, as the Neanderthal anticipation of the modern democratic state. A time may come when people will regard the contrivances and machinery of the American constitution as the political equivalents of the implements and contrivances of Neolithic man. They have served their purpose well, and under their protection the people of the States have grown into one of the greatest, most powerful and most civilized communities that the world has yet seen; but there is no reason in that for regarding the American constitution as a thing more final and inalterable than the elevated railways that used to overshadow many New York thoroughfares, or the excellent and homely type of house architecture that still prevails in Philadelphia. These things also have served a purpose well, they have their faults, and they can be improved. Our political contrivances, just as much as our domestic and mechanical contrivances need to undergo constant revision as knowledge and understanding grow.

Since the American constitution was planned, our conception of history and our knowledge of collective psychology have undergone very considerable development. We are beginning to see many things in the problem of government to which the men of the eighteenth century were blind; and, courageous as their constructive disposition was in relation to whatever political creation had gone before, it fell far short of the boldness which we in these days realize to be needful if this great human problem of establishing a civilized community of will in the earth is to be solved. They took many things for granted that now we know need to be made the subject of the most exacting scientific study and the most careful adjustment. They thought it was only necessary to set up schools and colleges, with a grant of land for maintenance, and that they might then be left to themselves. But education is not a weed that will grow lustily in any soil, it is a necessary and delicate crop that may easily wilt and degenerate. We learn nowadays that the under-development of universities and educational machinery is like some under-development of the brain and nerves, which hampers the whole growth of the social body. By European standards, by the standard of any state that has existed hitherto, the level of the common education of America is high; but by the standard of what it might be, America is an uneducated country. And those fathers of America thought also that they had but to leave the Press free, and everyone would live in the light. They did not realize that a free Press could develop a sort of constitutional venality due to its relations with advertisers, and that large newspaper proprietors could become buccaneers of opinion and insensate wreckers of good beginnings. And, finally, the makers of America had no knowledge of the complexities of vote manipulation. The whole science of elections was beyond their ken, they knew nothing of the need of the transferable vote to prevent the "working" of elections by specialized organizations, and the crude and rigid methods they adopted left their political system the certain prey of the great party machines that have robbed American democracy of half its freedom and most of its political soul. Politics became a trade, and a very base trade; decent and able men, after the first great period, drifted out of politics and attended to "business," and the sense of the State declined. Private enterprise ruled in many matters of common concern, because political corruption made collective enterprise impossible.

Yet the defects of the great political system created by the Americans of the revolutionary period did not appear at once. For several generations the history of the United States was one of rapid expansion and of an amount of freedom, homely happiness, and energetic work unparalleled in the world's history. And the record of America for the whole last century and a half, in spite of many reversions towards inequality, in spite of much rawness and much blundering, is nevertheless as bright and honourable a story as that of any other contemporary people.

In this brief account of the creation of the United States of America we have been able to do little more than mention the names of some of the group of great men who made this new departure in human history. We have named casually or we have not even named such men as Thomas Paine, Benjamin Franklin, Patrick Henry, Thomas Jefferson, the Adams cousins, Madison, Alexander Hamilton, and George Washington. It is hard to measure the men of one period of history with those in another. Some writers, even American writers, impressed by the artificial splendours of the European courts and by the tawdry and destructive exploits of a Frederick the Great or a Great Catherine, display a snobbish shame of something homespun about these makers of America. They feel that Benjamin Franklin at the Court of Louis

Benjamin Franklin

XVI, with his long hair, his plain clothes, and his pawky manner, was sadly lacking in aristocratic distinction. But, stripped to their personalities, Louis XVI was hardly gifted enough or noble-minded enough to be Franklin's valet. If human greatness is a matter of scale and glitter, then no doubt Alexander the Great is at the apex of human greatness. But is greatness that? Is not a great man rather one who, in a great position or amidst great opportunities—and great gifts are no more than great opportunities—serves God and his fellows with a humble heart? And quite a number of these Americans of the revolutionary time do seem to have displayed much disinterestedness and devotion. They are limited men, fallible men; but on the whole they seem to have cared more for the commonweal they were creating than for any personal end or personal vanity. It is impossible not to concede them a distinguished greatness of mind.

True they were limited in knowledge and outlook; they were limited by the limitations of the time. They were, like all of us, men of mixed motives; good impulses arose in their minds, great ideas swept through them, and also they could be jealous, lazy, obstinate, greedy, vicious. If one were to write a true, full, and particular history of the making of the United States, it would have to be written with charity and high spirits as a splendid comedy rising to the noblest ends. And in no other regard do we find the rich, tortuous humanity of the American story so finely displayed as in regard to slavery. Slavery, having regard to the general question of labour, is the test of this new soul in the world's history, the American soul.

Washington

Slavery began very early in the European history of America, and no European people who went to America can be held altogether innocent in the matter. At a time when the German is still the moral whipping-boy of Europe, it is well to note that the German record is in this respect the best of all. Almost the first outspoken utterances against negro slavery came from German settlers in Pennsylvania. But the German settler was working with free labour upon a temperate country-side well north of the plantation zone; he was not under serious temptation in this matter. American slavery began with the enslavement of Indians for gang work in mines and upon plantations, and it is curious to note that it was a very good and humane man indeed, Las Casas, who urged that negroes should be brought to America to relieve his tormented Indian protégés. The need for labour upon the plantations of the West Indies and the south was imperative. When the supply of Indian captives proved inadequate, the planters turned not only to the negro, but to the jails and poorhouses of Europe, for a supply of toilers. The reader of Defoe's *Moll Flanders* will learn how the business of Virginian white slavery looked to an intelligent Englishman in the early eighteenth century. But the negro came very early. The year (1620) that saw the Pilgrim Fathers landing at Plymouth in New England, saw a Dutch sloop disembarking the first cargo of negroes at Jamestown in Virginia. Negro slavery was as old as New England; it had been an American institution for over a century and a half before the War of Independence. It was to struggle on for the better part of a century more.

But the conscience of thoughtful men in the colonies was never quite easy upon this score, and it was one of the accusations of Thomas Jefferson against the crown and lords of Great Britain that every attempt to ameliorate or restrain the slave trade on the part of the colonists had been checked by the great proprietary interests in the mother-country. In 1776 Lord Dartmouth wrote that the colonists could not be allowed "to check or discourage a traffic so beneficent to the nation." With the moral and intellectual ferment of the Revolution, the question of negro slavery came right into the foreground of the public conscience. The contrast and the challenge glared upon the mind. "All men are by nature free and equal," said the Virginia Bill of Rights; and outside in the sunshine, under the whip of the overseer, toiled the negro slave.

It witnesses to the great change in human ideas since the Roman Imperial system dissolved under the barbarian inrush, that there could be this heart-searching. Conditions of industry, production, and land tenure had long prevented any recrudescence of gang slavery; but now the cycle had come round again, and there were enormous immediate advantages to be reaped by the owning and ruling classes in the revival of that ancient institution, in mines, upon plantations, and upon great public works. It was revived—but against great opposition. From the beginning of the revival there were protests, and they grew. The revival was counter to the new conscience of mankind. In some respects the new gang slavery was worse than anything in the ancient world. Peculiarly horrible was the provocation by the trade of slave wars and man hunts in Western Africa, and the cruelties of the long Transatlantic voyage. The poor creatures were packed on the ships often with insufficient provision of food and water, without proper sanitation, without medicines. Many who could tolerate slavery upon the plantations found the slave trade too much for their moral digestions. Three European nations were chiefly concerned in this dark business, Britain, Spain and Portugal, because they were the chief owners of the new lands in America. The comparative innocence of the other European powers is to be ascribed largely to their lesser temptations. They were similar communities; in parallel circumstances they would have behaved similarly.

Throughout the middle part of the eighteenth century there was an active agitation against negro slavery in Great Britain as well as in the States. It was estimated that in 1770 there were fifteen thousand slaves in Britain, mostly brought over by their owners from the West Indies and Virginia. In 1771 the issue came to a conclusive test in Britain before Lord Mansfield. A negro named James Somersett had been brought to England from Virginia by his owner. He ran away, was captured, and violently taken on a ship to be returned to Virginia. From the ship he was extracted by a writ of *habeas corpus*. Lord Mansfield declared that slavery was a condition unknown to English law, an "odious" condition; and Somersett walked out of the court a free man.

The Massachusetts constitution of 1780 had declared that "all men are born free and equal." A certain negro, Quaco, put this to the test in 1783, and in that year the soil of Massachusetts became like the soil of Britain, intolerant of slavery; to tread upon it was to become free. At that time no other state in the Union followed this example. At the census of 1790, Massachusetts, alone of all the states, returned "no slaves."

The state of opinion in Virginia is remarkable, because it brings to light the peculiar difficulties of the southern states. The great Virginian statesmen, such as Washington and Jefferson, condemned the institution, yet, because there was no other form of domestic service, Washington owned slaves. There was in Virginia a strong party in favour of emancipating slaves; but they demanded that the emancipated slaves should leave the state within a year or be outlawed! They were naturally alarmed at the possibility that a free barbaric black community, many of its members African-born and reeking with traditions of cannibalism and secret and dreadful religious rites, should arise beside them upon Virginian soil. When we consider that point of view, we can understand why it was that a large number of Virginians should be disposed to retain the mass of blacks in the country under control as slaves, while at the same time they were bitterly opposed to the slave trade and the importation of any fresh blood from Africa. The free blacks, one sees, might easily become a nuisance; indeed, the free state of Massachusetts presently closed its borders to their entry.

The question of slavery, which in the ancient world was usually no more than a question of status between individuals racially akin, merged in America with the different and profounder question of relationship between two races at opposite extremes of the human species and of the most contrasted types of tradition and culture. If the black man had been white, there can be little doubt that negro slavery would have vanished from the United States within a generation of the Declaration of Independence as a natural consequence of the statements in that declaration.

§ 7

We have told of the War of Independence in America as the first great break away from the system of European monarchies and foreign offices, as the repudiation by a new community of Machiavellian statecraft as the directive form of human affairs. Within a decade there came a second and much more portentous revolt against this strange game of Great Powers, this tangled interaction of courts and policies which obsessed Europe. But this time it was no breaking away at the outskirts. In France, the nest and home of Grand Monarchy, the heart and centre of Europe, came this second upheaval. And, unlike the American colonists, who simply repudiated a king, the French, following in the footsteps of the English revolution, beheaded one.

Like the British Revolution and like the revolution in the United States, the French Revolution can be traced back to the ambitious absurdities of monarchy. The schemes of aggrandizement, the aims and designs of the Grand Monarch, necessitated an expenditure upon war equipment throughout Europe out of all proportion to the taxable capacity of the age. And even the splendours of monarchy were enormously costly, measured by the productivity of the time. In France, just as in Britain and in America, the first resistance was made not to the monarch as such and to his foreign policy as such, nor with any clear recognition of these things as the roots of the trouble, but merely to the inconveniences and charges upon the individual life caused by them. The practical taxable capacity of France must have been relatively much less than that of England because of the various exemptions of the nobility and clergy. The burthen resting directly upon the common people was heavier.

That made the upper classes the confederates of the Court, instead of the antagonists of the Court as they were in England, and so prolonged the period of waste further; but when at last the bursting-point did come, the explosion was more violent and shattering.

During the years of the War of American Independence there were few signs of any impending explosion in France. There was much misery among the lower classes, much criticism and satire, much outspoken liberal thinking, but there was little to indicate that the thing as a whole, with all its customs, usages, and familiar discords, might not go on for an indefinite time. It was consuming beyond its powers of production, but as yet only the inarticulate classes were feeling the pinch. Gibbon, the historian, knew France well; Paris was as familiar to him as London; but there is no suspicion to be detected in the passage we have quoted that days of political and social dissolution were at hand. No doubt the world abounded in absurdities and injustices, yet never-theless, from the point of view of a scholar and a gentleman, it was fairly comfortable, and it seemed fairly secure.

There was much liberal thought, speech, and sentiment in France at this time. Parallel with and a little later than John Locke in England, Montesquieu (1689–1755) in France, in the earlier half of the eighteenth century, had subjected social, political, and religious institutions to the same searching and fundamental analysis, especially in his *Esprit des Lois*. He had stripped the magical prestige from the absolutist monarchy in France. He shares with Locke the credit for clearing away many of the false ideas that had hitherto prevented deliberate and conscious attempts to reconstruct human society. It was not his fault if at first some extremely unsound and impermanent shanties were run up on the vacant site. The generation that followed him in the middle and later decades of the eighteenth century was boldly speculative upon the moral and intellectual clearings he had made. A group of brilliant writers, the "Encyclopædists," mostly rebel spirits from the excellent schools of the Jesuits, set themselves under the leadership of Diderot to scheme out, in a group of works, a new world (1766). The glory of the Encyclopædists, says Mallet, lay "in their hatred of things unjust, in their denunciation of the trade in slaves, of the inequalities of taxation, of the corruption of justice, of the wastefulness of wars, in their dreams of social progress, in their sympathy with the rising empire of industry which was beginning to transform the world." Their chief error seems to have been an indiscriminate hostility to religion. They believed that man was naturally just and politically competent, whereas his impulse to social service and self-forgetfulness is usually developed only through an education essentially religious, and sustained only in an atmos-phere of honest co-operation. Unco-ordinated human initiatives lead to nothing but social chaos.

Side by side with the Encyclopædists were the Economists or Physiocrats, who were making bold and crude inquiries into the production and distribu-tion of food and goods. Morally, the author of the *Code de la Nature* de-nounced the institution of private property and proposed a communistic organization of society. He was the precursor of that large and various school of collectivist thinkers in the nineteenth century who are lumped together as Socialists.

Both the Encyclopædists and the various Economists and Physiocrats demanded a considerable amount of hard thinking in their disciples. An easier and more popular leader to follow was Rousseau (1712–78). He displayed a curious mingling of logical rigidity and sentimental enthusiasm. He preached the alluring doctrine that the primitive state of man was one of virtue and happiness, from which he had declined through the rather inexplicable activities of priests, kings, lawyers, and the like. Rousseau's intellectual influence was on the whole demoralizing. It struck not only at the existing social fabric, but at any social organization. When he wrote of the *Social Contract,* he seemed rather to excuse breaches of the covenant than to emphasize its necessity. Man is so far from perfect, that a writer who apparently sustained the thesis that the almost universal disposition, against which we all have to fortify ourselves, to repudiate debts, misbehave sexually, and to evade the toil and expenses of education for ourselves and others, is not after all a delinquency, but a fine display of Natural Virtue, was bound to have a large following in every class that could read him. Rousseau's tremendous vogue did much to popularize a sentimental and declamatory method of dealing with social and political problems.

We have already remarked that hitherto no human community had begun to act upon theory. There must first be some breakdown and necessity for direction that lets theory into her own. Up to 1788 the republican and anarchist talk and writing of French thinkers must have seemed as ineffective and politically unimportant as the æsthetic socialism of William Morris in England at the end of the nineteenth century. There was the social and political system going on with an effect of invincible persistence, the French king hunting and mending his clocks, the Court and the world of fashion pursuing their pleasures, the financiers conceiving continually more enterprising extensions of credit, business blundering clumsily along its ancient routes, much incommoded by taxes and imposts, the peasants worrying, toiling and suffering, full of a hopeless hatred of the nobleman's château. Men talked—and felt they were merely talking. Anything might be said, because, it seemed, nothing would ever happen.

§ 8

The first jar to this sense of the secure continuity of life in France came in 1787. Louis XVI (1774–93) was a dull, ill-educated monarch, and he had the misfortune to be married to a silly and extravagant woman, Marie Antoinette, the sister of the Austrian emperor. The question of her virtue is one of profound interest to a certain type of historical writer, but we need not discuss it here. She lived, as Paul Wiriath[1] puts it, "side by side, but not at the side" of her husband. She was rather heavy-featured, but not so plain as

---

[1] Article "France," *Encyclopædia Britannica.*

to prevent her posing as a beautiful, romantic and haughty queen. When the exchequer was exhausted by the war in America, when the whole country was uneasy with discontents, she set her influence to thwart the attempts at economy of the king's ministers, to encourage every sort of aristocratic extravagance, and to restore the church and the nobility to the position they had held in the great days of Louis XIV. Nonaristocratic officers were to be weeded from the army; the power of the church over private life was to be extended. She found in an upper-class official, Calonne, her ideal minister of finance. From 1783 to 1787 this wonderful man produced money as if by magic—and as if by magic it disappeared again. Then in 1787 he collapsed. He had piled loan on loan, and now he declared that the monarchy, the Grand Monarchy that had ruled France since the days of Louis XIV, was bankrupt. No more money could be raised. There must be a gathering of the notables of the kingdom to consider the situation.

To the gathering of notables, a summoned assembly of leading men, Calonne propounded a scheme for a subsidy to be levied upon all landed property. This roused the aristocrats to a pitch of great indignation. They demanded the summoning of a body roughly equivalent to the British parliament—the States General, which had not met since 1614. Regardless of the organ of opinion they were creating for the discontents below them, excited only by the proposal that they should bear part of the weight of the financial burthens of the country, the French notables insisted. And in May, 1789, the States General met.

It was an assembly of the representatives of three orders, the nobles, the clergy, and the Third Estate, the commons. For the Third Estate the franchise was very wide, nearly every taxpayer of twenty-five having a vote. (The parish priests voted as clergy, the small noblesse as nobles.) The States General was a body without any tradition of procedure. Inquiries were sent to the antiquarians of the Academy of Inscriptions in that matter. Its opening deliberations turned on the question whether it was to meet as one body or as three, each estate having an equal vote. Since the Clergy numbered 308, the Nobles 285, and the Deputies 621, the former arrangement would put the commons in an absolute majority, the latter gave them one vote in three. Nor had the States General any meeting-place. Should it meet in Paris or in some provincial city? Versailles was chosen, "because of the hunting."

It is clear that the king and queen meant to treat this fuss about the national finance as a terrible bore, and to allow it to interfere with their social routine as little as possible. We find the meetings going on in salons that were not wanted, in orangeries and tennis-courts, and so forth.

The question whether the voting was to be by the estates or by head was clearly a vital one. It was wrangled over for six weeks. The Third Estate, taking a leaf from the book of the English House of Commons, then declared that it alone represented the nation, and that no taxation must be levied henceforth without its consent. Whereupon the king closed the hall in which it was sitting, and intimated that the deputies had better go home. Instead, the deputies met in a convenient tennis-court, and there took oath—the Oath of the

Tennis Court—not to separate until they had established a constitution in France.

The king took a high line, and attempted to disperse the Third Estate by force. The soldiers refused to act. On that the king gave in with a dangerous suddenness, and accepted the principle that the Three Estates should all deliberate and vote together as one National Assembly. Meanwhile, apparently at the queen's instigation, foreign regiments in the French service, who could be trusted to act against the people, were brought up from the provinces under the Marshal de Broglie, and the king prepared to go back upon his concessions. Whereupon Paris and France revolted. Broglie hesitated to fire on the crowds. A provisional city government was set up in Paris and in most of the other large cities, and a new armed force, the National Guard, a force designed primarily and plainly to resist the forces of the crown, was brought into existence by these municipal bodies.

The revolt of July, 1789, was really the effective French Revolution. The grim-looking prison of the Bastille, very feebly defended, was stormed by the people of Paris, and the insurrection spread rapidly throughout France. In the east and north-west provinces many châteaux belonging to the nobility were burnt by the peasants, their title-deeds carefully destroyed, and the owners murdered or driven away. The insurrection spread throughout France. In a month the ancient and decayed system of the aristocratic order had collapsed. Many of the leading princes and courtiers of the queen's party fled abroad. The National Assembly found itself called upon to create a new political and social system for a new age.

§ 9

The French National Assembly was far less fortunate in the circumstances of its task than the American Congress. The latter had half a continent to itself, with no possible antagonist but the British Government. Its religious and educational organizations were various, collectively not very powerful, and on the whole friendly. King George was far away in England, and sinking slowly towards an imbecile condition. Nevertheless, it took the United States several years to hammer out a working constitution. The French, on the other hand, were surrounded by aggressive neighbours with Machiavellian ideas, they were encumbered by a king and court resolved to make mischief, and the church was one single great organization inextricably bound up with the ancient order. The queen was in close correspondence with the Count of Artois, the Duke of Bourbon, and the other exiled princes who were trying to induce Austria and Prussia to attack the new French nation. Moreover, France was already a bankrupt country, while the United States had limitless undeveloped resources; and the Revolution, by altering the conditions of land tenure and marketing, had produced an economic disorganization that had no parallel in the case of America.

These were the unavoidable difficulties of the situation. But in addition the Assembly made difficulties for itself. There was no orderly procedure. The

English House of Commons had had more than five centuries of experience in its work, and Mirabeau, one of the great leaders of the early Revolution, tried in vain to have the English rules adopted. But the feeling of the times was all in favour of outcries, dramatic interruptions, and such-like manifestations of Natural Virtue. And the disorder did not come merely from the Assembly. There was a great gallery, much too great a gallery, for strangers; but who would restrain the free citizens from having a voice in the national control? This gallery swarmed with people eager for a "scene," ready to applaud or shout down the speakers below. The abler speakers were obliged to play to the gallery, and take a sentimental and sensational line. It was easy at a crisis to bring in a mob to kill debate.

So encumbered, the Assembly set about its constructive task. On the Fourth of August it achieved a great dramatic success. Led by several of the liberal nobles, it made a series of resolutions, abolishing serfdom, privileges, tax exemptions, tithes and feudal courts. (In many parts of the country, however, these resolutions were not carried into effect until three or four years later.) Titles went with their other renunciations. Long before France was a republic it was an offence for a nobleman to sign his name with his title. For six weeks the Assembly devoted itself, with endless opportunities for rhetoric, to the formulation of a Declaration of the Rights of Man—on the lines of the Bills of Rights that were the English preliminaries to organized change. Meanwhile the Court plotted for reaction, and the people felt that the Court was plotting. The story is complicated here by the scoundrelly schemes of the king's cousin, Philip of Orleans, who hoped to use the discords of the time to replace Louis on the French throne. His gardens at the Palais-Royal were thrown open to the public, and became a great centre of advanced discussion. His agents did much to intensify the popular suspicion of the king. And things were exacerbated by a shortage of provisions—for which the king's government was held guilty.

Presently the loyal Flanders regiment appeared at Versailles. The royal family was scheming to get farther away from Paris—in order to undo all that had been done, to restore tyranny and extravagance. Such constitutional monarchists as General Lafayette were seriously alarmed. And just at this time occurred an outbreak of popular indignation at the scarcity of food, that passed by an easy transition into indignation against the threat of royalist reaction. It was believed that there was an abundance of provisions at Versailles; that food was being kept there away from the people. The public mind had been much disturbed by reports, possibly by exaggerated reports, of a recent banquet at Versailles, hostile to the nation. Here are some extracts from Carlyle descriptive of that unfortunate feast.

"The Hall of the Opera is granted; the Salon d'Hercule shall be drawing-room. Not only the Officers of Flandre, but of the Swiss, of the Hundred Swiss; nay of the Versailles National Guard, such of them as have any loyalty, shall feast; it will be a Repast like few.

"And now suppose this Repast, the solid part of it, transacted; and the first bottle over. Suppose the customary loyal toasts drunk; the King's health, the

Queen's with deafening vivats; that of the nation 'omitted,' or even 'rejected.'
Suppose champagne flowing; with pot-valorous speech, with instrumental music; empty featherheads growing ever the noisier, in their own emptiness, in
each other's noise. Her Majesty, who looks unusually sad to-night (His Majesty sitting dulled with the day's hunting), is told that the sight of it would
cheer her. Behold! She enters there, issuing from her State-rooms, like the
Moon from clouds, this fairest unhappy Queen of Hearts; royal Husband by
her side, young Dauphin in her arms! She descends from the Boxes, amid
splendour and acclaim; walks queen-like round the Tables; gracefully nod-
ding; her looks full of sorrow, yet of gratitude and daring, with the hope of
France on her mother-bosom! And now, the band striking up, *O Richard, O
mon Roi, l'univers t'abandonne* (O Richard, O my king, the world is all for-
saking thee), could man do other than rise to height of pity, of loyal valour?
Could featherheaded young ensigns do other than—by white Bourbon Cockades, handed them from fair fingers; by waving of swords, drawn to pledge the
Queen's health; by trampling of National Cockades; by scaling the Boxes,
whence intrusive murmurs may come; by vociferation, sound, fury and distraction, within doors and without—testify what tempest-tost state of vacuity
they are in? . . .

"A natural Repast; in ordinary times, a harmless one: now fatal. . . . Poor
ill-advised Marie Antoinette; with a woman's vehemence, not with a sovereign's foresight! It was so natural, yet so unwise. Next day, in public speech
of ceremony, Her Majesty declares herself 'delighted with Thursday.' "

And here to set against this is Carlyle's picture of the mood of the people.

"In squalid garret, on Monday morning Maternity awakes, to hear children weeping for bread. Maternity must forth to the streets, to the herb-
makers and bakers'-queues; meets there with hunger-stricken Maternity, sympathetic, exasperative. O we unhappy women! But, instead of bakers'-queues,
why not to Aristocrats' palaces, the root of the matter? *Allons!* Let us assemble.
To the Hôtel-de-Ville; to Versailles. . . ."

There was much shouting and coming and going in Paris before this latter
idea realized itself. One Maillard appeared with organizing power, and assumed a certain leadership. There can be little doubt that the revolutionary
leaders, and particularly General Lafayette, used and organized this outbreak
to secure the king, before he could slip away—as Charles I did to Oxford—to
begin a civil war. As the afternoon wore on, the procession started on its
eleven-mile tramp. . . .

Again we quote Carlyle:

"Maillard has halted his draggled Menads on the last hill-top; and now
Versailles, and the Château of Versailles, and far and wide the inheritance of
Royalty opens to the wondering eye. From far on the right, over Marly and
Saint-Germain-en-Laye; round towards Rambouillet, on the left, beautiful all;
softly embosomed; as if in sadness, in the dim moist weather! And near before
us is Versailles, New and Old; with that broad frondent *Avenue de Versailles*
between, stately frondent, broad, three hundred feet as men reckon, with its
four rows of elms; and then the Château de Versailles, ending in royal parks

and pleasances, gleaming lakelets, arbours, labyrinths, the *Ménagerie*, and Great and Little Trianon. High-towered dwellings, leafy pleasant places; where the gods of this lower world abide: whence, nevertheless, black care cannot be excluded; whither Menadic hunger is even now advancing, armed with pike-thyrsi!"

Rain fell as the evening closed.

"Behold the Esplanade, over all its spacious expanse, is covered with groups of squalid dripping women; of lank-haired male rascality, armed with axes, rusty pikes, old muskets, iron-shod clubs (*baton ferrés*, which end in knives or swordblades, a kind of extempore billhook); looking nothing but hungry revolt. The rain pours; Gardes-du-Corps go caracoling through the groups 'amid hisses'; irritating and agitating what is but dispersed here to reunite there. . . .

"Innumerable squalid women beleaguer the President and Deputation; insist on going with him: has not his Majesty himself, looking from the window, sent out to ask, What we wanted? 'Bread, and speech with the King,' that was the answer. Twelve women are clamorously added to the deputation; and march with it, across the Esplanade; through dissipated groups, caracoling bodyguards, and the pouring rain."

"Bread, and not too much talking!" Natural demands.

"One learns also that the Royal Carriages are getting yoked, as if for Metz. Carriages, royal or not, have verily showed themselves at the back gates. They even produced, or quoted, a written order from our Versailles Municipality —which is a monarchic not a democratic one. However, Versailles patrols drove them in again; as the vigilant Lecointre had strictly charged them to do. . . .

"So sink the shadows of night, blustering, rainy; and all paths grow dark. Strangest night ever seen in these regions; perhaps since the Bartholomew Night, when Versailles, as Bassompierre writes of it, was a *chétif château*.

"O for the lyre of some Orpheus, to constrain, with touch of melodious strings, these mad masses into Order! For here all seems fallen asunder, in wide-yawning dislocation. The highest, as in down-rushing of a world, is come in contact with the lowest: the rascality of France beleaguering the royalty of France; 'iron-shod batons' lifted round the diadem, not to guard it! With denunciations of bloodthirsty anti-national bodyguards, are heard dark growlings against a queenly name.

"The Court sits tremulous, powerless: varies with the varying temper of the Esplanade, with the varying colour of the rumours from Paris. Thick-coming rumours; now of peace, now of war. Necker and all the Ministers consult; with a blank issue. The Œil-de-Bœuf is one tempest of whispers: We will fly to Metz; we will not fly. The royal carriages again attempt egress —though for trial merely; they are again driven in by Lecointre's patrols."

But we must send the reader to Carlyle to learn of the coming of the National Guard in the night under General Lafayette himself, the bargaining between the Assembly and the King, the outbreak of fighting in the morning between the bodyguard and the hungry besiegers, and how the latter stormed into the palace and came near to a massacre of the royal family. Lafayette and his troops turned out in time to prevent that, and timely cartloads of loaves arrived from Paris for the crowd.

At last it was decided that the king should come to Paris.

"Processional marches not a few our world has seen; Roman triumphs and ovations, Cabric cymbal-beatings, Royal progresses, Irish funerals; but this of the French Monarchy marching to its bed remained to be seen. Miles long, and of breadth losing itself in vagueness, for all the neighbouring country crowds to see. Slow: stagnating along, like shoreless Lake, yet with a noise like Niagara, like Babel and Bedlam. A splashing and a tramping; a hurrahing, uproaring, musket-volleying; the truest segment of Chaos seen in these latter Ages! Till slowly it disembogue itself, in the thickening dusk, into expectant Paris, through a double row of faces all the way from Passy to the Hôtel-de-Ville.

"Consider this: Vanguard of National troops; with trains of artillery; of pikemen and pikewomen, mounted on cannons, on carts, hackney-coaches, or on foot. . . . Loaves stuck on the points of bayonets, green boughs stuck in gun-barrels. Next, as main-march, 'fifty cart-loads of corn,' which have been lent, for peace, from the stores of Versailles. Behind which follow stragglers of the Garde-du-Corps; all humiliated, in Grenadier bonnets. Close on these comes the royal carriage; some royal carriages; for there are a hundred national deputies too, among whom sits Mirabeau—his remarks not given. Then finally, pell-mell, as rear-guard, Flandre, Swiss, Hundred Swiss, other bodyguards, brigands, whosoever cannot get before. Between and among all which masses flows without limit Saint-Antoine and the Menadic cohort. Menadic especially about the royal carriage. . . . Covered with tricolor; singing 'allusive songs'; pointing with one hand to the royal carriage, which the allusions hit, pointing to the provision-wagons with the other hand, and these words: 'Courage, Friends! We shall not want bread now; we are bringing you the Baker, the Bakeress and Baker's boy.' . . .

"The wet day draggles the tricolor, but the joy is inextinguishable. Is not all well now? 'Ah, Madame, notre bonne Reine,' said some of these Strong-women some days hence, 'Ah, Madame, our good Queen, don't be a traitor any more and we will all love you!' . . ."

This was October the 6th, 1789. For nearly two years the royal family dwelt unmolested in the Tuileries. Had the Court kept common faith with the people, the king might have died there, a king.

From 1789 to 1791 the early Revolution held its own; France was a limited monarchy, the king kept a diminished state in the Tuileries, and the National Assembly ruled a country at peace. The reader who will glance back to the maps of Poland we have given in the previous chapter will realize what occupied Russia, Prussia, and Austria at this time. While France experimented with a crowned republic in the west, the last division of the crowned republic of the east was in progress. France could wait.

When we consider its inexperience, the conditions under which it worked, and the complexities of its problems, one must concede that the Assembly did a very remarkable amount of constructive work. Much of that work was sound and still endures, much was experimental and has been undone. Some was disastrous. There was a clearing up of the penal code; torture, arbitrary imprisonment, and persecutions for heresy were abolished. The ancient provinces of France, Normandy, Burgundy, and the like, gave place to eighty departments. Promotion to the highest ranks in the army was laid open to men of every class. An excellent and simple system of law courts was set up, but its value was much vitiated by having the judges appointed by popular election for short periods of time. This made the crowd a sort of final court of appeal, and the judges, like the members of the Assembly, were forced to play to the gallery. And the whole vast property of the church was seized and administered by the State; religious establishments not engaged in education or works of charity were broken up, and the salaries of the clergy made a charge upon the nation. This in itself was not a bad thing for the lower clergy in France, who were often scandalously underpaid in comparison with the richer dignitaries. But in addition the choice of priests and bishops was made elective, which struck at the very root idea of the Roman Church, which centred everything upon the Pope, and in which all authority is from above downward. Practically the National Assembly wanted at one blow to make the church in France Protestant, in organization if not in doctrine. Everywhere there were disputes and conflicts between the state priests created by the National Assembly and the recalcitrant (nonjuring) priests who were loyal to Rome. . . .

One curious thing the National Assembly did which greatly weakened its grip on affairs. It decreed that no member of the Assembly should be an executive minister. This was in imitation of the American constitution, where, also, ministers are separated from the legislature. The British method has been to have all ministers in the legislative body, ready to answer questions and account for their interpretation of the laws and their conduct of the nation's business. If the legislature represents the sovereign people, then it is surely necessary for the ministers to be in the closest touch with their sovereign. This severance of the legislature and executive in France caused misunderstandings and mistrust; the legislature lacked control and the executive lacked moral force. This led to such an ineffectiveness in the central government that in many districts at this time communes and towns were to be found that were practically self-governing communities; they accepted or rejected the commands of Paris as they thought fit, declined the payment of taxes, and divided up the church lands according to their local appetites.

§ 10

It is quite possible that, with the loyal support of the crown and a reasonable patriotism on the part of the nobility, the National Assembly, in spite of its noisy galleries, its Rousseauism, and its inexperience, might have blundered through to a stable form of parliamentary government for France. In Mirabeau it had a statesman with clear ideas of the needs of the time; he knew the strength and the defects of the British system, and apparently he had set himself to establish in France a parallel political organization upon a wider, more honest franchise. He had, it is true, indulged in a sort of Ruritanian flirtation with the queen, seen her secretly, pronounced her very solemnly the "only *man*" about the king, and made rather a fool of himself in that matter, but his schemes were drawn upon a much larger scale than the scale of the back stairs of the Tuileries. By his death in 1791 France certainly lost one of her most constructive statesmen, and the National Assembly its last chance of any co-operation with the king. When there is a Court there is usually a conspiracy, and royalist schemes and royalist mischief-making were the last straw in the balance against the National Assembly. The royalists did not care for Mirabeau, they did not care for France; they wanted to be back in their lost paradise of privilege, haughtiness, and limitless expenditure, and it seemed to them that if only they could make the government of the National Assembly impossible, then by a sort of miracle the dry bones of the ancient regime would live again. They had no sense of the other possibility, the gulf of the republican extremists, that yawned at their feet.

One June night in 1791, between eleven o'clock and midnight, the king and queen and their two children slipped out of the Tuileries disguised, threaded their palpitating way through Paris, circled round from the north of the city to the east, and got at last into a travelling-carriage that was waiting upon the road to Châlons. They were flying to the army of the east. The army of the east was "loyal," that is to say, its general and officers at least were prepared to betray France to the king and Court. Here was adventure at last after the queen's heart, and one can understand the pleasurable excitement of the little party as the miles lengthened between themselves and Paris. Away over the hills were reverence, deep bows, and the kissing of hands. Then back to Versailles. A little shooting of the mob in Paris—artillery, if need be. A few executions—but not of the sort of people who matter. A White Terror for a few months. Then all would be well again. Perhaps Calonne might return too, with fresh financial expedients. He was busy just then gathering support among the German princes. There were a lot of châteaux to rebuild, but the people who burnt them down could hardly complain if the task of rebuilding them pressed rather heavily upon their grimy necks. . . .

All such bright anticipations were cruelly dashed that night at Varennes. The king had been recognized at Sainte-Menehould by the landlord of the post-house, and as the night fell the eastward roads clattered with galloping messengers rousing the country and trying to intercept the fugitives. There were fresh horses waiting in the upper village of Varennes—the young officer in charge had given the king up for the night and gone to bed—while for half an hour in the lower village the poor king, disguised as a valet, disputed with his postilions, who had expected reliefs in the lower village and refused to go farther. Finally they consented to go on. They consented too late. The little party found the postmaster from Sainte-Menehould, who had ridden past while the postilions wrangled, and a number of worthy republicans of Varennes whom he had gathered together, awaiting them at the bridge between the two parts of the town. The bridge was barricaded. Muskets were thrust into the carriage: "Your passports!"

The king surrendered without a struggle. The little party was taken into the house of some village functionary. "Well," said the king, "here you have me!" Also he remarked that he was hungry. At dinner he commended the wine, "quite excellent wine." What the queen said is not recorded. There were royalist troops at hand, but they attempted no rescue. The tocsin began to ring, and the village "illuminated itself," to guard against surprise. . . .

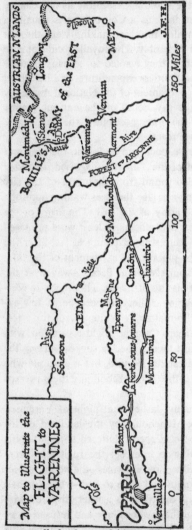

Map to illustrate the FLIGHT to VARENNES

A very crestfallen coachload of royalty returned to Paris, and was received by vast crowds—*in silence.* The word had gone forth that whoever insulted the king should be thrashed, and whoever applauded him should be killed. . . .

It was only after this foolish exploit that the idea of a republic took hold of the French mind. Before this flight to Varennes there was, no doubt, much abstract republican sentiment, but there was scarcely any expressed disposition to abolish monarchy in France. Even in July, a month after the flight, a great meeting in the Champ de Mars, supporting a petition for the dethronement of the king, was dispersed by the authorities, and many people were killed. But such displays of firmness could not prevent the lesson of that flight soaking into men's minds. Just as in England in the days of Charles I, so now in France, men realized that the king could not be trusted—he was dangerous. The Jacobins grew rapidly in strength. Their leaders, Robespierre, Danton, Marat, who had hitherto figured as impossible extremists, began to dominate French affairs.

These Jacobins were the equivalents of the American radicals, men with untrammelled advanced ideas. Their strength lay in the fact that they were unencumbered and downright. They were poor men with nothing to lose. The party of moderation, of compromise with the relics of the old order, was led by such men of established position as General Lafayette, who had distinguished himself as a young man by fighting for the American colonists as a volunteer, and Mirabeau, an aristocrat who was ready to model himself on the rich and influential aristocrats of England. But Robespierre was a needy but clever young lawyer from Arras, whose most precious possession was his faith in Rousseau; Danton was a scarcely more wealthy barrister in Paris, a big, gesticulating, rhetorical figure; Marat was an older man, a Swiss of some scientific distinction, but equally unembarrassed by possessions. He had spent several years in England, he was an honorary M.D. of St. Andrews, and had published some valuable contributions to medical science in English. Both Benjamin Franklin and Goethe were interested in his work in physics. This is the man who is called by Carlyle "rabid dog," "atrocious," "squalid," and "Dog-leech"—this last by way of tribute to his science.

The Revolution called Marat to politics, and his earliest contributions to the great discussion were fine and sane. There was a prevalent delusion in France that England was a land of liberty. His *Tableau des Vices de la Constitution d'Angleterre* showed the realities of the English position. His last years were maddened by an almost intolerable skin disease which he caught while hiding in the sewers of Paris to escape the consequences of his denunciation of the king as a traitor after the flight to Varennes. Only by sitting in a hot bath could he collect his mind to write. He had been treated hardly and suffered, and he became hard; nevertheless, he stands out in history as a man of distinguished honesty. His poverty particularly seems to have provoked the scorn of Carlyle.

"What a road he has travelled; and sits now, about half-past seven of the clock, stewing in slipper-bath; sore afflicted; ill of Revolution Fever. . . . Excessively sick and worn, poor man: with precisely elevenpence halfpenny of ready-money, in paper, with slipper-bath; strong three-footed stool for writing on, the while: and a squalid Washerwoman for his sole household . . . that is his civic establishment in Medical-School Street; thither and not elsewhere has his road led him. . . . Hark, a rap again! A musical woman's voice, refusing to be rejected: it is the Citoyenne who would do France a service. Marat, recognizing from within, cries, Admit her. Charlotte Corday is admitted."

The young heroine offered to give him some necessary information about the counter-revolution at Caen, and as he was occupied in making a note of her facts, she stabbed him with a large sheath-knife (1792). . . .

Such was the quality of most of the leaders of the Jacobin party. They were men of no property—untethered men. They were more dissociated and more elemental, therefore, than any other party; and they were ready to push the ideas of freedom and equality to a logical extremity. Their standards of patriotic virtue were high and harsh. There was something inhuman even in their humanitarian zeal. They saw without humour the disposition of the moderates to ease things down, to keep the common folk just a little needy and respectful, and royalty (and men of substance) just a little respected. They were blinded by the formulæ of Rousseauism to the historical truth that man is by nature oppressor and oppressed, and that it is only slowly by law, education, and the spirit of love in the world that men can be made happy and free.

And while in America the formulæ of eighteenth-century democracy were on the whole stimulating and helpful because it was already a land of open-air practical equality so far as white men were concerned, in France these formulæ made a very heady and dangerous mixture for the town populations, because considerable parts of the towns of France were slums full of dispossessed, demoralized, degraded, and bitter-spirited people. The Parisian crowd was in a particularly desperate and dangerous state, because the industries of Paris had been largely luxury industries, and much of her employment parasitic on the weaknesses and vices of fashionable life. Now the fashionable world had gone over the frontier, travellers were restricted, business disordered, and the city full of unemployed and angry people.

But the royalists, instead of realizing the significance of these Jacobins with their dangerous integrity and their dangerous grip upon the imagination of the mob, had the conceit to think they could make tools of them. The time for the replacement of the National Assembly under the new-made constitution by the "Legislative Assembly," was drawing near; and when the Jacobins with the idea of breaking up the moderates, proposed to make the members of the National Assembly ineligible for the Legislative Assembly, the royalists supported them with great glee, and carried the proposal. They perceived that the Legislative Assembly, so clipped of all experience, must certainly be a politically incompetent body. They would "extract good from the excess of evil," and presently France would fall back helpless into the hands of her legitimate masters. So they thought. And the royalists did more than this. They backed the election of a Jacobin as Mayor of Paris. It was about as clever as if a man brought home a hungry tiger to convince his wife of her need of him. There stood another body ready at hand with which these royalists did not reckon, far better equipped than the Court to step in and take the place of an ineffective Legislative Assembly, and that was the strongly Jacobin Commune of Paris installed at the Hôtel de Ville.

So far France had been at peace. None of her neighbours had attacked her, because she appeared to be weakening herself by her internal dissensions. It was Poland that suffered by the distraction of France. But there seemed no reason why they should not insult and threaten her, and prepare the way for a later partition at their convenience. At Pilnitz, in 1791, the King of Prussia and the Emperor of Austria met, and issued a declaration that the restoration of order and monarchy in France was a matter of interest to all sovereigns. And an army of émigrés, French nobles and gentlemen, an army largely of officers, was allowed to accumulate close to the frontier.

It was France that declared war against Austria. The motives of those who supported this step were conflicting. Many republicans wanted it because they wished to see the kindred people of Belgium liberated from the Austrian yoke. Many royalists wanted it because they saw in war a possibility of restoring the prestige of the crown. Marat opposed it bitterly in his paper *L'Ami du Peuple* because he did not want to see republican enthusiasm turned into war fever. His instinct warned him of Napoleon. On April 20th, 1792, the king came down to the Assembly and proposed war amidst great applause.

The war began disastrously. Three French armies entered Belgium; two were badly beaten, and the third, under Lafayette, retreated. Then Prussia declared war in support of Austria, and the allied forces, under the Duke of Brunswick, prepared to invade France. The duke issued one of the most foolish proclamations in history; he was, he said, invading France to restore the royal authority. Any further indignity shown the king he threatened to visit upon the Assembly and Paris with "military execution." This was surely enough to make the most royalist Frenchman a republican—at least for the duration of the war.

The new phase of revolution, the Jacobin revolution, was the direct outcome of this proclamation. It made the Legislative Assembly, in which orderly republicans (Girondins) and royalists prevailed, it made the government which had put down that republican meeting in the Champ de Mars and hunted Marat into the sewers, impossible. The insurgents gathered at the Hôtel de Ville, and on the 10th of August the Commune launched an attack on the palace of the Tuileries.

The king behaved with a clumsy stupidity, and with that disregard for others which is the prerogative of kings. He had with him a Swiss guard of nearly a thousand men as well as National Guards of uncertain loyalty. He held out vaguely until firing began, and then he went off to the adjacent Assembly to place himself and his family under its protection, leaving his Swiss fighting. No doubt he hoped to antagonize Assembly and Commune, but the Assembly had none of the fighting spirit of the Hôtel de Ville. The royal refugees were placed in a box reserved for journalists (out of which a small room opened), and there they remained for sixteen hours while the Assembly debated their fate. Outside there were the sounds of a considerable battle; every now and then a window would break. The unfortunate Swiss were fighting with their backs to the wall because there was now nothing else for them to do. . . .

The Assembly had no stomach to back the government's action of July in the Champ de Mars. The fierce vigour of the Commune dominated it. The king found no comfort whatever in the Assembly. It scolded him and discussed his "suspension." The Swiss fought until they received a message from the king to desist, and then—the crowd being savagely angry at the needless bloodshed and out of control—they were for the most part massacred.

The long and tedious attempt to "Merovingianize" Louis, to make an honest crowned republican out of a dull and inadaptable absolute monarch, was now drawing to its tragic close. The Commune of Paris was practically in control of France. The Legislative Assembly—which had apparently undergone a change of heart—decreed that the king was suspended from his office, confined him in the Temple, replaced him by an executive commission, and summoned a National Convention to frame a new constitution.

The tension of patriotic and republican France was now becoming intolerable. Such armies as she had were rolling back helplessly towards Paris (see map). Longwy had fallen, the great fortress of Verdun followed, and nothing seemed likely to stop the march of the Allies upon the capital. The sense of

royalist treachery rose to panic cruelty. At any rate the royalists had to be
silenced and stilled and scared out of sight. The Commune set itself to hunt
out every royalist that could be found, until the prisons of Paris were full.
Marat saw the danger of a massacre. Before it was too late he tried to secure
the establishment of emergency tribunals to filter the innocent from the guilty
in this miscellaneous collection of schemers, suspects, and harmless gentlefolk.
He was disregarded, and early in September the inevitable massacre occurred.

Suddenly, first at one prison and then at others, bands of insurgents took
possession. A sort of rough court was constituted, and outside gathered a wild
mob armed with sabres, pikes, and axes. One by one the prisoners, men and

women alike, were led out from their cells, questioned briefly, pardoned with
the cry of "Vive la Nation!" or thrust out to the mob at the gates. There
the crowd jostled and fought to get a slash or thrust at a victim. The condemned were stabbed, hacked, and beaten to death, their heads hewn off,
stuck on pikes, and carried about the town, their torn bodies thrust aside.
Among others, the Princess de Lamballe, whom the king and queen had left
behind in the Tuileries, perished. Her head was carried on a pike to the Temple
for the queen to see.

In the queen's cell were two National Guards. One would have had her look
out and see this grisly sight; the other, in pity, would not let her do so.

Even as this red tragedy was going on in Paris, the French general Dumouriez, who had rushed an army from Flanders into the forests of the Argonne, was holding up the advance of the Allies beyond Verdun. On September 20th occurred a battle, mainly an artillery encounter, at Valmy. A not very resolute Prussian advance was checked, the French infantry stood firm, their artillery was better than the allied artillery. For ten days after this repulse the Duke of Brunswick hesitated, and then he began to fall back towards the Rhine. The sour grapes of Champagne had spread dysentery in the Prussian army. This battle at Valmy—it was little more than a cannonade—was one of the decisive battles in the world's history. The Revolution was saved.

The National Convention met on September 21st, 1792, and immediately proclaimed a republic. The trial and execution of the king followed with a sort of logical necessity upon these things. He died rather as a symbol than as a man. There was nothing else to be done with him; a poor man, he cumbered the earth. France could not let him go to hearten the emigrants, could not keep him harmless at home; his existence threatened her. Marat had urged this trial relentlessly, yet with that acid clearness of his he would not have the king charged with any offence committed before he signed the constitution, because before then he was a real monarch, super-legal, and so incapable of being illegal. Nor would Marat permit attacks upon the king's counsel. . . . Throughout Marat played a bitter and yet often a just part; he was a great man, a fine intelligence, in a skin of fire; wrung with that organic hate in the blood that is not a product of the mind but of the body.

Louis was beheaded in January, 1793. He was guillotined—for since the previous August the guillotine had been in use as the official instrument in French executions.

Danton, in his leonine rôle, was very fine upon this occasion. "The kings of Europe would challenge us," he roared. "We throw them the head of a king!"

§ 11

And now followed a strange phase in the history of the French people. There arose a great flame of enthusiasm for France and the Republic. There was to be an end to compromise at home and abroad: at home, royalists and every form of disloyalty was to be stamped out; abroad, France was to be the protector and helper of all revolutionaries. All Europe, all the world, was to become republican. The youth of France poured into the republican armies; a new and wonderful song spread through the land, a song that still warms the blood like wine, the "Marseillaise." Before that chant and the leaping columns of French bayonets and their enthusiastically-served guns the foreign armies rolled back. Before the end of 1792 the French armies had gone far beyond the utmost achievements of Louis XIV; everywhere they stood on foreign soil. They were in Brussels, they had overrun Savoy, and they had raided to Mayence; they had seized the Scheldt from Holland. Then the French Government did an unwise thing. It had been exasperated by the expulsion of its representative from England upon the execution of Louis, and it declared war against England. It was an unwise thing to do, because the Revolution, which had given France a new enthusiastic infantry and a brilliant artillery released from its aristocratic officers and many cramping traditions, had destroyed the discipline of its navy, and the English were supreme upon the sea. And this provocation united all England against France, whereas there had been at first a very considerable liberal movement in Great Britain in sympathy with the Revolution.

Of the fight that France made in the next few years against a European coalition we cannot tell in any detail. She drove the Austrians for ever out of Belgium, and made Holland a republic. The Dutch fleet, frozen in the Texel, surrendered to a handful of cavalry without firing its guns. For some time the French thrust towards Italy was hung up, and it was only in 1796 that a new general, Napoleon Bonaparte, led the ragged and hungry republican armies in triumph across Piedmont to Mantua and Verona. An *Outline of History* cannot map out campaigns; but of the new quality that had come into war it is bound to take note. The old professional armies had fought for the fighting, as slack as workers paid by the hour; these wonderful new armies fought, hungry and thirsty, for victory. Their enemies called them the "New French." Says C. F. Atkinson,[1] "What astonished the Allies most of all was the number and the velocity of the Republicans. These improvised armies had, in fact, nothing to delay them. Tents were unprocurable for want of money, untransportable for want of the enormous number of wagons that would have been required, and also unnecessary, for the discomfort that would have caused wholesale desertion in professional armies was cheerfully borne by the men of 1793–94. Supplies for armies of then unheard-of size could not be carried in convoys, and the French soon became familiar with 'living on the country.' Thus 1793 saw the birth of the modern system of war—rapidity of movement, full development of national strength, bivouacs, requisitions, and force, as against cautious manœuvring, small professional armies, tents and full rations, and chicane. The first represented the decision-compelling spirit, the second the spirit of risking little to gain a little. . . ."

And while these ragged hosts of enthusiasts were chanting the "Marseillaise" and fighting for *la France,* manifestly never quite clear in their minds whether they were looting or liberating the countries into which they had poured, the republican enthusiasm in Paris was spending itself in a far less glorious fashion. Marat, the one man of commanding intelligence among the Jacobins, was now frantic with an incurable disease, and presently he was murdered; Danton was a series of patriotic thunderstorms; the steadfast fanaticism of Robespierre dominated the situation. This man is difficult to judge; he was a man of poor physique, naturally timid, and a prig. But he had that most necessary gift for power, faith. He believed not in a god familiar to men, but in a certain Supreme Being, and that Rousseau was his prophet. He set himself to save the Republic as he conceived it, and he imagined it could be saved by no

---

[1] In his article "French Revolutionary Wars," in the *Encyclopædia Britannica* Twelfth Edition.

other man than he. So that to keep in power was to save the republic. The living spirit of the republic, it seemed, had sprung from a slaughter of royalists and the execution of the king. There were insurrections: one in the west, in the district of La Vendée, where the people rose against conscription and against the dispossession of the orthodox clergy, and were led by noblemen and priests; one in the south, where Lyons and Marseilles had risen and the royalists of Toulon had admitted an English and Spanish garrison. To which there seemed no more effectual reply than to go on killing royalists.

Nothing could have better pleased the fierce heart of the Paris slums. The Revolutionary Tribunal went to work, and a steady slaughtering began.

In the thirteen months before June, 1794, there were 1,220 executions; in the following seven weeks there were 1,376. The invention of the guillotine was opportune to this mood. The queen was guillotined, and most of Robespierre's antagonists were guillotined; atheists who argued that there was no Supreme Being were guillotined; Danton was guillotined because he thought there was too much guillotine; day by day, week by week, this infernal new machine chopped off heads and more heads and more. The reign of Robespierre lived, it seemed, on blood, and needed more and more, as an opium-taker needs more and more opium.

Danton was still Danton, leonine and exemplary, upon the guillotine. · "Danton," he said, "no weakness!"

And the grotesque thing about the story is that Robespierre was indubitably honest. He was far more honest than any of the group of men who succeeded him. He was inspired by a consuming passion for a new order of human life. So far as he could contrive it, the Committee of Public Safety, the emergency government of twelve which had now thrust aside the Convention, *constructed*. The scale on which it sought to construct was stupendous. All the intricate problems with which we will struggle to-day were met by swift and shallow solutions. Attempts were made to equalize property. "Opulence," said St. Just, "is infamous." The property of the rich was taxed or confiscated in order that it should be divided among the poor. Every man was to have a secure house, a living, a wife and children. The labourer was worthy of his hire, but not entitled to an advantage. There was an attempt to abolish *profit* altogether, the rude incentive of most human commerce since the beginning of society. Profit is the economic riddle that still puzzles us to-day. There were harsh laws against "profiteering" in France in 1793; England in 1940 found it necessary to make quite similar laws. And the Jacobin government not only replanned— in eloquent outline—the economic but also the social system. Divorce was made as easy as marriage; the distinction of legitimate and illegitimate children was abolished. . . . A new calendar was devised, with new names for the months, a week of ten days, and the like—that has long since been swept away; but also the clumsy coinage and the tangled weights and measures of old France gave place to the simple and lucid decimal system that still endures. . . . There was a proposal from one extremist group to abolish God among other institutions altogether, and to substitute the worship of Reason. There was, indeed, a Feast of Reason in the cathedral of Notre Dame, with a pretty actress as the Goddess of Reason. But against this Robespierre set his face; he was no atheist. "Atheism," he said, "is aristocratic. The idea of a Supreme Being who watches over oppressed innocence and punishes triumphant crime is essentially the idea of the people."

So he guillotined Hébert, who had celebrated the Feast of Reason, and all his party.

A certain mental disorder became perceptible in Robespierre as the summer of 1794 drew on. He was deeply concerned with his religion. (The arrests and executions of suspects were going on now as briskly as ever. Through the streets of Paris every day rumbled the Terror with its carts full of condemned people.) He induced the Convention to decree that France believed in a Supreme Being, and in that comforting doctrine the immortality of the soul. In June he celebrated a great festival, the festival of his Supreme Being. There was a procession to the Champ de Mars, which he headed, brilliantly arrayed, bearing a great bunch of flowers and wheat-ears. Figures of inflammatory material, which represented Atheism and Vice, were solemnly burnt; then, by an ingenious mechanism, and with some slight creakings, an incombustible statue of Wisdom rose in their place. There were discourses—Robespierre delivered the chief one—but apparently no worship. . . .

Thereafter Robespierre displayed a disposition to brood aloof from affairs. For a month he kept away from the Convention.

One day in July he reappeared and delivered a strange speech that clearly foreshadowed fresh prosecutions. "Gazing on the multitude of vices which the torrent of Revolution has rolled down," he cried, in his last great speech in the Convention, "I have sometimes trembled lest I should be soiled by the impure neighbourhood of wicked men. . . . I know that it is easy for the leagued tyrants of the world to overwhelm a single individual; but I know also what is the duty of a man who can die in the defence of humanity." . . .

And so on to vague utterances that seemed to threaten everyone.

The Convention heard this speech in silence; then when a proposal was made to print and circulate it, broke into a resentful uproar and refused permission. Robespierre went off in bitter resentment to the club of his supporters, and *re-read his speech to them!*

That night was full of talk and meetings and preparations for the morrow, and the next morning the Convention turned upon Robespierre. One Tallien threatened him with a dagger. When he tried to speak he was shouted down, and the President jingled the bell at him. "President of Assassins," cried Robespierre, "I demand speech!" It was refused him. His voice deserted him; he coughed and spluttered. "The blood of Danton chokes him," cried someone.

He was accused and arrested there and then with his chief supporters.

Whereupon the Hôtel de Ville, still stoutly Jacobin, rose against the Convention, and Robespierre and his companions were snatched out of the hands of their captors. There was a night of gathering, marching, counter-marching; and at last, about three in the morning, the forces of the Convention faced the forces of the Commune outside the Hôtel de Ville.

Henriot, the Jacobin commander, after a busy day, was drunk upstairs; a parley ensued, and then, after some indecision, the soldiers of the Commune went over to the Government. There was a shouting of patriotic sentiments, and someone looked out from the Hôtel de Ville. Robespierre and his last companions found themselves betrayed and trapped.

Two or three of these men threw themselves out of a window, and injured themselves frightfully on the railings below without killing themselves. Others attempted suicide. Robespierre, it seems, was shot in the lower jaw by a gendarme. He was found, his eyes staring from a pale face whose lower part was blood.

Followed seventeen hours of agony before his end. He spoke never a word during that time; his jaw being bound up roughly in dirty linen. He and his companions, and the broken, dying bodies of those who had jumped from the windows, twenty-two men altogether, were taken to the guillotine instead of the condemned appointed for that day. Mostly his eyes were closed, but, says Carlyle, he opened them to see the great knife rising above him, and struggled. Also it would seem he screamed when the executioner removed his bandages. Then the knife came down, swift and merciful.

The Terror was at an end. From first to last there had been condemned and executed about four thousand people.

§ 12

It witnesses to the immense vitality and the profound rightness of the flood of new ideals and intentions that the French Revolution had released into the world of practical endeavour, that it could still flow in a creative torrent after it had been caricatured and mocked in the grotesque personality and career of Robespierre. He had shown its deepest thoughts, he had displayed anticipations of its methods and conclusions, through the green and distorting lenses of his preposterous vanity and egotism; he had smeared and blackened all its hope and promise with blood and horror; and yet the power of these ideas was not destroyed. They had stood the extreme tests of ridiculous and horrible presentation. After his downfall, the Republic still ruled unassailable. Leaderless, for his successors were a group of crafty or commonplace men, the European republic struggled on, and presently fell and rose again, and fell and rose and still struggles, entangled but invincible.

And it is well to remind the reader here of the real dimensions of this phase of the Terror, which strikes so vividly upon the imagination and which has therefore been enormously exaggerated relatively to the rest of the Revolution. From 1789 to late in 1791 the French Revolution was an orderly process, and from the summer of 1794 the Republic was an orderly and victorious state. The Terror was not the work of the whole country, but of the town mob which owed its existence and its savagery to the misrule and social injustice of the ancient regime; and the explosion of the Terror could have happened only through the persistent treacherous disloyalty of the royalists, which, while it raised the extremists to frenzy, disinclined the mass of moderate republicans from any intervention. The best men were busy fighting the Austrians and royalists on the frontier.

Altogether, we must remember, the total of the killed in the Terror amounted to a few thousands, and among those thousands there were certainly a great number of active antagonists whom the Republic, by all the standards of that time, was entitled to kill. It included such traitors and mischief-makers as Philip, Duke of Orleans, of the Palais-Royal, who had voted for the death of Louis XVI. More lives were wasted by the British generals alone on the opening day of what is known as the Somme offensive of July, 1916, than in the whole French Revolution from start to finish.

We hear so much about the martyrs of the French Terror because they were notable, well-connected people, and because there has been a sort of propaganda of their sufferings. But let us balance against them in our minds what was going on in the prisons of the world, generally at that time. In Britain and America, while the Terror ruled in France, far more people were slaughtered for offences—very often quite trivial offences—against property than were condemned by the Revolutionary Tribunal for treason against the State. Of course, they were very common people indeed, but in their rough way they suffered. A girl was hanged in Massachusetts in 1789 for forcibly taking the hat, shoes, and buckles of another girl she had met in the street. Again, Howard the philanthropist (about 1773) found a number of perfectly innocent people detained in the English prisons who had been tried and acquitted but were unable to pay the gaoler's fees. And these prisons were filthy places under no effective control. Torture was still in use in the Hanoverian dominions of his Britannic Majesty King George III. It had been in use in France up to the time of the National Assembly. These things mark the level of the age.

It is not on record that anyone was deliberately tortured by the French revolutionaries during the Terror. Those few hundreds of French gentlefolk fell into a pit that most of them had been well content should exist for others. It was tragic, but not, by the scale of universal history, a great tragedy. The common man in France was more free, better off, and happier during the "Terror" than he had been in 1787.

The story of the Republic after the summer of 1794 becomes a tangled story of political groups aiming at everything from a radical republic to a royalist reaction, but pervaded by a general desire for some definite working arrangement even at the price of considerable concessions. There was a series of insurrections of the Jacobins and of the Royalists: there seems to have been what we should call nowadays a hooligan class in Paris which was quite ready to turn out to fight and loot on either side; nevertheless the Convention produced a government, the Directory of five members, which held France together for five years. The last, most threatening revolt of all, in October, 1795, was suppressed with great skill and decision by a rising young general, Napoleon Bonaparte.

The Directory was victorious abroad, but uncreative at home; its members were far too anxious to stick to the sweets and glories of office to prepare a constitution that would supersede them, and far too dishonest to handle the task of financial and economic reconstruction demanded by the condition of France. We need only note two of their names—Carnot, who was an honest republican; and Barras, who was conspicuously a rogue. Their reign of five years formed a curious interlude in this history of great changes. They took things as they found them. The propagandist zeal of the Revolution carried the French armies into Holland, Belgium, Switzerland, south Germany, and north Italy. Everywhere kings were expelled and republics set up.

But such propagandist zeal as animated the Directorate did not prevent the looting of the treasures of the liberated peoples to relieve the financial embarrassment of the French Government. Their wars became less and less the holy war of freedom, and more and more like the aggressive wars of the ancient regime. The last feature of Grand Monarchy that France was disposed to discard was her foreign policy. One discovers it still as vigorous under the Directorate as if there had been no revolution.

§ 13

The ebb of this tide of revolution in the world, this tide which had create the great republic of America and threatened to submerge all European monarchies, was now at hand. It is as if something had thrust up from beneath the surface of human affairs, made a gigantic effort, and for a time spent itself. It swept many obsolescent and evil things away, but many evil and unjust things remained. It solved many problems, and it left the desire for fellowship and order face to face with much vaster problems that it seemed only to have revealed. Privilege of certain types had gone, many tyrannies, much religious persecution. When these things of the ancient regime had vanished, it seemed as if they had never mattered. What did matter was that for all their votes and enfranchisement, and in spite of all their passion and effort, common men were still not free and not enjoying an equal happiness; that the immense promise and air of a new world with which the Revolution had come remained unfulfilled.

Yet, after all, this wave of revolution had realized nearly everything that had been clearly thought out before it came. It was not failing now for want of impetus, but for want of finished ideas. Many things that had oppressed mankind were swept away for ever. Now that they were swept away it became apparent how unprepared men were for the creative opportunities this clearance gave them. And periods of revolution are periods of action; in them men reap the harvests of ideas that have grown during phases of interlude, and they leave the fields cleared for a new season of growth, but they cannot suddenly produce ripened new ideas to meet an unanticipated riddle.

The sweeping away of king and lord, of priest and inquisitor, of landlord and tax-gatherer and task-master, left the mass of men face to face for the first time with certain very fundamental aspects of the social structure, relationships they had taken for granted, and had never realized the need of thinking hard and continuously about before. Institutions that had seemed to be in the nature of things, and matters that had seemed to happen by the same sort of necessity that brought round the dawn and springtime, were discovered to be artificial, controllable, were they not so perplexingly intricate, and—now that the old routines were abolished and done away with—in urgent need of control. The New Order found itself confronted with three riddles which it was quite unprepared to solve: Property, Currency, and International Relationship.

Let us take these three problems in order, and ask what they are and how they arose in human affairs. Every human life is deeply entangled in them, and concerned in their solution. The rest of this history becomes more and more clearly the development of the effort to solve these problems; that is to say, so to interpret property, so to establish currency, and so to control international relations as to render possible a world-wide, progressive and happy community of will. They are the three riddles of the sphinx of fate, to which the human commonweal must find an answer or perish.

The idea of property arises out of the combative instincts of the species. Long before men were men, the ancestral ape was a proprietor. Primitive property is what a beast will fight for. The dog and his bone, the tigress and her lair, the roaring stag and his herd, these are proprietorship blazing. No more nonsensical expression is conceivable in sociology than the term "primitive communism." The Old Man of the family tribe of early Palæolithic times insisted upon his proprietorship in his wives and daughters, in his tools, in his visible universe. If any other man wandered into his visible universe he fought him, and if he could he slew him. The tribe grew in the course of ages, as Atkinson showed convincingly in his *Primal Law,* by the gradual toleration by the Old Man of the existence of the younger men, and of their proprietorship in the wives they captured from outside the tribe, and in the tools and ornaments they made and the game they slew. Human society grew by a compromise between this one's property and that. It was largely a compromise and an alliance forced upon men by the necessity of driving some other tribe out of its visible universe. If the hills and forests and streams were not *your* land or *my* land, it was because they had to be *our* land. Each of us would have preferred to have it *my* land, but that would not work; and in that case the other fellows would have destroyed us. Society, therefore, is from its beginnings the mitigation of ownership. Ownership in the beast and in the primitive savage was far more intense a thing than it is in the civilized world to-day. It is rooted more strongly in our instincts than in our reason.

In the natural savage and in the untutored man to-day—for it is well to keep in mind that no man to-day is more than four hundred generations from the primordial savage—there is no limitation to the sphere of ownership. Whatever you can fight for, you can own; womenfolk, spared captive, captured beast, forest glade, stone pit, or what not. As the community grew and a sort of law came to restrain internecine fighting, men developed rough and ready methods of settling proprietorship. Men could own what they were the first to make or capture or claim. It seemed natural that a debtor who could not pay up should become the property of his creditor. Equally natural was it that, after claiming a patch of land, a man should exact payments from anyone else who wanted to use it. It was only slowly, as the possibilities of organized life dawned on men, that this unlimited property in anything whatever began to be recognized as a nuisance. Men found themselves born into a universe all owned and claimed—nay, they found themselves born owned and claimed. The social struggles of the earlier civilization are difficult to trace now, but the history we have told of the Roman republic shows a community waking up to the idea that debt may become a public inconvenience and should then be repudiated, and that the unlimited ownership of land is also an inconvenience. We find that later Babylonia severely limited the rights of property in slaves. Finally, we find in the teaching of that great revolutionist, Jesus of Nazareth, such an attack upon property as had never been before. Easier it was, he said, for a camel to go through the eye of a needle than for the owner of great possessions to enter the kingdom of heaven.

A steady, continuous criticism of the permissible scope of property seems to have been going on in the world for the last twenty-five or thirty centuries. Nineteen hundred years after Jesus of Nazareth we find all the world that has come under the Christian teaching persuaded that there could be no property in persons. There has been a turnover in the common conscience in that matter. And also the idea that "a man may do what he likes with his own" was clearly very much shaken in relation to other sorts of property. But this world of the closing eighteenth century was still only in the interrogative stage in this matter. It had got nothing clear enough, much less settled enough, to act upon. One of its primary impulses was to protect property against the greed and waste of kings and the exploitation of noble adventurers. It was to protect private property that the Revolution began. But its equalitarian formulæ carried it into a criticism of the very property it had risen to protect. How can men be free and equal when numbers of them have no ground to stand upon and nothing to eat, and the owners will neither feed nor lodge them unless they toil? Excessively—the poor complained.

To which riddle the Jacobin reply was to set about "dividing up." They wanted to intensify and universalize property. Aiming at the same end by another route, there were already in the eighteenth century certain primitive socialists—or, to be more exact, communists—who wanted to "abolish" private property altogether. The State was to own all property. It was only as the nineteenth century developed that men began to realize that property was not one simple thing, but a great complex of ownerships of different values and consequences, that many things (such as one's own body, the implements of an artist, clothing, tooth-brushes) are very profoundly and incurably personal property, and that there is a very great range of things—railways, machinery of various sorts, homes, cultivated gardens, pleasure-boats, for example—which need each to be considered very particularly to determine how far and under what limitations it may come under private ownership, and how far it falls into the public domain and may be administered and let out by the state in the collective interest.

We have to-day the advantage of a hundred and thirty years of discussion over the first revolutionary generation, but even now this criticism of property is still a vast and passionate ferment rather than a science. Under the circumstances it was impossible that eighteenth-century France should present any other spectacle than that of vague and confused popular movements seeking to dispossess owners, and classes of small and large owners holding on grimly, demanding, before everything else, security of ownership.

Closely connected with the vagueness of men's ideas about property was the vagueness of their ideas about currency. Both the American and the French republics fell into serious trouble upon this score. Here, again, we deal with something that is not simple, a tangle of usages, conventions, laws, and prevalent mental habits, out of which arise problems which admit of no solution in simple terms, and which yet are of vital importance to the everyday life of the community. The validity of the acknowledgment a man is given for a day's work is manifestly of quite primary importance to the working of the social machine. The growth of confidence in the precious metals and of coins, until the assurance became practically universal that good money could be trusted to have its purchasing power anywhere, must have been a gradual one in human history. And being fairly established, this assurance was subjected to very considerable strains and perplexities by the action of governments in debasing currency and in substituting paper promises to pay for the actual metallic coins. So soon as serious political and social dislocation occurred, the money mechanism began to work stiffly and inaccurately.

The United States and the French Republic both started their careers in a phase of financial difficulty. Both governments had been borrowing and issuing paper promises to pay interest, more interest than they could conveniently raise. Both revolutions led to much desperate public spending and borrowing, and at the same time to an interruption of cultivation and production that further diminished real taxable wealth. Both governments, being unable to pay their way in gold, resorted to the issue of paper money, promising to pay upon the security of undeveloped land (in America) or recently confiscated church lands (France). In both cases the amount of issue went far beyond the confidence of men in the new security. Gold was called in, hidden by the cunning ones, or went abroad to pay for imports; and people found themselves with various sorts of bills and notes in the place of coins, all of uncertain and diminishing value.

However complicated the origins of currency, its practical effects and the end it has to serve in the community may be stated roughly in simple terms. The money a man receives for his work (mental or bodily) or for relinquishing his property in some consumable good, must ultimately be able to purchase for him for his use a fairly equivalent amount of consumable goods. ("Consumable goods" is a phrase we would have understood in the widest sense to represent even such things as a journey, a lecture or theatrical entertainment, housing, medical advice, and so forth.) When everyone in a community is assured of this, and assured that the money will not deteriorate in purchasing power, then currency—and the distribution of goods by trade—is in a healthy and satisfactory state. Then men will work cheerfully, and only then.

The imperative need for that steadfastness and security of currency is the fixed datum, therefore, from which the scientific study and control of currency must begin. But under the most stable conditions there will always be fluctuations in currency value. The sum total of saleable consumable goods in the world and in various countries varies from year to year and from season to season; autumn is probably a time of plenty in comparison with spring; with an increase in the available goods in the world the purchasing power of currency will increase, unless there is also an increase in the amount of currency. On the other hand, if there is a diminution in the production of consumable goods or a great and unprofitable destruction of consumable goods, such as occurs in a war, the share of the total of consumable goods represented by a sum of money will diminish, and prices and wages will rise. In modern war the explosion of a single big shell, even if it hits nothing, destroys labour and material roughly equivalent to a comfortable cottage or a year's holiday for a man. If the shell hits anything, then that further destruction has to be added to the diminution of consumable goods. Every shell that burst in the first World War diminished by a little fraction the purchasing value of every coin in the whole world. If there is also an increase of currency during a period when consumable goods are being used up and not fully replaced—and the necessities of revolutionary and war-making governments almost always require this— then the enhancement of prices and the fall in the value of the currency paid in wages is still greater.

Usually, also, governments under these stresses borrow money—that is to say, they issue interest-bearing paper, secured on the willingness and ability of the general community to endure taxation.

Such operations would be difficult enough if they were carried out frankly by perfectly honest men, in the full light of publicity and scientific knowledge. But hitherto this has never been the case; at every point the clever egotist, the bad sort of rich man, is trying to deflect things a little to his own advantage. Everywhere, too, one finds the stupid egotist ready to take fright and break into panic. Consequently we presently discover the State encumbered by an excess of currency, which is in effect a noninterest-paying debt, and also with a great burthen of interest upon loans. Both credit and currency begin to fluctuate wildly with the evaporation of public confidence. They are, we say, demoralized.

The ultimate consequence of an entirely demoralized currency would be to end all work and all trade that could not be carried on by payment in kind and barter. Men would refuse to work, except for food, clothing, housing, and payment in kind. The immediate consequence of a partially demoralized currency is to drive up prices and make trading feverishly adventurous and workers suspicious and irritable. A sharp man wants under such conditions to hold money for as brief a period as possible; he demands the utmost for his reality, and buys a reality again as soon as possible in order to get this perishable stuff, the currency paper, off his hands. All who have fixed incomes and saved accumulations suffer by the rise in prices, and the wage-earners find, with a gathering fury, that the real value of their wages is continually less.

Here is a state of affairs where the duty of every clever person is evidently to help adjust and reassure. But all the traditions of private enterprise, all the ideas of the later eighteenth century, went to justify the action of acute-minded and dexterous people who set themselves to accumulate claims, title, and tangible property in the storms and dislocations of this currency breakdown. The number of understanding people in the world who were setting themselves sincerely and simply to restore honest and workable currency and credit conditions were few and ineffectual. Most of the financial and speculative people of the time were playing the part of Cornish wreckers—not apparently with any conscious dishonesty, but with the completest self-approval and the applause of their fellow-men. The aim of every clever person was to accumulate as much as he could of really negotiable wealth, and then, and only then, to bring about some sort of stabilizing political process that would leave him in advantageous possession of his accumulation. Here were the factors of a bad economic atmosphere, suspicious, feverish, greedy, and speculative. . . .

In the third direction in which the Revolution had been unprepared with clear ideas, the problem of international relationships, developments were to occur that interacted disastrously with this state of financial and economic adventure, this scramble and confusion, this preoccupation of men's minds with the perplexing slipperiness of their private property and their monetary position at home. The Republic at its birth found itself at war. For a time that war was waged by the new levies with a patriotism and a zeal unparalleled in the world's history. But that could not go on. The Directory found itself at the head of a conquering country, intolerably needy and embarrassed at home, and in occupation of rich foreign lands, full of seizable wealth and material and financial opportunity. We have all double natures, and the French in particular seem to be developed logically and symmetrically on both sides. Into these conquered regions France came as a liberator, the teacher of Republicanism to mankind. Holland and Belgium became the Batavian Republic, Genoa and its Riviera the Ligurian Republic, north Italy the Cisalpine Republic, Switzerland was rechristened the Helvetian Republic, Mülhausen, Rome, and Naples were designated republics. Grouped about France, these republics were to be a constellation of freedom leading the world. That was the ideal side. At the same time the French Government, and French private individuals in concert with the Government, proceeded to a complete and exhaustive exploitation of the resources of these liberated lands.

So, within ten years of the meeting of the States General, New France begins to take on a singular likeness to the old. It is more flushed, more vigorous; it wears a cap of liberty instead of a crown; it has a new army—but a damaged fleet; it has new rich people instead of the old rich people, a new peasantry working even harder than the old and yielding more taxes; a new foreign policy curiously like the old foreign policy disrobed; and—there is no Millennium.

XXXVI

THE CAREER OF NAPOLEON BONAPARTE

§ 1. *The Bonaparte Family in Corsica.* § 2. *Bonaparte as a Republican General.* § 3. *Napoleon First Consul, 1799–1804.* § 4. *Napoleon I, Emperor, 1804–14.* § 5. *The Hundred Days.* § 6. *The Map of Europe in 1815.* § 7. *Empire Style.*

§ 1

AND now we come to one of the most illuminating figures in modern history, the figure of an adventurer and a wrecker, whose story seems to display with an extraordinary vividness the universal subtle conflict of egotism, vanity, and personality with the weaker, wider claims of the common good. Against this background of confusion and stress and hope, this strained and heaving France and Europe, this stormy and tremendous dawn, appears this dark little archaic personage, hard, compact, capable, unscrupulous, imitative, and neatly vulgar. He was born (1769) in the still half-barbaric island of Corsica, the son of a rather prosaic father, a lawyer who had been first a patriotic Corsican against the French monarchy which was trying to subjugate Corsica, and who had then gone over to the side of the invader. His mother was of sturdier stuff, passionately patriotic and a strong and managing woman. (She birched her sons; on one occasion she birched Napoleon when he was sixteen.) There were numerous brothers and sisters, and the family pursued the French authorities with importunities for rewards and jobs. Except for Napoleon, it seems to have been a thoroughly commonplace, "hungry" family. He was clever, bad-tempered, and overbearing. From his mother he had acquired a romantic Corsican patriotism.

Through the patronage of the French governor of Corsica he got an education first at the military school of Brienne and then at the military school of Paris, from which he passed into the artillery in 1785. He was an industrious student both of mathematics and history, his memory was prodigiously good, and he made copious note-books which still exist. These note-books show no very exceptional intelligence, and they contain short pieces of original composition—upon suicide and similar adolescent topics. He fell early under the spell of Rousseau; he developed sensibility and a scorn for the corruptions of civilization. In 1786 he wrote a pamphlet against a Swiss pastor who had attacked Rousseau. He dreamt of an independent Corsica, freed from the French. With the Revolution he became an ardent republican and a supporter of the new French regime in Corsica. For some years, until the fall of Robespierre, he remained a Jacobin.

§ 2

He soon gained the reputation of a useful and capable officer, and it was through Robespierre's younger brother that he got his first chance of distinction at Toulon. Toulon had been handed over to the British and Spanish by the royalists, and an allied fleet occupied its harbour. Bonaparte was given the command of the artillery, and under his direction the French forced the allies to abandon the port and town.

He was next appointed commander of the artillery in Italy, but he had not taken up his duties when the death of Robespierre seemed likely to involve his own; he was put under arrest as a Jacobin, and for a time he was in danger of the guillotine. That danger passed. He was employed as artillery commander in an abortive raid upon Corsica, and then went to Paris (1795) rather down at heel. Madame Junot in her *Memoirs* describes his lean face and slovenly appearance at this time, "his ill-combed, ill-powdered hair hanging down over his grey overcoat," his gloveless hands and badly blacked boots. It was a time of exhaustion and reaction after the severities of the Jacobite republic. "In Paris," says Holland Rose, "the star of Liberty was paling before Mercury, Mars, and Venus"—finance, uniforms, and social charm. The best of the common men were in the armies, away beyond the frontiers. We have already noted the last rising of the royalists in this year (1795). Napoleon had the luck to be in Paris, and found his second opportunity in this affair. He saved the Republic—of the Directory.

His abilities greatly impressed Carnot, the most upright of the Directors. Moreover, he married a charming young widow, Madame Josephine de Beauharnais, who had great influence with Barras. Both these things probably helped him to secure the command in Italy.

We have no space here for the story of his brilliant campaigns in Italy (1796–97), but of the spirit in which that invasion of Italy was conducted we must say a word or two, because it illustrates so vividly the double soul of France and of Napoleon, and how revolutionary idealism was paling before practical urgencies. He proclaimed to the Italians that the French were coming to break their chains—*and they were!* He wrote to the Directory: "We will levy 20,000,000 francs in exactions in this country; it is one of the richest in the world." To his soldiers he said, "You are famished and nearly naked. . . . I lead you into the most fertile plain in the world. There you will find great towns, rich provinces, honour, glory, riches. . . ."

We are all such mixed stuff as this; but these passages, written by a young man of twenty-seven, seem to show the gilt of honourable idealism rubbed off at an unusually early age.

His successes in Italy were brilliant and complete. He had wanted to go into Italy because there lay the most attractive task; he had risked his position in the army by refusing to take up the irksome duties of a command against the rebels in La Vendée. He had been a great reader of Plutarch's *Lives* and of Roman History, and his extremely active imagination was now busy with dreams of a revival of the eastern conquests of the Roman Empire. He got the republic of Venice out of his way by cutting it up between the French and Austria, securing the Ionian Islands and the Venetian fleet for France. This peace, the Peace of Campo Formio, proved a bad bargain for both sides. The new republic of France assisted in the murder of an ancient republic— Napoleon carried his point against a considerable outcry in France—and Austria got Venetia, in which land in 1918 she was destined to bleed to death. There were also secret clauses by which both France and Austria were later to acquire south German territory. And it was not only the Roman push eastward that was now exciting Napoleon's brain. This was the land of Cæsar— and Cæsar was a bad example for the successful general of a not very stable republic.

Cæsar had come back to Rome from Gaul a hero and conqueror. His imitator would come back from Egypt and India—Egypt and India were to

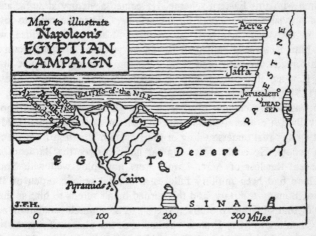

be his Gaul. The elements of failure stared him in the face. The way to Egypt and India was by sea, and the British, in spite of two recent naval mutinies, were stronger than the French at sea. Moreover, Egypt was a part of the Turkish Empire, by no means a contemptible power in those days. Nevertheless, he persuaded the Directory, which was dazzled by his Italian exploits, to let him go. An Armada started from Toulon in May, 1798, captured Malta, and had the good luck to evade the British fleet and arrive at Alexandria. He landed his troops hurriedly, and the Battle of the Pyramids made him master of Egypt.

The main British fleet at that time was in the Atlantic outside Cadiz, but the admiral had detached a force of his best ships, under Vice-Admiral Nelson —as great a genius in naval affairs as was Napoleon in things military—to chase and engage the French flotilla. For a time Nelson sought the French fleet in vain; finally, on the evening of the 1st of August, he found it at anchor in Aboukir Bay. He had caught it unawares; many of the men were ashore and a council was being held in the flagship. He had no charts, and it was a hazardous thing to sail into the shallow water in a bad light. The French admiral concluded, therefore, that his adversary would not attack before morning, and so made no haste in recalling his men aboard until it was too late to do so. Nelson, however, struck at once—against the advice of some of his captains. One ship only went aground. She marked the shoal for the rest of the fleet. He sailed to the attack in a double line about sundown, putting the French between two fires. Night fell as the battle was joined; the fight thundered and crashed in the darkness, until it was lit presently by the flames of burning French ships, and then by the flare of the French flagship, the *Orient,* blowing up. . . . Before midnight the Battle of the Nile was over, and Napoleon's fleet was destroyed. Napoleon was cut off from France.

Says Holland Rose, quoting Thiers, this Egyptian expedition was "the rashest attempt history records." Napoleon was left in Egypt with the Turks gathering against him and his army infected with the plague. Nevertheless, he went on for a time with this Eastern scheme. He gained a victory at Jaffa, and, being short of provisions, *massacred all his prisoners.* Then he tried to take Acre, where his own siege artillery, just captured at sea by the British, was used against him. Returning baffled to Egypt, he gained a brilliant victory over a Turkish force at Aboukir, and then, deserting the army of Egypt—it held on till 1801, when it capitulated to a British force—made his escape back to France (1799), narrowly missing capture by a British cruiser off Sicily.

Here was failure enough to discredit any general—had it been known. But the very British cruisers which came so near to catching him helped him by preventing any real understanding of the Egyptian situation from reaching the French people. He could make a great flourish over the Battle of Aboukir and conceal the loss of Acre. Things were not going well with France just then. There had been military failures at several points; much of Italy had been lost, Bonaparte's Italy, and this turned men's minds to him as the natural saviour of that situation; moreover, there had been much peculation, and some of it was coming to light. France was in one of her phases of financial scandal, and Napoleon had not filched; the public was in that state of moral fatigue when a strong and honest man is called for, a wonderful, impossible healing man who will do everything for everybody. People persuaded themselves that this specious young man with the hard face, so providentially back from Egypt, was the strong and honest man required—another Washington.

With Julius Cæsar rather than Washington at the back of his mind, Napoleon responded to the demand of his time. A conspiracy was carefully engineered to replace the Directory by three "Consuls"—everybody seems to have been reading far too much Roman history just then—of whom Napoleon was to be the chief. The working of that conspiracy is too intricate a story for our space: it involved a Cromwell-like dispersal of the Lower House (the Council of Five Hundred), and in this affair Napoleon lost his nerve. The deputies shouted at him and hustled him, and he seems to have been frightened. He nearly fainted, stuttered, and could say nothing, but the situation was saved by his brother Lucien, who brought in the soldiers and dispersed the council. This little hitch did not affect the final success of the scheme. The three Consuls were installed at the Luxembourg Palace, with two commissioners, to reconstruct the constitution.

With all his confidence restored, and sure of the support of the people, Napoleon took a high hand with his colleagues and the commissioners. A constitution was produced in which the chief executive officer was to be called the First Consul, with enormous powers. He was to be Napoleon; this was part of the constitution. He was to be re-elected or replaced at the end of ten years. He was to be assisted by a Council of State, appointed by himself, which was to initiate legislation and send its proposals to two bodies, the Legislative Body (which could vote but not discuss) and the Tribunate (which could discuss but not vote), which were *selected* by an appointed Senate from a special class, the "notabilities of France," who were elected by the "notabilities of the departments," who were elected by the "notabilities of the commune," who were elected by the common voters. The suffrage for the election of the notabilities of the commune was universal. This was the sole vestige of democracy in the astounding pyramid.

This constitution was chiefly the joint production of a worthy philosopher, Siéyès, who was one of the three Consuls, and Bonaparte. But so weary was France with her troubles and efforts, and so confident were men in the virtue and ability of this man of destiny, that when, at the birth of the nineteenth century, this constitution was submitted to the country, it was carried by 3,011,007 votes to 1,562. France put herself absolutely in Bonaparte's hands, and prepared to be peaceful, happy, and glorious.

§ 3

Now surely here was opportunity such as never came to man before. Here was a position in which a man might well bow himself in fear of himself, and search his heart, and serve God and man to the utmost. The old order of things was dead or dying, strange new forces drove through the world seeking form and direction; the promise of a world republic and an enduring world peace whispered in a multitude of startled minds. France was in his hand, his instrument, to do with as he pleased, willing for peace, but tempered for war like an exquisite sword. There lacked nothing to this great occasion but a noble imagination. Failing that, Napoleon could do no more than strut upon the crest of this great mountain of opportunity like a cockerel on a dunghill. The figure he makes in history is one of almost incredible self-conceit, of callous contempt and disregard of all who trusted him, and of a grandiose aping of Cæsar, Alexander, and Charlemagne which would be purely comic if it were not caked over with human blood. Until, as Victor Hugo said in his tremendous way, "God was bored by him," and he was kicked aside into a corner to end his days, explaining and explaining how very clever his worst blunders had been, prowling about his dismal hot island shooting birds and squabbling meanly with an underbred jailer who failed to show him proper "respect."

His career as First Consul was perhaps the least dishonourable phase in his career. He took the crumbling military affairs of the Directory in hand, and after a complicated campaign in North Italy brought matters to a head in the victory of Marengo, near Alessandria (1800). It was a victory that at some moments came very near disaster. In the December of the same year General Moreau, in the midst of snow, mud, and altogether abominable weather, inflicted an overwhelming defeat upon the Austrian army at Hohenlinden. If Napoleon had gained this battle, it would have counted among his most characteristic and brilliant exploits. These things made the hoped-for peace possible. In 1801 the preliminaries of peace with England and Austria were signed. Peace with England, the Treaty of Amiens, was concluded in 1802, and Napoleon was free to give himself to the creative statecraft of which France, and Europe through France, stood in need. The war had given the country extended boundaries, the treaty with England restored the colonial empire of France and left her in a position of security beyond the utmost dreams of Louis XIV. It was open to Napoleon to work out and consolidate the new order of things, to make a modern State that should become a beacon and inspiration to Europe and all the world.

He attempted nothing of the sort. His little, imitative imagination was full of the dream of being Cæsar over again. He was scheming to make himself a real emperor, with a crown upon his head and all his rivals and schoolfellows and friends at his feet. This could give him no fresh power that he did not already exercise, but it would be more splendid—it would astonish his mother. What response was there in a head of that sort for the splendid creative challenge of the time?

But first France must be prosperous. France hungry would certainly not endure an emperor. He set himself to carry out an old scheme of roads that Louis XV had approved; he developed canals in imitation of the English canals; he reorganized the police and made the country safe; and, preparing the scene for his personal drama, he set himself to make Paris look like Rome,

Napoleon as Emperor

with classical arches, with classical columns. Admirable schemes for banking development were available, and he made use of them. In all these things he moved with the times; they would have happened—with less autocracy, with less centralization—if he had never been born. And he set himself to weaken the republicans whose fundamental convictions he was planning to outrage. He recalled the émigrés, provided they gave satisfactory assurances to respect the new regime. Many were very willing to come back on such terms, and let Bourbons be bygones. And he worked out a great reconciliation, a Concordat, with Rome. Rome was to support him, and he was to restore the authority of Rome in the parishes. France would never be obedient and manageable, he thought, she would never stand a new monarchy, without religion. "How can you have order in a state," he said, "without religion? Society cannot exist without inequality of fortunes, which cannot endure apart from religion. When one man is dying of hunger near another who is ill of surfeit, he cannot resign himself to this difference unless there is an authority which declares—'God wills it thus: there must be poor and rich in the world: but hereafter and during all eternity the division of things will take place differently.'" Religion—and especially of the later Roman brand—was, he thought, excellent stuff for keeping the common people quiet. In his early Jacobin days he had denounced it for that very reason.

Another great achievement which marks his imaginative scope and his estimate of human nature was the institution of the Legion of Honour, a scheme for decorating Frenchmen with bits of ribbon which was admirably calculated to divert ambitious men from subversive proceedings.

And, also, Napoleon interested himself in Christian propaganda. Here is the Napoleonic view of the political uses of Christ, a view that has tainted all French missions from that time forth. "It is my wish to re-establish the institution for foreign missions; for the religious missionaries may be very useful to me in Asia, Africa, and America, as I shall make them reconnoitre all the lands they visit. The sanctity of their dress will not only protect them but serve to conceal their political and commercial investigations. The head of the missionary establishment shall reside no longer at Rome, but in Paris."

These are the ideas of a roguish merchant rather than a statesman. His treatment of education shows the same blindness to the realities of the dawn about him. Elementary education he neglected almost completely; he left it to the conscience of the local authorities, and he provided that the teachers should be paid out of the fees of the scholars; it is clear he did not want the common people to be educated; he had no glimmering of any understanding why they should be; but he interested himself in the provision of technical and higher schools because his State needed the services of clever, self-seeking, well-informed men. This was an astounding retrogression from the great scheme, drafted by Condorcet for the Republic in 1792, for a complete system of free education for the entire nation. Slowly but steadfastly the project of Condorcet comes true; the great nations of the world are being compelled to bring it nearer and nearer to realization, and the devices of Napoleon pass out of our interest. As for the education of the mothers and wives of our race, this was the quality of Napoleon's wisdom: "I do not think that we need trouble ourselves with any plan of instruction for young females; they cannot be better brought up than by their mothers. Public education is not suitable for them, because they are never called upon to act in public. Manners are all in all to them, and marriage is all they look to."

The First Consul was no kinder to women in the *Code Napoléon*. A wife, for example, had no control over her own property; she was in her husband's hands. This code was the work very largely of the Council of State. Napoleon seems rather to have hindered than helped its deliberations. He would

invade the session without notice, and favour its members with lengthy mono-
logues, frequently quite irrelevant to the matter in hand. The Council listened
with profound respect; it was all the Council could do. He would keep his
councillors up to unearthly hours, and betray a simple pride in his superior
wakefulness. He recalled these discussions with peculiar satisfaction in his later
years, and remarked on one occasion that his glory consisted not in having
won forty battles, but in having created the *Code Napoléon*. . . . So far as
it substituted plain statements for inaccessible legal mysteries his *Code* was a
good thing; it gathered together, revised and made clear a vast disorderly
accumulation of laws old and new. Like all his constructive work, it made
for immediate efficiency, it defined things and relations so that men could get
to work upon them without further discussion. It was of less immediate practical importance that it frequently defined them wrongly. There was no intellectual power, as distinguished from intellectual energy, behind this codification.
It took everything that existed for granted: "Sa Majesté ne croit que ce qui
est."[1] The fundamental ideas of the civilized community and of the terms
of human co-operation were in process or reconstruction all about Napoleon
—and he never perceived it. He accepted a phase of change, and tried to fix
it for ever. To this day France is cramped by this early nineteenth-century
strait-waistcoat into which he clapped her. He fixed the status of women, the
status of labourers, the status of the peasant, they all struggle to this day in
the net of his hard definitions.

So briskly and forcibly Napoleon set his mind, hard, clear and narrow, to
brace up France. That bracing up was only a part of the larger schemes that
dominated him. His imagination was set upon a new Cæsarism. In 1802 he
got himself made First Consul for life with the power of appointing a successor, and his clear intention of annexing Holland and Italy, in spite of his
treaty obligations to keep them separate, made the Peace of Amiens totter
crazily from the very beginning. Since his schemes were bound to provoke a
war with England, he should have waited, at any cost, until he had brought
his navy to a superiority over the British navy. He had the control of great
resources for shipbuilding, the British government was a weak one, and three
or four years would have sufficed to shift that balance. But, in spite of his
rough experiences in Egypt, he had never mastered the importance of sea
power. In 1803 his occupation of Switzerland precipitated a crisis, and war
broke out again with England. The weak Addington in England gave place to
the greater Pitt. The rest of Napoleon's story turns upon that war.

During the period of the Consulate the First Consul was very active in
advancing the fortunes of his brothers and sisters. This was quite human, very
clannish and Corsican, and it helps us to understand just how he valued his
position and the opportunities before him. A large factor in the making of
Napoleon was the desire to amaze, astonish, and subdue the minds of the
Bonaparte family, and their neighbours. He promoted his brothers ridiculously
—for they were the most ordinary of men. But one person who knew him

---

[1] Gourgaud, quoted by Holland Rose.

well was neither amazed nor subdued. This was his mother. He sent her money to spend and astonish the neighbours; he exhorted her to make a display, to live as became the mother of so marvellous, so world-shaking a son.

But the good lady, who had birched the Man of Destiny at the age of sixteen for grimacing at his grandmother, was neither dazzled nor deceived by him at the age of thirty-two. All France might worship him, but she had no illusions. She put by the money he sent her; she continued her customary economies. "When it is all over," she said, "you will be glad of my savings."

§ 4

We will not detail the steps by which Napoleon became Emperor. His coronation was the most extraordinary revival that it is possible to imagine. Cæsar was no longer the model; Napoleon was now Charlemagne. He was crowned emperor, not indeed at Rome, but in the cathedral of Notre Dame in Paris; the Pope (Pius VII) had been brought from Rome to perform the ceremony; and at the climax Napoleon I seized the crown, waved the Pope aside, and crowned himself. The injunction of Charlemagne to Louis had at last borne fruit. In 1806 Napoleon revived another venerable antiquity, and, still following the footsteps of Charlemagne, crowned himself with the iron crown of Lombardy in the cathedral of Milan.

The four daughter republics of France were now to become kingdoms: in 1806 he set up brother Louis in Holland and brother Joseph in Naples. But the story of the subordinate kingdoms he created in Europe, helpful though this free handling of frontiers was towards the subsequent unification of Italy and Germany, is too complex and evanescent for this *Outline*.

The pact between the new Charlemagne and the new Leo did not hold good for very long. In 1807 he began to bully the Pope, and in 1811 he made him a close prisoner at Fontainebleau. There does not seem to have been much reason in these proceedings. They estranged Catholic opinion, as his coronation had estranged liberal opinion. He ceased to stand either for the old or the new. The new he had betrayed; the old he had failed to win. He stood at last for nothing but himself.

There seems to have been as little reason in the foreign policy that now plunged Europe into a fresh cycle of wars. Having quarrelled with Great Britain too soon, he (1804) assembled a vast army at Boulogne for the conquest of England, regardless of the naval situation. He even struck a medal and erected a column at Boulogne to commemorate the triumph of his projected invasion. In some "Napoleonic" fashion the British fleet was to be decoyed away, this army of Boulogne was to be smuggled across the Channel on a flotilla of rafts and boats, and London was to be captured before the fleet returned. At the same time his aggressions in south Germany forced Austria and Russia steadily into a coalition with Britain against him. In 1805 two fatal blows at any hope he may have entertained of ultimate victory were struck by the British admirals Calder and Nelson. In July the former inflicted a serious reverse upon the French fleet in the Bay of Biscay; in October the latter destroyed the joint fleets of France and Spain at the Battle of Trafalgar. Nelson died splendidly upon the *Victory,* victorious. Thereafter Napoleon was left with Britain in pitiless opposition, unattainable and unconquerable, able to strike here or there against him along all the coasts of Europe.

For some years the mortal wound of Trafalgar was hidden from the French mind altogether. They heard merely that "storms have caused us to lose some ships of the line after an imprudent fight." After Calder's victory, Napoleon snatched his army from Boulogne, rushed it across Europe, and defeated the Austrians at Ulm and Austerlitz. Under these inauspicious circumstances Prussia came into the war against him, and was utterly defeated and broken at the Battle of Jena (1806). Although Austria and Prussia were broken, Russia was still a fighting power, and the next year was devoted to this tougher and less accessible antagonist. We cannot trace in any detail the difficulties of the Polish campaign against Russia; Napoleon was roughly handled at Pultusk —which he announced in Paris as a brilliant victory—and again at Eylau. Then the Russians were defeated at Friedland (1807). As yet he had never touched Russian soil, the Russians were still as unbeaten as the British; but now came an extraordinary piece of good fortune for Napoleon. By a mixture of boasting, subtlety and flattery he won over the young and ambitious Tsar Alexander I—he was just thirty years old—to an alliance. The two emperors met on a raft in the middle of the Niemen at Tilsit, and there came to an understanding.

Alexander had imbibed much liberalism during his education at the Court of Catherine II, and was all for freedom, education, and the new order of the world—subject to his own pre-eminence. "He would gladly have everyone free," said one of his early associates, "provided that everyone was prepared to do freely exactly what he wished." And he declared that he would have abolished serfdom if it had cost him his head—if only civilization had been more advanced. He made war against France, he said, because Napoleon was a tyrant, to free the French people. After Friedland he saw Napoleon in a different light. These two men met eleven days after that rout—Alexander no doubt in the state of explanatory exaltation natural to his type during a mood of change.

Tsar Alexander I.

To Napoleon the meeting must have been extremely gratifying. This was his first meeting with an emperor upon terms of equality. Two imaginations soared together upon the raft at Tilsit. "What is Europe?" said Alexander. "*We* are Europe." They discussed the affairs of Prussia and Austria in that spirit, they divided Turkey in anticipation, they arranged for the conquest of India, and, indeed, of most of Asia, and that Russia should take Finland from the Swedes; and they disregarded the disagreeable fact that the greater part of the world's surface is sea, and that on the seas the British fleets sailed now unchallenged. Close at hand was Poland, ready to rise up and become the passionate ally of France had Napoleon but willed it so. But he was blind to Poland. It was a day of visions without vision. Napoleon even then, it seems, concealed the daring thought that he might one day marry a Russian princess, a real princess. But that, he was to learn in 1810, was going a little too far.

After Tilsit there was a perceptible deterioration in Napoleon's quality; he became rasher, less patient of obstacles, more and more the fated master of the world, more and more intolerable to everyone he encountered.

In 1808 he committed a very serious blunder. Spain was his abject ally, completely under his control, but he saw fit to depose its Bourbon king in order to promote his brother Joseph from the crown of the two Sicilies. Portugal he had already conquered, and the two kingdoms of Spain and Portugal were to be united. Thereupon the Spanish arose in a state of patriotic fury, surrounded a French army at Baylen, and compelled it to surrender. It was an astonishing break in the French career of victory.

The British were not slow to seize the foothold this insurrection gave them. A British army under Sir Arthur Wellesley (afterwards the Duke of Wellington) landed in Portugal, defeated the French at Vimiero, and compelled them to retire into Spain. The news of these reverses caused a very great excitement in Germany and Austria, and the Tsar assumed a more arrogant attitude towards his ally.

There was another meeting of these two potentates at Erfurt, in which the Tsar was manifestly less amenable to the dazzling tactics of Napoleon than he had been. Followed four years of unstable "ascendancy" for France, while the outlines on the map of Europe waved about like garments on a clothes-line on a windy day. Napoleon's personal empire grew by frank annexations to include Holland, much of Western Germany, much of Italy, and much of the eastern Adriatic coast. But one by one the French colonies were falling to the British, and the British armies in the Spanish peninsula, with the Spanish auxiliaries, slowly pressed the French northwards. All Europe was getting very weary of Napoleon; his antagonists now were no longer merely monarchs and ministers, but whole peoples also. The Prussians, after the disaster of Jena in 1806, had set to work to put their house in order. Under the leadership of Freiherr von Stein they had swept aside their feudalism, abolished privilege and serfdom, organized popular education and popular patriotism, accomplished, in fact, without any internal struggle, nearly everything that France had achieved in 1789. By 1810 a new Prussia existed, the nucleus of a new Germany. And now Alexander, inspired, it would seem, by dreams of world ascendancy, was posing again as the friend of liberty. In 1810 fresh friction was created by Alexander's objection to Napoleon's matrimonial ambitions. For Napoleon was now divorcing his old helper Josephine, because she was childless, in order to secure the "continuity" of his "dynasty." Napoleon, thwarted of a Russian princess, snubbed, indeed, by Alexander, turned to Austria and married the archduchess Marie Louise. The Austrian statesmen read him aright. They were very ready to throw him their princess. By that marriage Napoleon was captured for the dynastic system. He might have been the maker of a new world, he preferred to be the son-in-law of the old.

In the next two years his affairs crumbled apace. He was no longer the leader and complement of the Revolution; no longer the embodied spirit of a world reborn; he was just a new and rawer sort of autocrat. He had estranged all free-spirited men, and he had antagonized the church. Kings and Jacobins were at one when it came to the question of his overthrow. Britain was now his inveterate enemy; Spain was blazing with a spirit that a Corsican should have understood; it needed only a breach with Alexander I to set this empire

The EMPIRE of NAPOLEON about 1810

of bluff and stage scenery swaying towards its downfall. The quarrel came. Alexander's feelings for Napoleon had always been of a very mixed sort; he envied Napoleon as a rival and despised him as an upstart. Moreover, there was a kind of vague and sentimental greatness about Alexander; he was given to mystical religiosity, he had the conception of a mission for Russia and himself to bring peace to Europe and the world—by destroying Napoleon. But bringing peace to Europe seemed to him quite compatible with the annexation of Finland, of most of Poland, and of great portions of the Turkish Empire. And particularly he wanted to resume trading with Britain, against which Napoleon had set his face. For all the trade of Germany had been dislocated and the mercantile classes embittered by the Napoleonic "Continental System," which was to ruin Britain by excluding British goods from every country in Europe. Russia had suffered even more than Germany.

The breach came in 1811, when Alexander withdrew from the "Continental System." In 1812 a great mass of armies, amounting altogether to 600,000

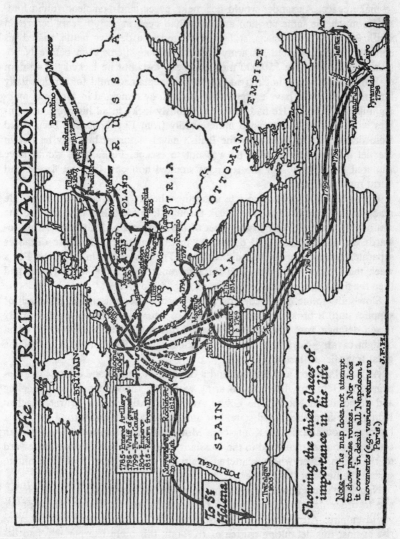

men, began to move towards Russia under the supreme command of the new emperor. About half this force was French; the rest was drawn from the French allies and subject peoples. It was a conglomerate army like the army of Darius or the army of Kavadh. The Spanish war was still going on; Napoleon made no attempt to end it. Altogether, it drained away a quarter of a million men from France. He fought his way across Poland and Russia to Moscow before the winter—for the most part the Russian armies declined battle—and even before the winter closed in upon him his position became manifestly dangerous. He took Moscow, expecting that this would oblige Alexander to make peace. Alexander would not make peace, and Napoleon found himself in much the same position as Darius had been in, 2,300 years before, in south Russia. The Russians, still unconquered in a decisive battle, raided his communications, wasted his army—disease helping them; even before Napoleon reached Moscow 150,000 men had been lost. But he lacked the wisdom of Darius, and would not retreat. The winter remained mild for an unusually long time—he could have escaped; but, instead, he remained in Moscow, making impossible plans. He had been marvellously lucky in all his previous gambles with fate; he had escaped undeservedly from Egypt, he had been saved from destruction in Britain by the British naval victories; but now he was in the net again, and this time he was not to escape. Perhaps he would have wintered in Moscow, but the Russians smoked him out; they set fire to and burnt most of the city.

It was late in October, too late altogether, before he decided to return. He made an ineffectual attempt to break through to a fresh line of retreat to the south-west, and then turned the faces of the survivors of his Grand Army towards the country they had devastated in their advance. Immense distances separated them from any friendly territory. The winter was in no hurry. For a week the Grand Army struggled through mud; then came sharp frosts, and then the first flakes of snow, and then snow and snow. . . .

Slowly discipline dissolved. The hungry army spread itself out in search of supplies until it broke up into mere bands of marauders. The peasants, if only in self-defence, rose against them, waylaid them, and murdered them; a cloud of light cavalry—Scythians still—hunted them down. That retreat is one of the great tragedies of history.

At last Napoleon and his staff and a handful of guards and attendants reappeared in Germany, bringing no army with him, followed only by straggling and demoralized bands. The Grand Army, retreating under Murat, reached Königsberg in a disciplined state, but only about a thousand strong out of six hundred thousand. From Königsberg Murat fell back to Posen. The Prussian contingent had surrendered to the Russians; the Austrians had gone homeward to the south. Everywhere scattered fugitives, ragged, lean, and frost-bitten, spread the news of the disaster.

Napoleon's magic was nearly exhausted. He fled post-haste to Paris. He began to order new levies and gather fresh armies amidst the wreckage of his world empire. Austria turned against him (1813); all Europe was eager to rise against this defaulting trustee of freedom, this mere usurper. He had betrayed the new order; the old order he had saved and revived now destroyed him. Prussia rose, and the German "War of Liberation" began. Sweden joined his enemies. Later, Holland revolted. Murat had rallied about 14,000 Frenchmen round his disciplined nucleus in Posen, and this force retreated through Germany, as a man might retreat who had ventured into a cageful of drugged lions and found that the effects of the drug were evaporating. Napoleon, with fresh forces, took up the chief command in the spring, won a great battle at Dresden, and then for a time he seems to have gone to pieces intellectually and morally. He became insanely irritable, with moods of inaction. He did little or nothing to follow up the Battle of Dresden. In September the "Battle of the Nations" was fought round and about Leipzig, after which the Saxons, who had hitherto followed his star, went over to the Allies. The end of the year saw the French beaten back into France.

1814 was the closing campaign. France was invaded from the east and the south. Swedes, Germans, Austrians, Russians, crossed the Rhine; British and Spanish came through the Pyrenees. Once more Napoleon fought brilliantly, but now he fought ineffectually. The eastern armies did not so much defeat him as push past him, and Paris capitulated in March. A little later at Fontainebleau the emperor abdicated.

In Provence, on his way out of the country, his life was endangered by a royalist mob.

§ 5

This was the natural and proper end of Napoleon's career. At last he was suppressed. And had there been any real wisdom in the conduct of human affairs, we should now have to tell of the concentration of human science and will upon the task his career had interrupted, the task of building up a world-system of justice and free effort in the place of the bankrupt ancient order. But we have to tell of nothing of the sort. Science and wisdom were conspicuously absent from the great council of the Allies. Came the vague humanitarianism and dreamy vanity of the Tsar Alexander, came the shaken Habsburgs of Austria, the resentful Hohenzollerns of Prussia, the aristocratic traditions of Britain, still badly frightened by the Revolution and its conscience all awry with stolen commons and sweated factory children. No peoples came to the Congress, but only monarchs and foreign ministers. The Congress had hardly assembled before the diplomatists set to work making secret bargains and treaties behind each other's backs. Nothing could exceed the pomp and splendour of the Congress which gathered at Vienna after a magnificent ceremonial visit of the allied sovereigns to London. The social side of the Congress was very strong; pretty ladies abounded, there was a galaxy of stars and uniforms, endless dinners and balls, a mighty flow of bright anecdotes and sparkling wit. The brightest spirit of the gathering was a certain Talleyrand, one of Napoleon's princes, a very brilliant man indeed, who had been a pre-revolutionary cleric, who had proposed the revolutionary confiscation of the church estates, and who was now for bringing back the Bourbons.

The Allies frittered away precious time in more and more rapacious disputes; the Bourbons returned to France. Back came all the remainder of the *émigrés* with them, eager for restitution and revenge. One great egotism had been swept aside—only to reveal a crowd of meaner egotists. The new king was the brother of Louis XVI; he had taken the title of Louis XVIII very eagerly so soon as he learnt that his little nephew (Louis XVII) was dead in the Temple. He was gouty and clumsy, not perhaps ill-disposed, but the symbol of the ancient system; all that was new in France felt the heavy threat of reaction that came with him. This was no liberation, only a new tyranny—a heavy and inglorious tyranny instead of an active and splendid one.

Was there no hope for France but this? The Bourbons showed particular malice against the veterans of the Grand Army, and France was now full of returned prisoners of war, who found themselves under a cloud. Napoleon had been packed off to a little consolation empire of his own, upon the island of Elba. He was still to be called Emperor and keep a certain state. The chivalry or whim of Alexander had insisted upon this treatment of his fallen rival. The Habsburgs had taken away his Habsburg empress—she went willingly enough—to Vienna, and he never saw her again.

After eleven months at Elba, Napoleon judged that France had had enough of the Bourbons; he contrived to evade the British ships that watched his island, and reappeared at Cannes in France for his last gamble against fate. His progress to Paris was a triumphal procession; he walked on white Bourbon cockades. Then for a hundred days, "the Hundred Days," he was master of France again.

His return created a perplexing position for any honest Frenchman. On the one hand there was this adventurer who had betrayed the republic; on the other the dull weight of old kingship restored. The Allies would not hear of any further experiments in republicanism; it was the Bourbons or Napoleon. Is it any wonder that, on the whole, France was with Napoleon? And he came back professing to be a changed man; there was to be no more despotism; he would respect the constitutional regime.

He gathered an army, he made some attempts at peace with the Allies; when he found these efforts ineffectual, he struck swiftly at the British, Dutch and Prussians in Belgium, hoping to defeat them before the Austrians and Russians could come up. He did very nearly manage this. He beat the Prussians at Ligny, but not sufficiently; and then he was hopelessly defeated by the tenacity of the British under Wellington at Waterloo (1815), the Prussians, under Blücher, coming in on his right flank as the day wore on. Waterloo ended in a rout; it left Napoleon without support and without hope. France fell away from him again. Everyone who had joined him was eager now to attack him, and so efface that error. A provisional government in Paris ordered him to leave the country, was for giving him twenty-four hours to do it in.

He tried to get to America, but Rochefort, which he reached, was watched by British cruisers. France, now disillusioned and uncomfortably royalist again, was hot in pursuit of him. He went aboard a British frigate, the *Bellerophon,* asking to be received as a refugee, but being treated as a prisoner. He was taken to Plymouth, and from Plymouth straight to the lonely tropical island of St. Helena.

There he remained until his death from cancer in 1821, devoting himself chiefly to the preparation of his memoirs, which were designed to exhibit the chief events of his life in an attractive light; and two of the men with him recorded his conversations and set down their impressions of him.

These works had a great vogue in France and Europe. The Holy Alliance of the monarchs of Russia, Austria, and Prussia (to which other monarchs were invited to adhere) laboured under the delusion that in defeating Napoleon they had defeated the Revolution, turned back the clock of fate, and restored Grand Monarchy for evermore. The cardinal document of the scheme of the Holy Alliance is said to have been drawn up under the inspiration of the Baroness von Krüdener, who seems to have been a sort of spiritual director to the Russian emperor. It opened, "In the name of the Most Holy and Indivisible Trinity," and it bound the participating monarchs, "regarding themselves towards their subjects and armies as fathers of families," and "considering each other as fellow-countrymen," to sustain each other, protect true religion, and urge their subjects to strengthen and exercise themselves in Christian duties. Christ, it was declared, was the real king of all Christian peoples, a very Merovingian king, one may remark, with those reigning sovereigns as his mayors of the palace. The British king had no power to sign this document, the Pope and the sultan were not asked; the rest of the European monarchs, including the king of France, adhered. But the king of Poland did not sign because there was no king in Poland; Alexander, in a mood of pious abstraction, had annexed the greater part of Poland. The Holy Alliance never became an actual legal alliance of states; it gave place to a real league of nations, the Concert of Europe, which France joined in 1818, and from which Britain withdrew in 1822.

There followed a period of peace and oppression in Europe. Many people in those hopeless days were disposed to regard even Naopleon with charity, and to accept his claim that in some inexplicable way he had, in asserting himself, been asserting the Revolution and France. A cult of him, as of something mystically heroic, grew up after his death.

§ 6

For nearly forty years the idea of the Holy Alliance, the Concert of Europe which arose out of it, and the series of congresses and conferences that succeeded the concert, kept an insecure peace in war-exhausted Europe. Two main things prevented that period from being a complete social and international peace, and prepared the way for the cycle of wars between 1854 and 1871. The first of these was the tendency of the royal Courts concerned towards the restoration of unfair privilege and interference with freedom of thought and writing and teaching. The second was the impossible system of boundaries drawn by the diplomatists of Vienna.

The disposition of monarchy to march back towards past conditions was first and most particularly manifest in Spain. Here even the Inquisition was restored. Across the Atlantic the Spanish colonies had followed the example of the United States and revolted against the European Great Power system, when Napoleon set up his brother Joseph upon the Spanish throne in 1810.

The Washington of South America was General Bolivar. Spain was unable to suppress this revolt, it dragged on much as the United States' War of Independence had dragged on, and at last the suggestion was made by Austria, in accordance with the spirit of the Holy Alliance, that the European monarchs should assist Spain in this struggle. This was opposed by Britain in Europe, but it was the prompt action of President Monroe of the United States in 1823 which conclusively warned off this projected monarchist restoration. He announced that the United States would regard any extension of the European system in the Western Hemisphere as a hostile act. Thus arose the Monroe Doctrine, which has kept the Great Power system out of America for nearly a hundred years, and permitted the new states of Spanish America to work out their destinies along their own lines. But if Spanish monarchism lost its colonies, it could at least, under the protection of the Concert of Europe, do what it chose in Europe. A popular insurrection in Spain was crushed by a French army in 1823, with a mandate from a European congress, and simultaneously Austria suppressed a revolution in Naples.

In 1824 Louis XVIII died, and was succeeded by that Count d'Artois whom we have seen hovering as an *émigré* on the French frontiers in 1789; he took the title of Charles X. Charles set himself to destroy the liberty of the Press and universities, and to restore absolute government; the sum of a billion francs was voted to compensate the nobles for the château-burnings and sequestrations of 1789. In 1830 Paris rose against this embodiment of the ancient regime, and replaced him by Louis Philippe, the son of that Philip, Duke of Orleans, who was executed during the Terror. The other continental monarchies, in face of the open approval of the Revolution by Great Britain and a strong liberal ferment in Germany and Austria, did not interfere in this affair. After all, France was still a monarchy. This young man, Louis Philippe (1830–48), remained the constitutional king of France for eighteen years. He went down in 1848, a very eventful year for Europe, of which we shall tell in the next chapter.

Such were the uneasy swayings of the peace of the Congress of Vienna, which were provoked by the reactionary proceedings of the monarchists. The stresses that arose from the unscientific map-making of the diplomatists gathered force more deliberately, but they were even more dangerous to the peace of mankind. It is extraordinarily inconvenient to administer together the affairs of peoples speaking different languages and so reading different literatures and having different general ideas, especially if those differences are exacerbated by religious disputes. Only some strong mutual interest, such as the common defensive needs of the Swiss mountaineers, can justify a close linking of peoples of dissimilar languages and faiths; and even in Switzerland there is the utmost local autonomy. Ultimately, when the Great Power tradition is dead and buried, those Swiss populations may gravitate towards their natural affinities in Germany, France, and Italy. When as in Macedonia, populations are mixed in a patchwork of villages and districts, the cantonal system is imperatively needed. But if the reader will look at the map of Europe as the Congress of Vienna drew it, he will see that this gathering seems almost as if it had planned the maximum of local exasperation. It destroyed the Dutch Republic, quite needlessly it lumped together the Protestant Dutch with the French-speaking Catholics of the old Spanish (Austrian) Netherlands, and set up a kingdom of the Netherlands. It handed over not merely the old republic of Venice but all of North Italy as far as Milan to the German-speaking Austrians. French-speaking Savoy it combined with pieces of Italy to restore the kingdom of Sardinia. Austria and Hungary, already a sufficiently explosive mixture of discordant nationalities, Germans, Hungarians, Czechoslovaks, Jugo-Slavs, Roumanians, and now Italians, was made still more impossible by 1772 and 1795. The Catholic and republican-spirited Polish people were

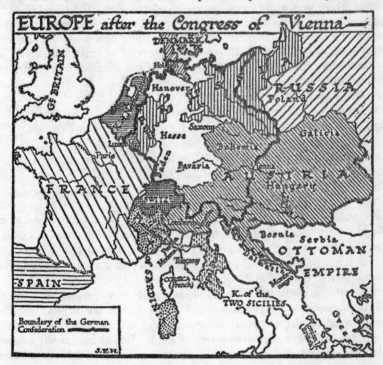

chiefly given over to the less civilized rule of the Greek-Orthodox Tsar, but important districts went to Protestant Prussia. The Tsar was also confirmed in his acquisition of the entirely alien Finns. The very dissimilar Norwegian and Swedish peoples were bound together under one king. Germany, the reader will see, was left in a particularly dangerous state of muddle. Prussia and Austria were both partly in and partly out of a German confederation which included a multitude of minor states. The King of Denmark came into the German confederation by virtue of certain German-speaking possessions in Holstein. Luxembourg was included in the German confederation, though its ruler was also king of the Netherlands, and though many of its people talked French. Here was a complete disregard of the fact that the people who talk

German and base their ideas on German literature, the people who talk Italian and base their ideas on Italian literature, and the people who talk Polish and base their ideas on Polish literature, will all be far better off and most helpful and least obnoxious to the rest of mankind if they conduct their own affairs in their own idiom within the ring-fence of their own speech. Is it any wonder that one of the most popular songs in Germany during this period declared that wherever the German tongue was spoken there was the German Fatherland?

Even to-day men are still reluctant to recognize that areas of government are not matters for the bargaining and interplay of tsars and kings and foreign offices. There is *a natural and necessary political map of the world* which transcends these things. There is *a best way possible* of dividing any part of the world into administrative areas, and a best possible kind of government for every area, having regard to the speech and race of its inhabitants, and it is our common concern to secure those divisions and establish those forms of government quite irrespective of diplomacies and flags, "claims" and melodramatic "loyalties," and the existing political map of the world. The natural political map of the world insists upon itself. It heaves and frets beneath the artificial political map like some misfitted giant. In 1830 French-speaking Belgium, stirred up by the current revolution in France, revolted against its Dutch association in the kingdom of the Netherlands. The Powers, terrified at the possibilities of a republic or of annexation to France, hurried in to pacify this situation and gave the Belgians a monarch, Leopold I of Saxe-Coburg-Gotha. There were also ineffectual revolts in Italy and Germany in 1830, and a much more serious one in Russian Poland. A republican government held out in Warsaw for a year against Nicholas I (who succeeded Alexander in 1825), and was then stamped out of existence with great violence and cruelty. The Polish language was banned, and the Greek Orthodox church was substituted for the Roman Catholic as the State religion. . . .

An outbreak of the natural political map of the world, which occurred in 1821, ultimately secured the support of England, France, and Russia. This was the insurrection of the Greeks against the Turks. For six years they fought a desperate war, while the governments of Europe looked on. Liberal opinion protested against this inactivity; volunteers from every European country joined the insurgents, and at last Britain, France, and Russia took joint action. The Turkish fleet was destroyed by the French and English at the Battle of Navarino (1827), and the Tsar invaded Turkey. By the treaty of Adrianople (1829) Greece was declared free, but she was not permitted to resume her ancient republican traditions. A German king was found for Greece, one Prince Otto of Bavaria—he gave way to delusions about his divine right, and was ejected in 1862—and Christain governors were set up in the Danubian provinces (which are now Roumania) and Serbia (a part of the Jugo-Slav region). This was a partial concession to the natural political map, but much blood had still to run before the Turk was altogether expelled from these lands. A little later the natural political map was to assert itself in Italy and Germany.

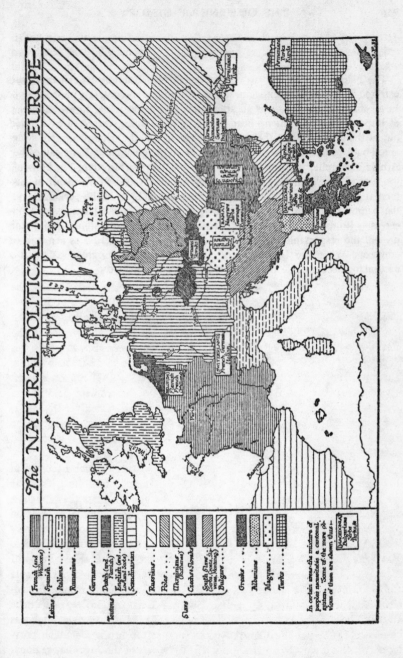

The NATURAL POLITICAL MAP of EUROPE

Latins	French (and Walloons)
	Spanish
	Italians
	Roumanian

Teutons	German
	Dutch (and Flemish)
	English (and Lowland Scots)
	Scandinavian

Slavs	Russian
	Poles
	Ukrainian (Ruthenian)
	Czecho-Slovaks
	South Slavs (Serbs, Croats, Slovenes, Montenegrin)
	Bulgarian

Greeks
Albanians
Magyars
Turks

In certain areas the mixture of peoples necessitates a sectional system. Some of the more obvious of them are shown thus:— Macedonians Bulgarians Serbs Turks

The Napoleonic attempt to restore the Roman Empire was reflected with extreme fidelity in the architecture, dress, furniture, and painting of the period. In all these things there was an attempt to revive the actual forms and spirit of Imperial Rome. Women's head-dresses and costumes seemed to have flitted out of the museums into the streets; the colonnade, the triumphal arch, swaggered back to the commanding positions of all the great cities. Paris gained her Arc de Triomphe, and London, duly imitative, her Marble Arch. The baroque, the rococo developments of Renaissance building vanished in favour of austerer façades. Canova, the Italian, was the great sculptor of the period. David, the painter, delighted in heroic nudes, Ingres immortalized Bonaparte princesses as Roman matrons and Roman goddesses. The public statues of London present the respectable statesmen and monarchs of the period as senators or emperors. When the United States chose a design for its great seal, it was natural to select an eagle and put in its claws the bolt of Jove.

XXXVII

THE REALITIES AND IMAGINATIONS OF
THE NINETEENTH CENTURY

§ 1

THE career and personality of Napoleon I bulks disproportionately in the nineteenth-century histories. He was of little significance to the broad onward movement of human affairs; he was an interruption, a reminder of latent evils, a thing like the bacterium of some pestilence. Even regarded as a pestilence, he was not of supreme rank; he killed far fewer people than the influenza epidemic of 1918, and produced less political and social disruption than the plague of Justinian.

Some such interlude had to happen, and some such patched-up settlement of Europe as the Concert of Europe, because there was no worked-out system of ideas upon which a new world could be constructed. And even the Concert of Europe had in it an element of progress. It did at least set aside the individualism of Machiavellian monarchy and declare that there was a human or at any rate a European commonweal. If it divided the world among the kings, it made respectful gestures towards human unity and the service of God and man.

The permanently effective task before mankind which had to be done before any new and enduring social and political edifice was possible, the task upon which the human intelligence is, with many interruptions and amidst much anger and turmoil, still engaged, was, and is, the task of working out and applying a Science of Property as a basis for freedom and social justice, a Science of Currency to ensure and preserve an efficient economic medium, a Science of Government and Collective Operations whereby in every community men may learn to pursue their common interests in harmony, a Science of World Politics through which the stark waste and cruelty of warfare between races, peoples, and nations may be brought to an end and the common interests of mankind brought under a common control, and, above all, a world-wide System of Education to sustain the will and interest of men in their common human adventure.

The real makers of history in the nineteenth century, the people whose consequences will be determining human life a century ahead, were those who advanced and contributed to this fivefold constructive effort. Compared to them, the foreign ministers and "statesmen" and politicians of this period were no more than a number of troublesome and occasionally incendiary schoolboys —and a few metal thieves—playing about and doing transitory mischief amidst the accumulating materials upon the site of a great building whose nature they did not understand.

And while throughout the nineteenth century the mind of Western civilization, which the Renascence had released, gathered itself to the task of creative social and political reconstruction that still lies before it, there swept across the world a wave of universal change in human power and the material conditions of life that the first scientific efforts of that liberated mind had made possible.

The prophecies of Roger Bacon began to live in reality. The accumulating knowledge and confidence of the little succession of men who had been carrying on the development of science, now began to bear fruit that common men could understand. The most obvious firstfruit was the steam-engine. The first steam-engines in the eighteenth century were pumping engines used to keep water out of the newly opened coal mines. These coal mines were being worked to supply coke for iron-smelting, for which wood-charcoal had previously been employed. It was James Watt, a mathematical instrument maker of Glasgow, who improved this steam pumping-engine and made it available for the driving of machinery. The first engine so employed was installed in a cotton mill in Nottingham in 1785.

In 1804 Trevithick adapted the Watt engine to transport, and made the first locomotive. In 1825 the first railway, between Stockton and Darlington, was opened for traffic. The original engine (Locomotion No. 1, 1825) still adorns Darlington platform. By the middle of the century a network of railways had spread all over Europe.

Here was a sudden change in what had long been a fixed condition of human life, the maximum rate of land transport. After the Russian disaster, Napoleon travelled from near Vilna to Paris in 312 hours. This was a journey of about 1,400 miles. He was travelling with every conceivable advantage, and he averaged under five miles an hour. An ordinary traveller could not have done this distance in twice the time. These were about the same maximum rates of travel as held good between Rome and Gaul in the first century A.D., or between Sardis and Susa in the fourth century B.C.

Then suddenly came a tremendous change. The railways reduced this journey for any ordinary traveller to less than forty-eight hours. That is to say, they reduced the chief European distances to about a tenth of what they had been. They made it possible to carry out administrative work in areas ten times as great as any that had hitherto been workable under one administration. The full significance of that possibility in Europe still remains to be realized. Europe is still netted in boundaries drawn in the horse and road era. In America the effects were immediate. To the United States of America, sprawling westward, it meant the possibility of a continuous access to Washington, however far the frontier travelled across the continent. It meant unity, sustained on a scale that would otherwise have been impossible.

The steamboat was, if anything, a little ahead of the steam-engine in its earlier phases. There was a steamboat, the *Charlotte Dundas,* on the Forth and Clyde Canal in 1802; and in 1807 an American named Fulton had a paying steamer, the *Clermont,* with British-built engines, upon the Hudson River above New York. The first steamship to put to sea was also an American, the *Phœnix,* which went from New York (Hoboken) to Philadelphia. So, too, was the first ship using steam (she also had sails) to cross the Atlantic, the *Savannah* (1819). All these were paddle-wheel boats, and paddle-wheel boats are not adapted to work in heavy seas. The paddles smash too easily, and the boat is then disabled.

The screw steamship followed rather slowly. Many difficulties had to be surmounted before the screw was a practicable thing. Not until the middle of the century did the tonnage of steamships upon the sea begin to overhaul that of sailing-ships. After that the evolution in sea transport was rapid. For the first time men began to cross the seas and oceans with some certainty as to the date of their arrival. The Transatlantic crossing, which had been an uncertain adventure of several weeks—which might stretch to months—was accelerated, until in 1910 it was brought down, in the case of the fastest boats, to under five days, with a practically notifiable hour of arrival. All over the oceans there was the same reduction in the time and the same increase in the certainty of human communications.

Concurrently with the development of steam transport upon land and sea a new and striking addition to the facilities of human intercourse arose out of the investigations of Volta, Galvani, and Faraday into various electrical phenomena. The electric telegraph came into existence in 1835. The first underseas cable was laid in 1851 between France and England. In a few years the telegraph system had spread over the civilized world, and news which had hitherto travelled slowly from point to point became practically simultaneous throughout the earth.

These things, the steam railway and the electric telegraph, were to the popular imagination of the middle nineteenth century the most striking and revolutionary of inventions, but they were only the most conspicuous and clumsy firstfruits of a far more extensive process. Technical knowledge and skill were developing with an extraordinary rapidity, and to an extraordinary extent, measured by the progress of any previous age.

Far less conspicuous at first in everyday life, but finally far more important, was the extension of man's power over various structural materials. Before the middle of the eighteenth century iron was reduced from its ores by means of wood-charcoal, was handled in small pieces, and hammered and wrought into shape. It was material for a craftsman. Quality and treatment were enormously dependent upon the experience and sagacity of the individual ironworker. The largest masses of iron that could be dealt with under those conditions amounted at most (in the sixteenth century) to two or three tons. (There was a very definite upward limit, therefore, to the size of cannon.) The blast furnace arose in the eighteenth century, and developed with the use of coke. Not before the eighteenth century do we find rolled sheet iron (1728) and rolled rods and bars (1783). Nasmyth's steam hammer came as late as 1839.

The ancient world, because of its metallurgical inferiority, could not use steam. The steam-engine, even the primitive pumping-engine, could not develop before sheet iron was available. The early engines seem to the modern eye very pitiful and clumsy bits of ironmongery, but they were the utmost that the metallurgical science of the time could do. As late as 1856 came the Bessemer process, and presently (1864) the open-hearth process, in which steel and every sort of iron could be melted, purified, and cast in a manner and upon a scale hitherto unheard of. To-day in the electric furnace one may see tons of incandescent steel swirling about like boiling milk in a saucepan.

Nothing in the previous practical advances of mankind is comparable in its consequences to the complete mastery over enormous masses of steel and iron and over their texture and quality which man has now achieved. The railways and early engines of all sorts were the mere first triumphs of the new metallurgical methods. Presently came ships of iron and steel, vast bridges, and a new way of building with steel upon a gigantic scale. Men realized too late that they had planned their railways with far too timid a gauge, that they could have organized their travelling with far more steadiness and comfort upon a much bigger scale.

Before the nineteenth century there were no ships in the world much over 2,000 tons burthen; now there is nothing wonderful about a 50,000-ton liner. There are people who sneer at this kind of progress as being a progress in "mere size," but that sort of sneering merely marks the intellectual limitations of those who indulge in it.

The great ship or the steel-frame building is not, as they imagine, a magnified version of the small ship or building of the past; it is a thing different in kind, more lightly and strongly built, of finer and stronger materials; instead of being a thing of precedent and rule-of-thumb, it is a thing of subtle and intricate calculation. In the old house or ship, matter was dominant—the material and its needs had to be slavishly obeyed; in the new, matter has been captured, changed, coerced. Think of the coal and iron and sand dragged out of the banks and pits, wrenched, wrought, molten and cast, to be flung at last, a slender, glittering pinnacle of steel and glass, six hundred feet above the crowded city!

We have given these particulars of the advance in man's knowledge of the metallurgy of steel and its results by way of illustration. A parallel story could be told of the metallurgy of copper and tin, and a multitude of metals, nickel and aluminium to name but two, unknown before the nineteenth century dawned.

It is in this great and growing mastery over substances, over different sorts of glass, over rocks and plasters and the like, over colours and textures, that the main triumphs of the mechanical revolution have thus far been achieved. Yet we are still in the stage of the firstfruits in the matter. We have the power, but we have still to learn how to use our power. Many of the first employments of these gifts of science have been vulgar, tawdry, stupid, or horrible. The artist and the adapter have still hardly begun to work with the endless variety of substances now at their disposal.

Parallel with this extension of mechanical possibilities the new science of electricity grew up. It was only in the eighties of the nineteenth century that this body of inquiry began to yield results to impress the vulgar mind. Then suddenly came electric light and electric traction; and the transmutation of forces, the possibility of sending *power,* that could be changed into mechanical motion or light or heat as one chose, along a copper wire, as water is sent along a pipe, began to come through to the ideas of ordinary people. . . .

The British and the French were at first the leading peoples in this great proliferation of knowledge; but presently the Germans, who had learnt humility under Napoleon showed such zeal and pertinacity in scientific inquiry as to overhaul these leaders. British science was largely the creation of Englishmen and Scotchmen[1] working outside the ordinary centres of erudition.

We have told how in England the universities after the Reformation ceased to have a wide popular appeal, how they became the educational preserve of the nobility and gentry, and the strongholds of the established church. A pompous and unintelligent classical pretentiousness dominated them, and they dominated the schools of the middle and upper classes. The only knowledge recognized was an uncritical textual knowledge of a selection of Latin and Greek classics, and the test of a good style was its abundance of quotations, allusions, and stereotyped expressions.

The early development of British science went on, therefore, in spite of the formal educational organization, and in the teeth of the bitter hostility of the teaching and clerical professions. French education, too, was dominated by the classical tradition of the Jesuits, and consequently it was not difficult for the Germans to organize a body of investigators, small indeed in relation to the possibilities of the case, but large in proportion to the little band of British and French inventors and experimentalists. And though this work of research and experiment was making Britain and France the most rich and powerful countries in the world, it was not making scientific and inventive men rich and powerful. There is a necessary unworldliness about a sincere scientific man; he is too preoccupied with his research to plan and scheme how to make money out of it.

The economic exploitation of his discoveries falls very easily and naturally, therefore, into the hands of a more acquisitive type; and so we find that the

---

[1] But note Boyle and Sir Wm. Hamilton as conspicuous scientific men who were Irishmen.

crops of rich men which every fresh phase of scientific and technical progress has produced in Great Britain, though they have not displayed quite the same passionate desire to insult and kill the goose that laid the national golden eggs as the scholastic and clerical professions, have been quite content to let that profitable creature starve. Inventors and discoverers came by nature, they thought, for cleverer people to profit by.

In this matter the Germans were a little wiser. The German "learned" did not display the same vehement hatred of the new learning. They permitted its development. The German business man and manufacturer, again, had not quite the same contempt for the man of science as had his British competitor. Knowledge, these Germans believed, might be a cultivated crop, responsive to fertilizers. They did concede, therefore, a certain amount of opportunity to the scientific mind; their public expenditure on scientific work was relatively greater, and this expenditure was abundantly rewarded.

By the latter half of the nineteenth century the German scientific worker had made German a necessary language for every science student who wished to keep abreast with the latest work in his department, and in certain branches, and particularly in chemistry, Germany acquired a very great superiority over her western neighbours. The scientific effort of the sixties and seventies in Germany began to tell after the eighties, and the Germans gained steadily upon Britain and France in technical and industrial prosperity.

In an Outline of History such as this it is impossible to trace the network of complex mental processes that led to the incessant extension of knowledge and power that is now going on; all we can do here is to call the reader's attention to the most salient turning-points that finally led the toboggan of human affairs into its present swift ice-run of progress.

We have told of the first release of human curiosity, and of the beginnings of systematic inquiry and experiment. We have told, too, how, when the plutocratic Roman system and its resultant imperialism had come and gone again, this process of inquiry was renewed. We have told of the escape of investigation from ideas of secrecy and personal advantage to the idea of publication and a brotherhood of knowledge, and we have noted the foundation of the British Royal Society, the Florentine Society, and their like as a consequence of this socializing of thought. These things were the roots of the mechanical revolution, and so long as the root of pure scientific inquiry lives that revolution will progress.

The mechanical revolution itself began, we may say, with the exhaustion of the wood supply for the ironworks of England. This led to the use of coal, the coal mine led to the simple pumping-engine, the development of the pumping-engine by Watt into a machine-driving engine led on to the locomotive and the steamship. This was the first phase of a great expansion in the use of steam. A second phase in the mechanical revolution began with the application of electrical science to practical problems and the development of electric lighting, power-transmission, and traction.

A third phase is to be distinguished when, in the eighties, a new type of engine came into use, an engine in which the expansive force of an explosive

mixture replaced the expansive force of steam. The light, highly efficient engines that were thus made possible were applied to the automobile, and developed at last to reach such a pitch of lightness and efficiency as to render flight—
long known to be possible—a practical achievement.

The work of the Wright brothers in America was of primary importance
in this field. A flying-machine—but not a machine large enough to take up a
human body—was made by Professor Langley, of the Smithsonian Institution
of Washington, as early as 1897. His next effort, a full-size aeroplane, failed
on its early trials, but after very extensive alterations was successfully flown
by Curtiss a few years later. By 1909 the aeroplane was available for human
locomotion.

There had seemed to be a pause in the increase of human speed with the
perfection of railways and automobile road traction, but with the flying
machine came fresh reductions in the effective distance between one point
of the earth's surface and another. In the eighteenth century the distance
from London to Edinburgh was an eight days' journey; in 1918 the British
Civil Air Transport Commission reported that the journey from London to
Melbourne, half-way round the earth, would probably, in a few years' time
be accomplished in that same period of eight days.

Too much stress must not be laid upon these striking reductions in the
time distances of one place from another. They are merely one aspect of a
much profounder and more momentous enlargement of human possibility.
The science of agriculture and agricultural chemistry, for instance, made quite
parallel advances during the nineteenth century. Men learnt so to fertilize the
soil as to produce quadruple and quintuple the crops got from the same area
in the seventeenth century. There was a still more extraordinary advance in
medical science; the average duration of life rose, the daily efficiency increased, the waste of life through ill-health diminished.

Now, here altogether we have such a change in human life as to constitute
a fresh phase of history. In a little more than a century this mechanical revolution has been brought about. In that time man made a stride in the material
conditions of his life faster than he had done during the whole long interval
between the Palæolithic stage and the age of cultivation, or between the days
of Pepi in Egypt and those of George III. A new gigantic material framework
for human affairs has come into existence. Clearly it demands great readjustments of our social, economical, and political methods. But these readjustments have necessarily waited upon the development of the mechanical
revolution, and they are still only in their opening stage to-day.

§ 2

There is a tendency in many histories to confuse together what we have
here called the *mechanical revolution*, which was an entirely new thing in
human experience arising out of the development of organized science, a new
step like the invention of agriculture or the discovery of metals, with something
else, quite different in its origins, something for which there was already an

historical precedent, the social and financial development which is called the *industrial revolution.*

The two processes were going on together, they were constantly reacting upon each other, but they were in root and essence different. There would have been an industrial revolution of sorts if there had been no coal, no steam, no machinery; but in that case it would probably have followed far more closely upon the lines of the social and financial developments of the later years of the Roman republic. It would have repeated the story of dispossessed free cultivators, gang labour, great estates, great financial fortunes, and a socially destructive financial process.

Even the factory method came before power and machinery. Factories were the product, not of machinery, but of the "division of labour." Drilled and sweated workers were making such things as millinery, cardboard boxes, and furniture, and colouring maps and book illustrations, and so forth, before even water-wheels had been used for industrial processes. There were factories in Rome in the days of Augustus. New books, for instance, were dictated to rows of copyists in the factories of the booksellers. The attentive student of Defoe and of the political pamphlets of Fielding will realize that the idea of herding poor people into establishments to work collectively for their living was already current in Britain before the close of the seventeenth century. There are intimations of it even as early as More's *Utopia* (1516). It was a social and not a mechanical development.

Up to past the middle of the eighteenth century the social and economic history of Western Europe was, in fact, retreading the path along which the Roman State had gone in the last three centuries B.C. America was in many ways a new Spain, and India and China a new Egypt. But the political disunions of Europe, the political convulsions against monarchy, the recalcitrance of the common folk, and perhaps, also, the greater accessibility of the Western European intelligence to mechanical ideas and inventions, turned the process into quite novel directions. Ideas of human solidarity, thanks mainly to Christianity, were far more widely diffused in this newer European world, political power was not so concentrated, and the man of energy anxious to get rich turned his mind, therefore, very willingly from the ideas of the slave and of gang labour to the idea of mechanical power and the machine.

The mechanical revolution, the process of mechanical invention and discovery, was a new thing in human experience, and it went on regardless of the social, political, economic, and industrial consequences it might produce. The industrial revolution, on the other hand, like most other human affairs, was and is more and more profoundly changed and deflected by the constant variation in human conditions caused by the mechanical revolution. And the essential difference between the amassing of riches, the extinction of small farmers and small business men, and the phase of big finance in the latter centuries of the Roman Republic on the one hand, and the very similar concentration of capital in the eighteenth and nineteenth centuries on the other, lies in the profound difference in the character of labour that the mechanical revolution was bringing about.

The power of the Old World was human power; everything depended ultimately upon the driving power of human muscle, the muscle of ignorant and subjugated men. A little animal muscle, supplied by draft oxen, horse traction, and the like, contributed. Where a weight had to be lifted, men lifted it; where a rock had to be quarried, men chipped it out; where a field had to be ploughed, men and oxen ploughed it; the Roman equivalent of the steamship was the galley with its banks of sweating rowers.

A vast proportion of mankind in the early civilizations was employed in purely mechanical drudgery. At its onset, power-driven machinery did not seem to promise any release from such unintelligent toil. Great gangs of men were employed in excavating canals, in making railway cuttings and embankments, and the like. The number of miners increased enormously. But the extension of facilities and the output of commodities increased much more. And as the nineteenth century went on, the plain logic of the new situation asserted itself more clearly. Human beings were no longer wanted as a source of mere indiscriminated power. What could be done mechanically by a human being could be done faster and better by a machine. The human being was needed now only where choice and intelligence had to be exercised. Human beings were wanted only as human beings. The *drudge,* on whom all the previous civilizations had rested, the creature of mere obedience, the man whose brains were superfluous, had become unnecessary to the welfare of mankind.

This was as true of such ancient industries as agriculture and mining as it was of the newest metallurgical processes. For ploughing, sowing and harvesting, swift machines came forward to do the work of scores of men. Here America led the Old World. The Roman civilization was built upon cheap and degraded human beings; modern civilization is being rebuilt upon cheap mechanical power. For a hundred years power has been getting cheaper and labour dearer. If for a generation or so machinery has had to wait its turn in the mine, it is simply because for a time men were cheaper than machinery. In Northumberland and Durham, in the early days of coal-mining, they were so cheaply esteemed that it was unusual to hold inquests on the bodies of men killed in mine disasters. Trade Unionism was needed to alter that state of affairs.

But this general trend towards the supplementing and supersession of manual labour by machinery was a change-over of quite primary importance in human affairs. The chief solicitude of the rich and of the ruler in the old civilization had been to keep up a supply of drudges. There was no other source of wealth. As the nineteenth century went on, it became more and more plain to the intelligent directive people that the common man had now to be something better than a drudge. He had to be educated—if only to secure "industrial efficiency." He had to understand what he was about.

From the days of the first Christian propaganda, popular education had been smouldering in Europe, just as it has smouldered in Asia wherever Islam has set its foot, because of the necessity of making the believer understand a little of the belief by which he is saved, and of enabling him to read a little in the sacred books by which his belief is conveyed. Christian controversies, with their competition for adherents, ploughed the ground for the harvest of popular education.

In England, for instance, by the thirties and forties of the nineteenth century, the disputes of the sects and the necessity of catching adherents young had produced an abundance of night schools, Sunday schools, and a series of competing educational organizations for children, the "undenominational" British schools, the church National schools, and even Roman Catholic elementary schools.

The earlier, less enlightened manufacturers, unable to take a broad view of their own interests, hated and opposed these schools. But here again needy Germany led her richer neighbours. The religious teacher in Britain presently found the profit-seeker at his side, unexpectedly eager to get the commonalty, if not educated, at least "trained" to a higher level of economic efficiency.

The second half of the nineteenth century was a period of rapid advance in popular education throughout all the Westernized world. There was no parallel advance in the education of the upper classes—some advance, no doubt, but nothing to correspond—and so the great gulf that had divided that world hitherto into the readers and the non-reading mass became little more than a slightly perceptible difference in educational level. At the back of this process was the mechanical revolution, apparently regardless of social conditions, but really insisting inexorably upon the complete abolition of a totally illiterate class throughout the world.

The economic revolution of the Roman republic had never been clearly apprehended by the common people of Rome. The ordinary Roman citizen never saw the changes through which he lived clearly and comprehensively as we see them. But the industrial revolution, as it went on towards the end of the nineteenth century, was more and more distinctly *seen* as one whole process by the common people it was affecting, because presently they could read and discuss and communicate, and because they went about and saw things as no commonalty had ever done before.

In this *Outline of History* we have been careful to indicate the gradual appearance of the ordinary people as a class with a will and ideas in common. It is the writer's belief that massive movements of the "ordinary people" over considerable areas only became possible as a result of the propagandist religions, Christianity and Islam, and their insistence upon individual self-respect.

We have cited the enthusiasm of the commonalty for the First Crusade as marking a new phase in social history. But, before the nineteenth century, even these massive movements were comparatively restricted. The equalitarian insurrections of the peasantry, from the Wycliffe period onward, were confined to the peasant communities of definite localities, they spread only slowly into districts affected by similar forces. The town artisan rioted, indeed, but only locally.

The château-burning of the French Revolution was not the act of a peasantry who had overthrown a government, it was the act of a peasantry released by the overthrow of a government. The Commune of Paris was the first effective appearance of the town artisan as a political power, and the Parisian crowd of the First Revolution was a very mixed, primitive-thinking, and savage crowd compared with any Western European crowd after 1830.

But the mechanical revolution was not only pressing education upon the whole population, it was leading to a big-capitalism and to a large-scale reorganization of industry that was to produce a new and distinctive system of ideas in the common people in the place of the mere uncomfortable recalcitrance and elemental rebellions of an illiterate commonalty.

We have already noted how the industrial revolution had split the manufacturing class, which had hitherto been a middling and various sort of class, into two sections—the employers, who became rich enough to mingle with the financial, merchandizing, and land-owning classes; and the employees, who drifted to a status closer and closer to that of mere gang and agricultural labour. As the manufacturing employee sank, the agricultural labourer, by the introduction of agricultural machinery and the increase in his individual productivity, rose.

By the middle of the nineteenth century, Karl Marx (1818–83), a German Jew of great scholarly attainments, was pointing out that the organization of the working classes by the steadily concentrating group of capitalist owners was developing a new social classification to replace the more complex class systems of the past. Property, so far as it was power, was being gathered together into relatively few hands, the hands of the big rich men, the capitalist class; while there was a great mingling of workers with little or no property, whom he called the "expropriated," or "proletariat"—a misuse of this word—who were bound to develop a common "class consciousness" of the conflict of their interests with those of the rich men.

Differences of education and tradition between the various older social elements, which were in process of being fused up into the new class of the expropriated, seemed for a time to contradict this sweeping generalization; the traditions of the professions, the small employers, the farmer peasant and the like, were all different from one another and from the various craftsman traditions of the workers; but, with the spread of education and the cheapening of literature, this "Marxian" generalization became more acceptable.

These classes, who were linked at first by nothing but a common impoverishment, were and are being reduced or raised to the same standard of life, forced to read the same books and share the same inconveniences. A sense of solidarity between all sorts of poor and propertyless men, as against the profit-amassing and wealth-concentrating class, became more evident by the end of the nineteenth century. Old differences were fading away, the difference between craftsman and open-air worker, between black coat and overall, between poor clergyman and elementary schoolmaster, between policeman and bus-driver. They had all to buy the same cheap furnishings and live in similar cheap houses; their sons and daughters began to mingle and marry; success at the upper levels by and large was impossible for the rank and file. Marx, who did not so much advocate the class-war, the war of the expropriated mass against the appropriating few, as foretell it, was to some extent at least justified by events. It was sometimes argued against Marx that the proportion of people who have savings invested had increased in many modern communities. These savings are technically "capital" and their owners "capitalists" to that extent, and this was supposed to contradict the statement of Marx that property concentrates into few and fewer hands. Marx used many of his terms carelessly and chose them ill, and his ideas were better than his words. When he wrote property he meant "property so far as it is power." The small investor has remarkably little power over his invested capital.

§ 3

To trace any broad outlines in the fermentation of ideas that went on during the mechanical and industrial revolution of the nineteenth century is a very difficult task. But we must attempt it if we are to link what has gone before in this history with the condition of our world to-day.

It will be convenient to distinguish two main periods in the hundred years between 1814 and 1914. First came the period 1814–48, in which there was a very considerable amount of liberal thinking and writing *in limited circles*, but during which there were no great changes or development of thought in the general mass of the people. Throughout this period the world's affairs were living, so to speak, on their old intellectual capital, they were going on in accordance with the leading ideas of the Revolution and the counter-revolution. The dominant liberal ideas were freedom and a certain vague equalitarianism; the conservative ideas were monarchy, organized religion, social privilege, and obedience.

Until 1848 the spirit of the Holy Alliance, the spirit of Metternich, struggled to prevent a revival of the European revolution that Napoleon had betrayed and set back. In America, both North and South, on the other hand, the revolution had triumphed and nineteenth-century liberalism ruled unchallenged. Britain was an uneasy country, never quite loyally reactionary nor quite loyally progressive, neither truly monarchist, nor truly republican, the land of Cromwell and also of the Merry Monarch Charles; anti-Austrian, anti-Bourbon, anti-papal, yet weakly repressive. We have told of the first series of liberal storms in Europe in and about the year 1830; in Britain in 1832 a Reform Bill, greatly extending the franchise and restoring something of its representative character to the House of Commons, relieved the situation.

Round and about 1848 came a second and much more serious system of outbreaks, that overthrew the Orleans monarchy and established a second republic in France (1848–52), raised North Italy and Hungary against Austria, the Poles in Posen against the Germans, and sent the Pope in flight from the republicans of Rome. A very interesting Pan-Slavic conference held at Prague foreshadowed many of the territorial readjustments of 1919. It dispersed after an insurrection at Prague had been suppressed by Austrian troops. The Hungarian insurrection was more vigorous and maintained the struggle for two years. Its great leader was Louis Kossuth; defeated and in exile he still maintained a vigorous propaganda for the liberty of his people.

Ultimately all these insurrections failed; the current system staggered, but kept its feet. There were, no doubt, serious social discontents beneath these revolts, but as yet, except in the case of Paris, these had no very clear form; and this 1848 storm, so far as the rest of Europe was concerned, may be best described, in a phrase, as a revolt of the natural political map against the artificial arrangements of the Vienna diplomatists and the system of suppressions those arrangements entailed.

The history of Europe, then, from 1815 to 1848 was, generally speaking, a sequel to the history of Europe from 1789 to 1814. There were no really new *motifs* in the composition. The main trouble was still the struggle, though often a blind and misdirected struggle, of the interests of ordinary men against the Great Power system which cramped and oppressed the life of mankind.

But after 1848, from 1848 to 1914, though the readjustment of the map still went on towards a free and unified Italy and a unified Germany, there began a fresh phase in the process of mental and political adaptation to the new knowledge and the new material powers of mankind. Came a great irruption of new social, religious, and political ideas into the general European mind. In the next three sections we will consider the origin and quality of these irruptions. They laid the foundations upon which we base our political thought to-day, but for a long time they had no very great effect on contemporary politics. Contemporary politics continued to run on the old lines, but with a steadily diminishing support in the intellectual convictions and consciences of men.

We have already described the way in which a strong intellectual process undermined the system of Grand Monarchy in France before 1789. A similar undermining process was going on throughout Europe during the Great Power period of 1848–1914. Profound doubts of the system of government and of the liberties of many forms of property in the economic system spread throughout the social body. Then came the greatest and most disorganizing war in history, so that it was impossible for those who lived immediately after it to estimate the power and range of the accumulated new ideas of those sixty-six years. They had been through a far greater catastrophe than the Napoleonic catastrophe, and were in a slackwater period corresponding to the period 1815–1830. But neither an 1830 nor an 1848 came to show them where they stood.

§ 4

We have traced throughout this history the gradual restriction of the idea of property from the first unlimited claim of the strong man to possess everything and the gradual realization of brotherhood as something transcending personal self-seeking. Men were first subjugated into more than tribal societies by the fear of monarch and deity. It is only within the last three or at most four thousand years that we have any clear evidence that voluntary self-abandonment to some greater end, without fee or reward, was an acceptable idea to men, or that anyone had propounded it.

Then we find spreading over the surface of human affairs, as patches of sunshine spread and pass over the hill-sides upon a windy day in spring, the idea that there is a happiness in self-devotion greater than any personal gratification or triumph, and a life of mankind different and greater and more important than the sum of all the individual lives within it. We have seen that idea become vivid as a beacon, vivid as sunshine caught and reflected dazzlingly by some window in the landscape, in the teachings of Buddha, Lao Tse, and, most clearly of all, of Jesus of Nazareth.

Through all its variations and corruptions, Christianity has never completely lost the suggestion of a devotion to God's commonweal that makes the personal pomps of monarchs and rulers seem like the insolence of an overdressed servant, and the splendours and gratifications of wealth like the waste of robbers. No man living in a community which such a religion as Christianity or Islam has touched can be altogether a slave; there is an ineradicable quality in these religions that compels men to judge their masters and to realize their own responsibility for the world.

As men have felt their way towards this new state of mind from the fierce self-centred greed and instinctive combativeness of the early Palæolithic family group, they have sought to express the drift of their thoughts and necessities very variously. They have found themselves in disagreement and conflict with old-established ideas, and there has been a natural tendency to contradict these ideas flatly, to fly over to the absolute contrary.

Faced by a world in which rule and classes and order seem to do little but give opportunity for personal selfishness and unrighteous oppression, the first impatient movement was to declare for a universal equality and a practical anarchy. Faced by a world in which property seemed little more than a protection for selfishness and a method of enslavement, it was natural to repudiate all property.

Our history shows an increasing impulse to revolt against rulers and against ownership. We have traced it in the Middle Ages burning the rich men's châteaux and experimenting in theocracy and communism. In the French revolutions this double revolt is clear and plain. In France we find side by side, inspired by the same spirit and as natural parts of the same revolutionary movement, men who, with their eyes on the ruler's taxes, declared that property should be inviolable, and others who, with their eyes on the employer's hard bargains, declared that property should be abolished. But what they are really revolting against in each case is that the ruler and the employer, instead of becoming servants of the community, still remain, like most of mankind, self-seeking, oppressive individuals.

Throughout the ages we find this belief growing in men's minds: that there can be such a rearrangement of laws and powers as to give rule and order while still restraining the egotism of any ruler and of any ruling class that may be necessary, and such a definition of property as will give freedom without oppressive power. We begin to realize nowadays that these ends are only to be attained by a complex constructive effort; they arise through the conflict of new human needs against ignorance and old human nature; but throughout the nineteenth century there was a persistent disposition to solve the problem by some simple formula. (And be happy ever afterwards, regardless of the fact that all human life, all life, is throughout the ages nothing but the continuing solution of a continuous synthetic problem.)

The earlier half of the nineteenth century saw a number of experiments in the formation of trial human societies of a new kind. Among the most important historically were the experiments and ideas of Robert Owen (1771–1858), a Manchester cotton-spinner. He is very generally regarded as the founder of modern Socialism; it was in connection with his work that the word "socialism" first arose (about 1835).

He seems to have been a thoroughly competent business man; he made a number of innovations in the cotton-spinning industry, and acquired a fair fortune at an early age. He was distressed by the waste of human possibilities among his workers, and he set himself to improve their condition and the relations of employer and employed. This he sought to do first at his Manchester factory, and afterwards at New Lanark, where he found himself in practical control of works employing about two thousand people.

Between 1800 and 1828 he achieved very considerable things; he reduced the hours of labour, made his factory sanitary and agreeable, abolished the employment of very young children, improved the training of his workers, provided unemployment pay during a period of trade depression, established a system of schools, and made New Lanark a model of a better industrialism, while at the same time sustaining its commercial prosperity. He wrote vigorously to defend the mass of mankind against the charges of intemperance and improvidence which were held to justify the economic iniquities of the time. He held that men and women are largely the product of their educational environment, a thesis that needs no advocacy to-day. And he set himself to a propaganda of the views that New Lanark had justified.

He attacked the selfish indolence of his fellow-manufacturers, and in 1819, largely under his urgency, the first Factory Act was passed, the first attempt to restrain employers from taking the most stupid and intolerable advantages of their workers' poverty. Some of the restrictions of that Act amaze us to-day. It seems incredible now that it should ever have been necessary to protect little children of *nine* (!) from work in factories, or to limit the nominal working day of such employees to *twelve hours!*

Peoples are perhaps too apt to write of the industrial revolution as though it led to the enslavement and overworking of poor children who had hitherto been happy and free. But this misinterprets history. From the very beginnings of civilization the little children of the poor had always been obliged to do whatever work they could do. But the factory system gathered up all this infantile toil and made it systematic, conspicuous, and scandalous. The factory system challenged the quickening human conscience on that issue. The British Factory Act of 1819, weak and feeble though it seems to us, was the Magna

Charta of childhood; thereafter the protection of the children of the poor, first from toil and then from bodily starvation and ignorance, began.

We cannot tell here in any detail the full story of Owen's life and thought. His work at New Lanark had been, he felt, only a trial upon a small working model. What could be done for one industrial community could be done, he held, for every industrial community in the country; he advocated a resettlement of the industrial population in townships on the New Lanark plan.

For a time he seemed to have captured the imagination of the world. *The Times* and *Morning Post* supported his proposals; among the visitors to New Lanark was the Grand Duke Nicholas, who succeeded Alexander I as Tsar; a fast friend was the Duke of Kent, son of George III and father of Queen Victoria. But all the haters of change, and all—and there are always many such—who were jealous of the poor, and all the employers who were likely to be troubled by his projects, were waiting for an excuse to counter-attack him, and they found it in the expression of his religious opinions, which were hostile to official Christianity, and through those he was successfully discredited. But he continued to develop his projects and experiments, of which the chief was a community at New Harmony in Indiana (U.S.A.), in which he sank most of his capital. His partners bought him out of the New Lanark business in 1828.

Owen's experiments and suggestions ranged very widely, and do not fall under any single formula. There was nothing doctrinaire about him. His New Lanark experiment was the first of a number of "benevolent businesses" in the world; Lord Leverhulme's Port Sunlight, the Cadburys' Bournville, and the Ford businesses in America are contemporary instances, and an approach towards communism. His proposals for State settlements were what we should call State socialism to-day. His American experiment and his later writings point to a completer form of socialism, a much wider departure from the existing state of affairs.

It is clear that the riddle of currency exercised Owen. He understood that we can no more hope for real economic justice while we pay for work with money of fluctuating value, than we could hope for a punctual world if there was a continual inconstant variability in the length of an hour. One of his experiments was an attempt at a circulation of labour notes representing one hours, five hours, or twenty hours of work. The co-operative societies of to-day—societies of poor men which combine for the collective buying and distribution of commodities or for collective manufacture or dairying or other forms of agriculture—arose directly out of his initiatives, though the pioneer co-operative societies of his own time ended in failure. Their successors have spread throughout the whole world, and number to-day some hundred millions of adherents; but they have been much more successful in distribution than production.

A point to note about this early socialism of Owen's is that it was not at first at all "democratic." The democratic idea was mixed up with it later. Its initiative was benevolent, its early form patriarchal; it was something up to which the workers were to be educated by liberally disposed employers and leaders. The first socialism was not a workers' movement; it was a masters' movement. Throughout its history the ideology of socialism has been the work mainly of men not workers. Marx is described by Beer as an "aristocrat"; Engels was a merchant, Lenin an exiled member of a landowning family.

Concurrently with this work of Owen's, another and quite independent series of developments was going on in America and Britain which was destined to come at last into relation with his socialistic ideas. The English law had long prohibited combinations in restraint of trade, combinations to raise prices or wages by concerted action. There had been no great hardship in these prohibitions before the agrarian and industrial changes of the eighteenth century let loose a great swarm of workers living from hand to mouth and competing for insufficient employment. Under these new conditions the workers in many industries found themselves intolerably squeezed. They were played off one against another; day by day and hour by hour none knew what concession his fellow might not have made, and what further reduction of pay or increase of toil might not ensue.

It became vitally necessary for the workers to make agreements—illegal though they were—against such underselling. At first these agreements had to be made and sustained by secret societies. Or clubs established ostensibly for quite other purposes, social clubs, funeral societies, and the like, served to mask the wage-protecting combination. The fact that these associations were illegal disposed them to violence; they were savage against "blacklegs" and "rats" who would not join them, and still more savage with traitors.

In 1824 the House of Commons recognized the desirability of relieving tension in these matters by conceding the right of workmen to form combinations for "collective bargaining" with the masters. This enabled Trade Unions to develop with a large measure of freedom. At first very clumsy and primitive organizations and with very restricted freedoms, the Trade Unions have risen gradually to be a real Fourth Estate in the country, a great system of bodies representing the mass of industrial workers.

Arising at first in Britain and America, they have, with various national modifications, and under varying legal conditions, spread to France, Germany, and all the Westernized communities.

Organized originally to sustain wages and restrict intolerable hours, the Trade Union movement was at first something altogether distinct from socialism. The Trade Unionist tried to make the best for himself of the existing capitalism and the existing conditions of employment; the Socialist proposed to change the system.

It was the imagination and generalizing power of Karl Marx which brought these two movements into relationship. He was a man with the sense of history very strong in him; he was one of the first to perceive that the old social classes which had endured since the beginning of civilization were in process of dissolution and regrouping. His racial Jewish commercialism made the antagonism of property and labour very plain to him. And his upbringing in Germany—where, as we have pointed out, the tendency of class to harden into caste was more evident than in any other European country—made him conceive of labour as presently becoming "Class conscious" and collectively antagonistic to the property-concentrating classes. In the Trade Union movement, which was spreading over the world, he believed he saw this development of class-conscious labour.

What, he asked, would be the outcome of the "class war" of the capitalist and proletariat? The capitalist adventurers, he alleged, because of their inherent greed and combativeness, would gather power over capital into fewer and fewer hands, until at last they would concentrate all the means of production, transit, and the like into a form seizable by the workers, whose class consciousness and solidarity would be developed *pari passu* by the process of organizing and concentrating industry.

They would seize this capital and work it for themselves. This would be the social revolution. Then individual property and freedom would be restored, based upon the common ownership of the earth and the management by the community as a whole of the great productive services which the private capitalist had organized and concentrated. This would be the end of the "capitalist" system, but not the end of the system of capitalism. State capitalism would replace private-owner capitalism.

This marks a great stride away from the socialism of Owen. Owen (like Plato) looked to the common sense of men of any or every class to reorganize the casual and faulty political, economic, and social structure. Marx found something more in the nature of a driving force in class hostility based on expropriation and injustice. And he was not simply a prophetic theorist; he was also a propagandist of the revolt of labour, the revolt of the so-called "proletariat." Labour, he perceived, had a common interest against the capitalist everywhere, though under the test of the Great Power wars of the time, and particularly of the liberation of Italy, he showed that he failed to grasp the fact that labour everywhere has a common interest in the peace of the world. But with the social revolution in view he did succeed in inspiring the formation of an international league of workers, the First International.

The subsequent history of socialism was chequered between the British tradition of Owen and the German class-feeling of Marx. What was called Fabian Socialism, the exposition of socialism by the London Fabian Society, made its appeal to reasonable men of all classes. What was called "Revisionism" in German Socialism inclined in the same direction. But, on the whole, it was Marx who carried the day against Owen, and the general disposition of socialists throughout the world was to look to the organization of labour, and labour only, to supply the fighting forces that would disentangle the political and economic organization of human affairs from the hands of the more or less irresponsible private owners and adventurers who controlled it.

§ 5[1]

While the mechanical revolution which the growth of physical science had brought about was destroying the ancient social classification of the civilized state which had been evolved through thousands of years, and producing new possibilities and new ideals of a righteous human community and a righteous world-order—a change at least as great and novel was going on in the field of religious thought. That same growth of scientific knowledge from which sprang the mechanical revolution was the moving cause of these religious disturbances.

Now, upon that matter, the teller of modern history is obliged to be at once cautious and bold. He has to pick his way between cowardly evasion on the one hand, and partisanship on the other. As far as possible he must confine himself to facts and restrain his opinions. Yet it is well to remember that no opinions can be altogether restrained. The writer has his own very strong and definite persuasions, and the reader must bear that in mind.

It is a fact in history that the teaching of Jesus of Nazareth had in it something profoundly new and creative; he preached a new Kingdom of Heaven in the hearts and in the world of men. There was nothing in his teaching, so far as we can judge it at this distance of time, to clash or interfere with any discovery or expansion of the history of the world and mankind. But it is equally a fact in history that St. Paul and his successors added to or completed or imposed upon or substituted another doctrine for—as you may prefer to think—the plain and profoundly revolutionary teachings of Jesus, by expounding a subtle and complex theory of salvation, a salvation which could be attained very largely by belief and formalities, without any serious disturbance of the believer's ordinary habits and occupations, and that this Pauline teaching *did* involve very definite beliefs about the history of the world and man.

It is not the business of the historian to controvert or explain these matters; the question of their ultimate significance depends upon the theologian; the historian's concern is merely with the fact that official Christianity throughout the world adopted St. Paul's view, so plainly expressed in his epistles and so untraceable in the Gospels, that the meaning of religion lay not in the future, but in the past, and that Jesus was not so much a teacher of wonderful new things, as a predestinate divine blood sacrifice of deep mystery and sacredness made in atonement of a particular historical act of disobedience to the Creator committed by our first parents, Adam and Eve, in response to the temptation of a serpent in the Garden of Eden. Upon that belief in that Fall as a fact, and not upon the personality of Jesus of Nazareth, upon the theories of Paul, and not upon the injunctions of Jesus, doctrinal Christianity built itself.

We have already noted that this story of the special creation of the world, and of Adam and Eve and the serpent, was also an ancient Babylonian story,

---

[1] For a closely parallel view of religion to that given here, see *Outspoken Essays*, by Dean Inge, Essays viii and ix on *St. Paul* and on *Institutionalism and Mysticism.*

and probably a still more ancient Sumerian story, and that the Jewish sacred books were the medium by which this very ancient and primitive "heliolithic" serpent legend entered Christianity. Wherever official Christianity has gone, it has taken this story with it. It has tied itself up to that story.

Until a century ago and less, the whole Christianized world felt bound to believe, and did believe, that the universe had been specially created in the course of six days by the word of God a few thousand years before—according to Bishop Ussher, 4,004 B.C. (The *Universal History*, in forty-two volumes, published in 1779 by a group of London booksellers, discusses whether the precise date of the first day of Creation was March 21st or September 21st, 4,004 B.C., and inclines to the view that the latter was the more probable season.)

Upon this historical assumption rested the religious fabric of the Western and Westernized civilization, and yet the whole world was littered, the hills, mountains, deltas, and seas were bursting, with evidence of its utter absurdity. The religious life of the leading nations, still a very intense and sincere religious life, was going on in a house of history built upon sand.

There is frequent recognition in classical literature of a sounder cosmogony. Aristotle was aware of the broad principles of modern geology, they shined through the speculations of Lucretius, and we have noted also Leonardo da Vinci's (1452–1519) lucid interpretation of fossils. The great Frenchman Descartes (1596–1650) speculated boldly upon the incandescent beginnings of our globe, and a Dane, Steno (1631–86), began the collection of fossils and the description of strata. But it was only as the eighteenth century drew to its close that the systematic study of geology assumed such proportions as to affect the general authority of the Bible version of the ancient Sumerian narrative.

Contemporaneously with the *Universal History* quoted above, a great French naturalist, Buffon, was writing upon the Epochs of Nature (1778), and boldly extending the age of the world to 70,000 or 75,000 years. He divided his story into six epochs to square with the six days of the Creation story. These days, it was argued, were figurative days; they were really ages. By that accommodating device, geology contrived to make a peace with orthodox religious teaching that lasted until the middle of the nineteenth century.

We cannot trace here the contributions of such men as Hutton and Playfair and Sir Charles Lyell, and the Frenchmen Lamarck and Cuvier, in unfolding and developing the record of the rocks. It was only slowly that the general intelligence of the Western world was awakened to two disconcerting facts: firstly, that the succession of life in the geological record did not correspond to the acts of the six days of creation; and, secondly, that the record, in harmony with a mass of biological facts, pointed away from the Bible assertion of a separate creation of each species, straight towards a genetic relation between all forms of life, *in which even man was included!* The importance of this last issue to the existing doctrinal system was manifest. If all the animals and man had been evolved in this ascendant manner, then there had been no first parents, no Eden, and no Fall. And if there had been no fall, then the entire historical fabric of Christianity, the story of the first sin and the reason for an atonement, upon which the current teaching based Christian emotion and morality, collapsed like a house of cards.

It was with something like horror, therefore, that great numbers of honest and religious-spirited men followed the work of the English naturalist Charles Darwin (1809–82). In 1859 he published his *Origin of Species by Means of Natural Selection,* a powerful and permanently valuable exposition of that conception of the change and development of species which we have sketched briefly in Chapter II; and in 1871 he completed the outline of his work with the *Descent of Man,* which brought man definitely into the same scheme of development with the rest of life.

Many men and women are still living who can remember the dismay and distress among ordinary intelligent people in the Western communities as the invincible case of the biologists and geologists against the orthodox Christian cosmogony unfolded itself. The minds of many resisted the new knowledge instinctively and irrationally. Their whole moral edifice was built upon false history; they were too old and set to rebuild it; they felt the practical truth of their moral convictions, and this new truth seemed to them to be incompatible with that. They believed that to assent to it would be to prepare a moral collapse for the world. And so they produced a moral collapse by not assenting to it.

The universities in England particularly, being primarily clerical in their constitution, resisted the new learning very bitterly. During the seventies and eighties a stormy controversy raged throughout the civilized world. The quality of the discussions and the fatal ignorance of the church may be gauged by a description in Hackett's *Commonplace Book* of a meeting of the British Association in 1860, at which Bishop Wilberforce assailed Huxley, the great champion of the Darwinian views, in this fashion.

Facing "Huxley with a smiling insolence, he begged to know *was it through his grandfather or grandmother that he claimed his descent from a monkey?* Huxley turned to his neighbour and said, 'The Lord hath delivered him into my hands.' Then he stood before us and spoke these tremendous words: 'He was not ashamed to have a monkey for his ancestor; but he would be ashamed to be connected with a man who used great gifts to obscure the truth.'" (Another version has it: "I have certainly said that a man has no reason to be ashamed of having an ape for his grandfather. If there were an ancestor whom I should feel ashamed in recalling, it would rather be a man of restless and versatile intellect who plunges into scientific questions with which he has no real acquaintance, only to obscure them by an aimless rhetoric and distract the attention of his audience from the real point at issue by eloquent digressions and skilled appeals to prejudice.") These words were certainly spoken with passion. The scene was one of great excitement. A lady fainted, says Hackett. . . . Such was the temper of this controversy.

The Darwinian movement took formal Christianity unawares, suddenly. Formal Christianity was confronted with a clearly demonstrable error in her theological statements. The Christian theologians were neither wise enough nor mentally nimble enough to accept the new truth, modify their formulæ, and insist upon the living and undiminished vitality of the religious reality those formulæ had hitherto sufficed to express. For the discovery of man's descent from sub-human forms does not even remotely touch the teaching of the Kingdom of Heaven. Yet priests and bishops raged at Darwin; foolish attempts were made to suppress Darwinian literature and to insult and discredit the exponents of the new views. There was much wild talk of the "antagonism" of religion and science.

Now, in all ages there have been sceptics in Christendom. The Emperor Frederick II was certainly a sceptic; in the eighteenth century Gibbon and Voltaire were openly anti-Christian, and their writings influenced a number of scattered readers. But these were exceptional people. . . . Now the whole of Christendom became, as a whole, sceptical. This new controversy touched everybody who read a book or heard intelligent conversation. A new generation of young people grew up, and they found the defenders of Christianity in an evil temper, fighting their cause without dignity or fairness. It was the orthodox theology that the new scientific advances had compromised, but the angry theologians declared that it was religion.

In the end men may discover that religion shines all the brighter for the loss of all its doctrinal wrappings, but to the young it seemed as if, indeed, there had been a conflict of science and religion, and that in that conflict science had won.

The immediate effect of this great dispute upon the ideas and methods of people in the prosperous and influential classes throughout the Westernized world was very detrimental indeed. The new biological science was bringing nothing constructive as yet to replace the old moral stand-bys. A real *demoralization* ensued.

The general level of social life in those classes was far higher in the early twentieth than in the early seventeenth century, but in one respect—in respect to disinterestedness and conscientiousness in these classes—it is probable that the tone of the earlier age was better than the latter. In the owning and active classes of the seventeenth century, in spite of a few definite "infidels," there was probably a much higher percentage of men and women who prayed sincerely, who searched their souls to find if they had done evil, and who were prepared to suffer and make great sacrifices for what they conceived to be right, than in the opening years of the twentieth century.

There was a real loss of faith after 1859. The true gold of religion was in many cases thrown away with the worn-out purse that had contained it for so long, and it was not recovered. Towards the close of the nineteenth century a crude misunderstanding of Darwinism had become the fundamental mind-stuff of great masses of the "educated" everywhere. The seventeenth-century kings and owners and rulers and leaders had had the idea at the back of their minds that they prevailed by the will of God; they really feared him, they got priests to put things right for them with him; when they were wicked, they tried not to think of him. But the old faith of the kings, owners and rulers of the opening twentieth century had faded under the actinic light of scientific criticism.

Prevalent peoples at the close of the nineteenth century believed that they prevailed by virtue of the Struggle for Existence, in which the strong and cunning get the better of the weak and confiding. And they believed further that they had to be strong, energetic, ruthless, "practical," egotistical, because God was dead, and had always, it seemed, been dead—which was going altogether further than the new knowledge justified.

They soon got beyond the first crude popular misconception of Darwinism, the idea that every man is for himself alone. But they stuck at the next level. Man, they decided, is a social animal like the Indian hunting dog. He is much more than a dog—but this they did not see. And just as in a pack it is necessary to bully and subdue the younger and weaker for the general good, so it seemed right to them that the big dogs of the human pack should bully and subdue. Hence a new scorn for the ideas of democracy that had ruled the earlier nineteenth century, and a revived admiration for the overbearing and the cruel.

It was quite characteristic of the times that Mr. Kipling should lead the children of the middle and upper-class British public back to the Jungle, to learn "the law," and that in his book *Stalky and Co.* he should give an appreciative description of the torture of two boys by three others, who have by a subterfuge tied up their victims helplessly before revealing their hostile intentions.

It is worth while to give a little attention to this incident in *Stalky and Co.*, because it lights up the political psychology of the British Empire at the close of the nineteenth century very vividly. The history of the last half-century is not to be understood without an understanding of the mental twist which this story exemplifies. The two boys who are tortured are "bullies," that is the excuse of the tormentors, and these latter have further been incited to the orgy by a clergyman. Nothing can restrain the gusto with which they (and Mr. Kipling) set about the job. Before resorting to torture, the teaching seems to be, see that you pump up a little justifiable moral indignation, and all will be well. If you have the authorities on your side, then you cannot be to blame. Such, apparently, is the simple doctrine of this typical imperialist. But every bully has to the best of his ability followed that doctrine since the human animal developed sufficient intelligence to be consciously cruel.

Another point in the story is very significant indeed. The head master and his clerical assistant are both represented as being privy to the affair. They *want* this bullying to occur. Instead of exercising their own authority, they use these boys, who are Mr. Kipling's heroes, to punish the two victims. Head master and clergyman turn a deaf ear to the complaints of an indignant mother. All this Mr. Kipling represents as a most desirable state of affairs.

In this we have the key to the ugliest, most retrogressive, and finally fatal idea of modern imperialism; the idea of a *tacit conspiracy between the law and illegal violence*. Just as the Tsardom wrecked itself at last by a furtive encouragement of the ruffians of the Black Hundreds, who massacred Jews and other people supposed to be inimical to the Tsar, so the good name of the

British Imperial Government has been tainted—and is still tainted—by an illegal raid made by Doctor Jameson into the Transvaal before the Boer War, by the adventures, which we shall presently describe, of Sir Edward Carson (afterwards Lord Carson) in Ireland, and by the tacit connivance of the British Government in Ireland with the so-called "reprisals" undertaken by the loyalists against the perpetrators, or alleged perpetrators, of Sinn Fein outrages.

By such treasons against their subjects, empires destroy themselves. The true strength of rulers and empires lies not in armies and navies, but in the belief of men that they are inflexibly open and truthful and legal. So soon as a government departs from that standard, it ceases to be anything more than "the gang in possession," and its days are numbered.

§ 6

We have already pointed out that there must be a natural political map of the world which gives the best possible geographical divisions for human administrations. Any other political division of the world than this natural political map will necessarily be a misfit, and must produce stresses of hostility and insurrection tending to shift boundaries in the direction indicated by the natural political map.

These would seem to be self-evident propositions were it not that the diplomatists at Vienna evidently neither believed nor understood anything of the sort, and thought themselves as free to carve up the world as one is free to carve up such a boneless structure as a cheese. Most of the upheavals and conflicts that began in Europe as the world recovered from the exhaustion of the Napoleonic wars were quite obviously attempts of the ordinary common men to get rid of governments that were such misfits as to be in many cases intolerable. Generally, the existing governments were misfits throughout Europe because they were not socially representative, and so they were hampering production and wasting human possibilities; but when there were added to these universal annoyances, differences of religion and racial culture between rulers and ruled (as in most of Ireland), differences in race and language (as in Austrian North Italy and throughout most of the Austrian Empire), or differences in all these respects (as in Poland and the Turkish Empire in Europe), the exasperation drove towards bloodshed.

Europe was a system of governing machines abominably adjusted. From the stresses of this maladjustment the various "nationalist" movements that played so large a part in the history of the nineteenth century drew their driving force.

What is a nation? What is nationality? If our story of the world has demonstrated anything, it has demonstrated the mingling of races and peoples, the instability of human divisions, the swirling variety of human groups and human ideas of association. A nation, it has been said, is an accumulation of human beings who think they are one people; but we are told that Ireland is a nation, and Protestant Ulster certainly does not share that idea; and Italy did not think it was one people until long after its unity was accomplished. When the writer was in Italy in 1916, people were saying: "This war will make us one nation."

Again, are the English a nation or have they merged into a "British nationality"? Scotsmen do not seem to believe very much in this British nationality.

Tribal Gods — national symbols for which men would die — of the 19th Century

John Bull   Britannia   Germania   France   Cathleen ní Houlihan

It cannot be a community of race or language that constitutes a nation, because the Gaels and the Lowlanders make up the Scottish "nation"; it cannot be a common religion, for England has scores; nor a common literature, or why is Britain separated from the United States, and the Argentine Republic from Spain? We may suggest that a nation is in effect any assembly, mixture, or confusion of people which is either afflicted by or wishes to be afflicted by a foreign office of its own, in order that it should behave collectively as if its needs, desires, and vanities were beyond comparison more important than the general welfare of humanity.

We have already traced the development of the Machiavellian monarchies into the rule of their foreign offices playing the part of "Powers." The "nationality" which dominated the political thought of the nineteenth century was really no more than the romantic and emotional exaggeration of the stresses produced by the discord of the natural political map with unsuitable political arrangements in the interests of such "Powers."

Throughout the nineteenth century, and particularly throughout its latter half, there has been a great working up of this nationalism in the world. All men are by nature partisans and patriots, but the natural tribalism of men in the nineteenth century was unnaturally exaggerated, it was fretted and over-stimulated and inflamed and forced into the nationalist mould.

Nationalism was taught in schools, emphasized by newspapers, preached and mocked and sung into men. It became a monstrous cant which darkened all human affairs. Men were brought to feel that they were as improper without a nationality as without their clothes in a crowded assembly. Oriental peoples, who had never heard of nationality before, took to it as they took to the cigarettes and bowler hats of the West. India, a galaxy of contrasted races, religions, and cultures, Dravidian, Mongolian, and Aryan, became a "nation." There were perplexing cases, of course, as when a young Whitechapel Jew had to decide whether he belonged to the British or the Jewish nation.

Caricature and political cartoons played a large part in this elevation of the cult of these newer and bigger tribal gods—for such, indeed, the modern "nations" are—to their ascendancy over the imagination of the nineteenth century. If one turns over the pages of *Punch*, that queer contemporary record of the British soul, which has lasted now since 1841, one finds the figures of Britannia, Hibernia, France, and Germania embracing, disputing, reproving, rejoicing, grieving.

It greatly helped the diplomatists to carry on their game of Great Powers to convey politics in this form to the doubting general intelligence. To the common man, resentful that his son should be sent abroad to be shot, it was made clear that instead of this being merely the result of the obstinacy and greed of two foreign offices, it was really a necessary part of a righteous inevitable gigantic struggle between two of these dim vast divinities. France had been wronged by Germania, or Italia was showing a proper spirit to Austria.

The boy's death ceased to appear an outrage on common sense; it assumed a sort of mythological dignity. And insurrection could clothe itself in the same romantic habiliment as diplomacy. Ireland became a Cinderella goddess, Cathleen ni Houlihan, full of heartrending and unforgivable wrongs; and young India transcended its realities in the worship of Bande Mataram.

The essential idea of nineteenth-century nationalism was the "legitimate claim" of every nation to complete sovereignty, the claim of every nation to manage all its affairs within its own territory, regardless of any other nation.

The flaw in this idea is that the affairs and interests of every modern community extend to the uttermost parts of the earth. The assassination of Sarajevo in 1914, for example, which caused the first World War, produced the utmost distress among the Indian tribes of Labrador, because that war interrupted the marketing of the furs upon which they relied for such necessities as ammunition, without which they could not get sufficient food.

A world of independent sovereign nations means, therefore, a world of perpetual injuries, a world of states constantly preparing for or waging war. But concurrently and discordantly with the preaching of this nationalism there was, among the stronger nationalities, a vigorous propaganda of another set of ideas, the ideas of imperialism, in which a powerful and advanced nation was conceded the right to dominate a group of other less advanced nations or less politically developed nations or peoples whose nationality was still undeveloped, who were expected by the dominating nation to be grateful for its protection and dominance.

This use of the word empire was evidently a different one from its former universal significance. The new empires did not even pretend to be a continuation of the world empire of Rome. They had lost the last connection between the idea of the empire and the peace of the world.

These two ideas of nationality and, as the crown of national success, "empire," ruled European political thought, ruled, indeed, the political thought of the world, throughout the latter half of the nineteenth century, and ruled it to the practical exclusion of any wider conception of a common human welfare. They were plausible and dangerously unsound working ideas. They represented nothing fundamental and inalterable in human nature, and they failed to meet the new needs of world controls and world security that the mechanical revolution was every day making more imperative.

They were accepted because people in general had neither the sweeping views that a study of world history can give, nor had they any longer the comprehensive charity of a world religion. Their danger to all the routines of ordinary life was not realized until it was too late.

§ 7

After the middle of the nineteenth century, this world of new powers and old ideas, this fermenting new wine in the old bottles of diplomacy, broke out through the flimsy restraints of the Treaty of Vienna into a series of wars. But by an ironical accident the new system of disturbances was preceded by a peace festival in London, the Great Exhibition of 1851. This exhibition deserves a paragraph or so.

The moving spirit in this exhibition was Prince Albert of Saxe-Coburg-Gotha, the nephew of Leopold I, the German king who had been placed upon the Belgian throne in 1831, and who was also the maternal uncle of the young Queen Victoria of England. She had become queen in 1837 at the age of eighteen. The two young cousins—they were of the same age—had married in 1840 under their uncle's auspices, and Prince Albert was known to the

British as the "Prince Consort." He was a young man of sound intelligence and exceptional education, and he seems to have been greatly shocked by the mental stagnation into which England had sunken.

Oxford and Cambridge, those once starry centres, were still recovering but slowly from the intellectual ebb of the later eighteenth century. At neither university did the annual matriculations number more than four hundred. The examinations were for the most part mere *viva voce* ceremonies. Except for two colleges in London (the University of London) and one in Durham, this was all the education on a university footing that England had to offer.

It was very largely the initiative of this scandalized young German who had married the British queen which produced the University Commission of 1850, and it was with a view to waking up England further that he promoted the first International Exhibition, which was to afford some opportunity for a comparison of the artistic and industrial products of the various European nations.

The project was bitterly opposed. In the House of Commons it was prophesied that England would be overrun by foreign rogues and revolutionaries who would corrupt the morals of the people and destroy all faith and loyalty in the country.

The exhibition was held in Hyde Park in a great building of glass and iron —which afterwards was re-erected as the Crystal Palace. Financially it was a great success. It made many English people realize for the first time that theirs was not the only industrial country in the world, and that commercial prosperity was not a divinely appointed British monopoly. There was the clearest evidence of a Europe recovering steadily from the devastation of the Napoleonic wars, and rapidly overtaking the British lead in trade and manufacture. It was followed directly by the organization of a Science and Art Department (1853), to recover, if possible, the educational lee-way that Britain had lost.

§ 8

The Great Exhibition of 1851 released a considerable amount of international talk and sentiment. It had already found expression in the work of such young poets as Tennyson, who had glanced down the vista of the future.

> "Till the war-drums throb'd no longer, and
> the battle-flags were furl'd,
> In the Parliament of man, the Federation
> of the world."

The vision was premature. Beneath the apparent peace of that brief interval of liberalism and superficial enlightenment the seeds of a new crop of international conflicts were germinating. France was nominally a liberal republic. But her president was a Bonaparte, the nephew of the First Napoleon, he was a person of great cunning and enterprise, and he was destined to bring upon France and Europe even greater disasters than those his uncle had achieved half a century before.

The French republic, which had replaced the Orleans monarchy in 1848, had had a brief and troubled career. From the outset it was embarrassed by crude socialistic proposals which produced much economic disorganization and even more business anxiety. The new Napoleon Bonaparte, posing as a liberal "safe" man, who would restore confidence and stabilize affairs, was able to secure his election as President in the October of that year. He took an oath as President to be faithful to the democratic republic, and to regard as enemies all who attempted to change the form of government. In four years' time (December, 1852) he was Emperor of the French.

At first he was regarded with considerable suspicion by Queen Victoria, or rather by Baron Stockmar, the friend and servant of King Leopold of Belgium,

Map of EUROPE, 1848–1871

Prussia to 1866 ....
..territory seized 1866-7.......
N. German Confederation, 1866..
German Empire, 1871 ....
France..territory acquired (Savoy & Nice, 1860)..
territory lost (Alsace-Lorraine, 1871..
Austria. territory lost (Lombardy, 1859, Venetia, 1866)
[For Italy see also separate map]

and the keeper of the international conscience of the British queen and her consort. All this group of Saxe-Coburg-Gotha people had a reasonable and generous enthusiasm for the unity and well-being of Germany—upon liberal lines—and they were disposed to be alarmed at this Bonapartist revival. Lord Palmerston, the British foreign minister, was, on the other hand, friendly with the usurper from the outset; he offended the queen by sending amiable dispatches to the French President without submitting them for her examination and so giving her sufficient time to consult Stockmar upon them, and he was obliged to resign. But subsequently the British Court veered round to a more cordial attitude to the new adventurer.

The opening years of his reign promised a liberal monarchy rather than a Napoleonic career—a government of "cheap bread, great public works, and holidays,"[1] and he expressed himself warmly in favour of the idea of nationalism, which was naturally a very acceptable idea to any liberal German intelligence. There had been a brief all-German parliament at Frankfort in 1848, which was overthrown in 1849 by the Prussian monarchy.

Before 1848 all the great European Courts of the Vienna settlement had been kept in a kind of alliance by the fear of a second and more universal democratic revolution. After the revolutionary failures of 1848 and the restoration of monarchy in France, this fear was lifted, and they were free to resume the scheming and counter-scheming of the days before 1789—with the vastly more powerful armies and fleets the first Napoleonic phase had given them. The game of Great Powers was resumed with zest, after an interval of sixty years, and it continued until it produced the catastrophe of 1914.

For a time the new Napoleon went warily. It was the Tsar of Russia, Nicholas I, who made the first move towards war. He resumed the traditional thrust of Peter the Great towards Constantinople. Nicholas invented the phrase of the "sick man of Europe" for the Sultan, and, finding an excuse in the misgovernment of the Christian population of the Turkish empire, he occupied the Danubian principalities in 1853.

It was a real international retrocession. European diplomatists found themselves with a "question" of quite the eighteenth-century pattern. The designs of Russia were understood to clash with the designs of France in Syria, and to threaten the Mediterranean route to India of Great Britain, and the outcome was an alliance of France and England to bolster up Turkey, and a war, the Crimean War, which ended in the repulse of Russia. One might have thought that the restraint of Russia was rather the business of Austria and Germany, but the passion of the foreign offices of France and England for burning their fingers in Russian affairs has always been very difficult to control. And the new Napoleon saw in this war an opportunity of cementing his insecure friendship with Britain and the British Court, which had so far held aloof from him.

The next phase of interest in this revival of the Great Power drama was the exploitation, by the Emperor Napoleon III and the king of the small kingdom of Sardinia in North Italy, of the inconveniences and miseries of the divided state of Italy, and particularly of the Austrian rule in the north. The King of Sardinia, Victor Emmanuel, made an old-time bargain for Napoleon's help in return for the provinces of Nice and Savoy. France was to have these, and Sardinia was to be compensated in Italy. The war between France and Sardinia on the one hand and Austria on the other broke out in 1859, and was over in a few weeks. The Austrians were badly beaten at Magenta and Solferino. Then, being threatened by Prussia on the Rhine, Napoleon made peace, leaving Sardinia the richer for Lombardy.

The next move in the game of Victor Emmanuel and of his chief minister

---

[1] Albert Thomas, in the *Encyclopædia Britannica*.

Cavour was an insurrectionary movement in Sicily led by the great Italian patriot Garibaldi. Sicily and Naples were liberated, and all Italy, except only Rome (which remained loyal to the Pope) and Venetia (which was held by the Austrians), fell to the king of Sardinia. A general Italian parliament met at Turin in 1861, and Victor Emmanuel became the first king of Italy.

But now the interest in this game of European diplomacy shifted to Germany. Already the common sense of the natural political map had asserted itself. In 1848 all Germany, including, of course, German Austria, was for a time united under the Frankfort parliament. But that sort of union was particularly offensive to all the German courts and foreign offices; they did not

The KINGDOM of ITALY, 1861.

want a Germany united by the will of its people, they wanted Germany united by regal and diplomatic action—as Italy was being united.

In 1848 the German parliament had insisted that the largely German provinces of Schleswig-Holstein, which had been in the German Bund, must belong to Germany. It had ordered the Prussian army to occupy them, and the king of Prussia had refused to take his orders from the German parliament, and so had precipitated the downfall of that body. Now the King of Denmark, Christian IX, for no conceivable motive except the natural folly of kings, embarked upon a campaign of annoyance against the Germans in these two duchies. Prussian affairs were then very much in the hands of a minister of the seventeenth-century type, von Bismarck (count in 1865, prince in 1871), and he saw brilliant opportunities in this trouble. He became the champion of the German nationality in these duchies—it must be remembered that the king of Prussia had refused to undertake this rôle for democratic Germany in 1848—and he persuaded Austria to side with Prussia in a military intervention.

Denmark had no chance against these Great Powers; she was easily beaten and obliged to relinquish the duchies.

Then Bismarck picked a quarrel with Austria for the possession of these two small states. So he brought about a needless and fratricidal war of Germans for the greater glory of Prussia and the ascendancy of the Hohenzollern dynasty in Germany. He consolidated Germany under the Prussian Hohenzollerns. German writers of a romantic turn of mind represent Bismarck as a great statesman planning the unity of Germany; but, indeed, he was doing nothing of the kind. The unity of Germany was a reality in 1848. It was and is in the nature of things. The Prussian monarchy was simply delaying the inevitable in order to seem to achieve it in Prussian fashion. That is why, when at last Germany was unified, instead of bearing the likeness of a modern civilized people, it presented itself to the world with the face of this archaic Bismarck, with a fierce moustache, huge jack-boots, a spiked helmet, and a sword.

In this war between Prussia and Austria, Prussia had for an ally Italy, while most of the smaller German states, who dreaded the schemes of Prussia, fought on the side of Austria. The reader will naturally want to know why Napoleon III did not grasp this admirable occasion for statecraft and come into the war to his own advantage. All the rules of the Great Power game required that he should. He was allowing a dangerous rival to France to arise in Europe in the shape of Prussia. He should have done something to prevent this. But Napoleon, unhappily for himself, had got his fingers in a trap on the other side of the Atlantic, and was in no position just then to intervene.

He had been sorely tempted by America. The discord between the interests of the southern and northern states in the North American union, due to the economic differences based on slavery, had at last led to open civil war. In our next section we will deal with this civil war more fully; here we will only say that it lasted four years, and ended at last in a reunited United States. All the elements of reaction in Europe rejoiced during the four years of republican dissension; the British aristocracy openly sided with the confederate states, and the British Government permitted several privateers, and particularly the *Alabama,* to be launched in England to attack the federal shipping.

Napoleon III was even more rash in his assumption that, after all, the new world had fallen before the old. Hitherto the United States had forbidden European interference upon the continent of America. This was, so to speak, a fixed rule of American policy. The sure shield of this Monroe Doctrine, it seemed to Napoleon, was now thrust aside for good, the Great Powers might meddle again in America, and the blessings of adventurous monarchy be restored there.

A pretext for interference was found in certain liberties taken with the property of foreigners by the Mexican president. A joint expedition of French, British, and Spanish occupied Vera Cruz, but Napoleon's projects were too bold for his allies, and they withdrew when it became clear that he contemplated nothing less than the establishment of a Mexican empire. This he did, after much stiff fighting, making the Archduke Maximilian of Austria Emperor of Mexico in 1864. The French forces, however, remained in effectual possession of the country, and a crowd of French speculators poured into Mexico to exploit its mines and resources.

But in April, 1865, the civil war in the United States was brought to an end, and the little group of eager Europeans in possession of Mexico found themselves faced by the victorious United States government in a thoroughly grim mood, with a large, dangerous-looking army in hand. The French imperialists were bluntly given the alternative of war with the United States or clearing out of America. In effect, this was an instruction to go. This was the entanglement which prevented Napoleon III from interference between Prussia and Austria in 1866, and this was the reason why Bismarck precipitated his struggle with Austria.

While Prussia was fighting Austria, Napoleon III was trying to escape with dignity from the briars of Mexico. He invented a shabby quarrel upon financial grounds with Maximilian and withdrew the French troops. Then, by all the rules of kingship, Maximilian should have abdicated. But, instead, he made a fight for his empire; he was defeated by his recalcitrant subjects, caught, and shot as a public nuisance in 1867. So the peace of President Monroe was restored to the new world.

But while Napoleon was busy with his American misadventure, Prussia and Italy were snatching victory over the Austrians (1866). Italy, it is true, was badly beaten at Custozza and in the naval battle of Lissa, but the Austrian army was so crushed by the Prussian at the battle of Sadowa that Austria made an abject surrender. Italy gained the province of Venetia, so making one more step towards unity—only Rome and Trieste and a few small towns on the north and north-western frontiers remained outside the kingdom—and Prussia became the head of a North German Confederation, from which Bavaria, Württemberg, Baden, Hesse, and Austria were excluded.

This victory of Prussia, this supersession of Austria as even the nominal head of things German, this restoration of the predominance of the kingdom of Frederick the Great, brought Prussia and France face to face. A great rivalry had become clear, a rivalry that was to produce the first World War. It was only a question of time before France and Prussia clashed. Each armed, but Prussia had better schoolmasters and a higher standard of obedience and efficiency than France.

The war almost came in 1867, when, so soon as he was free from Mexico, Napoleon sought to pick a quarrel with Prussia over Luxembourg. It came in 1870 quite on eighteenth-century grounds, with a dispute about the candidates for the vacant throne of Spain. Napoleon had some theory in his mind that Austria, Bavaria, Württemburg, and the other states outside the North German

Bismarck

Confederation would side with him against Prussia. He probably thought this would happen because he wanted it to happen. But since 1848 the Germans, so far as foreign meddling was concerned, had been in spirit a united people; Bismarck had merely imposed the Hohenzollern monarchy, with pomp, ceremony, and bloodshed, upon accomplished facts. All Germany sided with Prussia against France.

Early in August, 1870, the united German forces invaded France. In numbers, discipline, equipment, and leading they proved better than the French. The debacle of France was swift and complete. After the battles of Wörth and Gravelotte, one French army under Bazaine was forced into Metz and surrounded there, and on September 1st a second, with which was Napoleon, was defeated and obliged to capitulate at Sedan. Napoleon became a prisoner. Paris found herself bare to the invader. For a second time the promises of Napoleonism had failed France disastrously.

On September 4th France declared herself a republic again and, thus regenerated, prepared to fight for existence against triumphant Prussianism. For, though it was a united Germany that had overcome French imperialism, it had Prussia in the saddle. The army in Metz capitulated in October; Paris, after a siege and bombardment, surrendered in January, 1871, and France sued for peace.

With pomp and ceremony, in the Hall of Mirrors at Versailles, amidst a great array of military uniforms, the King of Prussia was declared German Emperor, and Bismarck and the sword of the Hohenzollerns claimed the credit for that German unity which a common language and literature had long since assured.

The peace of Frankfort which followed was a Hohenzollern peace. Bismarck had availed himself of the national feeling of Germany to secure the aid of the South German states, but he had no grasp of the essential forces that had given victory to him and to his royal master. The power that had driven Prussia to victory was the power of the natural political map of Europe insisting upon the unity of the German-speaking peoples. In the east, Germany was already sinning against that natural map by her administration of Posen and other Polish districts. Now greedy for territory, and particularly for iron mines, she annexed a considerable area of French-speaking Lorraine, including Metz, and Alsace, which, in spite of its German speech, was largely French in sympathy.

Inevitably there was a clash between German rulers and French subjects in these annexed provinces; inevitably the wrongs and bitterness of the subjugated France of Lorraine echoed in Paris and kept alive the passionate resentment of the French.

How at last that flared up in a great Revanche we shall tell later. . . .

Napoleon III hid his diminished head in England, and died there a year or so after his collapse.

So ended the second Bonapartist regime in France.

§ 9

It is a relief to turn from the disastrous exploits of this Bonapartist adventurer in France, and the temporary triumph of the Hohenzollern family over the popular movement in Germany, to an altogether greater and more significant figure, the figure of Abraham Lincoln, about which the incidents of the great war of secession in America may very conveniently be grouped.

The opening half of the nineteenth century, which had been an age of reaction and recovery in Europe, was in America a period of extravagant growth. The new means of communication, the steamboat and the railway and presently the electric telegraph, came just in time to carry forward the movement of the population across the continent. But for these mechanical aids, the United States even to-day might not reach westward beyond the Rocky Mountains and an entirely different people might be in possession of the western coast.

It is still very imperfectly grasped by politicians how dependent are the areas enclosed by governmental and administrative boundaries upon the means of communication available and the character of the country in relation to transport. Given roads and writing, open valleys tend to become consolidated under one government. Mountainous barriers separated not only peoples but rulers; the Roman empire was an empire of highroad and wheel, and its divisions and separations and fall were due to the impossibility of maintaining swift communications between part and part. The Western Europe that emerged from the Napoleonic storm was divided into national states that were perhaps as large as they could become without loss of solidarity with highroad horse traction as their swiftest linking method.

Had the people of the United States spread over the American continent with only horse traction, rough road, and letter-writing to keep them together, it seems inevitable that differences in local economic conditions would have developed different social types, that wide separation would have fostered differences of dialect and effaced sympathy, that the inconvenience of attending Congress at Washington would have increased with every advance of the frontier westward, until at last the States would have fallen apart into a loose league of practically independent and divergent nations. Wars, for mineral wealth, for access to the sea, and so forth, would have followed, and America would have become another Europe.

But the river steamboat, the railway, and the telegraph arrived in time to prevent this separation, and the United States became the first of a new type of modern transport state, altogether larger, more powerful, and more conscious of its unity than any state the world had ever seen before. For the tendency now in America is not to diverge but assimilate, and citizens from various parts of the States grow not more but less unlike each other in speech and thought and habit. The United States is really not comparable to a European power such as France or Italy. It is a new and bigger type of political organization.

Empires there have been before in the world comparable in area and population to the United States, but they were merely accumulations of diverse tribute-paying peoples united only by a government. The unity of the United States is inherent. It is a community of outlook of over one hundred million men. The railways which intensified the conflicts and congestions of Europe, the inventions that diminished the striking distance of the European armies and gave them ever greater destructive power, so that now there seems no choice for Western Europe between voluntary unification or forcible unification under some one predominant power, or chaos and destruction, confirmed the free unity of republican America. To Europe steam brought congestion, to America opportunity.

But on the way to this present greatness and security the American people passed through one phase of dire conflict. The river steamboats, the railways, the telegraph, and their associate facilities, did not come soon enough to avert the deepening conflict of interests and ideas between the southern slave-holding states and the free industrial north. The railways and steamboats at first did but bring into sharper conflict an already established difference. There was a profound difference in spirit between the two sections of the United States, and the increasing unification due to the new means of transport made the question whether the southern spirit or the northern should prevail an ever more urgent one. There was little possibility of compromise. The northern spirit was free and individualistic; the southern made for great estates and a conscious gentility ruling over a dusky subject multitude. The sympathies of British liberalism and radicalism were for the north; the sympathies of the British landlords and the British ruling class were for the south.

Every territory that was organized into a state, every new incorporation into the fast-growing American system, became a field of conflict between the two ideas, whether it should become a state of free citizens or whether the estate system should prevail. The issue crept slowly to predominance in American affairs after the establishment of Missouri (1821) and Arkansas (1836) as slave-holding states. From 1833 an American anti-slavery society was not merely resisting the extension of the institution, but agitating the whole country for its complete abolition. The issue flamed up into conflict over the admission of Texas to the union. Texas had originally been a part of the republic of Mexico, but it was largely colonized by Americans from the slave-holding states, and it seceded from Mexico and established its independence in 1836. A vigorous agitation for the annexation of Texas followed, and Texas was annexed in 1844 and admitted as a state in 1845. Under the Mexican law slavery had been forbidden in Texas, but now the south claimed Texas for slavery—and got it.

Moreover, a war with Mexico arising out of the Texas annexation had added New Mexico and other areas to the United States, and in these regions also slavery was permitted and a Fugitive Slave Bill increased the efficiency of the methods of catching and returning slaves who had fled to free states. But, meanwhile, the development of ocean navigation was bringing a growing swarm of immigrants from Europe to swell the spreading population of the northern states, and raising of Iowa, Wisconsin, Minnesota and Oregon, all northern farm lands, to state level gave the anti-slavery north the possibility of predominance both in the Senate and the House of Representatives. The cotton-growing south, irritated by the increasing threat of the Abolitionist movement, and fearing this predominance in Congress, began to talk of secession from the Union. Southerners began to dream of annexations to the south of them in Mexico and the West Indies, and of a great slave state, detached from the north and reaching from the Mason and Dixon line to Panama.

Kansas became the region for the final decision. The slavery issue plunged the territory of Kansas into what was practically a civil war between settlers from the free and immigrants from the slave states, a war that continued until 1857 and ended in the victory of the anti-slavery settlers. But until 1861 Kansas was not raised to statehood. The extension of slavery was the chief issue before the country in the presidential election of 1860, and the return of Abraham Lincoln as an anti-extension President decided the south to split the union.

South Carolina passed an "ordinance of secession," and prepared for war. Mississippi, Florida, Alabama, Georgia, Louisiana and Texas joined her early in 1861, and a convention met at Montgomery in Alabama, elected Jefferson Davis president of the "Confederate States" of America, and adopted a constitution similar to that of the United States but specifically upholding "the institution of negro slavery."

Such was the political situation with which Abraham Lincoln was called to deal as president of the Union. He was, it chanced, a man entirely typical of the new people that had grown up after the War of Independence. His people were quite common folk; his father could not read or write until after his marriage, and his mother, it is said, was an illegitimate child. She was a woman of exceptional intellect and character.

His early years had been spent as a drifting particle in the general westward flow of the population. He was born in Kentucky (1809), was taken to Indiana as a boy, and later on to Illinois. Life was rough in the backwoods of Indiana in those days; the house was a mere log cabin in the wilderness, and his schooling was poor and casual. But his mother taught him to read early, and he became a voracious reader.

At seventeen he was a big athletic youth, a great wrestler and runner. At nineteen he went down river to New Orleans as a hired hand on a flat boat. He worked for a time as clerk in a store, served as a volunteer in an Indian war, went into business as a storekeeper with a drunken partner, and contracted debts that he did not fully pay off for fifteen years. Finally, when he was about twenty-four, he got a job as a deputy to the county surveyor of Sangamon County, which, he said, "kept body and soul together."

All this time he was reading hard. His earlier books—those early books that make the mind—seem to have been few but good; he read all he could get; he knew his Shakespeare and Burns well, the life of Washington, a history of the United States, and so forth. He had the instinct for expression, and from his boyhood he wrote as well as studied, producing verse, essays, and the like. Much of this was coarse, homely stuff. Politics soon attracted him. In 1834, when he was still only five-and-twenty, he was elected member of the House of Representatives for the state of Illinois; he read for the bar, and was admitted in 1836. For a time he worked rather at law than politics.

But the great question before the people of the United States insisted upon the attention of every able man. This big, capable, self-educated man, typically a man of the middle west, could not fail to be profoundly stirred by the steady development of the issues of slavery and secession. In Illinois particularly the question flamed because the great leader in Congress of the party for the extension of slavery was Senator Douglas of Illinois. There was a personal rivalry between the two; they had both courted the lady who became Mrs. Lincoln. Douglas was a man of great ability and prestige, and for some years Lincoln fought against him by speech and pamphlet, first in Illinois and then throughout the eastern states, rising steadily to the position of his most formidable and finally victorious antagonist. Their culminating struggle was the presidential campaign of 1860, and on the 4th of March, 1861, Lincoln was inaugurated president, with the southern states already in active secession and committing acts of war.

The first proceeding of the secessionists was the seizure of all Federal forts and stores within their boundaries. These Federal posts were built on territory belonging to the states in which they stood, and these states claimed the right to "resume" their property. The garrison of Fort Sumter at Charlestown resisted, and the war began with the bombardment of this fort on the 12th of April, 1861. America at that time had only a very small regular army; it remained loyal to the president, and these opening operations of the Confederacy were conducted by state levies. President Lincoln at once called for 75,000 men, and Tennessee, Arkansas, North Carolina, and Virginia immediately went over to the Confederacy, which had now hoisted its own flag, the "Stars and Bars," against the Stars and Stripes.

So began the civil war in America. It was fought by improvised armies that grew steadily from a few score thousands to hundreds of thousands—until at last the Federal forces exceeded a million men; it was fought over a vast area between New Mexico and the eastern sea. Washington and Richmond were the chief objectives. It is beyond our scope here to tell of the mounting energy of that epic struggle that rolled to and fro across the hills and woods of Tennessee and Virginia and down the Mississippi. There was a terrible waste and killing of men. Thrust was followed by counter-thrust; hope gave way to despondency, and returned and was again disappointed. Sometimes Washington seemed within the Confederate grasp; again the Federal armies were driving towards Richmond.

The Confederates, outnumbered and far poorer in resources, fought under a general of supreme ability, General Lee. The generalship of the Union was far inferior. For long Lincoln clung to General McClellan, the "Young Napoleon," a pedantic, dilatory, and disappointing commander. Generals were dismissed, new generals appointed, until at last, under Sherman and Grant, came victory over the ragged and depleted south. In October, 1864, a Federal army under Sherman broke through the Confederate left and marched down from Tennessee through Georgia to the coast, right across the Confederate country, and then turned up through the Carolinas, coming in upon the rear of the Confederate armies. Meanwhile Grant held Lee before Richmond until Sherman closed on him.

On April 2nd, 1865, the Confederate troops evacuated Richmond; on April 9th, Lee and his army surrendered at Appomattox Court House, and within a month all the remaining secessionist armies had laid down their arms and the Confederacy was at an end.

But this four years' struggle had meant an enormous physical and moral strain for the people of the United States. In many states, in Maryland and Kentucky for example, opinion upon the war was acutely divided. The principle of state autonomy was very dear to many minds, and the north seemed in effect to be forcing abolition upon the south. Many men were against slavery, but also against interference with the free power of each individual state over its own people. In the border states brothers and cousins, even fathers and sons, would take opposite sides and find themselves in antagonistic armies. The north felt its cause a righteous one, but for great numbers of people it was not a full-bodied and unchallenged righteousness.

But for Lincoln there was no doubt. He was a clear-minded man in the midst of such confusion. He stood for the Union; he stood for the great peace of America. He was opposed to slavery, but slavery he held to be a secondary issue. His primary purpose was that the United States should not be torn into two contrasted and jarring fragments. So through the long four years of struggle he stood out an inflexible conviction, a steadfast will.

When in the opening stages of the war Congress and the Federal generals embarked upon a precipitate emancipation, Lincoln opposed and mitigated their enthusiasm. He was for emancipation by stages and with compensation. It was only in January, 1865, that the situation had ripened to a point when Congress could propose to abolish slavery for ever by a constitutional amendment; and the war was already over before this amendment was ratified by the state.

As the war dragged on through 1862 and 1863, the first passions and enthusiasms waned, and America learnt all the phases of war weariness and war disgust. Conscription replaced volunteering and changed the spirit of the fighting both in the south and the north. The war became a prolonged, dismal, fratricidal struggle.

July, 1863, saw New York rioting against the drafts, and the Democratic party in the north sought to win the presidential election on the plea that the war was a failure and should be discontinued. This would, of course, have meant a practical victory for the south. There were organized conspiracies to defeat the draft. The gaunt, tall man at the White House found himself with defeatists, traitors, dismissed generals, tortuous party politicians and a doubting and fatigued people behind him, and uninspired generals and depressed troops before him; and his chief consolation must have been that Jefferson Davis at Richmond could be in little better case.

The English government had misbehaved, and permitted the Confederate agents in England to launch and man three swift privateer ships—the *Alabama* is the best-remembered of them—which were chasing United States shipping from the seas. The French army in Mexico was trampling the Monroe Doctrine in the dirt. Came subtle proposals from Richmond to drop the war, leave the issues of the war for subsequent discussion, and turn, Federal and Confederate in alliance, upon the French in Mexico. But Lincoln would not listen to such proposals unless the supremacy of the Union was maintained. The Americans might do such things as one people but not as two.

He held the United States together through long weary months of reverses and ineffective effort, through black phases of division and failing courage; and there is no record that he ever faltered in his purpose. There were times when there was nothing to be done, when he sat in the White House silent and motionless, a grim monument of resolve; times when he relaxed his mind by jesting and broad anecdotes. He was full of sardonic humour, but very tender with the pain of others. When some enemies of Grant came to tell him that general drank, he asked for the brand of his whisky—"for the others." He was himself a man very abstemious in his habits, capable of either an immense industry or an immense patience.

At last in the early months of 1865 it was plain that victory was coming, and he set himself with all his force to make surrender easy and the treatment of the vanquished the beginning of a reconciliation. Still his watchword was "Union." He was soon in conflict with the extremists of his own side who wished for a vindictive peace.

He saw the Union triumphant. He entered Richmond the day after its surrender and heard of Lee's capitulation. He returned to Washington, and on April 11th made his last public address. His theme was reconciliation and the reconstruction of loyal government in the defeated states. On the evening of April 15th he went to Ford's Theatre in Washington, and as he sat looking at the stage he was shot in the back of the head and cruelly murdered by an actor named Booth, who had some sort of grievance against him, and who crept into the box unobserved.

If the work of healing was impaired and if the United States had more trouble and bitterness in the years following the war than there was need for, it was because Lincoln was dead. But his work was done, and the Union was saved, and saved for good. At the beginning of the war there was no railway to the Pacific coast; now the railways spread like a swiftly growing plant until they had clutched and held and woven all the vast territories of the United States into one now indissoluble mental and material unity.

From that time the consolidation of the United States has gone on steadfastly. Within half a century its population had passed the hundred million mark. And there is no sign that growth and development have yet reached any limitation. This titanic democracy, without king or elaborate foreign policy, is, we repeat, a new thing in the world's experience. It is not a "Great Power" in the sense in which that phrase is used in Europe. It is something more modern in its nature, and greater, and with a greater destiny.

§ 10

A fresh upthrust of, what we have here called, the natural map against the diplomatic arrangements of the treaty of Vienna began in 1875, when the Christian races in the Balkans, and particularly the Bulgarians, became restless and insurgent. The Turks adopted violent repressive measures, and embarked upon massacres of the Bulgarians on an enormous scale.

Thereupon Russia intervened (1877), and after a year of costly warfare obliged the Turks to sign the treaty of San Stefano, which was, on the whole, a sensible treaty, breaking up the artificial Turkish Empire, and to a large extent establishing the natural map. But it had become the tradition of British policy to thwart "the designs of Russia"—heaven knows why!—whenever Russia appeared to have a design, and the British foreign office, under the premiership of Lord Beaconsfield, intervened with a threat of war if a considerable restoration of the Turks' facilities for exaction, persecution and massacre was not made. For a time war seemed very probable. The British music-halls, those lamps to British foreign policy, were lit with patriotic fire, and the London errand-boy going his rounds was inspired to chant, with the simple dignity of a great people conscious of its high destinies, a song declaring that:

> "We don't want to fight, but, by Jingo,[1] if we do,
> We got the ships, we got the men, we got the
> munn-aye too" . . .

and so on to a climax:

> "The Russ'ns shall not 'ave Con-stan-te-no . . . ple."

In consequence of this British opposition, a conference was assembled in 1878 at Berlin to revise the treaty of San Stefano, chiefly in the interests of the Turkish and Austrian monarchies; the British acquired the island of Cyprus, to which they had no sort of right whatever, and which has never been of the slightest use to them; and Lord Beaconsfield returned triumphantly from the Berlin Conference, with what the British were given to understand at the time was "Peace with Honour."

---

[1] Hence "Jingo" for any rabid patriot.

This treaty of Berlin was the second main factor, the peace of Frankfort being the first, in bringing about the great war of 1914–18.

§ 11

We have suggested that in the political history of Europe between 1848 and 1878 the mechanical revolution was not yet producing any very revolutionary changes. The post-revolutionary Great Powers were still going on within boundaries of practically the same size and with much the same formalities as they had done in pre-revolutionary times. But where the increased

speed and certainty of transport and telegraphic communications were already producing very considerable changes of condition and method was in the overseas enterprises of Britain and the other European powers, and in the reaction of Asia and Africa to Europe.

The end of the eighteenth century was a period of disrupting empires and disillusioned expansionists. The long and tedious journey between Britain and Spain and their colonies in America prevented any really free coming and going between the home land and the daughter lands, and so the colonies separated into new and distinct communities, with distinctive ideas and interests and even modes of speech. As they grew, they strained more and more at the feeble and uncertain link of shipping that joined them. Weak trading-

posts in the wilderness, like those of France in Canada, or trading establishments in great alien communities, like those of Britain in India, might well
cling for bare existence to the nation which gave them support and a reason
for their existence. That much and no more seemed to many thinkers in the
early part of the nineteenth century to be the limit set to overseas rule.

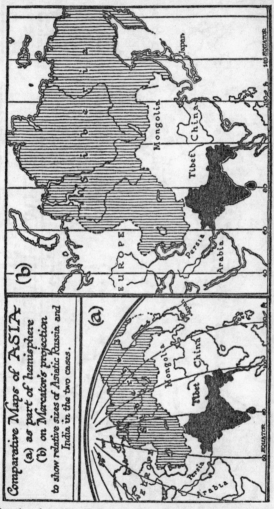

In 1820 the sketchy great European "empires" outside of Europe, that had
figured so bravely in the maps of the middle eighteenth century, had shrunken
to very small dimensions. Only the Russian sprawled as large as ever across
Asia. It sprawled much larger in the imaginations of many Europeans than in
reality, because of their habit of studying the geography of the world upon
Mercator's projection, which enormously exaggerated the size of Siberia.

The British Empire in 1815 consisted of the thinly populated coastal river and lake regions of Canada, and a great hinterland of wilderness in which the only settlements as yet were the fur-trading stations of the Hudson Bay Company; about a third of the Indian peninsula, under the rule of the East India

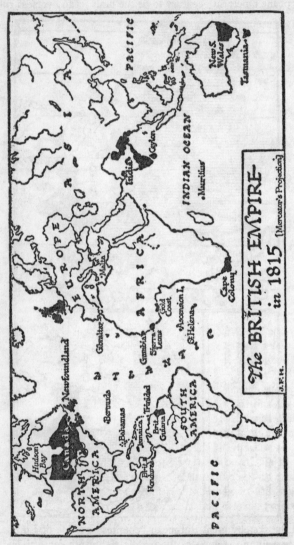

Company; the coast districts of the Cape of Good Hope, inhabited by blacks and rebellious-spirited Dutch settlers; a few trading stations on the coast of West Africa, the rock of Gilbraltar, the island of Malta, Jamaica, a few minor slave-labour possessions in the West Indies, British Guiana in South America, and, on the other side of the world, two dumps for convicts at Botany Bay in Australia and in Tasmania.

Spain retained Cuba and a few settlements in the Philippine Islands. Portugal had in Africa some vestiges of her ancient claims. Holland had various islands and possessions in the East Indies and Dutch Guiana, and Denmark an island or so in the West Indies. France had one or two West India Islands and French Guiana. This seemed to be as much as the European powers needed, or were likely to acquire, of the rest of the world. Only the East India Company showed any spirit of expansion.

In India, as we have already told, a peculiar empire was being built up, not by the British peoples nor by the British Government, but by this company of private adventurers with their monopoly and royal charter. The company had been forced to become a military and political power during the years of Indian division and insecurity that followed the break-up of India after the death of Aurungzeb in 1707. It had learnt to trade in states and peoples during the eighteenth century. Clive founded, and Warren Hastings organized, this strange new sort of empire; French rivalry was defeated, as we have already told; and by 1798 Lord Mornington, afterwards the Marquis Wellesley, the elder brother of that General Wellesley who became the Duke of Wellington, became Governor-General of India, and set the policy of the company definitely upon the line of replacing the fading empire of the Grand Mogul by its own rule.

Napoleon's expedition to Egypt was a direct attack upon the empire of this British company. While Europe was busy with the Napoleonic wars, the East India Company, under a succession of governors-general, was playing much the same rôle in India that had been played before by Turkoman and such-like invaders from the north, but playing it with greater efficiency and far less violence and cruelty. And after the peace of Vienna it went on, levying its revenues, making wars, sending ambassadors to Asiatic powers, a quasi-independent state—a state, however, with a marked disposition to send wealth westward.

In a previous chapter, we have sketched the break-up of the empire of the Great Mogul and the appearance of the Mahratta states, the Rajput principalities, the Moslem kingdoms of Oudh and Bengal, and the Sikhs. We cannot tell here in any detail how the British company made its way to supremacy, sometimes as the ally of this power, sometimes of that, and finally as the conqueror of all. Its power spread to Assam, Sind, Oudh. The map of India began to take on the outlines familiar to the English schoolboy of fifty years ago, a patchwork of native states embraced and held together by the great provinces under direct British rule. . . .

Now, as this strange unprecedented empire of the company grew in the period between 1800 and 1858, the mechanical revolution was quietly abolishing the great distance that had once separated India and Britain. In the old days the rule of the company had interfered little in the domestic life of the Indian states; it had given India foreign overlords, but India was used to foreign overlords, and had hitherto assimilated them; these Englishmen came into the country young, lived there most of their lives, and became a part of its system. But now the mechanical revolution began to alter this state of affairs. It became easier for the British officials to go home and to have holidays in Europe, easier for them to bring out wives and families; they ceased to be Indianized; they remained more conspicuously foreign and western—and there were more of them. And they began to interfere more vigorously with Indian customs. Magical and terrible things like the telegraph and the railway arrived. Christian missions became offensively busy. If they did not make very many converts, at least they made sceptics among the adherents of the older faiths. The young men in the towns began to be "Europeanized," to the great dismay of their elders.

India had endured many changes or rulers before, but never the sort of changes in her ways that these things portended. The Moslem teachers and the Brahmins were alike alarmed, and the British were blamed for the progress of mankind. Conflicts of economic interests grew more acute with the increasing nearness of Europe; Indian industries, and particularly the ancient cotton industry, suffered from legislation that favoured the British manufacturer.

A piece of incredible folly on the part of the company precipitated an outbreak. To the Brahmin a cow is sacred; to the Moslem the pig is unclean. A new rifle, needing greased cartridges—which the men had to bite—was served out to the company's Indian soldiers; the troops discovered that their cartridges were greased with the fat of cows and swine. This discovery precipitated a revolt of the company's Indian army, the Indian Mutiny (1857). First the troops mutinied at Meerut. Then Delhi rose to restore the empire of the Great Mogul. . . .

The British public suddenly discovered India. They became aware of that little garrison of British people, far away in that strange land of fiery dust and wearying sunshine, fighting for life against dark multitudes of assailants. How they got there and what right they had there, the British public did not ask. The love of one's kin in danger overrides such questions. There were massacres and cruelties. 1857 was a year of passionate anxiety in Great Britain. With mere handfuls of troops the British leaders, and notably Lawrence and Nicholson, did amazing things. They did not sit down to be besieged while the mutineers organized and gathered prestige; that would have lost them India forever. They attacked, often against overwhelming odds. "Clubs, not spades, are trumps," said Lawrence.

The Sikhs, the Gurkhas, the Punjab troops stuck to the British. The south remained tranquil. Of the massacres of Cawnpore and Lucknow in Oudh, and how a greatly outnumbered force of British troops besieged and stormed Delhi, other histories must tell. By April, 1859, the last embers of the blaze had been stamped out, and the British were masters of India again. In no sense had the mutiny been a popular insurrection; it was a mutiny merely of the Bengal Army, due largely to the unimaginative rule of the company officials. Its story abounds in instances of Indian help and kindness to British fugitives. But it was a warning.

The direct result of the mutiny was the annexation of the Indian Empire to the British Crown. By the Act entitled *An Act for the Better Government of India,* the Governor-General became a Viceroy representing the Sovereign, and the place of the company was taken by a Secretary of State for India responsible to the British Parliament. In 1877 Lord Beaconsfield, to complete this work, caused Queen Victoria to be proclaimed Empress of India.

Upon these extraordinary lines India and Britain were linked until after the second World War. India was still the empire of the Great Mogul, expanded, but the Great Mogul had been replaced by the "crowned republic" of Great Britain. India became an autocracy without an autocrat. Its rule combined the disadvantage of absolute monarchy with the impersonality and irresponsibility of democratic officialdom. The Indian with a complaint to make had no visible monarch to go to; his Emperor was a golden symbol; he must circulate pamphlets in England or inspire a question in the British House of Commons. The more occupied Parliament was with British affairs, the less attention India received and the more she was at the mercy of her small group of higher officials.

This was manifestly impossible as a permanent state of affairs. Indian life, whatever its restraints, was moving forward with the rest of the world; India had an increasing service of newspapers, an increasing number of educated people affected by Western ideas, and an increasing sense of common grievance against her government. There had been little or no corresponding advance in the education and quality of the British official in India during the century. His tradition was a high one; he was often a man of exceptional quality, but the system was unimaginative and inflexible. Moreover, the military power that stood behind these officials had developed neither in character nor intelligence during the century. No other class has been so stagnant intellectually as the British military caste. Confronted with a more educated India, the British military man, uneasily aware of his educational defects and constantly apprehensive of ridicule, displayed a growing disposition towards spasmodic violence that has had some very lamentable results. A sort of countenance was given to the lack of knowledge and self-control by the forceful teachings of Mr. Kipling to which we have already made allusion.

The growth of the British Empire in directions other than that of India was by no means so rapid during the earlier half of the nineteenth century. A considerable school of political thinkers in Britain was disposed to regard overseas possessions as a source of weakness to the kingdom. The Australian settlements developed slowly until in 1842 the discovery of valuable copper mines, and in 1851 of gold, gave them a new importance. Improvements in transport were also making Australian wool an increasingly marketable commodity in Europe. Canada, too, was not remarkably progressive until 1849; it was troubled by dissensions between its French and British inhabitants, there were several serious revolts, and it was only in 1867 that a new constitution creating a Federal Dominion of Canada relieved its internal strains. It was the railway that altered the Canadian outlook. It enabled Canada, just as it enabled the United States, to expand westward, to market its corn and other produce in Europe, and, in spite of its swift and extensive growth, to remain in language and sympathy and interests one community. The railway, the steamship, and the telegraphic cable were indeed changing all the conditions of colonial development.

Before 1840 English settlements had already begun in New Zealand, and a New Zealand Land Company had been formed to exploit the possibilities of the island. In 1840 New Zealand, also, was added to the colonial possessions of the British crown.

Canada, as we have noted, was the first of the British possessions to respond richly to the new economic possibilities the new methods of transport were

AFRICA
about the middle
of the 19th Century

opening. Presently the republics of South America, and particularly the Argentine Republic, began to feel, in their cattle trade and coffee growing, the increased nearness of the European market. Hitherto the chief commodities that had attracted the European powers into unsettled and barbaric regions had been gold or other metals, spices, ivory, or slaves. But in the latter quarter of the nineteenth century the increase of the European populations was obliging their governments to look abroad for staple foods; and the growth of scientific industrialism was creating a demand for new raw materials, fats and greases of every kind, rubber, and other hitherto disregarded substances. It was plain that Great Britain and Holland and Portugal were reaping a great and growing commercial advantage from their very considerable control of tropical and sub-tropical products. After 1871 Germany, and presently France, and later Italy, began to look for unannexed raw-material areas, or for Oriental countries capable of profitable modernization.

So began a fresh scramble all over the world, except in the American region where the Monroe Doctrine now barred such adventures, for politically unprotected lands. Close to Europe was the continent of Africa, full of vaguely known possibilities. In 1850 it was a continent of black mystery; only Egypt and the coast were known. A map must show the greatness of the

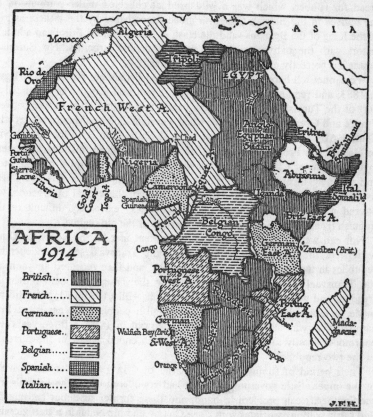

European ignorance at that time. It would need a book as long as this *Outline* to do justice to the amazing story of the explorers and adventurers who first pierced this cloud of darkness, and to the political agents, administrators, traders, settlers, and scientific men who followed in their track. Wonderful races of men like the pigmies, strange beasts like the okapi, marvellous fruits and flowers and insects, terrible diseases, astounding scenery of forest and mountain, enormous inland seas and gigantic rivers and cascades, were revealed—a whole new world. Even remains (at Zimbabwe) of some unrecorded and vanished civilization, the southward enterprise of an early people, were discovered.

Into this new world came the Europeans, and found the rifle already there in the hands of the Arab slave-traders, and negro life in disorder. By 1900, all Africa was mapped, explored, estimated, and divided between the European powers; divided with much snarling and disputation into portions that left each power uneasy or discontented, but which (see map) remained much the same till 1914. Little heed was given to the welfare of the natives in this scramble. The Arab slaver was, indeed, curbed rather than expelled; but the greed for rubber, which was a wild product collected under compulsion by the natives in the Belgian Congo—a greed exacerbated by the pitiless avarice of the King of the Belgians—and the clash of inexperienced European administrators with the native population, led to horrible atrocities. No European power has perfectly clean hands in this matter.

We cannot tell here in any detail how Great Britain got possession of Egypt in 1883, and remained there in spite of the fact that Egypt was technically a part of the Turkish Empire, nor how nearly this scramble led to war between France and Great Britain in 1898, when a certain Colonel Marchand, crossing Central Africa from the west coast, tried at Fashoda to seize the Upper Nile. In Uganda the French Catholic and the British Anglican missionaries disseminated a form of Christianity so heavily charged with the spirit of Napoleon, and so finely insistent upon the nuances of doctrine, that a few years after its first glimpse of European civilization, Mengo, the capital of Uganda, was littered with dead "Protestants" and "Catholics" extremely difficult to distinguish from the entirely unspiritual warriors of the old regime.

Nor can we tell how the British Government first let the Boers, or Dutch settlers, of the Orange River district and the Transvaal set up independent republics in the inland parts of South Africa, and then repented and annexed the Transvaal Republic in 1877; nor how the Transvaal Boers fought for freedom and won it after the Battle of Majuba Hill (1881). Majuba Hill was made to rankle in the memory of the English people by a persistent Press campaign. A war with both republics broke out in 1899, a three years' war enormously costly to the British people, which ended at last in the surrender of the two republics.

Their period of subjugation was a brief one. In 1907, after the downfall of the imperialistic government which had conquered them, the Liberals took the South African problem in hand, and these former republics became free and fairly willing associates with Cape Colony and the Natal in a confederation of all the states of South Africa as one self-governing republic under the British crown.

In a quarter of a century the partition of Africa was completed. There remained unannexed three comparatively small countries: Liberia, a settlement of liberated negro slaves on the west coast; Morocco, under a Moslem sultan; and Abyssinia, a barbaric country, with an ancient and peculiar form of Christianity, which had successfully maintained its independence against Italy at the battle of Adowa in 1896.

§ 12

It is difficult to believe that any large number of people really accepted this headlong painting of the map of Africa in European colours as a permanent new settlement of the world's affairs, but it is the duty of the historian to record that it was so accepted.

There was but a shallow historical background to the European mind in the nineteenth century, hardly any sense of what constitutes an enduring political system, and no habit of penetrating criticism. The quite temporary advantages that the onset of the mechanical revolution in the west had given the European Great Powers over the rest of the Old World were regarded by people, blankly ignorant of the great Mongol conquests of the thirteenth and following centuries, as evidences of a permanent and assured European leadership of mankind. They had no sense of the transferability of science and its fruits. They did not realize that Chinamen and Indians could carry on the work of research as ably as Frenchmen or Englishmen. They believed that there was some innate intellectual drive in the west, and some innate indolence and conservatism in the east, that assured the Europeans a world predominance for ever.

The consequence of this infatuation was that the various European foreign offices set themselves not merely to scramble with the British for the savage and undeveloped regions of the world's surface, but also to carve up the populous and civilized countries of Asia as though these peoples, also, were no more than raw material for European exploitation. The inwardly precarious but outwardly splendid imperialism of the British ruling class in India, and the extensive and profitable possessions of the Dutch in the East Indies, filled the ruling and mercantile classes of the rival Great Powers with dreams of similar glories in Persia, in the disintegrating Ottoman Empire, and in Further India, China and Japan.

In the closing years of the nineteenth century it was assumed, as the reader may verify by an examination of the current literature of the period, to be a natural and inevitable thing that all the world should fall under European dominion. With a reluctant benevolent air the European mind prepared itself to take up what Mr. Rudyard Kipling called "the White Man's Burthen"—that is to say, the lordship of the earth. The Powers set themselves to this enterprise in a mood of jostling rivalry, with half-educated or illiterate populations at home, with a mere handful of men, a few thousand at most, engaged in scientific research, with their internal political systems in a state of tension or convulsive change, with a creaking economic system of the most provisional sort, and with their religions far gone in decay. They really believed that the vast population of eastern Asia could be permanently subordinated to such a Europe.

Even to-day there are many people who fail to grasp the essential facts of this situation. They do not realize that in Asia the average brain is not one whit inferior in quality to the average European brain; that history shows

Asiatics to be as bold, as vigorous, as generous, as self-sacrificing, and as capable of strong collective action as Europeans; and that there are, and must continue to be, a great many more Asiatics than Europeans in the world.

It has always been difficult to restrain the leakage of knowledge from one population to another, and now it becomes impossible. Under modern conditions world-wide economic and educational equalization is in the long run inevitable. An intellectual and moral rally of the Asiatics began in the twentieth century and is still going on. Even now, for one Englishman or American who knows Chinese thoroughly, or has any intimate knowledge of Chinese life and thought, there are hundreds of Chinamen conversant with everything the English know.

In India, the balance was even worse throughout the earlier years of this century. To Britain, India sent students; to India, Britain sent officials—for the most part untrained in scientific observation. Even in 1955 there was still no organization for the sending of European students, as students, to examine and inquire into Indian history, archæology, and current affairs, or for bringing learned Indians into contact with British students in Britain.

Since the year 1898—the year of the seizure of Kiau-Chau by Germany and of Wei-hai-wei by Britain, and the leasing of Port Arthur to Russia— events in China have moved more rapidly than in any other country except Japan. A great hatred of Europeans swept like a flame over China, and a political society for the expulsion of Europeans, the Boxers, grew up and broke out into violence in 1900. This was an outbreak of rage and mischief on quite old-fashioned lines. In 1900 the Boxers murdered 250 Europeans and, it is said, nearly 30,000 Christians; China, not for the first time in history, was under the sway of a dowager empress. She was an ignorant woman, but of great force of character and in close sympathy with the Boxers. She supported them, and protected those who perpetrated outrages on the Europeans. All that, again, is what might have happened in 500 B.C. or thereabouts against the Huns.

Things came to a crisis in 1900. The Boxers became more and more threatening to the Europeans in China. Attempts were made to send up additional European guards to the Peking legations, but this only precipitated matters. The German minister was shot down in the streets of Peking by a soldier of the Imperial Guard. The rest of the foreign representatives gathered together and made a fortification of the more favourably situated legations and stood a siege of two months. A combined allied force of 20,000 under a German general then marched up to Peking and relieved the legations, and the empress fled to Sian-fu, the old capital of Tai-tsung in Shensi. Some of the European troops committed grave atrocities upon the Chinese civil population. That brings one up to about the level of 1850, let us say.

There followed the practical annexation of Manchuria by Russia, a squabble among the powers, and in 1904 a British invasion of Tibet, hitherto a forbidden country. But what did not appear on the surface of these events, and what made all these events fundamentally different, was that China now contained a considerable number of able people who had a European education and European knowledge.

The Boxer insurrection subsided, and then the influence of this new factor began to appear in talk of a constitution (1906), in the suppression of opium-smoking, and in educational reforms. A constitution of the Japanese type came into existence in 1909, making China a limited monarchy. But China was not to be moulded to the Japanese pattern, and the revolutionary stir continued. Japan, in her own reorganization, and in accordance with her temperament, had turned her eyes to the monarchist West, but China was looking across the Pacific. In 1911 the first Chinese revolution began. In 1912 the emperor abdicated, and the greatest community in the world became a republic. The overthrow of the emperor was also the overthrow of the Manchus, and the Mongolian pigtail, which had been worn by the Chinese since 1644, ceased to be compulsory upon them. But the disappearance of this emblem of servitude was the least of the changes. In the hopes of the revolutionaries and of many outside China, the revolution was to release all the latent powers of her vast population. A great network of railways would be built, universities would be founded, the Chinese script would be modernized, and women would be freed. Western inventions would be assimilated, while the ancient Chinese civilization would be preserved. Few observers commented that China was still a land of poor peasants, untouched by any republican ideas, knowing of no authority but an emperor who had been removed, and thinking only of their day to day living. Dotted about the vast expanse were some huge cities and in them the coolie population was almost equally ignorant. Most of what was written about China's future, in this history as much as elsewhere, makes pathetic reading to-day.

§ 13

The pioneer country, however, in the recovery of the Asiatic peoples was not China but Japan. We have outrun our story in telling of China. Hitherto Japan has played but a small part in this history; her secluded civilization has not contributed very largely to the general shaping of human destinies; she has received much, but she has given little. The original inhabitants of the Japanese islands were probably a northern people with remote Nordic affinities, the Hairy Ainu. But the Japanese proper are of the Mongolian race. Physically they resemble the Amerindians, and there are many curious resemblances between the prehistoric pottery and so forth of Japan and similar Peruvian products. It is not impossible that they are a back-flow from the trans-Pacific drift of the Neolithic culture, but they may also have absorbed from the south a Malay and even a Negrito element.

Whatever the origin of the Japanese, there can be no doubt that their civilization, their writing, and their literary and artistic traditions are derived from the Chinese. They were emerging from barbarism in the second and third century of the Christian era, and one of their earliest acts as a people outside their own country was an invasion of Korea under a queen Jingo, who seems to have played a large part in establishing their civilization. Their history is an interesting and romantic one; they developed a feudal system and a tradition of chivalry; their attacks upon Korea and China are an Eastern equivalent of the English wars in France.

Japan was first brought into contact with Europe in the sixteenth century. In 1542 some Portuguese reached it in a Chinese junk, and in 1549 a Jesuit missionary, Francis Xavier, began his teaching there. The Jesuit accounts describe a country greatly devastated by perpetual feudal war. For a time Japan welcomed European intercourse, and the Christian missionaries made a great number of converts. A certain William Adams, of Gillingham in Kent, became the most trusted European adviser of the Japanese, and showed them how to build big ships. There were voyages in Japanese-built ships to India and Peru.

Then arose complicated quarrels between the Spanish Dominicans, the Portuguese Jesuits, and the English and Dutch Protestants, each warning the Japanese against the evil political designs of the others. The Jesuits, in a phase of ascendancy, persecuted and insulted the Buddhists with great acrimony. These troubles interwove with the feudal conflicts of the time. In the end the Japanese came to the conclusion that the Europeans and their Christianity were an intolerable nuisance, and that Catholic Christianity in particular was a mere cloak for the political dreams of the Pope and the Spanish monarchy —already in possession of the Philippine Islands; there was a great and conclusive persecution of the Christians; and in 1638 Japan, with the exception of one wretched Dutch factory on the minute island of Deshima in the harbour of Nagasaki, was absolutely closed to Europeans, and remained closed for over 200 years.

The Dutch on Deshima were exposed to almost unendurable indignities. They had no intercourse with any Japanese except the special officials appointed to deal with them. During two centuries the Japanese remained as completely cut off from the rest of the world as though they lived upon another planet. It was forbidden to build any ship larger than a mere coasting boat. No Japanese could go abroad, and no European enter the country.

For two centuries Japan remained outside the main current of history. She lived on in a state of picturesque feudalism enlivened by blood feuds, in which about five per cent. of the population, the *samurai*, or fighting men, and the nobles and their families, tyrannized without restraint over the rest of the population. All common men knelt when a noble passed; to betray the slightest disrespect was to risk being slashed to death by his *samurai*. The elect classes lived lives of romantic adventure without one redeeming gleam of novelty; they loved, murdered, and pursued fine points of honour—which probably bored the intelligent ones extremely. We can imagine the wretchedness of a curious mind, tormented by the craving for travel and knowledge, cooped up in these islands of empty romance.

Meanwhile, the great world outside went on to wider visions and new powers. Strange shipping became more frequent, passing the Japanese headlands; sometimes ships were wrecked and sailors brought ashore. Through

Deshima, their one link with the outer universe, came warnings that Japan was not keeping pace with the power of the Western world. In 1837 a ship sailed into Yedo Bay flying a strange flag of stripes and stars, and carrying some Japanese sailors she had picked up far adrift in the Pacific. She was driven off by a cannon shot.

This flag presently reappeared on other ships. One in 1849 came to demand the liberation of eighteen shipwrecked American sailors. Then in 1853 came four American warships under Commodore Perry, and refused to be driven away. He lay at anchor in forbidden waters, and sent messages to the two rulers who at that time shared the control of Japan. In 1854 he returned with ten ships, amazing ships propelled by steam and equipped with big guns, and he made proposals for trade and intercourse that the Japanese had no power to resist. He landed with a guard of 500 men to sign the treaty. Incredulous crowds watched this visitation from the outer world marching through the streets.

Russia, Holland, and Britain followed in the wake of America. Foreigners entered the country, and conflicts between them and Japanese gentlemen of spirit ensued. A British subject was killed in a street brawl, and a Japanese town was bombarded by the British (1863). A great nobleman, whose estates commanded the Straits of Shimonoseki, saw fit to fire on foreign vessels, and a second bombardment by a fleet of British, French, Dutch, and American warships destroyed his batteries and scattered his swordsmen. Finally, an allied squadron (1865), at anchor off Osaka, imposed a ratification of the treaties which opened Japan to the world.

The humiliation of the Japanese by these events was intense, and it would seem that the salvation of peoples lies largely in such humiliations. With astonishing energy and intelligence they set themselves to bring their culture and organization up to the level of the European powers. Never in all the history of mankind did a nation make such a stride as Japan then did. In 1866 she was a mediæval people, a fantastic caricature of the extremist romantic feudalism: in 1899 hers was a completely Westernized people, on a level with the most advanced European powers, and well in advance of Russia. She completely dispelled the persuasion that Asia was in some irrevocable way hopelessly behind Europe. She made all European progress seem sluggish and tentative by comparison.

We cannot tell here in any detail of Japan's war with China in 1894–95. It demonstrated the extent of her Westernization. She had an efficient Westernized army and a small yet sound fleet. But the significance of her renascence, though it was appreciated by Britain and the United States, who were already treating her as if she were a European state, was not understood by the other Great Powers engaged in the pursuit of new Indias in Asia. Russia was pushing down through Manchuria to Korea, France was already established far to the south in Tonkin and Annam, Germany was prowling hungrily on the look-out for some settlement. The three powers combined to prevent Japan reaping any fruits from the Chinese war, and particularly from establishing herself on the mainland at the points commanding the Japan sea. She was exhausted by her war with China, and they threatened her with war.

In 1898 Germany descended upon China, and, making the murder of two missionaries her excuse, annexed a portion of the province of Shantung. Thereupon Russia seized the Liaotung peninsula, and extorted the consent of China

to an extension of her trans-Siberian railway to Port Arthur; and in 1900 she occupied Manchuria. Britain was unable to resist the imitative impulse, and seized the port of Wei-hai-wei (1898).

How alarming these movements must have been to every intelligent Japanese a glance at the map will show. They led to a war with Russia which marks an epoch in the history of Asia, the close of the period of European arrogance. The Russian people were, of course, innocent and ignorant of this trouble that was being made for them half-way round the world, and the wiser Russian statesmen were against these foolish thrusts; but a gang of financial adventurers surrounded the Tsar, including the Grand Dukes, his cousins. They had gambled deeply in the prospective looting of Manchuria and China, and they would suffer no withdrawal. So there began a transportation of great armies of Japanese soldiers across the sea to Port Arthur and Korea, and the sending of endless trainloads of Russian peasants along the Siberian railway to die in those distant battlefields.

The Russians, badly led and dishonestly provided, were beaten on sea and land alike. The Russian Baltic Fleet sailed round Africa to be utterly destroyed in the Straits of Tsushima. A revolutionary movement among the common people of Russia, infuriated by this remote and reasonless slaughter, obliged the Tsar to end the war (1905); he returned the southern half of Saghalien, which had been seized by Russia in 1875, evacuated Manchuria, and resigned Korea to Japan. The white man was beginning to drop his load in eastern Asia. For some years, however, Germany remained in uneasy possession of Kiau-Chau.

§ 14

We have already noted how the enterprise of Italy in Abyssinia had been checked at the terrible Battle of Adowa (1896), in which over 3,000 Italians were killed and more than 4,000 taken prisoner. The phase of imperial expansion at the expense of organized non-European states was manifestly drawing to a close. It had entangled the quite sufficiently difficult political and social problems of Great Britain, France, Spain, Italy, Germany and Russia with the affairs of considerable alien, unassimilable, and resentful populations: Great Britain had Egypt (not formally annexed as yet), India, Burma, and a variety of such minor problems as Malta and Shanghai; France had cumbered herself with Tonkin and Annam in addition to Algiers and Tunis; Spain was newly entangled in Morocco; Italy had found trouble for herself in Tripoli; and German overseas imperialism, though its "place in the sun" seemed a poor one, derived what satisfaction it could from the thought of a prospective war with Japan over Kiau-Chau.

All these "subject" lands had populations at a level of intelligence and education very little lower than those of the possessing country; the development of a native press, of a collective self-consciousness, and of demands for self-government was in each case inevitable, and the statesmen of Europe had been far too busy achieving these empires to have any clear ideas of what they would do with them when they got them.

The Western democracies, as they woke up to freedom, discovered themselves "imperial," and were considerably embarrassed by the discovery. The East came to the Western capitals with perplexing demands. In London the common Englishman, much preoccupied by strikes, by economic riddles, by questions of nationalization, municipalization, and the like, found that his path was crossed and his public meetings were attended by a large and increasing number of swarthy gentlemen in turbans, fezes, and other strange headgear, all saying in effect: "You have got us. The people who represent your government have destroyed our own government, and prevent us from making a new one. What are you going to do with us?"

§ 15

We may note here briefly the very various nature of the constituents of the British Empire in 1914. It was already a quite unique political combination; nothing of the sort had ever existed before. It was a new thing in political history, just as the United States is a new thing. It was a larger and a more complicated thing than such nationalist states as France, Holland or Sweden.

First and central to the whole system was the "crowned republic" of the United British Kingdoms, including (against the will of a considerable part of the Irish people) Ireland. The majority of the British Parliament, made up of the three united parliaments of England, Scotland, and Ireland, determined the headship, the quality and policy of the ministry, and determined it largely on considerations arising out of British domestic politics. It was this ministry which was the effective supreme government, with powers of peace and war, over all the rest of the empire.

Next in order of political importance to the British states were the "crowned republics" of Australia, Canada, Newfoundland (the oldest British possession, 1583), New Zealand, and South Africa, all practically independent and self-governing states in alliance with Great Britain, but each with a representative of the Crown appointed by the Government in office;

Next, the Indian Empire, an extension of the empire of the Great Mogul, with its dependent and "protected" states reaching now from Baluchistan to Burma, and including Aden, in all of which empire the British Crown *and* the India Office (under Parliamentary control) played the rôle of the original Turkoman dynasty;

Then the ambiguous possession of Egypt, still nominally a part of the Turkish Empire and still retaining its own monarch, the Khedive, but under almost despotic British official rule. Egypt, be it noted, was however no regular part of the Empire, for while the Khedive was there it could have no allegiance to the Crown. Nor was any endeavour made to replace the Khedive by King George V, even after Turkish suzerainty was ended.

Then the still more ambiguous "Anglo-Egyptian" Sudan province, occupied and administered jointly by the British and by the Egyptian Government;

Then a number of partially self-governing communities, some British in origin and some not, with elected legislatures and an appointed executive, such as Jamaica, the Bahamas, Bermuda, Malta.

Then the Crown colonies, in which the rule of the British Home Government (through the Colonial Office) verged on autocracy, as in Ceylon, Trinidad, and Fiji (where there was an appointed council), and Gibraltar and St. Helena (where there was a governor);

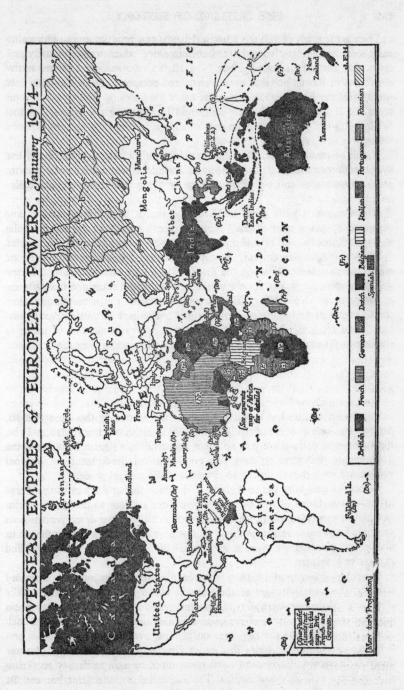

OVERSEAS EMPIRES of EUROPEAN POWERS, January 1914.

British   French   German   Dutch   Belgian   Italian   Portuguese   Russian   Spanish

[Mercator's Projection]

J.F.H.

Then great areas of (chiefly) tropical lands, raw-product areas, with politically weak and under-civilized native communities, which were nominally pro-
tectorates, and administered either by a High Commissioner set over native
chiefs (as in Basutoland) or over a chartered company (as in Rhodesia). In
some cases the Foreign Office, in some cases the Colonial Office, and in some
cases the India Office had been concerned in acquiring the possessions that
fell into this last and least definite class of all, but for the most part the Colonial
Office was now responsible for them.

It will be manifest, therefore, that no single office and no single brain had
ever comprehended the British Empire as a whole. It was a mixture of growths
and accumulations entirely different from anything that had ever been called
an empire before.

It guaranteed a wide peace and security; that is why it was endured and
sustained by many men of the "subject" races—in spite of official tyrannies
and insufficiencies, and of much negligence on the part of the "home" public.

Like the "Athenian empire," it was an overseas empire; its ways were sea
ways, and its common link was the British Navy. Like all empires, its cohesion
was dependent physically upon a method of communication; the development
of seamanship, shipbuilding, and steamships between the sixteenth and nineteenth centuries had made it a possible and convenient Pax—the "Pax Britannica"—and fresh developments of air or swift land transport or of undersea
warfare might at any time make it inconvenient or helplessly insecure.

§ 16

We have been writing of the nineteenth century because that is a convenient
existing term to use, but it will be plain to the reader by this time that the
period of this chapter is not really from 1800 to 1900, but from 1815 to 1914.
Between these dates there was no great catastrophe, no great breaking-point.
The changes that went on were very considerable indeed, but they were not
sudden nor were they in any sense reversals of the general process.

Before we deal with the convulsion with which this century of progress and
invention concluded, it will be well to give three sections to the artistic forms
in which it expressed itself. We have already dealt with the development of its
scientific knowledge and its political philosophy; we will now glance first at its
plastic and pictorial art, then at its musical life, and then at its creative and
expressive literature.

The story of European painting in the opening half of the nineteenth century
reflected the social changes of the time. It was a time in which the middle
class, the serious commercial type, was increasing very rapidly in wealth and
importance; it was a time of enriched manufacturers and new financial successes. Presently came the railways, steamships, overseas trade in staples and
the large speculative fortunes that arose directly and indirectly out of these
things. The restored European Courts were tinged by a disposition to propitiate
and associate with this new wealth. The successful manufacturer became the
typical patron of painting and architecture. He was trying to assimilate himself

to the gentlefolk. He desired rather pictures made by gentlemen for gentlemen, than disturbing power or disconcerting beauty. He desired pictures before which he could eat his dinner or drink his tea in comfort and satisfaction, and he was prepared to pay liberally for them. The versatile and wonderful Spaniard Goya (1746–1828), the great English landscape painters Constable (1776–1837) and Turner (1775–1851), David and Ingres, of whom we have spoken as expressing the spirit of the French Empire, passed and left no equals. But the painting of pictures became a very considerable profession. The British Royal Academy, the French Salon, held annual exhibitions of pictures painted to please, and artists bought large distinguished houses and lived lives of respectable luxury. In England many were even knighted. Sculpture followed in the same direction. The appreciation of pictures, if it ceased to be very intense, became very wide. For large sections of the English public, an annual pilgrimage to London "to see the Academy" became almost obligatory.

But as the century passed on beyond its middle years, the same tendency to unrest that had disturbed the religious and social routines of Europe appeared in the world of art. In England Ruskin (1819–1900) and William Morris (1834–1896) criticized the academic inanities of art and contemporary decoration with a disturbing effectiveness. There were schisms in the profession of painting; there appeared new schools, and notably the Pre-Raphaelites who sought for precedents and methods in the work of those earlier days before painting became elegant. Under the approval of Ruskin and Morris they turned their eyes back to the Middle Ages and painted Arthurian heroes and Blessed Damosels. Other, still more rebellious, spirits turned their eyes towards the world about them. Corot (1796–1875) had maintained his vigour of vision throughout this period of dullness, and after the disaster of 1870–71 France saw a great resumption of the precedents of Rembrandt and Velasquez in the work of such masters as Degas, Manet and Renoir. With them must be named the great American Whistler (1834–1903). People tired, almost unconsciously, of the polite picture, and a style of domestic architecture came into vogue which tolerated no surrender of wall-space to the framed oil-painting. As the period closed, the output of easel pictures for buying and hanging up just anywhere was undergoing a sensible decline, and the unstanchable supply of art students was being directed with increasing success to the more modest and desirable pursuit of the decorative arts.

In the closing years of the nineteenth century there were many signs to show that a maximum of exact representativeness in art had passed. Representation of flowers and figures vanished from carpet and curtain and dress materials; representation became a secondary and subdued quality in painting and sculpture. We have already noted a previous period of realistic rendering in the time of Akhnaton in Egypt and another during the Græco-Roman period, and we have remarked how rapidly this latter phase passed into the stiffness, flatness and symbolism of Byzantine and Gothic work and the formal and geometrical methods of Moslem decoration. Still earlier the vivid impressionism of the later Palæolithic period had been followed by the formalism of the early Neolithic art. Now, again, in the first and second decades of the twentieth century we find art turning away, as if glutted, from reality, disregarding outer form for the traces of motion, becoming once more analytical and symbolical. This drift seems likely to continue. It is also helped now by the increasing efficiency of photography for merely circumstantial precision. The world wearies of undigested fact.

The century opened in a phase of architectural dullness. The classical tradition, sustained by the rule of classical pedants in the schools, had gradually dominated and checked the free development of the Renaissance style, and most new buildings betrayed their regret for an age gone by two thousand years before. Everywhere appeared white-faced colonnaded façades of stucco. Then, with the Romantic revival in literature upon which we will presently enlarge, and with the collapse of Napoleon's attempt to revive Imperial Rome, came a shifting of the attention of this most imitative period to the Middle Ages. There was a Gothic revival after the classic revival, which was particularly powerful in Britain, and produced, among many other remarkable exploits, the present Houses of Parliament. Then the period of Queen Anne, which had been distinguished by a special development of the still living Renaissance modes, was invoked. Architects in Britain would build you a hall or house in the classic, Gothic, Scotch baronial or Queen Anne style; the one style that did not appear anywhere was the Nineteenth Century style. The Englishmen went about in trousers and top-hats and dingy coloured clothes, severely modern and sober, but their houses and public buildings were dressed in the dispirited fashions of the past, as if for some cheerless and unpopular fancy dress ball.

In France and Germany there was much more architectural initiative; the Renaissance style still lived and developed in France. Such interesting problems in architecture, however, as were afforded by railway stations, railway bridges, warehouses, factories and so forth, were never seriously attempted anywhere—with the possible exception of Germany. An inefficient ugliness was the rule for such buildings. It was as if the rush of new needs, new materials, and new opportunities had overwhelmed the architectural courage of the age. One of the oddest, most typical products of this phase of dismay is the London Tower Bridge, in which a light and powerful fabric of steelwork is plastered over with suggestions of Flemish stonemasonry and memories of a mediæval drawbridge. But all the public buildings of nineteenth-century Britain reek with bad decaying history.

Domestic architecture degenerated even more than public, throughout a large part of the century. The gross increase in the European populations, that absorbed so much of the increased resources of the time, led to a frightful proliferation of low-grade housing about the growing towns; endless rows of mean small houses in Britain, gawky tenement houses in most other European countries. Only as the century closed, and the birth-rate fell and the automobile came into effect in redistributing the population that had been breeding and congesting about the railway stations, did any general interest in domestic architecture revive and pleasant modern types of cottage and country house appear.

America in colonial days had produced an extremely agreeable type of country house, more particularly in Virginia and the South, an adaptation to local conditions of British country-house architecture, which itself sprang from the fruitful Renaissance stem. We have already noted Sir Christopher Wren's contribution to this development. Apart from this domestic side, American architecture until the closing decades of the century was mainly transplanted European design. The Capitol at Washington for example, is French work. It might have been built in Paris or Brussels. Much of the domestic housing was flimsy and commonplace. When Britain adopted the sash window, America retained the continental casement. But in the eighties and nineties of the century the growing wealth and self-reliance of the new world broke out into new and vigorous architectural initiatives. America began to use steel, glass and concrete construction with an increasing boldness and success. These materials and the invention and perfection of the "elevator" rendered possible buildings of a hitherto unprecedented height and scale. In 1870 American architecture scarcely existed; by 1910 America was far in advance of any other country in the world in the freshness and courage of its new buildings. At an interval came Germany. The names of Richardson (1838–1886) and Stanford White (1853–1906) stand out among the American architects of this new period.

It is to the America of the twentieth century that we must look for the gradual expression in building and housing of the new powers and resources the nineteenth century revealed to mankind; and associated with this development of architecture we may count on new and remarkable developments there of sculpture, painting, mosaic and the decorative arts generally. In that continent will be the greater opportunity, the greater wealth, the greater freedom of mind.

§ 17

The flow of musical creation that was in progress during the eighteenth century suffered little let or hindrance throughout the period of this chapter. We have named Mozart and Beethoven as culminating figures of the eighteenth century. Beethoven carries us over into the nineteenth century, and beside him we must put his contemporary Weber (1786–1826) an experimentalist and innovator of cardinal importance, and a little later the very considerable figures of Schubert (1797–1828), Mendelssohn (1809–1847), and Schumann (1810–1856). Nor can we ignore César Franck's (1822–1890) "Cathedrals of Sound." Music was now passing more and more out of the domain of royal and noble patronage into the concert hall and the appeal to the suffrages of a specially cultivated public. Side by side with opera, there was an increasing production of song and pianoforte pieces for the refined home and of dance music for the social gathering. There was no corresponding advance in religious music after the days of Handel and Bach. But the royal patron was still of importance to the composer of great operas, and the courts of Bavaria and Russia especially were the fostering-places of a new "opera-drama" and a new conception of the ballet.

One can trace in the music of the century the broadening interests of the age. Composers began to seek for new themes and a new spirit amidst the folk-music of the east European and eastern peoples.

Chopin (1809–1849) utilized Polish, Liszt (1811–1886) and Joachim (1831–1897) Hungarian sources of inspiration, and Brahms (1833–1897) went still further afield to India for material to incorporate with his essentially classical fabric. Wagner was born in 1813 and died in 1883. He followed in the footsteps of Weber. He broke up the established tradition of opera, dramatized and broadened and expanded the range of instrumental music, charged it with new power and passion. Later, in Russia, Tchaikovsky (1840–1893), Moussorgsky (1835–1881), and Rimsky Korsakov (1844–1908) were to discover new realms of colour and delight.

Here, in the limited space at our disposal, we can but name the Czech Dvořák (1841–1904), the lively enterprise of Richard Strauss (born 1864), and the fresh beauty of Debussy (1862–1918).

So far America had contributed little to great music. What had come from the States, so far as other countries were aware, was either imitative or of a type which was regarded as essentially unimportant—whether it was received with indulgent hilarity or pedantic disapproval. Nobody considered that what was called "jazz" or more often merely "ragtime" could be more than a transitory fad. It was known to be negro in origin, but its New Orleans beginnings were not investigated, and the proposition that these new rhythms could have any bearing, let alone influence, upon musical composition would have been received with laughter. But there is no room here to trace its development; still less that of modern music in the common sense. The appreciation of this latter, and most of its development, was a postwar phenomenon, and the limits of this work will prevent us carrying on the history of music and the other arts beyond the year 1918. Not that the record is unimportant; indeed the development of the gramophone and radio industries brought music that was once the privilege of a cultivated class into the homes of uncountable millions.

§ 18

In the space at our disposal here it is impossible to give much more than the barest, most simplified account of the great flood of literary activities through which the new forces of this century of expansion sought expression. We have already dealt with the leading ideas of the founders and makers of Socialism and of the influence of the enlarging scientific vision upon religious, political and social ideas. But it is impossible for us to do full justice to the significance and continuing influence of such great practical thinkers as Adam Smith (1723–1790), Malthus (1766–1834), and their successors, or of such profound and penetrating speculations as those of Schopenhauer (1788–1860) and Nietzsche (1844–1900) in Germany. Hegel (1770–1831), again, is for us like a tempting item at the end of too long a menu. We must leave him. He deflected the current of modern thought very curiously, but it recovers from his deflection.

Nor can we discuss here the accidents of taste and absurdities of interpretation that made Lord Byron (1788–1824), that doggerel satirist with the philosophy of a man-about-town, into a great figure in the nineteenth-century conception of literature throughout Europe, nor weigh the value of Goethe (1749–1832), who was for many years the intellectual and æsthetic god of Germany. He has that prominence no longer. He littered the German mind with a great wealth of uprooted and transplanted classicism. He was great, elegant and industrious. He was the noble collector in literature as Byron was the noble rebel.

The century opened with a considerable outburst of poetry, particularly in Britain. It was poetry with characteristics of its own; there was a new realization of nature as being in emotional relationship with man, an unconscious disregard of creeds and an unrestrained approach to the deepest questions about life, as though almost unawares the poet had gone out of the fabric of established and accepted beliefs into a free universe. The poems of this phase had generally a narrative thread that was reduced at times to a shadow —and they rambled gracefully, argumentatively, variously. Shelley (1792–1822), Keats (1795–1821), Wordsworth (1770–1850), are the outstanding names of this age of English poetic expression. Wordsworth with a very variable artistry gave voice to a mystical pantheism, a deep sense of God in Nature. Shelley was the first and greatest of modern poets. His thought was saturated with scientific ideas and his perception of the transitory nature of the political institutions of his time was far in advance of any contemporary. The poetic impulse was sustained in England in the succeeding generation with greater melody and beauty and less far-reaching implications by Tennyson (1809–1892), who achieved a great popularity, flattered Queen Victoria, and was the first among British poets to be made a peer for his poetry. His *Morte d'Arthur* is worthy to stand beside the architecture of the time. The fame of Longfellow (1807–1882) was not so much an American equivalent as an American retort to Tennyson.

Developing more slowly and against discouragement of the scholastic, academic and critical worlds, the form of prose fiction rose by degrees to equality with and then to a predominance over poetry. That was what people were really reading, that was what the times required. The great prose book about life, with a narrative progression in its substance, already foreshadowed by Rabelais and developed by the discursive novels of Fielding and Sterne, emerged slowly to completion and recognition as the century progressed. As it grew in length and power, the short novel and the short story appeared beside it.

The earlier novels were stories of events and studies of manners. Fanny Burney (1752–1840) takes us back to the world of Dr. Johnson. Jane Austen (1775–1817), working within narrow limits, carried on the tradition of feminine observation finely expressed. From the restraints and limitations of this sort of tale about manners and feelings, we find the English novel gradually breaking bounds as the mind of the century broke bounds.

A very great and central figure in the enlargement of the novel was the

German writer Jean Paul Richter (1763–1825). His narrative is a mere thread for jewelled and decorated digressions. Another great German writer was Heine (1797–1856). Richter affected the work of the English writer Thomas Carlyle very profoundly. Through Carlyle the discursive and enriching influence of Richter reached Charles Dickens (1812–1870) and George Meredith (1828–1909). Thackeray (1811–1863), the great rival of Dickens, wandered and philosophized and buttonholed his reader, but in a fashion that derives rather from Sterne than from the Germans. Charles Reade (1814–1884), in his *Cloister and the Hearth,* presented the still living issues between Protestantism and Catholicism in Europe in the fabric of a great romance. Both Thackeray and Carlyle found their disposition to discuss life freely leading them away from the form of frank fiction towards the interpretation of historical phases. There is a natural and necessary connection between the great novel of the English type and history. Carlyle's *French Revolution* and his *Frederick the Great* were read like novels, and an immense success was made by Macaulay (1800–1859) with his history of the later Stuart period. More scientific, but also duller historians succeeded to them; but in the new century their tradition was taken up by Lytton Strachey, J. L. & Barbara Hammond, and others.

In France, the same necessities and curiosities that broadened the English novel from a mere story to a picture and interpretation of life, inspired Balzac (1797–1850) to the vast enterprise of his *Comédie Humaine.* At a great distance below him, his successor, Zola (1840–1902), wrote his kindred Rougon-Macquart cycle, a group of novels tracing the fortunes of a copious French family through several generations. Victor Hugo (1802–1885) stands by himself, an exuberant, bold, florid and sometimes rather tawdry mind, erupting plays, poems, novels and political disquisitions. But in France the influence of the Academy, the classical tradition, the tradition of scholastic discipline, though it could not restrain these exceptional cases, did on the whole tame and subdue the art of fiction. It must have "form," said the pedagogues. It must be "correct." It must not digress. It must be politely impersonal in its manner. So the French novel was obstructed on its way to the limitless freedoms of experiment that the British school enjoyed. Within the limits thus fixed, Flaubert (1821–1880) is the most subtle and finished of French writers.

Thomas Hardy (1840–1928), the last of the great Victorian novelists, belongs rather to this French classical school than the British tradition in fiction. He rebelled in his later years against the limitations he had set himself, abandoned the novel form altogether, and in *The Dynasts,* a representation of the whole Napoleonic adventure in the form of a drama, he achieved his crowning masterpiece, another instance of the close affinity of the great novelists to the interpretative historian.

The desire to know about life and what is happening to it, the disposition to question life closely and keenly, that made the British impatient of the formal restrictions of poetry and elevated the novel and its cognate forms to literary predominance, spread through all the European countries. Germany, Russia, Scandinavia, in particular, produced great literature in this form. The outstanding name amidst a multitude of excellent German novelists is that of Gustav Freytag (1816–1895). Norway produced its Björnson (1832–1910); Russia a great galaxy of splendid writers from Gogol (1809–1852) to Dostoievsky (1821–1881), Turgeniev (1818–1883), Tolstoy (1828–1900), and Tchehof (died 1904).

But not all readers in the nineteenth century were eager and curious. Intermingled with the types and classes whose minds were filled with doubts and progress, were types and social strata in active resistance to progressive ideas. Side by side with a great and growing literature that provoked and stimulated, there was in Europe and America alike a vast output of written matter at every level of technical achievement, which was designed to amuse and soothe and reassure. People had learnt to read, there was much time and need for reading, and they read to stanch their minds rather than encourage their flow.

Sir Walter Scott is a figure whose enormous contemporary prestige will, like Lord Byron's, perplex posterity. He began his literary career as a poet, and wrote two long, glib narrative poems; he then wrote a series of historical romances, glorifying the romantic past, exalting the loyalties of monarchy, the richness of tradition. These appealed enormously to gentlefolks and prosperous people, alarmed by the cold uncertainties of the changing and questioning present. He was the begetter of a wave of romantic and regretful fiction, not only throughout the English-speaking world, but throughout Europe.

Upon the Continent, these two writers, strangely translated or paraphrased, were used as symbols of a vague large wave of influences, complex in origin, incoherent in aim and quality, and now happily dispersed and done with—the Romantic Movement. It meant mediævalism, it meant rich and florid colour, it meant gestures towards adventure in armour and a disapproval of contemporary fashions and interests. It meant instinct against reason and emotion against science. Its tendency to archaic language was tempered by the indolence of its exponents. It had more of the nature of a drinking bout followed by a riot than of a phase in intellectual and æsthetic progress. It was opposed not only to the realities of the present, but to the classic past. It was catholic, it was individualistic, it revived the fairies and wallowed in sham legends: it was anything: it was, in the final reckoning, nothing.

In Germany it was written about enormously and heavily, but it pervaded all Europe. Shakespeare was claimed as a Romantic; there was a woolly-brained "Romantic Philosophy" and a "Romantic Theology." There was a vast production of costume novels in English, the mental parallel of the English revival of Gothic architecture, and stockbrokers and tired business men could forget the responsibilities of their business activities and the question of where, if anywhere, they thought they were going, by dreaming themselves the gallant crusaders, soldiers, highwaymen and rescuers of distressed damsels, who figured as the heroes of these stories. There was no pretence to analyze the appearances and significance of the period in this costume stuff. That was its charm. It was the refuge of minds passionately anxious not to think. The mentality of the characters was the mentality of the prosperous middle-class, purified and idealized.

R. L. Stevenson (1850–1894), the last of the Scott dynasty of romantic writers, confessed himself capable of better things and called himself a mental prostitute—as, indeed, he was. The costume novel was written on the Continent, but it never became a serious industry there as it did in the English-speaking system, because the rapid development of a prosperous reading middle-class came later upon the Continent and under circumstances that were mentally more stimulating.

As a later development, we may note that after a pause in the growth of the novel, marked by a tendency to group novels in trilogies or extend them with sequels, there came in the 20's a fresh expansion of this form. The novel seemed likely to become a picture of the whole world seen through the eyes of some typical individual. The most remarkable of these new long novels was the *Jean Cristophe* of Romain Rolland (born 1866), which was published in ten successive volumes. Closely associated with this enlargement was the appearance of vast, formless, endless books of reminiscence, comment and description, of which the typical writer is Proust (died 1922). A figure standing almost alone in the world's literature of this age is Anatole France (1844–1924), whose Bergeret series displayed the same tendency to replace the isolated *roman* by a running commentary on things in general.

An interesting change in the novel as the nineteenth century passes into the twentieth is the steady increase of social, political and religious discussion. Novelists of the Dickens and Thackeray period wrote for a public whose ideas and social values were definitely settled. They do not discuss; they assume the moral scenery and concentrate upon character, upon personal idiosyncrasies. Thackeray did not discuss; he preached, a very different thing to do. In the nineteenth-century novel, "characters" and their behaviour constitute the entire substance of the fabric. But the intellectual unsettlement of the nineteen-twenties found itself reflected in the novel as a discussion of ideas. Thoughts and theories enter into the drama. They amplify the interest but they obscure that emphatic "characterization" more living than life, which is the supreme excellence of Victorian fiction.

Anticipations of all these developments of the modern novel in the direction of a roving and easy criticism of life and views about life can, no doubt, be found in the literature of earlier times, from the *Golden Ass* onward; but none of these anticipations of its form and scale appeared in anything like the variety and bulk of the nineteenth-century writings that are more or less novels, and hardly any had the peculiar quality of free, undirected judgment upon life in bulk and detail which distinguishes the nineteenth-century mind from all preceding phases.

The drama had depended hitherto for its support on the existence of a settled society, with fixed habits and convictions, which could supply regular and sympathetic audiences. In a century of social disorganization and reconstruction, the settled routines of theatre-going were broken up, and for half a century and more the varied multitude of people who thought and discussed and sought for new things was hardly represented at all in the audiences of the time. The European theatre passed through a phase of triviality and insignificance; it paralleled the popular novels and romances in its disposition to waste time agreeably.

The French drama was neat but empty. In England the drama was equally empty, but by no means so neat. Very gradually and against an immense critical opposition, the great forces that demanded discussion and ideas came into operation in the dramatic world. Ibsen, the Norwegian (1828–1906), was the central figure in the return of the drama towards the discussion of contemporary reality. Barrie's agreeable fantasy did much to smash the stiff tradition of the "well-made play" in England, and slowly Bernard Shaw (born 1856) struggled into predominance and influence. Hauptmann (born 1862) and Sudermann (born 1857) are prominent among the German dramatists of this new phase of sincerity and power. The war checked dramatic enterprise for a time, but its end released a great abundance of living and hopeful energy upon both sides of the Atlantic. But the development of drama after 1918 is a story for which, as has already been explained, there is no room here.

When we turn to the development of American literature we must distinguish between two sharply contrasted phases, the phase of European predominance, English and French, and the phase of release. For a long period the literary activities of America concentrated in New England and were merely a branch, albeit a very vigorous branch, of the general English and European literature. It centred upon Boston. The writers of this phase talked a lot about the Declaration of Independence, but so far as form and method went they did not seem to realize it had happened. America had its distinctive tastes; it was quicker to take up Carlyle than England was; it sounded a note of its own in the essays of Emerson (1803–1882); but Longfellow was merely an English poet who happened to have been born in America and who wrote about American themes. Edgar Allan Poe (1809–1849) was less English than European in his methods, and Hawthorne (1804–1864) showed a touch of self-conscious Teutonic glamour. W. D. Howells (1837–1920), again, wrote a series of fine austere novels in a manner that would put him beside Thomas Hardy under the French school in a general classification of the novel. Henry James (1843–1916) was an American who wrote neither like an Englishman nor an American, but like an American transplanted to European conditions; his scene was always European, and his favourite theme was the clash of the naïve American with the complexities of the older civilizations. Perhaps the most essentially American of all nineteenth-century writers was Mark Twain (1835–1910). Signs of the appearance of an independent American literature could have been observed well before the outbreak of the first World War, but it was not till after the war that American writing exploded, as it were, into full development. To describe this there is no room here; indeed the effort to carry the story of literature up to 1914 has begun to result in little more than a jejune catalogue of names.

But enough has been said, it is hoped, to provide a basis for reflection upon the nature of the civilization on which fell the catastrophe of 1914. That war has been described as "the second worst disaster in human history," the first being the fall of the Roman empire. But, though comparable, it was a different sort of disaster. The disappearance of ancient civilization and the beginning of the Dark Ages was certainly a calamity, but it was a foreseeable and unavoidable calamity. Ancient civilization was almost dead already; the empire had fallen in upon itself before the barbarians gave the final pushes. It was exhausted; if its end is to be compared to anything in nature it is to the death of a very old man. But the disaster of 1914 is more like the slaughter of a young and strong man; science, art, literature and all that makes up civilization were rising to greater heights than ever before when they were checked and in some cases driven back by a man-made catastrophe. For the slaughter that started in 1914 was a selective slaughter, unlike a Black Death; it was the young and healthy that were killed and maimed, and that on a scale never known before. No man can travel in France to-day, for example, and not notice the numberless war memorials on which are engraved an unending series of names—more, sometimes, in number than the present population of the villages. There were three young poets in England of outstanding promise —Brooke, Sorley, Owen—and all were killed; how many others unknown, artists, scientists, writers, lawyers and statesmen, were also slain? It was a commonplace to speak of "a missing generation" for the next quarter of a century; the second rate and colourless took control and Europe had as leaders Baldwin and Chamberlain, Ebert and Bruening, Millerand and Tardieu, Giolitti and Victor Emmanuel. To the lack of able men was added the destruction of the sense of an international community which had begun to arise. The Socialist International was torn in pieces, never to reunite. New States were erected in Europe, each with trade barriers against the next. National hatreds were deliberately fanned, dying dialects anxiously revived, censorships established and passport controls made universal. The mean-minded who were in control politically tried to extend their control to art and science, to divide the human mind into compartments and separate British, Russian, American, and French learning and civilization each from the other. Up till the year 1914 it was possible to view the history of the world as a progress, interrupted but always resumed, towards peace and freedom. In most of the states of the world political and parliamentary freedom was extending, personal rights were more protected, liberty of thought and of speech was expanding, and states were beginning to be less irresponsible in their foreign policy. It seemed to be not perhaps a Liberal, but at least a liberating century. That illusion was over in 1918; whatever men might hope for, they now knew that progress was not automatic. It must be fought for, not even the most elementary rights were secure.

XXXVIII

THE CATASTROPHE OF MODERN IMPERIALISM

§ 1. *The Armed Peace Before the first World War.* § 2. *Imperial Germany.* § 3. *The Spirit of Imperialism in Britain and Ireland.* § 4. *Imperialism in France, Italy and the Balkans.* § 5. *Russia a Grand Monarchy.* § 6. *The United States and the Imperial Idea.* § 7. *The Immediate Causes of the first World War.* § 8. *A Summary of the first World War up to 1917.* § 9. *The first World War from the Russian Collapse to the Armistice.*

§ 1

FOR thirty-six years after the Treaty of San Stefano and the Berlin Conference, Europe maintained an uneasy peace within its borders; there was no war between any of the leading states during this period. They jostled, browbeat, and threatened one another, but they did not come to actual hostilities. There was a general realization after 1871 that modern war was a much more serious thing than the professional warfare of the eighteenth century, an effort of peoples as a whole that might strain the social fabric very severely, an adventure not to be rashly embarked upon. The mechanical revolution was giving constantly more powerful (and expensive) weapons by land and sea, and more rapid methods of transport; and making it more and more impossible to carry on warfare without a complete dislocation of the economic life of the community. Even the foreign offices felt the fear of war.

But although war was dreaded as it had never been dreaded in the world before, nothing was done in the way of setting up a federal control to prevent human affairs drifting towards war. In 1898, it is true, the young Tsar Nicholas II (1894–1917) issued a rescript inviting the other Great Powers to a conference of states "seeking to make the great idea of universal peace triumph over the elements of trouble and discord." His rescript recalls the declaration of his predecessor, Alexander I, which gave its tone to the Holy Alliance, and it is vitiated by the same assumption that peace can be established between sovereign governments rather than by a broad appeal to the needs and rights of the one people of mankind. The lesson of the United States of America, which showed that there could be neither unity of action nor peace until the thought of the "people of Virginia" and the "people of Massachusetts" had been swept aside by the thought of the "people of the United States," went entirely disregarded in the European attempts at pacification.

Two conferences were held at The Hague in Holland, one in 1899 and another in 1907, and at the second nearly all the sovereign states of the world were represented. They were represented diplomatically, there was no direction of the general intelligence of the world to their deliberations, the ordinary common man did not even know that these conferences were sitting, and for the most part the assembled representatives haggled cunningly upon points of international law affecting war, leaving aside the abolition of war as a chimera. These Hague Conferences did nothing to dispel the idea that international life is necessarily competitive. They accepted that idea. They did nothing to develop the consciousness of a world commonweal overriding sovereigns and foreign offices. The international lawyers and statesmen who attended these gatherings were as little disposed to hasten on a world commonweal on such a basis as were the Prussian statesmen of 1848 to welcome an all-German parliament overriding the rights and "policy" of the King of Prussia.

In America a series of three Pan-American conferences in 1889, 1901, and 1906 went some way towards the development of a scheme of international arbitration for the whole American continent.

The character and good faith of Nicholas II, who initiated these Hague gatherings, we will not discuss at any length here. He may have thought that time was on the side of Russia. But of the general unwillingness of the Great Powers to face the prospect of a merger of sovereign powers, without which permanent peace projects are absurd, there can be no sort of doubt whatever. It was no cessation of international competition with its acute phase of war that they desired, but rather a cheapening of war, which was becoming too costly. Each wanted to economize the wastage of minor disputes and conflicts, and to establish international laws that would embarrass its more formidable opponents in war-time without incommoding itself. These were the practical ends they sought at the Hague Conference. It was a gathering they attended to please Nicholas II, just as the monarchs of Europe had subscribed to the evangelical propositions of the Holy Alliance to please Alexander I; and as they had attended it, they tried to make what they conceived to be some use of it.

§ 2

The peace of Frankfort had left Germany Prussianized and united, the most formidable of all the Great Powers of Europe. France was humiliated and crippled. Her lapse into republicanism seemed likely to leave her without friends in any European Court. Italy was as yet a mere stripling; Austria sank now rapidly to the position of a confederate in German policy; Russia was vast but undeveloped; and the British Empire was mighty only on the sea. Beyond Europe the one power to be reckoned with by Germany was the United States of America, growing now into a great industrial nation, but with no army nor navy worth considering by European standards.

The new Germany which was embodied in the empire that had been created at Versailles was a complex and astonishing mixture of the fresh intellectual and material forces of the world, with the narrowest political traditions of the European system. She was vigorously educational; she was by far the most educational state in the world; she made the educational pace for all her neighbours and rivals.

Nowhere was this competition more salutary than in Britain. What a German Prince Consort had been unable to do, the German commercial rival did.

That mean jealousy of the educated common man on the part of the British ruling class, which no patriotic pride or generous impulse had ever sufficed to overcome, went down before a growing fear of German efficiency. And Germany took up the organization of scientific research and of the application of scientific method to industrial and social development with such a faith and energy as no other community had ever shown before.

Throughout all this period of the armed peace she was reaping and sowing afresh and reaping again the harvests, the unfailing harvests, of freely disseminated knowledge. She grew swiftly to become a great manufacturing and trading power; her steel output outran the British; in a hundred new fields of production and commerce, where intelligence and system were of more account than mere trader's cunning, in the manufacture of optical glass, of dyes and of a multitude of chemical products, and in endless novel processes, she led the world.

To the British manufacturer who was accustomed to see inventions come into his works—he knew not whence nor why—begging to be adopted, this new German method of keeping and paying scientific men seemed abominably unfair. It was compelling fortune, he felt. It was packing the cards. It was encouraging a nasty class of intellectuals to interfere in the affairs of sound business men. Science went abroad from its first home like an unloved child. The splendid chemical industry of Germany was built on the work of the Englishman Sir William Perkins, who could find no "practical" English business man to back him.

And Germany also led the way in many forms of social legislation. Germany realized that labour is a national asset, that it deteriorates through unemployment, and that, for the common good, it has to be taken care of outside the works. The British employer was still under the delusion that labour had no business to exist outside the works, and that the worse such exterior existence was, the better somehow for him. Moreover, because of his general illiteracy, he was an intense individualist: his was the insensate rivalry of the vulgar mind; he hated his fellow-manufacturers about as much as he hated his labour and his customers. German producers, on the other hand, were persuaded of the great advantages of combination and civility; their enterprises tended to flow together and assume more and more the character of national undertakings.

This educating, scientific, and organizing Germany was the natural development of the liberal Germany of 1848; it had its roots far back in the recuperative effort that drew its impulse from the shame of the Napoleonic conquest. All that was good, all that was great in this modern Germany, she owed indeed to her schoolmasters.

But this scientific organizing spirit was only one of the two factors that made up the new German Empire. The other factor was the Hohenzollern monarchy which had survived Jena, which had tricked and bested the revolution of 1848, and which, under the guidance of Bismarck, had now clambered to the legal headship of all Germany outside Austria. Except the Tsardom, no other European state had so preserved the tradition of the Grand Monarchy of the eighteenth century as the Prussian. Through the tradition of Frederick the Great, Machiavelli now reigned in Germany. In the head of this fine new modern state, therefore, there sat no fine modern brain to guide it to a world predominance in world service, but an old spider lusting for power. Prussianized Germany was at once the newest and the most antiquated thing in Western Europe. She was the best and the wickedest state of her time.

The psychology of nations is still but a rudimentary science. Psychologists have scarcely begun to study the citizen side of the individual man. But it is of the utmost importance to our subject that the student of universal history should give some thought to the mental growth of the generations of Germans educated since the victories of 1871. They were naturally inflated by their sweeping unqualified successes in war, and by their rapid progress from comparative poverty to wealth. It would have been more than human in them if they had not given way to some excesses of patriotic vanity. But this reaction was deliberately seized upon and fostered and developed by a systematic exploitation and control of school and college, literature and press, in the interests of the Hohenzollern dynasty.

A teacher, a professor, who did not teach and preach, in and out of season, the racial, moral, intellectual, and physical superiority of the Germans to all other peoples, their extraordinary devotion to war and their dynasty, and their inevitable destiny under that dynasty to lead the world, was a marked man, doomed to failure and obscurity. German historical teaching became an immense systematic falsification of the human past, with a view to the Hohenzollern future. All other nations were represented as incompetent and decadent; the Prussians were the leaders and regenerators of mankind.

The young German read this in his school-books, heard it in church, found it in his literature, had it poured into him with passionate conviction by his professor. It was poured into him by all his professors; lecturers in biology or mathematics would break off from their proper subject to indulge in long passages of patriotic rant. Only minds of extraordinary toughness and originality could resist such a torrent of suggestion. Insensibly there was built up in the German mind a conception of Germany and its emperor as of something splendid and predominant as nothing else had ever been before, a godlike nation in "shining armour" brandishing the "good German sword" in a world of inferior—and badly disposed—peoples.

We have told our story of Europe; the reader may judge whether the glitter of the German sword is exceptionally blinding. Germania was deliberately intoxicated, she was systematically kept drunk, with this sort of patriotic rhetoric. It is the greatest of the Hohenzollern crimes that the Crown constantly and persistently tampered with education, and particularly with historical teaching. No other modern state had so perverted education. The oligarchy of the crowned republic of Great Britain may have crippled and starved education, but the Hohenzollern monarchy corrupted and prostituted it.

It cannot be too clearly stated, it is the most important fact in the history of the last half-century, that the German people were methodically indoctrinated with the idea of a German world-predominance based on might, and with the theory that war was a necessary thing in life. The key to German historical teaching is to be found in Count Moltke's dictum: "Perpetual peace is a dream, and it is not even a beautiful dream. War is an element in the order of the world ordained by God. Without war the world would stagnate and lose itself in materialism." And the German philosopher Nietzsche found himself quite at one with the pious field-marshal.

"It is mere illusion and pretty sentiment," he observes, "to expect much (even anything at all) from mankind if it forgets how to make war. As yet no means are known which call so much into action as a great war, that rough energy born of the camp, that deep impersonality born of hatred, that conscience born of murder and cold-bloodedness, that fervour born of effort in the annihilation of the enemy, that proud indifference to loss, to one's own existence, to that of one's fellows, that earthquake-like soul-shaking which a people needs when it is losing its vitality."

This sort of teaching, which pervaded the German Empire from end to end, was bound to be noted abroad, bound to alarm every other power and people in the world, bound to provoke an anti-German confederation, and it was accompanied by a parade of military, and presently of naval, preparation that threatened France, Russia, and Britain alike. It affected the thoughts, the manners, and morals of the German people.

After 1871 the German abroad thrust out his chest and raised his voice. He threw a sort of trampling quality even into the operations of commerce. His machinery came on the markets of the world, his shipping took the seas, with a splash of patriotic challenge. His very merits he used as a means of offence. (And probably most other peoples, if they had had the same experiences and undergone the same training, would have behaved in a similar manner.)

By one of those accidents in history that personify and precipitate catastrophes, the ruler of Germany, the Emperor William II, embodied the new education of his people and the Hohenzollern tradition in the completest form. He came to the throne in 1888 at the age of twenty-nine; his father, Frederick III, had succeeded his grandfather, William I, in the March, to die in the June of that year. William II was the grandson of Queen Victoria on his mother's side, but his temperament showed no traces of the liberal German tradition that distinguished the Saxe-Coburg-Gotha family. His head was full of the frothy stuff of the new imperialism. He signalized his accession by an address to his army and navy; his address to the people followed three days later. A high note of contempt for democracy was sounded: "The soldier and the army, not parliamentary majorities, have welded together the German Empire. My trust is placed in the army." So the patient work of the German schoolmasters was disowned, and the Hohenzollern declared himself triumphant.

The next exploit of the young monarch was to quarrel with the old Chancellor Bismarck, who had made the new German Empire, and to dismiss him (1890). There were no profound differences of opinion between them, but, as Bismarck said, the Emperor intended to be his own chancellor.

These were the opening acts of an active and aggressive career. This Wil-

liam II meant to make a noise in the world, a louder noise than any other
monarch had ever made. The whole of Europe was soon familiar with the
figure of the new monarch, invariably in military uniform of the most glittering
sort, staring valiantly, fiercely moustached, and with a withered left arm in-
geniously minimized. He affected silver shining breastplates and long white
cloaks. A great restlessness was manifest. It was clear he conceived himself
destined for great things, but for a time it was not manifest what particular
great things these were. There was no Oracle at Delphi to tell him that he
was destined to destroy a great empire.

The note of theatricality about him and the dismissal of Bismarck alarmed
many of his subjects, but they were presently reassured by the idea that he
was using his influence in the cause of peace and to consolidate Germany.
He travelled much, to London, Vienna, Rome—where he had private conversations with the Pope—to Athens, where his sister married the king in 1889,
and to Constantinople. He was the first Christian sovereign to be a sultan's
guest. He also went to Palestine. A special gate was knocked through the
ancient wall of Jerusalem so that he could ride into that place; it was beneath
his dignity to walk in. He induced the Sultan to commence the reorganization
of the Turkish army upon German lines and under German officers.

In 1895 he announced that Germany was a "world power," and that "the
future of Germany lay upon the water"—regardless of the fact that the British

The Emperor William II.

considered that they were there already—and he began to interest
himself more and more in the building up of a great navy. He also took
German art and literature under his
care; he used his influence to retain
distinctive and blinding German
blackletter against the Roman type
used by the rest of western Europe,
and he supported the Pan-German
movement, which claimed the
Dutch, the Scandinavians, the
Flemish Belgians, and the German
Swiss as members of a great German brotherhood—as, in fact, good
assimilable stuff for a hungry young
empire which meant to grow. All
other monarchs in Europe paled before him.

He used the general hostility
against Britain aroused throughout
Europe by the war against the Boer
Republics to press forward his
schemes for a great navy, and this,
together with the rapid and chal-

lenging extension of the German colonial empire in Africa and the Pacific Ocean, alarmed and irritated the British extremely. British liberal opinion in particular found itself under the exasperating necessity of supporting an ever-increasing British Navy. "I will not rest," he said, "until I have brought my navy to the same height at which my army stands." The most peace-loving of the islanders could not ignore that threat.

In 1890 he had acquired the small island of Heligoland from Britain. This he made into a great naval fortress.

As his navy grew, his enterprise increased. He proclaimed the Germans "the salt of the earth." They must not "weary in the work of civilization; Germany, like the spirit of Imperial Rome, must expand and impose itself." This he said on Polish soil, in support of the steady efforts the Germans were making to suppress the Polish language and culture, and to Germanize their share of Poland. God he described as his "Divine Ally." In the old absolutisms the monarch was either God himself or the adopted agent of God; the Kaiser took God for his trusty henchman. "Our old God," he said affectionately. When the Germans seized Kiau-Chau he spoke of the German "mailed fist." When he backed Austria against Russia, he talked of Germany in her "shining armour."

The disasters of Russia in Manchuria in 1905 released the spirit of German imperialism to bolder aggressions. The fear of a joint attack from France and Russia seemed lifting. The emperor made a kind of regal progress through the Holy Land, landed at Tangier to assure the Sultan of Morocco of his support against the French, and inflicted upon France the crowning indignity of compelling her by a threat of war to dismiss Delcassé, her foreign minister. He drew tighter the links between Austria and Germany, and in 1908 Austria, with his support, defied the rest of Europe by annexing from the Turk the Yugo-Slav provinces of Bosnia and Herzegovina. So by his naval challenge to Britain and these aggressions upon France and the Slavs he forced Britain, France, and Russia into a defensive understanding against him. The Bosnian annexation had the further effect of estranging Italy, which had hitherto been his ally.

Such was the personality that the evil fate of Germany set over her to stimulate, organize, and render intolerable to the rest of the world the natural pride and self-assertion of a great people who had at last, after long centuries of division and weakness, escaped from a jungle of princes to unity and the world's respect. It was natural that the commercial and industrial leaders of this new Germany who were now getting rich, the financiers intent upon over-seas exploits, the, officials and the vulgar, should find this leader very much to their taste. Many Germans, who thought him rash or tawdry in their secret hearts, supported him publicly because he had such an air of success. *Hoch der Kaiser!*

Yet Germany did not yield itself without a struggle to the strong-flowing tide of imperialism. Important elements in German life struggled against this swaggering new autocracy. The old German nations, and particularly the Bavarians, refused to be swallowed up in Prussianism. And, with the spread of education and the rapid industrialization of Germany, organized labour developed its ideas and a steady antagonism to the military and patriotic clattering of its ruler. A new political party was growing up in the State, the Social Democrats, professing the doctrines of Marx. In the teeth of the utmost opposition from the official and clerical organizations, and of violently repressive laws against its propaganda and against combinations, this party grew.

The Kaiser denounced it again and again; its leaders were sent to prison or driven abroad. Still it grew. When he came to the throne it polled not half a million votes; in 1907 it polled over three millions. He attempted to concede many things, old age and sickness insurance, for example, as a condescending gift, things which it claimed for the workers as their right. His conversion to socialism was noted, but it gained no converts to imperialism. His naval ambitions were ably and bitterly denounced; the colonial adventures of the new German capitalists were incessantly attacked by this party of the common sense of the common man. But to the army the Social Democrats accorded a moderate support, because, much as they detested their home-grown autocrat, they hated and dreaded the barbaric and retrogressive autocracy of Russia on their eastern frontier more.

The danger plainly before Germany was that this swaggering imperialism would compel Britain, Russia, and France into a combined attack upon her, an offensive-defensive. The Kaiser wavered between a stiff attitude towards Britain and clumsy attempts to propitiate her, while his fleet grew and while he prepared for a preliminary struggle with Russia and France. When in 1913 the British government proposed a cessation on either hand of naval construction for a year, it was refused.

The Kaiser was afflicted with a son and heir more Hohenzollern, more imperialistic, more Pan-Germanic than his father. He had been nurtured upon imperialist propaganda. His toys had been soldiers and guns. He snatched at a premature popularity by outdoing his father's patriotic and aggressive attitudes. His father, it was felt, was growing middle-aged and over-careful. The Crown Prince renewed him. Germany had never been so strong, never so ready for a new great adventure and another harvest of victories. The Russians, he was instructed, were decayed, the French degenerate, the British on the verge of civil war.

This young Crown Prince was but a sample of the abounding upper-class youth of Germany in the spring of 1914. They had all drunken from the same cup. Their professors and teachers, their speakers and leaders, their mothers and sweethearts, had been preparing them for the great occasion that was now very nearly at hand. They were full of the tremulous sense of imminent conflict, of a trumpet call to stupendous achievements, of victory over mankind abroad, triumph over the recalcitrant workers at home. The country was taut and excited like an athletic competitor at the end of his training.

§ 3

Throughout the period of the armed peace Germany was making the pace and setting the tone for the rest of Europe. The influence of her new doctrines of aggressive imperialism was particularly strong upon the British mind, which was ill-equipped to resist a strong intellectual thrust from abroad. The educational impulse the Prince Consort had given had died away after his death; the universities of Oxford and Cambridge were hindered in their task of effective revision of upper-class education by the fears and prejudices the so-called "conflict of science and religion" had aroused in the clergy who dominated them through Convocation; popular education was crippled by religious squabbling, by the extreme parsimony of the public authorities, by the desire of employers for child labour, and by individualistic objection to "educating other people's children."

The old tradition of the English, the tradition of plain statement, legality, fair play, and a certain measure of republican freedom, had faded considerably during the stresses of the Napoleonic wars; romanticism, of which Sir Walter Scott, the great novelist, was the chief promoter, had infected the national imagination with a craving for the florid and picturesque. "Mr. Briggs," the comic Englishman of *Punch* in the fifties and sixties, getting himself into highland costume and stalking deer, was fairly representative of the spirit of the new movement.

It presently dawned upon Mr. Briggs, as a richly-coloured and creditable fact he had hitherto not observed, that the sun never set on his dominions. The country which had once put Clive and Warren Hastings on trial for their unrighteous treatment of Indians was now persuaded to regard them as entirely chivalrous and devoted figures. They were "empire builders." Under the spell of Disraeli's Oriental imagination, which had made Queen Victoria "empress," the Englishman turned readily enough towards the vague exaltations of modern imperialism.

The perverted ethnology and distorted history which was persuading the mixed Slavic, Keltic, and Teutonic Germans that they were a wonderful race apart was imitated by English writers, who began to exalt a new ethnological invention, the "Anglo-Saxon." This remarkable compound was presented as the culmination of humanity, the crown and reward of the accumulated effort of Greek and Roman, Egyptian, Assyrian, Jew, Mongol, and such-like lowly precursors of its white splendour. The senseless legend of German superiority did much to exacerbate the irritations of the Poles in Posen and the French in Lorraine. The even more ridiculous legend of the superior Anglo-Saxon did not merely increase the irritations of English rule in Ireland, but it lowered the tone of British dealings with "subject" peoples throughout the entire world. For the cessation of respect and the cultivation of "superior" ideas are the cessation of civility and justice.

The imitation of German patriotic misconceptions did not end with this "Anglo-Saxon" fabrication. The clever young men at the British universities in the eighties and nineties, bored by the flatness and insincerities of domestic politics, were moved to imitation and rivalry by this new teaching of an arrogant, subtle, and forceful nationalist imperialism, this combination of Machiavelli and Attila, which was being imposed upon the thought and activities of young Germany. Britain, too, they thought, must have her shining armour and wave her good sword.

The new British imperialism found its poet in Mr. Kipling and its practical support in a number of financial and business interests whose way to monopolies and exploitations was lighted by its glow. These Prussianizing Englishmen carried their imitation of Germany to the most extraordinary lengths. Central Europe is one continuous economic system, best worked as one; and the new Germany had achieved a great customs union, a Zollverein of all its constituents. It became naturally one compact system, like a clenched fist. The British Empire sprawled like an open hand throughout the world, its members different in nature, need, and relationship, with no common interest except the common guarantee of safety. But the new imperialists were blind to that difference. If new Germany had a Zollverein, then the British Empire must be in the fashion; and the natural development of its various elements must be hampered everywhere by "imperial preferences" and the like. . . .

Yet the imperialist movement in Great Britain never had the authority nor the unanimity it had in Germany. It was not a natural product of any of the three united but diverse British peoples. It was not congenial to them. Queen Victoria and her successors, Edward VII and George V, were indisposed, either by sex, figure, temperament or tradition, to wear "shining armour," shake "mailed fists," and flourish "good swords" in the Hohenzollern fashion. They had the wisdom to refrain from any overt meddling with public ideas. And this "British" imperialistic movement had from the first aroused the hostility of the large number of English, Welsh, Irish, and Scotch writers who refused to recognize this new "British" nationality or to accept the theory that they were these "Anglo-Saxon" supermen. And many great interests in Britain, and notably the shipping interest, had been built up upon free trade, and regarded the fiscal proposals of the new imperialists, and the new financial and mercantile adventurers with whom they were associated, with a justifiable suspicion.

On the other hand, these ideas ran like wildfire through the military class, through Indian officialdom and the like. Hitherto there had always been something apologetic about the army man in England. He was not native to that soil. Here was a movement that promised to make him as splendidly important as his Prussian brother in arms. And the imperialist idea also found support in the cheap popular Press that was now coming into existence to cater for the new stratum of readers created by elementary education. This Press wanted plain, bright, simple ideas adapted to the needs of readers who had scarcely begun to think.

In spite of such support, and its strong appeal to national vanity, British imperialism never saturated the mass of the British peoples. The English are not a mentally docile people, and the noisy and rather forced enthusiasm for imperialism and higher tariffs of the old Tory Party, the army class, the country clergy, the music-halls, the assimilated alien, the vulgar rich, and the new large employers, inclined the commoner sort, and particularly organized labour, to a suspicious attitude. If the continually irritated sore of the Majuba defeat permitted the country to be rushed into the needless, toilsome, and costly conquest of the Boer republics in South Africa, the strain of that adventure produced a sufficient reaction towards decency and justice to reinstate the Liberal Party in power, and to undo the worst of that mischief by the creation of a South African confederation.

Considerable advances continued to be made in popular education, and in the recovery of public interests and the general wealth from the possession of the few. And in these years of the armed peace the three British peoples came very near to a settlement, on fairly just and reasonable lines, of their long-standing misunderstanding with Ireland. The first World War, unluckily for them, overtook them in the very crisis of this effort.

Like Japan, Ireland has figured but little in this *Outline of History,* and for the same reason, because she is an extreme island country, receiving much, but hitherto giving but little back into the general drama. Her population is a very mixed one, its basis, and probably its main substance, being of the dark "Mediterranean" strain, pre-Nordic and pre-Aryan, like the Basques and the people of Portugal and south Italy. Over this original basis there flowed, about the sixth century B.C.—we do not know to what degree of submergence—a wave of Keltic peoples, in at least sufficient strength to establish a Keltic language, the Irish Gaelic. There were comings and goings, invasions and counter-invasions of this and that Keltic or Kelticized people between Ireland, Scotland, Wales and England. The island was Christianized in the fifty century. Later on, the east coast was raided and settled by Northmen, but we do not know to what extent they altered the racial quality.

The Norman-English came in 1169, in the time of Henry II and onward. The Teutonic strain may be as strong or stronger than the Keltic in modern Ireland. Hitherto Ireland had been a tribal and barbaric country, with a few centres of security wherein the artistic tendencies of the more ancient race found scope in metal-work and the illumination of holy books. Now, in the twelfth century there was an imperfect conquest by the English crown, and scattered settlements by Normans and English in various parts of the country. From the outset profound temperamental differences between the Irish and English were manifest, differences exacerbated by a difference of language, and these became much more evident after the Protestant Reformation. The English became Protestant; the Irish, by a natural reaction, rallied about the persecuted Catholic church.

The English rule in Ireland had been from the first an intermittent civil war due to the clash of languages and the different laws of land tenure and inheritance of the two peoples. The rebellions, massacres, and subjugations of the unhappy island during the reigns of Elizabeth and James I we cannot tell of here; but under James came a new discord with the confiscation of large areas of Ulster and their settlement with Presbyterian Scotch colonists. They formed a Protestant community in necessary permanent conflict with the Catholic remainder of Ireland.

In the political conflicts during the reign of Charles I and the Commonweal, and of James II and William and Mary, the two sides in English affairs found sympathizers and allies in the Irish parties. There is a saying in Ireland that England's misfortune is Ireland's opportunity, and the English civil trouble that led to the execution of Strafford, was the occasion also of a massacre of the English in Ireland (1641). Later on Cromwell was to avenge that massacre by giving no quarter to any men found under arms, a severity remembered by the Irish Catholics with extreme bitterness. Between 1689 and 1691 Ireland was again torn by civil war. James II sought the support of the Irish Catholics against William III, and his adherents were badly beaten at the battles of the Boyne (1690) and Aughrim (1691).

There was a settlement, the Treaty of Limerick, a disputed settlement in which the English Government promised much in the way of tolerance for Catholics and the like, and failed to keep its promises. Limerick is still a cardinal memory in the long story of Irish embitterment. Comparatively few English people have ever heard of this Treaty of Limerick; in Ireland it rankles to this day.

The eighteenth century was a century of accumulating grievance. English commercial jealousy put heavy restraints upon Irish trade, and the development of a wool industry was destroyed in the south and west. The Ulster Protestants were treated little better than the Catholics in these matters, and they were the chief of the rebels. There was more agrarian revolt in the north than in the south in the eighteenth century.

Let us state as clearly as our space permits the parallelisms and contrasts of the British and Irish situation at this time. There was a parliament in Ireland, but it was a Protestant parliament, even more limited and corrupt than the contemporary British Parliament, there was a considerable civilization in and about Dublin, and much literary and scientific activity, conducted in English and centring upon the Protestant university of Trinity College. This was the Ireland of Swift, Goldsmith, Burke, Berkeley and Boyle. It was essentially a part of the English culture. It had nothing distinctively Irish about it. The Catholic religion and the Irish language were outcast and persecuted things in the darkness at this time.

It was from this Ireland of the darkness that the recalcitrant Ireland of the twentieth century arose. The Irish Parliament, its fine literature, its science, all its culture, gravitated naturally enough to London, because they were inseparably a part of that world. The more prosperous landlords went to England to live, and had their children educated there. This meant a steady drain of wealth from Ireland to England in the form of rent, spent or invested out of the country. The increasing facilities of communication steadily enhanced this tendency, depleted Dublin and bled Ireland white. The Act of Union (January 1st, 1801) was the natural coalescence of two entirely kindred systems, of the Anglo-Irish Parliament with the British Parliament, both oligarchic, both politically corrupt in the same fashion. There was a vigorous opposition to the Union on the part not so much of the outer Irish as of Protestants settled in Ireland, and a futile insurrection under Robert Emmet in 1803. Dublin, which had been a fine Anglo-Irish city in the middle eighteenth century, was gradually deserted by its intellectual and political life, and invaded by the outer Irish of Ireland. Its fashionable life became more and more official, centring upon the Lord Lieutenant in Dublin Castle; its intellectual life flickered and for a time nearly died.

But while the Ireland of Swift and Goldsmith was part and lot with the England of Pope, Dr. Johnson, and Sir Joshua Reynolds, while there has never been and is not now any real definable difference except one of geography between the "governing class" in Ireland and in Britain, the Irish underworld and the English underworld were essentially dissimilar.

The upward struggle of the English "democracy" to education, to political recognition, was different in many respects from the struggle of the Irish underworld. Britain was producing a great industrial population, Protestant or sceptical; she had agricultural labourers, indeed, but no peasants. Ireland with no coal, with a poorer soil, and landlords who lived in England, had become a land of rent-paying peasants. Their cultivation was allowed to degenerate more and more into a growing of potatoes and a feeding of pigs. The people married and bred; except for the consumption of whisky when it could be got, and a little fighting, family life was their only amusement. Here are the appalling consequences. The population of Ireland

in 1785 was 2,845,932,
in 1803 was 5,536,594,
in 1845 was 8,295,061,

at which date the weary potato gave way under its ever-growing burthen and there was a frightful famine. Many died, many emigrated, especially to the United States; an outflow of emigration began that made Ireland for a time a land of old people and empty nests.

Now, because of the Union of the Parliaments, the enfranchisement of the English and Irish populations went on simultaneously. Catholic enfranchisement in England meant Catholic enfranchisement in Ireland. The British got votes because they wanted them; the Irish commonalty got votes because the English did. Ireland was over-represented in the Union Parliament, because originally Irish seats had been easier for the governing class to manipulate than English; and so it came about that this Irish and Catholic Ireland, which had never before had any political instrument at all, and which had never sought a political instrument, suddenly found itself with the power to thrust a solid body of members into the legislature of Great Britain.

After the general election of 1874 the old type of venal Irish member was swept aside and the newly enfranchised "democracy" of Britain found itself confronted by a strange and perplexing Irish "democracy," different in its religion, its traditions, and its needs, telling a tale of wrongs of which the common English had never heard, clamouring passionately for a separation which they could not understand and which impressed them chiefly as being needlessly unfriendly.

The national egotism of the Irish is intense; their circumstances have made it intense; they were incapable of considering the state of affairs in England; the new Irish party came into the British Parliament to obstruct and disorder English business until Ireland became free, and to make themselves a nuisance to the English. This spirit was only too welcome to the oligarchy which still ruled the British Empire; they allied themselves with the "loyal" Protestants in the north of Ireland—loyal, that is, to the Imperial Government because of their dread of a Catholic predominance in Ireland—and they watched and assisted the gradual exasperation of the British common people by this indiscriminate hostility of the common people of Ireland.

The story of the relation of Ireland to Britain for the last half-century is one that reflects the utmost discredit upon the governing class of the British Empire, but it is not one of which the English commons need be ashamed. Again and again they have given evidences of good will. British legislation in relation to Ireland for nearly half a century shows a series of clumsy attempts on the part of Liberal England, made in the face of a strenuous opposition from the Conservative Party and the Ulster Irish, to satisfy Irish complaints and get to a footing of fellowship.

The name of Parnell, an Irish Protestant, stands out as that of the chief leader of the Home Rule movement. In 1886 Gladstone, the great Liberal Prime Minister, brought political disaster upon himself by introducing the first Irish Home Rule Bill, a genuine attempt to give over Irish affairs *for the first time in history* to the Irish people. The Bill broke the Liberal Party asunder; and a coalition government, the Unionist Government, replaced that of Mr. Gladstone.

This digression into the history of Ireland now comes up to the time of infectious imperialism in Europe. The Unionist Government, which ousted Mr. Gladstone, had a predominantly Tory element, and was in spirit "imperialist" as no previous British Government had been. The British political history of the subsequent years is largely a history of the conflict of the new imperialism, through which an arrogant "British" nationalism sought to override the rest of the empire against the temperamental liberalism and reasonableness of the English, which tended to develop the empire into a confederation of free and willing allies.

Naturally, the "British" imperialists wanted a subjugated Irish; naturally, the English Liberals wanted a free, participating Irish. In 1892 Gladstone struggled back to power with a small Home Rule majority; and in 1893 his second Home Rule Bill passed the Commons, and was rejected by the Lords. It was not, however, until 1895 that an imperialist government took office. The party which sustained it was called not Imperialist, but "Unionist"—an odd name when we consider how steadily and strenuously it has worked to destroy any possibility of an Empire commonweal. These Imperialists remained in power for ten years. We have already noted their conquest of South Africa. They were defeated in 1906 in an attempt to establish a tariff wall on the Teutonic model. The ensuing Liberal Government then turned the conquered South African Dutch into contented fellow-subjects by creating the self-governing Dominion of South Africa. After which it embarked upon a long-impending struggle with the persistently imperialist House of Lords.

This was a very fundamental struggle in British affairs. On the one hand was the Liberal majority of the people of Great Britain honestly and wisely anxious to put this Irish affair upon a new and more hopeful footing, and, if possible, to change the animosity of the Irish into friendship; on the other were all the factors of this new British Imperialism resolved at any cost and in spite of every electoral verdict—legally, if possible, but if not, illegally—to

The English 'Pale', 1494....

ditto , time of Elizabeth & James I

Districts 'planted' (i.e. confiscated & settled by English & Scots) time of Elizabeth & James I

ULSTER

Londonderry

Belfast

CONNAUGHT

Kells

Drogheda

Dublin

Galway

Aughrim

LEINSTER

Limerick

Wexford

MUNSTER

Waterford

Cork

IRELAND

J.F.H.

maintain their ascendancy over the affairs of the English, Scotch, and Irish and all the rest of the empire alike.

It was, under new names, the age-long internal struggle of the English community; that same conflict of a free and liberal-spirited commonalty against powerful "big men" and big adventurers and authoritative persons which we have already dealt with in our account of the liberation of America. Ireland was merely a battleground as America had been. In India, in Ireland, in England, the governing class and their associated adventurers were all of one mind; but the Irish people, thanks to their religious difference, had little sense of solidarity with the English. Yet such Irish statesmen as Redmond, the leader of the Irish party in the House of Commons, transcended this national narrowness for a time, and gave a generous response to English good intentions.

Slowly yet steadily the barrier of the House of Lords was broken down, and a third Irish Home Rule Bill was brought in by Mr. Asquith, the Prime Minister, in 1912. Throughout 1913 and the early part of 1914 this Bill was fought and refought through Parliament. At first it gave Home Rule to all Ireland; but an amending Act, excluding Ulster on certain conditions, was promised. This struggle lasted right up to the outbreak of the first World War. The royal assent was given to this Bill after the actual outbreak of war, and also to a Bill suspending the coming into force of Irish Home Rule until after the end of the war. These Bills were put upon the Statute Book.

But from the introduction of the Third Home Rule Bill onward, the opposition to it had assumed a violent and extravagant form. Sir Edward Carson, a Dublin lawyer who had become a member of the English Bar, and who had held a legal position in the ministry of Mr. Gladstone (before the Home Rule split) and in the subsequent imperialist government, was the organizer and leader of this resistance to a reconciliation of the two peoples. In spite of his Dublin origin, he set up to be a leader of the Ulster Protestants; and he brought to the conflict that contempt for law which is all too common a characteristic of the successful barrister, and those gifts of persistent, unqualified, and uncompromising hostility which distinguished a certain type of Irishman. He was the most "un-English" of men, dark, romantic, and violent; and from the opening of the struggle he talked with gusto of armed resistance to this freer reunion of the English and Irish which the Third Home Rule Bill contemplated.

A body of volunteers had been organized in Ulster in 1911, arms were now smuggled into the country, and Sir Edward Carson and a rising lawyer named F. E. Smith, trapped up in semimilitary style, toured Ulster, inspecting those volunteers and inflaming local passion. The arms of these prospective rebels were obtained from Germany, and various utterances of Sir Edward Carson's associates hinted at support from "a great Protestant monarch." Contrasted with Ulster, the rest of Ireland was at that time a land of order and decency, relying upon its great leader Redmond and the good faith of the three British peoples.

Now, these threats of civil war from Ireland were not in themselves anything very exceptional in the record of that unhappy island; what makes them significant in the world's history at this time is the vehement support they found among the English military and governing classes, and the immunity from punishment and restraint of Sir Edward Carson and his friends.

The virus of reaction which came from the success and splendour of German imperialism had spread widely, as we have explained, throughout the prevalent and prosperous classes in Great Britain. A generation had grown up forgetful of the mighty traditions of their forefathers, and ready to exchange the greatness of English fairness and freedom for the tawdriest of imperialisms. A fund of a million pounds was raised, chiefly in England, to support the Ulster Rebellion, an Ulster Provisional Government was formed, prominent English people mingled in the fray and careered about Ulster in automobiles, assisting in the gun-running, and there is evidence that a number of British officers and generals were prepared for a *pronunciamento* upon South American lines rather than obedience to the law.

The natural result of all this upper-class disorderliness was to alarm the main part of Ireland, never a ready friend to England; that Ireland also began in its turn to organize "National Volunteers" and smuggle arms. The military authorities showed themselves much keener in the suppression of the Nationalist than of the Ulster gun importation, and in July, 1914, an attempt to run guns at Howth, near Dublin, led to fighting and bloodshed in the Dublin streets. The British Isles were on the verge of civil war.

Such in outline is the story of the imperialist revolutionary movement in Great Britain up to the eve of the first World War. For revolutionary this movement of Sir Edward Carson and his associates was. It was plainly an attempt to set aside parliamentary government and the slow-grown, imperfect liberties of the British peoples, and, with the assistance of the army, to substitute a more Prussianized type of rule, using the Irish conflict as the point of departure. It was the reactionary effort of a few score thousand people to arrest the world movement towards democratic law and social justice, strictly parallel to and closely sympathetic with the new imperialism of the German junkers and rich men. But in one very important respect British and German imperialism differed. In Germany it centred upon the crown; its noisiest, most conspicuous advocate was the heir-apparent. In Great Britain the king stood aloof. By no single public act did King George V betray the slightest approval of the new movement; and the behaviour of the Prince of Wales, his son and heir, was equally correct.

In August, 1914, the storm of the first World War burst upon the world. In September, Sir Edward Carson was denouncing the placing of the Home Rule Bill upon the Statute Books. Its operation was suspended until after the war. On same day, Mr. John Redmond, the leader of the Irish majority, the proper representative of Ireland, was calling upon the Irish people to take their equal part in the burthen and effort of the war. For a time Ireland played her part in the war side by side with England faithfully and well, until in 1915 the Liberal Government was replaced by a coalition, in which, through the moral feebleness of Mr. Asquith, the Prime Minister, this Sir Edward Carson figured as Attorney-General (with a salary of £7,000 and fees), to be replaced presently by his associate in the Ulster sedition, Sir F. E. Smith.

Grosser insult was never offered to a friendly people. The work of reconciliation, begun by Gladstone in 1886, and brought so near to completion in 1914, was completely and finally wrecked.

In the spring of 1916 Dublin revolted unsuccessfully against this new government. The ringleaders of this insurrection, many of them mere boys, were shot, with a deliberate and clumsy sternness that, in view of the treatment of the Ulster rebel leaders, impressed all Ireland as atrociously unjust. A traitor, Sir Roger Casement, who had been knighted for previous services to the empire, was tried and executed, no doubt deservedly, but his prosecutor was Sir F. E. Smith of the Ulster insurrection—a shocking conjunction.

The Dublin revolt had had little support in Ireland generally, but thereafter the movement for an independent republic grew rapidly to great proportions. Against this strong emotional drive there struggled the more moderate ideas of such Irish statesmen as Sir Horace Plunkett, who wished to see Ireland become a Dominion, a "crowned republic," that is, within the empire, on an equal footing with Canada and Australia.

§ 4

Our studies of modern imperialism in Germany and Britain bring out certain forces common to the two countries, and we shall find these same forces at work in variable degrees and with various modifications in the case of the other great modern communities at which we shall now glance. This modern imperialism is not a synthetic world-uniting movement like the older imperialism; it is essentially a *megalomaniac nationalism*, a nationalism made aggressive by prosperity; and always it finds its strongest support in the military and official castes, and in the enterprising and acquisitive strata of society, in new money, that is, and big business; its chief critics in the educated poor, and its chief opponents in the peasantry and the labour masses. It accepts monarchy where it finds it, but it is not necessarily a monarchist movement. It does, however, need a foreign office of the traditional type for its full development. Its origin, which we have traced very carefully in this book of our history, makes this clear. Modern imperialism is the natural development of the Great Power system which arose, with the foreign office method of policy, out of the Machiavellian monarchies after the break-up of Christendom. It will only come to an end when the intercourse of nations and peoples through embassies and foreign offices is replaced by a federal assembly.

French imperialism during the period of the Armed Peace in Europe was naturally of a less confident type than the German. It called itself "nationalism" rather than imperialism, and it set itself, by appeals to patriotic pride, to thwart the efforts of those socialists and rationalists who sought to get into touch with liberal elements in German life. It brooded upon the *Revanche,* the return match with Prussia. But in spite of that preoccupation it set itself to the adventure of annexation and exploitation in the Far East and in Africa, narrowly escaping a war with Britain upon the Fashoda clash (1898), and it never relinquished a dream of acquisitions in Syria.

Italy, too, caught the imperialist fever. The blood-letting of Adowa cooled her for a time, and then she resumed in 1911 with a war upon Turkey and the annexation of Tripoli. The Italian imperialists exhorted their countrymen to forget Mazzini and remember Julius Cæsar; for were they not the heirs of the Roman Empire? Imperialism touched the Balkans; little countries not a hundred years from slavery began to betray exalted intentions; King Ferdinand of Bulgaria assumed the title of Tsar, the latest of the pseudo-Cæsars; and in the shop windows of Athens the curious student could study maps showing the dream of a vast Greek empire in Europe and Asia.

In 1912 the three states of Serbia, Bulgaria, and Greece fell upon Turkey, already weakened by her war with Italy, and swept her out of all her European possessions except the country between Adrianople and Constantinople; the following year they quarrelled among themselves over the division of the spoils. Roumania joined in the game and helped to crush Bulgaria. Turkey recovered Adrianople. The greater imperialisms of Austria, Russia, and Italy watched that conflict and one another. . . .

The BALKAN STATES
after the Wars of
1912-13

RUSSIA

AUSTRIA - HUNGARY

RUMANIA
Bucharest°

Bosnia
Sarajevo°

Danube

Belgrade

SERBIA

M.NEGRO

BULGARIA
°Sofia

ITALY

ALBANIA
Valona

°Adrianople

Salonica ⊘

ASIA
MINOR
°Smyrna

AEGEAN

GREECE

°Athens

J.F.H.

| Turkish territory acquired by Serbia | ⊞ | by Montenegro | ≡ | New autonomous princip! of Albania... | ⊠ |
| by Greece | ⊘ | by Bulgaria | ▨ | Bulgarian territory acquired by Rumania | ⠿ |

§ 5

While all the world to the west of her was changing rapidly, Russia throughout the nineteenth century changed very slowly indeed. At the end of the nineteenth century, as at its beginning, she was still a Grand Monarchy of the later seventeenth-century type standing on a basis of barbarism, she was still at a stage where Court intrigues and imperial favourites could control her international relations. She had driven a great railway across Siberia, to find the disasters of the Japanese war at the end of it; she was using modern methods and modern weapons so far as her undeveloped industrialism and her small supply of sufficiently educated people permitted; such writers as Dostoievsky had devised a sort of mystical imperialism based on the idea of

Holy Russia and her mission, coloured by racial illusions and anti-Semitic passion; but, as events were to show, this had not sunken very deeply into the imagination of the Russian masses.

A vague, very simple Christianity pervaded the illiterate peasant life, mixed with much superstition. It was like the pre-reformation peasant life of France or Germany. The Russian moujik was supposed to worship and revere his Tsar and to love to serve a gentleman; in 1913 reactionary English writers were still praising his simple and unquestioning loyalty. But, as in the case of the Western European peasant of the days of the peasant revolts, this reverence for the monarchy was mixed up with the idea that the monarch and the nobleman had to be good and beneficial; and this simple loyalty could, under sufficient provocation, be turned into the same pitiless intolerance of social injustice that burnt the château in the Jacquerie and set up the theocracy in Münster. Once the commons were moved to anger, there were no links of understanding in a generally diffused education in Russia to mitigate the fury of the outbreak. The upper classes were as much beyond the sympathy of the lower as a different species of animal. These Russian masses were three centuries away from such nationalist imperialism as Germany displayed.

And in another respect Russia differed from modern Western Europe and paralleled its mediæval phase, and that was in the fact that her universities were the resort of many very poor students quite out of touch and out of sympathy with the bureaucratic autocracy. Before 1917 the significance of the proximity of these two factors of revolution, the fuel of discontent and the march of free ideas, was not recognized in European thought, and few people realized that in Russia more than in any other country lay the possibilities of a fundamental revolution.

§ 6

When we turn from these European Great Powers, with their inheritance of foreign offices and national policies, to the United States of America, which broke away completely from the Great Power System in 1776, we find a most interesting contrast in the operation of the forces which produced the expansive imperialism of Europe.

For America as for Europe the mechanical revolution had brought all the world within the range of a few days' journey. The United States, like the Great Powers, had world wide financial and mercantile interests; a great industrialism had grown up and was in need of overseas markets; the same crisis of belief that had shaken the moral solidarity of Europe had occurred in the American world. Her people were as patriotic and spirited as any. Why, then, did not the United States develop armaments and an aggressive policy? Why was not the stars and stripes waving over Mexico, and why was there not a new Indian system growing up in China under that flag? It was the American who had opened up Japan. After doing so, he had let that power Europeanize itself and become formidable without a protest. That alone was enough to make Machiavelli, the father of modern foreign policy, turn in his grave.

If a Europeanized Great Power had been in the place of the United States, Great Britain would have had to fortify the Canadian frontier from end to end—it is now absolutely unarmed—and to maintain a great arsenal in the St. Lawrence. All the divided states of Central and South America would long since have been subjugated and placed under the disciplinary control of United States officials of the "governing class." There would have been a perpetual campaign to Americanize Australia and New Zealand, and yet another claimant for a share in tropical Africa.

And by an odd accident America had produced in President Roosevelt (president 1901–1909) a man of an energy as restless as the German Kaiser's, as eager for large achievements, as florid and eloquent, an adventurous man with a turn for world politics and an instinct for armaments, the very man, we might imagine, to have involved his country in the scramble for overseas possession.

There does not appear to be any other explanation of this general restraint and abstinence on the part of the United States, except in their fundamentally different institutions and traditions. In the first place, the United States Government had no foreign office and no diplomatic corps of the European type, no body of "experts" to maintain the tradition of an aggressive policy. The president has great powers, but they are checked by the powers of the Senate, which is directly elected by the people. Every treaty with a foreign power must first receive the assent of the Senate. The foreign relations of the country are thus under open and public control. Secret treaties are impossible under such a system, and foreign powers complain of the difficulty and uncertainty of "understandings" with the United States—a very excellent state of affairs. The United States is constitutionally incapacitated, therefore, from the kind of foreign policy that has kept Europe for so long constantly on the verge of war.

And, secondly, there has hitherto existed in the United States no organization for and no tradition of what one may call nonassimilable possessions. Where there is no crown there cannot be crown colonies. In spreading across the American continent, the United States had developed a quite distinctive method of dealing with new territories, admirably adapted for unsettled lands, but very inconvenient if applied too freely to areas already containing an alien population. This method was based on the idea that there cannot be in the United States system a permanently subject people.

The first stage of the ordinary process of assimilation had been the creation of a "territory" under the federal government, having a considerable measure of self-government, sending a delegate (who could not vote) to Congress, and destined, in the natural course of things, as the country became settled and population increased, to flower at last into full statehood. This had been the process of development of all the newer states of the Union; the latest territories to become states being Arizona and New Mexico in 1912. The frozen wilderness of Alaska, bought from Russia, remained politically undeveloped simply because it had an insufficient population for state organization.

As the annexations of Germany and Great Britain in the Pacific threatened to deprive the United States navy of coaling stations in that ocean, a part of the Samoan Islands (1900) and the Sandwich Islands (Hawaii) were annexed (1898). Here for the first time the United States had real subject populations to deal with. But, in the absence of any class comparable to the Anglo-Indian officials who sway British opinion, the American procedure followed the territorial method. Every effort was made to bring the educational standards of Hawaii up to the American level, and a domestic legislature on the territorial pattern was organized so that these dusky islanders seemed destined ultimately to obtain full United States citizenship. (The small Samoan Islands were taken care of by a United States naval administrator.)

In 1895 occurred a quarrel between the United States and Britain upon the subject of Venezuela, and the Monroe Doctrine was upheld stoutly by President Cleveland. Then Mr. Olney made this remarkable declaration: "To-day the United States is practically sovereign on this continent, and its fiat is law upon the subjects to which it confines its interposition." This, together with the various Pan-American congresses that have been held, points to a real open "foreign policy" of alliance and mutual help throughout America. Treaties of arbitration were extended over all that continent, and the future seemed to point to a gradual development of inter-state organization, a Pax Americana, of the English-speaking and Spanish-speaking peoples, the former in the rôle of elder brother. There was to be something which was not an empire, something going far beyond the great alliance of the British Empire in the open equality of its constituent parts.

Consistently with this idea of a common American welfare, the United States in 1898 intervened in the affairs of Cuba, which had been in a state of chronic insurrection against Spain for many years. A brief war ended in the acquisition of Cuba, Porto Rico, and the Philippine Islands. Cuba is now an independent self-governing republic. Porto Rico and the Philippines were given a special sort of government, with a popularly elected lower house and an upper body containing members appointed in the beginning by the United States senate. What exactly was to be the constitutional future of either, however, was not clear; discussions on this point remained uneasy.

Both Cuba and Porto Rico welcomed the American intervention in their affairs, but in the Philippine Islands there was a demand for complete and immediate freedom after the Spanish war, and a considerable resistance to the American military administration. There it was that the United States came nearest to imperialism of the Great Power type, and that her record is most questionable. There was much sympathy with the insurgents in the States. Here is the point of view of ex-President Roosevelt as he wrote it in his *Autobiography* (1913):

"As regards the Philippines, my belief was that we should train them for self-government as rapidly as possible, and then leave them free to decide their own fate. I did not believe in setting the time-limit within which we would give them independence, because I did not believe it wise to try to forecast how soon they would be fit for self-government; and once having made the promise, I would have felt that it was imperative to keep it. Within a few months of my assuming office we had stamped out the last armed resistance in the Philippines that was not of merely sporadic character; and as soon as peace was secured we turned our energies to developing the islands in the interests of the natives. We established schools everywhere; we built roads; we administered an even-handed justice; we did everything possible to encourage agriculture and industry; and in constantly increasing measure we employed natives to do their own governing, and finally provided a legislative chamber. . . .

"We are governing, and have been governing, the islands in the interests of the Filipinos themselves. If after due time the Filipinos themselves decide that they do not wish to be thus governed, then I trust that we will leave; but when we do leave, it must be distinctly understood that we retain no protectorate—and above all that we take part in no joint protectorate—over the islands, and give them no guarantee, of neutrality or otherwise; that, in short, we are absolutely quit of responsibility for them, of every kind and description."

This is an entirely different outlook from that of a British or French foreign office or colonial office official. But it is not very widely different from the spirit that created the commonweals of Canada, South Africa, and Australia, and brought forward the three Home Rule Bills for Ireland. It is in the older and more characteristic English tradition from which the Declaration of Independence derives. It sets aside, without discussion, the detestable idea of "subject peoples."

Here we will not enter into political complications attendant upon the making of the Panama Canal, for they introduce no fresh light upon this interesting question of the American method in world politics. The history of Panama is American history purely. But manifestly, just as the internal political structure of the Union was a new thing in the world, so, too, were its relations with the world beyond its borders.

§ 7

We have been at some pains to examine the state of mind of Europe and of America in regard to international relations in the years that led up to the world tragedy of 1914 because, as more and more people are coming to recognize, that great war or some such war was a natural consequence of the mentality of the period. All the things that men and nations do are the outcome of instinctive motives reacting upon the ideas which talk and books and newspapers and schoolmasters and so forth have put into people's heads. Physical necessities, pestilences, changes of climate, and the like outer things may deflect and distort the growth of human history, but its living root is thought.

All human history is fundamentally a history of ideas. Between the man of to-day and the Cro-Magnard the physical and mental differences are very slight; their essential difference lies in the extent and content of the mental background which we have acquired in the five or six hundred generations that intervene.

We are too close to the events of the first World War to pretend that this *Outline* can record the verdict of history thereupon, but we may hazard the guess that, when the passions of the conflict had faded, it will be Germany that will be most blamed for bringing it about, and she will be blamed not because she was morally and intellectually very different from her neighbours, but because she had the common disease of imperialism in its most complete and energetic form. No self-respecting historian, however superficial and popular his aims may be, can countenance the legend, produced by the stresses of the war, that the German is a sort of human being more cruel and abominable than any other variety of men. All the great states of Europe before 1914 were in a condition of aggressive nationalism and drifting towards war; the government of Germany did but lead the general movement. She fell into the pit first, and she floundered deepest. She became the dreadful example at which all her fellow-sinners could cry out.

For long, Germany and Austria had been seeking an extension of German influence eastward through Asia Minor to the East. The German idea was crystallized in the phrase "Berlin to Bagdad." Antagonized to the German dreams were those of Russia, which was scheming for an extension of the Slav ascendancy to Constantinople and through Serbia to the Adriatic. These lines of ambition lay across one another and were mutually incompatible. The feverish state of affairs in the Balkans was largely the outcome of the intrigues and propagandas sustained by the German and Slav schemes. Turkey turned for support to Germany, Serbia to Russia. Roumania and Italy, both Latin in tradition, both nominally allies of Germany, pursued remoter and deeper schemes in common. Ferdinand, the Tsar of Bulgaria, was following still darker ends; and the mysteries of the Greek Court, whose king was the German Kaiser's brother-in-law, are beyond our present powers of inquiry.

But the tangle did not end with Germany on the one hand and Russia on the other. The greed of Germany in 1871 had made France her inveterate enemy. The French people, aware of their inability to recover their lost provinces by their own strength, had conceived exaggerated ideas of the power and helpfulness of Russia. The French people had subscribed enormously to Russian loans. France was the ally of Russia. If the German powers made war upon Russia, France would certainly attack them.

Now, the short eastern French frontier was very strongly defended. There was little prospect of Germany repeating the successes of 1870–71 against that barrier. But the Belgian frontier of France was longer and less strongly defended. An attack in overwhelming force on France through Belgium might repeat 1870 on a larger scale. The French left might be swung back south-eastwardly on Verdun as a pivot, and crowded back upon its right, as one shuts an open razor.

This scheme the German strategists had worked out with great care and elaboration. Its execution involved an outrage upon the law of nations, because Prussia had undertaken to guarantee the neutrality of Belgium and had no quarrel with her, and it involved the risk of bringing in Great Britain (which power was also pledged to protect Belgium) against Germany. Yet the Germans believed that their fleet had grown strong enough to make Great Britain hesitate to interfere, and with a view to possibilities they had constructed a great system of strategic railways to the Belgian frontier, and made every preparation for the execution of this scheme. So they might hope to strike down France at one blow, and deal at their leisure with Russia.

In 1914 all things seemed moving together in favour of the two Central

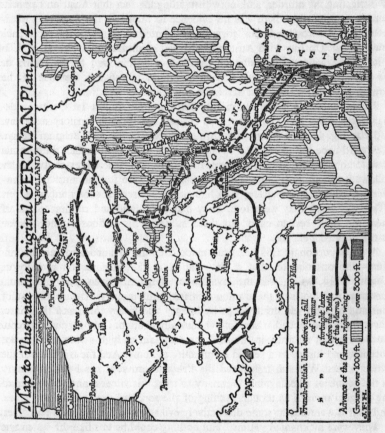

Powers. Russia, it is true, had been recovering since 1906, but only very slowly. France was distracted by financial scandals. The astounding murder of M. Calmette, the editor of the *Figaro*, by the wife of M. Caillaux, the minister of finance, brought these to a climax in March. Britain, all Germany was assured, was on the verge of a civil war in Ireland. Repeated efforts were made both by foreign and English people to get some definite statement of what Britain would do if Germany and Austria assailed France and Russia; but the British foreign secretary, Sir Edward Grey, maintained a front of heavy ambiguity up to the very day of the British entry into the war. As a consequence, there was a feeling on the Continent that Britain would either not fight or delay fighting, and this may have encouraged Germany to go on threatening France.

Events were precipitated on June 28th by the assassination of the Archduke Francis Ferdinand, and heir to the Austrian Empire, when on a State visit to Sarajevo, the capital of Bosnia. Here was a timely excuse to set the armies marching. "It is now or never," said the German Emperor. Serbia was accused of instigating the murder, and, notwithstanding the fact that Austrian commissioners reported that there was no evidence to implicate the Serbian government, the Austro-Hungarian government contrived to press this grievance towards war. On July 23rd Austria discharged an ultimatum at Serbia, and, in spite of a practical submission on the part of Serbia, and of the efforts of Sir Edward Grey, the British foreign secretary, to call a conference of the powers, declared war against Serbia on July 28th.

Russia mobilized her army on July 30th, and on August 1st Germany declared war upon her. German troops crossed into French territory next day, and the big flanking movement through Luxembourg and Belgium began. Westward rode the scouts and advance guards. Westward rushed a multitude of automobiles packed with soldiers. Enormous columns of grey-clad infantry followed; round-eyed, fair young Germans they were for the most part—law-abiding, educated youngsters who had never yet seen a shot fired in anger. "This was war," they were told. They had to be bold and ruthless. Some of them did their best to carry out these militarist instructions at the expense of the ill-fated Belgians.

A disproportionate fuss has been made over the detailed atrocities in Belgium—disproportionate, that is, in relation to the fundamental atrocity of August, 1914, which was the invasion of Belgium. Given that, the casual shootings and lootings, the wanton destruction of property, the plundering of inns and of food and drink shops by hungry and weary men, and the consequent rapes and incendiarism, follow naturally enough. Only very simple people believe that an army in the field can maintain as high a level of honesty, decency, and justice as a settled community at home. And the tradition of the Thirty Years' War still influenced the Prussian army. It has been customary in the countries allied against Germany to treat this vileness and bloodshed of the Belgian months as though nothing of the sort had ever happened before, and as if it were due to some distinctively evil strain in the German character.

They were nicknamed "Huns." But nothing could be less like the systematic destructions of these nomads (who once proposed to exterminate the entire Chinese population in order to restore China to pasture) than the German crimes in Belgium. Much of that crime was the drunken brutality of men who for the first time in their lives were free to use lethal weapons, much of it was the hysterical violence of men shocked at their own proceedings and in deadly fear of the revenge of the people whose country they had outraged, and much of it was done under duress because of the theory that men should be terrible in warfare and that populations are best subdued by fear. The German common people were bundled from an orderly obedience into this war in such a manner that atrocities were bound to ensue. Any people who had been worked up for war and led into war as the Germans were would have behaved in a similar manner.

On the night of August 4th, while most of Europe, still under the tranquil inertias of half a century of peace, still in the habitual enjoyment of such a widely diffused plenty, cheapness and freedom as no man living will ever see again, was thinking about its summer holidays, the little Belgian village of Visé was ablaze, and stupefied rustics were being led out and shot because it was alleged someone had fired on the invaders. The officers who ordered these acts, the men who obeyed, must surely have felt scared at the strangeness of the things they did. Most of them had never yet seen a violent death. And they had set light not to a village, but a world. It was the beginning of the end of an age of comfort, confidence, and gentle and seemly behaviour in Europe.

So soon as it was clear that Belgium was to be invaded, Great Britain ceased to hesitate, and (at eleven at night on August 4th) declared war upon Germany. The following day a German mine-laying vessel was caught off the Thames mouth by the cruiser *Amphion* and sunk—the first time that the British and Germans had ever met in conflict under their own national flags upon land or water. . . .

All Europe still remembers the strange atmosphere of those eventful sunny August days, the end of the Armed Peace. For nearly half a century the Western world had been tranquil and had seemed *safe*. Only a few middle-aged and ageing people in France had had any practical experience of warfare. The newspapers spoke of a world catastrophe, but that conveyed very little meaning to those for whom the world had always seemed secure, who were, indeed, almost incapable of thinking it as otherwise than secure.

In Britain particularly, for some weeks the peace-time routine continued in a slightly dazed fashion. It was like a man still walking about the world unaware that he has contracted a fatal disease which will alter every routine and habit in his life. People went on with their summer holidays; shops reassured their customers with the announcement "Business as usual." There was much talk and excitement when the newspapers came, but it was the talk and excitement of spectators who have no vivid sense of participation in the catastrophe that was presently to involve them all.

§ 8

We will now review very briefly the main phases of the world struggle which had thus commenced. Planned by Germany, it began with a swift attack designed to "knock out" France while Russia was still getting her forces together in the East. For a time all went well. Military science is never up to date under modern conditions, because military men are as a class unimaginative, there are always at any date undeveloped inventions, capable of disturbing current tactical and strategic practice, which the military intelligence has declined.

The German plan had been made for some years; it was a stale plan; it could probably have been foiled at the outset by a proper use of entrenchments and barbed wire and machine guns, but the French were by no means as advanced in their military science as the Germans, and they trusted to methods of open warfare that were at least fourteen years behind the times. They had a proper equipment neither of barbed wire nor machine guns, and there was a ridiculous tradition that the Frenchman did not fight well behind earthworks.

The Belgian frontier was defended by the fortress of Liége, ten or twelve

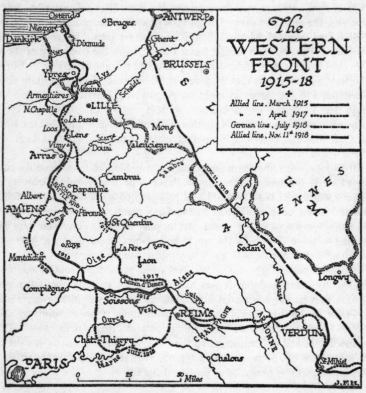

years out of date, with forts whose armament had been furnished and fitted in many cases by German contractors; and the French north-eastern frontier was very badly equipped. Naturally, the German armament firm of Krupp had provided nutcrackers for these nuts in the form of exceptionally heavy guns firing high-explosive shell. These defences proved, therefore, to be mere traps for their garrisons.

The French attacked and failed in the southern Ardennes. The German hosts swung round the French left with an effect of being irresistible; the last fort at Liége fell on August 16th, Brussels was reached on August 20th, and the small British army of about 70,000, which had arrived in Belgium, was struck at Mons in overwhelming force, and driven backward in spite of the very deadly rifle tactics it had learnt during the South African War. The little British force was pushed southward, and the German right swept down so as to leave Paris to the west and crumple the entire French army back upon itself.

So confident was the German high command at this stage of having won the war, that by the end of August German troops were already being withdrawn for the Eastern front, where the Russians were playing havoc in East and West Prussia. And then came the Allied counter-attack. The French produced an unexpected army on their left, and the small British army, shaken but reinforced, was still fit to play a worthy part in the counter-stroke. The German right overran itself, lost in cohesion, and was driven back from the Marne to the Aisne (Battle of the Marne, September 6th to 10th). It would have been driven back farther had it not had the art of entrenchment in reserve. Upon the Aisne it stood and dug itself in. The heavy guns, the high-explosive shells, the tanks, needed by the Allies to smash up these entrenchments, did not yet exist.

The Battle of the Marne shattered the original German plan. For a time France was saved. But the German was not defeated; he had still a great offensive superiority in military skill and equipment. His fear of the Russian in the East had been relieved by a tremendous victory at Tannenberg.

His next phase was a headlong, less elaborately planned campaign to outflank the left of the Allied armies and to seize the Channel ports and cut off supplies coming from Britain to France. Both armies extended to the west in a sort of race to the coast. Then the Germans, with a great superiority of guns and equipment, struck at the British round and about Ypres. They came very near to a break through, but the British held them.

The war on the Western front settled down to trench warfare. Neither side had the science and equipment needed to solve the problem of breaking through modern entrenchments and entanglements, and both sides were now compelled to resort to scientific men, inventors, and such-like unmilitary persons for counsel and help in their difficulty. At that time the essential problem of trench warfare had already been solved; there existed in England, for instance, the model of a tank which would have given the Allies a swift and easy victory before 1916; but the professional military mind is by necessity an inferior and unimaginative mind; no man of high intellectual quality would willingly imprison his gifts in such a calling; nearly all supremely great soldiers have been either inexperienced, fresh-minded young men like Alexander, Napoleon, and Hoche, politicians turned soldiers like Julius Cæsar, nomads like the Hun and Mongol captains, or amateurs like Cromwell and Washington: whereas this war after fifty years of militarism was a hopelessly professional war; from first to last it was impossible to get it out of the hands of the regular generals, and neither the German nor Allied headquarters was disposed to regard with toleration an invention that would destroy their traditional methods.

The Germans, however, did make some innovations. In February (28th) they produced a rather futile novelty, the flame projector, the user of which was in constant danger of being burnt alive; and in April, in the opening of a second great offensive upon the British (second Battle of Ypres, April 22nd to May 24th), they employed a cloud of poison gas. This horrible device was used against Algerian and Canadian troops; it shook them by the physical torture it inflicted, and by the anguish of those who died, but it failed to break through them. For some weeks chemists were of more importance than soldiers on the Allied front, and within six weeks the defensive troops were already in possession of protective methods and devices.

For a year and a half, until July, 1916, the Western front remained in a state of indecisive tension. There were heavy attacks on either side that ended in bloody repulses. The French made costly thrusts at Arras and in Champagne in 1915, the British at Loos.

From Switzerland to the North Sea there ran two continuous lines of entrenchment, sometimes at a distance of a mile or more, sometimes at a distance of a few feet (at Arras, *e.g.*), and in and behind these lines of trenches millions of men toiled, raided their enemies, and prepared for sanguinary and foredoomed offensives. In any preceding age these stagnant masses of men would have engendered a pestilence inevitably, but here again modern science had altered the conditions of warfare. Certain novel diseases appeared, trench feet for instance, caused by prolonged standing in cold water, new forms of dysentery, and the like, but none developed to an extent to disable either combatant force.

Behind this front the whole life of the belligerent nations was being turned more and more to the task of maintaining supplies of food, munitions, and, above all, men to supply the places of those who day by day were killed or mangled. The Germans had had the luck to possess a considerable number of big siege guns intended for the frontier fortresses; these were now available for trench smashing with high explosives, a use no one had foreseen for them. The Allies throughout the first years were markedly inferior in their supply of big guns and ammunition, and their losses were steadily greater than the German.

There was a tremendous German onslaught upon the French throughout the first half of 1916 round and about Verdun. The Germans suffered enormous losses and were held, after pushing in the French lines for some miles. The French losses were as great or greater. *"Ils ne passeront pas,"* said and sang the French infantry—and kept their word.

The Eastern German front was more extended and less systematically entrenched than the Western. For a time the Russian armies continued to press westward in spite of the Tannenberg disaster. They conquered nearly the whole of Galicia from the Austrians, took Lemberg on September 2nd, 1914, and the great fortress of Przemysl on March 22nd, 1915. But after the Germans had failed to break the Western front of the Allies, and after an ineffective Allied offensive made without proper material, they turned to Russia, and a series of heavy blows, with a novel use of massed artillery, were struck first in the south and then at the north of the Russian front. On June 3rd Przemysl was retaken, and the whole Russian line was driven back until Vilna (September 18th) was in German hands.

In May, 1915 (23rd), Italy joined the Allies and declared war upon Austria. (Not until a year later did she declare war on Germany.) She pushed over her eastern boundary towards Goritzia (which fell in the summer of 1916), but her intervention was of little use at that time to either Russia or the two Western powers. She merely established another line of trench warfare among the high mountains of her picturesque north-eastern frontier.

While the main fronts of the chief combatants were in this state of exhaustive deadlock, both sides were attempting to strike round behind the front of their adversaries. The Germans made a series of Zeppelin, and later of aeroplane, raids upon Paris and the east of England. Ostensibly these aimed at depots, munition works, and the like targets of military importance, but practically they bombed promiscuously at inhabited places.

At first these raiders dropped not very effective bombs, but later the size and quality of these missiles increased, considerable numbers of people were killed and injured, and very much damage was done. The English people were roused to a pitch of extreme indignation by these outrages. Although the Germans had possessed Zeppelins for some years, no one in authority in Great Britain had thought out the proper methods of dealing with them, and it was not until late in 1916 that an adequate supply of anti-aircraft guns was brought into play and that these raiders were systematically attacked by aeroplanes.

Then came a series of Zeppelin disasters, and after the spring of 1917 their use for any purpose but sea scouting declined, and their place as raiders was taken by large aeroplanes (the Gothas). The visits of these latter machines to London and the east of England became systematic after the summer of 1917. All through the winter of 1917–18 London on every moonlight night became familiar with the banging of warning maroons, the shrill whistles of the police alarm, the hasty clearance of the streets, the distant rumbling of scores and hundreds of anti-aircraft guns growing steadily to a wild uproar of thuds and crashes, the swish of flying shrapnel, and at last, if any of the raiders got through the barrage, with the dull heavy bang of the bursting bombs. Then presently, amidst the diminuendo of the gun-fire, would come the inimitable rushing sound of the fire-brigade engines and the hurry of the ambulances. . . . War was brought home to every Londoner by these experiences.

While the Germans were thus assailing the nerve of their enemy home population through the air, they were also attacking the overseas trade of the British by every means in their power. At the outset of the war they had various trade-destroyers scattered over the world, and a squadron of powerful modern cruisers in the Pacific, namely the *Scharnhorst,* the *Gneisenau,* the *Leipzig,* the *Nürnberg,* and the *Dresden.* Some of the detached cruisers, and particularly the *Emden,* did a considerable amount of commerce-destroying before they were hunted down, and the main squadron caught an inferior British force off the coast of Chile and sank the *Good Hope* and the *Monmouth* on November 1st, 1914. A month later these German ships were themselves pounced upon by a British force, and all (except the *Dresden*) sunk by Admiral Sturdee in the Battle of the Falkland Isles. After this conflict the Allies remained in undisputed possession of the surface of the sea, a supremacy which the great naval Battle of Jutland (May 31st, 1916) did nothing to shake.

The Germans concentrated their attention more and more upon submarine warfare. From the beginning of the war they had had considerable submarine successes. On one day, September 22nd, 1914, they sank three powerful cruisers, the *Aboukir,* the *Hogue,* and the *Cressy,* with 1,473 men. They continued to levy a toll upon British shipping throughout the war; at first they hailed and examined passenger and mercantile shipping, but this practice they discontinued for fear of traps, and in the spring of 1915 they began to sink ships without notice.

In May, 1915, they sank the great passenger liner the *Lusitania,* without any warning, drowning a number of American citizens. This embittered American feeling against them, but the possibility of injuring and perhaps reducing Britain by a submarine blockade was so great that they persisted in a more and more intensified submarine campaign, regardless of the danger of dragging the United States into the circle of their enemies.

Meanwhile, Turkish forces, very ill-equipped, were making threatening gestures at Egypt across the desert of Sinai.

And while the Germans were thus striking at Britain, their least accessible and most formidable antagonist, through the air and under the sea, the French and British were also embarking upon a disastrous flank attack in the east upon the Central Powers through Turkey. The Gallipoli campaign was finely imagined, but disgracefully executed. Had it succeeded, the Allies would have captured Constantinople in 1915. But the Turks were given two months' notice of the project by a premature bombardment of the Dardanelles in February; the scheme was also probably betrayed through the Greek Court, and when at last British and French forces were landed upon the Gallipoli peninsula, in April, they found the Turks well entrenched and better equipped for trench warfare than themselves.

The Allies trusted for heavy artillery to the great guns of the ships, which were comparatively useless for battering down entrenchments, and among every other sort of thing that they had failed to foresee, they had not foreseen hostile submarines. Several great battleships were lost; they went down in the same clear waters over which the ships of Xerxes had once sailed to their fate at Salamis. The story of the Gallipoli campaign from the side of the Allies is at once heroic and pitiful, a story of courage and incompetence, and of life, material, and prestige wasted, culminating in a withdrawal in January, 1916.

Linked up closely with the vacillation of Greece throughout this time was the entry of Bulgaria into the war (October 12th, 1915). The king of Bulgaria had hesitated for more than a year to make any decision between the two sides. Now the manifest failure of the British at Gallipoli, coupled with a strong Austro-German attack in Serbia, swung him over to the Central Powers. While the Serbs were hotly engaged with the Austro-German invaders upon the Danube he attacked Serbia in the rear, and in a few weeks the country had been completely overrun. The Serbian army made a terrible retreat through the mountains of Albania to the coast, where its remains were rescued by an Allied fleet.

An Allied force landed at Salonika in Greece, and pushed inland towards Monastir, but was unable to render any effectual assistance to the Serbians. It was the Salonika plan which sealed the fate of the Gallipoli expedition.

To the east, in Mesopotamia, the British, using Indian troops chiefly, made a still remoter flank attack upon the Central Powers. An army, very ill provided for the campaign, was landed at Basra in the November of 1914, and pushed up towards Bagdad in the following year. It gained a victory at Ctesiphon, the ancient Arsacid and Sassanid capital, within twenty-five miles of Bagdad, but the Turks were heavily reinforced, there was a retreat to Kut, and there the British army, under General Townshend, was surrounded and starved into surrender on April 29th, 1916.

All these campaigns in the air, under the seas, in Russia, Turkey, and Asia, were subsidiary to the main front, the front of decision, between Switzerland and the sea; and there the main millions lay entrenched, slowly learning the necessary methods of modern scientific warfare. There was a rapid progress in the use of the aeroplane. At the outset of the war this had been used chiefly for scouting, and by the Germans for the dropping of marks for the artillery. Such a thing as aerial fighting was unheard of. In 1916 the aeroplanes carried machine guns and fought in the air; their bombing work was increasingly important, they had developed a wonderful art of aerial photography, and all the aerial side of artillery work, both with aeroplanes and observation balloons, had been enormously developed. But the military mind was still resisting the use of the tank, the obvious weapon for decision in trench warfare.

Many intelligent people outside military circles understood this quite clearly. The use of the tank against trenches was an altogether obvious expedient. Leonardo da Vinci invented an early tank. Soon after the South African War, in 1903, there were stories in magazines describing imaginary battles in which tanks figured; and a complete working model of a tank, made by Mr. J. A. Corry, of Leeds, was shown to the British military authorities, who of course rejected it in 1911. Tanks had been invented and re-invented before the war began. But had the matter rested entirely in the hands of the military there would never have been any use of tanks.

It was Mr. Winston Churchill, who was at the British Admiralty in 1915–16, who insisted upon the manufacture of the first tanks, and it was in the teeth of the grimmest opposition that they were sent to France. To the British navy, and not to the army, military science owes the use of these devices. The German military authorities were equally set against them. In July, 1916, Sir Douglas Haig, the British commander-in-chief, began a great offensive which failed to break through the German line. In some places he advanced a few miles; in others he was completely defeated. There was a huge slaughter of the new British armies. And he did not use tanks.

In September, when the season was growing too late for a sustained offensive, tanks first appeared in warfare. A few were put into action by the British generals in a not very intelligent fashion. Their effect upon the German was profound, they produced something like a panic, and there can be little doubt that had they been used in July in sufficient numbers, and handled by a general of imagination and energy, they would have ended the war there and then. At that time the Allies were in greater strength than the Germans upon the Western front. The odds were roughly 7 to 4. Russia, though fast approaching exhaustion, was still fighting, Italy was pressing the Austrians hard, and Roumania was just entering the war on the side of the Allies. But the waste of men in this disastrous July offensive brought the Allied cause to the very brink of disaster.

Directly the British failure of July had reassured the Germans, they turned on the Roumanians, and the winter of 1916 saw the same fate overtake Roumania that had fallen upon Serbia in 1915. The year that had begun with the retreat from Gallipoli and the surrender of Kut, ended with the crushing of Roumania and with volleys fired at a landing party of French and British marines by a royalist crowd in the port of Athens. It looked as though King Constantine of Greece meant to lead his people in the footsteps of King Ferdinand of Bulgaria. But the coast line of Greece is one much exposed to naval action. Greece was blockaded, and a French force from Salonika joined hands with an Italian force from Valona to cut the king of Greece off from his Central European friends. (In June, 1917, Constantine was forced to abdicate by the Allies, and his son Alexander was made king in his place.)

On the whole, things looked much less dangerous for the Hohenzollern imperialism at the end of 1916 than they had done after the failure of the first great rush at the Marne. The Allies had wasted two years of opportunity. Belgium, Serbia, and Roumania, and large areas of France and Russia, were occupied by Austro-German troops. Counter-stroke after counter-stroke had failed, and Russia was now tottering towards a collapse. It was the obvious moment for Germany to make an offer of peace; and in fact negotiations were started towards that end. But they were half-hearted and were received with an equally timid negation from the Allied side. Indeed the Lloyd George and Clemenceau governments which in Britain and France replaced less "firm" governments were pledged to fight to the bitter end.

§ 9

Early in 1917 Russia collapsed.

By this time the enormous strain of the war was telling hardly upon all the European populations. There had been a great disorganization of transport everywhere, a discontinuance of the normal repairs and replacements of shipping, railways, and the like, a using-up of materials of all sorts, a dwindling of food production, a withdrawal of greater and greater masses of men from industry, a cessation of educational work, and a steady diminution of the ordinary securities and honesties of life.

More and more of the European population was being transferred from surroundings and conditions to which it was accustomed, to novel circumstances which distressed, stimulated, and demoralized it. But Russia suffered first and most from this universal pulling up of civilization from its roots. The Russian autocracy was dishonest and incompetent. The Tsar, like several of his ancestors, had now given way to a crazy pietism, and the Court was dominated by a religious imposter, Rasputin, whose cult was one of unspeakable foulness, a reeking scandal in the face of the world. Beneath the rule of this dirty mysticism, indolence and scoundrelism mismanaged the war.

The Russian common soldiers were sent into battle without guns to support them, without even rifle ammunition; they were wasted by their officers and generals in a delirium of militarist enthusiasm. For a time they seemed to be suffering mutely as the beasts suffer; but there is a limit to the endurance even of the most ignorant. A profound disgust for the Tsardom was creeping through these armies of betrayed and wasted men. From the close of 1915 onwards Russia was a source of deepening anxiety to her Western allies. Throughout 1916 she remained largely on the defensive, and there were rumours of a separate peace with Germany. She gave little help to Roumania.

On December 29th, 1916, the monk Rasputin was murdered at a dinner party in Petrograd, and a belated attempt was made to put the Tsardom in order. By March things were moving rapidly; food riots in Petrograd developed into a revolutionary insurrection; there was an attempted suppression of the Duma, the representative body, attempted arrests of liberal leaders, the formation of a provisional government under Prince Lvoff, and an abdication (March 15th) by the Tsar.

For a time it seemed that a moderate and controlled revolution might be possible—perhaps under a new Tsar. Then it became evident that the destruction of confidence in Russia had gone too far for any such adjustments. The Russian people were sick to death of the old order of things in Europe, of Tsars and of wars and great powers; it wanted relief, and that speedily, from unendurable miseries. The Allies had no understanding of Russian realities; their diplomatists were ignorant of Russian; genteel persons, with their attention directed to the Russian Court rather than Russia, they blundered steadily with the new situation. There was little goodwill among the diplomatists for republicanism, and a manifest disposition to embarrass the new government as much as possible. At the head of the Russian republican government was an eloquent and picturesque leader, Kerensky, who found himself assailed by the deep forces of a profounder revolutionary movement, the "social revolution," at home and cold-shouldered by the Allied governments abroad. His allies would neither let him give the Russian people land nor peace beyond their frontiers. The French and the British Press pestered their exhausted ally for a fresh offensive, but when presently the Germans made a strong attack by sea and land upon Riga, the British Admiralty quailed before the prospect of a Baltic expedition in relief.

The new Russian republic had to fight unsupported. In spite of their great naval predominance and the bitter protests of the English admiral, Lord Fisher (1841–1920), it is to be noted that the Allies, except for some submarine attacks, left the Germans the complete mastery of the Baltic throughout the war.

The Russian masses were resolute to end the war. There had come into existence in Petrograd a body representing the workers and common soldiers, the Soviet, and this body clamoured for an international conference of socialists at Stockholm. Food riots were occurring in Berlin at this time, war-weariness in Austria and Germany was profound, and there can be little doubt, in the light of subsequent events, that such a conference would have precipitated a reasonable peace on democratic lines in 1917 and a German revolution.

Kerensky implored his Western allies to allow this conference to take place, but, fearful of a world-wide outbreak of socialism and republicanism, they refused, in spite of the favourable response of a small majority of the British Labour Party. Without either moral or physical help from the Allies, the "moderate" Russian republic still fought on and made a last desperate offensive effort in July. It failed after some preliminary successes and another great slaughtering of Russians.

The limit of Russian endurance was reached. Mutinies now broke out in the Russian armies, and particularly upon the northern front, and on November 7th, 1917, Kerensky's government was overthrown and power was seized by the Soviet Government, dominated by the Bolshevik socialists under Lenin, and pledged to make peace regardless of the Western powers. Russia passed definitely "out of the war."

In the spring of 1917 there had been a costly and ineffective French attack upon the Champagne front, which had failed to break through and sustained enormous losses. Here, then, by the end of 1917, was a phase of events altogether favourable to Germany, had her government been fighting for security and well-being rather than for pride and victory. But to the very end, to the pitch of final exhaustion, the people of the Central Powers were held to the effort to achieve a complete victory.

To that end it was necessary that Britain should be not merely resisted, but subjugated, and in order to do that Germany had already dragged America into the circle of her enemies. Throughout 1916 the submarine campaign had been growing in intensity, but hitherto it had respected neutral shipping. In January, 1917, a completer "blockade" of Great Britain and France was proclaimed, and all neutral powers were warned to withdraw their shipping from the British seas. An indiscriminate sinking of the world's shipping began, which compelled the United States to enter the war in April (6th), 1917. Throughout 1917, while Russia was breaking up and becoming impotent, the American people were changing swiftly and steadily into a great military nation. And the unrestricted submarine campaign, for which the German imperialists had accepted the risk of this fresh antagonist, was far less successful than had been hoped. The British navy proved itself much more inventive and resourceful than the British army; there was a rapid development of anti-submarine devices under water, upon the surface, and in the air; and after a month or so of serious destruction, the tale of the submarine sinkings declined. The British found it necessary to put themselves upon food rations; but the regulations were well framed and ably administered, the public showed an excellent spirit and intelligence, and the danger of famine and social disorder was kept at arm's length.

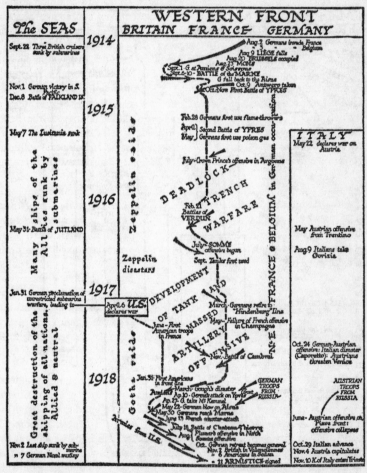

Yet the German imperial government continued to fight. If the submarine was not doing all that had been expected, and if the armies of America gathered like a thunder-cloud, yet Russia was definitely down; and in October the same sort of autumn offensive that had overthrown Serbia in 1915 and Roumania in 1916 was now turned with crushing effect against Italy. The Italian front collapsed after the Battle of Caporetto, and the Austro-German armies poured down into Venetia and came almost within gunfire of Venice. Germany felt justified, therefore, in taking a high line with the Russian peace proposals, and the peace of Brest-Litovsk (March 2nd, 1918) gave the Western Allies some intimation of what a German victory would mean to them. It was a crushing and exorbitant peace, dictated with the utmost arrogance of confident victors.

All through the winter German troops had been shifting from the Eastern

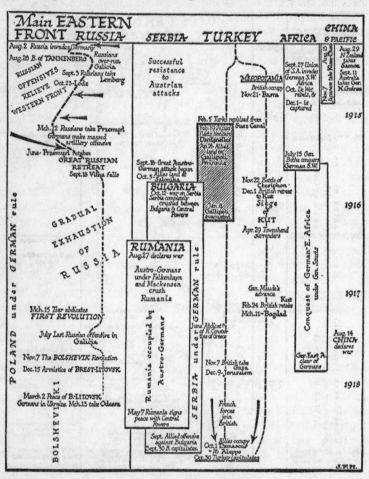

to the Western front, and now, in the spring of 1918, the jaded enthusiasm of hungry, weary, and bleeding Germany was lashed up for the one supreme effort that was really and truly to end the war. For some months American troops had been in France, but the bulk of the American army was still across the Atlantic. It was high time for the final conclusive blow upon the Western front, if such a blow was ever to be delivered.

The first attack was upon the British in the Somme region. The not very brilliant cavalry generals who were still in command of a front upon which cavalry was a useless encumbrance, were caught napping; and on March 21st, in "Gough's Disaster," the fifth British army was driven back in disorder almost to Amiens. The jealousies of the British and French generals had prevented any unified command of the Allied armies in France, and there was no general reserve whatever behind Gough. Nearly a thousand guns were lost by the Allies, and scores of thousands of prisoners. Throughout April and May the Germans rained offensives on the Allied front. They came near to a break through in the north, and they made a great drive back to the Marne, which they reached again on May 30th, 1918.

This was the climax of the German effort. Behind it was nothing but an exhausted homeland. Marshal Foch was put in supreme command of all the Allies' armies. Fresh troops were hurrying from Britain across the Channel, and America was now pouring men into France by the hundred thousand. In June the weary Austrians made a last effort in Italy, and collapsed before an Italian counter-attack. Early in June Foch began to develop a counter-attack. By July the tide was turning, and the Germans were reeling back. The Battle of Château-Thierry (July 18th) proved the quality of the new American armies. In August the British opened a great and successful thrust, and the bulge of the German lines towards Amiens wilted and collapsed. "August 8th," said Ludendorff, "was a black day in the history of the German army." The British attack on the Hindenburg line in September ensured the Allied victory.

Germany had finished. The fighting spirit passed out of her army, and October was a story of defeat and retreat along the entire Western front. Early in November British troops were in Valenciennes and Americans in Sedan. In Italy also the Austrian armies were in a state of disorderly retreat. But everywhere now the Hohenzollern and Habsburg forces were collapsing. The smash at the end was amazingly swift. Frenchmen and Englishmen could not believe their newspapers as day after day they announced the capture of more hundreds of guns and more thousands of prisoners.

In September a great Allied offensive against Bulgaria had produced a revolution in that country and peace proposals. Turkey had followed with a capitulation at the end of October, and Austro-Hungary on November 3rd. There was an attempt to bring out the German fleet for the last fight, but the sailors mutinied (November 7th).

The Kaiser and the Crown Prince bolted hastily, and without a scrap of dignity, into Holland. On November 11th an armistice was signed and the war was at an end. . . .

For four years and a quarter the war had lasted, and gradually it had drawn nearly everyone, in the Western world at least, into its vortex. Upwards of eight millions of people had been actually killed through the fighting, another twenty or twenty-five millions had died through the hardships and disorders entailed. Scores of millions were suffering and enfeebled by undernourishment and misery. A vast proportion of the living were now engaged in war work, in drilling and armament, in making munitions, in hospitals, in working as substitutes for men who had gone into the armies and the like. Business men had been adapting themselves to the more hectic methods necessary for profit in a world in a state of crisis. The war had become, indeed, an atmosphere, a habit of life, a new social order. Then suddenly it ended.

In London the armistice was proclaimed about 11 A.M. on November 11th. It produced a strange cessation of every ordinary routine. Clerks poured out of their offices and would not return, assistants deserted their shops, omnibus drivers and the drivers of military lorries set out upon journeys of their own devising with picked-up loads of astounded and cheering passengers going nowhere in particular and careless whither they went. Vast vacant crowds presently choked the streets, and every house and shop that possessed such adornments hung out flags. When night came, many of the main streets, which had been kept in darkness for many months because of the air raids, were brightly lit. It was very strange to see thronging multitudes assembled in an artificial light again. Everyone felt aimless, with a kind of strained and aching relief. It was over at last. There would be no more killing in France, no more air raids—and things would get better.

People wanted to laugh, and weep—and could do neither. Youths of spirit and young soldiers on leave formed thin noisy processions that shoved their way through the general drift, and did their best to make a jollification. A captured German gun was hauled from the Mall, where a vast army of such trophies had been set out, into Trafalgar Square, and its carriage burnt. Squibs and crackers were thrown about. But there was little concerted rejoicing. Nearly everyone had lost too much and suffered too much to rejoice with any fervour.

XXXIX

TWENTY YEARS OF INDECISION
AND ITS OUTCOME

§ 1. *A Phase of Moral Exhaustion.* § 2. *President Wilson at Versailles.* § 3. *Constitution of the League of Nations.* § 4. *The Treaties of 1919–20.* § 5. *Bolshevism in Russia.* § 6. *The Irish Free State.* § 7. *The Far and Near East.* § 8. *Debts, Money, and Stabilization.* § 9. *The Great Crash of 1929.* § 10. *The Spanish Tragedy.* § 11. *The Rise of Nazism.* § 12. *The World Slides to War.*

§ 1

THE world of the Western European civilizations in the years that followed the end of the first World War was like a man who has had some very vital surgical operation very roughly performed, and who is not yet sure whether he can now go on living or whether he has not been so profoundly shocked and injured that he will presently fall down and die. It was a world dazed and stunned. Militarist imperialism had been defeated, but at an overwhelming cost. It had come very near to victory. Everything went on, now that the strain of the conflict had ceased, rather laxly, rather weakly, and with a gusty and uncertain temper. There was a universal hunger for peace, a universal desire for the lost liberty and prosperity of pre-war times, without any power of will to achieve and secure these things.

In many respects there had been great deterioration. Just as with the Roman Republic under the long strain of the Punic Wars, so now there had been a great release of violence and cruelty, and a profound deterioration in financial and economic morality. Generous spirits had sacrificed themselves freely to the urgent demands of the war, but the sly and base of the worlds of business and money had watched the convulsive opportunities of the time and secured a firm grip upon the resources and political power of their countries. Everywhere, men who would have been regarded as shady adventurers before 1914 had acquired power and influence, while better men had toiled unprofitably. In the phase of post-war exhaustion it was difficult to restrain these newly rich and newly powerful men.

In the course of the war there had been extraordinary experiments in collective management in nearly all the belligerent countries. It had been realized that the common expedients of peace-time commerce, the higgling of the market, the holding out for a favourable bargain, was incompatible with the swift needs of warfare. Transport, fuel, food supply, and the distribution of the raw materials not only of clothing, housing and the like, but of everything needed for war munitions, had been brought under public control.

No longer had farmers been allowed to underfarm; cattle had been put upon deer-parks and grasslands ploughed up, with or without the owners' approval. Luxury building and speculative company promotion had been restrained. In effect, a sort of emergency socialist state had been established throughout most of belligerent Europe. It was rough-and-ready and wasteful, but it was more effective than the tangled incessant profit-seeking, the cornering and forestalling and incoherent productiveness of "private enterprise."

In the earliest years of the war there had also been in all the belligerent states a very widespread feeling of brotherhood and of the need for service in the common interest. The common men were everywhere sacrificing life and health for what they believed to be the common good of the State. In return, it was promised, there would be less social injustice after the war, a more universal devotion to the common welfare. In Great Britain, for instance, Mr. Lloyd George was particularly insistent upon his intention to make the after-war Britain "a land fit for heroes." He foreshadowed the continuation of this new war-socialism into the peace period in discourses of great fire and beauty.

In Great Britain there was created a Ministry of Reconstruction, which was understood to be planning a new and more generous social order, better labour conditions, better housing, extended education, a complete and scientific revision of the economic system. And the word "Reconstruction" coloured the lives and sustained the hopes of the distressed multitude everywhere. Similar promises of a better world sustained the common soldiers of France and Germany and Italy. It was premature disillusionment that caused the Russian collapse. So that two mutually dangerous streams of anticipation were running through the minds of men in Western Europe towards the end of the war. The rich and adventurous men, and particularly the new war profiteers, were making their plans to prevent such developments as, for example, that air transport should become a State property, and to snatch back manufactures, shipping, land transport, the trade in staples, and the public services generally, from the hands of the commonweal into the grip of private profit—they were securing possession of newspapers and busying themselves with party caucuses and the like to that end; while, on the other hand, the masses of common men were looking forward naïvely to a new state of society planned almost entirely in their interest and according to generous general ideas. The history of 1919 is largely the clash of these two streams of anticipation. There was a hasty selling off, by the "business" government in control, of every remunerative public enterprise to private speculators. . . .

By the middle of 1919 the labour masses throughout the world were manifestly disappointed and in a thoroughly bad temper. The British "Ministry of Reconstruction" and its foreign equivalents were exposed as a soothing sham. The common man felt he had been cheated. There was to be no reconstruction, but only a restoration of the old order—in a bleaker form necessitated by the poverty of the new time.

For four years the drama of the war had obscured the social question which had been developing in the Western civilizations throughout the nineteenth century. Now that the war was over, this question reappeared gaunt and bare, as it had never been seen before.

And the irritations and hardships and the general insecurity of the new time were exacerbated by a profound disturbance of currency and credit. Money, a complicated growth of conventions rather than a system of values, had been deprived within the belligerent countries of the support of a gold standard. Gold had been retained only for international trade, and every government had produced excessive quantities of paper money for domestic use. With the breaking down of the war-time barriers the international exchange became a wildly fluctuating confusion, a source of distress to everyone except a few gamblers and speculators. Prices rose and rose—with an infuriating effect upon the wage-earner. On the one hand was his employer resisting his demands for more pay; on the other hand, food, house-room, and clothing were being cornered against him. And—which was the essential danger of the situation— he began to lose whatever confidence he had ever possessed that any patience or industrial willingness he displayed would really alleviate the shortages and inconveniences by which he suffered.

In most of the European countries there was an urgent need of houses. Throughout the war there had been a cessation not only of building but of repairs. The shortage of houses in the last months of 1919 amounted to between 250,000 and a million homes in Britain alone. Conditions in France and Germany were even worse. Multitudes of people were living in a state of exasperating congestion, and the most shameless profiteering in apartments and houses was going on. It was a difficult but not an impossible situation. Given the same enthusiasm and energy and self-sacrifice that had tided over the monstrous crisis of 1916, the far easier task of providing a million houses could have been performed in a year or so. But there had been corners in building materials, transport was in a disordered state, and it did not *pay* private enterprise to build houses at any rents within the means of the people who needed them. Private enterprise, therefore, so far from bothering about the public need of housing, did nothing but corner and speculate in rents and sub-letting. It now demanded grants in aid from the State—in order to build at a profit.

And as another example of the inadequacy of a profiteering system to solve the problems of the time, there was a great crowding and dislocation of goods at the depots because there was insufficient road transport. There was an urgent want of cheap automobiles to move about goods and workers. But private enterprise in the automobile industry imagined it would be far more profitable to produce splendid and costly cars for those whom the war had made rich. The munition factories built with ready money could have been converted very readily into factories for the mass production of cheap auto- mobiles, but private enterprise had insisted upon these factories being sold by the State, and would neither meet the public need itself nor let the State do so.

So, too, with the world in the direst discomfort for need of shipping, private enterprise insisted upon the shutting down of the newly-constructed State ship- yards.

Currency was dislocated everywhere, but private enterprise was busy buying and selling francs or marks and intensifying the trouble.

These are facts that the historian of mankind is obliged to note with as little comment as possible. Private enterprise in Europe in 1919 and 1920 displayed neither will nor capacity for meeting the urgent needs of the time. So soon as it was released from control, it ran naturally into speculation, cornering, and luxury production. It followed the line of maximum profit. It displayed no sense of its own dangers; and it resisted any attempt to restrain and moderate its profits and make itself serviceable, even in its own interest.

And this went on in the face of the most striking manifestations of the extreme recalcitrance on the part of the European masses to the prolonged continuance of the privations and inconveniences they suffered. In 1913 these masses were living as they had lived since birth; they were habituated to the life they led. The masses of 1919, on the other hand, had been uprooted everywhere, to go into the armies, to go into munition factories, and so on. They had lost their habits of acquiescence, and they were hardier and more capable of desperate action. Great multitudes of men had gone through such brutalizing training as, for instance, bayonet drill; they had learnt to be ferocious, and to think less either of killing or being killed. Social unrest had become, therefore, much more dangerous.

It was not that the masses had or imagined that they had the plan of a new social, political, and economic system. They had not, and they did not believe they had. The defects we have pointed out in the socialist scheme were no secret from them. It was a much more dangerous state of affairs than that. It was that they were becoming so disgusted with the current system, with its luxury, its waste, and its general misery, that they did not care what happened afterwards so long as they could destroy it. It was a return to a state of mind comparable to that which had rendered possible the debacle of the Roman Empire.

Everywhere in Europe the forces of social revolution began to stir, and most notably in Italy and Germany. Communism displayed exceptional aggressiveness in Italy. In various parts of Italy there appeared communist mayors, and in Bologna there was a forcible attempt to put communist principles into operation. In July, 1920, Giolitti, a neutralist who had opposed the war, replaced Signor Nitti as head of the government. He made various experiments in co-partnership between the industrial workers and their employers. In September many steel works and other factories were seized by the workers, who began to operate them on socialist lines. These proceedings received the support and endorsement of the government.

The slide towards communism continued during 1921 in the face of a gathering opposition, and there was rioting and violence in Florence, Trieste, Puglia, Pisa and many other places. The socializing measures of Giolitti had produced a violent reaction among the classes interested in private property, and an organization of young men had grown up, the Fascisti, who affected shock heads, black shirts, nationalism of the intensest sort, and anti-socialism. They met violence with violence, they carried it to new extremes, they established an anti-socialist terror. They found a leader of great energy and slight scruples, Benito Mussolini, formerly a radical journalist. Under his skilful direction the Fascisti speedily outdistanced the sporadic and sentimental outrages of the communists. Liberal leaders and writers were waylaid and beaten with clubs. A favourite method of the Fascisti was the administration of over-doses of castor oil to those who criticized their proceedings unfavourably. Murder, beatings, torture, the burning of the private property of liberal thinkers, became the methods of social control in Italy. The shadow of communism was replaced by the reality of brigand rule.

By October, 1922, the Fascisti had grown to such strength that they constituted a veritable army and could march upon Rome. The Cabinet proclaimed martial law and prepared to fight, but the king refused his assent to these measures and invited Mussolini to take control of affairs. This he did. He became head of the government, and agreed to disband his blackshirts—a promise which was never kept. The Fascisti were put in control of the police and armed forces of the country, the freedom of the Press was destroyed, elections became a farce, political opponents continued to be assaulted, terrorized, murdered; and Mussolini, under the title of Il Duce, became virtual dictator, the king falling back into relative obscurity.

For a time a certain rough economic efficiency was restored to Italy, greatly applauded in some circles abroad. But the true interest of the Italian situation to the rest of the world lay in the fact that it manifested in the harshest and crudest forms the quality of the extreme left and the extreme right in contemporary human affairs, the impracticability and incapacity of the former and the readiness with which private ownership and enterprise when put upon the defensive, can degenerate into violence and brigandage. Italy, like Russia, had become a jail for every free-minded person. The creeping disease of illegality, upon which we have already animadverted in our criticism of *Stalky and Co.*, was in full flower in both these countries. But Italy did not stand alone in this matter; it was merely the most fully developed instance of a universal tendency of the times. In Germany, France and Great Britain the Fascisti were to find rivals and imitators, but for a time their activities in these countries were a nuisance rather than a tyranny.

§ 2

We have noted the general social and economic disorder of the European communities in the years following the war, before giving any account of the work of world settlement that centred on the Peace Conference at Paris, because the worried and preoccupied state of everyone concerned with private problems of income, prices, employment and the like goes far to explain the jaded atmosphere in which that conference addressed itself to the vast task before it. One cannot expect a vigorous public life when individual lives are confused and distressed.

The story of the conference turns very largely upon the adventure of one particular man, one of those men whom accident or personal quality picks out as a type to lighten the task of the historian. We have in the course of this history found it very helpful at times to focus our attention upon some individual—Buddha, Alexander the Great, Yuan Chwang, the Emperor Frederick II, Charles V, and Napoleon I, for example—and let him by reflection illuminate the period in which he lived. The conclusion of the first World War can be seen most easily as the rise of the American president, President Wilson, to predominant importance in the world's hopes and attention, and his failure to justify that predominance.

President Wilson (1856–1924) had previously been a prominent student and teacher of constitutional law and the political sciences generally. He had held various professorial chairs, and had been President of Princeton University (New Jersey). There is a long list of books to his credit, and they show a mind rather exclusively directed to American history and American politics. He retired from academic life, and was elected Democratic Governor of New Jersey in 1910. In 1912 he became the Democratic presidential candidate, and as a consequence of a violent quarrel between ex-President Roosevelt and President Taft, which split the dominant Republican party, President of the United States.

The events of August, 1914, seem to have taken President Wilson, like the rest of his fellow-countrymen, by surprise. We find him cabling an offer of his services as a mediator on August 3rd. Then, for a time, he and America watched the conflict. At first neither the American people nor their President seem to have had a very clear or profound understanding of that long-gathered catastrophe. Their tradition for a century had been to disregard the problems of the Old World, and it was not to be lightly changed. The imperialistic arrogance of the German Court and the alleged inclination of the German military authorities towards melodramatic "frightfulness," their invasion of Belgium, their use of poison gas, and the nuisance of their submarine campaign, created a deepening hostility to Germany in the United States as the war proceeded; but the tradition of political abstinence and the deep-rooted persuasion that America possessed a political morality altogether superior to European conflicts, restrained the President from active intervention. He adopted a lofty tone. He professed to be unable to judge the causes and justice of the first World War. It was largely his high pacific attitude that secured his re-election as President for a second term.

But the world is not to be mended by merely regarding evildoers with an expression of rather undiscriminating disapproval. By the end of 1916 the Germans had been encouraged to believe that under no circumstances whatever would the United States fight, and in 1917 they began their unrestricted submarine warfare and the sinking of American ships without notice. President Wilson and the American people were dragged into the war by this supreme folly. And, also, they were dragged into a reluctant attempt to define their relations to Old-World politics in some other terms than those of mere aloofness. Their thoughts and temper changed very rapidly. They came into the war side by side with the Allies, but not in any pact with the Allies. They came into the war, in the name of their own modern civilization, to punish and end an intolerable political and military situation.

Slow and belated judgments are sometimes the best judgments. In a series of "notes," too long and various for detailed treatment in this *Outline*, thinking aloud, as it were, in the hearing of all mankind, President Wilson sought to state the essential differences of the American State from the Great Powers of the Old World. He unfolded a conception of international relationships that came like a gospel, like the hope of a better world, to the whole eastern hemisphere.

Secret agreements were to cease, "nations" were to determine their own destinies, militarist aggression was to cease, the seaways were to be free to all mankind. These commonplaces of American thought, these secret desires of every sane man, came like a great light upon the darkness of anger and conflict in Europe. At last, men felt, the ranks of diplomacy were broken, the veils of Great Power "policy" were rent in twain. Here, with authority, with the strength of a powerful new nation behind it, was the desire of the common man throughout the world, plainly said.

President Wilson

Manifestly there was needed some overriding instrument of government to establish world law and maintain these broad and liberal generalizations upon human intercourse. A number of schemes had floated in men's minds for the attainment of that end. In particular, there was a movement for some sort of world league, a "League of Nations." The American President adopted this phrase and sought to realize it. An essential condition of the peace he sought was he declared to be this federal organ. This League of Nations was to be the final court of appeal in international affairs. It was to be the substantial realization of the peace. Here, again, he awakened a tremendous echo.

President Wilson was for a time the spokesman of a new age. Throughout the war, and for some little time after it had ended, he held, so far as the Old World was concerned, that exalted position. But in America where they knew him better there were doubts, and, writing as we do now, with the wisdom of subsequent events, we can understand these doubts. America, throughout a century and more of detachment and security had developed new ideals and formulæ of political thought, without realizing with any intensity that, under conditions of stress and danger, these ideals and formulæ might have to be passionately sustained. To her community many things were platitudes that had to the Old-World communities, entangled still in ancient political complications, the quality of a saving gospel. President Wilson was responding to the thought and conditions of his own people and his own country, based on a liberal tradition that had first found its full expression in English speech; but to Europe and Asia he seemed to be thinking and saying, for the first time in history, things hitherto undeveloped and altogether secret. And that misconception he may have shared.

We are dealing here with an able and successful professor of political science, who did not fully realize what he owed to his contemporaries and the literary and political atmosphere he had breathed throughout his life; and who passed very rapidly, after his re-election as President, from the mental attitudes of a political leader to those of a Messiah. His "notes" are a series of explorations of the elements of the world situation. When at last, in his address to Congress of January 8th, 1918, he produced his Fourteen Points as a definite statement of the American peace intentions, they were as a statement, far better in their spirit than in their arrangement and matter.

This document demanded open agreements between nations and an end to secret diplomacy, free navigation of the high seas, free commerce, disarmament, and a number of political readjustments upon the lines of national independence. Finally, in the Fourteenth Point, it required "a general association of nations" to guarantee the peace of the world. He sought "peace without victory."

These Fourteen Points had an immense reception throughout the world. Here at last seemed a peace for reasonable men everywhere, as good and acceptable to honest and decent Germans and Russians as to honest and decent Frenchmen and Englishmen and Belgians; and for some months the whole world was lit by faith in Wilson. Could they have been made the basis of a world settlement in 1919, they would forthwith have opened a new and more hopeful era in human affairs.

But, as we must tell, they did not do that. There was about President Wilson a certain narrow egotism; there was in the generation of people in the United States to whom this great occasion came—a generation born in security, reared in plenty and, so far as history goes, in ignorance—a generation remote from the tragic issues that had made Europe grave—a certain superficiality and lightness of mind. It was not that the American people were superficial by nature and necessity, but that they had never been deeply stirred by the idea of a human community larger than their own. It was an intellectual, but not a moral, conviction with them. One had on the one hand these new people of the New World, with their new ideas, their finer and better ideas, of peace and world righteousness, and on the other the old, bitter, deeply entangled peoples of the Great Power system; and the former were crude and rather childish in their immense inexperience, and the latter were seasoned and bitter and intricate.

The theme of this clash of the raw idealist youthfulness of a new age with the experienced ripeness of the old was treated years ago by that great novelist, Henry James, in a very typical story called *Daisy Miller*. It is the pathetic story of a frank, trustful, high-minded, but rather simple-minded American girl, with a real disposition towards righteousness and a great desire for a "good time," and how she came to Europe and was swiftly entangled and

M. Clemenceau

put in the wrong, and at last driven to welcome death by the complex tortuousness and obstinate limitations of the older world. There have been a thousand variants of that theme in real life, a thousand such transatlantic tragedies and the story of President Wilson is one of them. But it is not to be supposed, because the new thing succumbs to the old infections, that is the final condemnation of the new thing.

Probably no fallible human being manifestly trying to do his best amidst overwhelming circumstances has been subjected to such minute, searching, and pitiless criticism as President Wilson. He is blamed for conducting the war and ensuing peace negotiations on strictly party lines. He remained, it is charged against him, the President representing the American Democratic Party, when circumstances conspired to make him the representative of the general interests of mankind. He made no attempt to incorporate with himself such great American leaders as ex-President Roosevelt, ex-President Taft, and the like. He did not draw fully upon the moral and intellectual resources of the States; he made the whole issue too personal, and he surrounded himself with merely personal adherents. And a grave error was his decision to come to the Peace Conference himself. Nearly every experienced critic seems to be of opinion that he should have remained in America, in the rôle of America, speaking occasionally as if a nation spoke. Throughout the concluding years of the war he had, by that method, achieved an unexampled position in the world.

Says Doctor Dillon:[1] "Europe, when the President touched its shores, was as clay ready for the creative potter. Never before were the nations so eager to follow a Moses who would take them to the long-promised land where wars are prohibited and blockades unknown. And to their thinking he was that great leader. In France men bowed down before him with awe and affection. Labour leaders in Paris told me that they shed tears of joy in his presence, and that their comrades would go through fire and water to help him to realize his noble schemes. To the working classes in Italy his name was a heavenly clarion at the sound of which the earth would be renewed. The Germans regarded him and his humane doctrine as their sheet-anchor of safety. The fearless Herr Muehlon said: 'If President Wilson

Mr. Lloyd George

---

[1] *The Peace Conference.*

were to address the Germans, and pronounce a severe sentence upon them, they would accept it with resignation and without a murmur and set to work at once.' In German-Austria his fame was that of a saviour, and the mere mention of his name brought balm to the suffering and surcease of sorrow to the afflicted. . . ."

Such was the overpowering expectation of the audience to which President Wilson prepared to show himself. He reached France on board the *George Washington* in December, 1918.

He brought his wife with him. That seemed, no doubt, a perfectly natural and proper thing to an American mind. Quite a number of the American representatives brought their wives. Unhappily, a social quality, nay, almost a tourist quality, was introduced into the world settlement by these ladies. Transport facilities were limited, and most of them arrived in Europe with a radiant air of privilege. They came as if they came to a treat. They were, it was intimated, seeing Europe under exceptionally interesting circumstances. They would visit Chester, or Warwick, or Windsor, *en route*—for they might not have a chance of seeing these celebrated places again. Important interviews would be broken off to get in a visit to some "old historical mansion." This may seem a trivial matter to note in a History of Mankind, but it was such small human things as this that drew a miasma of futility over the Peace Conference of 1919. In a little while one discovered that Wilson, the Hope of Mankind, had vanished, and that all the illustrated fashion papers contained pictures of a delighted tourist and his wife, grouped smilingly with crowned heads and such-like enviable company. . . . It is so easy to be wise after the event, and to perceive that he should not have come over.

The men he had chiefly to deal with, for example M. Clemenceau (France), Mr. Lloyd George and Mr. Balfour (Britain), Baron Sonnino and Signor Orlando (Italy), were men of widely dissimilar historical traditions. But in one respect they resembled him and appealed to his sympathies. They, too, were party politicians, who had led their country through the war. Like himself they had failed to grasp the necessity of entrusting the work of settlement to more specially qualified men.

"They were the merest novices in international affairs. Geography, ethnology, psychology, and political history were sealed books to them. Like the Rector of Louvain University, who told Oliver Goldsmith that, as he had become the head of that institution without knowing Greek, he failed to see why it should be taught there, the chiefs of State, having obtained the highest position in their respective countries without more than an inkling of international affairs, were unable to realize the importance of mastering them or the impossibility of repairing the omission as they went along. . . .[1]

"What they lacked, however, might in some perceptible degree have been supplied by enlisting as their helpers men more happily endowed than themselves. But they deliberately chose mediocrities. It is a mark of genial spirits

---

[1] Dillon, *The Peace Conference.*

that they are well served, but the plenipotentiaries of the Conference were not characterized by it. Away in the background some of them had families or casual prompters to whose counsels they were wont to listen, but many of the adjoints who moved in the limelight of the world-stage were gritless and pithless.

"As the heads of the principal Governments implicitly claimed to be the authorized spokesmen of the human race, and endowed with unlimited powers, it is worth noting that this claim was boldly challenged by the people's organs in the Press. Nearly all the journals read by the masses objected from the first to the dictatorship of the group of Premiers, Mr. Wilson being excepted. . . ."

The restriction upon our space in this *Outline* will not allow us to tell here how the Peace Conference shrank from a Council of Ten to a Council of Four (Wilson, Clemenceau, Lloyd George, and Orlando), and how it became a conference less and less like a frank and open discussion of the future of mankind, and more and more like some old-fashioned diplomatic conspiracy. Great and wonderful had been the hopes that had gathered to Paris. "The Paris of the Conference," says Dr. Dillon, "ceased to be the capital of France. It became a vast cosmopolitan caravanserai teeming with unwonted aspects of life and turmoil, filled with curious samples of the races, tribes, and tongues of four continents who came to watch and wait for the mysterious to-morrow.

"An Arabian Nights' touch was imparted to the dissolving panorama by strange visitants from Tartary and Kurdistan, Korea and Azerbeijan, Armenia, Persia, and the Hedjaz—men with patriarchal beards and scimitar-shaped noses, and others from desert and oasis, from Samarkand and Bokhara. Turbans and fezes, sugar-loaf hats and head-gear resembling episcopal mitres, old military uniforms devised for the embryonic armies of new states on the eve of perpetual peace, snowy-white burnouses, flowing mantles and graceful garments like the Roman toga, contributed to create an atmosphere of dreamy unreality in the city where the grimmest of realities were being faced and coped with.

"Then came the men of wealth, of intellect, of industrial enterprise, and the seed-bearers of the ethical new ordering, members of economic committees from the United States, Britain, Italy, Poland, Russia, India, and Japan, representatives of naphtha industries and far-off coal mines, pilgrims, fanatics and charlatans from all climes, priests of all religions, preachers of every doctrine, who mingled with princes, field-marshals, statesmen, anarchists, builders-up and pullers-down. All of them burned with desire to be near to the crucible in which the political and social systems of the world were to be melted and recast.

"Every day, in my walks, in my apartment, or at restaurants, I met emissaries from lands and peoples whose very names had seldom been heard of before in the West. A delegation from the Pont-Euxine Greeks called on me, and discoursed of their ancient cities of Trebizond, Samsoun, Tripoli, Kerassund, in which I resided many years ago, and informed me that they, too, desired to become welded into an independent Greek Republic, and had come to have their claims allowed. The Albanians were represented by my old friend Turkhan Pasha on the one hand, and by my friend Essad Pasha on the other—the former desirous of Italy's protection, the latter demanding complete independence. Chinamen, Japanese, Koreans, Hindus, Kirghizes, Lesghiens, Circassians, Mingrelians, Buryats, Malays, and Negroes and Negroids from Africa and America were among the tribes and tongues forgathered in Paris to watch the rebuilding of the political world system and to see where they 'came in.' . . ."

To this thronging, amazing Paris, agape for a new world, came President Wilson, and found its gathering forces dominated by a personality narrower, in every way more limited and beyond comparison more forcible than himself: the French Premier, M. Clemenceau. At the instance of President Wilson, M. Clemenceau was elected President of the Conference. "It was," said President Wilson, "a special tribute to the sufferings and sacrifices of France." And that, unhappily, sounded the keynote of the Conference, whose sole business should have been with the future of mankind.

Georges Benjamin Clemenceau was an old journalist politician, a great denouncer of abuses, a great upsetter of governments, a doctor who had, while a municipal councillor, kept a free clinic, and a fierce, experienced duellist. None of his duels ended fatally, but he faced them with great intrepidity. He had passed from the medical school to republican journalism in the days of the Empire. In those days he was an extremist of the Left. He was for a time a teacher in America, and he married, and was afterwards divorced from, an American wife. He was thirty in the eventful year 1871. He returned to France after Sedan, and flung himself into the stormy politics of the defeated nation with great fire and vigour. Thereafter, France was his world, the France of vigorous journalism, high-spirited personal quarrels, challenges, confrontations, scenes, dramatic effects, and witticisms at any cost. He was what people call "fierce stuff," he was nicknamed the "Tiger," and he seems to have been rather proud of his nickname. Professional patriot rather than statesman and thinker, this was the man whom the war had flung up to misrepresent the fine mind and the generous spirit of France.

His limitations had a profound effect upon the Conference, which was further coloured by the dramatic resort, for the purpose of signature, to the very Hall of Mirrors at Versailles in which Germany had triumphed and proclaimed her unity. There the Germans were to sign.

To M. Clemenceau and to France, in that atmosphere, the war ceased to seem a world war; it was merely the sequel of the previous conflict of the Terrible Year, the downfall and punishment of offending Germany. "The world had to be made safe for democracy," said President Wilson. That from M. Clemenceau's expressed point of view was "talking like Jesus Christ." The world had to be made safe for Paris. "Talking like Jesus Christ" seemed a very ridiculous thing to many of those brilliant rather than sound diplomatists and politicians who made the year 1919 supreme in the history of human insufficiency.

(Another flash of the "Tiger's" wit, it may be noted, was that President Wilson with his Fourteen Points was "worse" than God Almighty. "Le bon dieu" only had ten. . . .)

M. Clemenceau sat with Signor Orlando in the more central chairs of the semicircle of four in front of the fire, says Keynes. He wore a black frockcoat and grey suède gloves, which he never removed during these sessions. He was, it is to be noted, the only one of these four reconstructors of the world who could understand and speak both French and English.

The aims of M. Clemenceau were simple and in a manner attainable. He wanted all the settlement of 1871 undone. He wanted Germany punished as though she was a uniquely sinful nation and France a sinless martyr land. He wanted Germany so crippled and devastated as never more to be able to stand up to France. He wanted to hurt and humiliate Germany more than France had been hurt and humiliated in 1871. He did not care if in breaking Germany Europe was broken; his mind did not go far enough beyond the Rhine to understand that possibility. He accepted President Wilson's League of Nations as an excellent proposal if it would guarantee the security of France whatever she did, but he preferred a binding alliance of the United States and England to maintain, uphold, and glorify France under practically any circumstances. He wanted wider opportunities for the exploitation of Syria, North Africa, and so forth by Parisian financial groups.

He wanted indemnities to recuperate France, loans, gifts, and tributes to France, glory and homage to France. France had suffered, and France had to be rewarded. Belgium, Russia, Serbia, Poland, Armenia, Britain, Germany, and Austria had all suffered, too; all mankind had suffered, but what would you? That was not his affair. These were the supers of a drama in which France was for him the star. . . . In much the same spirit Signor Orlando seems to have sought the welfare of Italy.

Mr. Lloyd George brought to the Council of Four the subtlety of a Welshman, the intricacy of a European, and an urgent necessity for respecting the nationalist egotism of the British imperialists and capitalists who had returned him to power. Into the secrecy of that council went President Wilson with the very noblest aims for his newly discovered American world-policy, his rather hastily compiled Fourteen Points, and a project rather than a scheme for a League of Nations.

"There can seldom have been a statesman of the first rank more incompetent than the President in the agilities of the Council Chamber."[1] From the whispering darknesses and fireside disputes of that council, and after various comings and goings we cannot here describe, he emerged at last with his Fourteen Points pitifully torn and dishevelled, but with a little puling infant of a League of Nations, which could die or which might live and grow—no one could tell. But that much, at least, he had saved. . . .

[1] Keynes.

§ 3

This homunculus in a bottle which it was hoped might become at last Man ruling the Earth, this League of Nations as it was embodied in the Covenant of April 28th, 1919, was not a League of Peoples at all; it was, the world discovered, a league of "states, dominions, or colonies." It was stipulated that these should be "fully self-governing," but there was no definition whatever of this phrase. There was no bar to a limited franchise and no provision for any direct control by the people of any state. India figured—presumably as a "fully self-governing state"! An autocracy would no doubt have been admissable as a "fully self-governing" democracy with a franchise limited to one person. The League of the Covenant of 1919 was, in fact, a league of "representatives" of foreign offices, and it did not even supersede embassies at every capital.

The British Empire appeared once as a whole, and then India (!) and the four dominions of Canada, Australia, South Africa and New Zealand appeared as separate sovereign states. Later, Ireland attained a separate status. The Indian representative was, of course, sure to be merely a British nominee; the dominion representatives would be colonial politicians. But if the British Empire was to be thus dissected, a representative of Great Britain should have been substituted for the imperial representative, and Egypt should also have been given representation. Moreover, either New York State or Virginia was historically and legally as much a sovereign state as New Zealand or Canada. The inclusion of India raised logical claims for French Africa and French Asia. One French representative did propose a separate vote for the little principality of Monaco.

There was to be an assembly of the League in which every member state was to be represented and to have equal voice, but the working directorate of the League was to vest in a Council, which was to consist of the representatives of the United States, Britain, France, Italy, and Japan, with four other members elected by the Assembly. The Council was to meet once a year; the gatherings of the Assembly were to be at "stated intervals," not stated.

Except in certain specified instances the league of this Covenant could make only unanimous decisions. One dissentient on the council could bar any proposal—on the lines of the old Polish *liberum veto*. This was quite a disastrous provision. To many minds it made the Covenant League rather less desirable than no league at all. It was a complete recognition of the unalienable sovereignty of states, and a repudiation of the idea of an overriding commonweal of mankind. This provision practically barred the way to all amendments to the league constitution in future except by the clumsy expedient of a simultaneous withdrawal of the majority of member states desiring to change, to form the league again on new lines. The Covenant made inevitable such a final winding-up of the league it created, and that was perhaps the best thing about it.

The following powers, it was proposed, should be excluded from the original league: Germany, Austria, Russia, and whatever remains there were of the

Turkish Empire. But any of these might subsequently be included with the assent of two-thirds of the Assembly. The original membership of the league as specified in the projected Covenant was: the United States of America, Belgium, Bolivia, Brazil, the British Empire (Canada, Australia, South Africa, New Zealand, and India), China, Cuba, Ecuador, France, Greece, Guatemala, Haiti, the Hedjaz, Honduras, Italy, Japan, Liberia, Nicaragua, Panama, Peru, Poland, Portugal, Roumania, the Serb-Croat-Slovene State, Siam, Czecho-slovakia and Uruguay. To which were to be added by invitation the following powers which had been neutral in the war: the Argentine Republic, Chile, Colombia, Denmark, Holland, Norway, Paraguay, Persia, Salvador, Spain, Sweden, Switzerland, and Venezuela.

Such being the constitution of the league, it is scarcely to be wondered at that its powers were special and limited. It was given a seat at Geneva and a secretariat. It had no powers even to inspect the military preparations of its constituent states, or to instruct a military and naval staff to plan out the armed co-operation needed to keep the peace of the world.

The French representative in the League of Nations Commission, M. Léon Bourgeois, insisted lucidly and repeatedly on the logical necessity of such powers. As a speaker he was rather copious and lacking in "spice" of the Clemenceau quality. The final scene in the plenary session of April 28th, before the adoption of the Covenant, is described compactly by Mr. Wilson Harris: the crowded Banqueting Hall at the Quai d'Orsay, with its "E" of tables for the delegates, with secretaries and officials lining the walls, and a solid mass of journalists at the lower end of the room. "At the head of the room the 'Big Three' *diverted themselves in undertones* at the expense of the worthy M. Bourgeois, now launched, with the help of what must have been an entirely superfluous sheaf of notes, on the fifth rendering of his speech in support of his famous amendments."

They were so often "diverting themselves in undertones," those three men whom God had mocked with the most tremendous opportunity in history. Keynes gives other instances of the levities, vulgarities, disregards, inattentions and inadequacies of these meetings.

This poor Covenant, arrived at in this fashion, returned with President Wilson to America, and there it met all the resentful opposition of the Republican Party and all the antagonism of the men who had been left out of the European excursion. The Senate refused to ratify the Covenant, and the first meeting of the League Council was held, therefore, without American representatives.

The close of 1919 and the opening months of 1920 saw a very curious change come over American feeling after the pro-French and pro-British enthusiasms of the war period. The peace negotiations reminded the Americans, in a confused and very irritating way, of their profound differences in international outlook from any European power, that the war had for a time helped them to forget. They felt they had been "rushed" into many things without due consideration. They experienced a violent revulsion towards that policy of isolation that had broken down in 1917. The close of 1919 saw a phase, a very understandable phase, of passionate and even violent "Americanism," in which European imperialism and European socialism were equally anathema. There may have been a sordid element in the American disposition to "cut" the moral responsibilities the United States had incurred in the affairs of the Old World, and to realize the enormous financial and political advantages the war had given the New World; but the broad instinct of the American people seems to have been sound in its distrust of the proposed settlement.

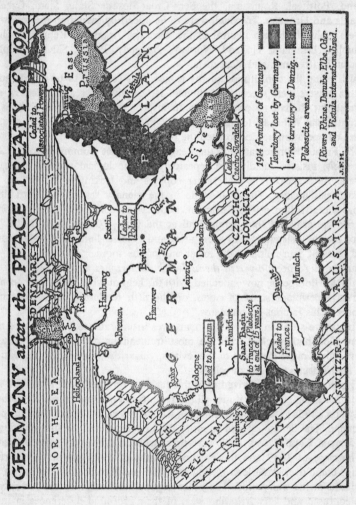

§ 4

A group of treaties embodied the decisions of Versailles. We give here first a map of the territorial aspects of the Peace Treaty with Germany. Mr. Horrabin's lucid pen gives the essential facts much more plainly than any dissertation can do. In addition it was stipulated that Germany should be extensively disarmed, should surrender her fleet, pay a great war indemnity, and great sums for the reparation of war damages. An allied commission was to observe the disarmament. The fleet was to have been handed over to the British upon June 21st, 1919, but the officers and men aboard could not endure to do this, and instead scuttled and sank their ships at Scapa Flow within sight of the British.

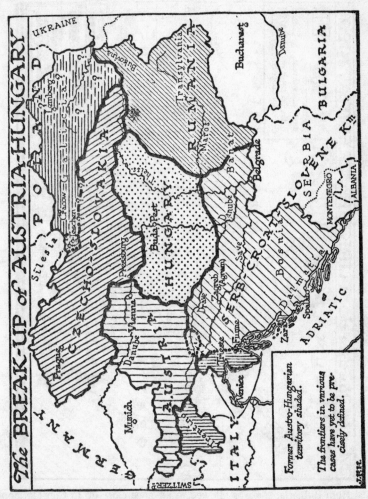

The Austro-Hungarian Empire was broken up altogether. A little Austria was left, pledged not to unite with Germany; a clipped and mutilated Hungary; Roumania expanded far beyond its legitimate boundaries into Transylvania; Poland received most of Galicia; Bohemia, with Slovak and Moravian extensions, reappeared as Czechoslovakia. The Serbs, Croats and the Montenegrins

(these latter feebly protesting) became a new Jugo-Slav state, and at once fell
into violent conflict with Italy over the port of Fiume, which the Italians quite
unrighteously claimed.

Bulgaria survived, with the loss to Greece of recently acquired territory in
Thrace. Greece, in spite of her betrayal of the Gallipoli expedition, was for
a time the pet child of the diplomatists at Versailles. She was given territory

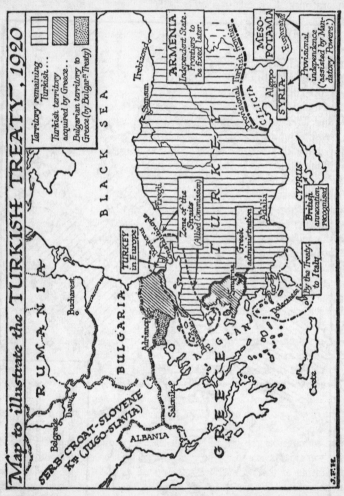

taken from Bulgaria, she was allowed to advance close up to Constantinople,
and a large piece of country round Smyrna fell to her share. She was not,
however, given back Rhodes and the other islands of the Dodecanese, in spite
of their purely Greek character. These were to be part of the Italian loot; and
the British stuck to Cyprus.

The Turkish treaty was hard to make and impossible to enforce. A nominal

Turkish government in Constantinople signed it, but a second real Turkish government established itself at Angora and refused to sign. A Greek army invaded the Smyrna district, and a second Turkish treaty, the Treaty of Sèvres (August, 1920), replaced the first. Complicated shiftings of control followed. An Interallied Control was set up in Constantinople (January, 1921), the Constantinople Turkish government evaporated, and the vital Turkish government at Angora opened up relations with the Bolsheviks in Moscow. The Greeks became more and more aggressive, with all sorts of vague encouragement behind them. The Greeks in this period of inflated ambitions made an attempt to seize Constantinople. They embarked upon a great offensive against Angora that was to end the Turk for ever. It got near to Angora and it staggered and collapsed. From August, 1922, onward there was nothing but retreat and flight from before the Turks. A terrified population of Asiatic Greeks fled with the armies. Nothing was held in Asia. Smyrna was evacuated before the end of September, and nearly a million fugitives of Greek race and language left Asia, never to return.

The vitality of the Turk in this phase was remarkable. He was not only driving back the attacking Greek, but he was, after his age-long tradition, massacring Armenians, and he was driving the French out of Cilicia. Among other startling intimations of modernity, the Turks got rid of the Sultan and adopted a republican form of government. They showed fight in the zone of the Straits and recovered Constantinople. It was clearly a source of strength to them, rather than weakness, that they were cut off altogether from their age-long ineffective conflict with the Arab. Syria, Mesopotamia, were entirely detached from Turkish rule. Palestine was made a separate state within the British sphere, earmarked as a national home for the Jews. A flood of poor Jewish immigrants poured into the promised land and was speedily involved in serious conflicts with the Arab population. The Arabs had been consolidated against the Turks and inspired with a conception of national unity through the exertions of a young Oxford scholar, Colonel Lawrence. His dream of an Arab kingdom with its capital at Damascus was speedily shattered by the hunger of the French and British for mandatory territory, and in the end his Arab kingdom shrank to the desert kingdom of the Hedjaz and various other small and insecure imamates, emirates and sultanates. Unity was to come to Arabia not from the West but from a revival of Moslem puritans, the Wahhabis, led by a desert king, Ibn Saud.

When we consider the transitoriness of the settlements effected by the diplomatists, we are impressed at once by the feebleness of their diplomacy and the realization of the strong intractable forces that defeated their manœuvres and arrangements. We are still more impressed by the uninstructed ineffectiveness of the new international idealism imported into European interchanges by President Wilson. His Fourteen Points were left by these treaties like a row of ruined and tattered houses in a bombarded village. Some had gone altogether; others were twisted out of recognition. The first attempt to produce a world law had passed away like a burst of laughter in a tavern.

Chief among the fixed obstacles that for a time brought the great project of world unity, the world-wide desire for an organized peace, to nothing, was the complete unpreparedness and unwillingness of that pre-existing league of nations, subjected states and exploited areas, the British Empire, to submit to any dissection and adaptation of its system, or to any control of its naval and aerial armament. A kindred contributory cause was the equal unpreparedness of the American mind for any interference with the ascendancy of the United States in the New World.

Neither of those Great Powers, who were necessarily dominant and leading powers at Paris, had properly thought out the implications of a League of Nations in relation to these older arrangements, and so their support of that project had to most European observers a curiously hypocritical air; it was as if they wished to retain and ensure their own vast predominance and security while at the same time restraining any other power from such expansions, annexations, and alliances as might create a rival and competitive imperialism. Their failure to set an example of international confidence destroyed all possibility of international confidence in the other nations represented at Paris.

Even more unfortunate was the refusal of the Americans to assent to the Japanese demand for a recognition of racial equality.

Moreover, the foreign offices of the British, the French, and the Italians were haunted by traditional schemes of aggression entirely incompatible with the new ideas. The French view and the Italian view were far behind even the British and American in the intensity of their national egotism. A league of Nations that is to be of any appreciable value to mankind must supersede imperialisms; it is either a super-imperialism, a liberal world-empire of united states, participant or in tutelage, or it is nothing; but few of the people at the Paris Conference had the mental vigour even to assert this obvious consequence of the League proposal.

They wanted to be at the same time bound and free; to ensure peace for ever, but to keep their weapons in their hands. Accordingly, the old annexation projects of the Great Power period were hastily and thinly camouflaged as proposed acts of this poor little birth of April 28th. The newly born and barely animate League was represented to be distributing, with all the reckless munificence of a captive pope, "mandates" to the old imperialisms that, had it been the young Hercules we desired, it would certainly have strangled in its cradle. Britain was to have extensive "mandates" in Mesopotamia and East Africa; France was to have the same in Syria; Italy was to have all her holdings to the west and south-east of Egypt consolidated as mandatory territory.

Clearly, if the weak thing that was being nursed by its Secretary, in its cradle at Geneva, into some semblance of life did presently succumb to the infantile weakness of all institutions born without passion, all these "mandates" would become frank annexations. Moreover, all the Powers fought tooth and nail at the Conference for "strategic" frontiers—the ugliest symptom of all. Why should a state want a strategic frontier unless it contemplates war? On that plea Italy, for example, insisted upon a subject population of Germans in the southern Tyrol and a subject population of Yugo-Slavs in Dalmatia.

Much graver in the long run than these territorial maladjustments was the imposition of a charge for "reparations" upon Germany far beyond her power of payment, and in contravention of the plain understandings upon which she had surrendered. She was put in a position of economic serfdom. She was saddled with a liability for impossibly immense periodic repayments, she was disarmed, and her inevitable default would leave her open to practically any aggression on the part of her creditors. The full potentialities of this arrangement only became apparent a year or so later. Then, German payments failed, and in January, 1923, the French marched into the Ruhr Valley, and remained there until August, 1925, working the mines as well as they could, administering the railways, and keeping open the resentful sores of the Germans by a hundred petty inevitable tyrannies and acts of violence.

We will not enter here into any detailed account of certain further consequences of the haste and assurance at Versailles—how President Wilson gave way to the Japanese and consented to their replacing the Germans at Kiau Chau, which is Chinese property; how the almost purely German city of Danzig was practically, if not legally, annexed to Poland; and how the Powers disputed over the claim of the Italian imperialists, a claim strengthened by these instances, to seize the Yugo-Slav port of Fiume and deprive the Yugo-Slavs of a good Adriatic outlet. Italian volunteers under the rhetorical writer D'Annunzio occupied this city and sustained a rebel republic there, until it was finally annexed to Italy in January, 1921.

Nor will we do more than note the complex arrangements and justifications that put the French in possession of the Saar valley, which is German territory, or the entirely iniquitous breach of the right of "self-determination" which practically forbade German Austria to unite—as it was natural and proper that she should unite—with the rest of Germany.

§ 5

We have already noted the two Russian revolutions of 1917. The time has now come for us to deal more fully with the extraordinary change of orientation that appeared in Russia at that time. It was nothing less than a collapse of the modern western civilization so far as Russia was concerned. But it was far more than a socialist experiment that had taken hold of the Russian people. It had an air, a deceitful air, of being a final and conclusive trying out of the Western socialist idea in practice. It did, in fact, demonstrate those insufficiencies of socialist theory to which we have already drawn attention, and particularly did it demonstrate the sterility of the Marxist school of socialism. It proved again the soundness of the principle that *a revolution can create nothing that has not been fully discussed, planned, thought out, and explained beforehand.* Otherwise a revolution merely destroys a government, a dynasty, an organization, as the case may be. A revolution is an excretory operation, not a creative one.

We have given an account of the growth of socialist ideas in the latter half of the nineteenth century, and of the large part played in that development by the "class war" ideas of Karl Marx. These ideas flattered the pride and stimulated the ambition of the more energetic and discontented personalities in all the industrial regions of the world. Marxism became the creed of the restless industrial worker everywhere. But since there is no great appeal in the socialist formula to the peasant, who owns or wants to own the land he culti-vates, and since the great town communities of Western Europe and America are middle-class rather than industrial in their mentality, the Marxists soon came to see that the social and economic revolution they contemplated could not wait for parliamentary methods and majority votes, it would have in the first place to be the work of a minority, a minority of industrial workers, who would seize power, establish communist institutions, and so train the rest of the world to the happiness of the millennium that would ensue. This phase of minority rule which was to bring about the millennium was called in the Marx-ist phraseology the "dictatorship of the proletariat."

Everywhere, with an intense propagandist energy, unpaid fanatical men spent their lives and energies in spreading this idea. In the opening decade of the twentieth century there were a large number of men in the world con-vinced that, if this vaguely conceived "dictatorship of the proletariat" could be brought about, a new and better social order would follow almost automati-cally. Others, who still used Marxist phrases, had begun in fact to rely on constitutionalism; but war and postwar conditions are hostile to constitutional-ists.

The Marxists had no clear and settled plans either for the payment of the worker, or for public discussion, or for economic administration, when "capi-talism" was destroyed. All these things had been provided for in what was, no doubt, a very empirical and unjust fashion, but which was nevertheless a work-ing fashion, in the individualist capitalist system. The Marxists had never worked out an alternative method of doing these things, and did not seem to be aware that an alternative method was needed. They said in effect to the workers: "Give us power, and everything shall be done." And Russia, tortured, wasted, and betrayed by the Allies she had served so well, gave herself over, in despair, to the "dictatorship of the proletariat."

The Communist party in Russia had fluctuated in numbers; until after the revolution it had never claimed more than 800,000 adherents and at the out-break it had no more than thirty thousand. But this comparatively little organi-zation, because it was resolute and devoted, and because there was nothing else honest or resolute or competent enough in the whole of that disorganized country to stand against it, was able to establish itself in Petersburg, Moscow, and most of the towns of Russia, to secure the adhesion of the sailors of the fleet (who killed most of their officers and occupied the fortresses of Sevas-topol and Kronstadt), and to become *de facto* rulers of Russia.

There was a phase of Terroristic government. The Bolsheviks claim that it was inevitable that at first they should rule by terror. The social disorganization of the country was extreme. Over large areas the peasants had risen against the landowners, and there was a cutting up of the estates and château-burning going on very like the parallel process of the first French revolution. There were many abominable atrocities. The peasants took over the land and divided it up among themselves, being in entire ignorance of the teachings of Karl Marx in that matter. At the same time hundreds of thousands of soldiers with arms in their hands were wandering back from the war zone to their homes. The Tsarist government had conscripted over eight million men altogether— far more men than it could ever equip or handle at the front—it had torn them up by the roots from their own villages, and great multitudes of these conscripts were now practically brigands living upon the countryside. Moscow in October and November, 1917, swarmed with such men. They banded themselves together, they went into houses and looted and raped, no one interfering. Law and administration had vanished. Robbed and murdered men lay neglected in the streets for days together.

This we have to remember was the state of affairs when the Bolsheviks came into power; it was not brought about by their usurpation. For a time in their attempts to restore order anyone found bearing arms was shot. Thousands of men were seized and shot, and it is doubtful if Moscow could have been restored to even a semblance of order without some such violence. The debacle of Tsarist Russia was so complete that the very framework and habit of public order had gone. "They had to shoot," President Masaryk once told the writer. And then he added, "They went on shooting—unreasonably, cruelly."

In the spring of 1918 the Bolsheviks had secured control of the large towns, the railways and the shipping of most of Russia. A Constituent Assembly had been dissolved and dispersed in January; the Bolsheviks could not work with it; it was too divided in its aims and counsels, they alleged, for vigorous action; and in March peace, a very submissive peace, with Germany was signed at Brest-Litovsk.

At the head of the Bolshevik dictatorship, which now set itself to govern Russia, was Lenin, a very energetic and clear-witted man who had spent most of his life in exile in London and Geneva, engaged in political speculations and the obscure politics of the Russian Marxist organizations. He was a quite honest revolutionary, simply living and indefatigable, with no experience whatever of practical administration. Associated with him was Trotsky, an exile from New York, who was presently to develop considerable practical military ability. Radek, Lunarcharsky, Zinoviev, Zorin, Kamenev, Krassin, were other conspicuous members of the small group which now set itself to reorganize Russia and steer it straight out of its disastrous position to a communist millennium. And in the end they did restore its social integrity.

At first the ideas of the Bolshevik leaders went far beyond Russia. The world, they realized, was becoming one system, in which it would be impossible to have more than one social and economic order. They called on the workers everywhere to unite, overthrow the capitalist system, and so bring about the planless, shapeless, Marxist millennium. But this procedure naturally brought them into conflict with all other existing governments. It added to their task of establishing communism in Russia the task of maintaining her against a series of counter-attacks to which this denunciation of foreign governments exposed her.

In two or three years the failure of the Bolsheviks so far as the establishment of a working communism went, and their demonstration of the uncreative barrenness of the Marxist doctrine, was complete. They did not get Russia to her feet again. They were quite unable to get the shattered Russian industry going. Most of their leaders were of the writing, talking type, without any managerial experience.

At the outset of their rule their narrow class-hatred inspired them to destroy most of what remained in Russia of the class of works-managers, technical experts, foremen, and the like. They had no systematic knowledge—and the conceit of the Marxist doctrinaires prompted them to despise any knowledge they did not possess—of the psychology of the worker at work. They had not even the practical working knowledge of the old capitalist they despised. All they knew about that sort of thing was the psychology of the worker in a mass meeting. They tried to run Russia by exhortation, and neither the worker when he returned to the factory nor the peasant when he got back to his plough responded with any practical results. Transport and mechanical production in the towns fell steadily into dislocation and decay, and the peasant produced for his own needs and hid his surplus.

When the writer visited Petersburg in 1920 he beheld an astonishing spectacle of desolation. It was the first time a modern city had collapsed in this fashion. Nothing had been repaired for four years. There were great holes in the streets where the surface had fallen into the broken drains; lamp-posts lay as they had fallen; not a shop was open, and most were boarded up over their broken windows. The scanty drift of people in the streets wore shabby and incongruous clothing, for there were no new clothes in Russia, no new boots. Many people wore bast wrappings on their feet. People, city, everything were shabby and threadbare. Even the Bolshevik commissars had scrubby chins, for razors and such-like things were neither being made nor imported. The death-rate was enormous, and the population of this doomed city was falling by the hundred thousand every year.

There are many reasons for believing that even in 1918 and 1919 the Bolshevik dictatorship would have recognized the error of its ways and begun to adapt itself to the unanticipated factors in the situation in which it found itself. They were narrow and doctrinaire, but many of them were men of imagination and intellectual flexibility, and there can be no disputing that, in all the evil they did, they were honest in intention and devoted in method. Manifestly they were attempting to work out an experiment of great value to mankind and should have been left in peace. They would have been forced to link their system on to the slowly evolved tradition of the monetary system, and to come to dealings with the incurable individualism of the peasant cultivator. But they were not left to themselves. From the outset of their career they raised a frenzy of opposition in Western Europe and America. None of the tolerance that had been shown the almost equally incapable and disastrous regime of the Tsar was shown to the Marxist adventurers. They were universally boycotted, and the reactionary governments of France and Great Britain subsidized and assisted every sort of adventurer within and without Russia to assail them.

A Press campaign confused the public mind by a stream of fantasies and evil suggestions about the Bolsheviks. They were, it is true, doctrinaire men with an incomplete social theory, muddling along in a shattered country. Among their subordinates were brutish and vile men. Any government in Russia would have had poor material in its administration and feeble powers of control over it. But anti-Bolshevik propaganda represented the Moscow adventurers as an abomination unparalleled in the world's history, and implied that their mere removal would be sufficient to restore happiness and hope to Russia. Something like a crusade against the Bolsheviks was preached, and a vivid reaction in their favour was produced in the minds of liberal thinkers who might otherwise have remained more critical.

As a consequence of this organized hostility, the Bolsheviks in Russia were forced from the very beginning into an attitude of defence against foreign aggression. The persistent hostility of the Western governments to them strengthened them greatly in Russia. In spite of the internationalist theories of the Marxists, the Bolshevik government in Moscow became a patriotic government defending the government against foreigners, and in particular defending the peasant against the return of the landowner and debt-collector. It was a paradoxical position; communism in Russia created peasant proprietors. And Trotsky, who had been a pacifist, was educated until he became a great general in spite of himself.

But this militarism, and this patriotism which was thus forced upon Lenin's government, this concentration of attention upon the frontiers, hampered any effective reconstruction of police and disciplinary method within, even had the Bolsheviks been capable of such reconstruction. The old inquisitorial and tyrannous Tsarist police was practically continued under the new government. A clumsy and inaccurate detective system with summary powers and bloodthirsty traditions struggled against foreign emissaries from abroad and against sedition, fear, and betrayal within, and incidentally gratified its ugly craving for punishment. In July, 1918, the Tsar and his family—there being some danger of their being rescued by reactionary troops—were massacred at the instance of a minor official. In January, 1919, four Grand Dukes, uncles of the Tsar, were executed at Petersburg by the police commission, in flat defiance of Lenin's reprieve.

For five years the Russian people, under this strange and unprecedented rule, maintained its solidarity against every attempt to divide and subjugate it. In August, 1918, British and French forces landed at Archangel; they were withdrawn in September, 1919. The Japanese made strenuous attempts from 1918 onward to establish themselves in Eastern Siberia. In 1919 the Russians were fighting not only the British at Archangel and the Japanese, but they had a reactionary force under Admiral Koltchak against them in Siberia, Roumanians in the south with French and Greek contingents, and General Denikin with an army of Russian reactionaries and enormous supplies of British and French war material and the support of the French fleet in the Crimea.

In July Koltchak and Denikin had united and held South-eastern Russia from Odessa to Ufa, and an Esthonian army under General Yudenitch was marching on Petersburg. It seemed as though the end of Bolshevism could be but a question of weeks or days. Yet by the end of the year Yudenitch was routed and forgotten, Koltchak was in full retreat to Siberia, and Denikin to the Black Sea. Denikin and the remnant of his forces were taken off by British and French ships in the early part of 1920, and Koltchak was captured and shot in Siberia.

But Russia was to have no respite. The Poles, incited by the French, opened a new campaign in April, 1920, and a fresh reactionary raider, General Wrangel, resumed the task of Denikin in invading and devastating his own country. The Poles, after being driven back upon Warsaw, recovered, with French assistance and supplies, and made a victorious advance into Russian territory; and a treaty, much to the territorial advantage of Poland, was made at Riga in October, 1920. Wrangel, after destroying the crops and food over great areas, suffered the fate of Denikin, and retired upon the hospitality of the Western powers at the end of the year. In March, 1921, the Bolshevik government had to suppress, and did suppress, an insurrection of the sailors in Kronstadt, "the Pretorian Guard of Bolshevism."

Throughout 1920 the hostility to the Bolsheviks in Western Europe and America was slowly giving way to saner conceptions of the situation. There were many difficulties in the way of "recognizing" the Bolshevik government fully and completely, difficulties largely due to the unreason that also prevailed on the Bolshevik side, but by the end of 1920 a sort of uncivil peace existed between Russia and most of the rest of the world, and American, British, and French inquirers were able to go in and out of the country. Early in 1921 both Britain and Italy made Trade Agreements with Russia; Russian representatives in the form of "Trade Delegations" reopened communications between that outcast land and the rest of the world.

But now a new and still more frightful disaster was preparing for the Russian people. In 1921 there was an unusual drought. The attentive reader of this history will have noted already what a precarious and fluctuating thing is the climate of the great land areas about the Caspian Sea. Naturally these are nomadic lands; it is doubtful if they will ever be safe for a mainly agricultural population. Now, with the drought, the crops over vast areas of South-eastern Russia failed absolutely, and the most terrible famine in the whole recorded history of our race ensued. Millions perished. Multitudes, whole villages, and townships sat down in their homes to die, and died. Many ate hay and earth and indescribable filth. Men dug in the graveyards and became cannibals. Great areas were depopulated.

Yet there was corn to burn not only in America but even in the Ukraine and Roumania and Hungary. But the communications of this country had been hopelessly shattered by the operations of Koltchak, Denikin, and Wrangel, and the Bolshevik government had neither the resources nor the ability to cope with this monstrous disaster. An American commission and a commission under Dr. Nansen, the great Arctic explorer, organized relief with the assent and assistance of the government, and fairly generous American supplies were poured into the country. But the chief European governments responded grudgingly or not at all to the extreme appeal of the situation. The British government, which had spent a hundred millions in illegitimate military operations against her former ally, smirched the good name of Britain in the world by refusing any contribution to the work of relief. So little, as yet, had the lesson of human solidarity that the first World War should have taught mankind been learnt.

While the hapless multitudes perished in Russia, corn wasted in the granaries a few hundred miles away, and in Western Europe ships lay up for want of freight, steel works where rails and engines could have been made stood idle, and millions of workmen were unemployed because, said the business men, "there was nothing for them to do." And thousands of square miles of South-eastern Russia became a desert of abandoned fields and of towns and villages of the dead.

Yet amidst this desolation the Bolshevik government remained. And gradually the necessity of recognizing and dealing with this strange new sort of state, however uncongenial it might be, was borne in upon the European mind. To this day the Western world still wrestles with that necessity. At the time of writing, the problem of correlating a capitalist system with a communist system upon one planet, from which the separations of great distances are vanishing, remains unsolved.

Bolshevik propaganda, turning away from the hostile West, shows itself increasingly disposed to appeal to the masses of indigent population in India and China. There had always been two sides to the Bolsheviks, a side of "Westernizers" who wanted to use science, machinery and big productive organization, of whom Lenin and Trotsky were typical, and a side of "Easternizers," whose disposition was militant and primitive and mystical, of whom Zinoviev was the chief. The policies of the British and French governments were turning the Bolshevik government steadily eastward. Under the influence of its example, the world of Islam seemed to be resuming its long arrested development. More and more in this period did the attitude of the Bolshevik regime towards the Atlantic civilizations, which have dominated the world for two and a half centuries, assimilate to that of Islam. It became implacable and obstructive. The Western powers, divided among themselves by bitter rivalries and conflicting interests, encountered also a steadily increasing resistance to their methods and exploitations in Russia, Turkey, North Africa and all Asia. This gathering resistance, and the waning energy of the thrust against it, give the true measure of the catastrophe of 1914–1918. The days of Western European world-predominance were drawing to their close.

Until the death of Lenin in 1924, the innate contradictions inside the Bolshevik party were concealed. He had dominated his colleagues as no one else could, partly because of his unique personality, but even more because he had been their leader before the Revolution, chosen in a free and equal society where (unlike under Stalin) nothing but merit counted. He was, to the end of his life, first among equals. When he was outvoted, as he was on his original proposal to make peace with Germany, he was content to wait, democratically, until events brought the majority round to his side. His mind was agile enough, after the Kronstadt revolt of 1921, to realize that a swift reversal of policy was necessary, and persuasive enough to carry the party with him in instituting the "New Economic Policy", which restored large areas of the less important forms of production and distribution to small private enterprise. This was never intended, of course, as more than an interim programme, a temporary backward step in the march towards Socialism; but for the moment it provided a great relief to a famine stricken land. His personal life was austere, no easier than that of the workers around him, and so long as he was alive there was no ostentation among Russian rulers; no city was named after him while he was alive. But as soon as he was dead the standards of the elite which he had led began to depreciate; the strain on them was too great. There were only a few thousand who had been trained in the pre-war school of international Socialism and underneath them were millions of dark people who had till recently been living in the Middle Ages; it was probably inevitable that there would be in some form or other, a great falling away from Leninist ideals. For no new generation of rebels was coming to reinforce the old rulers; the enrolled Communists came immediately under a strict discipline; the last Party conference at which there was any freedom of speech met soon after Lenin's death. The process of restoring an oligarchy, if not in deed an autocracy, was slow; and the Bolshevik slogans remained unchanged. The first step was even represented as a defence of democracy; Trotsky, Lenin's most eminent colleague, was accused of dictatorial ambitions and deprived of his offices. He was manœuvred out by three of his colleagues, two of whom, Zinovieff and Kameneff, were well-known; the third, Stalin, had played a relatively small part in the revolution, but was in charge of the party machine. Lenin, in his last "testament" had warned that he should be moved to some other post, but the warning came too late. It was not long before all but one of the members of the Central Committee bitterly regretted their inattention.

§ 6

The British Empire emerged from the first World War very severely strained physically and morally. The cream of the younger generation was dead, or weakened by wounds and the distortions of military subjugation. Her routines of government and her habits of freedom had been greatly disorganized by the emergency legislation necessary in the struggle, and her Press had been badly disordered by its devotion to propaganda. The news of things foreign had deteriorated notably. The general public was not only badly informed upon its imperial responsibilities but too preoccupied by business cataclysms to attend to them. It was a time of opportunity for the foolish and self-important official, and everywhere he made the most of his opportunities.

Everywhere throughout the empire, except in those portions that were already self-governing, there was a parallel process at work—an almost systematic exasperation of the subject populations by restraints, unreasonable regulations, slights, arbitrary arrests, and such-like interferences with liberty.

Everywhere the military and the official class were out of hand. Everywhere the old Tory element seems to have been bent upon provoking an explosion.

This was equally true of India and Egypt and Ireland. In these years of neglect and weakened central control a policy of repression, broken promises to the native, and of illusory reforms to still the uneasy conscience at home, stirred even the pacific Indian population to something close upon rebellion. Warnings and remonstrances went for a time unheeded. The clumsy recruiting methods of the administration of the Punjab had changed this part of India from one of the most loyal to one of the most unsettled of Indian provinces. There was rioting and attacks on Europeans, and a sort of official Terror culminated in the massacre of Amritsar (April, 1919), when a large crowd, for the most part unarmed, was fired upon and 379 people killed and over a thousand injured. The news of this outrage did not reach the conscience of the British public at home until the publication of the Hunter Report, late in 1919. Then for a time the better elements in English life asserted themselves. A regime of conciliation under Lord Reading as Viceroy was, however, thwarted and falsified by the reactionary elements in the government. In 1922 Mr. Gandhi, a saint-like preacher of passive resistance, was sentenced to six years' incarceration, and so made into a martyr.

A similar conflict went on in Egypt. A disposition to conciliation was crippled and thwarted by the pervading impulse to suppress. But the most tragic and pitiful story in all this melancholy record of British inadequacy in a time of magnificent opportunities is the story of the widening breach between the Irish and the English peoples.

In the days of those great and generous Irish statesmen, the brothers Redmond, it had still seemed possible for the two islands to live side by side, co-operating freely and willingly in a state of friendly and equal unity, sharing the imperial responsibilities of Britain and facing the world together. Their close proximity demands so close a bond. The prosperity of Ireland and England is like the prosperity of the Siamese Twins, whose bodies were linked arterially. Past wrongs and religious conflicts should not be sufficient to prevent an intelligent and wholesome co-operation. But it was not past wrongs, but present wrongs, which drove Ireland towards separation. We have told already how Sir Edward Carson, that evil genius of the British peoples, first introduced arms into Ireland and set going a horrible process of violence and reprisal in the land; how at the outset of the war Ireland was cheated of her Home Rule, and how the British Government, of which Mr. Asquith was the head, blindly or deliberately insulted Ireland by including this man of blood and sedition in the Coalition Government. We have told, too, how the Dublin rebellion was suppressed and punished, and how Ireland was further embittered. The results are plain upon the page of history.

In 1914 Ireland came into the first World War as freely and gallantly as England. It was still an orderly and civilized country. By the end of that struggle Ireland was a rebel country forcibly held. Extreme imperialism had produced its reaction in an extreme nationalism. Ireland was now set upon becoming a republic entirely independent of Great Britain.

A new Home Rule Bill passed the British parliament in 1920. It established two separate parliaments, one in Ulster and one in the rest of Ireland, but with arrangements for their co-operation and possible fusion. It was by the standard of previous Home Rule Bills a generous measure. But the Irish would have none of it. The Sinn Feiners who had been elected to the parliament of 1919 would not even appear at Westminster to discuss it. And meanwhile methods of insurrection and exasperation on the one hand and a policy of repression on the other were making the whole country a field of guerrilla warfare. The insurgents raided, ambushed, assassinated, and at length fought little pitched battles with small detachments of troops. The English troops, well-behaved at first, were presently tempted and encouraged to embark upon "reprisals." A special auxiliary police, the "Black and Tans," was organized, and distinguished itself by its rough-handed methods.

There was a steady crescendo of outrages. Every murder led to fresh murders on one side or the other. If a soldier or a Black and Tan was killed then someone on the other side was killed, who might or might not have been privy to the initial killing. Each side in this feud sought to outdo the other in ruthlessness. At last no one was safe in his home and his bed. In the night men of one faction or the other might come knocking at the door with some real or fancied accusation. Men were shot at their own doors; presently whole families were massacred. In December, 1920, in revenge for the ambushing of a party of eleven military cadets near Cork, the military broke out, killing and looting, so that property to the value of £3,000,000 was destroyed. In such an atmosphere robbing and brigandage flourished.

The Home Rule Bill became law in 1921, creating two Irish parliaments, one for the north and one for the south. The northern parliament was duly elected, and opened by the King in state on May 22, 1921. The southern Irish would have nothing to do with the southern parliament, and it never assembled. Instead there met in Dublin a self-constituted body, the Dail Eireann, professing to be the parliament of independent Ireland, and electing as its president a Mr. De Valera, who had been its chief creator.

The King, in opening the northern parliament, had made an extremely conciliatory speech. Mr. Lloyd George, the British Prime Minister, seizing upon this, invited Mr. De Valera and Sir James Craig to a conference upon Irish affairs in London, a truce to violence was called, a truce that was kept as well as the already disorganized state of the country permitted, and on October 11th, 1921, a conference opened in London in which Mr. De Valera and his chosen colleagues from the Dail Eireann, practically in the character of men who have conducted an armed insurrection to a successful issue, treated with the representatives of the British Government upon the future status of Ireland.

This was a thing almost as agreeable to thoughtful Englishmen as it would have been to an American in 1863 to have seen Jefferson Davis treating with Abraham Lincoln in Washington upon the future status of the cotton states. For the complete separation of Ireland from Britain promised to be not a merely inconvenient thing, but a very dangerous and, it may be, a disastrous thing, for both countries. But this practical admission of defeat was a pill which the Englishman had allowed his chosen friends the Carsonites to make up for him, and he had to swallow it with as good a grace as possible. The spectacle in Whitehall in October, 1921, during the Downing Street conference was a very curious one. There was a great and defiant display of Irish flags and Irish national symbols, and the behaviour of the London crowd was not simply tolerant but friendly and sympathetic.

After much wrangling, a settlement was finally worked out and confirmed both by the British parliament and—with resistance and reluctance—by Dail Eireann. Subject to a final allegiance to the British crown and certain naval and aerial restrictions, all Ireland, with the exception of Protestant Ulster under the northern parliament, became an independent state, the Irish Free State. This was a great triumph of reasonableness and the desire for peace. It conceded a practical freedom; it reserved a formal union. But it was threatened on either side.

Mr. De Valera objected because it divided Ireland and was not sufficiently humiliating for Great Britain, and he incited his followers to revolt against the new Free State. Sir Edward Carson, now a judge and Lord Carson, also did his best, in spite of the decorum customary to judges, to keep alive the spirit of violence and bloodshed in Ulster. So that it was with difficulty and to the tune of nocturnal shots and screams that the Irish Free State struggled into being. The country was full of young men who had learnt no trade but guerrilla warfare, habits of disorder and violence had taken a deep hold upon the population, and a civil war between the Republicans under De Valera and the Free State army ensued.

Such briefly was the story of the practical separation of Ireland from England. All that followed was to widen and deepen that separation. Michael Collins and Kevin O'Higgins, the two Irish statesmen who might have been able and willing to bridge it, were murdered. De Valera, abandoning civil war, succeeded to power by Parliamentary means and devoted himself to widening it. A new constitution declared Ulster to be a part of what was now called "Eire"; the threat, fortunately, remained only verbal. But in 1936 De Valera took advantage of the abdication crisis to cut all constitutional connections with the British Commonwealth except the one that consisted in having Irish envoys accredited in the name of the King. So slight, however, was this connection that during the second World War Eire remained neutral, kept its envoy in Berlin and officially condoled with the Germans on the death of Hitler. When, after the war, a rival coalition unseated De Valera, it severed even this last formal bond.

This series of events, which to American and British people alike must be a source of profound anxiety and regret, was a foreseeable result of the methods used by the British governing class in the inter-war period in dealing with the Empire's subject populations.

At one time it had seemed as though the British Empire was to be the foster-mother of a great and exemplary confederation of free nations, either speaking English or using English as a *lingua franca,* and developing one great tradition of open speech, plain dealing, and justice throughout the world. At one time it had seemed that this great network, strengthened by a deepening understanding and a closer and closer co-operation with the United States of America, might play a leading part in binding all the world together into a still greater unity. But the British ruling class, between the wars, was unable or unwilling to take its opportunities. Its education was too limited and its courage too small. The Governments between the wars, but for two fleeting episodes, were Conservative or Conservative-led, and for them conservatism meant holding on to what they had. They resisted to the last what they still considered to be subject races; when they had to yield, they did so late and grudgingly, leaving contempt and division behind them where they might have had gratitude and co-operation. That nationalism in its crudest form still rules and poisons the minds of peoples in Asia and Africa as well as Europe is partly the fault of the British politicians of the twenties and thirties; an opportunity was offered to them that never recurred. The problems they evaded or tried to suppress were to return after the second World War, in a far more dangerous form; nor would there be any solutions as simple and obvious as those which were vainly advocated to them at the earlier date.

§ 7

We have already noted the downfall of the Manchu dominion over China in 1911. This marks the realization by the Chinese intelligence of the outworn nature of its ancient imperial system. The old garment was cast aside. But there was no new garment ready to wear. The great mass of the population went on as it had gone on through century after century, industrious, illiterate, prolific, poor, peaceful and conservative, and overhead the educated minority struggled to discover efficient new forms to replace the supreme government that had grown threadbare and vanished away.

In the south a westernizing republicanism spread under the leadership of Dr. Sun Yat-sen, and the new government set up in Peking was republican and parliamentary in form. The reality of power rested with those who had control of the armed forces of the country, and it seemed probable for a time that a new dynasty would be set up under a great statesman and official, Yuan Shih-K'ai. The monarchy was, indeed, actually restored in 1915, but it vanished again the next year. The Japanese took a diplomatic part in the inevitable dissensions among the Chinese; they supported first this party and then that, in a general policy of preventing the consolidation of a renascent China.

In a belated and ineffective way China joined the allies against Germany in 1917, in the hope of securing a status that would avail it against the inimical pressure of Japan.

From the death of Yuan Shih-K'ai onward the history of China becomes increasingly confused. A number of military leaders sprang up and seized large areas and struggled against each other for the supreme power. Rival Chinese governments sent their representatives to Europe. The United States, Japan and the chief European powers conducted complicated intrigues, supporting this man or that. Meanwhile, the general life continued along time-honoured lines, and there were considerable developments of factory production and banking. Education was modernized, and experiments were made in the simplification of the script. There is something profoundly stirring to the historical imagination in the spectacle of this vast population dissolving the ancient bonds of its administrative fabrics and seeking blindly and gropingly for the new possibilities of social organization and collective power.

China had been condemned after the Boxer troubles to pay heavy indemnities to the various powers whose subjects had suffered in these risings. The Americans, with great wisdom, had remitted the payments due to them on condition that they were earmarked for education, and a considerable number of Chinese students were sent to American colleges as the first-fruits of this generous idea. The French were more inclined towards banking and railway enterprise. The British and Japanese assigned their share vaguely between educational, sanitary, relief and economically beneficial works.

The Americans, at one time, seemed likely to be the spiritual fathers of a new China. But the young graduates who returned from the States with a wide knowledge of Western culture, and of Western industrial progress, almost without exception became followers of a native Chinese philosopher, Dr. Sun Yat-sen, already mentioned on a previous page. Dr. Sun for the Chinese became for a while as important a teacher and philosopher as Lenin did for Russians: for a quarter of a century his Will was ceremoniously read at public meetings, his picture was bowed to, and his "Three Principles" were assumed to be the basis of all political programmes. These Three Principles were: (1) Nationalism, by which he did not mean the ordinary nationalism, which has devastated Europe and Asia, but the substitution of devotion to the community for devotion to the family; he did, as was inevitable in China of that day, include in this first principle the need to remove foreigners from their privileged position; (2) Democracy—the rule of the people, including women, who had been till then assumed to be an inferior sex; (3) Social Justice, or Popular Livelihood—the word is difficult to translate. Eighty per cent. of the Chinese people were farmers; nearly all were indebted either to the moneylender, or the landlord, or both. The phrase may have been vague; its meaning to the average Chinaman, or to Dr. Sun, was not.

The principles of Dr. Sun and Nikolai Lenin were not far separated, neither were the needs of the Russian and Chinese revolutionaries. An agreement was easily come to, and in 1924 a member of the Russian Communist Party, Michael Borodin, assisted Dr. Sun to organize the Kuomintang, a party based upon his Three Principles. Local branches were opened, strict discipline was enforced, workers and peasants were enrolled, and a military section was organized in Canton (the only great city Dr. Sun controlled) under the direction of a young Chinese officer named Chiang Kai-Shek. All the rest of China was under the control of "war-lords," as Britain had been during the Heptarchy: they paid no attention to what was going on in the South. Yen, Wu, Feng, Lu, Chang were names which for some years seemed to have importance; there was a shadow of a government in Peking to cover their operations, but it did not even have enough power to stop them from making open war on each other when they chose. By 1926 the reorganized Kuomintang felt that it was ready to deal with them. Its newly trained troops swept aside the discontented and incompetent soldiers of the war-lords; "Marshals" fell down like Aunt Sallies. Within a few months all South China was in their hands. To cross to the North, and to take control of the Yang-tse-Kiang, the great river on which so much of Chinese trade depended, they had to deal with a more formidable enemy—the foreigners, of whom at the moment the British seemed the most arrogant and against whom a Kuomintang trade boycott had been operating for months. There was a tense moment when the Kuomintang troops captured Hankow, the enormous triple trading city far up the Yangtse, where there was a British "concession," and made it clear, by strikes as well as armed threats, that foreign control must end. Fortunately, the British Government was wiser than the "old China hands" in Shanghai who wrote articles calling for war: it opened negotiations and handed over to the Chinese the concessions in Hankow and Kiukiang. The foreigner had been defeated. The Kuomintang armies, directed by Chiang Kai-Shek, who had married Dr. Sun's sister-in-law, went north and captured Peking; there were now no independent war-lords left except Chang who had the isolated principality of Manchuria, and, just south of him, Feng, a once-famous "Christian general" (he was said to have baptized his armies with a hosepipe) who declared his complete conversion to Kuomintang principles.

But hopes for a peaceful and united China were to be dashed; Dr. Sun, the one man who could have held the Kuomintang together, had died in 1925. In 1927 the directors of the Communist International decided that the time had come to make the further step (logically necessary, in their view) from the confused "petty bourgeois and peasant" control by the Kuomintang to a proletarian dictatorship. Borodin himself, and Dr. Sun's widow, are said to have protested; but to no purpose. The attempt, based upon recent and turbulent trade unions, was made; the answer by General Chiang Kai-Shek was crushing. At the outset, the revolutionaries controlled Hankow while Chiang's base was the new capital, Nanking. Only a few weeks had passed before the Communists were flying remnants and Chiang was in control of the whole Chinese government machine. But to be in control of the machine was not to be in control of China: if Chiang had carried out the Three Principles all might have been well, but in order to break the Hankow revolutionaries he had had to rely upon the old class of landlords, officials, and employers; and anything in the nature of a social revolution was now impossible.

Roads were built, many miles of railroad were constructed, factories were started, much educational work was done, foreign powers were helpful, and foreign capital was invested. But the peasants found no relief from their indebtedness (let alone from their rents), and the town workers found their efforts to help themselves by trade union action simply forbidden. Of the Three Principles, the Chinese people received from the Kuomintang government something of the First ("Nationalism")—the foreigner had been sharply put back in his place and the worship of the family had been partly superseded—;

a very little of the second ("Democracy"), for though China was a Republic in which women were fairly treated, and some democratic formulæ were adhered to, the State was in fact a Party dictatorship headed by "Generalissimo" Chiang Kai-Shek; and nothing at all of the Third ("Social Justice"). The defeated Communists, who in their ruin learned to pay more attention to the peasants' demands and less to the theories of the Marx-Engels Institute in Moscow, found many supporters in the villages, and in two Central provinces, Kiang-si and Hu-nan, were able to set up units of government which for years defied Chiang's attempts to destroy them. This, and the almost greater nuisance of guerilla warfare, also prevented him from making China into a united State. Two war-lords remained: Chang was effectively independent in Manchuria, and the sly Christian General Feng north of Peking managed to keep his troops under his own hand. So long, however, as the world outside was at peace these things seemed not to matter greatly.

In the nearer East, Persia had before the first World War been a happy hunting ground for European diplomats and a very wretched land for men and women to live in. Russia pressed upon the unfortunate country from the north, Britain from the Persian Gulf; each did what it could to discredit and injure the other; great oil resources had been discovered and the American oil interests pursued devious paths of instigation and support. A parody of Western parliamentary government existed under a Shah, and the reality of power shifted between a number of scrambling feudal chiefs. They raided and murdered one another. The Russians had put in a Cossack brigade nominally to obey the government, but really to control it. The British had created a countervailing body, a *gendarmerie* officered by Swedes, which was understood to be international-spirited. These conflicting bodies muddled and murdered in the name of Western order. The Germans intrigued through the Turks to the detriment of both British and French.

The protection, diversion or destruction of oil pipe-lines is the key to the complex strategy of the situation. The first World War was for Persia a story of raids, marches, seizures and adventures by Cossacks, Germans, British and native tribal forces. As the victory swayed between Germany and her antagonists, the Persians, who cared nothing for these European disputes, propitiated or attacked the British. For a time after the war the British were ascendant in Persia, but in 1920 their position began to be seriously threatened by a Bolshevik invasion which resumed the ancient pressures of the Tsarist system. But gradually something more native and more detached from the conventions of diplomacy asserted itself. Persian national consciousness was growing, and the prestige of the West was fading. A strong man appeared, Riza Khan, who seized the government in 1921, retaining the nominal headship of the Shah. He made a treaty with Soviet Russia that established the country upon a footing of greater independence than it had enjoyed for many years. In 1926 he dispensed with the Shah and made himself ruler; the change was mostly one of names.

From Persia in the east to the Atlantic coast of Morocco, along the whole line of contact between ancient Christendom and the Muhammadan world, these post-war years display a complex of troubles and conflicts between Islam and the European powers and far more solidarity and unity of purpose, and even, at last, unity of action, is apparent upon the Islamic than the western side. The European powers, blind to their growing danger, continued to intrigue against each other, upon seventeenth and eighteenth century lines. The trade in armament, open or furtive, flourished. It became more and more difficult to retain the loyalty of native levies.

In Morocco, Spain sustained a wasteful unending war against a gathering insurrection equipped with European and American weapons. There were disasters, retreats and withdrawals, and a certain Abd-el-Krim rose to leadership over the Riffs. Meanwhile the French held Fez and spread and sustained their dominions to the south of the Riff tribes, refraining from any co-operation with the Spanish until in 1925 Abd-el-Krim turned his guns and rifles against them and opened the prospect of a long and dangerous war.

A hundred and twenty thousand men were speedily involved in the struggle on the French side. French checks in Morocco produced a repercussion in the mandatory territories of Syria. The Druses rose against the French and inflicted serious losses. The Arab population became unhelpful and dangerous. The danger to Fez became also a danger to Damascus. To the south, the Wahabite Arabs were able to force the British-protected King of the Hedjaz to a resignation (1923) and exile. They took Mecca and spread their power slowly and surely into the ear-marked territory. In Egypt there was almost incessant trouble; the Egyptians under British rule were like boiling milk beneath a lid.

Everywhere in the Moslem world, Italy, France, Britain and Germany were destroying the ancient prestige of the West by their propaganda activities, and arousing Islam to a new self-consciousness. Turks, Arabs, Egyptians and Moslem India discussed European Imperialism together and discovered a common interest in its supersession. The pressure on the French in Morocco was presently relieved by the military and administrative genius of Marshal Lyautey, and Abd-el-Krim was captured and sent into exile in 1926. The British Government, with its usual air of yielding ungraciously and under pressure what the natural liberalism of its home population was only too ready to concede, consented, after a long struggle against Zaghlul Pasha and the nationalist organization called the Wafd, to make the abolition of the British Protectorate and the Egyptian Declaration of Independence (1928) fully effective. The old protectorate was replaced by a treaty of offensive and defensive alliance, first projected in 1930 and signed in 1937, by which Egypt became eligible for admission to the League of Nations as an independent sovereign power. The situation in the Western Mediterranean was complicated for the British in Palestine because of that schizophrenia of the Foreign Office which had given contradictory promises to the Arabs and the Zionist Jews. The long and intricate struggle of a certain section of the world-wide community of Jews to return to a country that had ceased to be even nominally Jewish in the days of Alfred the Great and in which (see Chapter 18, §§ 2 and 3) it is highly probable the bulk of their ancestors had never lived at all, witnesses to the power of historical assertion over fact. The immigrants were from the first resented by the Arab natives, but for so long as the flow was small the problem seemed not insoluble. But the energy of Dr. Chaim Weizmann and his fellow-zealots was reinforced by the recrudescence of anti-Semitism in Europe which made it a matter of life and death to find a home for fleeing Jews. The Jewish settlers claimed with much truth that they cultivated the land better than the natives, and were introducing industries never before known; the Arab resistance and anger merely grew the greater. The Jewish colonists were united by religious habits and observances and a belief that they were a "Chosen People"; the backward and half-feudal Arabs were in no state to resist. When they tried open violence, the British Mandatory power put them down by force. But even before 1939 it was clear that worse was to come; it was also clear that the governing power had no plans with which to meet the impending disaster. Both sides based their claims on religion and refused to discuss them reasonably; both looked to support from outside, the one from Islam and the other to world Jewry.

§ 8

In our account of the first French Revolution we have already discussed the elementary relations of credit and currency to social life. But the social dislocation caused in France by the Revolution and the wars that ensued was trivial in comparison with the immense displacements in Europe after the first World War. The community of the end of the eighteenth century was altogether more simple and autonomous than the intricately interwoven European community of the present time. Its economic and social life was contained within its own borders. But the peculiar difficulty of the modern situation is that while economic relationships and reactions, because of the vast change in the means of communication, have long since transcended the boundaries of existing states, while now staple commodities and labour can be moved in mass from almost any part of the world to another—a thing never known before except in case of the food supply of imperial Rome—men still clung to the petty political divisions, the isolated sovereign states established under the superseded conditions.

The delusion of national sovereignty, with its attendant fanaticisms for "God, King and Country" and the like, is the most monstrous of all superstitions at present active in the world. Each state must be free to make its own money, regulate its own credit, hamper transport through its territory and set up tariff barriers to the flow of trade. Each must incur its own debts and remain obstructive, hostile and armed to the teeth against its essentially similar neighbours. Each must maintain its own educational system, teach a partial and lying history, and instil a poisonous national conceit and a poisonous hostility to foreigners in each new generation.

The consequence to Europe of this inherited curse of unfederalized sovereign states was that, when the process of economic confusion and exhaustion that had appeared in France after the French Revolution recurred in Europe

on a much vaster scale after the first World War, it was enormously complicated by the international tangle. Every state was impoverished, but every state
had figured up debts against every other state for national aid in the war in
which they were allies, and fantastic debt charges had been imposed upon the
vanquished. Although the United States in the later stages of the war had been
an antagonist of Germany and had suffered less than any European state concerned, American munitions had been supplied at exaggerated prices to all
her allies, and Europe was now stupendously indebted to America.

A frank repudiation of most of these war debts and war claims would have
cleared the air for all the world, but only a powerful federal government in Europe could have been so bold and frank. Europe had no federal government,
no world politicians, no broad-minded leaders, but only parochial-minded
kings, statesmen, politicians, tariff-sustained business leaders, newspapers
limited in outlook to their language and distribution areas, state-supported
teachers, national universities, and groups of "patriotic" financiers; and all
were terrified at the bare idea of any greater system that would obliterate
the abundant personal advantages they enjoyed at the expense of the European
commonweal. They would not have a common Europe; they would not hear
of it; they would rather have had Europe dead than denationalized. As soon
would flies abolish a manure-heap.

So all Europe west of Russia passed politically into a Shylock phase;
schemes for the repayment of those fantastic war debts consumed the public
mind, and meanwhile each sovereign state followed its own devices with
money. Many people were catastrophically impoverished, many became fantastically rich by speculation, and it seemed wiser to spend money than to
accumulate it. If there was a failure to produce houses for ordinary people
there was no let or hindrance to the building and improvement of luxury
hotels; there was never so much dancing in Europe and never so sedulous a
pursuit of sport and pleasure. The face of Europe showed the flush of a wasting fever.

The monetary collapse came first in Russia. There it was fostered and welcomed by the Communist government. Roubles were printed without restraint,
and exchange fell and prices rose until an egg or an apple was sold for 10,000
roubles and the peasant had no more inducement to hoard or to work for
hoarding. It was the intention of the stricter communists to abolish all free
buying and selling. Money was to be rendered valueless, and the work of the
citizen was to be recognized by periodically delivered cards not generally in-
terchangeable but bearing detachable coupons for food, clothing, books, travel
and so forth. But already in 1921 the Bolshevik government was convinced
of the need of recovering that economic fluidity that only money can give,
and a new rouble currency appeared, of which one rouble was worth 10,000
of the older dispensation. This was replaced in 1923 by the chervonetz, a gold
rouble equal in value to the Tsarist rouble before the war.

To the west of Russia there was no attempt to get rid of the use of money
altogether, but there was more or less inflation in every country. The monetary experiences of Germany were extreme, and give the general process in

its completest form. Unable to raise sufficient money by taxation to meet its foreign obligations and its internal necessities, the government resorted to the printing-press. As it increased the amount of marks in circulation, the cost of administration and the price of the foreign currency needed for reparation payments rose, and this necessitated a further resort to the printing-press. In January, 1923, the dollar, which at par had been worth five gold marks, had appreciated to 7,260. Then came a swift collapse. In February it was worth 21,210 paper marks. In July it passed the million point. By the end of the year it was worth four billion paper marks.

The social effects of this fantastic change of trustworthy money to worthless paper were profound. The whole class of people living on investments with fixed interest, retired people, widows and orphans with annuities and so forth, was pauperized and driven to the most abject expedients to live; all scientific, literary and educational activities dependent on endowments stopped. Officials, teachers, professional men and such-like persons living on fixed salaries or fixed fees were never able to increase their stipends in proportion to the rise in prices. There was, in fact, a sort of economic massacre of the poor educated. Rents vanished, but the prices of every necessity soared fantastically.

On the other hand, every mortgagor and every business company was in a position to pay off its debts with worthless paper, and the internal government debt and municipal loans evaporated. For a time export business was feverishly stimulated. Strong checks had to be imposed to prevent the exportation of everything valuable in the land. But the importation of food and raw materials sank to nothing, and employment after an initial spurt rapidly decreased. Food became scarce in the towns because the peasants, realizing the uselessness of money, would now only barter. Hunger, distress and worry were the lot of the mass of the middle classes and of the saving respectable poor. The suicide-rate rose steeply. The birth-rate fell 15 per cent. as compared with the previous year. In spite of this, the infant mortality increased 21 per cent.

Everywhere political trouble broke out, reactionary and insurrectionary movements. Perhaps no other people but the orderly, educated and disciplined Germans could have weathered this storm. In November the government created a new currency. It introduced a new "Rentenmark" secured on the general assets in the country, and it stopped the further printing of the old marks. A Rentenmark was worth a billion paper marks. By restraining the issue severely, the Rentenmark was gradually lifted to success, and so Germany was able to return, also, to its former allegiance to the gold standard. A gold Reichsmark replaced the Rentenmark in 1925, at equal value, and the Rentenmarks were gradually withdrawn.

In several countries, in Austria and Poland for example, the monetary story had been almost as tragic as in Germany. Both staggered back to their present new adjusted currency. The Austrians adopted a new coin of account, the schilling; the Poles, a zloty, both based on gold. Such countries as Czechoslovakia, Greece, Finland, though they inflated, inflated in moderation, and retained their original monetary unit in a kind of stability at about a fifth or a sixth of its former gold value. Italy, France and Belgium inflated within still more narrow limits. The lira sank from 25¼ to below 100 to the pound sterling before the time of Mussolini, and, after a phase of dubious security, went on sinking gradually to 110, 120, 130; it was then put through a regime of severe restriction and "stabilized" at a new level of rather more than a quarter of its original value. The French and Belgian franc and the Spanish peseta sank still more slowly. The franc passed the hundred to the pound limit in 1925, and then after a crisis and a panic was adjusted at about a fifth of its pre-war purchasing power.

The British sovereign fell away from its gold value after the war, but never to the extent of losing more than a third of its worth, and in 1924–25, after strenuous efforts, a restraint upon credit, a check to business enterprise and a grave crisis of unemployment, it was pulled back to its ancient parity with the gold dollar. The Scandinavian countries, Holland and Switzerland experienced relatively small currency exaltations and depressions.

This is history in an arithmetical form. The reader must imagine for himself the enormous volume of fears, anxieties, cruel disappointments, tragic distresses, hardships, privations, illnesses, despairs and deaths these barometric antics of the European currencies would mean if they could be translated into terms of human feeling.

Britain struggled back for a time to the gold standard. It did not give an ideal currency, but it seemed to be the only standard possible in the world while money was still controlled by a multitude of independent governments. Because there was no cosmopolitan government, no federal world government capable of controlling these affairs, it seemed necessary to hand over the economic lordship of the earth to a metal. It was dead stuff; it could not respond to increases and decreases of real wealth; it made every new productive activity pay tribute to the profits of the past; but at least it could not cheat and lie and it had no patriotic prejudices.

But it could be caught and imprisoned. The enormous war-debt payments made to America and France accumulated vast quantities of gold in these two countries. There it was hoarded so that the actual value of the coined dollar in gold became less than the normal "gold dollar" note. The return to the gold standard in a time when the production of commodities in general outran the release of gold for coinage was all to the advantage of the creditor. Prices fell. He reaped more than he had sown and enterprise was crippled.

§ 9

Up till the winter of 1929 the world had been slowly recovering. It was still suffering from the effects of the war, it was distracted in more senses than one, and it may well have been unconsciously hoping for an 1830 or 1848 to clarify its problems for it. However, it was to have something very different—not an upheaval directed by men who, however unpractical, had ideals to inspire them and ideas to offer to their followers, but an impersonal, uncontrolled and insensate disaster, whose origins it did not understand and whose effects were almost wholly evil. So much stress, in earlier sections of this history, has been laid on the defects and disappointments of the post-war world that a short time must be spent on showing why 1929 became for millions of people the last of the golden years to which they looked back.

Firstly, they had security against war. The League of Nations was still, it was true, only a League of some nations; the United States remained sulkily absent; Russia was neither willing nor allowed to come in. But even thus truncated, it had stopped promising little wars in the Aland Isles, Silesia, and Macedonia; it might not have strength to hold back major powers, but no major power had shown any desire to flout it. Italy, in particular, had declared Fascism was "not an article for export" and frequently paid more deference to League opinion than more democratic states. Secondly, there had been a great advance in scientific and industrial knowledge; particularly astonishing to the ordinary man were the adoption of flying as a normal means of travel and the universal use of the wireless for communication. Thirdly, there had at last come a period of prosperity for the ordinary man. There were many exceptions—there were countries like Britain where a foolish financial policy kept a million men unemployed, or like China where poverty was endemic— but on the whole the population of the world had more time for leisure and more to eat than it had had before. The population of the United States indeed seemed almost fantastically rich. These easier conditions were reflected in a greater political freedom. The eastern European nations did not cease persecuting their minorities, but they became milder. The League's Minorities and Mandates Commissions made oppressive practices more difficult and more unpopular. Near Eastern nations like Irak and Egypt did not, it is true, secure uncorrupt and truly democratic governments; but the governments they had were at least at the level of England of the 18th century, which was in the circumstances a great advance. There was even a rapprochement between the British and the Indian nationalists. The outside world had ceased to harry Russia; after a controversy between Trotsky and Stalin over the possibility of "Socialism in one country alone" the latter had won, and turned Trotsky out (1927) with his theory of "permanent revolution." Nobody but professional revolutionaries seemed distressed by this: the Soviet Union next year turned to a "Five Year Plan" for industrial re-equipment which seemed to be, if anything, a guarantee of peaceful intentions to its neighbours. The mildness with which the Bolsheviks treated their deposed leader, who was merely exiled, was frequently contrasted with the savagery of the French Revolution.

The collapse of 1929, as no one will forget who lived through it, began on the 24th October, in Wall Street. It signalized itself merely by the hasty selling, at rapidly falling prices, of securities which the wiser operators already knew were overpriced. But from that moment the panic spread until the whole surface of the world was affected by industrial paralysis: paralysis is an apt word, for it was like a disease, but a disease with no cause in nature. The starvation, the silent factories, the goods thrown away, the men standing idle were the results of human activities. There had been no famines, floods, or national disasters (indeed, at one time men even prayed for these to relieve their troubles); there had not even been wars or devastations. Nevertheless, in the richest country in the world, the United States, "nearly twenty million people were facing starvation in the early months of 1933" (Mr. Hampden Jackson). The condition of poorer countries was correspondingly worse. The crisis continued beyond 1933—indeed, it can be argued that it did not really cease until war and the preparations for war ended it.

There had been commercial crises for nearly a century. Economists, observing them dispassionately as if they had been uncontrollable phenomena (as they may well have been, while private ownership was uncontrolled), noted that they recurred roughly every ten years. None, however, had been quite so disastrous as this; for this one was intensified by the consequences of particular follies. Most of these have been enumerated, but the reader may need to be reminded of them. The first folly was the political and economic clauses of the Versailles Treaty: the predictions of Keynes and others were at last being realized. Old established units like the Austrian empire had been broken up, and feeble little states, each with its tariff wall, had taken their place. Even reforms which were desirable in themselves turned out to be dangerous; the substitution of peasant proprietors for semi-feudal landlords in the centre and east, for example, had caused a fall in agricultural production, and it was only by agriculture that these countries could live. Worse than this was the effect of "reparations"—the belief that the Allied countries could indefinitely live off Germany was having its inevitable results. The Dawes plan, it had been calculated, meant that Germany would pay 80 marks every second, or 288,000 marks an hour, for an unlimited time; the improvement of the Young plan limited the period—to fifty-nine years! Such avaricious dreams could only be realities so long as America was prepared to lend money lavishly to Germany to make payments possible; the moment this ceased to be so, not only Germany but all those leaning on her would collapse. Most disastrous of all, probably, was the financial policy of the United States. The States tried to enforce, by all the means they could short of war, the payment of the "war debts" of their Allies; at the same time their rulers, as blind as they were greedy, prevented the payments being made. Ultimately all international payments had to be made in goods or gold; successive American Congresses increased tariffs until foreign goods were effectively excluded. (The highest known tariff was actually enacted as late as 1930). For a while the problem was evaded by the piling up of a useless mass of gold at Fort Knox, drawn from all foreign countries; for a little longer, again, it was evaded by American loans to debtor countries, but so soon as these loans had to be called in, disaster was certain. As if to make sure that their people's suffering would be as acute as possible, United States businessmen developed instalment selling (hire-purchase) to such an extent that nearly every other family was in debt for some article or other, and gambling in stocks increased so much that in the larger cities even stenographers and labourers were in the game.

The political effects of this disaster, which is now seen to be a dividing line in history, were double. In countries where a change of government was constitutionally possible, the government was thrown out. If it was "Left," a "Right" government was installed, or *vice-versa*—it was almost a matter of chance. Where dictatorships ruled, governments became more ruthless at home, and abroad realized that they could at last act precisely as their narrowest greed suggested to them. The peace-loving powers had no longer the power or will to protect the beginnings of international organizations; the dictators could, and they did, attack their weaker neighbours and start on the path to the second World War.

Certain countries, as has been said, went "Left." Alfonso of Spain hurried out of the country in 1930 and left it to the Republicans. President Hoover and the Republican Party of the United States had so consistently claimed credit for American prosperity that they could not escape responsibility for the disaster: they were dismissed in 1932 by an electorate which was not to forgive them for very many years. The Siamese King was compelled to give up his autocracy the same year, and accept some sort of popular control. But these, at spots so widespread across the world, were almost the only cases where men reacted to the crisis by a new determination to control their own affairs: elsewhere, the story was one of despair, or of acquiescence in the revival of the old methods of tyranny and violence.

A new rash of dictators spotted the South American continent. Getulio Vargas installed himself in Brazil at the end of 1929. Bolivia, Peru, and the Argentine became dictatorships next year; Chile in 1931. In 1932, ignoring the League's appeals, Bolivia and Paraguay embarked on a long and bloody war for a jungle called the Gran Chaco; the war gave an opportunity for Fascist and Nazi agents to enter South America and practice their chosen profession. In India the short period of co-operation between British and Indians ended in 1930 in the resumption of "civil disobedience"; in the Near East King Fuad of Egypt chased out his Parliament, and the Iraki government in 1933 celebrated its new freedom from the British by quite coolly and deliberately massacring the Assyrians for being Christians.

In Europe, Pilsudski rigged the Polish elections so as to make himself dictator at the end of 1929; Kings Alexander of Yugoslavia and Carol of Roumania dispensed with Parliamentary control; a Bulgarian military dictatorship was set up in 1934 and a Greek (under Metaxas) in 1935. Estonia and Latvia became dictatorships in 1934; the Portuguese dictator, Salazar, presented himself with a new statutory authorization in 1933. Dollfuss, a Catholic politician, wiped out the Austrian Socialists by violence in Vienna, and installed a Catholic-Fascist regime, in February 1934. Probably the worst of all the results of the crisis, for the future, was the installation of the Nazis in power in Germany in 1933, to be described later; the most immediately shocking was the invasion of Manchuria by Japan in 1931. The existing pacific government of Japan was turned out by Army officers, and its more important members murdered methodically at later dates; the new government, deciding correctly that the League powers would not intervene, took a trivial pretext to invade Manchuria, a Chinese province that Chiang Kai-Shek had not succeeded in controlling, occupied it and refused to move.

What seemed to make the crises insoluble (though the causes were really deeper) was the course of events in Britain. London was still the financial centre of the world; the British government was a Labour government headed by an unusually vague-spoken politician, Ramsay MacDonald. It had no majority in Parliament; if it had wished to meet the crisis by a Socialist policy it would not have been allowed to do so; in the upshot it was able to do nothing.

American investment in Germany and Austria ceased in 1929. In 1930, as Wall Street became more and more desperate, American lenders began to call back their loans, and within a few months the Credit Anstalt, a bank that financed the majority of Austrian industry, faced bankruptcy. President Hoover suggested a moratorium on reparations payments, Chancellor Brüning of Germany a Customs Union with Austria. But France, whose government had been taken over by a politician named Tardieu who thought the Versailles treaty "too moderate," obstructed both proposals. British and German banks had to lend money to prop up the Austrian bank; in so doing they only transferred the danger to themselves. A run started on the German banks, and in July 1931 the famous Darmstadt Bank failed. The weight now fell wholly on London, and the run on gold was such that by August it was clear that the Bank of England could not survive without foreign aid. Gold was to be found only in Paris and New York; Paris would lend none, and New York insisted upon changes in British policy (notably reductions in unemployment pay) which the Cabinet would not accept. MacDonald, the Premier, in consultation with his Conservative opponents, turned his own party out and formed a "National Government" to save the pound. But the pound could not be saved: late in September an Act was passed abandoning the gold standard. The pound fell in value by a fifth, and all the countries which had confidently used London as their banker and conducted their trade in sterling found themselves forced off the gold standard as well. The old financial and trade arrangements of the world were in ruins.

The new British government succeeded in blaming the disaster wholly upon its predecessor; at the general election of 1931 the "National" coalition gained 570 seats to Labour's 46, and although the giant size of the majority was diminished in 1935, the election introduced nine continuous years of rule by a small Conservative group. The name "National" was retained for electoral purposes, there being small parties called "National Liberal" or "National Labour"; but the enormous majority was Conservative. The effective direction was in the hands of a circle around first Stanley Baldwin and then Neville Chamberlain; Winston Churchill and his followers were excluded. French politicians were less fortunate: in 1936 a coalition of Radicals, Socialists, and Communists called the "Popular Front" put the existing clique out of office.

The domestic policy of the United States was completely in the hands of a great empiricist. Neither Congress nor the people were disposed to oppose or even criticize any remedies that Franklin Delano Roosevelt proposed; he himself held no systematized philosophy and was deliberately trying one thing after another. So much did his hit-or-miss technique commend itself to his countrymen that despite furious opposition they would never desert him. First elected in 1932 and taking office in 1933, he was re-elected in 1936, 1940 and 1944; his reign (he is the only President to whom the word is appropriate) ended only with his death. His earliest devices included the Agricultural Adjustment Act (AAA) to force up farm prices by reducing production, and the National Industrial Recovery Act (NIRA) which attempted to revive industry by persuading employers to observe "codes" raising wages, shortening hours, improving conditions, and banning child labour. Both these Acts ran into difficulties, and the administration was more indignant than sorry when the Supreme Court in 1935 and 1936 declared them unconstitutional. Their objects seemed more likely to be achieved by a grand and continuing scheme of public works, already started in 1933 and carried on under various names until the approach of war made it unnecessary. Far different from the road-mending which had previously been dignified with the title of public works, it included schemes for even actors and writers, and one achievement that awed all but the angriest critics—the Tennessee Valley Authority, which, setting out to control a destructive river, proved to be the greatest and most successful example of regional planning in a free country. Flood control was the least of its benefits—cheap and universal electricity, reforestation, the restoration of eroded land and the introduction of new industries completely changed what had once been a poverty-stricken and despairing area. Less universal approval was secured by the Wagner Act (1935) which forced American businessmen, till then the most autocratic in the world, to recognize and negotiate with the trade unions, who now began to exercise a stronger and stronger influence in politics.

Russia, based on a Socialist economy, did not receive the same shock as other states: no inexplicable queues of unemployed appeared, no factories were closed down while materials were abundant. But the Soviet Union was affected almost as seriously in other ways. Lenin had explicitly laid it down that the suspension of freedom during the revolution was to be temporary, and would be followed by a state freer than anything possible under a *bourgeois* order. But so far from increasing personal liberties, the Soviet Union became politically more and more of a police state; from a turbulent and dictatorial democracy it was evolving into an oligarchy and seemed on the way to becoming an autocracy. There was great material progress which only the most biased observers could ignore. The Five Year Plan was very nearly completed in four years. Great power stations were erected—one very famous on the Dnieper—oil wells sunk, steel-plants erected, and wholly new industrial centres created at Kuznetzk in Siberia, Magnetogorsk in the Urals, and elsewhere. Illiteracy, in this vast and most backward of countries, was partly destroyed; in the outlying and more barbarian parts of the Union the advances in civilization were sensational. But peasant proprietorship, which was not permissible by Communist theory, was ended in 1929–31 in an unnecessarily brutal manner. All successful peasants were labelled "Kulaks," and were to be forced into collective farms or State farms. Many thousands were deported to Siberia; sabotage and resistance was widespread; it was stated that at one time half the livestock of Russia had been slaughtered.

The first Five Year Plan was succeeded in 1932 by the announcement of a second Plan, which was to concentrate upon housing, transport, the production of consumer goods and the raising of the standard of life of the people. In many ways it was successful, but it was accompanied by political changes that startled the outside world. Trotsky had been expelled by an alliance between Kamenev, Zinoviev, and Stalin; the first two of these triumvirs found that they had handed themselves over to the power of the third. Stalin, as secretary of the Communist Party, was the sole controller of political power; nor was he a man given to mercy. Over 110 people had been put to death to avenge the murder of his friend Kirov in 1930. His colleagues found themselves first extruded from power, and then put on trial. In 1936 fourteen of the most famous "comrades of Lenin," including Kamenev and Zinoviev, were charged with treason, and shot. Another batch followed a few months later; next year Tukhachevsky and many others of the higher officers of the Red Army were executed. Throughout the country these trials were paralleled by the execution or imprisonment of thousands of minor persons, until there was no one at all who opposed the policies of Stalin. Mr. Vishinsky, the chief prosecutor, secured 6,238 death sentences in open court. The accused, without so far as is known one exception, produced confessions admitting exactly what they were charged with, even when these offences were very improbable. By the end of the "purges" all the leaders of the 1917 revolution, bar one, were dead. This one was an eminence surrounded by younger men or men of the second rank: he now received an adoration very surprising to those who remembered the democratic traditions of the older socialism. Lenin was dead before men dared rename a city after him, but the Russian map now was spattered with Stalin, Stalino, Stalinsk, Stalingrad, Stalinogorsk, Stalinabad, and such-like.

The profound political change inside Russia had effects outside its borders. In 1927 there were revolutionary Communist parties in almost every Parliamentary country; they had to be brought to heel. The annual meetings of the Communist International were suspended for six years to allow of this. Trotskysts were first driven out: the abandonment of "permanent revolution" in favour of "Socialism in one country" naturally made the defence of that one country—Russia—more important than revolutionary aspirations at home. What had been individual revolutionary parties became instruments of Russian foreign policy; year by year the leaders or followers who did not acquiesce in this change were expelled. At first the "Party line" was to attack most venomously the Socialists and Liberals in democratic countries, describing them as "social-fascists" and, as in a Berlin tram-strike, co-operating with the Nazis against them. The disastrous consequences of this policy to Russia became clear soon after 1933; and it was suddenly reversed in 1935, after the "Stalin-Laval pact." To this, an abortive alliance between Russia and France, was attached a formal approval of French re-armament: the French Communist party was required almost overnight to abandon its anti-militarism and anti-imperialism. Soon this was translated into a universal policy of close co-operation with Socialists and Liberals, in what were called "Popular Fronts" against Fascism. Considerable political successes were secured, especially in

France, Spain and China. But the most permanent significance of the changes was that there were now in every Parliamentary country two Parties which were not indigenous groups, answerable to their fellow countrymen and shaping their policies by what they believed to be their country's needs, but representatives of an outside power. One set defended the interests of the Soviet Union; the other that of the Hitler-Mussolini alliance which now called itself the Axis. That the two could co-operate, however, seemed to everyone impossible.

§ 10

In April, 1931, the Spanish monarchy collapsed and Spain became a republic. The royal family retired unmolested, and there was very little armed conflict or violence.

Spain had been preparing for a liberal revolution for the better part of a century. So far we have told little of her experiences after the downfall of Napoleon. It is a story of decadence and humiliation, of nation-wide ignorance, miseducation and incompetence, under the domination of the Roman Catholic Church. So far it is the completest instance of imperialist decay and collapse. We have already told of General Bolivar, of the loss of the vast Spanish colonies in America, and how for once Britain and the United States came into intelligent co-operation for the protection of democracy in the New World. (Chapter 36, § 6.) That great British statesman Canning had called the new-world republics into being, he said, "to redress the balance of the old." Cuba only remained under Spanish rule. That same section tells of the counter-revolution in Europe for nearly forty years.

All over Europe the struggle for liberal thought and human freedom was an uphill struggle, less desperate perhaps in Great Britain than anywhere else in the world except America. In Spain the hand of oppression was at its heaviest and clumsiest; but the liberation of South America kept alive the spirit of revolt. Spain must have been very like hell for an intelligent patriot during that long interlude of aristocratic and pious decadence. Phases of indignant and not very intelligent revolt alternated with periods of suffocation and robbery. A great foolery of dynastic conflict between Bourbons of various complexions, Carlists and so forth, absolutist generals posing as "strong men," an intrusive elected King Amadeo from Savoy, and so forth, went on.

In 1897 the United States began to concern itself with the brutalities of a particularly stern repressionist, General Weyler, and to speak very plainly to the Spanish government. The latter became propitiatory, but suddenly war was precipitated by the unexplained blowing-up of a United States battleship, the *Maine,* in the port of Havana. The United States demanded the immediate evacuation of Cuba by the Spanish, and Spain declared war (1898). The eastern Spanish fleet was destroyed by Admiral Dewey in Manila Bay, the West Indian Spanish fleet, at Santiago de Cuba, Cuba surrendered to the Americans, and the war was at an end. The Spanish government, faithful child of the Church, appealed in vain to the Pope and various reactionary monarchies to intervene, and in the subsequent treaty Spain surrendered Cuba, Porto Rico, the Philippine Isles, the Sulu Isles and indeed everything she had left in the way of an overseas empire, except Morocco.

There were popular revolts in Barcelona and Saragossa, and they were dealt with by General Weyler. But the movement for a Spanish liberal renascence was growing in power, and a number of Spanish writers and thinkers were giving themselves to the problem of organizing a new Spain. Alfonso XIII became King in 1902. He married the English princess Victoria Eugénie, the granddaughter of Queen Victoria and the niece of King Edward VII, who was converted to Catholicism for that purpose and had bestowed upon her the "golden rose," as a mark of special favour, by the Pope. A clerical monarchy sustained by military men must naturally have a war going on somewhere, and Morocco was now almost the only field open to them and to the concession-aires with whom they are so apt to associate.

Morocco was using up a multitude of young soldiers who never came back, and with a demand for more taxes and more conscripts the popular patience gave way. There was a revolt in Barcelona, and the people, with a very clear appreciation of the source of their troubles, burnt convents and churches. The congregations, they knew, paid no taxes, the churches were the symbols of a crushing suppression of thought, and it was natural that they should be taken to symbolize the national decadence. In any forthcoming trouble in Spain, where people are so apt to be direct and violent, church and convent burning is likely to recur. It is regrettable but unavoidable.

The Barcelona revolt was spontaneous and ill-organized, and it was sup-pressed after three days' fighting. After it was all over, a very distinguished Spanish educationist, Ferrer, who had founded "lay schools" in Catalonia, but who had had no share in the insurrection, was arrested and shot (1909). At home the reactionaries could fight, but in Morocco the case was different. A few days before the murder of Ferrer, the Riff tribesmen had inflicted a heavy defeat on Marshal Marina. Before and after the war of 1914–1918, the Spanish people continued to bleed into Morocco, until in 1921 they en-countered a crowning disaster at the hands of Abd-el-Krim. An army of 19,-000 was defeated and slaughtered; only 9,000 escaped into French territory.

But enough has been told to explain why the Republican movement gath-ered force, why it won a great majority in the reassembled Cortes, which had not been called for eight years, and how King Alfonso felt the coming revolu-tion, and how at a sound of shouting in the streets he packed up and fled, leaving his British princess to follow in a day or so, quite unmolested, with her golden rose and her family (1931). A republican regime succeeded under President Zamorra, with Azaña as Prime Minister. They found themselves faced by a gigantic task of social sanitation.

The country had been bled white by the Church and the grandees; it was two hundred years behind the times. Thousands of elementary schools were needed, there had to be a complete educational reconstruction, the vast neg-lected estates of the grandees and of the Church had to be distributed among the peasants, and industry rescued from the clutches of monopolistic concessionaires. That alone was a stupendous undertaking. But the new government had also to make terms with Catalonian and Basque separatism and with the crude impatience of the illiterates they were liberating. Zamorra betrayed a reactionary disposition and there were monarchist revolts, which exacerbated the antagonism of right and left. Azaña embodied left liberal opinion. In 1934 he was under arrest. In 1936 he was President in the place of Zamorra. But now the leftward swing was getting more violent. It was impossible to keep the town crowds off the convents and churches. The dislike of the peasants for the parish priests was also vivid enough to be disconcerting. The new government found it impossible to deliver a millennium forthwith. It was attacked for not going fast enough and far enough. It had to face irrational strikes and in particular, Anarchist Syndicalism, a sort of impracticable Rousseauism with a taste for violent methods. (You will find an excellent account of its ruthless exaltation in Ramon Sender's *Seven Red Sundays,* a quite fundamental book.) Nevertheless this government held on stoutly, and if it had not been assailed by the gathering forces of reaction it might have pulled Spain into line and effective co-operation with the Atlantic democracies.

A military adventurer named Franco had attempted a republican pronunciamento under the monarchy (1930). He had been pardoned and entrusted with a command in Morocco. There also he found opportunity where an honest man would have found service. He revolted against the struggling government in Madrid (1936). He invaded Spain with Moorish troops, proposing to restore order, Christianity, the rights of property and anything else that seemed likely to appeal to the forces of reaction. He was openly supported by the totalitarian governments of Germany and Italy, which saw in Spain the possibilities of an effective outwork in the coming struggle against the quasi-liberal Atlantic powers. He also received the blessings of the Vatican and, what is now an undeniable fact despite brass-faced denials in Parliament, the effective sympathy of the reactionary elements in the British and French governments. From the outset they did their utmost to impede the flow of help and munitions to the lawful Spanish government, and Franco was recognized by all the gentlefolk as a "Christian gentleman." He made a headlong rush for Madrid, he was checked and held there, and Spain became, as it were, a demonstration table of the three main groups of force that distracted mankind then.

Taking them in their historical order; there was first the great complex of traditions, interests, prestige and privilege dating from the days before the Protestant Reformation, the American Declaration of Independence and the French Revolution. This, with its priestcraft, monarchy, armed force, rich and poor, we may call the Ancient Order. We have told in this history how the spirit of freedom in man had struggled to escape from the incubus of the past and how time after time the powers of reaction have sneaked back subtly and persistently to their former controls. And next in order in our survey is the second element, Militarism, the adventurer conqueror, the soldier gangster, who as a mercenary soldier, a nomad from without or a blatant patriot from within, has first of all organized a temporarily irresistible fighting force and then taken possession of the social system. He brings no constructive ideas with him; he insists upon nothing but servility and obedience, and sooner or later, the old order achieves a resurrection through him. This is the rhythm of history. He is only good in his uniform; he must buy the satisfaction of life at a price. The priests and concessionaires will serve him; aristocratic womanhood is all too ready to soften his manners. The Catholic Church, as ever, renders unto Cæsar the things that are Cæsar's. So, at the price of a few individual humiliations, the old regime reconciles itself to the new bravoes, and the dreaded reconstruction of the world and the emancipation of the common man is averted for another generation.

The third group of forces in human affairs is even more complicated than the other two. In this *Outline* we have traced its development from the dawn of the idea in Greece, in Palestine, in India, China and elsewhere that there was a *possible better life for men*. That indeed, linked to the progressive material enlargement of the human community, is the essential story of this entire book. This *Outline* was not planned so; it came out like that. But so far the aspiration for a greater brotherhood has never manifested itself except locally, intermittently and incoherently. Now upon the vivid Spanish stage these scattered and unorganized drives towards a greater life for men, were drawn together, to realize at once their common spirit and their lamentable need for a common formula for their desires. Volunteers to aid the Spanish Left poured in from every quarter of the earth, to discover themselves one in spirit and hopelessly diverse in method. Even in the face of a steadfast attack they would not consolidate. They fought among themselves behind the front. After the most heroic efforts they shared at last a common defeat.

So we distinguish the three main divisions in the human struggle to-day, as they revealed themselves in Spain. Not one of these divisions displays any really powerful unanimity of purpose. They are still divisions of instinct and prepossession rather than divisions of reasoned will. Everywhere there are possibilities of great interchanges of strength. Everywhere the issues remain obscured and the outcome indecisive.

And yet the human thrust towards that better order of freedom and brother-hood recurs with an undying obstinacy. It is blind, but there may come a time when it will be only purblind, a time when it will see and comprehend fully the common purpose of its impulse. To trace the history of mankind for the past ten thousand years, as we have done, makes us realize that, with an almost astronomical inevitability, we are moving *towards* a world unification based on a fundamental social revolution. Yet because of the almost universal indefiniteness of human thought to-day, that revolution seems likely still to cost our species an incalculable further depletion in waste and suffering. There may be a limit to human vitality. Conceivably that revolution may never accomplish itself, and our species may stagger half way to its goal and fall and fail. There is no reason in history to suppose that man is exempt from the universal law, that a failure of adaptation spells extinction. Are we adapting? Are we adapting fast enough in the face of our present disorders?

I have devoted this much space to a general discussion of the primary factors in the present situation, as the Spanish conflict laid them bare. The detailed history of that three years' struggle would be an epic of confused heroism beyond the compass of this *Outline*. Franco fought his way to the outskirts of Madrid and gained a footing in the new university quarter before the end of 1936, but there he was held until the end of the conflict in 1939. During this period the reactionary French and British Foreign Offices kept up a parade of legality and non-intervention that was of very great help to Franco. Franco was openly supported by Germany and Italy, and the legal government almost as openly by Russia. Spain became an arena in which those great powers with the utmost ruthlessness tried out new tactics and new machines. German and Italian troops fought openly side by side with the Sultan of Morocco's Moors, in the name of Spanish "Nationalism." Guernica, the sacred city of the Basques, was obliterated with its entire population by German bombers in 1937, so anticipating the great massacre of Rotterdam in 1940. The Basque people, who are sincere Roman Catholics, made a desperate, pathetic and quite useless appeal to the Vatican. The Republican government struggled on until April 1939. Then Franco entered Madrid in triumph.

<h2 style="text-align:center">§ 11</h2>

The state of mind of a young German in the years following the war is presented in a book, *Little Man What Now?* by Hans Fallada, one of those books in which the novelist outdoes the historian in his presentation of an atmosphere in which, and because of which, things happen. His "Little Man" is out of work, humiliated, exasperated, driven inevitably towards revolt. He loves, and his fatherhood is shameful and the outlook for any child he begets is undernourishment and servitude. There is no outlet for him, no world across the seas now in which a man can start life again. What has brought all this about? There is no one to tell him of the arrogant folly of 1914, and all he reads and hears is saturated with the suggestion that the retribution of Versailles was most unfair. And he would not be human if he did not accept the pleasing suggestion that the German armies were not defeated in 1918, as they certainly were; they were betrayed. They were betrayed by the insidious British propaganda and by treachery at home. And now all this poverty is due to the iniquitous blockade, to the monstrous burthen of the indemnities, to the machinations of cosmopolitan and mainly Jewish finance and to the greed of the Jews. Many of the employers to whom he goes so hopelessly, he finds are Jews—or they seem to be Jews. Jews hide in poverty and blossom in prosperity. Some may have bloomed a little too brightly in the years after the war. The "Little Man" who was a child in 1918, who heard of nothing but glorious victories until the collapse and starvation, peers into restaurants, studies shop windows. Shall he go Bolshevik? But the Social Democrats and the Communists were in the conspiracy that let down the home front! The Social Democrats make all sorts of concessions to the French and British, but they get nothing in return—*nothing that lets me out*. That was the state of mind of a whole new generation of Germans, of millions of pent-up, dis-comfited young men. It accumulated explosive force through the days of monetary collapse which precipitated all the younger bourgeoisie into the festering stratum of distress. The particular form the explosion took was a matter of individual accident. It took the form of the most disastrous war convulsion that mankind has hitherto experienced.

The particular brand that fired this overcharged human magazine was named Adolf Hitler, an excitable, garrulous creature with a vein of certifiable insanity in his composition. It was sometimes alleged that his name was origi-nally Schücklgruber, but this is a libel upon him. He was the son of a certain Alois Schücklgruber, who was the illegitimate son of a woman called Schücklgruber, but this Alois had been brought up in the house of his putative father, Hietler, a miller's hand, and subsequently, at the age of forty, took his name and became Schücklgruber-Hitler. Later the Schücklgruber dropped out, presumably for snobbish reasons. Alois was a person of some energy and ambition; he had three wives and a certain confusion of legitimate and ille-gitimate children, but he struggled up to the genteel position and title of Herr Oberofficial Hitler in the Customs Service. He insisted sternly upon the Herr Oberofficial. He died suddenly while his son was still a schoolboy, and he left his widow very ill-provided for.

These facts, and most of Adolf's early career, have been disinterred very carefully and impartially by Dr. Rudolf Olden (*Hitler the Pawn*). Most of the statements about his education, ambitions, military achievements and so forth, given in *Mein Kampf,* or made to privileged interviewers, are either absolute lies or bold distortions of fact. As a schoolboy Hitler was a complete failure; he was unable to qualify to enter the Art School of the Vienna Academy. Something obscure happened in his mind at the onset of adolescence, and he developed a well-known form of insanity characterized among other things by an obscene hatred of the stranger male. In the Southern United States it is chiefly found in relation to negroes and leads very frequently to homicide by individuals or lynching parties; in the case of Hitler the insane jealousy centred upon Jews. An obsession of this sort dehumanizes a man, canalizes his activities and becomes a source of morbid energy. He had been rejected by the Army before 1914, but he volunteered at the outbreak of war and became an orderly. He never rose above the rank of a corporal. He possessed an Iron Cross of the First Class, but his accounts of how he came by it varied widely. The Reichswehr dossier of his war record had been destroyed.

Through the dingy years before the war, this unstable creature had gone about dreaming and muttering to himself; he seems never to have earned a living by his industry, and to have sunk to rags and the common doss-house; he was rejected as unfit for the Austrian Army, but he volunteered in 1914; he became something of a ranter among his comrades at the front, and afterwards at Munich his growing flood of words was manifest. Bavaria, immediately after 1918, was in a ferment. There were two Soviet Republics and then a military reaction. The Bavarian General Staff organized political discussions to educate the people against communism and pacifism. At one of these meetings in an Army barracks Hitler was moved to deliver with great effectiveness and violence a tirade against the Jews. As a consequence he was appointed an "education officer." He ceased to be a mere irresponsible spouter.

He took up his new task with enthusiasm. He pervaded the barracks and cafés of Munich with his torrential eloquence. He formed in succession the German Workers' Party, the National Socialist German Workers' Party, which passed on into the National Socialist Party. Its blend of socialism, patriotism, Jew-baiting, terrorist activities and stupendous promises was all the Little Man felt he needed.

The Army had hatched a bigger egg than it had intended. In 1923 the National Socialist Party was growing to formidable proportions, and Hitler had formed an alliance with General Ludendorff, who was still keeping alive the idea of a war of revenge. There was a Putsch, an ill-conceived attempt to seize power in Munich and march on Berlin. It failed ignominiously, the National Socialists seized the Town Hall, squabbled, and marched on the military headquarters. Whereupon the police fired. Hitler threw himself flat, sprained his arm and ran. Göring, his close associate, was wounded and fled also. Vain, gallant old Ludendorff marched straight forward through the sharpshooters and was respectfully taken prisoner.

All that would be a trivial story and Hitler might well have vanished from history there and then, if it were not for all that gathering mass of young men in the background. Not merely in the background. They came to shout in the court on his behalf, they were shouting and marching all over Germany now, and Hitler went to prison in Landsberg on the Lech for six months and wrote *Mein Kampf,* a confused, illiterate, schoolboy production, a book as common as the swill of beer wiped from a café table, but one which was to be made compulsory reading throughout the German world.

From Hitler's imprisonment in 1924 to his political recrudescence in 1929, there intervenes the Stresemann period of German history. Gustav Stresemann began as a passionate German patriot; his earliest activities were devoted to the agitation for a German navy that would be an effective menace against Britain, if she should intervene in the war against France and Russia that was being planned before 1914. Stresemann carried his intense patriotism through the war, and until he began to realize the real opportunities and dangers of the German situation after 1918. Then, and largely through the able diplomacy of the British Ambassador, Lord D'Abernon, he adopted a line of toleration and compromise. He managed to secure progressive alleviations of the debt payments imposed on his country, and set himself to freeing the German soil from foreign occupation. His mind broadened with experience, and he became a close personal friend of Monsieur Briand and, so far as one can judge, a genuine advocate with him of European federation. The occupied territory was definitely to be freed of the last foreign troops in 1931. He did not live to see that day; he died in 1929. So that he scarcely felt the beginnings of the economic world storm which was gathering about him. Nor did he realize the portentousness of those restless gangs of young men who seethed in all the cities of the land. His mind was too set in the ideas of the old diplomacy.

We have told already in one of the earlier sections of this chapter of the post-war monetary collapse that culminated in 1923, how for a time there was an unstable rehabilitation of monetary methods, and how at last in 1930–31 the whole system crashed in a common world-wide financial disaster. With this came Hitler's second opportunity. His most immediate material was the various Youth Movements which, with considerable variations of spirit and objective, had flourished in Germany as long as the parallel Boy Scout movement in the British Empire. To organize an armed and uniformed force out of this material, he needed monetary support, and this he got from the financiers interested in the heavy industries, which needed rearmament in order to flourish, and who were therefore bitterly opposed to the Stresemann policy of pacification. He presented himself to these magnates chiefly as a competent strike-breaker and as a useful instrument in turning the unrest of the masses away from social revolution towards a Pan-German crusade. He secured the support of Hugenberg, the managing director of the great firm of Krupps, and creator and leader of the "German Nationalist Party." Hugenberg had bought up a vast network of newspapers, cinemas and the like; he was a little, grey-headed, overbearing dogmatist, and he thought he had bought Hitler. But there he was mistaken. Röhm too thought he had secured Hitler, to give him and his S.A. the control of the reviving and expanding army.

Hitler and his close associates, with the industrialists behind them, had now the amplest resources available for an intense campaign to restore the aggressive spirit in Germany, and they flung themselves into it with immense energy. All over the country violence was organized, against the Jews, against the intellectuals, against the Communists. These last were threatened with extermination. It was a close imitation of the campaign of brutality and terror upon which Fascism rose to power in Italy, but it was more systematic, extensive and brutal. In 1930 the National Socialist Party had twelve members in the Reichstag, shrunken from an original fourteen (1924). In the September election of 1930, it reappeared with one hundred and seven, representing six and a half million voters. And so Hitler clambered to the thirteen million who voted for him as President in 1932 against the nineteen million cast for old Marshal Hindenburg.

The political comings and goings that ensued are too complex for us to deal with in detail. In the January of 1933, President Hindenburg, who was now over eighty-five and in a state of extreme senile decay, went back upon his repeated declarations—"I give my word of honour as a Prussian general"— that he would do nothing of the sort, and made Hitler Imperial Chancellor. Probably the old man forgot.

But Hitler was still very much in the hands of the Army and the industrialists, and still very far from actual dictatorship. His group of intimates decided upon a coup. They set the Reichstag on fire on Feb. 27th, declared it was part of a nation-wide Communist conspiracy, and let loose a wild storm of anti-Communist and anti-Jewish violence. Trade Unions and Labour Banks were abolished. Eighty-one Communist members of the re-elected Reichstag were either put in prison or compelled to hide or go abroad. Their abolition left Hitler in an effective majority in the Reichstag.

There ensued a curious episode. The terroristic weapon of the National Socialist Party was the S.A., the Storm Detachment, the illegal Storm Troops, organized by Röhm in the days of Germany's general disarmament. Now that the country was boldly rearming in defiance of its treaty obligations, the S.A. became, from the point of view of the expanding regular army (the Reichswehr), unnecessary and troublesome. And Hitler decided to sacrifice it. Röhm, Gregor Strasser and a number of men who had been his closest and most loyal associates in his early days, General von Schleicher and his wife and a multitude of minor S.A. leaders, were murdered in the "blood bath" of the thirtieth of June (1934). Thereafter Hitler became not so much the leader as the ostensible divinity of the German people. And thereafter under the leadership of this demented, wordy being, Germany turned itself more and more definitely towards war.

§ 12

The world slid into the war which Hitler planned, with scarcely an effort to prevent it. The only serious endeavours were made by the Soviet Union, which regarded itself as directly threatened by the Nazis. It joined the League of Nations in 1934, reversing Lenin's policy, and in the following two years, as has been said, saw to it that the Communist parties about the world adopted a "united front" policy to strengthen anti-Fascism in other countries. As the catastrophe approached, Litvinov in its name more than once made suggestions for concerted resistance to the Axis advance, suggestions which the British and French governments always evaded.

The reasons for the inertia of the rest of the world were two. In the United States the reason was wishful thinking. The States had dealt the heaviest blow to world peace that they could by withdrawing from the League at its inception: since then it had become almost an article of national faith that America would avoid being involved in the next war by simply declining to take any part in foreign affairs. The President was almost the only American statesman of influence who saw in the growth of Nazism a thing which might threaten the States, but his pronouncements on this (such as his "quarantine" speech) were neither frequent nor vigorous; and they were very coldly received. Even as late as July 1939 when he proposed to amend the Neutrality Act, the Senate forbade it. The governments of Britain and France, however, could not pretend to themselves that the rise of Nazism was no affair of theirs. Yet over a number of years they took actions which built up the strength of the power which was going to ruin them. Their reason must even now be partly conjectural. It is not sufficient to say that they acted so because they were rich, and old, and frightened: in Britain in particular the policy was consistently carried through (after MacDonald and Baldwin had retired) by a group of four men, Neville Chamberlain, Lord Halifax, Sir John Simon, and

Sir Samuel Hoare, who were ageing, it is true, but disastrously vigorous, opinionated, and honest. What moved such men seems to have been an entire misconception of what they were facing, arising from a sort of inverted theory of the class war. They perceived that the Nazis and Fascisti when they were victorious stamped out first of all Communist organizations, all trade unions and socialist parties; that they put down "indiscipline" and various unhealthy modern tendencies in art and morals; that they trained young men admirably in vigorous military exercises; that they were supported by the subscriptions of energetic businessmen. The conservatives in Britain and France, on all these points, felt a fellow-feeling with the Nazis and Fascisti even if they deplored their crudities and brutalities (which they were assured were much exaggerated). They assumed the existence of a similar sympathy on the other side. They were sure that the Soviet Union and the Union only was the enemy of the Axis, and that they themselves could quite easily come to a businesslike arrangement with Hitler and his colleagues. They did not, in short, know anything about the nature of gangsterism, and had no idea that they were selected as the first and fattest victims.

No other theory seems to explain the complacency with which they watched and even assisted the series of events which first denuded them of all their potential allies and then led them into a disastrous war. At this distance, the sequence of occurrences seems too clear for any but self-deluded men to have missed. At first the war was organized separately in the East and West: the policies of Germany and Japan were only co-ordinated in principle in November 1936, and complete co-operation dated only from late 1937. Seeing that her invasion of Manchuria led to only verbal protests, Japan in 1933 left the League and invaded China proper, occupying the northern province of Jehol in face of very slight resistance. Chiang Kai-Shek was still mostly occupied with subduing the Communists; he had so much success that in 1934 they fled from their strongholds in central China, and after a surprising forced march of some thousands of miles reappeared in the western province of Kan-su, where it was more difficult to touch them. By then, however, the new Russian policy had reached China, and its results appeared in a peculiarly Chinese incident. Chiang Kai-Shek was kidnapped in 1936 by the son of the war-lord who had been expelled from Manchuria by the Japanese, and was carried by him to the headquarters of the Communist General Mao Tse-tung. Instead of executing him, Mao and his colleagues reasoned with him about the Japanese danger; his wife was fetched to join in the discussions. After some days of discussion and meditation both sides declared they had found enlightenment, and pledged themselves unitedly to resist the invasion. It was only just in time, for next year the Japanese launched a full-scale invasion of China, capturing Peking and bombing and burning Chinese cities. Fighting on unequal terms, the Chinese were forced back and in 1938 Hankow, Nanking, Shanghai, and Canton were all in Japanese hands. But the new alliance (though both sides were justifiably suspicious of each other) held firm; Chiang Kai-Shek retired to Chungking in the far interior and the Japanese found that they owned only the railways, waterways, and large cities. All round them the country was hostile and infested with guerrillas. What should have been a firm taking-off ground for further advances had proved to be a morass: the "China incident" (as the Japanese called it) seemed to be proving not a source of strength but a trap. One part of the war-plan had gone wrong.

But there were no such errors in the West. The year 1933, when Hitler took power, saw the dissolution of the last Disarmament Conference, the breakup (through American action) of a world conference to stabilize exchanges, and the resignation of Germany from the League of Nations. It was as if a line had been drawn underneath one page of history. Thereafter, in 1935, Hitler announced that the Versailles Treaty had ceased to exist, reintroduced conscription, and recommenced open rearmament in defiance of it. The British government protested, and then almost at once signed a naval pact regulating the size of the new German navy. The next move was Mussolini's. In October of that year his armies invaded the territory of a fellow-member of the League, Abyssinia. The grievances alleged were trivial border disputes; the real grievance was that in 1896 the Abyssinians had defeated an Italian invading army at Adowa. The direct breach of the peace shocked the world and galvanized the League of Nations: forty-two states agreed in condemning Italy and in applying "sanctions" under the presumed leadership of Britain and France. A once-famous speech by the Foreign Secretary, Sir Samuel Hoare, on September 11 had pledged Britain to stand by the League Covenant in the spirit and the letter, but in fact he came to an agreement with the French premier, Pierre Laval, to do no such thing. "Sanctions" were not applied to the materials needed by the Italian armies (oil, steel and coal), and poison gas was passed through the Suez Canal in shiploads. By May, 1936, the Italians were in Addis Ababa: the League of Nations, as a protective force, was destroyed. Hitler had meanwhile sent his troops into the Rhineland, from which they were by treaty excluded. The Franco rebellion in Spain, backed by Italy and Germany, also began in 1936; its history has already been given.

In March 1938 the Nazi troops occupied Austria, jailed Schuschnigg, the Catholic dictator who had succeeded Dollfuss, and started the usual massacres and imprisonments of Jews and anti-Fascists.

In September 1938 Hitler announced that the "oppression" of Germans in Czechoslovakia was intolerable; war appeared to be near, and France (though not Britain) was tied to Czechoslovakia by treaty. Chamberlain flew to Munich, and a quadruplicate conference of Britain, France, Germany, and Italy compelled Czechoslovakia to cede her frontier districts and with them her ability to defend herself. Chamberlain, returning from Munich, announced "I believe this is peace for our time." (All of these aggressions, it should be mentioned, were punctuated by statements from Hitler of his peaceful intentions and unwillingness to make any further claims. At the same time, usually, the Russians would make proposals for consultations to stop the Nazi advance, which would be ignored.)

In March 1939 the Nazis occupied the rest of Czechoslovakia and installed their usual regime; Hitler also seized Memel from the small state of Lithuania.

In April 1939 Italy invaded and conquered Albania. Hitler cancelled his non-aggression pact with Poland.

By this time even the Chamberlain government had realized what was approaching with great strides towards it. The Versailles Treaty was gone, the League of Nations had been destroyed, and there was only one possible ally of any strength left—Russia. A mission was at last sent to Moscow to negotiate a treaty. It was too late: a change of policy was occurring there, symbolized by the substitution of the "realist" Mr. Molotov for the old Bolshevik Litvinov.

The German plans for war, as even amateur strategists knew, were held up by the fear of having to fight on two fronts. It was the traditional anxiety of German generals: with Russian armies on the east and French on the west, and with Britain holding the seas, Germany was a nut in a nutcracker. So long as this threat existed, Hitler could not start on his "one-by-one" programme. When it was removed, war could begin. He opened negotiations to remove it.

With a blindness which seems even less explicable than Chamberlain's, Stalin and Molotov seem to have regarded the Allied and the German missions to Moscow as no more than rival suitors for their favour, and to have decided that the Nazis were to be preferred. On August 23rd, 1939, the Nazi-Soviet Pact was signed. On September 1st as a direct sequel, German troops invaded Poland and the second World War had begun.

XL

THE SECOND WORLD WAR

§ 1. *The Course of the War.*   § 2. *The Outlook for Mankind.*

§ 1

No GOVERNMENT, except the German government, had any idea of what was going to happen in September 1939. That Poland would be defeated many people expected; nobody expected that it would be destroyed in three weeks. Initially, as so often, the Nazis had the advantage of surprise, for the Polish army was not even completely mobilized. But the first defeats were followed by graver disasters; in guns, tanks, and aircraft the Poles were hopelessly outclassed. Where there was some protection available, as in Warsaw or in the Hela Peninsula outside Danzig, they fought desperately; but their main armies were massacred. Up till September 17th there were some hopes, possibly illusory, that they could hold a line along the San, Bug, and Narew rivers; but on that day the use of the Nazi-Soviet alliance was shown. The Russians invaded Poland in the East and the war was effectively over. The two allies met at Bialystock and, on September 29th, arranged a Fourth Partition of Poland; the last Polish troops surrendered on October 1st at Hela. Other effects of the alliance were seen in the next four weeks when the Baltic Republics of Esthonia, Latvia and Lithuania were compelled to sign pacts giving the Russians military bases in their countries, the Nazis obligingly evacuating all Germans from those areas.

During this disaster the Western Allies had done practically nothing. General Gamelin, the French commander-in-chief, had made a timid sortie from the Maginot Line, but retired as soon as he met the Siegfried Line. Their inertia was such that Hitler in October hopefully made a peace offer on the basis of the Allies accepting the conquest of Poland. It was refused; but for more tangible defiances the Allied peoples had to content themselves with such incidents as the dramatic cornering of the German battleship-raider *Graf Spee* by three small British ships in December, and the organization of an economic blockade. Their rulers, indeed, had still so little knowledge of their opponent's power that their eyes were elsewhere, on a part of the world where Soviet plans had gone astray. Finland had been presented with demands similar to those made on the Baltic States, but being a solid democratic state instead of a weak dictatorship, had civilly refused them. On the last day of November, in defiance of treaties as well as of the League of Nations Covenant, the Russians invaded the small republic, and bombed its capital, Helsinki. The odds were fantastic—50 or 60 to 1 in population, and something similar in arms and equipment—but to the universal astonishment heavy Russian attacks were beaten off. With no effective help but some surreptitious aid from Sweden the Finns held the invaders back for over three months; so great was the indignation at the Soviet invasion that the British and French governments prepared an expedition to aid them, and an entanglement in a second war was prevented only by the barring of the way by Norway and Sweden.

On March 12th, 1940 the Finnish war ended in the inevitable Russian victory; the Allies fell back into their old inertia, marked on April 5th by a complacent statement by Chamberlain: "Hitler has missed the bus." Four days after that pronouncement the Germans seized the whole of Denmark and the greater part of Norway—the first of these pacific states making no resistance, the other a disorganized and unsuccessful one. Chamberlain could not believe it: told that the Germans had taken Narvik in the far north he informed the Commons it could not be true—the place must be "Larvik" in the far south. British troops were hastily landed at the small ports of Namsos and Andalsnes to aid the struggling Norwegians. But they had no adequate air protection, no tanks, no big guns, and no plan comparable to the Germans'; they and the French who joined them seemed little more formidable than the Poles. Only the Navy's actions at Narvik seemed competent, and these could not save the campaign. By the end of the month Norway was conquered.

This was too much for the British House of Commons (the French reaction was weaker). Explosive debates, in which one of his own nominal followers said to him, "In the name of God, go!", convinced Chamberlain, after a hostile vote of 200 to 281, that he must resign; a coalition headed by Winston Churchill and including the Labour Party took office instead. It was only just in time: that very day (May 10) the Germans broke a fresh set of treaties by invading Belgium and Holland. Now the Western world saw "German might" at last in full action. "Panzer" divisions, a combination of tanks and infantry, forced their way through ordinary lines—the tanks breaking down weak places, the infantry behind them wiping up resistance. Bombers, including new things called dive bombers, were used as weapons to break up enemy formations—both they and tanks being radio-guided. (The telephone lines of 1918, so easily cut, were only a memory.)

Attacks were planned to the last detail: Eben Emael, the great fort which was the centre pin of Belgian defence, lasted just one day. But the attacks were not on soldiers only, for this was "total war." The tanks and screaming dive bombers drove packs of terrified civilians before them; the Allied forces, trying to march to aid the Belgians, found themselves entangled in a mass of panic-struck refugees stampeding to the west. Parachutists descended behind the lines and seized bridges: in Holland German spies, often old residents, set up machine gun posts. To add to the terror, the defenceless city of Rotterdam was raided by the Luftwaffe and many hundred people killed: the crime was deliberate for the world had got to learn a lesson.

Holland was conquered in five days; then while the Allied troops which had wheeled north to aid Belgium were slowly retreating to the coast, the Germans broke through an ill-defended sector in the Ardennes, near to the ominous town of Sedan. By May 15th the French 9th Army was a wreck and the panzers were pouring through a 50-mile gap well north of the useless Maginot

Line. Four days later they had reached the sea; the Belgian and British armies, and some French, were encircled in Flanders. The Belgian King surrendered; the British army and its French fellows were extracted from Dunkirk between May 28th and June 2nd by a suddenly assembled fleet of about 666 private boats and 222 naval vessels. By then, however, the French armies were beginning to collapse; the panzers were breaking through so fast that sometimes their tanks were 50 miles ahead of their infantry. Along the white roads, between "the lilacs and the roses," in the brilliant summer sun poured terrified crowds, part civilian, part in uniform, fleeing they did not know where, dragging incongruous pieces of their household goods, dive bombed and machine gunned if they ceased to stampede. A civilization seemed to be ending: no similar sights had been seen since the barbarians destroyed the Roman Empire. On June 17, ignoring a British offer of a complete Anglo-French Union, a new French government under the ancient Marshal Pétain announced it would give up the struggle.

Better armaments and generalship, the unwillingness of the French upper class to resist, the Communist propaganda among the workers had secured the Nazi victory. Now their allies took their pickings: Mussolini bravely declared war on the defeated Allies, the Soviet Union took Bessarabia from Roumania (previously covered by an Anglo-French guarantee) and annexed Esthonia, Latvia and Lithuania. There was a brief pause.

The battle which was to come ranks with Marathon and Salamis among those which changed history and saved a civilization. Had Britain not resisted, or had it been conquered, it is not difficult to estimate what would have followed. The Nazi plan is now fairly clear, and it is clear too how nearly it succeeded. The defeat of Britain was to be followed by the conquest of Russia: as it was, the Soviet forces came to the very edge of disaster in 1941 and 1942 and it is hardly likely they would have survived the attack of a Germany which had defeated Britain, had no need to defend its rear and had all the seas wide open to supply its armies. The defeat of Russia was to be followed by a triple attack on the credulous and half-armed United States—from Japan on the West, from all-Nazi Europe on the East, and from Latin-American allies already being prepared in the South. This vast, but not impracticable programme was thwarted by British resistance.

There were already many broken nations sheltering behind the British shield. For many months, before the reading of the evening news, the British Broadcasting Corporation played, after the British national anthem, the songs of all the other states whose governments had a ghostly existence in London. It was a long procession, as pathetic as it was gallant: Holland, Belgium, Norway, Denmark, Luxembourg, Abyssinia, Poland, Czechoslovakia, and France: soon joined by Yugoslavia and Greece. Few of them realized how thin the shield was. After Dunkirk (says John Brophy) there were in Britain "about one and a half infantry divisions, a few brigades of field artillery, and only sixty tanks." There was also, it is true, the Home Guard, a volunteer force which in a few weeks numbered over a million men, prepared to deal with the parachutists who had wrecked Dutch and Belgian resistance; but they were armed (if at all) only with shotguns, until the late autumn when 800,000 American rifles arrived. The Navy, indeed, was as formidable as ever; but the Royal Air Force was grossly outnumbered by the Luftwaffe.

Hitler fixed the date for the invasion of Britain—it was September 21st, 1940 —and the first step, which was to be the destruction of the British Air Force, began on the 8th of August. Heinkel and Dornier bombers, Junker dive bombers, and Messerschmidt fighters swept over south-eastern England. They were met by a small number of Spitfires and Hurricanes, aided by some eld-erly Defiants. So few were the defenders that no continuous patrols could be maintained: the crews must wait for the attackers, nor, when they were dis-covered, could the full force (such as it was) be sent up; squadrons must be held back to meet the third and fourth waves that the lavish invader could send. The Luftwaffe plan was fivefold: to destroy the coastal convoys that fed Britain, to sink or immobilize the Navy, to drive the R.A.F. from the sky, to paralyze the ports, and to wreck all the aerodromes from which planes could rise to bomb the invading flotillas. On August 12th, for example; 200 aircraft in waves attacked Dover, 150 Portsmouth and the Isle of Wight. The fight went on through August and September into October. Streaks of white smoke across the bright blue Kent skies, the quick rattle of machine guns, sudden dull explosions, swaying white parachutes with men clinging to them, blazing machines crashing into hillsides were all that men on the ground could see. But in September the issue was decided: the R.A.F. had driven the Luftwaffe from the daytime skies. The Prime Minister, Winston Churchill, whose speeches were in themselves part of the defences of Britain, said of the pilots, "never, in the field of human conflict, was so much owed by so many, to so few."

In October, the Luftwaffe turned to a fresh technique. (The invasion had been adjourned; the flatbottomed barges, like Napoleon's, had been dis-persed.) It had been foreshadowed; abandoning the attempt to wreck airfields and destroy the R.A.F., the Germans had on September 7th raided the London docks and the blaze could be seen twenty miles away. Throughout the winter, raids at night, when the R.A.F. could not find them, were carried out by the German pilots. The centre of Coventry was destroyed on November 15th (the Germans delightedly invented a verb, "to coventrate"). Ninety-six sepa-rate raids were made on London; one, on the 29th December, burning out the whole centre of the city. Fifty thousand high explosive bombs and un-counted incendiaries fell on the city. At first, some strategic plan seemed to direct the attacks: railways, stations, gas works, waterworks, sewage plants, docks, and power stations were aimed at; later the impulse seemed to be random anger. "Magnetic" mines, which rose from the sea bed to sink steel ships that passed, made harbours useless, until at the end of November a mine was found intact, pulled apart and examined; as a result a process called "degaussing" was devised which defeated this device.

Misfortune makes new bedfellows. The Germans had expected that their attack would produce the same results as elsewhere—indeed, they broadcast on the assumption that this had been so, and that streams of terrified refugees were packing the roads north from London; "Lord Haw-Haw" (William Joyce) kindly advised them that North Wales was their only safe refuge. But in fact the children had been removed in an orderly manner and billeted, with some grumbling but on the whole efficiently, on country householders; no crowds of refugees followed them. In London and the provincial cities all classes sheltered in the same air-raid shelters; moreover, Acts had been passed which enforced an equality which two years before would have been denounced as unforgivably socialistic. All property, including the land, was placed under government control by Acts passed immediately after the Churchill government took power. Banks were taken under control; foreign investments taken over; employers' books were opened to inspection; orders could be issued to enforce production of anything that was required. War profits were to be taxed; war damages were to be universally shared. Labour agreed to be directed, and this conscription was shortly extended to women too. There had been no such complete enrolment of all citizens since the days of Sparta, two and a half thousand years before.

But with all this the odds were against the British. Only 44 million British were opposed to 88 million Germans; and if to the 44 million islanders were added the Dominion supporters, Hitler could call upon the majority of the population of Europe. The Navy, indeed, was still unequalled; but one of the gravest limitations of sea power was shown by the news that 500,000 tons of shipping were sunk monthly by Nazi submarines early in 1941. Nevertheless, the navy was active. On July 3rd, 1940, it sunk or seized at Oran the French navy, which Marshal Pétain might have transferred to German control; and on Nov. 13 at Taranto the Fleet Air Arm wrecked 3 battleships and 4 cruisers and auxiliaries of the Italian navy, which had been expected to control the Mediterranean. Next month, the British and Dominion forces in Egypt under General Wavell started an offensive against the Italian forces in Libya which resulted in the complete occupation of Cyrenaica and the capture of prisoners far outnumbering the whole attacking force.

But these exploits were not decisive. The British could, as they did, reconquer the whole of Abyssinia and restore the Emperor; they could sink half the Italian fleet at the battle of Cape Matapan in March 1941; the balance was still against them. While the ceaseless bombardment of the island continued, fresh land defeats came in the Near East. Mussolini, seeking another cheap victory, had at the end of October 1940 invaded Greece from his colony Albania: to his great surprise his superior forces were steadily beaten by the smaller power, which actually began to conquer Albania. After a while Hitler (as it then seemed) came leisurely to his ally's aid; to clear the way Hungary, Roumania and Bulgaria were ordered to join the Axis; Prince Paul, the Regent of Yugoslavia, approved a Pact with Germany on March 25th. This the Yugoslavs would not have; two days later he was turned out and his boy nephew put on the throne as Peter II. On April 6th, with terrifying speed, the German armies attacked Yugoslavia. The Yugoslav army was unready and dispersed; Belgrade was partly destroyed in the usual terror raid; by the 17th all resistance, except from some rather ineffective Serbian guerrillas headed by a Colonel Mihailovitch, was over. The Germans now entered Greece. The panzers were a very different proposition from the Italian armies, and the Greeks called at once for British aid. All that could be spared from Wavell's forces—perhaps more than was wise—was sent, but once again German air superiority was victorious. Thermopylæ might perhaps have been held, but the main Greek army cut off in Epirus surrendered and the mainland had to be evacuated. An attempt was made to hold Crete; this too was taken by air power. Moreover, while the Navy was rescuing British forces in Greece, the Germans had shipped big reinforcements to Libya, and their army and the Italians, under General Rommel, drove the weakened British out of practically all Wavell's conquests.

Momentarily, it looked as if the disaster would spread. Rashid Ali, a Nazi supporter, seized power from the feeble Regent of Irak, and was supplied with Nazi planes via the Syrian aerodromes under the control of the Vichy French. But for once the reply was swift: Rashid Ali made his first attack on May 2nd and by June 1st the British had taken Bagdad. In the next five weeks they had reconquered all Irak and also occupied Syria.

One grave anxiety had been removed. Britain was an overpopulated island which lived only by its imports, paid for partly by overseas investments. These were being sold fast to purchase munitions, particularly in the States; and ruin was very near. President Roosevelt in 1939 had persuaded Congress to modify the Neutrality Act's embargo on arms by permitting "Cash and Carry" sales (which effectively meant sales to Britain and France only), but even to this, opposition was furious: Senator Borah declared it was the equivalent of taking up arms, Nye that nothing would be "ahead of America but hell," Clark that Britain and France were "the aggressors," Lundeen that the opportunity should be taken to enforce payment of the World War I debts or to seize the West Indies. In September 1940, 50 over-age destroyers were sold to Britain in return for naval bases. Contemporaneously, an "America First" committee was incorporated in Chicago; it was noisy and apparently influential. Nevertheless, at the end of 1940 a "Lease-Lend" Bill was proposed, and carried through on March 11th, 1941. It effectively meant that the large stream of munitions coming through to Britain was henceforward free of charge.

But wars cannot be won with money; it was perhaps fortunate for the world that Hitler became impatient now. He had been meditating for some while starting on the second portion of his great war-plan, leaving the first unfinished. In May his half-crazy second-in-command Hess even went secretly on a solo flight to Britain to see if the British government could not be induced to co-operate. What was in his mind became suddenly clear at four o'clock in the morning of June 22nd, when along all the vast frontier the German armies charged into the territory of the Soviet Union.

The Russians seemed taken by surprise. Barely a week earlier Tass, their official agency, had announced "there could be no misunderstanding between the two countries." Certainly, their frontier forces were all driven back: in eleven days the Germans had occupied an area larger than all France. But they then entered a deep zone of fortifications, loosely called "the Stalin Line" and stretching roughly along the 1938 frontier. Here the fighting became more stubborn; the fury of both sides was unmatched but their equipment more equal. But the result was the same: in August the line was pierced in three places—in the north by the capture of Pskov on the way to Leningrad, in the centre by the capture of Vitebsk on the way to Smolensk, in the south by the capture of Zhitomir on the way to Kiev. Throughout the summer the same story of Russian defeats and retreats continued. Leningrad was blockaded, the Finns avenging themselves by coming on it from the north; Smolensk was captured; in the south the Germans broke into the Ukraine, the great industrial and agricultural reserve of Russia, occupying almost everything west of the Dnieper.

Britain, which had immediately offered Russia a treaty of alliance, gave what help it could; so did the U.S.A., but it all was still small. The two English-speaking powers had endeavoured to clarify the objects of the war: at the beginning of the year President Roosevelt had spoken to Congress on the "four freedoms"—of speech and of worship, from want and from fear. In August he met Premier Churchill at sea and they drafted and signed an "Atlantic Charter," to enforce these—less clear, on the whole, than President Wilson's 14 points but with the same intentions. Stalin endorsed it, adding "our aim is to help those nations struggling against Hitler's tyranny and then leave it to them quite freely to organize their life as they see fit—there must be no interference whatever in the internal affairs of other nations."

But words, no more than money, win wars. The German army stamped forward. Kiev fell, Kharkov fell, all the Ukraine was occupied—the Russians burning or blowing up all they could as they left, to leave nothing for the conqueror. Savage brutality marked the German advance: in Western Europe the soldiers had (by the low standards now accepted) been fairly well behaved but they had no need to restrain themselves now. The Russian commanders Voroshilov and Budyenny were sent to the rear, but their successors were no luckier; the Don basin was occupied, the Crimea overrun, and the Germans were within nearly 20 miles of Moscow; government offices and foreign diplomats were sent to Kuibishev, 500 miles away.

Once again the Axis could not wait; it must pluck the fruit before it was ripe. On October 9th the Germans had, officially and clearly believing it, announced that the Soviet armies were in dissolution. This now seemed to be proved, to others than themselves, and the time to have arrived when the third phase of Axis conquest should commence. On December 7th, 1941, Japan attacked the American Pacific fleet at Pearl Harbour, sinking or putting out of action all 8 of its battleships, 3 out of its 7 cruisers, and 3 destroyers. America was now at war with the Axis.

During the months that followed Allied fortunes were at their lowest. The remaining naval forces in the Pacific, assembled under a Dutch admiral, were sunk off Java; two great British ships, the *Prince of Wales* and the *Repulse,* hurried to the East to save the situation, were sunk off Malaya for lack of air protection. The Philippines were conquered. Malaya was overrun and the great fortress of Singapore fell on February 15th, 1942. So far from aiding the Allies, the natives of south-eastern Asia were indifferent. Years of exploita-tion brought a foreseeable result: where they did not actively co-operate with the Japanese, they prevented (as at Penang) any efforts to "scorch the earth" as the Russians were doing. The only flash of hope came from Libya, where the British attacked Rommel in November and drove him right down to El Agheila, the turning point to Tripolitania. But it was only a flash; in January he counter-attacked and reconquered everything to Derna.

More hope, though it was to prove ephemeral, came from Russia. The Ger-mans were, strangely enough, not equipped for winter fighting and the hur-ried removal of Russian factories to sites beyond the Urals offset, to some extent, the loss of the Ukraine. General Timoshenko drove them back in the south, reaching Kharkov; Moscow was disengaged and Leningrad partially relieved. The news seemed overshadowed by the loss of another whole coun-try: the British were stampeded out of Burma, Rangoon falling on March 7th. In June the Germans attacked again in Libya; great hopes had been pinned on the reinforced 8th Army with its new U.S. tanks, but it was driven back to El Alamein, Rommel promising he would "pursue the beaten British into the Nile Valley." Next month the Japanese were swarming over New Guinea on the way to Australia, and the Germans broke Russian resistance in the south. Sevastopol fell, Rostov fell, and the Nazi troops pushed forward to-wards Grozny and Stalingrad, threatening to stop oil supplies in the first case and to cut the Volga line of supply in the second.

The British had made an attempt to rally the Indian people to their support. In March Sir Stafford Cripps was sent out to offer the Indian Congress Do-minion status after the war, with the right of secession; a constitution to be drafted by the Indians themselves; an executive Council immediately with the powers of a British Cabinet, the Viceroy's powers being held in reserve like the King's. But Mr. Gandhi sneered, "This is a post-dated cheque on a bank that is obviously crashing." Congress in July resolved on "a mass struggle" against the British; no resistance except soul-force would be opposed to the Japanese.

As if to mark their certainty of victory, the Germans in June had punished the death of Heydrich, the governor of Czechoslovakia, by killing 300 people and completely destroying the village of Lidice. But this murderousness was in fact a sign of weakness: ever since "Colonel Britton" in July 1941 had an-nounced on the British wireless the mobilization of the "V. army," resistance had been growing against the Germans. It was to be heartened by the news in the late summer, when at last the organization of Allied resources poured munitions into Britain and Russia. United States troops attacked the Japs on Guadalcanal in the Pacific in August; it was a slow and bloody fight, but it was an attack; and in New Guinea the Japs were pushed back to the sea. Though the Germans reached the Caucasus and hoisted the swastika on Mount Elbruz, the highest peak in Europe, they found it difficult to take Stalingrad; the Russian defence was unexpectedly obstinate.

Then, in November 1942, there seemed to come a sudden crack. On the morning of October 23rd, after long preparation, General Montgomery's 8th

Army attacked Rommel in Libya; the Axis air forces were swept from the skies; in the first days of November the battle of El Alamein was won and for the first time the world saw a Nazi army running helter-skelter, not to stop for hundreds of miles. The Soviet armies counter-attacked in South Russia; Stalingrad did not fall and the German force attacking it was encircled; and in January the world was to see for the first time a Nazi army marched off into captivity. A week after Montgomery's attack, American and British troops unexpectedly landed at Casablanca, Algiers, and Oran; after some half-hearted resistance by Pétain troops, a new front was established. The Allied difficulties were at first mainly political: the American commander-in-chief, General Eisenhower, first accepted as ruler a Pétainist admiral, Darlan, and after Darlan was assassinated a more reputable general, Giraud; Giraud's elevation was much resented by de Gaulle, a general who since July 1940 had been organizing French resistance from London. Eventually, de Gaulle's authority was recognized, but the ill-feeling left had a marked effect upon French policy in the future. Meanwhile, the Germans under von Arnim had had time to organize themselves in Tunisia; it was not until May 7th, 1943, that his forces and Rommel's, driven together as into a pen, surrendered and another great German army went to the prison camps. By now, too, the British Isles were no longer the victims of heavy bombardment; the R.A.F. by night and the U.S.A.A.F. by day were pounding and breaking German and European cities and military objectives, doing wide damage which may have helped greatly to shorten the war.

Submarine sinkings, however, remained alarming, and although the Russian armies were now becoming fully equipped the Stalingrad victory was not followed by any German debacle. The summer's fighting was to-and-fro—Russians advancing and being pushed back, and Germans doing the same; by August the Russians had a distinct advantage, especially in the South. Meanwhile the Western Allies, hopping from Africa, had conquered Sicily in July and entered Europe by the Italian "toe"; Mussolini, the first to fall, had been turned out of power on July 25th. Roosevelt and Churchill (who at Casablanca in January issued a statement demanding "unconditional surrender") now at Quebec received and accepted an Italian offer to change sides; but the ball seems to have been fumbled. The German reaction was the faster. The British forces who tried to take over the Greek islands abandoned by the Italians were once again defeated by German air power; very little ground was gained even in Italy, and an American landing further up the coast at Salerno was for a while in great danger; the Germans even rescued Mussolini and set up a "Fascist Republic" in the north.

The time had come to prevent dissensions between the Allies. The Russians had, nominally, dissolved the Communist International in May, but the month before (with an eye to the future) they had broken with the exiled Polish government in London. In many parts of Europe the Communist resistants were on poor terms with the others; in Yugoslavia indeed they were fighting, the active Communist Tito against the inert Royalist Mihailovitch. After consultations with Chiang Kai-Shek, in Cairo, Roosevelt and Churchill met Stalin at Teheran in Persia, at the end of November, for the first of three conferences whose decisions are still partly unknown. Later events seemed to show that the institution of a "United Nations" organization after the war was decided upon here, and that the military arrangements included an eventual Russian declaration of war on Japan, and the Russian right to liberate eastern Europe themselves, up to and including Prague. A co-ordination of resistance was arranged, involving the abandonment of Mihailovitch.

The turn from 1943 to 1944 saw the turn in the fortunes of the war. The Russians attacked all along the line and this time their gains were not lost again. Zhitomir was taken, Pskov was taken, Leningrad was relieved, Nikopol was taken, Odessa was taken; the Soviet forces were back to the 1938 border and soon over it. The "Gustav line" was broken at Cassino in Italy and after some nerve-racking days at a beachhead at Anzio, American troops entered Rome on June 4th. In the Far East, Japanese naval supremacy had been ended in March 1943 by the U.S. Navy in the battle of the Bismarck Sea; the slow but effective MacArthur-Nimitz "island-hopping" technique thus made possible had now cleared New Guinea and the Solomons and led to a devastating attack by a carrier task force on the formidable fortress-island of Truk. British and Chinese troops both entered Burma and at last began to drive the Japanese back.

But all this was overshadowed on the morning of June 6th by an event that will continue to be discussed as long as military history is written. The Western armies landed in France.

Long prepared, often adjourned (one actual false start was made), the gigantic expedition took place in a short lull in the worst storms June had seen in the Channel for twenty years. Despite the great armaments assembled, the landings were very hazardous; they are listed by the supreme commander, the American general Eisenhower, as one of the three crucial periods of his campaign. The "West-wall" had been declared impenetrable, and a gallant attack on it at Dieppe in 1942, largely by Canadians, had been disastrous. Eisenhower had 37 divisions under his hand, but von Rundstedt, his opponent, had 60. But bombing by 171 squadrons wrecked so many airfields, railways, and bridges that von Rundstedt could not collect his forces when he had realized where the main blow was being struck. Rejecting the Cotentin and the Pas de Calais where they were expected, the Allies had landed on the open beaches of Normandy, dropping parachute troops before them and bringing two artificial harbours called "mulberries." There were three separate landings, soon merged into one, the eastern end being manned by the British, the western by the Americans. Rommel (the commanders in the field were, to begin with, once again Rommel and Montgomery) concentrated all his armour and his best infantry at the east, around Caen, to save Paris and the Seine basin and protect the sites from which the Germans were now bombarding Britain (the Germans were using pilotless aircraft ["V-1"s] which blew up the buildings they struck—followed later by others faster than sound ["V-2"s] which fell onto their objectives from the upper air). Progress here was bloody and slow, but the United States troops pushed steadily westwards, until they first cut off the Cotentin peninsula and then captured Cherbourg, at last securing a big natural port. At the end of July they forced their way round the corner into Brittany by taking Avranches, opening the way for General Patton's army to fan out into its famous drive across north France. The French "Forces of the Interior" leapt to arms to meet him, and German rule began to fall to pieces. Dinan was taken on August 2nd, Rennes on the 4th, Mayenne on the 6th, Le Mans on the 9th, Nantes and Angers on the 10th—the Germans hurriedly fleeing into the fortified ports of Brest, St. Nazaire, St. Malo, and Lorient.

But this sensational advance seemed to the Germans to give them a chance: if Avranches could be retaken, Patton would be cut right off and immobilized. A powerful panzer attack was launched against it on August 7th. It was checked by the 12th, and the German generals held on too long. The whirling advance of Patton had now turned their positions into a long enclosed salient in the area of Falaise, which became what was hideously but correctly called a "killing ground." A few relics of the 5th and 7th panzer armies fled towards the bridgeless Seine; by the 22nd the rest of the German armies was dead or captive.

Meanwhile Patton's drive had swept on: Chartres, Dreux, Mantes on Seine, Orléans, Fontainebleau and Troyes all fell within a fortnight; and a fresh landing had been made in the South between Marseilles and Toulon which chased the Germans up the Rhone. But to a great extent France freed herself: Eisenhower estimated the value of the Resistance forces as "fifteen divisions"; the Germans ran because they had to, for all the country around them had suddenly become armed enemy territory. Paris freed itself by a revolt organized by the police, on August 19th, before the Allies arrived on the 25th.

Now came the turn of the British and Canadians; in a great northward sweep which stilled one by one the great ramps from which the "V-1"s were flying out towards Britain they poured across northern France and Belgium. On the 30th August the British were at Beauvais, next day at Amiens, then —day by day—at Arras, Tournai, Brussels, Antwerp, and Louvain. The Canadians and British on September 1st took Dieppe and Rouen; in the next four days they invested Le Havre, Boulogne and Calais; on the 6th they took Ostend. But now the great rush seemed to end; United States troops advanced to Luxembourg, French to the Rhine through the Vosges, but an attempt to carry on the invasion into Holland led to the loss of three quarters of a British parachute force at Arnhem. The first German city to fall, Aachen on the extreme border, was taken on October 21st; but heavy rains fell in November and the Allied armies seemed to have exhausted their impetus.

In eastern Europe the news also had been good, but there were some shadows. A heavy blow to the German armies had been struck in July by the recapture of Minsk; Vilna followed, and in August Russian troops crossed the East Prussian border near Mariampole; in Warsaw the Polish resistance forces rose in revolt to meet them. But the Russians failed to come to their aid; after three months of desperate struggle the Warsaw fighters were exterminated. The weight of the Soviet attack was shifted south; King Michael of

Roumania arrested his local Führer and changed sides; Bulgaria surrendered; Marshal Tito freed Yugoslavia; the Red Army entered Hungary. (Greece was freed by the British.)

In the Far East the Japanese fleet was shattered in the battle of the Philippines, and American troops landed on one of the islands (Leyte); British forces were slowly driving the Japanese back in Burma, but the going was very hard.

The winter of 1944 saw the last panzer attack in history. Fourteen infantry and ten panzer divisions, parachute troops and a restored Luftwaffe on December 12th attacked the Americans in the traditional area of the Ardennes. They broke through on a 45-mile front; the right and left of General Bradley's army were torn apart; the 101st U.S. Airborne Division was cut off in Bastogne on the way to Sedan; the Germans advanced 60 miles, almost to the Meuse. But they were first held and then driven back; a little more than a month later they were back where they were before, minus tanks, planes, and oil that they badly needed.

From then on the German ruin was precipitate. In January 1945 the Russians overran all Poland and Lithuania, entering Silesia and soon being a bare 30 miles from Berlin. In the West the Germans decided to fight west of the Rhine—the third crucial disaster in Eisenhower's opinion (the second being Falaise); by the first week in March they were crushed again and only the thin barrier of the Rhine remained. A second conference between Roosevelt, Churchill, and Stalin, in February at Yalta, co-ordinated plans for the final attack and for the political settlement of Europe and the Far East—successfully in the first case. Indeed, German military resistance was now only due to the will of one man, Adolf Hitler. An attempt to assassinate him on July 20, 1944 had failed, and while he still spoke the Nazis would still resist. But he could not alter the course of history; the Western armies were over the Rhine in March, the Ruhr was surrounded and soon after captured with its defenders. The Russians entered Vienna on April 13th, and shortly afterwards surrounded Berlin with the Führer within it; Patton drove towards Czechoslovakia stopping short of Prague; the British reached the Elbe. On that river on April 25th the Russian 58th Guards met the 69th U.S. division; and the Reich was cut in half.

It had been expected that Hitler would retire by air to a "redoubt" in the Alps where a last stand could be made, but he did not do so. Crazier than ever in his last days, and feeding himself to the end with delusions about German armies advancing to rescue him, he decided on a more melodramatic end; as the Russians fought their way to his air-raid shelter in Berlin he committed suicide on the last day of April with Eva Braun, and their bodies were afterwards burnt by his order. Mussolini two days before had been shot, with his mistress, by Italian partisans, and hanged upside down in the street.

The news ended resistance. On May 2nd Berlin surrendered; so did all the German armies in Italy; two days later the armies in Holland, northwest Germany, and Denmark did the same; on the 7th a general surrender was signed by Jodl, the German Chief of Staff. Nothing remained now to be done in Germany, except to co-ordinate the actions of the conquerors. As they over-

ran the Reich, and had seen Belsen, Dachau, Auschwitz and the other concentration camps, the Allies had realized that, unlike those of the first World
War, the stories of German crimes and savagery had been much below the
truth. They were not inclined for mercy, and meeting at Potsdam on July 17th,
agreed on economic and political arrangements for Germany which were
afterwards criticized as making it impossible for the country ever to be anything but a subsidized slum; moreover, the French, who occupied part of Germany, declined to co-operate in carrying out the plans. There were strange
faces at the conference. One of the architects of victory had died on the day
the Allies reached the Elbe, and an anxious President Truman took Roosevelt's
place. In the middle of the conference Churchill, who had linked his fortunes
with the Conservatives, disappeared; a general election had replaced him by
C. R. Attlee, the leader of the Labour Party. Stalin alone remained immovable
and inscrutable. But there was as yet no grave disagreement. The Russians
indeed seemed to favour (as might be expected) Communist parties in the
countries they had occupied, but other parties were not proscribed. Further-
more, a great step, as everyone agreed, had been taken towards unity on June
26th when the World Security Charter of the United Nations had been signed
at San Francisco by fifty nations. To placate both the Soviet and the United
States Senate a veto right for Great Powers had been incorporated in the new
organization.

But if there was no more fighting to be done in Germany, the war was
not over. The drama in Europe had played the Far Eastern struggle off the
stage; the Burma forces bitterly called themselves "the forgotten army." British and Indian forces had reopened the land road to China in January; in
March they had retaken Mandalay and the Burmese irregulars under Aung
San had crossed over from the Japanese side to the Allies; on May 5th Rangoon was taken and Burma was freed. In the Pacific the U.S. soldiers and
marines found that the vanishing of the Japanese navy made no difference in
the desperate fury with which the Japanese defended the vital Pacific islands.
The liberation of the Philippines was not completed until July 5th. The defenders of the island of Iwo Jima fought from February 19th to March 15th;
those of Okinawa, an island even more menacingly near to Japan, fought
with almost crazy recklessness from April 1st for nearly three months. Japan
seemed to have a great deal of energy left and a Russian declaration of war
still seemed to be a thing much to be desired.

But in fact Japan was far more exhausted than she appeared, and the use
of the most alarming of all "new weapons" was to bring her to a sudden
surrender. Early in the war, warned by Professor Einstein, among others, of
what the Nazis were doing, the Allies had been endeavouring to "split the
atom" and so release the ultimate energy of the universe. American, Canadian, and British scientists had worked on the problem and on July 16th,
1945, at six in the morning in a desert in New Mexico, an "atom bomb" had
been successfully exploded. Whether this mechanism should be used or not
depended, effectively, upon the new American President; he decided, as he
said afterwards, that two hundred thousand American lives might be saved if

it was, and probably even more of other nations. An atom bomb after what was, perhaps, a perfunctory warning, was dropped on the Japanese port of Hiroshima on August 6th. Broadly speaking, it destroyed the whole city and all living things therein. A similar result followed from the dropping of another atom bomb on Nagasaki three days later. (Between the two, the Russians had declared war on Japan and entered Manchuria; it seemed now a matter of small importance.) On August 14th the Japanese emperor surrendered unconditionally, and next day Mr. Truman and Mr. Atlee announced that "V-J Day," the ending of the second World War, might at last be officially celebrated.

§ 2

Whatever be the fate of the United Nations, there can be little question that the attainment of a federation of all humanity, together with a sufficient measure of social justice, to ensure health, education, and a rough equality of opportunity to most of the children born into the world, would mean such a release and increase of human energy as to open a new phase in human history. The enormous waste caused by the mutual injuries of competing great powers, and the still more enormous waste due to the under-productiveness of great masses of people, either because they are too wealthy for stimulus or too poor for efficiency, would cease. There would be a vast increase in the supply of human necessities, a rise in the standard of life and in men's ideas of what is considered a necessity, a development of transport and every kind of convenience; and a multitude of people would be transferred from low-grade production to such higher work as art of all kinds, teaching, scientific research, and the like. All over the world there would be a setting free of human capacity, such as has occurred hitherto only in small places and through precious limited phases of prosperity and security. Unless we are to suppose that spontaneous outbreaks of supermen have occurred in the past, it is reasonable to conclude that the Athens of Pericles, the Florence of the Medici, Elizabethan England, the great deeds of Asoka, the Tang and Ming periods in art, are but samples of what a whole world of sustained security would yield continuously and cumulatively. Without supposing any change in human quality, but merely its release from the present system of inordinate waste, history justifies this expectation.

We have seen how, since the liberation of human thought in the fifteenth and sixteenth centuries, a comparatively few curious and intelligent men, chiefly in Western Europe, have produced a vision of the world and a body of science that is now, on the material side, revolutionizing life. Mostly these men have worked against great discouragement, with insufficient funds and small help or support from the mass of mankind. It is impossible to believe that these men were the maximum intellectual harvest of their generation. England alone in the last three centuries must have produced scores of Newtons who never learnt to read, hundreds of Daltons, Darwins, Bacons, and

Huxleys who died stunted in hovels, or never got a chance of proving their quality.

All the world over, there must have been myriads of potential first-class investigators, splendid artists, creative minds, who never caught a gleam of inspiration or opportunity, for every one of that kind who had left his mark upon the world. In the present warfare thousands of potential great men are dying unfulfilled. But a world with something like a secure international peace, and something like social justice, will fish for capacity with the fine net of universal education, and may expect a yield beyond comparison greater than any yield of able and brilliant men that the world has known hitherto.

It is such considerations as this, indeed, which justify the concentration of effort in the near future upon the making of a new world state of righteousness out of our present confusions. War is a horrible thing, and constantly more horrible and dreadful, so that unless it is ended it will certainly end human society; social injustice, and the sight of the limited and cramped human beings it produces, torment the soul, but the strongest incentive to constructive political and social work for an imaginative spirit lies not so much in their mere hope of escaping evils as in the opportunity for great adventures that their suppression will open to our race. We want to get rid of the militarist, not simply because he hurts and kills, but because he is an intolerable thick-voiced blockhead who stands hectoring and blustering in our way to achievement. We want to abolish many extravagances of private ownership just as we should want to abolish some idiot guardian who refused us admission to a studio in which there were fine things to do.

There are people who seem to imagine that a world order and one universal law and justice would end human adventure. It would but begin it. But instead of the adventure of the past, the "romance" of the cinematograph world, the perpetual reiteration harping upon the trite reactions of sex and combat and the hunt for gold, it would be an unending exploration upon the edge of experience. Hitherto a man has been living in a slum, amidst quarrels, revenges, vanities, shames and taints, hot desires and urgent appetites. He has scarcely tasted sweet air yet, and the great freedoms of the world that science has enlarged for him.

To picture to ourselves something of the wider life that world unity would open to men is a very attractive speculation. Life will certainly go with a stronger pulse, it will breathe a deeper breath, because it will have dispelled and conquered a hundred infections of body and mind that now reduce it to invalidism and squalor. We have already laid stress on the vast elimination of drudgery from human life through the creation of a new race of slaves, the machines. This, and the disappearance of war and the smoothing out of endless restraints and contentions by juster social and economic arrangements, will lift the burthen of toilsome work and routine work, that has been the price of human security since the dawn of the first civilizations, from the shoulders of our children. Which does not mean that they will cease to work, but that they will cease to do irksome work under pressure, and will work freely, planning, making, creating, according to their gifts and instincts. They will fight nature no longer as dull conscripts of the pick and plough, but for a splendid conquest. Only the spiritlessness of our present depression blinds us to the clear intimations of our reason that in the course of a few generations every little country town could become an Athens, every human being could be gentle in breeding and healthy in body and mind, the whole solid earth man's mine and its uttermost regions his playground.

In this *Outline* we have sought to show two great systems of development interacting in the story of human society. We have seen that later special Neolithic culture giving rise in the warmer alluvial parts of the world to the great primordial civilizations, fecund systems of subjugation and obedience, vast multiplications of industrious and subservient men. We have shown the necessary relationship of these early civilizations to the early temples and to king-gods and god-kings. At the same time we have traced the development from a simpler Neolithic level of the wanderer peoples, who became the nomadic peoples, in those great groups the Nordic Aryans and the Hun-Mongol peoples of the north-west and the north-east and the Semites of the Arabian deserts. Our history has told of a repeated overrunning and refreshment of the originally brunet civilizations by these hardier, bolder, free-spirited peoples of the steppes and desert. We have pointed out how these constantly-recurring nomadic injections have steadily altered the primordial civilizations both in blood and in spirit; and how the world religions of to-day, and what we now call democracy, the boldness of modern scientific inquiry and a universal restlessness, are due to this "nomadization" of civilization. The old civilizations created tradition, and lived by tradition. To-day the power of tradition is destroyed. The body of our state is civilization still, but its spirit is the spirit of the nomadic world. It is the spirit of the great plains and the high seas.

So that it is difficult to resist the persuasion that so soon as one law runs in the earth and the fierceness of frontiers ceases to distress us, that urgency in our nature which stirs us in spring and autumn to be up and travelling will have its way with us. We shall obey the call of the summer pastures and the winter pastures in our blood, the call of the mountains, the desert, and the sea. For some of us, also, who may be of a different lineage, there is the call of the forest, and there are those who would hunt in the summer and return to the fields for the harvest and the plough. But this does not mean that men will have become homeless and all adrift. The normal nomadic life is not a homeless one, but a movement between homes. The Kalmucks to-day, like the swallows, go yearly a thousand miles from one home to another. The beautiful and convenient cities of the coming age, we conclude, will have their seasons when they will be full of life, and seasons when they will seem asleep. Life will ebb and flow to and from every region seasonally as the interest of that region rises or declines.

There will be little drudgery in this better-ordered world. Natural power harnessed in machines will be the general drudge. What drudgery is inevitable will be done as a service and duty for a few years or months out of each life; it will not consume nor degrade the whole life of anyone. And not only drudges, but many other sorts of men and ways of living which loom large in the current social scheme will necessarily have dwindled in importance or passed away altogether; there will be few professional fighting men or none at all, no custom-house officers; the increased multitude of teachers will have abolished large police forces and large jail staffs, mad houses will be rare or non-existent; a world-wide sanitation will have diminished the proportion of hospitals, nurses, sick-room attendants, and the like; a world-wide economic justice, the floating population of cheats, sharpers, gamblers, forestallers, parasites, and speculators generally. But there will be no diminution of adventure or romance in this world of the days to come. Sea fisheries and the incessant insurrection of the sea, for example, will call for their own stalwart types of men; the high air will clamour for manhood, the deep and dangerous secret places of nature.

Men will turn again with renewed interest to the animal world. In these disordered days a stupid, uncontrollable massacre of animal species goes on— from certain angles of vision it is a thing almost more tragic than human miseries; in the nineteenth century dozens of animal species, and some of them very interesting species, were exterminated; but one of the first fruits of an effective world state would be the better protection of what are now wild beasts. It is a strange thing in human history to note how little has been done since the Bronze Age in taming, using, befriending, and appreciating the animal life about us. But that mere witless killing, which is called sport to-day, would inevitably give place in a better-educated world community to a modification of the primitive instincts that find expression in this way, changing them into an interest not in the deaths but in the lives of beasts, and leading to fresh and perhaps very strange and beautiful attempts to befriend these pathetic, kindred lower creatures we no longer fear as enemies, hate as rivals, or need as slaves.

And a world state and universal justice do not mean the imprisonment of our race in any bleak institutional orderliness. There will still be mountains and the sea, there will be jungles and great forests, cared for, indeed, and treasured and protected; the great plains will still spread before us and the wild winds blow. But men will not hate so much, fear so much, nor cheat so desperately—and they will keep their minds and bodies cleaner.

The weaving of mankind into one community does not imply the creation of a homogeneous community, but rather the reverse; the welcome and the adequate utilization of distinctive quality in an atmosphere of understanding. It is the almost universal bad manners of the present age which make race intolerable to race. The community to which we may be moving will be more mixed—which does not necessarily mean more interbred—more various and more interesting than any existing community. Communities all to one pattern, like boxes of toy soldiers, are things of the past rather than the future.

But one of the hardest, most impossible tasks a writer can set himself, is to picture the life of people better educated, happier in their circumstances, more free and more healthy than he is himself. We know enough to-day to know that there is infinite room for betterment in every human concern. Nothing is needed but collective effort and mutual toleration. Our poverty, our restraints, our infections and indigestions, our quarrels and misunderstandings, are all things controllable and removable by concerted human action; but we know as little how life would feel without them as some poor, dirty, ill-treated, fierce-souled creature born and bred amidst the cruel and dingy surroundings of a European back street can know what it is to bathe every day, always to be clad beautifully, to climb mountains for pleasure, to fly, to meet none but agreeable, well-mannered people, to conduct researches or make delightful things. Yet a time when all such good things will be for all men may be coming more nearly than we think. Each one who believes that brings the good time nearer; each heart that fails delays it.

One cannot foretell the surprises or disappointments the future has in store. Before this chapter of the World State can begin fairly in our histories, other chapters as yet unsuspected may still need to be written, as long and as full of conflict as our account of the growth and rivalries of the Great Powers and the insurrection of gangster totalitarianism. There may be tragic economic struggles, grim grapplings of race with race and class with class. It may be that "private interprise" will refuse to learn the lesson of service without yet another catastrophic revolution. We do not know; we cannot tell. These are unnecessary disasters, but they may be unavoidable, monstrous disasters. Human history becomes more and more a race between education and catastrophe. Against the unifying effort of Christendom and against the unifying influence of the mechanical revolution, catastrophe won. We cannot tell yet how much of the winnings of catastrophe still remain to be gathered in, what vast harvests of wasted lives still await the reaper. New falsities, still undreamt of, may arise and hold men in some unrighteous and fated scheme of order for a time, before they collapse amidst the misery and slaughter of generations.

Yet, clumsily or smoothly, the world, it seems, progresses and will progress. In this *Outline*, in our account of Palæolithic men we have borrowed a description from Mr. Worthington Smith of the very highest life in the world some fifty thousand years ago. It was a bestial life. We have sketched, too, the gathering for a human sacrifice, some fifteen thousand years ago. That scene, again, is almost incredibly cruel to a modern civilized reader.

It is not more than five hundred years since the great empire of the Aztecs still believed that it could live only by the shedding of blood. Every year in Mexico hundreds of human victims died in this fashion: the body was bent like a bow over the curved stone of sacrifice, the breast was slashed open with a knife of obsidian, and the priest tore out the beating heart of the still living victim. The day may be close at hand when we shall no longer eat out the hearts of men, even for the sake of our national gods. Let the reader but refer to the earlier time charts we have given in this history, and he will see the true measure and transitoriness of all the conflicts, deprivations, and miseries of this present period of bleak and painful, and yet, on the whole, of hopeful change.

CHRONOLOGICAL TABLE

To CONCLUDE this Outline, we give here a Table of Leading events from the year 800 B.C. to A.D. 1953.

It is well that the reader should keep in mind an idea of the true proportions of historical to geological time. Let us quote from a recent book by J. H. Robinson: "In order to understand the light which the discovery of the vast age of mankind casts on our present position, our relation to the past, and our hopes for the future, let us borrow with some modifications (from Heinrich Schmidt, one of Haeckel's students) an ingenious device for illustrating modern historical perspective. Let us imagine the whole history of mankind crowded into twelve hours, and that we are living at noon of the long human day. Let us, in the interest of moderation and convenient reckoning, assume that man has been upright and engaged in seeking out inventions for only two hundred and forty thousand years. Each hour of our clock will represent twenty thousand years, each minute three hundred and thirty-three and a third years. For over eleven and a half hours nothing was recorded. We know of no persons or events; we only infer that man was living on the earth, for we find his stone tools, bits of his pottery, and some of his pictures of mammoths and bison. Not until twenty minutes before twelve do the earliest vestiges of Egyptian and Babylonian civilization begin to appear. The Greek literature, philosophy, and science, of which we have been accustomed to speak as 'ancient,' are not seven minutes old. At one minute before twelve Lord Bacon wrote his *Advancement of Learning,* and not half a minute has elapsed since man first began to make the steam engine do his work for him."

That is an excellent example of a small-scale time-representation of history.

Chronology only begins to be precise enough to specify the exact year of any event after the establishment of the eras of the First Olympiad and the building of Rome.

About the year 1,000 B.C. the Aryan peoples were establishing themselves in the peninsulas of Spain, Italy, and the Balkans, and they were established in North India, Cnossos was already destroyed, and the spacious times of Egypt, of Thothmes III, Amenophis III and Rameses II were three or four centuries away. Weak monarchs of the XXIst Dynasty were ruling in the Nile Valley. Israel was united under her early kings; Saul or David or possibly even Solomon may have been reigning. Sargon I (2,750 B.C.) of the Akkadian Sumerian Empire was a remote memory in Babylonian history, more remote than is Constantine the Great from the world of the present day. Hammurabi had been dead a thousand years. The Assyrians were already dominating the less military Babylonians. In 1,100 B.C. Tiglath Pileser I had taken Babylon. But there was no permanent conquest; Assyria and Babylonia were still separate empires. In China the new Chow dynasty was flourishing. Stonehenge in England was already a thousand years old.

The next two centuries saw a renascence of Egypt under the XXIInd Dynasty, the splitting up of the brief little Hebrew kingdom of Solomon, the spreading of the Greeks in the Balkans, South Italy and Asia Minor, and the days of Etruscan predominance in Central Italy. We may begin our list of ascertainable dates with—

B.C.

800. The building of Carthage.

790. The Ethiopian conquest of Egypt (founding the XXVth Dynasty).

776. First Olympiad.

753. Rome built.

745. Tiglath Pileser III conquered Babylonia and founded the New Assyrian Empire.

738. Menahem, king of Israel, bought off Tiglath Pileser III.

735. Greeks settling in Sicily.

722. Sargon II armed the Assyrians with iron weapons.

721. He deported the Israelites.

704. Sennacherib.

701. His army destroyed by a pestilence on its way to Egypt.

680. Esarhaddon took Thebes in Egypt (overthrowing the Ethiopian XXVth Dynasty).

667. Sardanapalus.

664. Psammetichus I restored the freedom of Egypt and founded the XXXVIth Dynasty (to 610). He was assisted against Assyria by Lydian troops sent by Gyges.

608. Necho of Egypt defeated Josiah, king of Judah, at the Battle of Megiddo.

606. Capture of Nineveh by the Chaldeans and Medes. Foundation of the Chaldean Empire.

604. Necho pushed to the Euphrates and was overthrown by Nebuchadnezzar II.

586. Nebuchadnezzar carried off the Jews to Babylon. Many fled to Egypt and settled there.

550. Cyrus the Persian succeeded Cyaxares the Mede.
     Cyrus conquered Crœsus.
     Buddha lived about this time. So also did Confucius and Lao Tse.

539. Cyrus took Babylon and founded the Persian Empire.

527. Peisistratus died.

525. Cambyses conquered Egypt. Æschylus born.

521. Darius I, the son of Hystaspes, ruled from the Hellespont to the Indus. His expedition to Scythia.

495. Sophocles born.

490. Battle of Marathon.

484. Herodotus born. Æschylus won his first prize for tragedy.

480. Battles of Thermopylæ and Salamis. Euripides born.

479. The Battles of Platæa and Mycale completed the repulse of Persia.

474. Etruscan fleet destroyed by the Sicilian Greeks.

B.C.

470. Voyage of Hanno.
466. Pericles.
465. Xerxes murdered.
438. Herodotus recited his History in Athens.
431. Peloponnesian War began (to 404).
429. Pericles died. Herodotus died.
427. Aristophanes began his career. Plato born. He lived to 347.
401. Retreat of the Ten Thousand.
390. Brennus sacked Rome.
366. Camillus built the Temple of Concord.
359. Philip became king of Macedonia.
338. Battle of Chæronia.
336. Macedonian troops crossed into Asia. Philip murdered.
334. Battle of the Granicus.
333. Battle of Issus.
332. Alexander in Egypt.
331. Battle of Arbela.
330. Darius III killed.
323. Death of Alexander the Great.
321. Rise of Chandragupta in the Punjab. The Romans completely beaten
      by the Samnites at the Battle of the Caudine Forks.
303. Chandragupta repulsed Seleucus.
285. Ptolemy Soter died.
281. Pyrrhus invaded Italy.
280. Battle of Heraclea.
279. Battle of Ausculum.
278. Gauls' raid into Asia Minor and settlement in Galatia.
275. Pyrrhus left Italy.
264. First Punic War. (Asoka began to reign in Behar—to 227.) First
      gladiatorial games in Rome.
260. Battle of Mylæ.
256. Battle of Ecnomus.
246. Shi-Hwang-ti became king of Ts'in.
241. Battle of Ægatian Isles. End of First Punic War.
225. Battle of Telamon. Roman armies in Illyria.
220. Shi-Hwang-ti became emperor of China.
219. Second Punic War.
216. Battle of Cannæ.
214. Great Wall of China begun.
210. Death of Shi-Hwang-ti.
202. Battle of Zama.
201. End of Second Punic War.
200–197. Duration of war between Rome and with Macedonia.
192. War with the Seleucids.
190. Battle of Magnesia.

B.C.

149. Third Punic War. (The Yueh-Chi came into Western Turkestan.)
146. Carthage destroyed. Corinth destroyed.
133. Attalus bequeathed Pergamum to Rome. Tiberius Gracchus killed.
121. Gaius Gracchus killed.
118. War with Jugurtha.
106. War with Jugurtha ended.
102. Marius drove back Germans.
100. Triumph of Marius. (Wu-ti conquering the Tarim valley.)
 91. Social war.
 89. All Italians became Roman citizens.
 86. Death of Marius.
 78. Death of Sulla.
 73. The revolt of the slaves under Spartacus.
 71. Defeat and end of Spartacus.
 66. Pompey led Roman troops to the Caspian and Euphrates. He encountered the Alani.
 64. Mithridates of Pontus died.
 53. Crassus killed at Carrhæ. Mongolian elements with Parthians.
 48. Julius Cæsar defeated Pompey at Pharsalos.
 44. Julius Cæsar assassinated.
 31. Battle of Actium.
 27. Augustus Cæsar princeps (until 14 A.D.).
  4. True date of birth of Jesus of Nazareth.

CHRISTIAN ERA

A.D.

  6. Province of Mœsia established.
  9. Province of Pannonia established. Imperial boundary carried to the Danube.
 14. Augustus died. Tiberius emperor.
 30. Jesus of Nazareth crucified.
 37. Caligula succeeded Tiberius.
 41. Claudius (the first emperor of the legions) made emperor by pretorian guard after murder of Caligula.
 54. Nero succeeded Claudius.
 61. Boadicea massacred Roman garrison in Britain.
 68. Suicide of Nero. (Galba, Otho, Vitellus, emperors in succession.)
 69. Vespasian began the so-called Flavian dynasty.
 79. Titus succeeded Vespasian.
 81. Domitian.
 84. North Britain annexed.
 96. Nerva began the so-called dynasty of the Antonines.
 98. Trajan succeeded Nerva.
102. Pan Chau on the Caspian Sea. (Indo-Scythians invading North India.)

A.D.

117. Hadrian succeeded Trajan. Roman Empire at its greatest extent.

138. Antoninus Pius succeeded Hadrian.
(The Indo-Scythians at this time were destroying the last traces of Hellenic rule in India.)

150. [About this time Kanishka reigned in India, Kashgar, Yarkand, and Kotan.]

161. Marcus Aurelius succeeded Antoninus Pius.

164. Great plague began and lasted to the death of Marcus Aurelius (180). This also devastated all Asia.

180. Death of Marcus Aurelius.
(Nearly a century of war and disorder began in the Roman Empire.)

220. End of the Han dynasty. Beginning of four hundred years of division in China.

226. Ardashir I (first Sassanid shah) put an end to Arsacid line in Persia.

242. Mani began his teaching.

247. Goths crossed Danube in a great raid.

251. Great victory of Goths. Emperor Decius killed.

260. Sapor I, the second Sassanid shah, took Antioch, captured the Emperor Valerian, and was cut up on his return from Asia Minor by Odenathus of Palmyra.

269. The Emperor Claudius defeated the Goths at Nish.

270. Aurelian became emperor.

272. Zenobia carried captive to Rome. End of the brief glories of Palmyra.

275. Probus succeeded Aurelian.

276. Goths in Pontus. The Emperor Probus forced back Franks and Alemanni.

277. Mani crucified in Persia.

284. Diocletian became emperor.

303. Diocletian persecuted the Christians.

306. Constantine the Great became emperor.

311. Galerius abandoned the persecution of the Christians.

314. Constantine presided over a Christian Council at Arles.

321. Fresh Gothic raids driven back.

323. Constantine presided over the Council of Nicæa.

337. Vandals driven by Goths obtained leave to settle in Pannonia.
Constantine baptized on his death-bed.

354. St. Augustine born.

361-3. Julian the Apostate attempted to substitute Mithraism for Christianity.

379. Theodosius the Great (a Spaniard) emperor.

390. The statue of Serapis at Alexandria broken up.

392. Theodosius the Great emperor of East and West.

395. Theodosius the Great died. Honorius and Arcadius redivided the empire with Stilicho and Alaric as their masters and protectors.

A.D.

410. The Visigoths under Alaric captured Rome.

425. Vandals settling in south of Spain. Huns in Pannonia, Goths in Dalmatia. Visigoths and Suevi in Portugal and North Spain. English invading Britain.

429. Vandals under Genseric invaded Africa.

439. Vandals took Carthage.

448. Priscus visited Attila.

451. Attila raided Gaul and was defeated by Franks, Alemanni, and Romans at Troyes.

453. Death of Attila.

455. Vandals sacked Rome.

470. Ephthalites' raid into India.

476. Odoacer, king of a medley of Teutonic tribes, informed Constantinople that there was no emperor in the West. End of the Western Empire.

480. St. Benedict born.

481. Clovis in France. The Merovingians.

483. Nestorian Church broke away from the Orthodox Christian Church.

493. Theodoric the Ostrogoth conquered Italy and became King of Italy, but was nominally subject to Constantinople.
(Gothic kings in Italy. Goths settled on special confiscated lands as a garrison.)

527. Justinian emperor.

528. Mihiragula, the (Ephthalite) Attila of India, overthrown.

529. Justinian closed the schools at Athens, which had flourished nearly a thousand years. Belisarius (Justinian's general) took Naples.

531. Chosroes I began to reign.

543. Great plague in Constantinople.

544. St. Benedict died.

553. Goths expelled from Italy by Justinian. Cassiodorus founded his monastery.

565. Justinian died. The Lombards conquered most of North Italy (leaving Ravenna and Rome Byzantine). The Turks broke up the Ephthalites in Western Turkestan.

570. Muhammad born.

579. Chosroes I died.
(The Lombards dominant in Italy.)

590. Plague raged in Rome. (Gregory the Great—Gregory I—and the vision of St. Angelo.) Chosroes II began to reign.

610. Heraclius began to reign.

618. Tang dynasty began in China.

619. Chosroes II held Egypt, Jerusalem, Damascus, and had armies on Hellespont.

622. The Hegira.

623. Battle of Badr.

A.D.

627. Great Persian defeat at Nineveh by Heraclius. The Meccan allies besieged Medina. Tai Tsung became Emperor of China.

628. Kavadh II murdered and succeeded his father, Chosroes II.
Muhammad wrote letters to all the rulers of the earth.

629. Yuan Chwang started for India. Muhammad returned to Mecca.

632. Muhammad died. Abu Bekr Caliph.

634. Omar second Caliph.

635. Tai Tsung received Nestorian missionaries.

636. Battle of the Yarmuk. Moslems took Syria.

637. Battle of Kadessia.

638. Jerusalem surrendered to Omar.

642. Heraclius died.

644. Othman third Caliph.

645. Yuan Chwang returned to Singan.

655. Defeat of the Byzantine fleet by the Moslems.

656. Othman murdered at Medina.

661. Ali murdered. Muawija Caliph. (First of the Omayyad caliphs.)

668. The Caliph Muawija attacked Constantinople by sea—Theodore of Tarsus became Archbishop of Canterbury.

675. Last of the sea attacks by Muawija on Constantinople.

687. Pepin of Hersthal, mayor of the palace, reunited Austrasia and Neustria.

711. Moslem army invaded Spain from Africa.

716–17. Suleiman, son and successor of Walid, failed to take Constantinople. The Omayyad line passed its climax.

721. Charles Martel mayor of the palace. The domains of the Caliph Walid I extended from the Pyrenees to China.

732. Charles Martel defeated the Moslems near Poitiers.

735. Death of the Venerable Bede.

743. Walid II Caliph—the unbelieving Caliph.

749. Overthrow of the Omayyads. Abul Abbas, the first Abbasid Caliph. Spain remained Omayyad. Beginning of the break-up of the Arab Empire.

751. Pepin crowned King of the French.

755. Martyrdom of St. Boniface.

768. Pepin died.

771. Charlemagne sole king.

774. Charlemagne conquered Lombardy.

776. Charlemagne in Dalmatia.

786. Haroun-al-Raschid Abbasid Caliph in Bagdad (to 809).

795. Leo III became Pope (to 816).

800. Leo crowned Charlemagne Emperor of the West.

802. Egbert, formerly an English refugee at the Court of Charlemagne, established himself as King of Wessex.

811. Krum of Bulgaria defeated and killed the Emperor Nicephorus.

A.D.

814. Charlemagne died; Louis the Pious succeeded him.

828. Egbert became first King of England.

843. Louis the Pious died, and the Carlovingian Empire went to pieces. Until 962 there was no regular succession of Holy Roman Emperors, though the title appeared intermittently.

850. About this time Rurik (a Northman) became ruler of Novgorod and Kieff.

852. Boris first Christian King of Bulgaria (to 884).

865. The fleet of the Russians (Northmen) threatened Constantinople.

886. The Treaty of Alfred of England and Guthrum the Dane establishing the Danes in the Danelaw.

904. Russian (Northmen) fleet off Constantinople.

911. Rolf the Ganger established himself in Normandy.

919. Henry the Fowler elected King of Germany.

928. Marozia imprisoned Pope John X.

931. John XI Pope (to 936).

936. Otto I became King of Germany in succession to his father, Henry the Fowler.

941. Russian fleet again threatened Constantinople.

955. John XII Pope.

960. Northern Sung dynasty began in China.

962. Otto I, King of Germany, crowned Emperor (first Saxon Emperor) by John XII.

963. Otto deposed John XII.

969. Separate Fatimite Caliphate set up in Egypt.

973. Otto II.

983. Otto III.

987. Hugh Capet became King of France. End of the Carlovingian line of French kings.

1016. Canute became King of England, Denmark, and Norway.

1037. Avicenna of Bokhara, the Prince of Physicians, died.

1043. Russian fleet threatened Constantinople.

1066. Conquest of England by William, Duke of Normandy.

1071. Revival of Islam under the Seljuk Turks. Battle of Melasgird.

1073. Hildebrand became Pope (Gregory VII) to 1085.

1077. Henry IV did penance at Canossa.

1079. Peter Abelard born.

1082. Robert Guiscard captured Durazzo.

1084. Robert Guiscard sacked Rome.

1087–99. Urban II Pope.

1094. Pestilence.

1095. Urban II at Clermont summoned the First Crusade.

1096. Massacre of the People's Crusade.

1099. Godfrey of Bouillon captured Jerusalem. Paschal II Pope (to 1118).

A.D.

1138. Kin Empire flourished. The Sung capital shifted from Nanking to Hang Chau.

1142. Peter Abelard died.

1147. The Second Crusade. Foundation of the Christian kingdom of Portugal.

1169. Saladin Sultan of Egypt.

1177. Frederick Barbarossa acknowledged supremacy of the Pope (Alexander III) at Venice.

1187. Saladin captured Jerusalem.

1189. The Third Crusade.

1193. Albertus Magnus born.

1198. Averroes of Cordoba, the Arab philosopher, died. Innocent III Pope (to 1216); Frederick II (aged four), king of Sicily, became his ward.

1202. The Fourth Crusade attacked the Eastern Empire.

1204. Capture of Constantinople by the Latins.

1206. Kutub founded Moslem state at Delhi.

1212. The Children's Crusade.

1214. Jengis Khan took Peking.

1215. Magna Charta signed.

1216. Honorius III Pope.

1218. Jengis Khan invaded Kharismia.

1221. Failure and return of the Fifth Crusade. St. Dominic died (the Dominicans).

1225. Thomas Aquinas born.

1226. St. Francis of Assisi died (the Franciscans).

1227. Jengis Khan, khan from the Caspian to the Pacific, died, and was succeeded by Ogdai Khan. Gregory IX Pope.

1228. Frederick II embarked upon the Sixth Crusade, and acquired Jerusalem.

1234. Mongols completed conquest of the Kin Empire with the help of the Sung Empire.

1239. Frederick II excommunicated for the second time.

1240. Mongols destroyed Kieff. Russia tributary to the Mongols.

1241. Mongol victory at Liegnitz in Silesia.

1244. The Egyptian Sultan recaptured Jerusalem. This led to the Seventh Crusade.

1245. Frederick II re-excommunicated. The men of Schwyz burnt the castle of New Habsburg.

1250. St. Louis of France ransomed. Frederick II, the last Hohenstaufen Emperor, died. German interregnum until 1273.

1251. Mangu Khan became Great Khan. Kublai Khan governor of China.

1258. Hulagu Khan took and destroyed Bagdad.

1260. Kublai Khan became Great Khan. Ketboga defeated in Palestine.

1261. The Greeks recaptured Constantinople from the Latins.

A.D.

1265. Dante Alighieri born.

1266. Giotto born.

1269. Kublai Khan sent a message of inquiry to the Pope by the older Polos.

1271. Marco Polo started upon his travels.

1273. Rudolph of Habsburg elected emperor. The Swiss formed their Ever-lasting League.

1274. Thomas Aquinas died.

1280. Kublai Khan founded the Yuan dynasty in China. Albertus Magnus died.

1292. Death of Kublai Khan.

1293. Roger Bacon, the prophet of experimental science, died.

1294. Boniface VIII Pope (to 1303).

1295. Marco Polo returned to Venice.

1303. Death of Pope Boniface VIII after the outrage of Anagni by Guil-laume de Nogaret.

1304. Petrarch born.

1305. Clement V Pope.

1308. Duns Scotus died.

1309. The papal Court set up at Avignon.

1318. Four Franciscans burnt for heresy at Marseilles.

1337. Giotto died.

1347. Occam died.

1348. The Great Plague, the Black Death.

1358. The Jacquerie in France.

1368. In China the Mongol (Yuan) dynasty fell, and was succeeded by the Ming dynasty (to 1644).

1369. Timurlane assumed the title of Great Khan.

1374. Petrarch died.

1377. Pope Gregory XI returned to Rome.

1378. The Great Schism. Urban VI in Rome, Clement VII at Avignon.

1381. Peasant revolt in England. Wat Tyler murdered in the presence of King Richard II.

1384. Wycliffe died.

1387. Fra Angelico da Fiesole born.

1398. Huss preached Wycliffism at Prague.

1400. Chaucer died.

1405. Death of Timurlane.

1414–18. The Council of Constance. Huss burnt (1415).

1417. The Great Schism ended. Martin V Pope.

1420. The Hussites revolted. Martin V preached a crusade against them.

1431. The Catholic Crusaders dissolved before the Hussites at Domazlice. The Council of Basel met. Villon born. Mantegna born.

1436. The Hussites came to terms with the church.

1439. Council of Basel created a fresh schism in the church.

A.D.

1445. Discovery of Cape Verde by the Portuguese.

1446. First printed books (Coster in Haarlem).

1449. End of the Council of Basel.

1452. Leonardo da Vinci born.

1453. Ottoman Turks under Muhammad II took Constantinople.

1471. Dürer born.

1473. Copernicus born.

1480. Ivan III, Grand-duke of Moscow, threw off the Mongol allegiance.

1481. Death of the Sultan Muhammad II while preparing for the conquest of Italy. Bayazid II Turkish Sultan (to 1512).

1486. Diaz rounded the Cape of Good Hope.

1492. Columbus crossed the Atlantic to America. Rodrigo Borgia, Alexander VI, Pope (to 1503).

1493. Maximilian I became emperor.

1498. Vasco da Gama sailed round the Cape to India.

1499. Switzerland became an independent republic.

1500. Charles V born.

1509. Henry VIII King of England.

1512. Selim Sultan (to 1520). He bought the title of Caliph. Fall of Soderini (and Machiavelli) in Florence.

1513. Leo X Pope.

1515. Francis I King of France.

1517. Selim annexed Egypt. Luther propounded his theses at Wittenberg.

1519. Leonardo da Vinci died. Magellan's expedition started to sail round the world. Cortez entered Mexico City.

1520. Suleiman the Magnificent, Sultan (to 1566), who ruled from Bagdad to Hungary. Charles V Emperor.

1521. Luther at the Diet of Worms. Loyola wounded at Pampeluna.

1525. Baber won the Battle of Panipat, captured Delhi, and founded the Mogul Empire.

1527. The German troops in Italy, under the Constable of Bourbon, took and pillaged Rome.

1528. Paul Veronese born.

1529. Suleiman besieged Vienna.

1530. Pizarro invaded Peru. Charles V crowned by the Pope. Henry VIII began his quarrel with the Papacy.

1532. The Anabaptists seized Münster.

1535. Fall of the Anabaptist rule in Münster.

1539. The Society of Jesus founded.

1545. The Council of Trent (to 1563) assembled to put the church in order.

1546. Martin Luther died.

1547. Ivan IV (the Terrible) took the title of Tsar of Russia. Francis I died.

1549. First Jesuit missions arrived in South America.

1552. Treaty of Passau. Temporary pacification of Germany.

A.D.

1556. Charles V abdicated. Akbar Great Mogul (to 1605). Ignatius of Loyola died.

1558. Death of Charles V.

1561. Francis Bacon (Lord Verulam) born.

1563. End of the Council of Trent and the reform of the Catholic Church.

1564. Shakespeare born.

1566. Suleiman the Magnificent died.

1567. Revolt of the Netherlands.

1568. Execution of Counts Egmont and Horn.

1573. Siege of Alkmaar.

1583. Sir Walter Raleigh's expedition to Virginia.

1603. James I King of England and Scotland.

1605. Jehangir Great Mogul.

1606. Virginia Company founded.

1609. Holland independent.

1618. Thirty Years' War began.

1620. *Mayflower* expedition founded New Plymouth. First negro slaves landed at Jamestown (Va.).

1625. Charles I of England.

1626. Sir Francis Bacon (Lord Verulam) died.

1628. Shah Jehan Great Mogul. The English *Petition of Right*.

1629. Charles I of England began his eleven years of rule without a parliament.

1632. Leeuwenhoek born. Gustavus Adolphus killed at the Battle of Lützen.

1634. Wallenstein murdered.

1638. Japan closed to Europeans (until 1865).

1640. Charles I of England summoned the Long Parliament.

1641. Massacre of the English in Ireland.

1643. Louis XIV began reign of seventy-two years.

1644. The Manchus ended the Ming dynasty.

1645. Swine pens in the inner town of Leipzig pulled down.

1648. Treaty of Westphalia. Thereby Holland and Switzerland were recognized as free republics and Prussia became important. The treaty gave a complete victory neither to the Imperial Crown nor to the Princes.

War of the Fronde; it ended in the complete victory of the French Crown.

1649. Execution of Charles I of England.

1658. Aurungzeb Great Mogul. Cromwell died.

1660. Charles II of England.

1674. Nieuw Amsterdam finally became British by treaty and was renamed New York.

1683. The last Turkish attack on Vienna defeated by John III of Poland.

1688. The British Revolution. Flight of James II. William and Mary began to reign.

A.D.

1689. Peter the Great of Russia (to 1725).

1690. Battle of the Boyne in Ireland.

1701. Frederick I first King of Prussia.

1707. Death of Aurungzeb. The empire of the Great Mogul disintegrated.

1713. Frederick the Great of Prussia born.

1733. Oglethorpe founded Georgia.

1736. Nadir Shah raided India. (The beginning of twenty years of raiding and disorder in India.)

1740. Accession of Frederick the Great, King of Prussia.

Maria Theresa began to reign. (Being a woman, she could not be empress. Her husband, Francis I, was emperor after 1745 until his death in 1765, when her son, Joseph II, succeeded him).

1741. The Empress Elizabeth of Russia began to reign.

1755–63. Britain and France struggled for America and India. France in alliance with Austria and Russia against Prussia and Britain (1756–63); the Seven Years' War.

1757. Battle of Plassey.

1759. The British general Wolfe took Quebec.

1760. George III of Britain.

1762. The Empress Elizabeth of Russia died. Murder of the Tsar Paul, and accession of Catherine the Great of Russia (to 1796).

1763. Peace of Paris; Canada ceded to Britain. British dominant in India.

1764. Battle of Buxar.

1766. Malthus born.

1769. Napoleon Bonaparte born.

1774. Louis XVI began his reign. Suicide of Clive. The American revolutionary drama began.

1775. Battle of Lexington. Turner born.

1776. Declaration of Independence by the United States of America.

1780. End of the reign of Maria Theresa. The Emperor Joseph (1765 to 1790) succeeded her in the hereditary Habsburg dominions.

1783. Treaty of Peace between Britain and the new United States of America. Quaco set free in Massachusetts.

1787. The Constitutional Convention of Philadelphia set up the Federal Government of the United States. France discovered to be bankrupt. The Assembly of the Notables.

1788. First Federal Congress of the United States at New York.

1789. The French States-General assembled. Storming of the Bastille.

1791. The Jacobin Revolution. Flight to Varennes.

1792. France declared war on Austria. Prussia declared war on France. Battle of Valmy. France became a Republic.

1793. Louis XVI beheaded.

1794. Execution of Robespierre and end of the Jacobin republic. Rule of the Convention.

A.D.

1795. The Directory. Bonaparte suppressed a revolt and went to Italy as commander-in-chief.

1797. By the Peace of Campo Formio Bonaparte destroyed the Republic of Venice.

1798. Bonaparte went to Egypt. Battle of the Nile.

1799. Bonaparte returned. He became First Consul with enormous powers.

1800. Legislative union of Ireland and England enacted January 1st, 1801. Napoleon's campaign against Austria. Battles of Marengo (in Italy) and Hohenlinden (Moreau's victory).

1801. Preliminaries of peace between France, England, and Austria signed.

1803. Bonaparte occupied Switzerland, and so precipitated war.

1804. Bonaparte became emperor. Francis II took the title of Emperor of Austria in 1805, and in 1806 he dropped the title of Holy Roman Emperor. So the "Holy Roman Empire" came to an end.

1805. Battle of Trafalgar. Battles of Ulm and Austerlitz.

1806. Prussia overthrown at Jena.

1807. Battles of Eylau and Friedland, and Treaty of Tilsit.

1808. Napoleon made his brother Joseph King of Spain.

1810. Spanish America became republican.

1811. Alexander withdrew from the "Continental System."

1812. Napoleon's retreat from Moscow.

1814. Abdication of Napoleon. Louis XVIII.

1815. The Waterloo campaign. The Treaty of Vienna.

1819. The First Factory Act passed through the efforts of Robert Owen.

1821. The Greek Revolt.

1824. Charles X of France.

1825. Nicholas I of Russia. First railway—Stockton to Darlington.

1827. Battle of Navarino.

1829. Greece independent.

1830. A year of disturbance. Louis Philippe ousted Charles X. Belgium broke away from Holland. Leopold of Saxe-Coburg-Gotha became king of this new country, Belgium. Russian Poland revolted ineffectually.

1832. The First Reform Bill in Britain restored the democratic character of the British Parliament.

1835. The word "Socialism" first used.

1837. Queen Victoria.

1840. Queen Victoria married Prince Albert of Saxe-Coburg-Gotha.

1848. Another year of disturbance. Republics in France and Rome. The Pan-slavic Conference at Prague. All Germany united in a parliament at Frankfort. German unity destroyed by the King of Prussia.

1851. The Great Exhibition of London.

1852. Napoleon III Emperor of the French.

1854. Perry (second expedition) landed in Japan. Nicholas I occupied the Danubian provinces of Turkey.

A.D.

1854–56. Crimean War.

1856. Alexander II of Russia.

1857. The Indian Mutiny.

1859. Franco-Austrian war. Battles of Magenta and Solferino.

1861. Victor Emmanuel first king of Italy. Abraham Lincoln became President U.S.A. The American Civil War began.

1863. British bombarded a Japanese town.

1864. Maximilian became Emperor of Mexico.

1865. Surrender of Appomattox Court House. Japan opened to the world.

1866. Prussia and Italy attacked Austria (and the south German states in alliance with her). Battle of Sadowa.

1867. The Emperor Maximilian shot.

1870. Napoleon II declared war against Prussia.

1871. Paris surrendered (January). The King of Prussia became William I, "German Emperor." The Peace of Frankfort.

1875. The "Bulgarian atrocities."

1877. Russo-Turkish War. Treaty of San Stefano. Queen Victoria became Empress of India.

1878. The Treaty of Berlin. The Armed Peace of 36 years began in Western Europe.

1881. The Battle of Majuba Hill. The Transvaal free.

1882. Charles Darwin died.

1883. Britain occupied Egypt. Karl Marx died.

1886. Gladstone's first Irish Home Rule Bill.

1888. Frederick III (March), William II (June), German emperors.

1890. Bismarck dismissed. Heligoland ceded to Germany by Lord Salisbury.

1894–95. Japanese war with China.

1895. "Unionist" (Imperialist) government in Britain.

1896. Battle of Adowa.

1898. The Fashoda quarrel between France and Britain. Germany acquired Kiau-Chau.

1899. The war in South Africa began (Boer War).

1900. The Boxer risings in China. Siege of the Legations at Peking.

1904. The British invaded Tibet.

1904–5. Russo-Japanese War.

1906. The "Unionist" (Imperialist) party in Great Britain defeated by the Liberals upon the question of tariffs.

1907. The Confederation of South Africa established.

1908. Austria annexed Bosnia and Herzegovina.

1909. M. Bleriot flew in an aeroplane from France to England.

1911. Italy made war on Turkey and seized Tripoli.

1912. China became a republic. The Balkan league made war on Turkey.

1913. Bloodshed at Londonderry in Ireland caused by "Unionist" gun-running.

A.D.

1914. The first World War in Europe began. (*See* Chart, pp. 863–64.)

1917. The two Russian revolutions. Establishment of the Bolshevik regime in Russia.

1918. The Armistice (Nov.).

1919. The Peace of Versailles.

1920. First meeting of League of Nations. Last invaders (Wrangel, Poles) expelled from Russia.

1922. Russian famine. Ataturk defeats Greeks. Irish Free State established.

1923. French occupy the Ruhr; collapse of German currency.

1924. Death of Lenin; first steps taken to Stalin's autocracy.

1929. American Wall-street crash starts world-wide slump.

1931. Spain becomes a republic.

1933. Inauguration of Roosevelt's "New Deal" in the U.S.A. Nazis take power in Germany.

1935. Italy invades and conquers Abyssinia; League of Nations fails to act.

1936. Franco rebels against Spanish republic, with aid of Nazis and Fascists.

1937. "Axis" formed (Germany, Italy, Japan; later Franco-Spain); Japan invades China.

1938. Germany annexes Austria; Munich conference.

1939. Germany annexes Czechoslovakia; Italy annexes Albania; Spanish civil war ends. Soviet-Nazi pact signed; Germany attacks Poland. War. Russia and Germany partition Poland; Russia annexes Baltic states and attacks Finland.

1940. Germany overruns Denmark, Norway, Holland and Belgium. Chamberlain replaced by Coalition government headed by Churchill. Fall of France. Battle of Britain.

1941. British beat off German air attacks; reconquer Abyssinia; Germany conquers Yugoslavia and Greece. Germans invade Russia. Japan attacks U.S. fleet at Pearl Harbour. The Atlantic Charter.

1942. Axis victories until late in year (El Alamein, New Guinea, Stalingrad, North African landings).

1943. Fall of Mussolini.

1944. Capture of Rome; Allied landings in Normandy; Germans expelled from Russia, France and Belgium.

1945. Suicide of Hitler; Nazi surrender. A-bomb devastates Hiroshima and Nagasaki, Japan surrenders. Charter of United Nations signed.

1946. Guerrilla war in Palestine. Beginning of British Welfare state. First Soviet "cold war" aggressions.

1947. India, Ceylon, Pakistan granted independence; Burma leaves British commonwealth. Marshall Plan. Soviet rejects atom control plan; eliminates opposition in Hungary and Bulgaria.

1948. British quit Palestine: Arab-Jew war. Chinese communists defeat Kuomintang. Soviet completes subjugation of Roumania and Czechoslovakia. Berlin blockade.

A.D.

1949. Atlantic pact signed. Soviet takes over Poland; Dutch ousted from Indonesia; Chiang from China.
1950. Korean war. Beginning of European army, under U.S. general.
1952. Mau Mau revolt. Egyptian revolution.
1953. Death of Stalin. Korean armistice. East Berlin revolt.

KEY TO PRONUNCIATION

VOWELS

a   as in far (far), father (fa' thėr), mikado (mi ka' dō).

ă   "   " fat (făt), ample (ămpl), abstinence (ăb' stin ėns).

ā   "   " fate (fāt), wait (wāt), deign (dān), jade (jād).

aw   "   " fall (fawl), appal (á pawl'), broad (brawd).

ä   "   " fair (fär), bear (bär), where (hwär).

e   "   " bell (bel), bury (ber'i).

ë   "   " her (hër), search (sërch), word (wërd), bird (bërd).

ē   "   " beef (bēf), thief (thēf), idea (ī dē' á), beer (bēr), casino (ká sē' nō).

i   "   " bit (bit), lily (lil' i), nymph (nimf), build (bild).

ī   "   " bite (bīt), analyze (ăn' á līz), light (līt).

o   "   " not (not), watch (woch), cough (kof), sorry (sor' i).

ō   "   " no (nō), blow (blō), brooch (brōch).

ö   "   " north (nörth), absorb (áb sörb').

oo   "   " food (food), do (doo), prove (proov), blue (bloo), strew (stroo).

u   "   " bull (bul), good (gud), would (wud).

ŭ   "   " sun (sŭn), love (lŭv), enough (é nŭf').

ū   "   " muse (mūz), stew (stū), cure (kūr).

ou   "   " bout (bout), bough (bou), crowd (kroud).

oi   "   " join (join), joy (joi), buoy (boi).

A dot placed over a, e, o, or u (á, ė, ó, ů) signifies that the vowel has an obscure indeterminate, or slurred sound, as in:—

advice (ád vīs'),   current (kŭr' ėnt),   sailor (sā' lór),

breakable (brā' kábl),   notion (nō' shŭn),   pleasure (plezh' ůr).

CONSONANTS

"s" is used only for the sibilant "s" (as in "toast," tōst, "place," plās); the sonant "s" (as in "toes," "plays") is printed "z" (tōz, plāz).

"c" (except in the combinations "ch" and "ch"), "q" and "x" are not used.

b, d, f, h (but see the combinations below), k, l, m, n (see n below), p, r, t, v, z and w and y when used as consonants have their usual values.

ch   as in church (chërch), batch (băch), capriccio (ka prē' chō).

ch   "   " loch (loch), coronach (kor' o nach), clachan (klăch' án).

g   "   " get (get), finger (fing' gėr).

j   "   " join (join), judge (jŭj), germ (jërm), ginger (jin' jėr).

gh (in proper names only) as in Ludwig (lut' vigh).

hl (in proper names only) as in Llandilo (hlăn dī' lo).

hw as in white (hwīt), nowhere (nō' hwär).

n   "   " cabochon (ka bō shon'), congé (kon' zhā).

sh   "   " shawl (shawl), mention (men' shŭn).

zh   "   " measure (mezh' ór), vision (vizh' ůn).

th   "   " thin (thin), breath (breth).

th   "   " thine (thīn), breathe (brēth).

The accent (') *follows* the syllable to be stressed.—CASSELL'S *New English Dictionary.*

INDEX

Maps, Diagrams, Portraits, and other Illustrations are indicated by italic figures.

403; races and peoples, 110, 111–12, 114,
123, 125, 141–42, 145, 215, 220–21, 241, 290,
372 *sqq.*, 403, 404–5, 442, 568, 582–83, 585,
665, 675–76, 809, *110*
Mongolian languages, 120, 125
Mongoloid tribes, 145, 621
Mongols, 402, 404–5, 411, 470, 489, 539, 556
sqq., 562–64, 566–67, 570–78, 583, 586, 601,
616, 624, 671, 809, *110*, 563
Monitors, lizards, 37
Monkeys, 47, 52–53
Monks, *see* Monasteries
Monmouth, ship, 857
Monosyllabic languages, 120–21
Monroe, James, President of U.S.A., 752
Monroe Doctrine, 752, 788, 796, 805, 848
Mons, 855
Montaigne, 612
Monte Cassino, 445–46
Montenegro, 883–84
Montesquieu, 708
Monteverde, Claudio, 660
Montezuma, 622
Montfort, Simon de, 644
Montgomery, Ala., 793
Montgomery, Field Marshal, 932–33, 934
Month, lunar, *see* Lunar month
Montreal, 671
Montserrat, 599
Moon, 11, 14, 15, 99; worship of, 167, 176
Moors, 361, 552, 595, 624
Moose, 56
Moral ideas, 217
Moravia, 409, 883
More, Sir Thomas, 636, 764
Moreau, J. V. M., 740
Morning Post, 772
Mornington, Lord (Marquis Wellesley), 801
Morocco, 155, 583, 806, 833, 901–2, 914–15,
917
Morris, William, 708, 817
Morte d'Arthur 224, 821
Mortillet, G. de, 74
Mosaic, 200, 819; Byzantine, 447–48; Roman,
397
Mosasaurs, 33, 37
Moscow, 577, 658, 675, 885, 888–89, 891;
Grand Duke of, 574; retreat from, 748
Moses, 140, 149, 174, 206, 214, 457
Moslem schools, 579; universities, 501–2
Moslems, the, 212, 485 *sqq.*, 498, 525, 530,
532, 537, 539, 555, 556, 562, 567–68, 569,
579–80, 582, 595, 672, 802, *487, 490, 491;*
in Europe, 495–96, 506, 510, 513, 517, 528,
543, 618, 659; *see also* Crusades; Islam;
Muhammad; Muhammadanism
Mosses, 27, 28
Most, 591
Mosul, 534, 575
Mother, the, 97
Motley, J. L., 641
Motor cars, *see* Automobiles
Mounds, 85–86, 96, 111, 218, 222, 225
Mountains, 14, 32, 43
Mouse, 88
Moussorgsky, M. P., 820
Mousterian Age and implements, 60, 66, 76,
64, 80
Mouth organs, early, 202
Mozart, W. A., 660, 819
Muawiya (Moawiya), 493, 495
Mudfish, 27, 47
Muehlon, Herr, 875
Munammad, prophet, 417, 420, 456, 464, 471,
475, 589; life of, 471 *sqq.*, 494–95; teaching
of, 484 *sqq.*, 496–97; *see also* Islam;
Moslems; Muhammadanism
Muhammad II, sultan, 570, 626
Muhammad Ali, 481
Muhammad-Ibn-Musa, 502
Muhammadan communistic movement, 594
Muhammadanism, 496, 506, 573; *see also*
Islam; Moslems; Muhammad

Mulberry tree, 389
Mülhausen, 734
Müller, Max, 168
Mummies, 113, 286
Munich, 609, 923
Münster, 593, 846
Munzuk, 412
Murad I, 569
Mural paintings, 458
Murat, 748
Murray, Gilbert, 6, 157, 224, 233, 237, 260,
268, 362, 430
Muscovites, 663
Muscovy, empire of, 658; *see also* Russia
Muses, 301
Museums, 267, 301 *sqq.*, 351, 361, 466; temples
as, 172
Music, 8, 89, 199, 200–3, 554, 655, 659–61,
819–20; Arab, 202; early Christian, 448, 520;
gipsy, 581; Greek, 202, 275
Musical instruments, 89, 202–3
Musk–ox, 49, 59, 77, *54*
Mussolini, Benito, 913, 923, 933, 936; *see also*
Italy, World War II
Mussel-shell, arrowheads of, 141
Mutations, 22
Mutilation of human body, 103–4
Mycale (mik' á lē), Mount, 257, 259
Mycenae (mī sē' nē), 83, 230, 239–42
Mycerinus, 138
Mylae, 347
Myos-hormos, 392
Myres, J. L., 224, 372
Myron, 261
Mysteries, religious, 280–81, 396
Myth-making, 99–100, 201, 268–69
Mythology, 268

Nabateans, 454
Nabonidus, 177, 180, 183, 204, 211, 214, 243,
246, 311
Nadir Shah, 672
Nagasaki, 810
Nalanda, 473
Nankin, 556
Nansen, 892
Naples, 334, 445, 543, 550, 609, 636, 734, 743,
752, 787
Napoleon I, 6, 635, 721, 724, 728, 735 *sqq.*,
751, 757, 758, 801, *737, 740, 746, 747*
Napoleon III, 6, 416, 784–90
Narbonne, 609
Naseby, 647
Nasmyth, James, 760
Natal, 806
Nathan, 210
National Assembly, French, 710 *sqq.*, 714–16,
719–21
National Convention, French, 723, 725–26, 728
National Guard, French, 711, 714
National Industrial Recovery Act, 911
National schools, 766
National Socialist Party, *see* Nazism
National Symbols, 782, *781*
Nationalism, 522–23, 780–83, 840 *sqq.*, 844,
899–901
Natural rights, 593; selection, 22–24
Nautilus, pearly, 39
Naval tactics, Roman, 346–49
Navarino, battle of, 754
Navigation, early, 149–55, 157, 197, 616 *sqq.*,
149, 150, 151
Nazarenes, 426, 429 *sqq.*
Nazi-Soviet Pact, 924, 925
Nazism, 909, 917–24; *see also* Germany,
World War II
Neanderthal man, 58, 59–67, 81, 84 *sqq.*, 94
sqq., 109, 198, 360, 363, 365, *61, 65, 80, 115*
Neanderthaloid men, 66, 95
Nebuchadnezzar II (the Great), 136, 140, 154,
204, 212–13, 243, 286, 288; map showing
relation of Median and Second Babylonian
Empires in reign of, *301*